Applying Ethics:
A Text with Readings

Applying Ethics:
A Text with Readings

Second Edition

Vincent Barry

Bakersfield College

Wadsworth Publishing Company
Belmont, California
A Division of Wadsworth, Inc.

Philosophy Editor: Kenneth King
Production: Stacey C. Sawyer, San Francisco
Designer: Andrew H. Ogus
Copy Editor: Anne Montague
Cover: Adriane Bosworth/Marie Carluccio
Typesetting: Graphic Typesetting Service, Los Angeles

Printed in the United States of America

3 4 5 6 7 8 9 10—89 88 87 86

Library of Congress Cataloging in Publication Data

Barry, Vincent E.
  Applying ethics.

  Includes bibliographies and index.
  1. Social ethics.   2. United States—Moral conditions. I. Title.
HM216.B18   1984   170   84-10445
ISBN 0-534-03687-2s

ISBN 0-534-03687-2

CONTENTS

9. WAR   374

INDEX   414

to Jim Wilson

PREFACE

The first edition of *Applying Ethics* was a text/reader that integrated moral theory and its application. That edition attempted to make students recognize and think about some of the important moral issues of our time. It also tried to get students to see the moral overtones in their own lives; experience the urgency of ethics; and understand, analyze, and resolve moral dilemmas for themselves. This new edition shares these goals.

Applying Ethics, Second Edition, is divided into two parts. Part I introduces the study of ethics, including moral reasoning, and examines important principles of morality and social ethics. Part II covers the following issues: pornography, abortion, euthanasia, capital punishment, job discrimination, world hunger, and war.

For each issue, sufficient background material is provided for readers to begin thinking intelligently about the moral concerns involved. Arguments for and against particular propositions (for example, "The rich nations have an obligation to help feed the world's starving masses") are presented in dialogue format, like everyday conversations people might have. This format is intended to air the arguments surrounding a moral issue in a way that facilitates understanding, stimulates discussion, and relates the issues to the lives of "ordinary" people.

Readings, case presentations, and bibliographies complete the chapters.

There is much that's new about the second edition of *Applying Ethics*:

1. *It makes a sharper distinction between morality and areas with which morality is often confused.* Chapter 1 examines the difference between morality and etiquette, and morality and law.

2. *It provides a section on moral development.* Students seem better able to grasp what's involved in moral reasoning if they have some understanding of how they develop morally. So before discussing the common patterns of moral reasoning, Chapter 1 introduces Lawrence Kohlberg's theory of moral development.

3. *It expands the coverage of informal fallacies.* Moral reasoning is no less susceptible to erroneous thinking than is nonmoral. Chapter 1, therefore, includes a well-illustrated treatment of the more common informal fallacies and shows

how they can arise in moral discourse. (The coverage here has been increased by about 50 percent.)

4. *It discusses major moral principles and types of normative theories.* Chapter 2 surveys the pre-eminent theories of value and obligation in Western philosophy: rational development (Aristotle), natural law (religious and secular), divine command, duty (Kant), self-interest (egoism), and utility (utilitarianism). Students make use of these principles in responding to the "Questions for Analysis," which follow both the readings and the case presentations.

5. *It examines social ethics.* Understanding and reacting thoughtfully to the crucial moral issues of the day require familiarity with some basic concepts of social ethics. So Chapter 2 inspects notions of justice, equality, and freedom, including the Marxist view.

6. *It comprehensively treats euthanasia.* Among other things, Chapter 5 examines the meanings of personhood, death, and ordinary vs. extraordinary treatment. It also raises the unique moral problems surrounding the treatment of defective newborns and the making of death decisions in the institutional setting. The hospice approach to care for the dying is also covered.

7. *It evaluates capital punishment as a deterrent.* Since both retentionists and abolitionists sometimes base their positions on an interplay between the death penalty and deterrence, Chapter 6 takes a close look at current data relating to this issue.

8. *It examines job discrimination.* Before tackling the arguments for and against reverse discrimination, Chapter 7 looks at the nature and forms of job discrimination and the statistical and attitudinal evidence of it.

9. *It considers core moral concerns relating to world hunger.* Most of Chapter 8 is devoted to a discussion of liberty and property rights and to international economic justice—productive as well as distributive.

10. *It discusses war.* As a moral issue, war is, sad to say, never passé. It is only more or less timely—today more than less. Chapter 9 examines the morality of war and attends especially to the issues of greatest moral concern: nuclear war and nuclear deterrence.

11. *It provides timely, provocative readings.* About half the essays are new or revised. They represent a cross-section of philosophical opinion on the issues. Each selection is preceded by an overview and followed by questions that test comprehension.

12. *It introduces actual cases for study and discussion.* Students seem more intrigued by actual than fictionalized cases. So the lion's share (eleven of fourteen) of the case presentations in the second edition really happened. Of these, several are very recent—for example, the cases of the tragically deformed "Baby Jane Doe," death-row inmate J. D. Autry, and the U.S. intervention in Grenada. Others, although not as fresh as yesterday's news, are nonetheless contemporary. Taken together with the cases that begin the issue chapters, these cases should spark many lively classroom debates and, when used with the

Questions for Analysis that follow them, form a basis for written assign-
ments, even research papers.

I hope these additions and revisions make *Applying Ethics, Second Edition,* an
even more useful tool than the first edition was reported to be.

Many individuals assisted in developing this new edition, chief among whom
are: Wadsworth philosophy editor Ken King; reviewers L. E. Andrade, Illinois
State University, Alvin Denman, Antioch College, Lynn Lindholm, University
of North Dakota, George Stengren, Central Michigan University, and Jeffrey
Watts, University of Hawaii; copy editor Anne Montague; and the Wadsworth
production staff. As always, errors of fact or omission are my responsibility.

Vincent Barry

Part I

Ethics and Ethical Principles

1

VALUES, ETHICS, REASONING

In the late 1950s and early 1960s, America's brew of racial unrest, which had been heating up for so long, finally boiled over. "Justice too long delayed is justice denied"; "We shall overcome"; "Freedom now!" These cries for racial equality echoed throughout the land. "Freedom riders," who traveled the roads of America's South to demonstrate opposition to racial injustices, became commonplace on the nightly news. So did the face of their leader, the velvet-voiced, inspirational president of the Southern Christian Leadership Conference, the Reverend Martin Luther King, Jr.

At the height of this period of vigorous racial protest, King was arrested in Birmingham, Alabama. The charge: "parading without a permit." The act instantly reminded some of the contrived charges brought against historic figures such as Socrates and Jesus. Others praised the Birmingham commissioner of public safety, Eugene "Bull" Connor, for keeping order and preventing violence. Among those applauding Connor were eight of King's fellow clergymen, who published a statement attacking King's action as unwise and untimely. Confined in the city jail, King responded in what has become known as his "Letter from Birmingham Jail."

In this important document in the history of civil rights, King defends his conduct. It was not only justified, he says, but obligatory. At one point in the long essay, King confronts the central issue of whether it is ever right willfully to break the law. He thinks it is. Here is why:

> You express a great deal of anxiety over our willingness to break laws. This is certainly a legitimate concern. Since we so diligently urge people to obey the Supreme Court's decision of 1954 outlawing segregation in the public schools, at first glance it may seem rather paradoxical for us consciously to break laws. One may well ask: "How can you advocate breaking some laws and obeying others?" The answer lies in the fact that there are two types of laws: just and unjust. I would be the first to advocate obeying just laws. One has not only a legal but a moral responsibility to obey just laws. Conversely, one has a moral

responsibility to disobey unjust laws. I would agree with St. Augustine that "an unjust law is no law at all."

Now, what is the difference between the two? How does one determine whether a law is just or unjust? A just law is a man-made code that squares with the moral law or the law of God. An unjust law is a code that is out of harmony with the moral law. To put it in the terms of St. Thomas Aquinas: An unjust law is a human law that is not rooted in eternal law and natural law. Any law that uplifts human personality is just. Any law that degrades human personality is unjust. All segregation statutes are unjust because segregation distorts the soul and damages the personality. It gives the segregator a false sense of superiority and the segregated a false sense of inferiority. Segregation, to use the terminology of the Jewish philosopher Martin Buber, substitutes an "I-it" relationship for an "I-thou" relationship and ends up relegating persons to the status of things. Hence segregation is not only politically, economically, and sociologically unsound; it is morally wrong and sinful. Paul Tillich has said that sin is separation. Is not segregation an existential expression of man's tragic separation, his awful estrangement, his terrible sinfulness? Thus it is that I can urge men to obey the 1954 decision of the Supreme Court, for it is morally right; and I can urge them to disobey segregation ordinances, for they are morally wrong.

Let us consider a more concrete example of just and unjust laws. An unjust law is a code that a numerical or power majority group compels a minority group to obey but does not make binding on itself. This is *difference* made legal. By the same token, a just law is a code that a majority compels a minority to follow and that it is willing to follow itself. This is *sameness* made legal.

Let me give another explanation. A law is unjust if it is inflicted on a minority that, as a result of being denied the right to vote, had no part in enacting or devising the law. Who can say that the legislature of Alabama which set up that state's segregation laws was democratically elected? Throughout Alabama all sorts of devious methods are used to prevent Negroes from becoming registered voters, and there are some counties in which, even though Negroes constitute a majority of the population, not a single Negro is registered. Can any law enacted under such circumstances be considered democratically structured?

Sometimes a law is just on its face and unjust in its application. For instance, I have been arrested on a charge of parading without a permit. Now, there is nothing wrong in having an ordinance which requires a permit for a parade. But such an ordinance becomes unjust when it is used to maintain segregation and to deny citizens the First Amendment privilege of peaceful assembly and protest.

I hope you are able to see the distinction I am trying to point out. In no sense do I advocate evading or defying the law, as would the rabid segregationist. That would lead to anarchy. One who breaks an unjust law must do so openly, lovingly, and with a willingness to accept the penalty. I submit that an individual who breaks a law that conscience tells him is unjust, and who willingly accepts the penalty of imprisonment in order to arouse the conscience of the community over its injustice, is in reality expressing the highest respect for law.[1]

1.   *From "Letter from Birmingham Jail, April 16, 1963," in* Why We Can't Wait *by Martin Luther King, Jr. Copyright ©1963 by Martin Luther King, Jr. Reprinted by permission of Harper & Row, Publishers, Inc.*

Two aspects of King's letter, which are evident even in this short excerpt, make it a lively springboard to our study of ethics. First, it illustrates the moral aspect of an individual's perspective. Second, it underscores the importance of justification in moral decision, especially in the public realm.

Both the moral aspect of an individual's perspective and the importance of justification in moral decision are focal points of this opening chapter, which introduces the study of ethics, including some basic terms and concepts.

Values and Justification

Although there is much debate about the precise nature of values, let us define a value simply as *an assessment of worth*. Defined as such, values constitute a large part of who we are and how we live. Clearly we make all sorts of assessments of worth. In automobiles, some of us value low-slung sports models, others conservative sedans. In books, some prefer science fiction, others historical nonfiction. Politically, some people value a democratic form of government, others a constitutional monarchy. Differences in values exist in religion, art, politics, education, in every area of human affairs. Most important, humans seem to be the only animals that can formulate and express a value (ads for cat food notwithstanding).

Where do values come from? How do they arise? Why does one person see beauty in an ocean, while another is unmoved? Why will one person risk life and limb to ensure justice, while another stands detached and indifferent? Our values are generally shaped and formed by experience. Thus the sea holds little beauty for an individual who has seen a loved one die in it. The person who has felt the sting of racial or sexual discrimination can understandably develop a passion for fair and just treatment, even at great personal risk. In brief, the values we hold, as individuals and as groups, are inseparable from the endlessly changing experiences of our lives.

History reveals that no society has ever been without some value system and that every individual has some code of values. The issue, therefore, is not whether we are to have values but what those values will be.

What we value in the realm of human conduct are called our moral values. Some people, for example, might value justice. They might contend that a person should always do the just thing and refrain from doing what is unjust. Others might value civil order. They might argue that we should always act in a way that promotes civil order and refrain from acting in a way that will produce disorder. Of course, we could speak of other moral values that people hold: honesty, truth, loyalty, love, and so on. But how do we know which values to hold? This is a tough question to answer, perhaps impossible to answer to everyone's satisfaction. The study of ethics involves a search for the answer.

Complicating the question of which moral values to hold is the inevitable situation of conflicting values. Martin Luther King was involved in precisely this dilemma. Should he prefer justice or order? By parading without a permit, King clearly stated that in the area of racial equality he valued justice over order. King believed that intentionally breaking the law was the right thing to do in that instance because such behavior would dramatize the inequities of segregation. Having given justice priority over order, King acted in accordance with that decision. Thus the King case well illustrates how a personal value can translate into a social position and into subsequent action. Indeed, our positions and actions on the issues of the day take root in the values that we hold for ourselves and our society. Moral positions and conduct cannot be separated from moral values.

But how do we know that King acted right? Can we ever know? Again, this is a difficult question to answer. However, the study of ethics also involves a search for what constitutes morally right human conduct.

In defending his action, Martin Luther King realized that it was not enough to express a moral value, to prefer justice to order in the case of racial inequality. He had to justify his position, to demonstrate why racial justice was a superior value to civil order. So often today people hold views without really knowing why. They may be against abortion and capital punishment, for euthanasia and premarital sex, or against censorship and reverse discrimination. On any issue you can find numerous people willing to give you a position. But ask the same people for their reasons, why they believe as they do, and they may not be able to say.

Of course, just because a person cannot give satisfactory reasons for his or her beliefs and positions it does not necessarily mean that those viewpoints lack validity. But if our opinions are to influence others, then at some point we must present well-reasoned arguments for them. If we want to ensure that our own views are the clearest and most compelling of the alternatives, then we must subject those views to rational analysis.

We shall talk considerably more about moral justification shortly. But first, let's find out what ethics involves.

Ethics

In the chapters ahead we'll focus on values that govern what is called good and bad conduct. *Ethics is the study of what constitutes good and bad conduct, including related action and values.*

The term *ethics* is sometimes used synonymously with *morals*. It would be more accurate, though, to use the terms *morals* and *moral* to refer to the conduct itself, and terms *ethics* and *ethical* to refer to the study of moral conduct or to the code one follows. So when we use the word *moral*, we refer to an action or person insofar as either is considered right or good. When we use the word *immoral*, we refer to an action or person insofar as either one is considered wrong or bad.

Sometimes in ethics the word *nonmoral* occurs. *Nonmoral* refers to something outside the sphere of moral concern. For example, whether your new sports car will "top out" at 120 or 130 mph is a nonmoral question. But whether you should top it out on Main Street on a Wednesday at high noon would probably be a moral question.

How do moral standards differ from other kinds of standards? Although there is some disagreement about precisely what distinguishes moral standards from others, at least two features are widely endorsed.

First, moral standards concern behavior that can be of serious consequence to human well-being, that can profoundly injure or benefit people. For example, moral norms against lying, stealing, murder, and so on deal with actions that can hurt people. Also, the moral principle that human beings should be treated with dignity and respect represents a critical interest of human beings. Thus the *seriousness* of moral standards sets them apart from standards that do not seem to deal as critically with the interests of human beings, such as grammatical and artistic standards.[2]

Second, the validity of moral standards rests on the adequacy of the reasons that support or justify them and not on the decisions of particular authoritative bodies. Laws and organizational codes of conduct, for example, can be established and altered by the decisions of legislatures, voters, company boards of directors, and so on. But moral standards are not made up by such bodies, although they can be and are endorsed or rejected by them. So long as the reasons used to support the standards remain adequate, the standards remain valid.[3] Of course, as we'll see, precisely what constitutes "adequate reasons" for a moral standard is problematic and indeed is at the base of considerable difference of opinion regarding the legitimacy of moral principles.

While these distinguishing features set moral standards apart from other standards, it would be useful to distinguish morality more specifically from two areas with which it's sometimes confused: etiquette and law. (Beyond these, morality is often confused with religion, in the sense that some think that morality must have a religious basis. We'll consider this view in the next chapter where we examine religious authoritarianism.)

Morality and Etiquette

Etiquette refers to any special code of behavior or courtesy. In our society, for example, it's considered bad etiquette to eat with one's fingers or to use obscene language in public. It's considered good etiquette to say "Please" when requesting and "Thank you" when receiving, to hold a door open for someone entering immediately behind us, and to offer an elderly person one's seat on a bus. It's commonplace to judge people's manners as "good" or "bad" and the conduct that reflects them "right" or "wrong." Thus, "The treasurer was wrong to use vulgar language at the board meeting"; "Jane was right to introduce her friend to her parents"; "It's bad to slurp your soup"; "It's good to wear dark clothes to a funeral." *Good, bad, right,* and *wrong* here simply mean "socially appropriate" or "socially inappropriate." In these contexts, such words are expressing judgments dealing with manners, not ethics—with matters of taste, not morality.

2. *See Manuel G. Velasquez,* Business Ethics: Concepts and Cases *(Englewood Cliffs, N.J.: Prentice-Hall, 1982), p. 10.*

3. *Velasquez,* Business Ethics: Concepts and Cases, *p. 10.*

So-called rules of etiquette that one might learn, say, in the syndicated "Miss Manners" column are prescriptions for behaving in what's thought to be a socially acceptable manner. If we want to "fit in," get along with others, and be thought well of by them, we should observe common rules of etiquette. If we don't, then we're rightly considered ill-mannered, boorish, uncivilized—but not necessarily immoral. By the same token, observing the conventions of etiquette does not of itself make one moral.

The rules of etiquette typically are nonmoral assertions: "Give the groom your 'congratulations' but the bride your 'best wishes' "; "Push your chair back into place upon leaving a dinner table." This doesn't mean, however, that what is considered bad taste couldn't also raise a moral question. For example, the male boss who refers to female subordinates as "honey" and "doll" shows bad manners. If such epithets have the effect of diminishing the worth of the women or perpetuating sexism, then they also raise moral issues concerning equal treatment and the denial of dignity to human beings. The key thing to remember is that if the man's behavior is immoral, it is so because it violates not a rule of etiquette but a moral ideal or principle—equal treatment, dignity of the human being, non-injury.

It's worth repeating that scrupulous observance of rules of etiquette does not necessarily make one moral. In fact, it can have the effect of camouflaging moral issues that only rule breaking can flush out. For example, not too long ago in some parts of America it was thought "bad manners" for blacks and whites to eat together. Those who obeyed the convention and were thus judged "well-bred" certainly had no grounds for feeling moral. The only way to dramatize the injustice underlying this practice was to violate the rule, in which case one would be judged, at the very least, "ill-mannered." For those in the '60s who conducted sit-ins, being considered boorish was small price to pay for dramatizing the unequal treatment and degradation of human beings that lay at the base of this rule of etiquette.

Etiquette, then, tells us how to behave in certain social situations if we want to be adjudged courteous and well-mannered. Ethical standards, however, prescribe what we ought to do if we are to be regarded as moral. Etiquette and ethics are not connected in such a way that following rules of etiquette is either a necessary or a sufficient condition for behaving morally.

Morality and Law

Before distinguishing between morality and law, it's useful to clarify what's meant by "law." Basically there are four kinds of law: statutes, regulations, common law, and constitutional law.

Statutes are laws enacted by legislative bodies. For example, the law that prohibits touching other people without their consent ("battery") is a statute. Statutes can be enacted by Congress or state legislatures. (Laws enacted by local governing bodies, such as city councils, generally are termed *ordinances.*) Statutes constitute a large part of the law and are what many of us mean when we speak of "laws." But there are other important forms of law.

Administrative regulations are a second form. Given the limitations on their expertise, legislative bodies often establish boards or agencies, one of whose functions is to issue detailed regulations of certain kinds of conduct. For example, state legislatures set up license boards to formulate regulations for the licensing and professional conduct of physicians and nurses. As long as these regulations don't exceed the board's statutory powers and don't conflict with other kinds of law, they are legally binding.

Common law refers to laws applied in the English-speaking world before there were any statutes. Courts frequently wrote opinions explaining the bases of their decisions in specific cases, including the legal principles they deemed appropriate. Each of these opinions became a precedent for subsequent decisions in similar cases. Over the years, a massive body of legal principles accumulated that is collectively referred to as common law. Like administrative regulations, common law is valid insofar as it is consistent with statutory law and with still another source, constitutional law.

Constitutional law refers to court rulings on any law. The courts are empowered by the U.S. Constitution to declare any law unconstitutional. So although courts cannot make laws, they have far-reaching powers to rule on a law's constitutionality and thereby declare it invalid. Invested with the greatest judiciary power is the U.S. Supreme Court, which, of course, rules on an array of cases, some of which we'll have occasion to mention elsewhere in our study of ethics.

Is the law, whatever its source, always a reliable standard for determining moral behavior? It is, if and only if: (1) what is legal is necessarily moral and (2) what is not prohibited by law is always moral. But both these propositions are incorrect.

Regarding the first proposition, that what is legal is necessarily moral, consider the actual case of a four-month-old baby suffering from diarrhea and fever.[4] The family physician prescribed medication on the second day of the child's illness and saw him during office hours on the third day. On the fourth day, the child's condition worsened. Knowing that the doctor was not in the office that day, the parents whisked the child to the emergency room of a nearby hospital, where they were told that hospital policy forbade treating anyone already under a doctor's care without first contacting the doctor. Unable to contact the doctor and thus denied emergency treatment, the parents took their child home, where he died later that day of what turned out to be bronchial pneumonia.

There was a time when hospitals had a legal right to accept for emergency treatment only those whom they chose to accept. In this case, then, the hospital was exercising its legal right. But was it *morally justified* in exercising the right, inasmuch as by doing so it in effect denied the child lifesaving care? Although moralists might differ in their replies, all would agree that the issue cannot be satisfactorily resolved solely by appeal to law. So even if the hospital did act legally, it didn't necessarily act morally. (As it happened, the case went to court

4. Wilmington General Hospital *v.* Manlove, *54 Delaware 15, 174A 2nd 135, 1961.*

and set a precedent of repudiation of the traditional discretionary powers given a hospital in operating its emergency facility. But even if the court had upheld the institution's right, profound moral questions of injury and fairness would still remain.)

What about the second proposition—that what is not expressly prohibited by law is always moral? Let's suppose that you're driving to work one day and see an accident victim on the side of the road, blood oozing from his leg. He is clearly in need of immediate medical attention, which you can provide since you just completed a course in first aid. *Should* you stop? (Notice that the question is *should*, not *would*, you stop.)

Legally speaking, you have no obligation to stop and offer aid. In fact, under common law, the prudent thing would be to drive on, since by stopping you implicitly would assume a duty to the victim to use reasonable care and thus would incur legal liability if you didn't and the victim suffered injury as a result. Even in states where so-called Good Samaritan laws have been enacted to provide immunity from damages to those rendering emergency aid (except for gross negligence or serious misconduct), one is not obliged to render such aid. And yet all moralists would agree that, regardless of the law, such self-defensive behavior raises serious moral questions of beneficence, non-injury, and justice. In short, if you sped away without rendering aid, your behavior would be morally suspect, although perfectly legal.

Let's consider still another example in health care that points up the distinction between morality and legality. Health-care providers are not legally prohibited from charging whatever they choose, from using drugs to make the institutionalized elderly and mentally ill more submissive, from denying powerful drugs on request to the gravely ill who are in excruciating pain. Surely, given the violations of autonomy and also the financial, physical, and mental injury that such practices involve, their moral propriety is debatable. But to argue that the absence of legal prohibitions makes these practices morally permissible has the effect of stifling the moral scrutiny they require.

What are we to say, then, of the relationship between law and morality? In theory and practice, law functions to codify customs, ideals, beliefs, *and* the moral values of a society. Therefore, law undoubtedly reflects changes in a society's way of thinking, in what it views as right or wrong at a particular time. But it's a mistake to look at the law as sufficiently establishing an individual's, profession's, or society's standards of morality. The law simply cannot cover the wide range of conduct that any individual or group exhibits. True, the law prohibits the most outrageous violations of what a society considers ethical standards. But what about the countless cases that do not involve a wanton breach of these standards?

For these reasons, law alone, although useful in alerting us to moral issues and informing us of our rights and responsibilities, cannot be taken as an adequate standard of moral conduct. Conformity with the law is neither requisite nor sufficient for determining moral behavior, any more than conformity to rules of etiquette is. By the same token, nonconformity with law is not necessarily immoral, for the law disobeyed may be unjust.

In ethics, then, we are concerned with questions of right and wrong, duty and obligation, and moral responsibility. When ethicists use words like *good* or *right* to describe a person or action, they generally mean that the person or action conforms with some moral standard. A good person or action has desirable qualities. Ethicists often disagree about the nature of these qualities and follow different paths in hopes of discovering them. For purposes of understanding, though, we can view ethics as divided into two fields: normative ethics and nonnormative ethics.

Normative Ethics

Normative ethics involves an attempt to determine what moral standards, that is, norms, to follow so that our actions may be morally right or good. There are two normative areas: applied and general. *Applied normative ethics is the attempt to explain and justify positions on specific moral problems,* such as sex outside marriage, capital punishment, euthanasia, reverse discrimination, and so on. This area of normative ethics is termed *applied* because the ethicist applies or uses the general ethical principles in an attempt to resolve the specific moral problems.

For example, in defending civil disobedience Martin Luther King applied the principles of justice and equality. When such general principles are arranged into an ethical theory, the second field of normative ethics, called general normative ethics, is involved.

General normative ethics is the reasoned search for principles of conduct, including a critical study of the major theories about what things are good, what acts are right, and what acts are blameworthy. It attempts to determine precisely what moral standards to follow so that our actions may be morally right or good. For most of us, ethical action springs from some standard: "Do unto others as you would have them do unto you"; "Act in such a way that you bring about the greatest good for the greatest number"; "Always act in your own best interests." What principle ought we to adopt? That is partially what general normative ethics tries to discover. It tries to formulate and defend a system of basic ethical principles that presumably are valid for everyone.

Nonnormative Ethics

Like normative ethics, nonnormative ethics consists of two fields: scientific and metaethical.

SCIENTIFIC OR DESCRIPTIVE.   *The scientific or descriptive study of morality involves factual investigation of moral behavior.* It is concerned with how people do in fact behave. This approach is used widely in the social sciences. For example, anthropologists and sociologists report on how moral attitudes and codes differ from society to society, investigating and describing the values and behaviors of different cultures. Anthropologists tell us that Eskimos used to abandon their elderly on the ice to die of starvation and exposure and that some African tribes kill infant twins and require that a man marry his brother's widow. The fact that societies often differ markedly in their values and conceptions of right and wrong has led many to advance a doctrine called ethical relativism.

In order to understand ethical relativism, one must first be familiar with ethical absolutism. *Ethical absolutism is the doctrine that there exists one and only one moral code.* Absolutists maintain that this code applies to everyone, at all times, everywhere. What is a moral duty for me must also be a moral duty for you. What is a moral duty for an American must also be a moral duty for an Asian, African, European, and aborigine. If euthanasia is wrong, it is wrong for everyone, at all times, everywhere. The fact that a society may see nothing wrong with euthanasia or lying or cannibalism in no way affects the rightness or wrongness of such actions. Ethical absolutists do not necessarily claim that their interpretation of the absolute standard is the true and valid one. But they do insist that there is a true moral code and that this code is the same for all people in all ages.

Ethical relativism is the doctrine that denies that there is a single moral standard that is universally applicable to all people at all times. Relativists deny that there exists only one moral code, law, principle, or standard. They insist that there are many moral codes that take root in diverse social soils. As the name implies, ethical relativists insist that any morality is relative to the time, place, and circumstances in which it occurs.

Ethical relativism is not the same as cultural relativism. Cultural relativism is a sociological fact: Research indicates the existence of many obviously different and often contradictory moral codes. Ethical relativists are not merely saying that what is thought right in one part of the world is frequently thought wrong in another. Scientific or descriptive ethics has established this fact, which even absolutists accept. Rather, ethical relativists assert that precisely the same action that is right in one society at one time can be wrong in another. Thus, putting to death anyone over eighty years old can be right in the jungles of New Guinea and wrong in the United States. Such a claim is quite different from saying that putting octogenarians to death is *thought* to be right in one place and *thought* to be wrong in another. In short, ethical relativists believe that what is *thought* right *is* right.

We won't take the time here to criticize these positions. Whether we go along with absolutism or with relativism, we still must decide what we ought to do individually and collectively. Presumably this requires some standard on which we base the decisions. So whether I am an absolutist or a relativist, the questions remain: How ought I behave and how ought my society behave?

METAETHICS.   The second field of nonnormative ethics is called metaethics. *Metaethics is the highly technical discipline investigating the meaning of ethical terms, including a critical study of how ethical statements can be verified.* Largely the province of philosophers, metaethics is concerned with the meanings of such important ethical terms as *right, obligation,* and *responsibility.* Metaethicists would be more concerned with the meanings of the words *good* and *bad* than with what we think is good and bad. If you maintained, for example, that Martin Luther King's behavior was right, the metaethicist might ask: Just what do you mean by "right"?

Metaethical positions are generally divided into what are sometimes called naturalism, nonnaturalism, and noncognitivism. *Naturalism maintains that ethical statements can be translated into nonethical statements.* One naturalistic position—autobiographical naturalism—contends that an ethical statement simply expresses the approval or disapproval of the speaker. For example, when you say that "King was right," you mean "I approve of King's action." Another naturalistic position—

sociological naturalism—contends that an ethical statement simply expresses the approval or disapproval of the majority. For example, "King was right" means "The majority approves of King's action." Still another naturalistic position—theological naturalism—holds that an ethical statement expresses divine approval or disapproval. In that case, "King was right" in effect means that "God (or some equivalent reference) approves of King's action."

Nonnaturalism, in contrast to naturalism, *is the position that an ethical statement defies translation into a nonethical form.* Nonnaturalists insist that at least some ethical words can be defined only in terms of other ethical words. They might argue that the statement "King was right" can only be translated into other ethical statements, such as "King's action was proper," or "King's action should have been performed," or "King's action was good." They claim that using naturalistic translations would be like trying to define *hour* in other than temporal terms, or *inch* in other than spatial terms. It just cannot be done. Clearly, then, nonnaturalists come close to asserting that ethical statements cannot be verified, that they cannot be determined true or false. How then does the nonnaturalist handle ethical statements? One of the foremost nonnaturalists, G. E. Moore, advises that we reflect on them and determine, as well as we can, whether we believe the statements are ture. As Moore puts it:

> There is no empirical observation and no mathematical or logical calculation which would enable us to discover the truth of ethical propositions. All we can do is to distinguish them carefully from all other propositions (especially some empirical ones with which they are apt to be confused), and then reflect upon them and see whether, after this reflection, we believe that they are true.[5]

In addition to naturalism and nonnaturalism there is a position sometimes called emotivism or noncognitivism. *Emotivism or noncognitivism can be broadly defined as a metaethical position which claims that ethical statements are used to evoke a predetermined response or to encourage a predetermined behavior.* In this view, then, ethical statements can be used, indeed are used, to make someone feel or behave in a certain way. For example, if a teacher says to a student, "Cheating is wrong," the teacher may not be expressing a moral position on cheating but is rather trying to instill in the student a certain attitude toward cheating. The teacher may also be trying to elicit a certain behavior. Ethical statements would therefore amount to commands such as "Don't cheat"; "Don't lie"; "Don't break promises." The essential difference between an autobiographical naturalist and a noncognitivist is that the former believes that ethical statements are subjective and verifiable, while the latter believes that they are subjective but not verifiable.

Focus on Normative

As the title of this text indicates, our emphasis is on applied ethics. The chapters raise issues of contemporary moral importance: pornography, abortion, euthanasia, capital punishment, reverse discrimination, world hunger and economic justice, and war. But the book also introduces basic or theoretical ethics (Chapters 2 and 3).

5.   *G. E. Moore,* Principia Ethica *(London: Cambridge University Press, 1903).*

There are several reasons for the focus on normative ethics, applied and theoretical. First, most of us approach ethics normatively. In our personal and social lives, we want to determine for ourselves some principles and standards of moral behavior. Although language analysis helps clarify meaning, at some point each of us must investigate normative ethics to determine our principles and standards.

Second, urgent moral issues face us today. These issues cry for resolution that must spring from serious, informed, and extensive debate. In recent years ethicists have indeed recognized the urgency of these issues by rekindling their traditional interest in normative ethics.

The third reason for concentrating on normative ethics rests on the fact that almost daily we make moral judgments—assessments of right and wrong, good and bad. These judgments inevitably are based on moral standards—that is, normative theories. If we are interested in giving reasons for a moral judgment, we must at some point appeal to and defend the moral standard on which it is based. This third point will become clearer when we discuss the processes by which moral standards are linked to moral judgments. But first let's see how our ability to employ these standards develops.

Moral Development

Just as individuals develop physically, they also develop morally. We are no more born with an ability to understand and apply moral standards than we are with an ability to ride a bicycle. Just as there are stages in physical development, so our ability to make reasoned moral judgments also develops step by step.

Think back to your childhood, to occasions of moral choice: the choice between lying and truth telling, for example, or between being honest or dishonest. Why, as a child, did you tell the truth on some occasions rather than lie? Why did you return something you found to its proper owner rather than keep it? Probably because you were told by your parents or by someone in authority that telling the truth and being honest were the right things to do, and lying or being dishonest were the wrong things. What's more, if you were caught lying or being dishonest, you probably would be punished—scolded, spanked, sent to bed without dinner, denied a privilege, and so on. However, if you told the truth or were honest, you likely would be rewarded—hugged, praised, given candy, and so on. Given such clear and decisive messages, you quickly realized that doing what you were told was in your own interest and disobeying wasn't. In short, you obeyed so as to avoid punishment and get reward. You acted out of self-interest.

As you grew into adolescence, these moral instructions probably were gradually internalized: They were no longer imposed from the outside under threat of punishment or promise of reward, and you didn't follow them exclusively out of self-interest. Rather, you began to see the implications of these moral lessons more clearly and followed them in part because they advanced the welfare of people you knew and cared for. At this stage, then, it could be said that your moral standards were based largely on loyalty to family and friends, and possibly even nation. This is not to say that you were no longer self-interested—adolescence, to be sure, is a period of intense self-centeredness. But it is also a time when the sphere of interests widens to include at least those with whom we have special relationships, especially family and peers.

It's only later as a mature adult that any of us is equipped to inspect the moral standards we have inherited and their consequences. We can then broaden our interest base to include not just our immediate circle of friends and relatives but all people. At this point, morality is grounded essentially in universal principles that impartially take into account the interests of everyone.

Some psychologists have identified the stages of moral development more precisely than we just did. The best known of these theories of moral development is the one advanced by psychologist Lawrence Kohlberg.

Kohlberg's Theory

Drawing on twenty years of research, Kohlberg has devised a sequence of six stages in the development of a person's ability to reason about moral matters. Although not all psychologists agree with Kohlberg's theory, most think that moral reasoning does develop more or less in the way that Kohlberg claims. Even if Kohlberg's theory needs some fine tuning, it does help us understand how we may internalize moral standards and how we become more sophisticated and critical in our use and understanding of these standards. Just as important, it helps explain why students often have difficulty "doing ethics"—that is, understanding and participating in the full-blown moral debates that occupy moral philosophers and often nonphilosophers as well. We'll say more about this point after considering Kohlberg's theory.

Kohlberg groups his stages of moral development into three levels, each containing two stages. The second stage is the more advanced form of the general orientation of each level. What follows is a summary of the six stages.[6]

LEVEL ONE: PRECONVENTIONAL STAGES. By the "preconventional stages" Kohlberg means the levels of moral development that are characterized by unquestioning obedience and the gratification of one's own needs. This is the level the child typically operates on. The child can respond to rules and social expectations and can apply moral labels—"good," "bad," "right," "wrong"—but sees them as imposed from the outside. Thus the child views right and wrong in terms of pleasant or painful consequences of actions, or in terms of the physical power of those who set the rules. Seeing situations solely from his or her own viewpoint and still lacking the ability to identify with others to any meaningful degree, the child's primary motivation is self-interest.

Stage One: Punishment and Obedience Orientation—At this stage of the first level, the physical consequences of an act wholly determine for the child the act's goodness or badness. The operative rule here might be stated as: "Do the 'right'

---

6. *Lawrence Kohlberg, "Moral Stages and Moralization: The Cognitive-Developmental Approach," in* Moral Development and Behavior: Theory, Research, and Social Issues, *ed. Thomas Lickona (New York: Holt, Rinehart & Winston, 1976), pp. 31–53. This account is based on the lucid summary presented by Manuel G. Velasquez,* Business Ethics: Concepts and Cases, *pp. 21–23.*

thing and defer to the superior physical power of authorities in order to avoid punishment." At this stage, there is little if any awareness that others have needs and desires similar to the child's own.

Stage Two: Instrument and Relativity Orientation—At this stage, the child generally regards as right whatever satisfies his or her own needs, or the needs of those the child cares about. This stage differs from the first in that the child is aware that others have needs and desires similar to his or her own. But still, the child defers to the needs and desires of others out of self-interest. Thus the operative rule for this stage might be: "Respect the needs and desires of others in order to get what you want."

LEVEL TWO: CONVENTIONAL STAGES.   By "conventional stages" Kohlberg means those levels of moral development at which individuals recognize that meeting the expectations of one's own family, peer group, or nation is valuable in its own right, regardless of the consequences to oneself. The individual not only conforms to expectations but exhibits loyalty to the group and its norms. He or she recognizes that others are similar to him or her and is motivated to conform to the group's norms even if it means subordinating his or her own needs.

Stage Three: Interpersonal Concordance Orientation—At this stage of Level Two, right conduct is viewed as what pleases and helps others and elicits social approval. Looked at this way, right action is conformity to what is generally expected of a "good" daughter or son, sister or brother, friend, employee, and so on. Kohlberg's example of Stage Three morality is Charlie Brown of *Peanuts.* The following rule seems to apply in Stage Three: "Do the right thing in order to be a 'good person' in the eyes of others, and thus in your own eyes."

Stage Four: Law and Order Orientation—At this stage, the sphere of interests broadens to include one's own nation. The individual is still authority-oriented but recognizes a personal stake in the maintenance of law and order. He or she is better able to see other people as parts of a larger social system that defines individual roles and obligations. He or she can separate the norms generated by the system from those generated by his or her interpersonal relationships and motives. So Stage Four morality is characterized by duty to society and respect for law, which is not yet perceived as a social contract open to change but as being fixed and immutable. Thus, racism may be wrong, but one shouldn't break the law to protest it, for that invites social chaos. The operative rule for Stage Four morality could be stated as: "Be dutiful to society's norms and respect the law in order to preserve social harmony."

LEVEL THREE: POSTCONVENTIONAL STAGES.   By "postconventional stages" Kohlberg means autonomous or principled stages. This level represents higher values and the questioning of the existing legal system in light of social utility and abstract principles, such as justice and human dignity. On this level, the person no longer blindly accepts the values and norms of the group but tries to see situations from a viewpoint that impartially takes everyone's interests into account. The person questions authorities and the laws and values of society, perhaps even redefining them in terms of self-chosen universal moral principles that seemingly can be justified to any rational individual, whatever the person's role in society.

Stage Five: Social Contract Orientation—At this stage, the individual recognizes an implicit agreement existing between individual and society—a social contract, whereby the state acquires its legitimacy through the consent of the governed. This social contract orientation is characterized by a recognition of the value of constitutional rights and legal procedures. Although the person implicitly recognized a social contract at Stage Four, at this stage he or she acknowledges possible change of the social contract based on social utility. In Kohlberg's view, this stage represents the "official morality" of the U.S. government and is expressed in the U.S. Constitution. Accordingly, breaking a law to protest racial inequality would be right if it helped change an unjust law. Kohlberg believes that some, but hardly a majority of, individuals reach this stage.

It's very difficult, perhaps impossible, to formulate an operative rule for Stage Five because the individual really is attempting to draw a line of demarcation between individual and society, a point we'll say considerably more about in Chapter 2, where we discuss ethics and society. The individual recognizes that this line is not fixed and immutable, but dynamic—always in need of redrawing, based on common agreement and due process.

Stage Six: Universal Ethical Principles Orientation—The final stage of Kohlberg's theory of moral development includes the formulation of abstract moral principles. Right action is defined in terms of these principles, chosen because of their logical comprehensiveness, their universality, and their consistency. These ethical principles are not concrete propositions, such as those found in the Ten Commandments or in civil statutes, but abstract universal principles dealing with justice, reciprocity, equality, and respect for all persons. At this stage, the person acts a certain way because that action conforms with moral principles that he or she views as legitimate criteria for evaluating all other moral rules and arrangements.

Kohlberg terms these six stages (which are summarized in Table 1-1) *sequential*—people do not enter a later stage until they have passed through each of the earlier ones. But there's no guarantee that a person will ever reach the later stages. In fact, Kohlberg believes much of the American population remains at Stages Three and Four.

If he's right, it's little wonder that many of us don't fully understand, let alone can intelligently participate in, the great moral debates that fly around issues such as abortion, capital punishment, pornography, affirmative action, world hunger, and nuclear war. Tackling these issues ultimately calls for a high level of abstract, moral thought, which Stages Three and Four, not to mention One and Two, do not require. It's no less surprising that many students taking introductory ethics are puzzled by the level of abstraction in which issues are framed. Fixated at Stages Three or Four, and not even recognizing the possibility of further stages of moral development, they can view the study of ethics and the debates about prominent moral issues as so much "blooming, buzzing confusion," to quote the American philosopher William James. And they can misinterpret the searching analyses of moral philosophers as idle philosophic curiosity, when in fact they represent, by Kohlberg's account, the highest stages of moral reasoning.

Table 1-1   Kohlberg's Stages of Moral Development

Stage	1	2	3	4	5	6
Universal Ethical Principles						Commitment to principles such as justice and human dignity
Social Contract					Recognition of possibility of change in social contract	
Law and Order				Loyalty to nation		
Interpersonal Concordance			Conformity to social expectations			
Instrument and Relativity		Satisfaction of own needs by deferring to others				
Punishment and Obedience	Physical consequences					

The fact is that one of the purposes of studying ethics, perhaps the main one, is to develop your ability to reason about moral issues. Studying ethics should help you acquire the more critical understanding of "right" and wrong" that defines Kohlberg's later, autonomous stages of moral development, Five and especially Six. One of the central aims of studying ethics, therefore, is to help you move beyond simple and often blind acceptance of the moral standards you have inherited from family, peers, profession, nation, and culture. Contrary to popular misconception, the study of ethics is *not* intended to get you to abandon or necessarily even to modify those standards but to enable you to examine them critically and, in the end, to determine for yourself a set of moral principles to which you can rationally assent. By discussing, analyzing, and criticizing your moral judgments and those of others, you can acquire the intellectual skills needed to develop a rational set of moral principles. We can get a better idea of these processes by inspecting the patterns of moral reasoning.

Patterns of Moral Reasoning

Although you are unlikely to find among ethicists a consensus on many issues of morality, you will find patterns of moral reasoning. An awareness of these patterns will help you understand what is involved in presenting or criti-

cizing a moral position and also how to begin formulating your own moral positions. Furthermore, you will be better able to understand the reading selections
provided at the end of each chapter.

To begin, it is useful to view patterns of moral reasoning in the context of
argument. An argument is a group of statements one of which—the conclusion—
is said to follow from the others—the premises. Here is a simple example of an
argument:

> If a person is a mother, the person is a female.
>
> Fran is a mother.
>
> Therefore, Fran is a female.

Notice that the first two statements, the premises, entail the last statement,
the conclusion. In other words, given the first two premises, the conclusion must
logically follow.

Regarding civil disobedience, consider these arguments:

> If an action violates the law, it is wrong.
>
> Civil disobedience violates the law.
>
> So civil disobedience is wrong.

> If an action violates the will of the majority, the action is wrong.
>
> Civil disobedience violates the will of the majority.
>
> Therefore, civil disobedience is wrong.

> If an action is an expression of one's commitment to a higher law, the action
> is moral.
>
> Civil disobedience can be an expression of one's commitment to a higher law.
>
> Thus, civil disobedience can be moral.

> If an action is the only practical alternative in a situation, the action is right.
>
> Civil disobedience may be the only practical alternative in a situation.
>
> Therefore, civil disobedience may be right.

These represent a wide range of arguments in opposition to or defense of
civil disobedience. Notice that each of these contains a particular moral judgment. *A particular moral judgment is a claim about what should be done or what was
done by a specific person or group of people in a specific historical situation.* For example,
"King's action was good"; "King's action was bad"; "King was right"; and "King
was wrong" are all particular moral judgments. Other examples of particular
moral judgments are: "The government should allow voluntary euthanasia";

"Abortion on demand ought not be legalized"; "It's right to help feed the world's starving masses." Certain moral words appear in particular moral judgments: *good, bad, right, wrong, should, should not*, and so forth. Although not all judgments using such words are moral judgments (for example, "King was a good speaker"; "Judging from the polls, the President should win the upcoming election"), these words frequently do indicate the presence of particular moral judgments. So do the words *duty, responsibility,* and *obligation.*

Even when moral words are absent, a particular moral judgment may be implied. For example, if the speaker was clearly suggesting moral disapproval in the statement "King broke the law!" that statement would be expressing a particular moral judgment, as well as a factual judgment. So the context of a statement, its physical and rhetorical surroundings, is important to consider in determining the presence of a particular moral judgment.

In contrast with particular moral judgments are general moral principles. *General moral principles are claims about what should be done in every case of a certain sort or by everyone in a certain sort of situation.* The first premise in each of the preceding civil disobedience arguments, the "if" premise, may be considered a general moral principle. Sometimes general moral principles are more global in scope. For example, "One should always treat people as one would want to be treated"; "One should always try to produce the greatest amount of happiness for the greatest number of people."

This distinction between particular moral judgments and general moral principles engenders a feature of defensible moral views that relates directly to our discussion of the patterns of moral reasoning. This feature is: If a particular moral judgment is defensible, then it must be supportable by a defensible general moral principle, usually together with additional facts.[7] *A general moral principle supports a particular moral judgment if the principle, together with facts, logically entails the particular moral judgment.* If someone argues that abortion on demand is wrong but cannot produce a supporting principle when asked, then that person's position is considerably weakened. And if the person does not see any need to support the judgment by appeal to a general principle, then we must conclude that the person simply does not understand how moral concepts are used or is using moral words such as *wrong* in a way much different from their common meaning.

Keeping this feature in mind—that if a particular moral judgment is defensible, then it must be supportable by a defensible general moral principle—will enormously aid your understanding of moral discourse, which can be highly complex and sophisticated. It will also sharpen your own critical faculties and improve your ability to formulate relevant moral arguments. The importance of this feature lies in the fact that much of what occurs in moral debates can be interpreted in the light of the feature itself.

For example, in all the preceding arguments about civil disobedience someone is trying to defend the morality or immorality of civil disobedience by appeal

7.   See: Stephen P. Stitch, "The Recombinant DNA Debate: Some Philosophical Considerations" in The Recombinant DNA Debate, eds. David A. Jackson and Stephen P. Stitch (Englewood Cliffs, N.J.: Prentice-Hall, 1979), p. 184.

to a general moral principle and some fact. Once the principle and facts are disclosed, discussion may focus on a number of points. If all parties are willing to grant the general moral principle, then they will concentrate on the factual claims. However, someone may object to the general moral principle; in that case whoever advanced the argument must defend the principle. Usually this defense can be conducted by appeal to an even more general principle, together with more facts, that buttresses the principle under attack.

Sometimes the proponent of the principle will try to show how the principle entails other particular moral judgments that the opponent accepts. For example, in the following dialogue, Wayne is questioning the moral principle "If an action violates the will of the majority, then the action is wrong." Jami is defending the principle.

Jami:	Okay, do you think the government should impose a national religion on all Americans?
Wayne:	If it tried to, I'd be the first to fight it.
Jami:	All right. How do you feel about legalizing pot?
Wayne:	I'm against it.
Jami:	And using kids in pornography?
Wayne:	There are and there should be laws against it.
Jami:	But the principle that you're objecting to leads to these judgments you agree with.

Of course Jami's argument is by no means a conclusive defense for the general moral principle under discussion. After all, other moral principles could just as easily entail the judgments agreed upon. Wayne points this out.

Wayne:	Now wait a minute. I oppose a state religion because it's unconstitutional, not because it violates the will of the majority. As for grass, I'm against legalizing it because we don't know enough about it yet. And using kids in pornography is wrong because it involves sexual exploitation and exposes kids to a lot of dangers.

Notice that, although Jami's strategy for defending the principle about majority rule proved inconclusive, it did serve to shift the burden of argument to Wayne. It forced him to counter with alternative principles that at least equally well supported the particular moral judgments raised.

In attacking a moral principle a common strategy is first to isolate particular moral judgments that the advocate of the principle rejects and then to demonstrate how the principle plus additional facts actually entail those unacceptable judgments. In the following dialogue, for example, Jami is attacking Wayne's advocacy of the principle "If an action is an expression of one's commitment to a higher law, then the action is moral."

Jami: What do you think of parents who for religious reasons won't allow their children to have necessary medical care?

Wayne: I've heard about that. In fact, there was a couple on our block who wouldn't let their kid have a blood transfusion when she needed it.

Jami: You think that's right?

Wayne: Of course not.

Jami: But they were obeying a "higher law," weren't they? I mean, they were probably acting on some religious conviction or on grounds of conscience.

Wayne: Maybe they were, but so what?

Jami: Well, the principle you're defending leads to a judgment you reject. How do you account for that?

At this point, Wayne, or anyone in a similar position, presumably has two alternatives: abandon the principle he is defending or change his view about the judgment. Either Wayne must abandon his view that any action that is an expression of one's commitment to a higher law is moral, or he can decide that parental denial of necessary medical services for children, on grounds of religion or conscience, is in fact right.

Recognizing thus the patterns of moral reasoning in ethical discourse and the need to support judgments with principles greatly aids in formulating and unraveling ethical arguments. Essential to moral argument, then, is justification. *Justification refers to reasons, the evidence that supports the position. Justification also refers to the reasoning process one follows to arrive at the position.* In justifying our moral positions to others, we must demonstrate that our premises (evidence or reasons) are true and that they logically entail the judgment (the position).

The previously mentioned strategies are common ways that people use to try to justify their moral judgments. However, while a knowledge of these strategies is useful in recognizing and understanding the anatomy of moral arguments, the strategies are not altogether satisfactory for dissecting an argument. In order to analyze an argument, we must first make a study of correct argument. Logic is such a study. Logic provides analytical methodology that enables us to detect flaws in the reasoning process. Obviously this text cannot provide complete logical training. But it can help you become familiar with some of the spurious emotional and psychological devices people often use to win us to their views. These devices are called logical fallacies. A simple acquaintance with some of these fallacies will help you detect any glaring deficiencies in moral arguments.

Fallacies

In the broadest sense, *a fallacy is an incorrect way of reasoning. More narrowly, a fallacy is any attempt to persuade emotionally or psychologically, but not logically.* In moral discourse, and nonmoral for that matter, fallacies are commonplace errors in reasoning that people fall into because of (1) careless use of language, which introduces ambiguity into argument and (2) inattention to subject matter, as a result of which the irrelevant or presumptuous is introduced.

The specific ways that people use language carelessly and disregard subject matter are far too numerous to exhaust here. But we can cover the most common of these fallacies, a knowledge of which will help you spot and avoid erroneous moral reasoning. More specifically, it will help you critically appraise the arguments and counterarguments that appear later in this book in connection with specific issues.

To illustrate some of these fallacies, let us fictionalize a civil disobedience case not too different from the one that involved Martin Luther King. This case concerns the highly controversial subject of forced busing. Some believe that in order to racially integrate and balance school enrollments, children should be bused to schools outside their neighborhoods. Others say that this is illegal as well as immoral.

In our fictitious case, Maria Josephson supports forced busing. So much does she favor it that, like King, she is organizing and planning to lead a demonstration in the heart of a major U.S. city without first obtaining a license to demonstrate. She hopes that by being arrested she and other demonstrators will dramatize to the country the injustice of racially imbalanced schools and the moral obligation to remedy that imbalance through forced busing. City officials are trying to dissuade Josephson from her proposed course. Charged with this responsibility is the city chief of police, Robert Dillon.

Ambiguity

When we're careless in our use of language, ambiguity often results. *The fallacy of ambiguity occurs when we use a word or phrase in such a way that its meaning is not clear or can be taken in more than one way.* Illustrative is the following conversation that occurs when Dillon visits Josephson in hopes of preventing the demonstration.

Dillon:	I can't impress on you enough, Ms. Josephson, that what you're about to do is wrong.
Josephson:	I disagree with you. Not only is it right, but it is absolutely obligatory.
Dillon:	You realize what will happen to you, don't you?
Josephson:	Of course I do. That doesn't frighten me. I've got right on my side.
Dillon:	And I've got the law on mine.
Josephson:	I disagree. If you really understood it, you would see that the law is on my side.

Unless Josephson and the chief quickly start defining their terms, their conversation will rapidly founder for lack of clarity. Terms like *wrong, right,* and *law* all need definition before Dillon and Josephson can hope to reach any accord.

Take just one word, *law*. Clearly, by *law* Dillon means statutes, human-made prescriptions for behavior. Josephson may mean the U.S. Constitution, or she may be appealing to some higher law, perhaps what she considers a principle of human rights, perhaps even some kind of divine prescription. It is hard to say. But they seem to be coming from different directions on this one point alone. In short, ambiguity *is* present.

Take, as another example, Dillon's assertion "What you're about to do is wrong." Probably by *wrong* Dillon means "against the law." On the other hand, Josephson understands wrong in a moral context. Undoubtedly she would agree that she is breaking the law, but she would contend that she is not doing "wrong"— that is, something immoral. But even used in a moral sense, a word like *wrong* is still ambiguous.

Consider the possible meanings that *wrong* could have in the statement "Civil disobedience is wrong." It may mean that the speaker disapproves of civil diso- bedience. It may mean that society disapproves of civil disobedience, or possibly it could mean that God, speaking through some book like the Bible or the Koran, disapproves of civil disobedience.

So in evaluating ethical arguments, it is important to try to determine what people mean by their ethical terms. Of course, it is just as important to define other terms that may appear in ethical discourse. If someone argues that abortion is wrong because it is the willful taking of an innocent human life, it is essential to define *innocent* and *human life* before attempting to evaluate that argument. This may seem like a tedious task, but in the long run it is the only way to avoid the fallacy of ambiguity.

Genetic Fallacy

There are several fallacies that can be called abusive because they attack something associated with the arguer rather than the argument itself. One of these abusive appeals is called the *genetic fallacy, which consists of attempting to discredit a position by condemning its source (genesis) or to estabish a position by con- demning the source of an opposed viewpoint.* How or where an idea originates, or who holds it, is irrelevant to an idea's worth. It's always fallacious to object to or reject a conclusion because of its source.

For example, suppose someone argues against a national health insurance program on the grounds that such a program "smacks of socialism." Perhaps guaranteeing all people access to medical care despite their inability to pay may be decidedly socialistic. But that in itself doesn't prove that the United States should not have such a program.

Suppose someone argues for gun control because the opposition is headed by the National Rifle Association (NRA). True enough, the NRA has a vested interest in opposing gun control law. But that's irrelevant to whether there should be such a law. Of course, it would be wise to withhold judgment pending further consideration of the facts as presented by a more objective body, but it would be fallacious to reject the anti-gun control position simply because the NRA drafted it or to endorse gun control for the same reason.

Ad Hominem

Ad hominem is Latin for "to the man." *The fallacy of ad hominem consists in attacking the person rather than the person's argument.* There are two ways that people argue ad hominem: abusively and circumstantially.

ABUSIVE.   The abusive ad hominem consists in a slur on the person's character—in short, character assassination. Like the genetic fallacy, the abusive ad hominem attacks the source of origin. But in addition, it heaps abuse on the source.

Josephson: People like you lack any moral sense. You're fascistic. It's not so much that you're bent on enforcing the law as perpetuating racism.

Josephson seeks to discredit Dillon with allegations of Nazi tendencies and ulterior motives to discredit the anti-demonstration position. Whether either charge is justified is irrelevant to the rightness or wrongness of the demonstration. Even if Dillon is a racist, that would suggest only that he's racially motivated, not that his anti-demonstration stand is without merit and that Josephson is thereby correct.

Regarding a proposal to halt the construction of nuclear power plants, an energy expert says: "The people behind this proposal are wild-eyed environmentalists and fanatics." The expert condemns the source of the position and heaps abuse on it as well. The charges are irrelevant to the issue and thus fallacious if they're intended or taken as grounds for concluding that the construction of nuclear power plants should not be halted.

Abusive ad hominems frequently crop up in moral discourse when the issues are emotionally charged. When one cares passionately about a cause, it's tempting to cast reason aside and name-call. Thus: "Those opposed to capital punishment are no more than bleeding-heart liberals who have no respect for the rights of victims"; "Those in favor of capital punishment are law-and-order fanatics bent on revenge, not justice." "Abortion on demand is proposed by those with no respect for the sanctity of life"; "People who want to outlaw abortion on demand are sexists who seek to deny women control over their own bodies." "Anyone in favor of disarmament is a communist dupe"; "Anyone opposing disarmament is a warmonger."

It's important to remember that not every argument that takes into account the character or motives of the disputants is fallacious. Personal considerations are certainly relevant in deciding a person's reliability and willingness to tell the whole truth. If people have proved unreliable, that is surely a basis for doubting what they say. But *suspecting* their words is different from *rejecting* them. Weighing the reliability of a witness differs from assuming that there is something about the witness that automatically discredits what the person says. Not accepting is *not* the same as rejecting.

CIRCUMSTANTIAL.   The circumstantial ad hominem consists of urging someone to accept or reject a particular position because of his or her special circumstances or self-interest. For example, Dillon tells Josephson: "I really don't see how you can favor forced busing when you have children who could be affected by such a policy." Dillon gives no consideration to the worth of the policy, but would have Josephson oppose forced busing strictly out of self-interest.

Another example of the circumstantial ad hominem: As a panelist discussing marriage, a Roman Catholic priest argues, for various reasons, that divorce is morally objectionable. Another panelist says to the priest: "Frankly, Father, I don't understand how you can speak so authoritatively on marriage. You are, needless to say, a celibate." Rather than address the priest's reasons for objecting to divorce, the panelist attacks an aspect of the priest's life, celibacy. But a celibate can have credible views on the social and spiritual impacts of divorce.

Invincible Ignorance

Perhaps you have heard someone argue, "I don't care what the President has done, he is still the President and therefore should not be impeached," or "No matter what medical authorities say, no one can convince me that cigarette smoking causes lung cancer." Such arguments rely on invincible ignorance. *Invincible ignorance is the fallacy of insisting on the legitimacy of an idea or principle despite contradictory facts.* The attitude of invincible ignorance is captured in the statement: "Don't confuse me with facts. My mind is already made up." The phrase "I don't care what you say" is a dead giveaway of invincible ignorance.

Moral arguments frequently rely on invincible ignorance. For example: "I don't care what you say, lying is always wrong"; "It doesn't matter what anyone thinks, abortion isn't right"; "I admit that there are more good reasons to remain sexually faithful than not. But I always do what I feel like"; "I don't care how many reasons there are for (or against) forced busing, you'll never convince me it's right (or wrong)."

Questionable Claim

Dillon: You're really convinced that what you're doing is right, aren't you?

Josephson: If I weren't, I wouldn't be here.

Dillon: Well, tell me—how can you be so sure?

Josephson: Because racial injustice is wrong, and forced busing is the only way to correct it.

Dillon: The *only* way?

Josephson: That's right.

Dillon: I doubt that.

Dillon doubts that forced busing is the *only* way to right racial injustice. He probably thinks that Josephson has overstated her case. Frequently people make claims so expansive that they lose credibility. Consider these two advertising claims, for example: "Dial is the most effective deodorant soap you can buy" and "Zest makes you feel cleaner than soap." Each of these statements involves the fallacy of questionable claim. *A questionable claim is one that cannot stand up under investigation because of the breadth of its assertion.* In other words, an argument posited on questionable claim founders for lack of demonstrative evidence. Words like *most* and *best* and other superlatives often signal questionable-claim fallacies.

In the moral sphere, people frequently rely on unquestioned assumptions as the foundations of their ethical codes. Thus: "What I believe is right *is* right"; "Whatever the Bible forbids is necessarily wicked"; "Whatever is good for society is always the right thing to do." Obviously these assumptions are morally controversial and need thoughtful examination before acceptance. Without justification, they are questionable claims.

Inconsistency

The fallacy of inconsistency occurs when we contradict ourselves in word or action without justification for the change of mind. An example of the inconsistency fallacy occurred during the 1976 presidential primaries. President Ford claimed that Ronald Reagan was too conservative to be president of the United States. Asked afterwards whether he could conceive of Reagan running on the Republican ticket as a vice-presidential candidate, Ford refused to rule out the possibility. How Reagan could be too conservative to be president and yet be put within a heartbeat of the presidency needed justification. Ford was being inconsistent.

In the moral sphere, parents frequently tell children it is wrong to lie or cheat, and yet they themselves turn around and do precisely that. More seriously, some people seem to act inconsistently when they contend that they believe in the golden rule (doing unto others as you would have them do unto you) while actually operating in their own best interests.

One ethicist, whom we will meet later, so highly regarded logical consistency that he established his ethical code using it as the main principle. Of course, there is no virtue in being consistent for consistency's sake. In the words of Ralph Waldo Emerson, "A foolish consistency is the hobgoblin of little minds." Naturally, when we have good and compelling reasons to change our minds, we obviously should. But when the reasons aren't good or aren't expressed or apparent, then inconsistency is present.

Begging the Question

Josephson: I think the demonstration is right because the goal is right.

Dillon: I don't mean to be rude, Ms. Josephson, but how do you know your goal is right?

Josephson: Because it's proper for our society to have racially integrated schools.

Josephson has begged the question. *Begging the question is the fallacy of answering a question with a variation of the very question asked* or *of assuming that the statement to be proved is true to make it look more plausible.* Obviously, the goal of forced busing is racially integrated schools and, ultimately, equal educational opportunity. So when Josephson replies to Dillon, she assumes the very thing he's asking her to prove—namely, that the integration of schools is a worthy social goal.

Consider this exchange as another example of begging the question.

A: How do you know God exists?

B: Because it says so in the Bible.

A: But how do you know the Bible speaks the truth?

B: Because it's the inspired word of God.

Note the circularity in the argument.

In the moral sphere, circular reasoning frequently undermines arguments. For example,

A: Lying in this instance is the right thing to do because it will produce the most good for the most people.

B: But how do you know that what produces the most good for the most people is the right thing to do?

A: Because that contention is consistent with the greatest-happiness principle.

This sounds good until you realize that the greatest-happiness principle is that the moral act is the one that produces the most good for the most people. So what produces the most good for the most people is not only consistent with the greatest-happiness principle, it *is* the principle! Speaker A is guilty of circularity, or begging the question.

Argument from Ignorance

Dillon: The fact is that you cannot prove that the demonstration is right.

Josephson: I'm sure I can't in any way that will satisfy you, because you've already made up your mind. But what if I can't? What does that prove?

Dillon: To me it proves that what you're about to do is wrong.

It is tempting to think that because something cannot be proved, it must not be the case. This is Chief Dillon's erroneous conviction, an argument from ignorance. *The argument from ignorance is the fallacy of insisting that a statement is true until proved false or false until proved true.* Perhaps you have heard someone argue like this: "Until you prove that God exists, he does not"; "Since no convincing evidence was brought against the senator, the senator obviously did not break any law"; "Women have never shown themselves to be as fast sprinters as men, so clearly they are not." All of these are arguments from ignorance.

In ethics, the argument from ignorance is tempting because of the seeming nonempirical character of ethical statements. Thus someone may argue that the doctrine that one should always act in one's own best long-term interests cannot be proved and, therefore, we should reject it. Or, since the doctrine that we have a moral obligation to honor our promises cannot be proved, it is all right to break promises. An even worse argument: Since no moral statement can be empirically verified, then no moral truth exists.

False Appeal to Authority

Dillon:	Besides, people don't want forced busing in this city.
Josephson:	What does that have to do with it?
Dillon:	Everything. It means that the majority of people disagree with you. They don't approve of what you're doing.
Josephson:	But I don't see how the views of the people affect the rightness or wrongness of racial integration.
Dillon:	Because this is a democracy. And in a democracy the will of the majority rules.
Josephson:	But that doesn't make the will of the majority right.
Dillon:	Doesn't it? When an overwhelming number of people are opposed to something, to me that's proof positive that the thing is wrong.

In attempting to justify his position, Dillon appeals to majority opinion, which is a form of authority. *Authority is an alleged expert source outside the agent on whom the agent is resting his or her claim to knowledge.* A simple example: "Cigarette smoking is hazardous to health because the surgeon general says so." In this claim to knowledge, the surgeon general is used as the expert outside the agent making the claim. Here the claim is legitimate, because the authority is indeed an expert in the area and there is general agreement among the experts. When these two criteria are present—expertise and general agreement among experts—you can feel secure in your appeal to authority. But when either is absent, then you have a false appeal to authority.

Suppose, for example, someone is drinking milk because a celebrity has endorsed it. Probably the celebrity is not a nutritionist or in any way qualified to speak about the virtues of milk. So the celebrity is *not* an expert in the field. Moreover, there is disagreement among experts about the value of milk: Milk is not good for everyone. So the claim that you should drink milk because the celebrity endorses it would be a *false appeal to authority.*

The false appeal to authority frequently crops up in ethics. The following appeals are probably false because of disagreement among experts: "Civil disobedience is an evil practice because civil authorities condemn it"; "Killing is wrong because it says so in the Bible"; "Wiretapping is moral because the President approves of it." Often the false appeal to authority appears as a version called *popularity,* or *democracy,* as in the preceding exchange between Dillon and Josephson.

POPULARITY, OR DEMOCRACY.   *The fallacy of popularity, or democracy, is a false appeal to authority that relies on numbers alone to support its claim.* For example: "Fifty million people have seen this film. Shouldn't you?" "This album has already sold 1 million copies. Get yours today!" Because we are so influenced by popular appeals, for some people such appeals may imply conclusions, as in: "The latest polls indicate that most Americans believe that abortion on demand is right." Possibly implied conclusion: "So it must be!" It's this fallacy that Dillon commits. Even if a majority opposed forced busing, that doesn't mean that forced busing is necessarily immoral.

APPEAL TO TRADITIONAL WISDOM.   Occasionally the false appeal to authority takes the form of the appeal to traditional wisdom. *Traditional wisdom is the fallacy of relying exclusively on the past to justify the present.* The phrase "This is how it has always been done" signals the traditional-wisdom appeal. A woman who insists on keeping her maiden name after marrying might be told that she cannot because it has never been done. In expressing his opposition to the Equal Rights Amendment, Senator Sam Ervin relied on traditional wisdom when he said the bill's having lain around Congress for over forty years without having been passed was conclusive proof it should not be passed at all. In the moral sphere, one might argue: "Traditionally in this society, individuals have always had the right to determine the size of their families. So it's immoral for the government to tell them how many children they can have."

In addition to the fallacies we have already mentioned, other fallacies frequently occur.

Provincialism

Provincialism is the fallacy of seeing things exclusively through the eyes of one's own group, organization, or affiliation. For example: "This automobile must be good because it's made in America." The fallacy of provincialism is especially evident in moral doctrines that insist the good act is the one that a particular group of people approves of. Evident in such reasoning is also an appeal to popularity or democracy.

Hasty Conclusion

As its name implies, *the fallacy of hasty conclusion occurs when we make a judgment based on insufficient evidence.* For example: "The last three teachers in the room were males. So all teachers at this college must be males"; "Since only 42 percent of those eligible actually voted, this proves that the majority of voters are apathetic." In ethics, someone may use atypical cases as a basis for a conclusion. For example: "Since it is right to lie if your life is threatened, it is unwise to hold to a rule that considers lying immoral."

Two-Wrongs-Make-a-Right

The fallacy of two-wrongs-make-a-right is the fallacy of defending what is considered wrongdoing by pointing to an instance of similar behavior. Thus if a traffic officer stops you for speeding, your defense might be: "Why stop me? A Jaguar just passed me as if I were standing still." Perhaps it did, but that does not justify your speeding.

Frequently we rely not on a single instance to justify wrongdoing but on a great number of instances. Thus: "Everybody is speeding! I'm just trying to keep up with traffic!" *A person who relies on numbers of instances to justify wrongdoing is guilty of a common-practice appeal.* Here are some examples of the common-practice appeal in moral arguments: "Cheating on your income tax is all right because just about everyone else does it"; "Premarital sex is moral because it has become pretty much an accepted practice"; "Political corruption is not necessarily immoral, for there is such a wide occurrence of it."

Straw Man

The straw-man fallacy consists of presenting a position in an altered version that is easier to attack than the original. An unsuspecting audience can easily infer that the original argument is demolished when the straw man is blown over.

See if you can spot the straw man in this exchange:

Dillon: The fact of the matter, Ms. Josephson, is that all the polls indicate that the majority of Americans, black and white, oppose busing.

Josephson: Since when is "right" determined by a head count?

Dillon: Since we've had a democracy. You know as well as I that in a democracy the people rule. What you're advocating is complete disregard of the people's will. And that's communistic.

The real issue here is forced busing; the straw is communism. It's easier to get Americans to oppose communism than forced busing. And that's the point: In rejecting communism, the audience is likely to reject forced busing. Maybe forced busing should be rejected, but not because it's "communistic." Even if communistic countries typically ignore or don't solicit the views of their people on public issues, that doesn't mean any policy that runs counter to majority opinion is thereby communistic or shares communism's motives.

Not all straw men are so obvious, however. For example, we will later see that a common argument against capital punishment is that it's racist. Proportionately more nonwhites are sentenced to death than whites. Therefore, the argument goes, capital punishment is immoral and shouldn't be legalized.

Although this argument is seductive, the race issue seems a straw man. It doesn't address the issue of whether capital punishment is moral and should be legalized. Rather, it addresses the fairness of administering capital punishment, which, although a question of utmost moral concern, is irrelevant to the issue being argued. Of course, one might attempt to salvage this particular anti-capital-punishment argument by insisting that capital punishment can *only* be administered unfairly, a point that would be relevant to the discussion. But then one would have to prove that this is the case. That capital punishment is unfairly administered does not prove that it can't be administered fairly.

As one final example of the straw man, consider this argument, advanced by the dean of a prestigious graduate school of business, against including business-ethics courses in the business curriculum. "Much can be said about the moral and ethical nature of our economic system," the dean admitted, "but by the time students get to graduate schools, their morality and ethical standards have long been set. And I think it's quite presumptuous of us to tell them what's right and what's wrong."

This argument is psychologically persuasive. Few of us want moral dogma dispensed in the classroom. And thus we're invited to conclude that we shouldn't want business-ethics courses because they're dogmatic.

But dogma is a straw man. The fact is that business-ethics courses need not indoctrinate. Quite the opposite: They can and do typically investigate the possible bases for a just economic system; explore the relationships between business and various parties, such as employees, stockholders, consumers, and government; and consider a variety of business issues within the framework of diverse ethical principles.

That the students' "morality and ethical standards have long been set" is another straw man. After all, if this is true, then a course in business ethics is really a waste of time, energy, and money. And no right-thinking taxpayer wants to incur such waste. But even if the moral and ethical standards of students have long been set, that doesn't mean they are set in cement, or that there aren't higher levels of moral reasoning for students to attain, or that students shouldn't be encouraged to critically examine their moral beliefs. Furthermore, it's highly improbable that students preparing to enter a profession have given much thought to the moral aspects of that profession.

Is/Ought

The fallacy of is/ought consists of assuming that because something is the case, it ought to or should be the case; or that because something is not the case, it ought or should not be the case. The is/ought fallacy frequently arises in arguments about value and social policy. Dillon might argue: "Look, we've never had forced busing in this country. That's proof positive that we shouldn't start now." The false assumption here is that prescription (*ought, should*) can legitimately be inferred from description (the *is*).

Some other examples of is/ought thinking: A parent argues, "Certainly there's something wrong with growing marijuana for sale [that is, one *shouldn't* do it]. If there weren't, it wouldn't be illegal." A nurse tells a colleague, "Nurses really shouldn't strike. After all, very few of us ever have, or even have an interest in that sort of thing." In both cases the reasoning makes an erroneous leap from the *is* to the *ought*. Simply because females have never been drafted doesn't mean that they *shouldn't* be drafted. Simply because we have always had a democratic form of government doesn't mean that we *should*. Simply because we're prohibited from carrying a concealed weapon without a license doesn't mean that we should be. There may be compelling reasons for not drafting females, for having a democratic form of government, for prohibiting people from carrying a concealed weapon without a license. But appealing to the status quo does not of itself demonstrate that.

Don't misunderstand. Ethical judgments typically take the form of *ought* as in "One ought to tell the truth"; "One ought to be honest"; "One ought not to steal or kill." Not every such assertion involves a leap from the *is* to the *ought*. For example, someone tells a young man: "You ought to register for the draft, because it's the law." Here the speaker isn't assuming that because there is a law that requires males to register for the draft at age eighteen, there *ought* to be such a law. If the *ought* is being used here in the sense of "moral obligation," then the speaker at the very least means that the registration law imposes on males a moral obligation to register. Thus, "You ought to register for the draft because you have a moral obligation to obey the law." However, if the speaker infers from the fact that there is a registration law that there ought to be one, then he or she would be committing the is/ought fallacy.

Although we're treating is/ought thinking as fallacious, we should hastily note that a famous and still not completely resolved metaethical dispute concerns the general question of whether a moral duty can be derived from a statement of what *is*, exclusive of normative premises. As we'll see in a later chapter, this is/ought dispute figures prominently in the development and criticism of some prominent normative themes.

Fallacies of Faulty Causation

A causal statement asserts a relationship between two things such that one is said to bring about the other. A causal statement can be reduced to the assertion "A causes B," as in "Cigarette smoking causes lung cancer"; "Capital punishment deters crime"; "The doctrine of nuclear deterrence makes nuclear war more possible." Note that the word *cause* has many cousins that convey the idea of causation: *Produce* means "to cause something to happen"; *deter* means "to cause not to happen"; *kill* means "to cause to die"; *vaporize* means "to cause a thing to change into a vapor," and so on. When causal statements are supported, causal arguments result—arguments that attempt to support a causal statement, as in "Capital punishment should be legalized, because it deters crime"; "Active euthanasia should not be permitted, because it will lead to abuses."

Many causation arguments are legitimate. But probably just as many are fallacious. In order to understand the fallacies connected with faulty causation, it helps to distinguish among three different meanings of *cause:* necessary, sufficient, contributory.

CAUSE AS A NECESSARY CONDITION.   *Cause* sometimes carries the meaning of "necessary condition"—that is, a condition that must be present if the effect is to occur. If in "A causes B" the term *cause* implies a necessary condition, then A *must* be present for B to occur. In the absence of A, B cannot occur; or simply, "If no A, then no B." In this sense, electricity is a cause for light in a bulb. If no electricity, then no light. Similarly, oxygen ordinarily can be considered a necessary condition for fire. If no oxygen, then no fire.

CAUSE AS A SUFFICIENT CONDITION.   *Cause* sometimes carries the meaning of "sufficient condition"—that is, a condition in whose presence the effect will always occur. If in "A causes B" the term *cause* implies a sufficient condition, then when A is present, B will always occur. In other words, the presence of A is always enough to bring about B, or simply: "If A, then B." In this sense, a blown fuse is a sufficient condition for a light to go out. If the fuse blows, the light will go out; no other condition is needed. But, of course, a blown fuse is not a necessary condition for the light to go out; the light could go out if the power company turned off the current when I failed to pay the electric bill.

CAUSE AS A CONTRIBUTORY CONDITION.   *Cause* sometimes carries the meaning of "contributory condition"—that is, a condition that helps create the total set of conditions, necessary or sufficient, for an effect. A violent storm can be a contributory cause to your room's suddenly being pitched into darkness. The storm can help create the conditions that cause the light to go off. But obviously the light may go off without a storm, and the light may remain on in the presence of a storm. So to say that A is a contributory cause of B is to say that B is more likely to occur when A occurs than when A does not occur. The lights in your room are more likely to go off in the presence of a violent storm than in its absence.

Usually we speak of contributory causes when we wish to emphasize the complexity of a problem. For example, in discussing the causes of the fall of the Roman Empire, historians generally cite a number of contributory causes: moral decay, economic chaos, effete leadership, the rise of Christianity, and so on. Of course, speaking of contributory causes doesn't rule out the possibility of focusing on one chief cause. Thus while mentioning a cluster of contributory causes, some historians might focus on the rise of Christianity, others on economic disorder, depending on their viewpoint.

With these distinctions in mind, we can now turn to some common fallacies associated with faulty causal reasoning.

CAUSAL OVERSIMPLIFICATION.   *Assuming that a necessary or contributory cause for an event is the sufficient cause is causal oversimplification.* For example, suppose Josephson tells Dillon: "Forced busing will have the effect of providing all races equal opportunity for education." Josephson seemingly thinks that busing of itself is enough to ensure equality of educational opportunity. But it isn't. Other things are necessary, including comparable quality of schools, teachers, educational services, and so on. Forced busing at best contributes to equal educational opportunity, it doesn't guarantee it. If Josephson says that it does, she's guilty of causal oversimplification, which in this case takes the form of treating a contributory cause as a sufficient one.

Similarly, if Josephson argues "Forced busing is justified because without it minorities cannot get equal educational opportunities," she is viewing forced busing as a necessary condition of equal educational opportunity. She's saying that without forced busing, there can be no equal opportunity. But why couldn't equal opportunity be available in the absence of forced busing? If, for example, education of comparable quality was made available to all students, wouldn't that provide roughly equal educational opportunity? If so, then Josephson is again guilty of causal oversimplification, in this case by treating a contributory cause (forced busing) as a necessary one.

As another example of a causal oversimplification, consider the common argument that if less violence was depicted in movies and on television, fewer real-life crimes of violence would be committed. Therefore, it's concluded, cinematic violence should be controlled—that is, censored. To contend that reducing cinematic violence will reduce real-life violence is to treat the relationship as a sufficient one. But, at most, cinematic violence is a contributory cause.

NEGLECT OF A COMMON CAUSE.   *This fallacy results from failing to recognize that two seemingly related events may be not causally related at all but rather are effects of a common cause.* Suppose, for example, a person suffers from both depression and alcoholism. It's tempting to infer that one is causing the other—the depression is causing the drinking, or the drinking is causing the depression. But both may be the effects of some underlying cause, such as a profound emotional disturbance. Some people are for strict control of pornography, even abolition of pornographic materials in order to reduce the number of sex crimes. They point out that in numerous cases of sex offenses, pornographic materials have been found in the possession of the offender. The implication here is that there's a causal relationship between pornography and sex offenses, such that reading or viewing salacious material induces the potential offender to rape, molest children, or commit other sex crimes. But it's possible that both the exposure to pornography *and* the sex offenses may be the effects of some underlying cause, such as hatred of women (in the case of rape), deep feelings of sexual inferiority, or sexual impotence.

POST HOC.   *Asserting that one event is the cause of another merely because the first preceded the second is the post hoc* (Latin for "after this") *fallacy.* For example, adolescent crime has increased since the arrival of punk rock from England, so someone concludes that punk rock is causing an increase in juvenile crime—from which it might further be concluded that punk rock should be banned. But that punk rock descended on the United States immediately before the juvenile crime wave doesn't of itself establish punk rock as the cause.

That murder may decline after the enactment of capital punishment doesn't demonstrate that the death penalty caused the decline. Don't think that the proximity of the two events—capital punishment and a decline in the murder rate—is being dismissed as irrelevant. There could well be a causal connection between them: The possibility of death as a punishment could deter serious crimes of violence like murder. But *to assume* such a connection based just on those two events is fallacious, because proximity of events does not of itself establish a causal relationship between them. The nearness of events in time may *suggest* an association that should be further investigated for a possible causal link, but it does not of itself demonstrate one.

SLIPPERY SLOPE.   *The slippery-slope fallacy consists in objecting to a particular action because it supposedly will lead inevitably to a similar but less desirable action, which in turn will lead to an even less desirable action, and so on down the "slippery slope" to some ultimate horror.* "Don't take the first drink," a father tells his son. "Otherwise you'll end up a drunk." But taking a first drink doesn't at all ensure that one will become an alcoholic. In fact, the majority of people who take the first drink, and quite a few afterward, don't become alcoholics. The error involved in slippery-slope thinking is not the presumption that one thing will lead to another, for sometimes it does. It is the presumption of *inevitability* between two events that is erroneous. The way to detect the slippery slope is to ask yourself

"Must A *inevitably* lead to Z?" If the answer is no, if the presumed chain can be broken at any one link along the way, then the slippery-slope fallacy is present.

Slippery-slope thinking finds its way into moral reasoning. Someone argues: "Euthanasia should not be legalized because that will lead to the murder of the mentally retarded, the congenitally diseased, the incorrigible criminal, and to the extermination of all sorts of so-called social undesirables." But legalized mercy deaths for the incurably ill and suffering do not necessarily lead to such morally dubious consequences at all. It's possible to allow euthanasia without legalizing any of the other acts.

CAUSAL INFERENCE FROM STATISTICAL CORRELATION.   One of the most common causal fallacies involves a leap from a statistical correlation to a causal correlation. *This is the fallacy of assuming that because two phenomena are related statistically, they must be related causally.*

A statistical correlation is a connection between properties that members of a group share. A study may indicate that users of a particular toothpaste have far fewer cavities than nonusers. It's tempting, but erroneous, to infer from this—as advertisers would have us do—that the particular toothpaste prevents cavities. Such statistical correlations of themselves are not enough to establish causal connections. The difference in the number of cavities may be explained by overall dental hygiene and diet.

A statistical correlation between the availability of handguns and crimes committed with handguns does not of itself establish that handgun availability leads to handgun-related crimes. Nor, on the other hand, would a statistical correlation between restricted availability of handguns and a decrease in handgun-related crimes necessarily show that the restriction of handguns reduces crimes committed with them.

Of course, a high degree of correlation between two sets of data may strongly *suggest* a causal connection. For example, medical scientists knew for some time that a statistical correlation existed between cigarette smoking and lung cancer—that the incidence of lung cancer in the smoking population was higher than in the nonsmoking population. Although this suggested a causal connection, researchers had to investigate the smoking process with special attention to its impact on the lungs. Carefully controlled studies involving animals and humans revealed that smoking not only injures lung tissue but produces malignant lesions. On the basis of this kind of hard evidence, researchers then could demonstrate a causal (that is, contributory) connection between smoking and lung cancer and had a basis for accepting the statistical correlation as having causal import. But the point remains: Statistical correlations are not necessarily causal correlations.

In moral discourse, one frequently has occasion to support moral judgments by appeal to various data. Under these conditions it's tempting to make a causal argument based exclusively on statistical correlations. For example, in arguing that premarital sex is immoral, one might claim that premarital sex has the effect of discouraging people from marrying, which the arguer views as a socially undesirable tendency. As a basis for the claim that having premarital sex discourages people from marrying, the person might point to a study showing that those who have premarital sex tend to marry in fewer numbers that those who don't. But this statistical correlation wouldn't demonstrate that premarital sex necessarily induces these people not to marry. Perhaps those who by temperament are not likely to marry are very likely to have premarital sex, or those who by temperament are most likely to marry are also most likely to eschew premarital sex. Of course, maybe the statistics do suggest a causal connection, that premarital sex tends to dissuade people from marrying. But the statistics themselves can only suggest, not demonstrate, the causal connection.

Although avoiding these and other fallacies will help us keep ethical discourse on a rational level, avoidance alone does not justify moral positions. Obviously Maria Josephson believes that demonstrating without a permit is in this instance moral, if not legal. But we really do not know why she believes this. Evidently her belief is connected with her conviction that racially imbalanced schools are immoral. She must justify this claim, after which she must then justify that intentionally breaking a law is moral. This she must do without relying on fallacies.

A similar problem faced Martin Luther King and faces all who must make a moral decision. It is one thing to claim, as King did, that segregationist laws are immoral; it is another to justify that claim. Opinions, beliefs, feelings, hunches, even convictions are relatively cheap commodities in the marketplace of ideas. But sound justification for them is rare. King attempted to provide such justification.

King's Moral Justification of Civil Disobedience

The core of the Martin Luther King case is civil disobedience, his willfull breaking of a city ordinance in order to dramatize its inequity and the inequity of racial segregation laws. The question is: Is King morally justified in breaking the ordinance? He believes that he is. More important, he thinks he can justify that belief as indicated in the excerpt presented at the beginning of this chapter.

At the outset King attempts to clarify, to avoid ambiguity. Thus in providing his justification, King distinguishes between two types of law: just and unjust. He says, "I would be the first to advocate obeying just laws. One has not only a legal but a moral responsibility to obey just laws. Conversely, one has a moral responsibility to disobey unjust laws.[8] At this point, you may wish to question this assumption. If not, you must still wonder what the difference is between a just and an unjust law. This is the crux of the civil disobedience issue. It is a question that Maria Josephson and all engaging in civil disobedience must ultimately answer. King realizes this.

In distinguishing between a just law and an unjust law, King provides four criteria. By so doing he provides grounds for a rational discussion of the civil

8.   King, "Letter from Birmingham Jail, April 16, 1963," p. 86.

disobedience issue, which, like most moral questions, could otherwise founder in emotionalism.

First, King contends that a just law is a human-made code that squares with the law of God. An unjust law does not. Again, you might question this contention; certainly you would if you did not believe in God. King further argues that a law that uplifts human personality is just and that a law that degrades human personality is unjust. Since all segregation laws, according to King, degrade human personality, they are unjust. We could construct King's first argument this way:

If a law does not respect personhood, it is unjust.

A segregation law does not respect personhood.

Therefore, a segregation law is unjust.

King further describes a just law as one that a majority compels a minority to obey and also binds itself to obey. Segregation laws are the opposite of this. They bind a minority but not the majority that has formulated them. So they are unjust. We can represent King's second argument thus:

If a majority formulates a law to bind a minority but not itself, that law is unjust.

Segregation laws are laws that a majority formulates to bind a minority but not itself.

Therefore, segregation laws are unjust.

In addition, King characterizes an unjust law as one that is inflicted on a minority that, as a result of having been denied the right to vote, had no voice in the law's devising or enactment. Again, since segregation laws are of this kind, they are unjust. Thus King's third argument is:

If a law is inflicted on a minority that, as a result of having been denied the right to vote, had no voice in formulating it, then that law is unjust.

Segregation laws are inflicted on a minority that, as a result of having been denied the right to vote, had no voice in formulating them.

Therefore, segregation laws are unjust.

Finally, King argues that a just law can be unjust in its application. This is crucial in this case because it is on this basis that he feels justified in willfully breaking the Birmingham ordinance. Remember, King has been arrested on a charge of parading without a permit. There is nothing intrinsically wrong with such an ordinance. But when the ordinance is used to deny citizens the First Amendment privilege of peaceful assembly and protest, and thereby to maintain segregation, then it is unjust. King's argument might be constructed to read:

If a law, which is not intrinsically unjust, is used to deny citizens constitutional rights, then it is an unjust law.

Birmingham's ordinance against parading without a permit is a law that, on its face, is not unjust, but in this case is being used to deny citizens constitutional rights.

Therefore, Birmingham's ordinance against parading without a permit in this case is an unjust law.

Of course, what is implied in King's stand is the third characteristic of all moral reasoning—that we should never do what is wrong. Obviously King believes that what is unjust is wrong. Therefore, he must not obey the law. To do so would be to act immorally. Conversely, to disobey it would be to act morally. Hence his demonstration.

At this point we may wonder about some of the assumptions King makes. For example, in his first argument King assumes that if a law uplifts personality, then it is just. But why is a law that uplifts personality necessarily just? We could also wonder precisely what *uplifting personality* means. We could ask similar questions about the assumptions King makes in the next three arguments. In doing so we are beginning to wonder how basic ethical judgments and principles are to be justified. After all, the first statement in each of King's arguments is an assumption. On what basis are these assumptions themselves to be justified? If they are not justified, then they are questionable claims.

In his essay it is clear that King is using a law of God as the basis for his assumptions. But not all ethical judgments are so defended. Some ethicists would agree with King's decision, but for different reasons. They might argue that segregation laws are immoral because they are not in the best long-term interests of all people. Others might claim that what King did was immoral because his action was not in his own best long-term interests. Still others might argue that his action was moral because it was in his own best long-term interests. Furthermore, metaethicists would probably wonder precisely what the word *just* and *unjust* mean to begin with. When we raise such questions, we inevitably engage in full-scale philosophical debate about moral issues.

Our coverage so far has emphasized the usefulness of proper reasoning in ethics. It is tempting to infer from our discussion of moral reasoning that right conduct in personal and social affairs always requires explicit thought and analysis, the careful weighing of arguments. Also, one might be tempted to infer that people in their practical moral decisions must always be able to give a satisfactory account of their reasons and that these reasons be "respectable." Actually, such analysis is only part of moral reasoning, a part that needs a counterweight in order to avoid an overdependence on logic in resolving ethical issues. To provide this balance we will examine briefly the role that intuition may play in moral evaluation.

Intuition

Subjecting moral positions to rational scrutiny is surely useful. Among other things, such analysis helps untangle confusions, minimize prejudice, and avoid superstitions. Probably the more deliberate and methodical our analysis is before a decision and consequent action, the less likely we are to be misled by others' opinions and confused thought. In addition, explicitness in moral reasoning can lead to explicit understanding of our reasons, which many would say is in itself an intellectual virtue. Indeed, explicit thought is crucial when we must explain, defend, and advocate positions, all inevitable procedures with social issues. For these reasons the theories and issues raised in this text are subject to critical analysis.

At the same time, it's important to recognize that human consciousness functions in ways other than discursive, or analytical, reasoning to apprehend the world and adjust to it. One of these ways is intuition.

Intuition is generally defined as the function of consciousness that apprehends directly and is not the result of conscious reasoning or of immediate sense perceptions. It is a nonsensuous apprehension, a direct vision of reason, although it does not rely on discursive reasoning. When we reason discursively, we draw conclusions in an orderly, step-by-step way, through logical inferences drawn from premises. When we reason intuitively, we recognize some truth immediately; we see without further evidence that something is true.

Intuition is frequently viewed as analogous to sensation, whereby we apprehend objects through the senses. For example, in seeing the color of the chalk, my eye is directly aware of the chalk. In a like way, the mind or intellect or consciousness can be directly confronted by some object, not a sensuous one but a nonsensuous one. When I know through intuition, I am aware, say, of truth or falsity, rightness or wrongness, not of colors, sounds, smells, tastes, or textures.

To understand precisely how some ethicists view the role of intuition in moral evaluation and judgment, we must be aware of the various positions that philosophers take on intuition generally. For example, some philosophers claim that intuition is present in all knowledge. Thus intuition may refer to any individual's awareness of the immediate data of consciousness, to the knowledge of oneself that appears present in all knowledge of other objects, to a grasp of the connection between statements in arguments, to an understanding of the axioms of mathematics, to the recognition of moral and aesthetic standards. Other philosophers hold that intuition is instead the result of subconscious discursive reasoning. They view intuition as the accumulated experience and thinking, together with persistent labor, which result in an insight into a situation. Still other philosophers believe that intuition is a higher form of knowledge, different in kind from knowledge disclosed by the senses or intellect. Intuition then is a knowledge that may result in a unique vision of reality. Whatever their position on intuition, philosophers agree that there does appear to be an element of intuition in knowledge, moral knowledge included.

Ethicists commonly observe that moral choice involves valuing. Valuing in turn involves an awareness of the pleasant or unpleasant, good or bad, better or worse nature of an object or situation. Such valuing appears to bear the element of intuition. It also may be crucial to our adjustment to life situations. Some philosophers have suggested the possibility that a "feeling" or "valuing" sense is a most important organ of knowledge, that a "feeling" response to a situation may augment knowledge disclosed through the senses and intellect. They connect intuition with basic life interest, as opposed to judgments that are complex. One such basic interest might be romantic love. People "fall in love" on the basis of some unanalyzable, unreconstructible appeal to their feelings. And on this basis they claim to know that they are in love and adopt appropriate courses of action and life-style regarding the object of their affection. Valuing in general is much the same; it involves intuition and cannot always be analyzed.

Recognizing this, a number of ethicists espouse *ethical intuitionism*, which views intuition as a reliable source of moral knowledge. However, just as there are various positions on intuition, so there are on ethical intuitionism. Some ethicists believe that a person knows which act is right by an intuition of the act. Thus when an individual act, such as one that involves hurting another person, is held before the mind, its rightness or wrongness, suitability or unsuitability to a situation can be grasped by intuition. Other ethicists claim that we intuit the rightness or wrongness not of individual acts but rather of basic moral principles. Such moral principles can take the form of all acts of a specific kind being right or all acts of a specific kind being wrong. We presumably recognize the truth of such moral principles by reflecting on their full meaning; we do not need further evidence to know they are true. When confronted with a particular act, therefore, we can deduce its rightness or wrongness by subsuming the act under the principle. For example, given that I intuit the truth of the moral principle that keeping a promise is right, when faced with an act that involves keeping a promise, I recognize an obligation to keep my promise. Still other ethical intuitionists claim that no such deductions are possible. While agreeing that we intuit moral principles, they claim that we do not infer the correct course of action from the rightness or wrongness of the act as much as from an "educated guess" about the act's morality. In this view, we know by intuition and with certainty the truth of the principle, but we do not know with certainty that a particular course of action is the right one.

Considerably more study must be done on the nature and function of intuition. We simply do not clearly understand what role intuition plays in consciousness and knowing. It seems indisputable, however, that intuition does play some role. And it is important at least to recognize this element of intuition while studying ethics, not only to understand the philosophical bases for some ethical theories but also to avoid creating a kind of tyranny of the intellect.

Summary

This chapter has dealt with the nature of ethics, moral reasoning, and the role of intuition in moral judgment. Ethics divides into normative and nonnormative fields. Normative ethics includes theory and application; nonnormative includes scientific or descriptive ethics and metaethics. This text will focus on normative ethics, which in part involves the reasoned search for principles of conduct. Ethics must be distinguished from etiquette and law.

Although ethicists rarely reach a moral consensus on many issues, there are patterns of moral reasoning which professional and nonprofessional ethicists use in arguing their positions. The heart of these patterns, and the feature of all defensible moral positions, consists in a moral judgment supported by a general moral principle. This feature allows for a number of strategies in arguing a moral position. Of course, people are not always logical in the way they argue. Frequently they try to persuade by using misleading emotional and psychological devices called *fallacies*. A knowledge of these fallacies can help one detect flaws in moral reasoning.

Finally, we tried to balance our discussion of moral reasoning by examining the role of intuition in acquiring moral knowledge. In the last analysis we must strive to effect a balance of the rational and the nonrational, the objective and the subjective.

Selections for Further Reading

Barry, Vincent E. *Invitation to Critical Thinking.* New York: Holt, Rinehart & Winston, 1984.

Castaneda, H. N. *The Structure of Morality.* Springfield, Ill.: Thomas, 1973.

Damer, Edward T. *Attacking Faulty Reasoning.* Belmont, Calif.: Wadsworth, 1980.

Engel, S. Morris. *Analyzing Informal Fallacies.* Englewood Cliffs, N.J.: Prentice-Hall, 1980.

Grice, G. R. *The Grounds of Moral Judgment.* New York: Cambridge University Press, 1962.

Hampshire, Stuart, et al. *Private and Public Morality.* New York: Cambridge University Press, 1978.

Kahane, Howard. *Logic and Contemporary Rhetoric,* 4th ed. Belmont, Calif.: Wadsworth, 1984.

Richards, D. A. *A Theory of Reasons for Actions.* Oxford: Clarendon Press, 1971.

Taylor, Richard. *Good and Evil: A New Direction.* New York: Macmillan, 1970.

Toulmin, Stephen. *An Examination of the Place of Reason in Ethics.* New York: Cambridge University Press, 1950.

2
PRINCIPLES

Frank Grogan wished he had never heard of Icarus Aircraft, let alone JLP-23. Why had he been assigned that particular project? After all, Icarus manufactured a whole fleet of executive aircraft that could keep a young engineer busy for years to come. Why JLP-23?

The irony was that Grogan had first seen the project as a rare opportunity to practice his specialty: aircraft fuselage and airfoil design. But ever since he'd become aware of some potentially dangerous wing-design specifications, the project had become a nightmare.

The whole thing was getting really sticky. Sometimes he wished he hadn't said anything, that he'd kept his mouth shut. But oh no, not him! Not getting any satisfaction from underlings, he had to go right to the top—to President Wendell Kravits himself. Kravits's reaction baffled Grogan. Kravits seemed to think that Grogan knew no more about wing design than a kid assembling a model plane.

"Precipitate." That's what Kravits had termed Grogan's alarm. "Not that I don't commend your vigilance, Frank," he had added, "but the danger you're talking about could materialize only under the most extreme and unrealistic conditions—conditions, in fact, more likely to occur in military flying than in civilian."

Maybe Kravits was right, Grogan thought. Kravits certainly had a lot more experience than he himself had. Still, that didn't make Kravits an authority on wing specifications. No, Grogan decided, Kravits was wrong. Given just the right conditions, the wing sections of the JLP-23 could separate from the fuselage.

So now Grogan had to decide whether to drop the whole matter or take it beyond Kravits, maybe to the stockholders or even to the press. More than anything else, he wanted to do the *right* thing. But what was that?

In Chapter 1 we explored this feature of defensible moral views: If a particular moral judgment is defensible, then it must be supportable by a defensible general moral principle. After deliberating, Grogan may decide to drop the whole issue or go to the board of directors or "blow the whistle" on Icarus by revealing the problem to the media. Whatever his judgment and subsequent action, a general moral principle should support them. In other words, if Grogan decides to press the issue no further, he should be able to provide some supporting principle which, together with additional facts, entails his moral judgment. If he cannot produce such a principle or sees no need to, then he simply does not understand how moral concepts are used. Or he is using moral words such as *right* and *wrong, good* and *bad* in a way far different from their common meanings in ethics. Moral principles, therefore, play a fundamental role in Grogan's forming a defensible moral judgment, indeed in anyone's forming any defensible moral judgment.

To understand better just how moral principles provide defense for moral judgments, it helps to grasp the distinction between what philosophers call statements of *fact* and statements of *value*. "The earth is roughly spherical" is a factual statement, whereas "Abortion is *wrong*" and "Grogan *should not* do the president's bidding" are statements of value, in these cases statements of moral value.

Something outside the speaker makes factual statements true or false. The statement "The earth is roughly spherical" is true because the earth *is* roughly spherical. The statement describes an actual state of affairs. By the same token, "The earth is flat" is false because the earth *isn't* flat; the statement does not describe an actual state of affairs.

Moral judgments are different from statements of fact. If I claim the earth is flat, and you say it isn't, we can check the shape of the earth (for example, by means of satellite-transmitted photos) and settle the matter. But if I argue that abortion is immoral, and you say it's sometimes perfectly all right, no appeal to ordinary facts (say, about the nature of the fetus, how abortions are performed, how much they cost, who performs them, and so on) can settle the dispute. Indeed, we might agree on all the ordinary facts pertaining to abortion but disagree on whether it's right or wrong.

So it appears that the truth or falsity of moral statements is to be judged in some way other than by examining some parts of the universe. How then *are* moral claims to be judged? Are there peculiarly *moral* facts that make moral statements true just as physical facts verify statements such as "At sea level, water boils at 212 degrees Fahrenheit" and "Lemons taste sour"? If not, what makes a moral statement true?

Moral principles are thought to provide the standard we can use to determine the truth of moral statements such as "Abortion is wrong (or right)"; "Lying is never (or sometimes) justifiable"; "One should never (or may under certain circumstances) steal."

This chapter deals with such principles. Although we can't cover all the types of ethical theory, we can provide representative samples that show the various possible approaches to moral problems and decisions. We will focus on the following views: rational development, natural law, divine command, duty, self-interest, and utility.

Rational Development: Aristotle

Aristotle (384–322 B.C.) is the pre-eminent philosopher of the type of morality associated with rational development. The presupposition of Aristotle's ethics is that each kind of thing has certain characteristic tendencies and that the good is the fulfillment of these tendencies. At the beginning of his monumental treatise on ethics, entitled *Nicomachean Ethics* (so named in honor of his son Nicomachus the Younger), he writes:

> Every art and every investigation, as well as every action and choice, may be said to aim at some particular good: as, for example, health is the end which is aimed at by the science of medicine, a vessel by the act of shipbuilding, victory by military strategy, and wealth by domestic economy.

If the good is the fulfillment of a thing's natural tendencies, what is the good at which human behavior aims? What is the primary goal proper for a human? Everyone would agree, said Aristotle, that it is what the Greeks called *eudaimonia*.

Eudaimonia

The usual translation of *eudaimonia* is happiness. By "happiness" Aristotle seems to mean "well-being," the fulfillment of our distinctive function.[1] Since the word "happiness" is used in a very different sense by utilitarians, whom we'll consider later, the word *eudaimonia* will be translated here to mean "well-being."

In Aristotle's view, then, well-being is the end or good that is proper to the essential nature of the person. Although people seek other goods—for example, wealth, power, pleasure, prestige—they do so because they think that through these means they will attain what all people aspire to, well-being. Well-being alone, Aristotle maintained, meets all the requirements for the proper goal of human action.

Rationality as the Distinguishing Human Characteristic

Granted that well-being is the person's ultimate end, how is it to be attained? Aristotle believed that the answer to this question could be deduced from human nature. In other words, by determining what distinguishes humans from other things, we can learn what we must do to attain well-being.

In Aristotle's view, the characteristic that is peculiar to the human being is rationality, the ability to reason. Since the human is a rational animal, Aristotle concluded that individuals attain well-being when they lead a life of reason.

For Aristotle, then, the general rule of morality is "to act in accordance with right reason." What this means is that the rational part of the self (or "soul," as Aristotle terms it) should control the irrational part. Implied here is Aristotle's belief that the self is characterized by an irrational and a rational part.

RATIONAL VS. IRRATIONAL SELF.   The irrational self is impulsive and passionate. It is the part that is influenced by things outside the self, such as objects and

---

1. *Philip Wheelwright,* A Critical Introduction to Ethics *(New York: Odyssey Press, 1959), pp. 136–137.*

persons. It typically reacts to these external factors emotionally. The irrational self leads the individual to desire things and other people or to avoid and destroy them. By themselves, said Aristotle, these capacities for love and hate, attraction and repulsion, creation and destruction can easily run amok, for, in themselves, they contain no principle of measure or selection. They can't tell us what we should desire, how much, or under what circumstances. In short, they provide no guide for how we should relate to things and other people.

In contrast, the rational self is capable of distinguishing between different kinds of things; it has the power of analysis. It can understand the relationships between things, thereby attaining scientific knowledge. Most important, the rational self has the power of deliberation, through which it discovers the guides for human behavior.

Virtue

By Aristotle's account, people don't automatically act the right way. Although we have a natural capacity for right behavior, we don't exercise it by nature. Morality, then, has to do with developing habits of right thinking, right choice, and right behavior.

Since the passions can lead to a variety of action, from too little to too much, Aristotle said a person must and can discover through reason the proper meaning of excess and deficiency, and thereby discover the golden mean. For example, I can feel the emotion of fear, lust, or anger too much or too easily, and in either case wrongly. To feel these emotions when I ought, toward whom, and as I should is the *golden mean;* this, said Aristotle, is the best state for a person to be in—the state of *virtue.* For Aristotle, then, virtue is a state of being, "a state apt to exercise deliberate choice, being in the relative mean, determined by reason, and as the man of practical wisdom would determine."

THE GOLDEN MEAN.   Aristotle did not think of the golden mean as the midpoint between two extremes which can be calculated easily like an arithmetic mean. The mean's position in relation to the extremes will vary according to circumstances. More courage is required of the soldier than the farmer; the courage of the soldier will more closely approximate the extreme of recklessness than that of the farmer. Regarding the virtue of generosity, a poor woman might act extravagantly in giving even a small sum to charity. But a wealthy woman who gave the same amount would be stingy.

Aristotle's theory of the golden mean, then, is no simple formula for moral perfection. The mean on any given occasion must be determined and applied with the greatest possible prudence. The mean is always relative to ourselves and to all other persons and events affected. Most important, the mean is determined by reason, that is, as a person of prudence and soundly developed character would determine it. The life of reason, then, is the highest good. It is the purpose of a person's conduct to establish on the basis of reason a life of happiness for all humankind.

VIRTUE AS PLEASURABLE.   Aristotle didn't believe that one becomes a virtuous person by performing a single act of moderation, by practicing the golden mean once, twice, or even a dozen times. One must form a habit of virtuous conduct, and since, when formed, a habit becomes pleasant rather than painful, pleasure and pain become a useful, though hardly a final, test of morality.

Thus if I perform an act of heroism with trembling hesitancy, my courage is not yet deeply ingrained. Should I act justly only with profound reluctance, perhaps only when coerced, justice is not yet a habit with me—I am not yet virtuous in regard to justice. In contrast, when acts of courage, justice, temperance, and wisdom (Aristotle's cardinal virtues) always bring me pleasure and joy, I have formed habits of these virtues and thus am a virtuous person. The relation of virtue to pleasure, then, is not that what is pleasurable is virtuous but that virtue, when it has become a habit, brings pleasure.

Philosophic Contemplation

If people are to attain their ultimate end, well-being, they must practice moral virtue. But, said Aristotle, that isn't enough; the achievement of moral virtue actualizes only one capacity of the self: controlling impulse and passion, taming the irrational self. The self also has the capacity to engage in what Aristotle termed reflective contemplation of the universe, or the enjoyment of reason for its own sake.

In the person of developed character, therefore, the disinterested enjoyment of reason may become an authentic expression of the entire self. Moral virtue remains a part of the ideal, for only after moral virtues have become habitual can a person engage in philosophic contemplation without bias. Pleasure, too, is part of the ideal, for, as noted, the habitual practice of virtue gives pleasure. And when the contemplative life too has become a habit, its pursuit provides the most intense pleasure. In the end, the good life, the life proper to a human being, is one of reflective contemplation.

Critical Inquiries

1. *Can the good be deduced from the nature of things?* As we saw, Aristotle's ethics presupposes that each kind of thing has certain characteristic tendencies and that the good is the fulfillment of these tendencies. Thus the human's good can be deduced from human nature. But this seemingly implies an optimistic and undemonstrated assumption: that fulfilled or actualized tendency is fully good. What basis is there for such an assumption?

    Aristotle's view allows the facts of the actual world to dictate our standards of value. But philosophers such as Immanuel Kant, as we will see, deny that the *ought* (the good and right) can be derived from the *is* (matters of fact) and thus attack Aristotle's ethics at its base.

2. *Is Aristotle's definition of human goodness correct?* Aristotle's definition of human goodness rests on two premises: (1) The good is to be found in the life and work peculiar to the human being. (2) Rationality is the distinguishing mark of the human being. Both premises can be challenged.

    Regarding the first, why must ethical superiority be attributed to a factor that appears to be peculiar to a species? If all human beings were exactly like other animals except that they alone had bowlegs, that wouldn't prove human good is bowleggedness.[2] Of course, one could reply that Aristotle is assuming the superiority of humans to other animals on the basis of the fact that only humans have reason. But some philosophers would challenge this view. Hedonists, for example, claim that good is pleasure. That a cat or dog can feel pleasure, they would claim, doesn't detract from human good.

3. *Is reason peculiar to humans?* Some psychologists have demonstrated that chimpanzees have the capacity to reason on a practical level. For example, chimps apparently can figure out ways of arranging and mounting boxes so as to reach bananas hanging at the top of their cage. While it's true that such behavior does not manifest theoretical reason—that which yields knowledge of fixed principles or philosophical wisdom—do we know that chimps, dolphins, or other animals don't have this capacity? Are we certain that they don't have curiosity and enjoy satisfying it? It could be argued, counter to Aristotle, that what primarily distinguishes the human creature is the whole development of human culture, and not just philosophy and science, as Aristotle seems to imply. In any event, critics who raise this point in effect are objecting to what they see as the bias of the philosopher: the exclusive emphasis on reason.

4. *Is moral virtue necessarily found in adherence to the mean between two extremes of excess and deficiency?* Critics of Aristotle's ethics sometimes question his doctrine of the golden mean. They say that "Be cautious; avoid extremes; follow the mean" is a counsel of prudence and not necessarily of morality. After all, even the wicked and crafty can find the golden mean useful.

Natural Law

Natural-law theory refers to the general view that moral principles are objective truths that can be discovered in the nature of things. Such a view has been extremely influential in the development of moral political theories.

At the outset, it's important not to confuse "natural law" as it pertains to morality with what modern science means by *"a* natural law," such as the law of gravity. Everyone is subject to the law of gravity and every other such scientific natural law. Such laws are descriptive generalizations and, as such, are not logically the sorts of things that can be broken or disobeyed.

Some moralists believe there is a moral natural law that operates throughout the universe as scientific natural laws do, except that the moral natural law is not automatically compulsory. Humans are obliged to obey it only by their reason and conscience. For example, natural-law theorists ordinarily believe that we should live in harmony with each other. But, of course, we don't always do this: We often prey on, war with, and destroy one another. Unlike a natural law in science, moral natural law can be violated by us in our interactions with others. In the moral sphere, then, natural law orders our conduct only to the extent that

2. *Melvin Rader,* The Enduring Questions, *3rd ed. (New York: Holt, Rinehart & Winston, 1976), p. 497.*

it is apprehended by our reason or is the result of an investigation of the universe and imposed by our will.

Notice there are two ways of considering knowledge of the natural: (1) We can know natural law through reason alone; (2) We can come to know it by studying human nature and the universe. By this latter account, the *ought* is based on the *is*. Norms are derived from facts. Each individual shares with other members of the species an essential nature, which determines the individual's most fundamental tendencies. To understand human nature is to recognize these tendencies. Think of an acorn. An acorn has a self-contained end to which it strives: to become an oak. All things, Aristotle said, have such self-contained ends, unique purposes to fulfill. Good resides in the fulfillment of these ends or natural tendencies, evil in their frustration. By this account, moral laws are not purely arbitrary. Even when it is broken, natural law remains a nonarbitrary standard, immutable in the sense of being eternally valid.

Whether natural law is discovered prior to experience (*a priori*) or is based on experience (*a posteriori*), it is considered a moral imperative, a description of what ought to happen in human relationships. Any ethical theory, then, that makes the following two basic assumptions can be called a natural-law theory: First, moral values and duties depend on the basic nature of human beings. Second, we can discover what humans are like by applying the processes of rational and scientific reflection, just as we do in other areas of human knowledge. These assumptions turn up in religious and secular versions of natural-law theory.

Religious Interpretations: Saint Thomas Aquinas

A good example of how natural-law theory operates in a religious context is the moral philosophy developed in the thirteenth century by Saint Thomas Aquinas (1225–1274). Aquinas's view of human nature, and his thought in general, was strongly influenced by the texts of Aristotle. A basic idea that Aquinas borrowed from Aristotle is that the universe is teleological, that is, governed by purposes or ends. Aquinas believed that movement toward an end characterizes everything in the universe, including people and their institutions. For Aquinas, the goals that permeate the universe are ordained by God.

As Aquinas conceived it, morality is not an arbitrary set of rules for behavior. Rather, it is part of the person's teleological nature. In other words, God has built the basis of moral obligation into the very nature of the human in the form of various inclinations, such as the preservation of life, the propagation of the species, and the search for truth and a peaceful society. Moral law is founded on these natural inclinations and the person's ability to discern the right course of conduct through reason. In Aquinas's view, then, natural law consists of precepts or rules of conduct corresponding to these natural inclinations.

Although the precepts themselves don't vary from place to place, their enforcement does. Since different societies are influenced by different topographies, climates, cultures, and social customs, Aquinas believed that different codes of justice are needed. He called these specific codes of justice *human law*.

The function of rulers is to formulate human law by informing themselves of the specific needs of their communities and then passing appropriate decrees. Whether human law is just depends on its conformity with natural law, which is the expression of the will of God applied to human situations.

Secular Interpretations: Cicero

Natural law need not be viewed as having divine origins. For example, the natural-law theory of the Roman statesman, orator, philosopher, and writer Cicero (106–43 B.C.) is based on the concept of a cosmic order as the ground of objective moral laws. Borrowing from the Stoics, a school of philosophers circulating about 300 B.C., Cicero viewed nature as the rational and animating force of all things. By means of reason, people can discover the fundamental laws of the universe and direct their conduct in conformity with these laws. To live according to nature is to develop one's essential faculties and, at the same time, be in tune with the order of the cosmos. Cicero's theory of natural law, then, is rooted in the concept of natural harmony. Embedded in the innermost nature of the person, the society, and the universe, natural law is independent of convention, legislation, and all other institutional devices. It is not based on human whim or decrees but is both a law of nature and a moral law—universal, irrevocable, and inalienable. It provides the ultimate standard of right conduct for individuals and states.

Fundamental to Cicero's doctrine of natural law is the doctrine of natural brotherhood and equality. All humans are by nature kin. By this Cicero didn't mean that we are all equal in learning or talents or that we should be made equal in worldly goods. Rather, all of us possess a similar psychological constitution and should, as a result, be treated with dignity and respect. In other words, natural law provides a basis for natural rights.

The concept of natural rights has often been linked with "the social contract." "Social contract" refers to the idea of an original covenant by which individuals, who possessed natural rights in a primeval, nonpolitical "state of nature," joined together and established government. One main reason for establishing the state is so that natural rights (e.g., "life, liberty, and the pursuit of happiness") may be better defined and protected. If the government fails to ensure these natural rights for its citizens, then it forfeits its right to rule. In this way, the theories of natural law, natural rights, and social contract combine to form the basis of democratic and even revolutionary tendencies.

Critical Inquiries

1. *Can morality be based on nature?* It seems that "good," in the sense of what ought to be, and "right," in the sense of what ought to be done, are not natural characteristics. This has led many philosophers to conclude that the concepts of "good" and "right" have a distinctly *ethical* meaning. This meaning, they say, must be grasped by intuition or *a priori* reason or some peculiarly moral sense rather than by empirical science or through theories of reality. As we'll see, Immanuel Kant, for one, affirmed the moral law but said it was known *intuitively,* not by reason, from human nature. Thus understood, there exists a moral law but not necessarily a *natural* one. If like-

minded philosophers are right, then any morality based on nature seems invalid.

2.   *In what sense is the "natural law" a law?* Although we may observe regularity in human behavior, this does not necessarily mean that we are morally obligated to act in definite ways. Yes, we can describe how person behave, but descriptions do not necessarily yield moral prescriptions or laws. To see a "moral law" in this behavior is the fallacy of mistaking the figurative for the literal. States may govern by law. But to view humans as also governed by their nature is a mere figurative expression personifying human nature as a lawgiver and represents no real government or real law.

3.   *Is natural law ultimately based on an erroneous concept of human nature, namely, that it is fixed?* Natural law seems to stem from a concept of a fixed essence or nature in human beings. But these concepts have been invalidated by the experimental method of modern science, which fails to discover any such hard-and-fast categories among things. On the contrary, the theory of biological evolution, for example, teaches that there are no invariable classes of living things. Moreover, so-called process philosophers see everything as on the move, becoming quite new, with no static patterns of behavior to be forever repeated. If there is no fixed human nature, there can be no obligations arising out of it. If, however, natural law is as reactive as human nature, then in what sense is natural law an absolute foundation of morality?

4.   *Why isn't natural law easily known by us?* Presumably moral natural law resides in our nature. If it does, shouldn't it be easily known by us? But people disagree not only on how to fulfill their obligations but also on what their obligations are and even whether they have any. And even those who argue for natural law don't agree on its content, interpretation, or application. So even if natural law exists, it will be virtually useless as a guide to morality.

Natural-law theorists might reply that it is not according to our nature to know such difficult and complex matters in a simple way. On the contrary, we're so constructed that we must think, reason, and argue matters out for ourselves. In this way, we arrive at the content, interpretation, and application of natural law.

But even granting that the content, interpretation, and application of the moral natural law must be worked out through collective human effort, there's still the matter of its existence. If natural law resides in our nature, how is it that we all don't at least recognize and acknowledge it, even those of us who have given the matter serious and prolonged deliberation? The study of human nature and nature itself turns up all manner of characteristics and tendencies that are widely acknowledged, although not always accounted for in the same way or emphasized to the same degree. But there isn't nearly a consensus about the *existence* of so-called natural law, let alone its content, interpretation, and application. Surely what is "natural" should at least be readily apparent to a large majority of rational beings.

Divine Command

Perhaps the most popular answer to the question "What makes true moral statements true?" is that God's commands (not to steal, not to lie, not to kill) make statements such as "Stealing is wrong," "Lying is wrong," "Killing is wrong" true. This theory ordinarily is called *divine command* or *theological voluntarism*.

Notice that this view does not state that we should obey God's law because we will therefore promote our own or the general good, or be faithful to some virtuous principles. Perhaps we will accomplish these ends, but the primary justification for obeying God's law is that God wills it. Also, the theory does not defend the morality of an action by promising some supernatural reward to the faithful, although this is typically assumed to follow upon obedience to God's will. Perhaps behaving righteously is in the faithful's best interests, and perhaps they will be rewarded. But divine-command theorists wouldn't justify moral actions primarily by appeal to such self-interest.

Understandably, divine-command theorists would see no intrinsic worth or value in such things as pleasure, power, or knowledge. Instead, they would propose something like union with God as taking the form of heavenly salvation.

What is of intrinsic value, then, is independent of what any individual thinks or likes and what any society happens to sanction. Moral laws are established by God; they are universally binding for all people and are eternally true, regardless of whether they are universally obeyed. Such God-established laws are generally interpreted in a religious tradition. The Ten Commandments are a good example. These laws, claim their adherents, apply to everybody everywhere, and their value does not depend on what produces human satisfaction, either individually or collectively.

Because the justification of such moral law is usually divine authority and its supposed expression through humans and their institutions, the Bible or the Koran may be invoked as authority, as may a religious institution or leader.

Critical Inquiries

1. *How do we know what God commands?* Aside from an appeal to faith, there are three standard answers to this question.

CONSCIENCE.   First, some say our conscience tells us what God commands. Thus we should "let our conscience be our guide."

But common experience teaches that what conscience tells one person can radically differ from what it tells another. The best examples of how inconsistent a moral guide conscience can be are found by comparing cultures. Eating human flesh, for example, seriously offends the conscience of most Westerners but doesn't bother New Guinea cannibals. Eating beef offends the conscience of most Hindus, and eating pork offends the conscience of Orthodox Jews. But neither dietary practice offends the conscience of most Christians.

Even within a culture, the dictates of one person's conscience can differ from another's. For some Christians, abortion always runs counter to what their conscience tells them is right. But for other Christians, abortion accords with the dictates of their conscience.

Moreover, even when we consult our conscience, we often fail to get an answer, or we get a contradictory one. For example, many people today are confused about the morality of birth control, abortion, premarital sex, capital punishment, smoking marijuana, and so on.

There emerges, then, serious reason for questioning the divine origin of conscience. Would God tell one group of us that killing and eating human beings is a terrible sin, while telling others it's an act of merit? Would he tell some of us that abortion is always a moral outrage, while informing others that it's all right?

Of course, it doesn't follow that we should ignore our conscience in determining what to do. How we feel about something is an important bit of information, and appealing to conscience, to moral intuitions, is a way of finding out. The point, then, is not that conscience isn't a valuable source of discovering our feelings about something but rather that in appealing to conscience, we can't be appealing to God's will, because conscience differs so radically from person to person and place to place.

RELIGIOUS AUTHORITIES.   A standard way to find out what God commands is to consult religious authorities or experts. Frequently voluntarists point to a holy book or scripture as evidence. The Ten Commandments are the likely source for Jews and Christians. Yet we are still left wondering how we know that scriptures represent the inspired word of God. Some would say because it says so in the scriptures. But this is circular reasoning. After all, how do we know that there is a God at all? And if there is, can we be sure that he expressed himself in one source and not in another?

The essential problem with consulting religious authorities is determining which authorities to turn to. Just think of the array of religions in the world, each with its own creed. Hindu priests, New Guinea shamans, Zen masters, Jewish rabbis, and Christian ministers all offer very different answers to questions about God's will. And even among Christians, Baptist pastors, Catholic priests, and Mormom elders often are at odds on these questions. Unless the preference is a matter of faith, religious authority has to be selected on the basis of evidence of reliability, as are selections about other authorities—in medicine, law, education, criminology, and so on. Yet there seems to be no compelling evidence to favor one religious authority over another.

Furthermore, if the decision is to be made on faith alone, that raises additional problems, for, like conscience, the leaps of faith that we make don't always land us on common moral ground.

THE BIBLE.   For Jews and Christians, another standard way of discovering what God commands is by appeal to the Bible. But what the Bible says about morality and God's commands is vague and requires human interpretation to enact.

Take, for example, the word *honor* in the commandment to honor our parents. Does *honor* mean that we should obey, respect, or love them? Does it mean all these things, or perhaps something else? If *honor* means *obey*, does the commandment mean that we should always obey our parents—even when they ask us to do something that goes against our conscience?

Often it's difficult to find any reasonably straightforward or literal interpretation of biblical moral teachings that is not inconsistent or contradictory. For example, in Exodus we are told "Thou shalt not suffer a witch to live" and "Whoever lieth with a beast shall surely be put to death." But these moral guidelines seem to contradict the commandment not to kill. Of course, if *kill* is taken to mean *murder*, there is no contradiction. But then other problems arise. Which sorts of killings are murders and which aren't? Answers to this question call for human interpretation, and those interpretations can vary. Is killing civilians during war murder, and thus prohibited? Some would say it all depends on whether the actions occur accidentally or by design. Even if this is a morally meaningful distinction, it again reflects human distinction, not one set forth in the Bible.

In addition to being sometimes inconsistent and contradictory, biblical moral teachings are incomplete—they don't cover every possible situation. They say little about the morality of abortion, inasmuch as they are silent on the key question of whether a fetus is a human being. Likewise, they say next to nothing about fair wages, war, pornography, and whether it's all right to cheat on our taxes. Even when the Bible is decisive, it often runs counter to strongly held moral intuitions. For example, the Bible condones slavery, forbids all lending of money at interest, and insists on second-class status for women.

There are those, to be sure, who say that when the Bible is interpreted *correctly*, its apparent inconsistencies, contradictions, and counterintuitive commandments are cleared up. But is there any good reason for accepting one interpretation over another as the word of God?

2. *Does divine-command theory satisfactorily explain why God commands something?* This question points to the philosophic issue of whether something is right because God commands it, or whether God commands something because it is right. If the latter, then the divine-command theory collapses because it contends that something is right because God commands it. This issue is one that Plato (427–347 B.C.) raised in his dialogue *Euthyphro*, which deals with the nature of piety. At one point in the dialogue, Socrates says to Euthyphro: "[a] Is what is holy holy because the gods approve it, or [b] do they approve it because it is holy?"[3]

If the answer is yes to *a* and no to *b*, then on what grounds is religion a solid basis and guide to morality? After all, if pure willing by God makes something right, then that makes right and wrong seem wholly arbitrary. For example, if God didn't approve benevolence because it is right, then God has no more reason to approve benevolence than to disapprove it. According to *a*, then, if God's will were that benevolence is evil, then it would be evil.

The answer to Socrates' question, therefore, appears to be *b*—that God says an act is right *because* the act is right. But this implies that the grounds for an act's being right exist independently of God's will, in which case God is not the author of morality, which further implies that not even a so-called true religion must be

3. Plato, "Euthyphro," trans. Lance Cooper, in Collected Dialogues of Plato, eds. Edith Hamilton and Huntington Cairns (Princeton, N.J.: Princeton University Press, 1973).

the basis of morality. Moreover, like the rest of us, God seemingly must use intellect to find out what the grounds of morality are, in order to know what to approve and disapprove. But if this is so, then morality exists independently of religion and is open to discovery by us and by God.

So whether one answers Socrates' question *a* or *b*, religion is not the foundation for morality. In the first instance, *a*, arbitrary willing doesn't provide a justifiable foundation. In the second, *b*, humans as well as God can discover morality, since we share rationality.

That religion need not be a basis for morality in no way implies that the moral teachings of religions are incorrect or worthless. On the contrary, historically one of religion's supreme contributions to moral development has resulted from its role as curator of our highest ideals and noblest principles. Indeed, in times like the present, religion is one of the few institutions willing to address the moral issues at the center of intense international debate.

Duty: Kant

Another type of ethics is termed *deontological,* derived from the Greek words *deon* (duty) and *logos* (science, or theory). A deontological ethics is one based on the theory of duty. As typically used, the term means an ethics of duty for duty's sake, expressed in its most undiluted form in the motto "Let me do right though the heavens fall."

The best example of a purely deontological ethics is found in the thought of the influential German philosopher Immanuel Kant (1724—1804). Kant was looking for moral principles that are inherently right or wrong apart from any particular circumstances. These moral principles or laws, Kant thought, are recognized immediately or directly as true and binding.

Kant inherited the Christian reverence for divine law and the worth of the individual. He was also deeply influenced by the Greeks' and his own century's respect for reason. But, while influenced by these traditions, Kant's ethics departs from them in significant ways.

First, according to Kant, there can be morality without religion. Individuals can recognize their moral duty without the idea of God, and they must obey the law simply out of respect for it, for duty's sake. Kant did hold that the moral universe compels us to postulate the existence of God, but he didn't believe that the idea of God is necessary to derive moral duty.

Second, regarding the Greek tradition, Kant did not believe as Aristotle did that we can discover moral principles by studying human nature. While such a study provides interesting information about how people *do* behave, it will not tell us, said Kant, how they *ought* to behave. For Kant, then, the *ought* cannot be derived from the *is,* as Aristotle said and, as we'll see, utilitarians agreed.

Still, we do make moral judgments, as when we say we *ought* to tell the truth and we *should never* steal. The question is: How do we arrive at such rules of behavior?

A Priori Judgments

For Kant, the moral rules that we ought to tell the truth and that we ought not to steal are, in principle, the same as the scientific rule "Every change must have a cause." What makes them similar is that both of these judgments come from our *reason* and not from the objects of experience. Just as reason brings out the category of causality to visible objects, and thereby explains the process of change, so reason can bring to given moral situations the concept of duty. As in science, so in moral philosophy we use concepts that go beyond any particular facts we experience at a given time, said Kant. In both cases, experience triggers the mind to think in universal terms. When we experience some example of change—for instance, an acorn turing into an oak—our minds bring to this event the category of causality, thereby enabling us to explain the relation of cause and effect not only in this case but in all cases of change. Likewise, in the context of human relations, reason can determine not only how we should behave at a particular moment but what the principle of behavior should be at all times.

For Kant, moral knowledge, like scientific knowledge, is based on *a priori judgments: reasoning based on knowledge that is logically prior to experience.* "The basis of obligation," he writes, "must not be sought in human nature, in the circumstances of the world in which man is placed [as Aristotle contended], but *a priori*."[4]

As a rational being, I ask not only "What shall I do?" but "What *should* I do?" I can assume, said Kant, that all rational beings are conscious of being under an obligation to act in particular ways. Thus when I answer the question "What should I do?" I am also considering what *all* rational beings must do, for if the moral law is valid for me as a rational being, it must be valid for you and all other rational beings. A major test of a morally good act, therefore, is whether its principle can be applied to all rational beings and be applied consistently. For Kant, moral philosophy is the quest for the principles that apply to all rational beings and that lead to behavior we call *good*.

Good Defined as the Good Will

Kant believed that nothing is good in itself except a good will. This doesn't mean that numerous facets of the human personality are not good and desirable—intelligence, sensitivity, talent, virtue, rational development, and so on. But their goodness, said Kant, resides in the will that makes use of them.

By will *Kant meant the uniquely human capacity to act according to principles.* Contained in a good will is the concept of duty. Only when we act from duty does our action have moral worth. When we act only out of feeling, inclination, or intended results, our actions—though otherwise identical with ones that spring from a sense of duty—have no true moral worth.

To illustrate, merchants have a duty not to shortchange their customers. But simply because merchants do not shortchange customers, need we say that they are acting from a good will? They may be acting from an inclination to promote

4. *Immanuel Kant,* Foundations of the Metaphysics of Morals, *trans. Lewis White (New York: Bobbs-Merrill, 1959), p. 41.*

business or to avoid legal entanglement. If so, they would be acting *in accordance with* duty but not *from* duty. Their apparently virtuous gesture just happens to coincide with duty. In Kant's view, if they have not willed the action from a sense of duty to be fair and honest, their action does not have true moral worth. For Kant, actions have true moral worth only when they spring from a recognition of a duty and a choice to discharge it.

Perfect and Imperfect Duties

Kant distinguished two kinds of duties: perfect and imperfect. A perfect duty is one that we must always observe; an imperfect duty is one that we must observe only on some occasions. *Perfect duty refers to negative obligations—things we must always refrain from doing. Imperfect duty refers to positive obligations—things that we must do only on some occasions.* For example, Kant would say that we have the perfect duty not to injure another person, but we have only an imperfect duty to show love and compassion. There are times, in other words, when we must indeed show love and compassion, but when, to whom, and how much remain unclear.

The nature of one's duties determines what others can claim as a right. Since I am always obligated to refrain from injuring you, you have a right to demand of me that I not injure you. But since I need not always show love and compassion, you have no right to demand that I do so.

Still, we are left wondering: What duties do we have, and how can we know them? Suppose Frank Grogan truly wishes to act from duty. What is his duty? And how can he discover it?

The Categorical Imperative

For Kant, an absolute moral truth must be logically consistent: free from internal contradiction. To say, for example, that a change does not have a cause or that a triangle has four sides is to state a contradiction. Kant aimed to ensure that his absolute moral law would avoid such contradictions. If he could formulate such a rule, he maintained, it would oblige everyone to follow it without exception. Kant believed that the categorical imperative is that rule.

Kant thought that there is just one command or imperative that is categorical, or presents an action as of itself necessary, regardless of any other considerations. He argued that from this one categorical imperative, this universal command, we can derive all commands of duty. Simply stated, *Kant's categorical imperative says that we should act in such a way that we could will the maxim of our action to become a universal law.*

By *maxim*, Kant meant the subjective principle of an action, the principle that people in effect formulate in determining their conduct. For example, suppose building contractor John Martin promises to install a sprinkling system in a project but is willing to break that promise if it suits his purposes. His maxim can be expressed: "I'll make promises that I'll break whenever keeping them no longer suits my purposes." This is the subjective principle, the maxim, that directs his action. Kant insisted that the morality of any maxim depends on whether we can logically will it to become a universal law. Could Martin's maxim be universally acted upon?

That depends on whether the maxim as law would involve a logical contradiction. In fact, the maxim "I'll make promises that I'll break whenever keeping them no longer suits my purposes" involves a contradiction. On the one hand, Martin wants it to be possible to make promises and have them honored. On the other, if people break promises when they so desire, then promises cannot be honored in the first place. It is the nature of promises that they can be believed. A law that allowed promise breaking would contradict the very nature of a promise. This is true even if desirable consequences resulted from breaking the promise.

Consider, as another example, a man who, in despair after suffering a series of serious setbacks, contemplates suicide. While still in possession of his reason, the man asks whether it would be contrary to his duty to himself to take his own life. He wonders whether the maxim of his actions could become a universal law of nature. Addressing just such a case, Kant writes:

> His maxim, however, is: For love of myself, I make it my principle to shorten my life when by a longer duration it threatens more evils than satisfaction. But it is questionable whether this principle of self-love could become a universal law of nature. One immediately sees a contradiction in a system of nature whose law would be to destroy life by the feeling whose special office is to impel the improvement of life. In this case, it would not exist as nature: hence the maxim cannot obtain as a law of nature, and thus it wholly contradicts the supreme principle of all duty.[5]

A closer look at examples like these reveals three formulations of the categorical imperative: the principle of universality; the principle of humanity as an end, never as merely a means; and the principle of autonomy.

THE PRINCIPLE OF UNIVERSALITY.   First, to be a moral rule, the rule of conduct must be consistently universalizable, for Kant's moral rule prescribes categorically, not hypothetically. A hypothetical prescription tells me what I should do if I desire certain consequences. For example, "If I want people to think well of me, I should keep promises." The goodness of promise keeping in a hypothetical prescription depends on consequences. But Kant's imperative is categorical; it commands unconditionally, regardless of consequences. A categorical imperative takes the form of "Do this" or "Don't do that," without if's, and's, or but's. Such a command must be universalizable and not determined on empirical grounds, hypothetically. Human experience varies, and thus the facts derived from it do, too; a rule based on empirical conditions, therefore, loses its inherent necessity and universality.

THE PRINCIPLE OF HUMANITY AS AN END, NEVER AS MERELY A MEANS.   The second formulation of the categorical imperative is that rational creatures should treat other rational creatures as ends in themselves, and not just as means to ends. For example, Kant would object to the practice of *forcing* people to be subjects in medical experiments to yield a cure for cancer—even though great social benefit

5. *Immanuel Kant,* Foundations of the Metaphysics of Morals, *6th ed., trans. T. K. Abbott (London: Longman's Green, 1909), p. 15.*

might result. The reason is that such experiments would be using the individuals as means to an end against their will. No matter how desirable that end, Kant would oppose this practice because it would be ignoring the right that rational human beings have to determine the disposition of their own bodies. In such experiments, then, Kant would require the subjects' informed consent.

THE PRINCIPLE OF AUTONOMY.   A third formulation of the categorical imperative concerns the autonomy or self-determination of the will. By this Kant meant, in part, that each person through his or her own act of will legislates the moral law. He distinguished autonomy from heteronomy, the determination of a law or action by someone or something other than the self. The heteronomous will is influenced, even determined, by desires or inclinations shaped by outside forces. In contrast, the autonomous will is free and independent; it is the supreme principle of morality. The moral laws that we obey, then, are not imposed on us from the outside. They are self-imposed and self-recognized. The sense of duty that we obey comes from within; it is an expression of our own higher selves.

Kant's concept of the autonomous will doesn't deny that many people act only on the level of conventional morality and, in so doing, they may act in conformity with the moral law. For example, the person who does not lie or steal acts in accordance with conventional morality. But to have true, personal moral worth, their actions should not only conform with the moral law but be done with consciousness of that law.

There are three aspects of morality in Kant's notion of autonomy, two of which are also implicit in Kant's first two formulations of the categorical imperative. They are: freedom, the self-imposition of the moral law, and the universal acceptability of the moral law.

Freedom—According to Kant, only rational beings can be bona fide members of the moral community, because morality requires both the possibility of conceiving and understanding the moral law and the possibility of knowingly and willingly acting from duty to it. Human beings, unlike other animals, can inhibit and control their instincts, passions, and drives. Just as important, they can examine their actions *before* performing them. The ability to so act imposes an obligation to do so. This is the freedom peculiar to the rational being: to override instincts and stimuli, to engage in moral reflection. It is the freedom of self-determination, which becomes moral freedom when we choose to act from moral duty. In acting this way, said Kant, rational beings perfect themselves morally.

Self-Imposition of the Moral Law—A second aspect of autonomy stresses the fact that moral beings give themselves the moral law. As ends in themselves (the second formulation of the categorical imperative), moral beings are not subservient to anyone else. We determine the moral law for ourselves and accept its demands on ourselves. But that doesn't mean we can prescribe anything we want, for we are bound by reason and *its* demands. Since reason is the same for all rational beings, we all give ourselves the *same* moral law. So while the categorical imperative is the same for all of us, it is imposed and recognized by each of us for himself or herself.

Universal Acceptability of the Moral Law—The third aspect of autonomy is the universal acceptability of the moral law. This is a function of the fact that each moral being gives himself or herself the moral law. To see whether a rule or principle is a moral law, said Kant, we should ask if what the rule commands would be acceptable to all rational beings acting rationally. In considering lying, theft, or murder, for example, I must consider the act not only from my viewpoint but from the perspective of the person lied to, robbed, or murdered. Presumably, rational beings will see that they don't want to be lied to, robbed, or murdered. They will reach this determination not merely from considering their own good but because, as rational beings, they accept limits on what they permit themselves to do as members of a community. The test of the morality of a rule is not whether people in fact accept it but whether all rational beings, thinking rationally, would accept it regardless of whether they are the agents or the receivers of the actions.

Critical Inquiries

1. *Are ethical principles* a priori? The impulse behind Kant's ethics is the discovery and justification of *a priori* forms, concepts, and principles. He draws a sharp distinction between *is* and *ought* and contends that the moral *ought* must be formulated in *a priori* principles. Is he correct?

Aristotle, for one, denied the sharp antithesis between *what is* and *what ought to be*—and on this point has received support from other moral philosophers, such as utilitarians. What ought to be, it can be argued, is what satisfies a genuine need. These needs can be determined scientifically, and plans devised to satisfy them according to the facts.

Kant would reject such an empirical procedure as question-begging. It *assumes*, he would say, that morality consists in the fulfillment of our needs, a most dubious assumption. If need is interpreted in a nonmoral sense, it isn't a moral concept and hence is irrelevant. If interpreted in a moral sense, then Kant would argue that it must be connected with obligation, and obligation is not the sort of thing that empirical science can ever discover and justify.

The problem here concerns whether or not the *ought* can be derived from the *is*. For the reasons stated, Kant believed it could not, that the *ought* must be formulated in *a priori* principles. But the issue is far from resolved. Indeed, as indicated, it is a problem that modern philosophers continue to debate.

2. *Is good will the exclusive and unconditional good?* To understand this inquiry, let's consider pleasure. According to Kant, pleasure is good if combined with a good will but evil if combined with a bad will. Hedonists would agree that pleasure can be bad, but not because it is disconnected from a good will. For example, they would concede that pleasure gained, say, from wanton sadism may be bad not in and of itself but because its bad effects greatly outweigh its intrinsic goodness. But *as pleasure*, it is intrinsically good. By this hedonistic account, what makes good will intrinsically good is simply the pleasure that it involves rather than the accompanying sense of duty.

For their part, nonhedonists might admit that the good will is intrinsically good. But they would add that there are other intrinsic goods, such as truth and beauty, that are no less ultimate and unconditional. Such a pluralistic theory of goodness raises the question of whether there is any unconditional good—pleasure, love, respect for duty, or anything else.

3. *Does Kant's ethics provide a sound test of right?* Kant's first formulation of the categorical imperative says the moral rule must function without exception. Critics wonder why the prohibition against actions such as lying, promise breaking, suicide, and so on must be exceptionless. They say that Kant failed to distinguish between saying that a person should not except himself or herself from a rule and that the rule itself has no exceptions.

If stealing is wrong, it's wrong for me as well as for you. "Stealing is wrong, except if I do it" is not universalizable, for then stealing would be right for all to do, which contradicts the assertion that stealing is wrong. But because no one may make of oneself an exception to a rule, it doesn't follow that the rule itself has no exceptions.

Suppose, for example, we decide that stealing is sometimes right, perhaps in the case of a person who is starving. Thus the rule becomes "Never steal except when starving." This rule seems just as universalizable as "Never steal." The phrase "except . . ." can be viewed not as an *exception* to the rule but as a *qualification* of it. In suggesting that Kant has drawn too sharp a distinction between a hypothetical and a categorical imperative, critics in effect are asking why a qualified rule is not just as good as an unqualified one. If it is, then we no longer need to state rules in the simple, direct, unqualfied manner that Kant did.

In fairness to Kant, it could be argued that his universalization formula, in fact, can be interpreted flexibly enough to meet commonsense objections. For example, perhaps we could universalize the principle that individuals should steal rather than starve to death, or lie in order to save an innocent person from the threat of murder, or take one's own life in order to extinguish unspeakable pain. However, to make exception to the prohibitions aginst stealing, lying, and taking one's life seems to invite a non-Kantian empirical analysis to morally justify the exceptions. Furthermore, making exceptions to these perfect duties seemingly contradicts presumed exceptionless character or at least calls for a further discussion of the interplay between them and imperfect duties (e.g., to keep oneself alive, to protect the innocent, to save pain). But can we reason this way without a more empirical approach to ethics than Kant would allow? Can we do so without setting aside his notion of "perfect duties"?

Similar problems arise when one tries to apply Kant's second formulation of the categorical imperative: that individuals must always be considered ends in themselves and never means. This formula expresses our sense of the intrinsic value of the human spirit and has profound moral appeal. But is it possible to implement this formula without a view to the effects of our actions? After all, to say that I should always treat you as an end in yourself presumes I have some positive idea of the ends of all rational creatures. If I must so treat you, then this second formulation of the categorical imperative seems inconsistent with the first in the sense that the first is a right-for-right's-sake principle and the second is a right-for-good's-sake principle. Is Kant consistent?[6]

Kant's third formulation of the categorical imperative means that every rational person determines the moral law for himself or herself but cannot morally pre-

6. *Rader,* The Enduring Questions, *p. 564.*

scribe anything because each person is bound by reason and its demands. We are both sovereign and subject, willing the universal laws of morality for ourselves and others. The moral law must be the person's own free choice but is nonetheless a universal law.

But is genuine freedom consistent with Kant's interpretation of universality? Existentialists, for example, argue that freedom doesn't consist merely in willing the dictates of universal abstract reason. It is more individualistic and creative. They would say that in conceiving of morality as obedience to universal law, Kant dissolves the individual personality in a sea of ethical abstraction. In so doing, he in effect undermines his very demands for a moral community of free and responsible human beings. Existentialists would further say the freedom that consists of choosing whether to obey the *ought* is a bogus freedom. True freedom, in contrast, is *determining* the *ought* of a situation without appeal to *a priori* knowledge.

Self-Interest (Egoism)

The view that associates morality with self-interest is generally referred to as *egoism. Egoism contends that an act is moral when it promotes the individual's best long-term interests.* In determining the morality of an action, egoists use their best long-term advantage to measure the action's rightness. If an action produces, will probaby produce, or is intended to produce a greater ratio of good to evil for the individual in the long run than any other alternative, then that action is the right one to perform. Indeed, the individual *must* take that course.

Ethicists often distinguish between two kinds of egoism: personal and impersonal. Personal egoists claim that they themselves should pursue their own best long-term interests, but they do not claim that others should necessarily do the same. In contrast, impersonal egoists believe that everyone should follow his or her best long-term interests.

Several misconceptions haunt egoism. One is that egoists do what they want, that they are believers of "eat, drink, and be merry." Not so. Undergoing unpleasant, even painful experience is compatible with egoism, provided such temporary sacrifice is consistent with the advancement of long-term happiness. Another misconception is that egoists necessarily eschew virtues like honesty, generosity, and self-sacrifice. Again, this isn't always so. Whatever is compatible with one's long-term best interests—which could include self-giving acts—is compatible with egoism. Still another misconception is that all egoists are exponents of hedonism, the view that the only good in life worth seeking is pleasure. Although some egoists are hedonistic—as was the ancient Greek philosopher Epicurus (341–270 B.C.)—other egoists identify the good with knowledge, power, rational self-interest, or with what some modern psychologists call self-actualization. In fact, ethical egoists may hold any theory of what is good and what is bad.

Perhaps the chief misconception about egoism, however, is that it disallows acts intended to benefit someone else at the expense of the doer. In fact, there are two sorts of cases in which egoism seemingly would *require* acts of generosity. The first is where we expect our generosity to be reciprocated. (For example, you might do favors for a political candidate, expecting favors in return if he or she is elected.) The other sort of case is simply where a person wants to help someone else, say a close relative or friend. Assuming that the person will derive satisfaction from this, it is an egoistic act.

So egoism doesn't preach that we should never act generously but that there is no *moral duty* requiring us to act in the interest of others, if we otherwise wouldn't want to. In short, egoism says that we have no moral obligations toward others. If we do have a moral duty, it is to ourselves: Always look out for Number One.

Ethical egoism can be connected with Aristotle's belief that how we ought to behave can be derived from some aspect of human nature, in this case the alleged fact that we are, by nature, selfish creatures. And, according to the doctrine of psychological egoism, human beings are, as a matter of fact, constructed so that they must behave selfishly. Psychological egoists claim that all actions are in fact selfishly motivated and that unselfish actions are therefore impossible. This would include even such apparently self-sacrificial acts as parents giving up their own lives in order to save the lives of their children. Such acts, say psychological egoists, are selfishly motivated because they're done to satisfy the parents' desires to benefit themselves—for example, to perpetuate their line or to avoid unbearable guilt feelings.

This psychological theory of human motivation is the basis of philosophical egoists' distinctive claim: Since all acts are done because of the desires or motives of those who do them, all actions are by their nature selfish; it cannot even be our moral duty to act unselfishly.

Critical Inquiries

1. *Is psychological egoism testable?* For a statement to have scientific worth, it must permit some experiment that would have the effect of discounting or supporting it. For example, the statement "Cars with dead batteries can't start" is testable. Just find a car with a dead battery that starts. If you can, then the statement's incorrect; if you can't, then there's good reason to accept the claim. On the other hand, if you say "Cars won't start if a demon has hexed them," there's no possible way to test this hypothesis; it's a nonscientific statement. So if statements or explanations are to be taken scientifically, they must be testable.

When psychological egoists claim that people always act out of self-interest, they offer a description of human motivation that defies any test of verification. For example, if you say to a psychological egoist: "What about the case of the passenger in a plane crash who allows others to be rescued before himself, and consequently dies? Doesn't that show that people are at least capable of acting selflessly?" No, psychological egoists would say, because "deep down" the person was motivated by self-interest. And they would similarly dismiss all other examples of such heroics. What possible circumstances or conditions, then, would have the effect of disproving psychological egoism? What test would psychological egoists allow that could in theory falsify their claim? None, for one can always appeal to egoistic motivation as the main impulse behind any action.

If this analysis is correct, psychological egoism cannot be taken as a *scientific* description of human motivation. If all conceivable human conduct fits in with psychological egoism, then no actual state of affairs, no observations, no experimental results can be claimed as supporting evidence, because there's no observable difference between the statement's being true and its being false. Of course, psychological egoists might say that they don't intend to convey any scientific information to begin with. But then precisely what kind of information are they conveying, such that we should dismiss the commonsense presumption that people can act out of self-denial? If there's no observable difference between the description's being true or false, just what kind of information is being conveyed? This raises questions not only about the acceptability of psychological egoism but also about the soundness of philosophical egoism, inasmuch as it is based on psychological egoism.

2. *Does philosophical egoism change the meaning of* selfish *and* unselfish *actions?* Confronted by examples of seemingly selfless behavior, philosophical egoists respond that such behavior is, in fact, selfishly motivated. The air-crash passenger who throws a lifeline to a fellow passenger rather than take it himself is motivated by a desire to help himself rather the other, although one may not know precisely what that benefit might be. Similar explanations of heroic deeds lead the philosophical egoist to conclude that since all actions are by their nature selfish, we cannot be morally bound to act unselfishly.

The strength of the philosophical egoist's arguments seems to depend on the meaning of "selfish actions" and "unselfish actions." Presumably the philosophical egoist would define "selfish actions" as actions people perform to satisfy their own desires. Conversely, "unselfish actions" (were they possible) would be actions entirely divorced from the doer's desires, done rather to satisfy the desires of others.

But is the crucial difference between "selfish" and "unselfish" actions that a selfish action is intended to satisfy the desires of the doer, but an unselfish action never is? In fact, this is how unselfish and selfish actions ordinarily are distinguished: unselfish actions are motivated by a desire to help someone else, while selfish actions are motivated by a desire to help oneself.[7] The common distinction between selfish and unselfish actions, then, lies in the motivation of the doer, and not in the fact that unselfish actions, unlike selfish ones, are completely divorced from the doer's desires.

In the light of this common understanding of "selfish" and "unselfish" actions, philosophical egoism loses its force. After all, if there are cases of unselfish actions (that is, actions done from the doer's desire to benefit others), then we aren't forced to conclude that egoism is right. Other types of normative theories and ethical principles are possible.

3. *Does egoism provide means for settling conflicts of interest?* Suppose that it is in Frank Grogan's best long-term interests to "blow the whistle" on Icarus and that it is in Kravits's best long-term interests to silence Grogan. Ethical egoists

---

7. *Howard Kahane,* Thinking about Basic Beliefs: An Introduction to Philosophy *(Belmont, Calif.: Wadsworth, 1983), p. 14.*

would have each man do whatever was necessary to promote his own best long-term self-interests. But what Grogan should do is incompatible with what Kravits supposedly should do. Apparently there are two opposing ethical obligations here. Are both right? Egoists insist that egoism is not intended to arbitrate ethical conflicts such as this. Nevertheless, critics insist that a moral code, by definition, must resolve such conflicts. If it cannot, how useful is it?

4. *Does egoism introduce inconsistency into moral counsel?* Suppose that Grogan goes to a board member for advice. The board member happens to be an impersonal egoist. Assuming that it is in Grogan's best interests to speak out publicly, the board member advises him to do everything possible to do just that. A few minutes later, Kravits calls the same board member for advice. Again, assuming that it is in Kravits's best interests to silence Grogan, the board member advises Kravits to do everything he can to accomplish that. The board member's counsel hardly seems to indicate a single, consistent attitude. True, the impersonal egoist would maintain that the board member is simply saying that both Grogan and Kravits should try to effect their own best interests and that the board member hopes both will win. But the objection remains: The board member is recommending as right two conflicting courses of action.

5. *Does egoism undermine the moral point of view?* Many ethicists claim that the moral point of view is a necessary part of moral decision making. The moral point of view, according to ethicists, is the attitude of one who sees or tries to see all sides of an issue without being committed to the interests of a particular individual or group. Thus the moral point of view demands detachment and impartiality. If we accept the moral point of view, then we must look for it in any proposed ethical standard, including ethical egoism.

But ethical egoists cannot take the moral point of view, for they are always influenced by their own best interests, regardless of the issue, principles, or circumstances involved. Consider in the preceding example the implications of the board member's own egoism. Since she is an egoist, she must advise Grogan and Kravits in *her own* best long-term interests, not theirs. In effect, the board member, as an egoist, must be committed to the narrowest form of moral provincialism.

6. *Does egoism ignore blatant wrongs?* This may be the most common objection to egoism, indeed to any normative theory based solely on a consideration of the consequences of actions. By reducing everything to the standard of the best long-term self-interest, egoism on principle takes no stand against seemingly outrageous acts: murder, discrimination, deliberately false advertising, and so on. All such actions are morally neutral to the egoist until the test of self-interest is applied.

Of course, the egoist might call this objection a case of question begging—using the assumption that the aforementioned are morally objectionable as grounds for repudiating egoism when, in fact, their morality is the very issue which normative theories, such as egoism, address. Still, egoism must respond to the widely observed human desire to be fair or just, a desire that seemingly is at least sometimes stronger than competing selfish desires. A moral theory that allows the possibility of murder in the cause of self-interest offends our basic moral intuitions about justice and non-injury.

Utility

Whereas egoism maintains that the promotion of one's own best long-term interests should be the standard of morality, utilitarianism insists that the promotion of the best long-term interests of everyone concerned should be the moral standard. Stated briefly, *the utilitarian doctrine asserts that we should always act so as to produce the greatest possible ratio of good to evil for everyone concerned.*

As developed by John Stuart Mill (1806–1873), utilitarianism maintained that what is intrinsically good is pleasure or happiness. More recent utilitarians, however, view things other than happiness as having intrinsic worth (for example, knowledge, power, beauty, and moral qualities). Their view is termed *pluralistic,* or *ideal, utilitarianism* and has attracted thinkers such as G. E. Moore[8] and Hastings Rashdall.[9] But since we will be primarily considering Mill's utilitarianism, we will be using *intrinsic good* to mean happiness. What we will say about Mill's position, however, applies equally to pluralistic utilitarianism, if for *happiness* or *pleasure* the phrase *intrinsic good* is substituted.

Before evaluating the utilitarian doctrine, let's clear up some points about utilitarianism that frequently lead to its misapplication. First, in speaking of right and wrong acts, utilitarians are speaking about those over which we exercise control, those that are voluntary. This does not mean, however, that we must have premeditated the action. For example, suppose that as you are walking down a street you observe a child standing in a driveway as a car is backing up. The child will surely be struck. Without deliberation you rush to the scene and snatch the child away from the path of the car. Although you did not premeditate this action, you could have acted otherwise; you could have chosen not to save the child. This is a voluntary action.

Second, in referring to the "greatest possible ratio of good to evil," utilitarians do not indicate a preference for immediate or remote good. The emphasis is on *greatest.* If the long-term good will be greater than the short-term, we should prefer it, and vice versa. Frequently, however, the long-term good is less certain that the immediate good. In such cases we may prefer the immediate good.

Third, in determining the "greatest possible ratio of good to evil for everyone," we must consider unhappiness or pain as well as happiness. For example, if it were possible to calculate pleasure and pain, then we should subtract from the total happiness our action would produce the total unhappiness it would produce. The result, in theory, will be an accurate measure of the action's worth. So if an action produces eight units of happiness and four units of unhappiness, its net worth is four units. If a second action produces ten units of happiness

8. *G. E. Moore,* Principia Ethica *(London: Cambridge University Press, 1903).*

9. *Hastings Rashdall,* A Theory of Good and Evil: A Treatise on Moral Philosophy, *2 vols. (New York: Kraus Reprint, reprint of 1924 edition).*

and seven units of unhappiness, its net worth is three units. In such a case we should choose the first action over the second. In the event that both acts lead not to happiness but to unhappiness, we should do the one that leads to fewer units of unhappiness.

Fourth, when choosing between two actions, one that you prefer and one that you do not prefer, choose the one that produces the greatest net happiness. Obviously you should not disregard your own preferences, but you should not give them added weight either. Count yourself as just one vote among the many.

Utilitarianism can take one of two forms: act or rule.

Act Utilitarianism

Act utilitarianism maintains that the right act is the one that produces the greatest ratio of good to evil for all concerned. In performing an action we must ask ourselves what the consequences of this particular act in this particular situation will be for all concerned. If the consequences produce more general good than those of any other alternative, then the action is the right one and the one we should perform.

If Frank Grogan is an act utilitarian, he will consider the consequences of his alternatives not only for himself but for the firm, the aircraft industry, business generally, customers, fellow employees, and society at large. He will let an evaluation of all the consequences to all the parties suggest the course of his action. Under other circumstances, he might take another course. In short, each situation is considered unique; each new set of circumstances calls for a fresh evaluation.

Act utilitarianism avoids a number of the faults found with egoism. First, it provides an objective way to resolve conflicts of self-interest. By proposing a standard outside self-interest, act utilitarianism greatly minimizes and may actually eliminate conflicts of self-interest such as that between Grogan and Kravits. Rather than considering only their own interests, which may conflict, parties appeal to a uniform standard: the general good. Second, act utilitarianism has the logical consistency that personal egoism lacks. And third, act utilitarians are able to take the moral point of view. But act utilitarianism, too, has weaknesses.

Critical Inquiries

1. *Are the consequences of actions certain?* We can never be sure of the consequences of our actions. Evaluation of the morality of those actions on any consequential basis is extremely problematic. Thus, any utilitarian stand seems essentially a questionable claim springing from an unknown fact. Act consequentialists might reply that morality is not so much in what the action produces as in what the agent intends that it produce. For example, if Grogan speaks publicly, it is not so important that he produce the most happiness for all concerned as it is important that he intend his action to do so. It is a safe bet, however, that not one of the Watergate conspirators *intended* his action to lead to what it did. But does this make their actions right? Ironically, in emphasizing intention here, the act utilitarian is not taking a consequential position at all but rather a nonconsequential one.

2. *Are some actions wrong, no matter how much good they produce?* What about actions that in themselves seem questionable? Suppose, for example, Grogan's calculations lead him to believe that the greatest good will be served if he takes no further action, despite his conviction that the faulty wing design could, in just the right conditions, kill people. Or suppose a used-car dealer sets back the odometer on a car in order to get a quick sale. The dealer is certain the car is in good shape and is convinced that the odometer reading played no part in setting the sticker price, which in fact is highly competitive. In short, whoever buys the car will undoubtedly get a good deal; indeed, both seller and buyer will get a good deal. Some critics of act utilitarianism would object that such actions, despite their consequences, are in themselves morally objectionable. These critics point out that an act may be wrong because it involves perpetrating an injustice, telling a lie, breaking a promise, or violating a rule. As a result, some ethicists, such as A. C. Ewing, conclude that "act utilitarian principles, logically carried out, would result in far more cheating, lying and unfair action than any good person would tolerate."[10]

3. *Does the principle of utility conflict with that of justice?* Critics of utilitarianism have pointed out that mere increase in total happiness is not of itself good. On the contrary, the *distribution* of happiness is a further and most important question. Surely it is not unreasonable to argue for a state of affairs in which the happy people are those who most deserve to be—even though they may be few in number. This objection relates to the preceding one; in both cases utilitarianism associates justice with efficiency rather than fair play. Utilitarians determine what is just by a calculation of total benefit, not by appeal to merit and desert. If an action is efficient—in the sense that it is calculated to produce more total good than any other alternative—then in the traditional utilitarian view, the action is thereby just. Critics dispute this concept by arguing that the total amount of good is not the most important measure of justice.

Rule Utilitarianism

Rule utilitarianism asserts that we should not consider the consequences of a particular action but rather the consequences of the rule under which the action falls. Reconsider the case of the used-car dealer. Even if the dealer's action produces more happiness than any other alternative, some utilitarians might still consider it wrong. In their evaluation, they would appeal not to the action itself but to the rule under which the action falls. The rule utilitarian could argue that the rule requiring dealers to represent a car's mileage accurately is a good rule because it generally produces a greater ratio of good to evil than misrepresentation of the mileage. Reasoning thus, they would call the dealer's action immoral, even though in this particular case the greatest good was served.

Rule utilitarians, then, ask us to determine the worth of the rule under which any action falls. If obeying the rule generally produces more total good than violating it, we should obey it, regardless of the consequences in any particular situation. In another example, suppose that the greatest common good would

10.   *A. C. Ewing,* Ethics *(New York: Free Press, 1965), p. 41.*

be served by imprisoning someone for a crime the person did not commit. While act utilitarians in theory could condone such an action, rule utilitarians probably could not. Such an action would violate a rule which, if followed, generally produces more good than if violated. The rule: Never imprison an innocent person.

Irish philosopher George Berkeley (1685–1753) offered one strong argument for rule utilitarianism. Berkeley reasoned that if each time a person must make a moral decision he or she must evaluate the consequences of a proposed action, then enormous difficulties would arise due to ignorance, prejudice, carelessness, lack of time, or indifference. The result would hardly be in the best interests of the general good. Rules, however, that everyone is aware of and attempts to implement simplify such problems, thereby advancing the common good. Just as we have traffic laws to promote the best interests of all drivers, so rules in the moral realm promote the general good. Although rule utilitarianism seems to resolve some of the problems of act utilitarianism, and today it is vigorously defended by philosophers such as Richard Brandt,[11] it is not an airtight ethical theory.

Critical Inquiries

1. *How does one formulate a satisfactory rule?* One problem that arises in dealing with any rule theory is the formulation of the rule itself. For example, is the rule "Never intentionally deceive anyone" a desirable one? One way to find out is to devise a situation testing its effectiveness.

For example, suppose that someone was holding a pistol to your head and threatened to pull the trigger unless you told the next person who entered the room that your name was something other than what it actually is. Should you in this circumstance deliberately deceive that person who enters the room? It would certainly be a healthy, if not moral, thing to do. So maybe such a rule needs to be qualified to read: "Never intentionally deceive someone *unless your life depends on it*." But still, problems persist.

Suppose that you have been captured by an enemy who is trying to extract from you vital troop movement information. If you divulge the information, 100 soldiers will most probably perish. If you misinform the enemy, you will save the soldiers' lives, although you will probably lose your own life. Here your own life may seem less worthy of preservation than the lives of 100 soldiers. So maybe the rule should be amended again to read: "Never intentionally deceive anyone unless your own life *or someone else's depends on it*."

The point is that it is difficult to establish rules of moral behavior. True, we can qualify them, but frequently such qualifications so weaken and compromise the rule that the result is more like act utilitarianism than rule.

2. *How does one decide between contradictory rules that appear to produce equally desirable results?* For example, one can legitimately argue that the rule "Never

---

11.   *Richard B. Brandt, "In Search of a Credible Form of Rule Utilitarianism," in* Morality and the Language of Conduct, *ed. G. Nakhnikian and H. Castaneda (Detroit: Wayne State University Press, 1961).*

intentionally deceive someone unless the truth will deeply pain that person" will produce as great a ratio of good to evil as "Never intentionally deceive anyone even if telling the truth will deeply pain someone else." Which of the two contradictory rules should rule utilitarians choose?

A consummate rule utilitarian supposedly could not prefer one rule to the other. Since both produce equally beneficial results, one rule is not better than the other, even though one appears unjust. If rule utilitarians reply that we must prefer the rule that does not allow the injustice, then they would be inconsistent—they would be introducing nonconsequential factors into their evaluation.

3. *Does rule utilitarianism ignore what appear to be blatant wrongs?* We have raised this objection before, in discussing act utilitarianism and egoism. To see how it applies to rule utilitarianism, let us look at another case illustration. Suppose that doctors and scientists could guarantee that they could relieve the suffering of millions of people if they were given a number of experimental patients on whom they would perform agonizingly painful and ultimately fatal operations. Would they be justified in performing these experiments on the "less desirable" and "less productive" members of society (that is, the convicted murderers, the permanently mentally ill, the terminally ill) without their consent? Such experiments would seemingly produce the greatest good for the greatest number. Yet critics of rule utilitarianism argue for the intrinsic worth of the individual and, consequently, consider any rule that would condone such behavior immoral.

Ethics and Society

So far we have been discussing ethical and moral questions mainly from the viewpoint of individual morality. We've asked, for example, whether individuals should decide what to do on the basis of reason, God's commands, social utility, or some other criterion. We've examined these questions primarily in terms of our individual relationship to a relatively small circle of associates.

But clearly we interact with other people besides our immediate acquaintances. There are millions of others whom we'll never meet or deal with directly but whose lives are connected to ours, and ours to theirs, because we are all members of a society.

Society *refers to the totality of relationships among people. A specific society consists of a group of human beings broadly distinguished from other groups by its interests, institutions, and culture.* Inasmuch as human beings are of necessity social animals, personal issues are bound to merge with social concerns. Many of the important moral issues that you and I face are not wholly or even largely private and personal, but social. For example, capital punishment, pornography and censorship, euthanasia, abortion, job discrimination—all raise important social and moral concerns not just for the individual, but for society as a whole.

Social ethics is the study of people in groups, with particular attention to the abstract claims they have on each other in the form of rights, duties, and privileges, and especially their demands for justice, equality, and freedom.

Justice

It's common to think of justice in terms of crime and punishment. Sometimes we read of a criminal's being sent to prison, and we infer that justice was meted out. Other times, we hear of someone's not being punished for apparent wrong-doing, and we bemoan the miscarriage of justice. In short, we often think of justice as retribution—punishment given for some wrongdoing.

But we can think of justice in terms other than retribution. Justice also deals with *distribution.* Given the relative scarcity of a society's wealth and goods, how should they be distributed? Should everyone receive the same amount? Ought those most in need receive the lion's share, or should the resources be distributed according to the individual's potential contributions to society? Should members of groups that have been unfairly discriminated against receive special consideration and treatment? Who should have access to medical care? Only those who can afford it? Everyone who needs it? Those who likely will benefit most?

The issues of distribution aren't confined to wealth and goods, however. Equally important is the distribution of privilege and power. Education raises such issues. Who should be educated? Everyone? Only those who can afford an education? Only those who promise benefit to society? Turning to other questions of privilege and power, we can ask: Who should be permitted to vote? To drive? To drink? Should everyone be treated the same under the law? Or should certain individuals (juveniles, for example) receive special consideration?

All these questions involve distributive justice. As its name implies, *distributive justice is concerned with the fair and proper distribution of public benefits and burdens among the members of a community.* While distributive justice operates in all organizations, it applies chiefly to the state's (the government's) relationship with its members.

Clearly, the subject of distributive justice touches many areas, from jobs to income, from taxes to medical services. What is the proper way of distributing what is available when there isn't enough for all? It's commonly claimed that jobs should be distributed on the basis of talent and ability. In the tax code of 1980, large corporations were given tax breaks because it was felt that they would reinvest their savings, thus increasing jobs and productivity, which in turn would benefit the whole of society. And some people believe that medical services should be provided on the basis of need, not ability to pay. Each of these assertions implies some standard that should be considered in the distribution of certain resources: merit, social benefit, need.

No matter which serves as the standard for distribution, it ordinarily can be traced, and ideally should be, to a fully developed theory of justice. The person who invokes talent and ability as the principle of job distribution probably views justice itself in terms of merit. The person who argues for tax breaks for large corporations likely is viewing justice in terms of social utility. And those who think that medical resources should be distributed on the basis of need typically view justice chiefly in terms of equality: If everyone were treated equally, all would get what they need. In fact, merit, social utility, and equality have historically served as focal points for various theories of justice and continue to exert profound influence on our current views of justice.

MERIT.   Plato (428–348 B.C.) and Aristotle proposed the first significant theory of justice, which is associated with giving people what is their due. In Plato's view, justice in the state is exactly what it is in the individual: a harmony between the various parts for the good of the whole. Social justice, then, requires cooperation among all members of a society. It follows that the interests of the individual must be subordinated to those of society.

Such a notion had a decided impact on the overwhelming majority of the Greek population, who were poor and powerless. The submissive role that these people played, especially the slaves, was considered vital to the overall success of Greek society. Consequently, their rights were kept to a minimum. They expected reward only insofar as their actions benefited their superiors. Such an attitude could be fostered only in a rigidly structured society, whose sharply drawn class divisions left no confusion as to one's place, role, or expectations in life. And this is precisely the kind of society that Plato erected in his immortal work, *The Republic*—one in which every individual has his or her place, and justice means that each acts and is treated accordingly. In Plato's view, then, justice is associated with merit: Individuals are treated and expected to act according to the kinds of persons they are, according to the roles that nature has fitted them to fulfill.

Apparent in *The Republic* is Plato's insistence not only on severe class distinctions but also on the *inequality* of individuals. Aristotle agreed, and thus for him, as for Plato, justice is giving to people what is their due. Indeed, in his *Politics*, Aristotle defended slavery, not only because of an economic benefit to society but because he believed that those who were slaves were naturally suited for that role and would be wretched and ineffectual were they made free.

It's interesting to speculate how Plato and Aristotle might react to some contemporary issues that raise questions of justice. For example, it seems that both would object to heterogeneous grouping in public schools (that is, the practice of placing students of diverse abilities in the same class, as opposed to homogeneous grouping, in which students of like ability are placed in a class). They would probably disapprove of giving aliens the same privileges as citizens (for example, education and medical care) and of treating men and women as equals. As for the draft, they wouldn't object to discriminating between males and females, but they might to subjecting every male of a certain age to the draft. The just thing, they might say, would be to conscript only those suited to be soldiers.

Even though we may not share the Greek view of inequaliy, our own concepts of justice are in other important ways deeply indebted to this Greek view. For example, like these two philosophical luminaries, we today hold that equals shoud be treated equally. The difference, of course, is that we espouse *egalitarianism, the view that all are equal by virtue of being human beings*. In his concern with the distribution of society's resources, Aristotle anticipated an issue of social justice of vital national and international concern today. Furthermore, despite his elitism, Aristotle clearly recognized the importance of justice for the poorest and least powerful members of society. Finally, much of the theorizing since the time of the Greeks has been, in effect, a response to Plato's claim that justice is giving everyone what is his or her due. Philosophers since Plato have attempted to spell out what an individual is entitled to and why. Inevitably, this has called for an inspection of the relationship between justice and equality, which we will see as we turn to the theory of justice associated with social utility.

SOCIAL UTILITY.   The theory that views justice in terms of social utility has its base in the social and political thought of a number of British philosophers of the eighteenth and nineteenth centuries. The foundation of their position differs from that of the Greeks in that it holds that everyone is equal.

The assumption of equality is one we can readily identify with, having been reared in a society founded on the premise that "all men are created equal." In the United States it is widely believed that everyone is entitled to a period of roughly the same kind of education; that the sexes should be treated equally; that individuals should be treated the same before the law; that everyone should have equal job opportunities and equal access to medical care; and that everyone should be allowed to practice religion, speak freely, travel, and so on. Similarly, we reject slavery in principle because it violates our belief in universal equality. We even object to (though practice) snobbery, presumably because we believe that one person is not necessarily better than another simply because of wealth, family, intelligence, or some other criterion. The point is that we needn't look far to see evidence that, at least in theory, our society is built on a commitment to egalitarianism. But this commitment raises problems of both a theoretical and an operational sort, of which you must be aware to understand the thrust of the social-utility theory.

Consider the practice of heterogeneous grouping in the classroom. Consistent with the belief that everyone is equal, we try to ensure that individuals have about the same educational opportunities, at least in their formative years. Thus thirty students of widely different ability and capacities typically are placed in the same class at the same time with the same instructor. Faced with such essential diversity, teachers often end up aiming at the nonexistent "average" pupil. Like as not, the instructional level will be too high for the slowest and too low for the swiftest. As a result, the slowest don't learn and the swiftest get bored; both "turn off." Is this just?

Medical technology has made the dream of organ transplant an astonishing reality. Corneas, hearts, kidneys, even livers can be transplanted with success. But demand exceeds supply. Who should get available organs when there aren't enough to go around? By a strict egalitarian calculation, everyone who needs a heart, say, should have an equal chance of getting it. But suppose two people are in need of the only available heart. One of them is an internationally renowned neurosurgeon in her forties whose survival promises to benefit countless persons. The other is a sixty-five-year-old derelict who for three decades has abused his body and whose survival promises little if any benefits to anyone, except possibly himself. Is it just to treat these individuals as equals in determining who will receive the heart? Or is it more just that they be treated as unequals?

Doubtless, the examples could be multiplied, but the point should already be clear: There are cases in which the public interest clashes with the requirements of equal treatement. For Greek theorists like Plato and Aristotle, this was no great problem, because they associated justice with merit, not equality. But for modern theorists, who largely take equality as a natural fact, the tension between public interest and demand for equal treatment poses an urgent conflict. Indeed, it is one that British social philosophers have discussed for several centuries and that has given rise to the social-utility view of justice.

The most explicit statement of the utility view is expressed by John Stuart Mill. In *Utilitarianism* (1863), Mill concedes that the notion of equality is often part of both our conception and practice of justice. But he does not believe that equality constitutes the essence of justice. While the conception of justice varies in different persons, says Mill, it always conforms to the individual's idea of utility: People believe that equality is the dictate of justice *except* when they feel that expediency requires inequality. They are likely to say, for example, that the famous surgeon and the skid-row bum should not be treated as equals in determining who of the two should get the available heart. Since preserving the life of the surgeon promises more social benefit, expediency requires inequality of treatment.

In Mill's view, then, expediency is the ever-present criterion in determining what is just and unjust. Whatever the institution, policy, or program, its justness depends ultimately on one's opinion about expediency in regard to the phenomenon. Is reverse discrimination just? It all depends on whether it serves the public interest better than any other alternative posed to ensure comparability of opportunity. Does a fee-for-service medical system best serve society's interests? Does a selective-service system that conscripts males but not females most effectively advance the common good? While individual answers may vary, each of them, according to Mill, will be based on opinion about expedience of the practice. What is considered expedient will be considered just; what is not considered expedient will not be considered just.

Since Mill's utility theory of justice is a logical extension of his ethical theory, it's understandable that it should invite some of the same critical inquiries. First, even if what we consider expedient we also consider just, *ought* we? For example, there are laws regulating the amount of marijuana one can possess. Even if such laws are expedient—productive of the most social good—ought we consider them just? There are laws prohibiting active euthanasia. Even if we assume the expediency of such laws, we can still ask whether they are just.

Another and operationally more troublesome problem with social-utility theory arises from the inevitable clash of individual and public interest. Surely there are cases when the general utility can be served only at the expense of a single individual, or perhaps a group of them. Take, for example, the currently volatile and socially divisive issue of installing commercial nuclear power plants. Even if (1) the plants are the most efficient source of energy available (which, of course, is debatable), and (2) they pose only remote and minimal hazards to individuals living near them (again debatable), is it *just* for the state to insist that these individuals must bear even a negligible risk or undergo dislocations for the good of society?

In recent years considerable money and domestic resources have been diverted from human services to national defense. Some individuals and groups (e.g., the poor, the young, the elderly, the infirm, racial minorities) seem to be directly injured as a result. The justification for the realignment of priorities largely takes the form of an appeal to the national interest. Even if the national interest is best served this way, is it fair to shore up national defense at the expense of the economically most vulnerable members of society? Of course, one could respond that the utility of a specific act by itself cannot give an adequate concept of justice, that what is needed is a theory of general practice along the lines of rule utilitarianism. But as we noted earlier, rule utilitarianism still allows the possibility of systematically increasing general utility at the expense of some individual or group. Is this just? Utility theorists would likely say it is, simply because justice ultimately has no concrete meaning apart from expediency.

But not all agree. In fact, a powerful contemporary theory of justice proposed by the American philosopher John Rawls attempts to reassert the primacy of individual rights by placing the emphasis on the advantages of a practice to the least advantaged members of society. In so doing, it clearly ties together the concepts of justice and equality.

EQUALITY.   By his own account, Rawls has presented his theory as a modern alternative to utilitarianism, one he hopes will be compatible with the belief that justice must be associated with equality. This alternative focuses primarily on the distribution of economic goods and services and attempts to alleviate the plight of the most disadvantaged. Economists refer to it as the *maximin principle:* Inequality is permissible only if it improves (*max*imizes) the lot of the worst off (the *min*imal sector) in society.

The heart of Rawls's theory of justice consists of two principles: equal liberty and difference. In developing the equal-liberty principle, Rawls admits that it is nothing new (nor is his theory of justice, for that matter); rather, it is a point on which all social philosophers and moralists agree. *The equal-liberty principle means that each person participating in a practice, policy, or regulation or affected by it has an equal right to the most extensive liberty compatible with a like liberty for all.* Rawls notes that the term *person* has various referents depending on the circumstances. Sometimes it will mean an individual, other times it may refer to a nation, business firm, church, team, or association. No matter the denotation of *person,* the principle applies in all instances, although there is a logical priority given to the case of individuals as opposed to, say, business firms or nations. Central to Rawls's equal-liberty principle is his conception of equality, by which he means the impartial and equitable administration and application of the rules that define a practice.

To illustrate the equal-liberty principle, let's suppose the federal government decides that every family of four should have an income of at least $7,500 a year. Any family with a subminimal income (that is, below $7,500) would be subsidized the difference. According to the equal-liberty principle, the rule must be administered to all families of four in the subminimal category without exception. Thus if a family of four making $6,000 a year were excluded, the rule would not be equitably administered. Nor would it be if legislators failed to recognize income reduced by factors outside the family's control. For example, suppose two families each earned $6,000 a year, but the first incurred medical bills totaling $2,000. An equitable distribution would involve a $3,500 subsidy to the first family and a $1,500 subsidy to the second. Naturally, any family with conditions similar to those of the first family would rightly expect the same treatment. Note Rawls is defining liberty with reference to the pattern of rights, duties, powers, and liabilities established by a practice. In this case, families making less than $7,500 a year have a *right* to expect equal treatment regarding governmental subsidies.

But should there be such a subsidy to begin with? After all, all those making more than $7,500 will end up paying for it out of their taxes. And isn't that an infringement on their personal liberty? In fact—and Rawls concedes this—any law or regulation, by definition, will restrict personal liberty. In an attempt to justify regulatory infringements on personal liberty, then, Rawls offers his second principle: the principle of difference.

According to the difference principle, "social and economic inequalities are to be arranged so that they are . . . to the greatest benefit of the least advantaged" (italics added).[12] This is why Rawls's view is identified with the interests of society's worst off.

In order to understand the implications of the difference principle, it's important to distinguish between contingent and noncontingent equality. *Contingent equality is equality that depends on something else for its justification; it is not justified in and of itself.* For example, utilitarians would justify equality on grounds of social improvement: People should be treated equally when and if the social good is advanced. When the social good is retarded, and more good can be realized by treating people unequally, the inequality is justified. In contrast, a noncontingent equality is not justified by appeal to consequences or to anything else. We should treat people equally not because equality leads to the greatest social benefit but because, in and of itself, it is the right and proper way to deal with people.

For Rawls, equality is not contingent. He would permit inequality only when the practice involving inequality in all likelihood works to the advantage of the worst off. Notice that the difference principle disallows inequalities generally justified on utilitarian grounds, that is, on the grounds that the greatest number will benefit. In Rawls's view, an inequality that helps most people but not the worst off is not justified.

As opposed to the emphasis on efficiency of classical utilitarianism's concept of justice, Rawls's, like Kant's, takes root in reciprocity. *Reciprocity is the principle that requires that a practice be such that all members, exercising rationality, could and would accept it and be bound by it.* Without reciprocity, there can be no basis for true community.

Now let's see how Rawls's theory might work in practice by relating it to the graduated income tax. Some economists argue that a sharply graduated income tax reduces work incentive—that the most productive and talented members of a society are discouraged from working and so cut back on their effort. If physicians lost their incentive to work, for example, all of us would probably end up worse off than we were originally, including the worst off. Under Rawls's

---

12. *John Rawls*, A Theory of Justice *(Cambridge, Mass.: Harvard University Press, 1972), p. 255.*

maximin rule, therefore, it seems defensible not to tax physicians so much as, say, artists of equal income, since the loss of the artists' work probably would not worsen the state of the worst off. It is conceivable, however, that the artists might be heavily taxed so long as such taxation reduced the economic gap between them and the poorest group in society. But wouldn't the artists, like the physicians, ultimately lose incentive? And, with that loss, wouldn't their tax dollars be lost to the poor? Presumably, at this point, Rawls would favor the unequal economic status of the groups, since such inequality would actually serve to improve the position of the lowliest group in the society. It is clear, then, that Rawls's maximin rule is compatible with considerable inequality, but only if it improves the status of the poorest members of society.

In his argument, Rawls relies on a traditional "patterned" distribution of goods. A patterned distribution is one that can be summed up in some formula like "To each according to his or her _____ ," where the blank may be filled in with *need, work, intelligence,* or *effort,* for example. It is highly unlikely that any society already reflects this formula for the distribution of wealth. Therefore, to achieve a just society, the goods must be redistributed until people's holdings correspond with what is thought to be the just pattern. Rawls believes the just pattern to be his maximin rule.

Rawls's Harvard colleague Robert Nozick, for one, disagrees. He thinks any theory of justice relying on a patterned distribution of wealth is inherently unjust because it coerces individuals and thus violates their basic rights. Such a theory deprives citizens of the free exercise of their preferences even when they are not hurting anyone else.

Nozick asks us to imagine a society in which the goods are distributed according to some patterned concept of justice, such as equality, whereby everyone has precisely the same holdings. Suppose, for example, basketball star Julius Erving signs a contract with a team under which he receives 25¢ from each game ticket sold. Excited by the prospect of seeing Erving play, fans gladly pay a surcharge on their tickets. In the course of the season, 1 million people attend Erving games. As a result, Erving ends up with $250,000—much more money than anyone else has in the hypothetical society. The transaction obviously has altered the patterned distribution of wealth, but is the new distribution unjust? If it is, why? Nozick argues that the source of the injustice cannot be that a million people freely chose to spend their money in this way and not some other. Since they knew where their money was going, they have no just claim against Erving. As for those who did not see him play, their holdings are unaffected. And if they had no claim against the goods of the transacting parties before this alteration occurred, they shouldn't have any afterward.

Embedded in this illustration are several objections to Rawls's maximin rule. One is that Rawls is using the better-off people in society to assure the welfare of the worst off. Some, like Nozick, regard this as a species of utilitarianism, which they consider fundamentally unjust. A related objection is that Rawls is not impartial, for he is seeing things only through the eyes of the worst off. Finally, Rawls has been criticized for his apparent claim that under certain circumstances individuals are not entitled to what they create.

In fairness to Rawls, it seems that in applying his difference principle to specific transactions, critics overburden it. After all, Rawls's difference principle is addressing the backdrop against which public policies and decisions about redressing inequalities are to be made. It is not speaking directly to specific, small-scale instances of the Julius Erving variety. More important, Rawls is *not* making the socialistic argument that all property should be shared. He says only that society must help the most disadvantaged members. This does not at all mean that everyone has a right to an equal share. In other words, Rawls's concept of justice does not equate fair distribution with equal distribution. Individuals have a just claim to whatever they have acquired so long as the acquisition occurred within the context of a fair social policy.

Rawls's theory is significant and controversial, not because it has connected justice with equality, for such a connection has a long history, but because it has enlarged the sphere of equality. While most, if not all, of us today would agree that people should have equal legal rights and opportunities, many would not extend equality to material goods and social services. Rawls is claiming that justice requires not only political and legal equality but an equality embracing the rights of individuals to material goods and social services. On this point he puts considerable distance between himself and both social utilitarians like Mill and the mainstream of today's conservative social and fiscal thinkers who would consider the distribution of goods and services a matter of utility. We will return to this matter shortly after discussing freedom, which it is closely linked to.

Freedom

Another central concern in social ethics is freedom. The kind of freedom we have in mind can be called political and social freedom, which includes the freedoms of speech, religion, and governance. History records many heroic battles fought to secure these freedoms as well as to win equality: the same treatment for all citizens in the state.

The classic description of freedom may be in Mill's essay *On Liberty* (1859). One of Mill's concerns in this essay is the freedom of the individual, specifically what actions individuals in society may rightly perform. Mill claims that society may interfere with the individual in matters involving other people but not in matters involving only the individuals themselves. In effect, he distinguishes between two spheres of interest, the outer and the inner. A matter belongs to the inner sphere if it involves only the self or a few others. The following excerpt from *On Liberty* captures the spirit of Mill's position:

> What, then, is the rightful limit to the sovereignty of the individual over himself? Where does the authority of society begin? How much of human life should be assigned to individuality, and how much to society?
>
> Each will receive its proper share, if each has that which more particularly concerns it. To individuality should belong the part of life in which it is chiefly the individual that is interested; to society, the part which chiefly interests society.
>
> Though society is not founded on a contract, and though no good purpose is answered by inventing a contract in order to deduce social obligations from

it, everyone who receives the protection of society owes a return for the benefit, and the fact of living in society renders it indispensable that each should be bound to observe a certain line of conduct towards the rest. This conduct consists, *first*, in not injuring the interests of one another; or rather certain interest, which either by express legal provision or by tacit understanding, ought to be considered as rights; and *secondly*, in each person's bearing his share (to be fixed on some equitable principle) of the labors and sacrifice incurred for defending the society or its members from injury and molestation. These conditions society is justified in enforcing, at all costs to those who endeavor to withhold fulfillment. Nor is that all that society may do. The acts of an individual may be unhurtful to others, or wanting in due consideration for their welfare, without going to the length of violating any of their constitutional rights. The offender may then be justly punished by opinion, though not by law. As soon as any part of a person's conduct affects prejudicially the interests of others, society has jurisdiction over it, and the question whether the general welfare will or will not be promoted by interfering with it, becomes open to discussion. But there is no room for entertaining any such question when a person's conduct affects the interests of no persons besides himself, or need not affect them unless they like (all the persons concerned being of full age, and the ordinary amounts of understanding). In all such cases, there should be perfect freedom, legal and social, to do the action and stand the consequences.[13]

Although Mill appears to have drawn some line of demarcation between society and individual, it's fuzzy. Just how many constitute "a few others"? Furthermore, Mill argues that since the individual and not society is the best judge of what advances self-interest, the individual should be free from interference in such pursuits. But do we always know our best interests? Suppose a woman who enjoys heroin shoots up every day. This matter might fall within the inner sphere, in which case she should be free from interference. Yet her behavior is probably not in her best interests. Therefore, it could easily be argued that her behavior should be interfered with. But should it?

When, if ever, should government interfere in cases of individual morality? Governments do legislate morality in the sense of passing laws to prevent great social harm—for example, passing laws against murder. There's little debate that governments must do this. But what about when no direct social harm is in question, such as the case of sex acts in private between consenting adults?

GOVERNMENT INTERFERENCE IN PRIVATE MORALITY.   Some say governments have no business legislating private morality because the purpose of government is completely social. People who hold this view, whom we'll call noninterventionists, often oppose laws prohibiting homosexual or any other private sexual behavior between adults; abortion; the use or sale of birth control devices; and the use or sale of drugs like marijuana, tobacco, and alcohol. (Of course, noninterventionists can be selective in their opposition; for example, some may oppose laws prohibiting the sale and use of alcohol but support one prohibiting the sale or use of marijuana.)

13.   *John Stuart Mill*, On Liberty *(London: J. M. Dent, 1910), pp. 77–78.*

Interventionists, in contrast, claim that few, if any, acts are totally private in their effects. Inasmuch as all human beings are social animals, what one person does inevitably affects others. In short, strictly individual or private morality doesn't really exist. For example, even if alcoholics drink privately, their alcoholism inevitably affects the people around them: when they fail to support dependents, when they're absent from work or inefficient if present, when they endanger their lives or others' on the highways, and so on.

While the interventionist view has appeal, it doesn't distinguish between legislating against harmful *public effects* of private behavior and legislating against the private behavior itself. For example, very few people who support severe punishments for drunk driving would support any punishment for the drinking in private that preceded the driving. Governments, say noninterventionists, should legislate against the harmful public effects of private acts but not against the acts themselves. When they do, they are unjustifiably invading privacy and limiting personal freedom.

Noninterventionists bolster their position further by pointing to the diverse opinions in society. Some people think abortion is always immoral; others believe it is sometimes all right. Likewise, some believe no pornographic materials should be made available even to adults; other believe that government has no right to restrict their availability; still others believe that government should exercise some control over the sale of pornographic materials, such as confining them to a specific location in a community. Given such diversity of opinion in our society, noninterventionists say that we must be tolerant of each person's or group's moral beliefs if we're to have the social cohesion and cooperation needed for a society to function well.

Embedded in the interventionist-noninterventionist debate is the broader question of governmental paternalism or benevolent interference. Should government interfere in the lives of adults "for their own good" even when the adults don't want it to? If a man chooses to drink himself into a daily stupor, do we have the obligation, even the right, to stop him if he is harming no one else, or if the people potentially affected have not requested intervention?

For utilitarians, the answer presumably must lie in a consideration of utility of one practice rather than another. But even Mill would confine government intervention in such cases to conduct negatively affecting the interests of others. Natural-rights theorists presumably can invoke the right of each individual to autonomy and self-determination in arguing against intervention. So whereas the man may be acting immorally, a government that interferes with his action is itself acting immorally by abridging his autonomy—an act some would say is the arch-villainy, for in undercutting individual autonomy it makes personal moral decisions impossible.

In the final analysis, interventionists must face up to a cluster of knotty issues. What basis is there for saying that governments have an obligation, even a right, for interfering in private acts that produce no apparent public harm? What concept of government and the proper relationship between government and individual underlies such a position, and on what grounds is the concept to be justified? Just how far should a government go in exercising paternalism?

Should it, for example, take steps to ensure that no one is reading "immoral" literature in the privacy of his or her home? That a couple have only "moral sex"? That individuals are not befouling their bodies with "junk" foods and their minds with "trashy" television programs? Some would say that such questions are extreme, that they in effect are unfairly discrediting the interventionist position with a slippery-slope argument. But even if interventionism is applied more selectively—for example, prohibit the private reading of salacious material but not the consumption of unhealthful foods—interventionists still must explain and *justify* such distinctions—why it's all right to abridge individual autonomy in one case but not another. Finally, and perhaps of ultimate importance, they must address the long-term implications of such governmental interference. Do we want a society in which government legislates private morality?

It is all well and good to defend such rights as freedom of speech and religion and of private morality, but what of the many people who find themselves far more concerned with eking out an existence—who can't afford proper medical care, good education, and a decent neighborhood for their families? Freedom from government persecution is not necessarily economic freedom. It is this latter freedom that Karl Marx, and his frequent collaborator Friedrich Engels, addressed.

THE MARXIST VIEW.   For Karl Marx (1818–1883) and like-minded socialists, the moral foundation of justice is the ideal of social equality described in the maxim "From each according to his abilities, to each according to his needs." Marx believed that one general, overriding fact distinguishes humans from other animals: Humans produce their own means of subsistence. According to Marx, it is natural and right for humans to work for their living; the life of productive activity is the right one for humans.

Granted that it's proper for humans to work for their living, what may be said about the product of that work? Like classical utilitarians and contemporary thinkers such as Rawls and Nozick, Marx believed that individuals have a legitimate claim to the product of their own labor. But he rejected the notion that they are entitled to own property they have not personally produced. Marx also did not believe that property ownership is licit when it functions to enrich the already affluent at the expense of other people, thereby forcing these people to work without benefit of the products of their labor. But this, according to Marx, is precisely what capitalism encourages: the exploitation of the large working class (proletariat) by the affluent few (bourgeoisie) who own the means of production. The result of exploitation is alienation, a key concept in Marx's notion of freedom.

Marx associated alienation with the ownership of private property. Individuals' alienation is the result of unfulfilling work. Because the work is imposed on them as a means of satisfying the needs of others, workers feel exploited and debased. What about those who are paid handsomely for their efforts? They too remain alienated, said Marx, because, since the fruits of their labor are enjoyed by someone else, the work ultimately proves meaningless to them. In his *Economic and Philosopical Manuscripts* (1844), Marx spoke of alienation as the separation of individuals from the objects they create, which in turn results in separation from other people, from oneself, and ultimately from the species itself.

In Marx's view, when workers are alienated they cannot be free. They may have the political and social freedoms of speech, religion, governance, and private morality, but even so, they still aren't free, because these freedoms don't necessarily guarantee freedom from economic exploitation.

How can people be free of alienation, of economic exploitation? Marx said they must first recognize the key to freedom lies in economics. Therefore, people must return to a "natural" state in which they and their labor are one. This natural state recognizes the corrupting influence of society and calls for a conception of the state that will allow people to be unselfish and nondestructive. But don't misunderstand—Marx did not advocate the end of work. On the contrary, he believed that work is humanizing and ennobling. He simply urged people to liberate themselves from alienating work.

Marx prescribed a fairer distribution of wealth as a means of combating alienation and ensuring freedom. Marx, unlike Rawls, equates fair distribution with equal distribution. This in part means no ownership of property except for those products a person makes directly. It also means an end to the worker/owner distinction, thereby making everyone a laborer who shares in the benefits of his or her labor. Marx called for nationalization as a way of attaining freedom from alienation—nationalization of land, factories, transport, and banks. But insofar as (1) the state presumably is the basis of all social ills, and (2) nationalization will exacerbate this by concentrating power in the hands of the state, it isn't at all clear how such institutional changes could affect freedom.

This observation has led philosophy professor Leslie Stevenson to suggest that we understand Marx as saying, at least in his early phase, that "alienation consists in the lack of community. In other words, since the State is not a real community, individuals cannot see their work as contributing to a group of which they are members. It would follow that freedom from alienation would be won by decentralizing, not nationalizing, the State in genuine communities or 'communes.' These entities would be characterized by the abolition of money, specialization, and private property."[14] Such entities would embody and implement the principle "From each according to his abilities, to each according to his needs."

Marx held that nothing less than a complete revolution of the economic system would effect the ideal of social equality. Piecemeal measures wouldn't do (e.g., higher wages, shorter work hours, better working conditions, etc.), for these do not alter the evil nature of the system. Moroever, legal and political institutions presumably are powerless to change conditions because they themselves are determined by the underlying economic system.

However, the development of capitalistic systems since Marx's time seems to belie these claims. Legal, political, and other institutions have modified the economic system of capitalism so that, in the United States, a "New Federalism" has been proposed in part to restore the "purity" of the system. The twentieth century has seen legislation curbing the worst, though not all, excesses of worker exploitation, guaranteeing a minimum wage (although this is currently under

14. *Leslie Stevenson*, Seven Theories of Human Nature (*New York: Oxford University Press, 1975*), p. 58.

attack for teenagers), and ensuring a comparatively safe and healthful work environment. Victories by labor unions have so increased the workers' share of the economic pie that workers in some airlines, rubber, automotive, and trucking industries have recently agreed to salary reductions in order to prop up these faltering enterprises and preserve their own jobs. Indeed, many of the specific measures proposed by Marx and Engels in the *Communist Manifesto* (1848) have been implemented in capitalistic countries: a program of graduated income tax, free education for all children in public schools, a concentration of considerable economic control in the hands of the state, and so on.

The indisputable fact is that the capitalism Marx experienced in the nineteenth century does not exist today. Changes have resulted not from a single-stroke, revolutionary rising of the masses but from a relatively orderly, step-by-step reform. The result is certainly far from perfect, but it does seem to discredit the Marxian repudiation of gradual reform. What's more, the well-documented suffering and dislocation that have followed on the heels of myriad revolutions mock the glib assumption that such upheavals inevitably will usher in social equality.

Finally, Marx's utopian vision of a truly classless society, one that embodies the principle "From each according to his abilities, to each according to his needs," at the very least seems wishful thinking. Why, critics have asked, will a communist society necessarily be classless? Won't those exercising dictatorship of the proletariat form a new governing class with ample opportunities to abuse their power?[15] If the history of Russia since the revolution is an indication, the emergence of such a new ruling class seems inevitable. Far from withering away, the state in communist countries has assumed monolithic dimensions, and the more entrenched it's become, the more it restricts the aforementioned freedoms from government persecution.

Summary and Conclusions

Rational development, natural law, divine command, duty, egoism, and utilitarianism are six important types of normative theory that attempt to provide grounds for accepting a moral judgment as true. Although each of these theories has weaknesses, they all nonetheless have a wide range of application for moral decision making.

A question inevitably arises here: "Which theory, if any, ought I endorse?" There is no principle that we can apply in choosing from among the array of ethical principles. So perhaps the whole enterprise of trying to formulate and justify moral principles is futile and should be abandoned. While such a reaction is understandable—especially from those beginning a study of ethics—there are good reasons not to act on this impulse of despair. After all, to say that an ethical theory is imperfect is not to say that it is empty or that the search for a satisfactory theory is futile. Human relationships present a tangled web of frequently subtle,

15. *Stevenson, p. 58.*

ill-defined problems. It is little wonder that we do not have a single theory that wins everyone's acceptance.

Each ethical theory discussed has an impressive range of application. In criticizing each theory, philosophers inevitably focus on its weaknesses. This approach is consistent with the philosophical enterprise of pursuing truth and certainty. Philosophers cite cases that tend to break the theory down, that test its strength at the most fundamental levels. Failing to grasp this aspect of the philosophical enterprise, one could conclude that there is little worth in these ethical theories. This judgment would be a gross overstatement that not even the theories' harshest critics would agree with. It would be as indefensible as scrapping the theory of biological evolution or of quantum mechanics because these are incomplete or unsatisfactory in important ways. As in the world of science, so in the realm of human relationships which ethics deals with, we face complex realities that by nature seem to preclude total success.

Granted that these theories, though imperfect, are extremely useful, is not a selection of one theory ultimately arbitrary? Since none can be proved correct, does it matter which one we choose? Again, such a reaction is totally understandable, but before deciding that the choice of an ethical theory is arbitrary, we should reflect on the meaning of the word *choice*.

It probably would be an arbitrary decision to conclude that since all ethical codes generally agree on basic ideals, it does not matter which code is followed. This position would be incorrect because each code commits us to different principles. The thoughtful person recognizes these differences and chooses. Such a choice, rooted as it is in a consideration of the alternatives, cannot be arbitrary. Instead, it is based on the best available evidence, on a consideration of everything it could possibly be founded on. In other words:

> To describe such ultimate decisions as arbitrary . . . would be like saying that a complete description of the universe was utterly unfounded, because no further fact could be called upon in corroboration of it. This is not how we use the words "arbitrary" and "unfounded." Far from being arbitrary, such a decision would be the most well-founded of decisions, because it would be based upon a consideration of everything upon which it could possibly be founded.[16]

The selection of an ethical theory is arbitrary only for frivolous and unthinking people who have never undertaken a serious investigation into ethical theory. For those persons who have, the choice—far from being arbitrary—is often slow, methodical, and agonizing. The process suggests not the impudence of those who say it does not matter but the courage of those who say it does. It is an individual choice, not an arbitrary one.

Finally, we should note that the fundamental worth of studying and understanding ethical thought is not that we thereby have definite guides to moral conduct. Rather, the value lies in becoming aware of the moral options available to us, of the general paradigm within which moral inquiry can take place as

---

16. R. M. Hare, *The Language of Morals (Oxford: Clarendon Press, 1952), p. 69.*

concrete human beings grapple with real-life issues. Individual moral choices are frequently not between obvious right or wrong, good or bad, but between actions and values that contain elements of both. The challenge, then, is not so much one of finding an ethical standard to use but of applying a defensible standard in a specific instance.

This challenge applies equally to matters of social ethics, which is the study of people in societies, with particular attention to the abstract claims they have on each other in the form of rights, duties, and privileges, and especially their demands for justice, equality, and freedom. Thus in issues involving distributive justice, we must decide which of several competing conceptions of justice—merit, social utility, or equality—is the most defensible. Likewise, in matters of freedom, we must decide whether freedom should be construed narrowly in the sense of freedoms of speech, religion, governance, and private morality, or more broadly in the sense of freedom from economic exploitation.

Selections for Further Reading

Broad, C. D. *Five Types of Ethical Theory.* New York: Harcourt, Brace, 1930.

Daniels, Norman, ed. *Reading Rawls.* New York: Basic Books, 1975.

Fried, Charles. *An Anatomy of Values: Problems of Personal and Social Choice.* Cambridge, Mass.: Harvard University Press, 1970.

Gewirth, Alan. *Reason and Morality.* Chicago: University of Chicago Press, 1978.

Kant, Immanuel. *Foundations of the Metaphysics of Morals,* Lewis White Beck, trans. New York: Bobbs-Merrill, 1959.

Ladd, J. *Ethical Relativism.* Belmont, Calif.: Wadsworth, 1973.

Mill, John Stuart. *Utilitarianism.* New York: Bobbs-Merrill, 1957.

Muller, Herbert J. *The Children of Frankenstein.* Bloomington: Indiana University Press, 1960.

Nietzsche, Friedrich. *Genealogy of Morals,* F. Golffing, trans. Garden City, N.Y.: Doubleday, 1956.

Oraison, Mafe. *Morality for Moderns,* J. F. Bernard, trans. New York: Doubleday, 1972.

Phelps, Edmund, ed. *Economic Justice.* Baltimore: Penguin Education, 1973.

Plato. *The Republic,* Benjamin Jowett, trans. New York: Random House, 1957.

Rawls, John. *A Theory of Justice.* Cambridge, Mass.: Harvard University Press, 1971.

Ross, W. D. *Foundations of Ethics.* New York: Oxford University Press, 1954.

Sen, Amartya. *On Economic Inequality*. Oxford: Clarendon Press, 1973.

Stace, W. T. *The Concept of Morals*. New York: Macmillan, 1965.

Warnock, Mary. *Existential Ethics*. New York: St. Martin's Press, 1968.

Part II

Issues

3
PORNOGRAPHY

In 1972 the state of Georgia sought an injunction against the showing of two films by the Paris Adult Theatres I and II of Atlanta. The state claimed that the films—*It All Comes Out in the End* and *Magic Mirror*—were obscene under relevant Georgia standards. The trial court demurred, saying an injunction could be granted only if it could be proved that the films were being shown to minors or nonconsenting adults. The state appealed the decision, and the Georgia Supreme Court reversed it. Eventually the U.S. Supreme Court upheld the reversal by a 5–4 majority.[1]

In writing the majority decision, Chief Justice Warren Burger argued that the state is justified in restricting consenting adults' access to obscene material in order to maintain public safety and a decent society, including a proper tone of commerce. In dissenting, Justice William Brennan wrote that state efforts to totally suppress obscene material inevitably would lead to erosion of protected free speech and overburden the nation's judicial machinery.

Were the films in question "obscene"? If they were, should their showing have been prohibited? Or should consenting adults have been allowed to see the films, even if the films were obscene? These are some of the prominent questions the Supreme Court addressed in *Paris I*, and has in many similar cases. And it's a safe bet that such issues will continue to appear on the Court's docket, for pornography is a multibillion-dollar-a-year business whose seemingly uncontrollable growth has individuals, institutions, and government agencies alarmed.

Among those concerned is the U.S. Congress, which has labeled traffic in pornographic materials a matter of national concern. In 1966 Congress established the Commission on Obscenity and Pornography. The commission's responsibility was to make recommendations based on a thorough study of pornographic and obscene materials. In 1970 the commission submitted its report to the President and Congress recommending that legislation prohibiting the sale, exhibition, and distribution of sexual material to consenting adults be repealed.

---

1.   Paris Adult Theatre I *v.* Slaton. *U.S. Supreme Court, 413, U.S. 49, 1973.*

The commission's report met with widespread executive, legislative, and popular disapproval. In fact, the commission itself was divided: Six of the eighteen members did not support its recommendation. As a result, implementation has been sporadic.

Whether there should be laws restricting the consenting adult's access to pornography or not is a key moral question in the pornography issue. But an even more basic question—and one that often intrudes on the discussions of the morality of restrictive pornography legislation—is whether there is anything morally objectionable about pornographic materials.

In this chapter we shall consider both questions: the morality of pornographic materials and the morality of restrictive pornography laws. Central to both questions is the definition of pornography, so we shall begin our discussion by considering the problem of defining it. We will then air some of the arguments relative to the two main moral concerns that the pornography issue involves.

The Meaning of Pornography

What is pornographic? Or, precisely, what material is rightly considered pornographic and why? The exact meanings of *pornographic* and *pornography* are a principal issue in the debate on the morality both of pornography and of the laws that would restrict its production and distribution.

Generally, pornography refers to literature, art, or photography that is "obscene." To understand the meaning of *pornography,* then, one must understand what *obscene* means.

The *Random House Dictionary* defines *obscene* as: "1. offensive to modesty or decency; 2. intended to cause sexual excitement or lust; 3. abominable or disgusting." Clearly such a definition is loaded with words that imply value judgments: "offensive," "abominable," "disgusting." Such descriptions refer to feelings or reactions in those who experience pornographic material. This is an important point, because it suggests that "obscenity" is not a property inherent in a book, film, or photograph but a tendency that the work may have to elicit feelings of revulsion in those who experience it.

The claim that the X-rated movie *Deep Throat* depicts various human sexual acts can be verified by observing the film. To call the same film "obscene" or "pornographic" is to express a personal evaluation the legitimacy of which depends, at least in part, on the perspective of the person or group making the judgment. If beauty is in the eye of the beholder, then obscenity and pornography seem to be, too.

Of course, perceptions change. To illustrate, few people today would consider Mark Twain's *Huckleberry Finn* obscene. And yet at the time of its publication, this American classic was condemned as obscene. So was Nathaniel Hawthorne's *The Scarlet Letter,* which today is assigned reading for many high school students.

We could add more examples, but there is no need. The point is that our reasons for calling something obscene or pornographic cannot be divorced from where and when we live. Moreover, our own personal judgments of pornography are as subject to change as those of the society in which we live. It is not at all uncommon to find oneself firmly convinced that a film or book is obscene or pornographic only to find oneself wondering, some time afterward, what was ever considered so objectionable about the material. And, of course, the reverse is possible, too: What once did not even make a person blink subsequently elicits a disapproving scowl.

Because of the highly idiosyncratic nature of judgments about pornography, many argue that it is impossible to assign any meaningful definition to the terms *obscene* and *pornographic*. Not everyone agrees, however. In the landmark case *Roth* v. *United States* (1957), the U.S. Supreme Court laid down a definition of obscenity that for more than two decades has been applied in cases of alleged pornography.

In defining obscene and pornographic material, the Court cited four basic characteristics. (1) The material must be considered in terms of its appeal to "the average person." This contrasted sharply with earlier definitions, which included material that might affect only those susceptible to it. (2) The material must be "patently offensive because it affronts contemporary community standards relating to the description or representation of sexual matters." (3) The work must be taken as a whole, not piecemeal; the dominant theme must be taken into account rather than material taken out of context. Thus the terms *pornographic* or *obscene* may be applied only to material whose *theme* satisfies the other elements of the definition. (4) The material must appeal only to "prurient interest." It must be totally lacking in any social value or importance. By the Court's account, then, a work is obscene or pornographic if, considered in terms of its appeal to the average person, it offends community standards because its theme, taken as a whole, appeals to prurient interests and is without social value.

Is such a definition operational? No, say its detractors. They point out, first, that "average person" is a hopelessly vague phrase. Who, after all, is this so-called average person? And even if we could isolate such a creature, we could not freeze that person's attitudes, outlooks, and appetites so that they never changed.

The Court's critics see similar operational problems in the phrase "contemporary community standards." Just what "community" should we have in mind? The village, town, city, county, state, region, country? And even if we could agree on the community, can we really determine what the community's standards are? Perhaps some citizens' group should represent the view of the community. Or maybe each member of the community should be polled: If more individuals think a work obscene than not, then by the community's standards it is. Of course, we would have no way of knowing that the people judged the work pornographic on "legitimate" grounds: on its appeal to the average person, on its appeal to prurience, on its lack of social value.

In addition, critics argue that any judgment about a work's "prurience" is so subjective as to be useless. In the last analysis, they say, all such judgments will be little more than expressions of someone's beliefs.

Finally, there is the matter of "social value." Who can say what has social value? Sometimes what appears to have no social value turns out to be extremely worthwhile. In a dynamic, evolving society such as ours, it is very difficult, if not impossible, to say with assurance what has value and what does not. Might not a reasonable criterion for judging whether material has any redeeming value be whether it "plays," that is, whether it finds any audience? If it does, then it serves some social purpose; it has some social value. Moreover, the fact that what is repugnant to the vast majority of people can still find a niche in society may itself be a social value in reaffirming the full and open nature of our society.

Of course, the Supreme Court's definition is a legal one. But other definitions have been proposed. In a religious vein, some have argued that any material calculated to arouse sexual passion is obscene. But such a definition ignores the nature of the material itself. Is patently asexual material to be taken as pornographic so long as it was *intended* to arouse sexual passion? By the same token, is material that has a high sexual content but that was not intended to arouse sexual passion not pornographic? From a psychological viewpoint, other definitions try to distinguish pornography from what is often termed "erotic realism." The latter supposedly provides an accurate picture of sex as a basic aspect of life. Pornography, on the other hand, is thought to lack such realism, often exaggerating the sexuality of the people it portrays, focusing exclusively on the physiological responses of the participants and frequently presenting what is widely considered deviant sexual behavior. Still, such a distinction seems to raise just as many questions of interpretation as it intends to dispel.

Still other definitions would view pornography in terms of dehumanization and depersonalization. An obscene work—as distinguished from an artistic one—presents a disgusting picture of human life, not for the readers' or viewers' contemplation, but for their enjoyment, even participation. In effect, while erotic works of art present sexual material for the spectators' consideration and edification, pornography invites them to wallow in it. Maybe so. But by what criteria are we to distinguish the work that invites contemplation from the one that invites sheer sexual indulgence?

Finally, there are those who, while admitting they cannot define pornography, nonetheless say they can recognize it. In the words of former Supreme Court Justice Potter Stewart: "I know it when I see it." Thus, in 1974, the Court, after due deliberation, ruled that the film *Carnal Knowledge* was not obscene, but that *The Illustrated Presidential Report of the Commission on Obscenity and Pornography* was.

Effects of Pornography

Since there is no universally agreed-upon definition of pornography, it seems futile to discuss the possible effects of pornography. This may explain why, until very recently, no scientific research had been done to discover these effects.

Despite the troublesome definitional problems, the Commission on Obscenity and Pornography did conduct a series of studies whose findings bear on the moral arguments we will consider shortly. At the outset, the commission avoided trying to define *pornographic* and *obscene*. Instead, it chose to discuss "erotic materials," which presumably deal with or arouse sexual feelings or desires. Without passing legal or moral judgment on such materials, the commission sought to determine what effects various erotic material had on people in a variety of contexts. Here are six of the commission's most important findings:

1. A significant number of persons masturbated more often after exposure to erotic materials.

2. Erotic dreams, sexual fantasies, and conversations about sexual matter tended to increase after exposure to erotic materials.

3. Where there was an increase in sexual activity, it generally tended to be temporary and didn't differ in kind from the sexual behavior the person was accustomed to engage in before exposure.

4. Some married couples reported more agreeable marital relations and a greater willingness to discuss sexual matters after exposure than before.

5. Both delinquent and nondelinquent youth have wide exposure to erotic materials.

6. There is no statistical correlation between sex crimes and exposure to erotic materials. (Incidentally, sex crimes decreased appreciably in Denmark after Danish law was changed to permit virtually unrestricted access to erotic materials.)

The commission's overall conclusion was that "empirical research designed to clarify the question has found no evidence to date that exposure to explicit sexual materials plays a significant role in the causation of delinquent or criminal behavior among youths or adults. The commission cannot conclude that exposure to erotic materials is a factor in the causation of sex crime or sex delinquency."[2]

It's worth noting that several commission members protested the commission's findings, and wrote a minority report to that effect. Among other things, the minority report claimed that the commission ignored or underrated important studies in its final report, such as the one that found a definite correlation between juvenile exposure to pornography and precocious heterosexual and deviant sexual behavior. Another study found a direct relation between the frequency with which adolescents saw movies depicting sexual intercourse and the extent to which they themselves engaged in premarital intercourse. Still another study found that rapists were the group reporting the highest rates of excitation to masturbation by pornography in both the adult and adolescent years. The significance of this last study, said the minority dissenters, is in its implication that exposure to pornography does not serve adequately as catharsis to prevent a sex crime, as some researchers have maintained. In fact, the dissenters claimed, it may do just the opposite. As evidence they again invoked this third study, which reported that 80 percent of prisoners who had been exposed to erotic materials said they "wished to try the act" they had seen. When asked whether they had acted on their desires, between 30 and 38 percent said they had. This

2.   *The Report of the Commission on Obscenity and Pornography* (New York: Bantam Books, 1970), p. 31.

figure is consistent with still another study, which reported that 39 percent of sex offenders said that pornography had something to do with their committing the crimes they were convicted of.[3]

What are we to make of these studies, whose findings often point to opposed conclusions regarding the effects of pornography? A completely satisfactory evaluation calls for analyses of the surveys' methods to ensure that they were genuinely scientific, a task we can't undertake here. Suffice it to say we should recall the fallacies of causation, especially those pertaining to inference of causation from statistical correlations and the post hoc fallacy: A statistical correlation between two phenomena does not of itself establish a causal connection between them, and simply because one event follows another doesn't necessarily mean that the first caused the second. This is not to say, apropos the minority's view, that there is no causal connection between erotic materials and sexual behavior, only that the jury is still out. We don't have sufficient grounds at present to say that exposure to erotic materials has socially undesirable effects on those exposed to them. By the same token, the presently available evidence does not prove that such materials do not have these effects.

Moral Issues

Pornography and obscenity raise numerous moral questions, two of which concern us here. The first may be phrased: Are pornographic materials in and of themselves morally objectionable, or are they not? We will call the various arguments connected with this question "Arguments against Pornographic Materials" and "Arguments for Pornographic Materials." The second question, which concerns the legality of pornography, may be stated: Is it right for the state to limit the consenting adult's access to obscene and pornographic material? In responding to this question, we will present "Arguments for Censorship" and "Arguments against Censorship."

It is most important to distinguish these two questions. Whether pornography is moral is a separate and distinct question from whether consenting adults should be allowed access to it. One could argue consistently that pornography is morally objectionable but that the state has no right to limit an adult's access to it. Or one might argue consistently that pornography is not morally objectionable but that the state ought to limit an adult's access to it.

There is another reason to keep the two issues separate. Often arguments for censorship assume that pornography is morally objectionable and, therefore, should be suppressed. Perhaps what is immoral ought to be suppressed, perhaps not. Whatever the view—and there are grounds for reasonable debate—the issue is strictly academic until it is established that pornography is, in fact, immoral. But often this is ignored; pornography is assumed to be immoral, and the argument moves inexorably toward its censorship.

So keep in mind the distinction between the morality of pornographic mate-

3. *Ibid., Part IV.*

rial and the morality of laws that restrict the adult's access to pornographic material. While obviously related by common subject, these important questions for the individual and society are significantly different, as we will see in the arguments connected with them.

Arguments against Pornographic Materials

1.   *Pornography degrades humans.*

POINT: "Nobody can deny that every piece of pornography shares one thing with every other piece of pornography: It degrades humans. It presents in graphic detail a depraved picture of human life; it portrays humans functioning in a way less than human, wallowing in some animal level of lust and depravity, and inviting the spectators to join them. What's wrong with pornography? It affronts human dignity; in its portrayal of humans, it dehumanizes them."

COUNTERPOINT: "Now, don't tell me you've never had a lustful thought. Why, even a U.S. President once admitted to having lusted in his heart. Let's not kid ourselves: Lust is as much a human emotion as fear, anger, or hatred. And, whether we like to admit it or not, some people do act in depraved ways—and, at times, a lot more than in the average 'porno' flick. So, frankly, I don't see what's so 'dehumanizing' about portraying these aspects of the human personality. Sure, I'd probably agree that they aren't as uplifting as showing the human in its finest hour, as in films like *Gandhi, Chariots of Fire,* and *The Right Stuff.* But that's really irrelevant. We're not judging art here, but morality. I might also agree that some people are scandalized, maybe even 'dehumanized,' by pornography. But that speaks more of their reaction to the material than to any feature of the material itself. Some people are amused by 'porn,' others bored by it. So what are we to say—that there's something inherently amusing or boring about pornography? No, simply that some people react to pornography in a bored or amused way."

2.   *Pornography separates sexual passion from affection or love.*

POINT: "In our culture, sexual intimacies generally have been associated with the most profound affection that one human being can show toward another. While it's true that sex doesn't always carry that symbolic meaning, our society still recognizes that it should. And individuals in many cases still expect sex to have that affectionate, caring, loving aspect. But you'll never find this side of sex in pornography. Quite the opposite. Every effort is made in pornography to separate sex from affection, caring, and love. 'Impersonal lust' is the order of the day. In the real world, sex without love is objectionable. It's no less objectionable when portrayed that way on the screen or in a book."

COUNTERPOINT: "Sure, sex with affection may be more enjoyable than affectionless sex. It may even be an ideal. But what falls short of the ideal isn't necessarily wrong. Nor is it wrong to portray what is less than the ideal. In fact, some people would say that without such portrayals we'd lose sight of the ideal. But for the sake of argument, let's assume that affectionless sex is wrong. Even so, it doesn't necessarily follow that to portray affectionless sex, even pornographically, is also wrong. Lots of things are wrong—kidnapping, rape, murder. That doesn't mean that it's wrong to portray these subjects in film or literature. Sure, you might say that a presentation that 'glorifies' these things, a presentation that does not categorically condemn them, is wrong. But what constitutes a 'glorifying' presentation? At what point does a film, for example, not only cease to portray affectionate sexual passion and begin to portray it as a depersonalized sexual desire, but also to glorify that presentation? I don't know; I don't think anybody does. I'm not even sure what criteria you'd use to make such a judgment. So how can you call something wrong when you can't even pin down what it is you're judging objectionable?"

3. *Pornography is anti-female.*

POINT: "Anyone who's seen even one pornographic film or read one obscene book realizes that the pornographic view is an anti-female view. Pornographic material generally portrays women as objects, not persons. They are playthings of a male, machinery to be tinkered with and manipulated. Why, pornography is as much a kind of group defamation as is Nazi propaganda, which degrades Jews. Just as we find anti-Semitic material objectionable on the grounds that it degrades a group of human beings and lessens the inherent respect and dignity they deserve, so we should object to pornography. After all, pornography undercuts respect for women, reinforces cultural prejudices, and encourages acts of violence against women."

COUNTERPOINT: "First of all, there's a big difference in intent between pornographic and anti-Semitic material. The latter is motivated by hate and aims not only to degrade Jews, but to incite others to join a loathsome genocidal cause. But hate isn't the impulse behind pornography. Money usually is, sometimes notoriety, even sheer pleasure. But not hate, and certainly not hate of women. Look at the material; study it. I think you'll find that if it does 'dehumanize,' it plays no favorites. Males are 'depersonalized' as much as females. And second, you don't have to get very far into anti-Semitic material before you find examples of viciously cruel, overt defamation. You never find that in pornography. And you won't find any singling out of a vulnerable minority group. On the contrary, porn deals with humans across the board: male and female, black and white, Jew and Gentile. And it certainly doesn't invite the sort of violence against women that anti-Semitic propaganda does against Jews. In fact, there's no evidence of a correlation between pornography and violence directed at women."

4. *Pornography breaks down protective barriers.*

POINT: "Our society subjects us to extensive conditioning on matters of sex. And for good reason: Sex is a most powerful appetite, which, if not carefully controlled, can produce a lot of hardship for ourselves and others. No wonder our families, schools, and churches take such pains to help us develop constructive attitudes toward sex and deal with sexual feelings and fantasies which, if pursued, would hurt us and society. If this process is effective, then by the time we're adults we have learned to channel our sexual drives properly and have developed certain barriers to help us do that. But pornography breaks down those barriers; it loosens the wildest of sexual feelings and fantasies. The result is behavior that is neither in the interest of the individual nor in the interest of society. So what makes pornography objectionable is that it threatens to undo the control that individuals exercise over their sexuality and leads to self-destructive and antisocial behavior."

COUNTERPOINT: "You make it sound like anybody who enjoys pornography will turn into some sort of sex fiend! That's absurd. In fact, there's some reason to believe that pornography can be healthful for some people and for society. But beyond this, you blithely assume that society's conditional process is above reproach, even that we must ensure that nothing happens to 'undo' it. Did it ever occur to you that society's sexual values and the way they're taught may in part explain the great popularity of pornography?"

Arguments for Pornographic Materials

1. *Pornography can be beneficial.*

POINT: "Not only is pornography not necessarily degrading, it can actually be beneficial. Obviously, those who produce and willingly participate in it feel neither degraded nor exploited. In fact, they often enjoy considerable financial and professional success as a result. They may even feel that they're contributing something worthwhile to society. But beyond this, pornographic material can be a useful source of information about human sexuality. Even more important, it can serve as a sexual release for those in society who, for one reason or another, can't find or have difficulty finding sexual fulfillment in the absence of such materials. Given these benefits, and that there's no solid evidence that pornography harms anyone, there's no reason to object to it."

COUNTERPOINT: "The fact that pornography may benefit the people involved with it says very little about the morality of pornography. Robbery, murder, and skyjacking may also benefit the participants, but that doesn't make those activities moral. Likewise, lots of people would enjoy the spectacle of a duel with pistols at dawn, but that doesn't make dueling right. As for those poor souls who can find sexual release only through pornography, don't you think it would make more sense for society to identify and help those individuals in ways that are more meaningful for both them and society? But even granting your 'benefits,' they don't nearly begin to offset the liabilities of pornography, including its depraved view of human sexuality and dehumanization of men and women."

2. *Sexually explicit material is morally neutral.*

POINT: "The word *pornography* is loaded. As soon as you use it, you're making a pejorative judgment. That's why I'd prefer to talk about 'sexually explicit material.' That phrase describes the material under discussion but doesn't judge it as offensive or disgusting, thereby biasing a moral evaluation of it. Now, it seems to me that the only way someone can find such material in and of itself objectionable is by finding human sexuality or human sexual passion morally objectionable, because this is what 'sexually explicit material' deals with. As far as I'm concerned, there's nothing dirty, sinful, or evil about sex. Like eating, exercising, or watching TV, sex is morally neutral. Certainly it can raise moral concerns, and so can 'explicit sexual material.' For example, if people were forced to view such material or to participate in it, I'd consider that a violation of their civil rights and therefore wrong. But the material itself is neither good nor bad. It's morally inert. Everything depends on how it's used: when, by whom, and with what results. To call sexually explicit material in and of itself morally objectionable doesn't make sense."

COUNTERPOINT: "You conveniently forget, or ignore, that 'explicit sexual material' serves up more than just human sexuality and sexual passion. It packages sex, and that package, more often than not, is colored by dehumanization, human exploitation, sadism, masochism, and other forms of behavior that degrade human sexuality and human beings. Also, sexually explicit material has a viewpoint, and part of the viewpoint usually is an invitation to the spectator to join the fun. Who are we kidding? 'Sexually explicit material,' as you use that term, is inseparable from debasing forms of sexual behavior. So when you say that such material is in itself morally neutral or inert, you're sadly mistaken. Its content *always* raises serious moral questions about the proper concept of human sexuality, the dignity of human beings, and the treatment that individuals accord one another."

Arguments for Censorship

1. *Pornography leads to crime.*

POINT: "Let's be clear about one thing: Pornography leads to crime. Take, for example, the case of the unstable young man who raped a girl after he'd been aroused by lurid scenes in an obscene comic book. Such cases could multiply. Why, the Gebhard study [1965] confirmed reports of police officers that sex offenders often have pornography in their possession or admit to having seen pornographic materials. If you're still not convinced, just use a little common sense. If good literature can have a salutary effect on readers, then why can't obscene and pornographic material have a harmful effect? It can. And that's why the state must regulate pornography—to help reduce the incidence of crime."

COUNTERPOINT: "I agree there's a large body of material dealing with the relation between pornography and sex crimes. But—and it's a big 'but'—no cause-and-effect relationship has ever been found. In fact, in the Gebhard studies the use of pornography by sex offenders was compared to the experiences of a control group of normal, nonoffender males, and to those of a group of prisoners who weren't sex offenders. Guess what? There was *no* difference among the groups in their use, possession of, or exposure to pornography. If there were any correlations to be drawn, they would be between the use of and exposure to pornography and the individual's age, socioeconomic class, and educational level. And as if that weren't enough, consider this: The study found that sex offenders weren't prone to any greater sexual arousal from viewing pornography than were other groups of males."

2. *The community has the right and obligation to enforce its moral standards.*

POINT: "Like it or not, most people today find pornography repugnant. Sure, there are some people who aren't offended by the obscene, and there are those who even enjoy it. But so what? Society is run by majority rule. When the consensus supports a moral standard, the community has every right to enforce that standard. Indeed, it has an obligation to."

COUNTERPOINT: "For a government to impose conventional moral standards on the individual amounts to a tyranny of the majority. In fact, nothing is more repugnant than to impose the moral standards of the community on all its members, even those who disagree with those decisions. It was the recognition of this fact that led the founding fathers to incorporate the Bill of Rights into the Constitution, and specifically to draft the First Amendment, which provides that 'Congress shall make no law . . . abridging the freedom of speech, or of the press.' 'No law abridging' means *no* law abridging, not even laws we happen to agree with, or anti-obscenity laws. What could be more clear? The supreme law of the land has fixed its own value on freedom of speech and press by putting these freedoms beyond the reach of federal power to abridge."

3. *The government has the right and duty to suppress views that are incompatible with the security and well-being of the community.*

POINT: "Nobody objects when the government polices individuals who don't maintain standards of health and who threaten society. By the same token, why shouldn't the government be concerned with the moral health of individuals, since this too can affect societal well-being? We all know that pornographic materials have the effect of preoccupying men and women with gratification of their own sensual desires. They also lead to impersonal expressions of sexuality, the destruction of love, and the psychological deprivation of children unfortunate enough to be under the guardianship of adults who indulge in pornography. Since all this can undermine the moral foundations of society, it seems clear to me that government has the right and duty to regulate pornographic and obscene materials."

COUNTERPOINT: "Sure, government has the right, even the obligation to secure and protect its citizens from physical harm if it is difficult or impossible for them to protect themselves. But physical threats are quite different from what you term moral threats, and the physical health of society differs markedly from its moral health. Yes, a government ought to ensure that diseases aren't spread by indifferent or uncaring individuals; it's justified in quarantining, even imposing treatment on certain individuals in order to protect society. But 'pornography' isn't smallpox; it's not a disease which, if unchecked, will rage and consume the population. The litany of 'effects' you say pornography produces just doesn't wash. Of course, viewing or reading erotic materials is sexually arousing for a large number of people. In your view, such sexual stimulation presumably will lead the normal individual to all sorts of unspeakable, unhealthful acts. But there's no reason, not one iota of evidence, for believing that the sexual stimulation of normal individuals leads to anything other than fantasies and normal sexual activity. Now, I find nothing inherently wrong with fantasies, even sexual ones; nor do I find anything objectionable about normal sexual activity."

4. *People need standards of decency and direction in sexual matters.*

POINT: "Generally speaking, people need direction, standards of decency, particularly regarding sex. The home, church, and school are unable to provide this necessary guidance alone. Law is needed. Law must hold up an authoritative standard for guidance of opinion and judgment. So laws that regulate pornography and obscenity perform a needed educative function. They alert people to the fact that the organized community draws a line between the decent and the indecent. In effect, such laws say: 'This is what we believe is decent, and this is what we believe is indecent; this is what's right, and this is what's wrong; this is what our community will permit, and this is what it will not permit.' The beneficial, long-term effect of such standards on people's moral values and attitudes can't be underestimated. By the same token, there's no calculating the negative long-term impact on values and attitudes in the absence of legal guidelines."

COUNTERPOINT: "Frankly, I resent the paternalistic cut of your argument. There's more than a hint of: 'Now, don't worry, folks, we're doing this for your own good.' Thank you, but no thanks. Certainly government has a right and duty to intervene in matters where there's a clear and present threat of harm. But in the case of pornography, there is none. Thus the government has no right to restrict our access to pornographic material, even for our own good. Individuals should be the judges of what's for their own good, not government. In short, I find the paternalistic principle you propose unacceptable justification for limiting personal liberty."

Arguments against Censorship

1. *No operationally meaningful definition of* obscene *is possible.*

POINT: "It's obvious that individuals bring to a film or a book their own concepts of offensiveness, which may differ from time to time in the same individuals. Also, there's no way of knowing the impact of materials on the public because of all the variables involved. What's more, in trying to define obscenity, one inevitably tries to do so in terms of the 'average person.' The fact is, there is no such animal, and so any definition or description of the obscene that ties it to an 'average person' is simply foolish. Another definitional problem arises in trying to define the 'community' whose standards we're supposed to use. Finally, it's impossible to determine with anything that even approaches objectivity which works have 'redeeming social value,' presumably a criterion for exempting material from censorship. The bottom line is that we don't have any meaningfully operational definition of *obscene* and *pornographic*. If you can't even define these terms, how can you write laws about them? You can't and you shouldn't."

COUNTERPOINT: "The problem with your argument is that it fails to distinguish between the impossibility of formulating a definition and the difficulty of applying one. I grant you that even the Supreme Court's definition of what's obscene may pose operational problems. But this isn't an uncommon problem in law. Law is, in part, based on a set of definitional assumptions. Whether or not a particular phenomenon falls within that definitional assumption always involves some interpretation. Certainly this is true of obscenity and pornography. Sometimes there's very little difficulty in applying the definition; other times considerably more interpretation is involved. If a law is difficult to interpret and apply, then we should refine it. But we shouldn't conclude that an operational difficulty proves that it's impossible to define terms in any meaningfully operational way and, therefore, that a law can't and shouldn't be formulated."

  2.   *Governmental abuse will follow such legislation.*

POINT: "Asking government to serve as censor to our films and literature is like asking a fox to guard the hen house. Why, if government is allowed to oversee what people can read and view in sexual matters, there's no telling what government will attempt to regulate next—and it won't wait to be asked, either. Invite government in, and don't be at all surprised if it then proceeds to limit our religious and political freedoms, using, again, deviations from the standards of the nonexistent 'average' person and 'the community' as its justification."

COUNTERPOINT: "Oh, come now. You know as well as I that the passage of anti-smut laws doesn't at all mean the end of our religious and political freedoms. There's no reason whatever to suspect that government will invade any other aspects of people's reading or viewing, as, for example, by censoring politically 'unorthodox' material. Don't you realize that during World War II the government was given wide-ranging liberty-limiting powers? Certainly it had far greater censorship prerogatives than it would under proposed obscenity and pornography legislation. What better opportunity did government have to extend these powers than it had after the war? But it never happened. In the end, each of your fears poses a separate and distinct issue from pornography and obscenity legislation. If the time ever came when political or religious censorship was a serious social consideration, then it would have to be debated on its own merits. In no way would it, or should it, necessarily be tied to anti-smut laws."

  3.   *Censorship raises insurmountable operational problems.*

POINT: "Think about the operational problems that censorship raises. The chief one is: Which works won't be censored? Some have said that the 'classics' will and should be exempt from censorship. Okay, but what's a 'classic'? Any traditional definition probably would exclude new works, since a work usually can't be recognized as a classic until some time after its release. Fine, but what does that mean? It means that the censor must determine which works will become classics—an absurdly impossible task. As a result, censors will have little choice but to ban these 'nonclassics' that smack of smut. You probably think this is an idle fear. Is it? Plenty of works of art and literature that today are considered classics once were banned: works by Chaucer, Shakespeare, Swift, and Twain, just to mention a few. And more recently, William Faulkner, Ernest Hemingway, and James Joyce found their works banned. Just imagine what creative artists would suffer, who must compose with the specter of the censor haunting their every move. One of the world's greatest writers, Leo Tolstoy, said it all. 'You would not believe,' wrote the Russian novelist, 'how from the very commencement of my activity that horrible censor question has tormented me. I wanted to write what I felt; but at the same time it occurred to me that what I wrote would not be permitted, and involuntarily I had to abandon the work. I abandoned and went on abandoning and meanwhile the years passed away.' "

COUNTERPOINT: "As an intelligent person who's interested in the arts generally and literature in particular, and as one who's sensitive to the state of the artist in society, I share your concerns. Like you, I don't want an atmosphere that inhibits our artists, nor do I want simpletons censoring works of merit. Furthermore, I don't for a minute deny that some abuses have accompanied anti-obscenity laws. Despite all that, let me ask you this: What law ever has been free from potential abuse at the hands of the overzealous, the narrow-minded, the ill-informed, and, yes, the lame-brained? My point is that the objections you raise really speak to the implementations of anti-obscenity laws and not to the justifiability of the laws themselves. To me what you say is like arguing against capital punishment legislation because capital punishment laws are unfairly applied. If there is inequity in the application of the law, then let's correct that. But let's not abolish the law. The problem isn't with the law, but with how it's implemented."

4.   *Government has no right to limit liberty where there is no danger of harm.*

POINT: "When is a government justified in limiting individual liberty? When there's evidence of harm to others. But there's no evidence that pornography presents a clear and present danger to members of society. So the government has no right to pass laws restricting an adult's access to pornography."

COUNTERPOINT: "I disagree that pornography presents no danger to society. Even if we are uncertain that pornography leads to crime, why assume that it doesn't? It seems to me more prudent to assume that it does, until the overwhelming weight of evidence proves otherwise. After all, assuming that pornography is innocuous is far riskier than assuming that it is harmful. Actually, I think there's pretty good reason for assuming that pornography probably is harmful. At the very least it often deals with things like exhibitionism, voyeurism, prostitution, sadism, child molestation, and other forms of sexual perversion, many of which involve harm to people. Besides, much of the stuff portrayed is illegal. So in trafficking in this smut, pornography encourages disrespect for and even disobedience of the law. Surely this is a threat to a peaceful society. But all this aside, I think that, freed of censorship, pornography poses a direct and immediate threat to the style and quality of life we want and value. To say, then, that pornography poses no threat or harm to society is incorrect. On the contrary, pornography threatens the peace, security, and values of our society. The government has a right and duty to prevent such harm through the passage of anti-obscenity laws."

5.   *Pornography can be beneficial.*

POINT: "Much that is positive may be said on behalf of pornography. For one thing, it can aid normal sexual development. For another, it can invigorate flagging sexual relations. Why, it's even been used successfully in sex therapy sessions, to treat various sexual dysfunctions. And there's little question that pornographic materials can provide some people release from sexual tensions. It can provide an acceptable sexual substitute for those who might otherwise be sexually frustrated. Finally, it's at least possible that exposure to pornography has prevented people from acting in a harmful way, perhaps from committing sex crimes."

COUNTERPOINT: "Regarding your last claim—that exposure to pornography may actually prevent antisocial acts—I suggest you read the minority report offered by several members of the Commission on Obscenity and Pornography. It mentions a study that finds the group reporting the highest rates of excitation to masturbation by pornography were rapists. Now, surely you can't say that pornography served as an adequate catharsis for these people. If it had, why did they go out and rape someone? In still another study, 39 percent of sex offenders reported that pornography had something to do with their committing the sex offense. As for your claim that pornography serves as a 'release' for some people, perhaps it does. But what kind of release? Escape might be a better term—escape from reality into fantasy and narcissism. Some release! Who knows that the darkly private, short-lived release you speak of doesn't eventuate in greater tension, frustration and, worst of all, despair and self-loathing?

Beyond the (Garbage) Pale, or Democracy, Censorship and the Arts

Walter Berns

About fifteen years ago, political scientist Walter Berns wrote an essay that referred to a New York Times *editorial (1 April 1969) entitled "Beyond the (Garbage) Pale." In effect, the editorial called for the censorship of explicit portrayal of sexual intercourse on the stage. Hence the title of Berns's essay, a part of which appears here.*

While Berns's argument for censorship of pornography is not a new one, it is not the most

From Walter Berns, "Beyond the (Garbage) Pale, or Democracy, Censorship and the Arts," in Censorship and Freedom of Expression, *Harry M. Clor, ed. (Chicago: Rand McNally, 1971). Reprinted by permission of Harry M. Clor.*

*common in contemporary pro-censorship literature. Pruned to its essentials, the argument goes
something like this: Pornography can have political consequences, intended or not. The chief
political consequence is that it makes us "shameless." Indeed, one of the purposes of pornography
seems to be to convince us that shame is unnatural. But, in Berns's view, shame is not only
natural but necessary for the proper functioning and stability of society. Without shame,
individuals are "unruly and unrulable." Having lost all measure of self-restraint, individuals will
have to be ruled by tyrants. Thus tyranny, not democracy, is the proper government for the
shameless and self-indulgent. Since pornography induces shamelessness and self-indulgence, it
undercuts democracy.*

*In support of his contention, Berns refers to a number of "thoughtful men" who were
familiar with this censorship argument at the time modern democracies were being constituted.
He, and presumably they, claims that censorship is not only compatible with a democracy but a
necessary part of it.*

The case for censorship is at least as old as the case against it, and, contrary to what is usually thought today, has been made under decent and democratic auspices and by intelligent men. To the extent to which it is known today, however, it is thought to be pernicious or, at best, irrelevant to the enlightened conditions of the twentieth century. It begins from the premise that the laws cannot remain indifferent to the manner in which men amuse themselves, or to the kinds of amusement offered them. "The object of art," as Lessing put the case, "is pleasure, and pleasure is not indispensable. What kind and what degree of pleasure shall be permitted may justly depend on the law-giver."[1] Such a view, especially in this uncompromising form, appears excessively Spartan and illiberal to us; yet Lessing was one of the greatest lovers of art who ever lived and wrote.

We turn to the arts—to literature, films, and the theatre, as well as to the graphic arts which were the special concern of Lessing—for the pleasure to be derived from them, and pleasure has the capacity to form our tastes and thereby to affect our lives, and the kind of people we become, and the lives of those with whom and among whom we live. Is it politically uninteresting whether men and women derive pleasure from performing their duties as citizens, parents, and spouses or, on the other hand, from watching their laws and customs and institutions ridiculed on the stage? Whether the passions are excited by, and the affections drawn to, what is noble or what is base? Whether the relations between men and women are depicted in terms of an eroticism wholly divorced from love and cal-

culated to destroy the capacity for love and the institutions, such as the family, that depend on love? Whether a dramatist uses pleasure to attach man to what is beautiful or to what is ugly? We may not be accustomed to thinking of these things in this manner, but it is not strange that so much of the obscenity from which so many of us derive our pleasure today has an avowed political purpose.[2] It would seem that these pornographers know intuitively what liberals—for example, Morris Ernst—have forgotten, namely, that there is indeed a "causal relationship . . . between word or pictures and human behavior." At least they are not waiting for behavioral science to discover this fact.

The purpose is sometimes directly political and sometimes political in the sense that it will have political consequences intended or not. This latter purpose is to make us shameless, and it seems to be succeeding with astonishing speed. Activities that were once confined to the private scene—to the "ob-scene," to make an etymological assumption are now presented for our delectation and emulation in [sic] center stage. Nothing that is appropriate to one place is inappropriate to any other place. No act, we are to infer, no human possibility, no possible physical combination or connection, is shameful. Even our lawmakers now so declare. "However plebeian my tastes may be," Justice Douglas asked somewhat disingenuously in the *Ginzburg* case, "who am I to say that others' tastes must be so limited and that others' tastes have no 'social importance'?" Nothing prevents a dog from enjoying sexual intercourse in the marketplace, and it is unnatural to deprive man of the same pleasure, either actively or as voyeurs in the theatre. Shame itself is unnatural, a convention devised by hypocrites to inhibit the pleasures of the body. We must get rid of our "hangups."

But what if, contrary to Freud and to what is generally assumed, shame is natural to man in the sense of being an original feature of human existence, and shamelessness unnatural in the sense of having to be acquired? What if the beauty that we are capable of knowing and achieving in our lives with each other derives from the fact that man is naturally a "blushing creature," the only creature capable of blushing? Consider the case of voyeurism, a case that, under the circumstances, comes quickly to mind. Some of us—I have even known students to confess to it—experience discomfort watching others on the stage or screen performing sexual acts, or even the acts preparatory to sexual acts, such as the disrobing of a woman by a man. This discomfort is caused by shame or is akin to shame. True, it could derive from the fear of being discovered enjoying what society still sees as a forbidden game. The voyeur who experiences shame in this sense is judging himself by the conventions of his society and, according to the usual modern account, the greater the distance separating him from his society in space or time, the less he will experience this kind of shame. This shame, which may be denoted as concealing shame, is a function of the fear of discovery by one's own group. The group may have its reasons for forbidding a particular act, and thereby leading those who engage in it to conceal it—to be ashamed of it—but these reasons have nothing to do with the nature of man. Voyeurism, according to this account, is a perversion only because society says it is, and a man guided only by nature would not be ashamed of it.

According to another view, however, not to be ashamed—to be a shameless voyeur—is more likely to require explanation, for voyeurism is by nature a perversion.

> Anyone who draws his sexual gratification from looking at another lives continuously at a distance. If it is normal to approach and unite with the partner, then it is precisely characteristic of the voyeur that he remains alone, without a partner, an outsider who acts in a stealthy and furtive manner. To keep his distance when it is essential to draw near is one of the paradoxes of his perversion. The

looking of the voyeur is of course also a looking at and, as such, is as different from the looks exchanged by lovers as medical palpation from the gentle caress of the hand.[3]

From this point of view, voyeurism is perversion not merely because it is contrary to convention, but because it is contrary to nature. Convention here follows nature. Whereas sexual attraction brings man and woman together seeking a unity that culminates in the living being they together create, the voyeur maintains a distance; and because he maintains a distance he looks at, he does not communicate; and because he looks at he objectifies, he makes an object of that with which it is natural to join. Objectifying, he is incapable of uniting and therefore of love. The need to conceal voyeurism—the concealing shame—is a corollary of the protective shame, the shame that impels lovers to search for privacy and for an experience protected from the profane and the eyes of the stranger. The stranger is "at odds with the shared unity of the [erotic couple], and his mere presence tends to introduce some objectification into every immediate relationship."[4] Shame, both concealing and protective, protects lovers and therefore love. And a polity without love—without the tenderness and the charming sentiments and the poetry and the beauty and the uniquely human things that depend on it and derive from it—a polity without love would be an unnatural monstrosity.[5]

To speak in a manner that is more obviously political, such a polity may even be impossible, except in a form unacceptable to free men. There is a connection between self-restraint and shame, and therefore a connection between shame and self-government or democracy. There is therefore a danger in promoting shamelessness and the fullest self-expression or indulgence. To live together requires rules and a governing of the passions, and those who are without shame will be unruly and unrulable; having lost the ability to restrain themselves by observing the rules they collectively give themselves, they will have to be ruled by others. Tyranny is the mode of government for the shameless and self-indulgent who have carried liberty beyond any restraint, natural and conventional.

Such was the argument made prior to the twentieth century, when it was generally understood that democracy, more than any other form of government, required self-restraint, which it would inculcate through moral education and impose on itself through laws, including laws governing the manner of public amusements. It was the tyrant who could usually allow the people to indulge themselves. Indulgence of the sort we are now witnessing did not threaten his rule, because his rule did not depend on a citizenry of good character. Anyone can be ruled by a tyrant, and the more debased his subjects the safer his rule. A case can be made for complete freedom of the arts among such people, whose pleasures are derived from activities divorced from their labors and any duties associated with citizenship. Among them a theatre, for example, can serve to divert the search for pleasure from what the tyrant regards as more dangerous or pernicious pursuits.[6]

Such an argument was not unknown among thoughtful men at the time modern democracies were being constituted. It is to be found in Jean-Jacques Rousseau's *Letter to M. d'Alembert on the Theatre*. Its principles were known by Washington and Jefferson, to say nothing of the antifederalists, and later on by Lincoln, all of whom insisted that democracy would not work without citizens of good character; and until recently no justice of the Supreme Court and no man in public life doubted the necessity for the law to make at least a modest effort to promote that good character, if only by protecting the effort of other institutions, such as the church and the family, to promote and maintain it. The case for censorship, at first glance, was made wholly with a view to the political good, and it had as its premise that what was good for the arts and sciences was *not* necessarily good for the polity.

Notes

1. *Laocoön* (New York: Noonday Press), ch. 1, p. 10.

2. *Che!* and *Hair*, for example, are political plays. . . .

3. Erwin W. Straus, *Phenomenological Psychology* (Basic Books, New York, 1966), p. 219. I have no doubt that it is possible to want to observe sexual acts for reasons unrelated to voyeurism. Just as a physi-cian has a clinical interest in the parts of the body, philosophers will have an interest in the parts of the soul, or in the varieties of human things which are manifestations of the body and the soul. Such a "looking" would not be voyeurism and would be unaccompanied by shame; or the desire to see and to understand would require the "seer" to overcome shame. (Plato, *Republic*, 439e) In any event, the case of the philosopher is politically irrelevant, and aesthetically irrelevant as well.

4. Straus, p. 221.

5. It is easy to prove that shamefulness is not the only principle governing the question of what may properly be presented on the stage; shamefulness would not, for example, govern the case of a scene showing the copulating of a married couple who love each other very much. That is not intrinsically shameful—on the contrary—yet it ought not to be shown. The principle here is, I think, an aesthetic one: Such a scene is dramatically weak because the response of the audience would be characterized by prurience and not by a sympathy with what the scene is intended to portray, a beautiful love. This statement can be tested by joining a college-town movie audience; it is confirmed unintentionally by a defender of nudity on the stage. . . .

6. The modern tyrant does not encourage passivity among his subjects; on the contrary, they are expected by him to be public-spirited: to work for the State, to exceed production schedules, to be citizen soldiers in the huge armies, and to love Big Brother. Indeed, in Nazi Germany and the Soviet Union alike, the private life was and is discouraged, and with it erotic love and the private attachments it fosters. Censorship in a modern tyrannical state is designed to abolish the private life to the extent that this is possible. George Orwell understood this perfectly. This severe censorship that characterizes modern tyranny, and distinguishes it sharply from premodern tyranny, derives from the basis of modern tyrannical rule: Both Nazism and Communism have roots in theory, and more precisely, a kind of utopian theory. The modern tyrant parades as a political philosopher, the heir of Nietzsche or Marx, with a historical mission to perform. He cannot leave his subjects alone.

Questions for Analysis

1. Do you agree with Berns that what is good for the arts and sciences is not necessarily good for society?

2.   *Do you agree that one of the purposes of pornography is to make us shameless?*

3.   *Why does Berns believe that shame is necessary for the protection of lovers and love, and what does that have to do with the justification of censorship?*

4.   *Would you call Berns's argument essentially utilitarian or not? Could his argument be termed Kantian? Explain.*

5.   *In what sense could Berns's argument be said to fly in the face of popular conceptions of democracy?*

Pornography and Respect for Women

Ann Garry

Recently some feminists and nonfeminists alike have argued that pornography is anti-female, that it's designed to humiliate women. Professor of philosophy Ann Garry agrees. Arguing in a Kantian way, Garry objects to most pornography because it encourages attitudes and behavior that violate the moral principle of respect for people. Does that mean that pornography is always evil? Not necessarily, says Garry. It is possible, she claims, for pornography to be nonsexist and nondegrading and, therefore, morally acceptable.

Pornography, like rape, is a male invention, designed to dehumanize women, to reduce the female to an object of sexual access, not to free sensuality from moralistic or parental inhibition. . . . Pornography is the undiluted essence of anti-female propaganda.
—Susan Brownmiller, *Against Our Will: Men, Women and Rape*[1]

It is often asserted that a distinguishing characteristic of sexually explicit material is the degrading and demeaning portrayal of the role and status of the human female. It has been argued that erotic materials describe the female as a mere sexual object to be exploited and manipulated sexually. . . . A recent survey shows that 41 percent of American males and 46 percent of the females believe that "sexual materials lead people to lose respect for women." . . . Recent experiments suggest that such fears are probably unwarranted.
—Presidential Commission on Obscenity and Pornography[2]

The kind of apparent conflict illustrated in these passages is easy to find in one's own thinking as well. For example, I have been inclined to think that pornography is innocuous and to dismiss "moral" arguments for censoring it because many such arguments rest on an assumption I do not share—that sex is an evil to be controlled. At the same time I believe that it is wrong to exploit or degrade human beings, particularly women and others who are especially susceptible. So if pornography degrades human beings, then even if I would oppose its censorship I surely cannot find it morally innocuous.

In an attempt to resolve this apparent conflict I discuss three questions: Does pornography degrade (or exploit or dehumanize) human beings? If so, does it degrade women in ways or to an extent that it does not degrade men? If so, must pornography degrade women, as Brownmiller thinks, or could genuinely innocuous, nonsexist pornography exist? Although much current pornography does degrade women, I will argue that it is possible

This article first appeared in Social Theory and Practice, *Vol. 4 (Summer 1978), pp. 395–421. Reprinted here by permission of the author as it appears in* Philosophy and Women, *edited by Sharon Bishop and Marjorie Weinzweig (Belmont, CA.: Wadsworth, 1979).*

to have nondegrading, nonsexist pornography. However, this possibility rests on our making certain fundamental changes in our conceptions of sex and sex roles. . . .

I

The . . . argument I will consider [here] is that pornography is morally objectionable, not because it leads people to show disrespect for women, but because pornography itself exemplifies and recommends behavior that violates the moral principle to respect persons. The content of pornography is what one objects to. It treats women as mere sex objects "to be exploited and manipulated" and degrades the role and status of women. In order to evaluate this argument, I will first clarify what it would mean for pornography itself to treat someone as a sex object in a degrading manner. I will then deal with three issues central to the discussion of pornography and respect for women: how "losing respect" for a woman is connected with treating her as a sex object; what is wrong with treating someone as a sex object; and why it is worse to treat women rather than men as sex objects. I will argue that the current content of pornography sometimes violates the moral principle to respect persons. Then, in [the concluding part] of this paper, I will suggest that pornography need not violate this principle if certain fundamental changes were to occur in attitudes about sex.

To many people, including Brownmiller and some other feminists, it appears to be an obvious truth that pornography treats people, especially women, as sex objects in a degrading manner. And if we omit "in a degrading manner," the statement seems hard to dispute: How could pornography *not* treat people as sex objects?

First, is it permissible to say that either the content of pornography or pornography itself degrades people or treats people as sex objects? It is not difficult to find examples of degrading content in which women are treated as sex objects. Some pornographic films convey the message that all women really want to be raped, that their resisting struggle is not to be believed. By portraying women in this manner, the content of the movie degrades women. Degrading women is morally objectionable. While seeing the movie need not cause anyone to imitate the behavior shown, we can call the content degrading to women because

of the character of the behavior and attitudes it recommends. The same kind of point can be made about films (or books or TV commercials) with other kinds of degrading, thus morally objectionable, content—for example, racist messages.

The next step in the argument is to infer that, because the content or message of pornography is morally objectionable, we can call pornography itself morally objectionable. Support for this step can be found in an analogy. If a person takes every opportunity to recommend that men rape women, we would think not only that his recommendation is immoral but that he is immoral too. In the case of pornography, the objection to making an inference from recommended behavior to the person who recommends is that we ascribe predicates such as "immoral" differently to people than to films or books. A film vehicle for an objectionable message is still an object independent of its message, its director, its producer, those who act in it, and those who respond to it. Hence one cannot make an unsupported inference from "the content of the film is morally objectionable" to "the film is morally objectionable." Because the central points in this paper do not depend on whether pornography itself (in addition to its content) is morally objectionable, I will not try to support this inference. (The question about the relation of content to the work itself is, of course, extremely interesting; but in part because I cannot decide which side of the argument is more persuasive, I will pass.[3]) Certainly one appropriate way to evaluate pornography is in terms of the moral features of its content. If a pornographic film exemplifies and recommends morally objectionable attitudes or behavior, then its content is morally objectionable.

Let us now turn to the first of our three questions about respect and sex objects: What is the connection between losing respect for a woman and treating her as a sex object? Some people who have lived through the era in which women were taught to worry about men "losing respect" for them if they engaged in sex in inappropriate circumstances find it troublesome (or at least amusing) that feminists—supposedly "liberated" women—are outraged at being treated as sex objects, either by pornography or in any other way. The apparent alignment between feminists and traditionally "proper" women need not surprise us when we look at it more closely.

The "respect" that men have traditionally

believed they have for women—hence a respect they can lose—is not a general respect for persons as autonomous beings; nor is it respect that is earned because of one's personal merits or achievements. It is respect that is an outgrowth of the "double standard." Women are to be respected because they are more pure, delicate, and fragile than men, have more refined sensibilities, and so on. Because some women clearly do not have these qualities, thus do not deserve respect, women must be divided into two groups—the good ones on the pedestal and the bad ones who have fallen from it. One's mother, grandmother, Sunday School teacher, and usually one's wife are "good" women. The appropriate behavior by which to express respect for good women would be, for example, not swearing or telling dirty jokes in front of them, giving them seats on buses, and other "chivalrous" acts. This kind of "respect" for good women is the sort that adolescent boys in the back seats of cars used to "promise" not to lose. Note that men define, display, and lose this kind of respect. If women lose respect for women, it is not typically a loss of respect for (other) women as a class but a loss of self-respect.

It has now become commonplace to acknowledge that, although a place on the pedestal might have advantages over a place in the "gutter" beneath it, a place on the pedestal is not at all equal to the place occupied by other people (i.e., men). "Respect" for those on the pedestal was not respect for whole, full-fledged people but for a special class of inferior beings.

If a person makes two traditional assumptions—that (at least some) sex is dirty and that women fall into two classes, good and bad—it is easy to see how that person might think that pornography could lead people to lose respect for women or that pornography is itself disrespectful to women. Pornography describes or shows women engaging in activities inappropriate for good women to engage in—or at least inappropriate for them to be seen by strangers engaging in. If one sees these women as symbolic representatives of all women, then all women fall from grace with these women. This fall is possible, I believe, because the traditional "respect" that men have had for women is not genuine, wholehearted respect for full-fledged human beings but half-hearted respect for lesser beings, some of whom they feel the need to glorify and purify.[4] It is easy to fall from a pedestal. Can

we imagine 41 percent of men and 46 percent of women answering "yes" to the question "Do movies showing men engaging in violent acts lead people to lose respect for men?"

Two interesting asymmetries appear. The first is that losing respect for men as a class (men with power, typically Anglo men) is more difficult than losing respect for women or ethnic minorities as a class. Anglo men whose behavior warrants disrespect are more likely to be seen as exceptional cases than are women or minorities (whose "transgressions" may be far less serious). Think of the following: women are temptresses; blacks cheat the welfare system; Italians are gangsters; but the men of the Nixon administration are exceptions—Anglo men as a class did not lose respect because of Watergate and related scandals.

The second asymmetry concerns the active and passive roles of the sexes. Men are seen in the active role. If men lose respect for women because of something "evil" done by women (such as appearing in pornography), the fear is that men will then do harm to women—not that women will do harm to men. Whereas if women lose respect for male politicians because of Watergate, the fear is still that male politicians will do harm, not that women will do harm to male politicians. This asymmetry might be a result of one way in which our society thinks of sex as bad—as harm that men do to women (or to the person playing a female role, as in a homosexual rape). Robert Baker calls attention to this point in " 'Pricks' and 'Chicks': A Plea for 'Persons.' "[5] Our slang words for sexual intercourse—'fuck,' 'screw,' or older words such as 'take' or 'have'—not only can mean harm but have traditionally taken a male subject and a female object. The active male screws (harms) the passive female. A "bad" woman only tempts men to hurt her further.

It is easy to understand why one's proper grandmother would not want men to see pornography or lose respect for women. But feminists reject these "proper" assumptions: good and bad classes of women do not exist; and sex is not dirty (though many people believe it is). Why then are feminists angry at the treatment of women as sex objects, and why are some feminists opposed to pornography?

The answer is that feminists as well as proper grandparents are concerned with respect. However, there are differences. A feminist's distinction between treating a woman as a full-fledged person and treating her as merely a sex object does not correspond to the good-bad woman distinction. In the latter distinction, "good" and "bad" are properties applicable to groups of women. In the feminist view, all women are full-fledged people—some, however, are treated as sex objects and perhaps think of themselves as sex objects. A further difference is that, although "bad" women correspond to those thought to deserve treatment as sex objects, good women have not corresponded to full-fledged people; only men have been full-fledged people. Given the feminist's distinction, she has no difficulty whatever in saying that pornography treats women as sex objects, not as full-fledged people. She can morally object to pornography or anything else that treats women as sex objects.

One might wonder whether any objection to treatment as a sex object implies that the person objecting still believes, deep down, that sex is dirty. I don't think so. Several other possibilities emerge. First, even if I believe intellectually and emotionally that sex is healthy, I might object to being treated *only* as a sex object. In the same spirit, I would object to being treated *only* as a maker of chocolate chip cookies or *only* as a tennis partner, because only one of my talents is being valued. Second, perhaps I feel that sex is healthy, but it is apparent to me that you think sex is dirty; so I don't want you to treat me as a sex object. Third, being treated as any kind of object, not just as a sex object, is unappealing. I would rather be a partner (sexual or otherwise) than an object. Fourth, and more plausible than the first three possibilities, is Robert Baker's view mentioned above. Both (1) our traditional double standard of sexual behavior for men and women and (2) the linguistic evidence that we connect the concept of sex with the concept of harm point to what is wrong with treating women as sex objects. As I said earlier, 'fuck' and 'screw,' in their traditional uses, have taken a male subject, a female object, and have had at least two meanings: harm and have sexual intercourse with. (In addition, a prick is a man who harms people ruthlessly; and a motherfucker is so low that he would do something very harmful to his own dear mother.)[6] Because in our culture we connect sex with harm that men do to women, and because we think of the female role in sex as that of harmed object, we can see that to treat a woman as a sex object is automatically to

treat her as less than fully human. To say this does not imply that no healthy sexual relationships exist; nor does it say anything about individual men's conscious intentions to degrade women by desiring them sexually (though no doubt some men have these intentions). It is merely to make a point about the concepts embodied in our language.

Psychoanalytic support for the connection between sex and harm comes from Robert J. Stoller. Stoller thinks that sexual excitement is linked with a wish to harm someone (and with at least a whisper of hostility). The key process of sexual excitement can be seen as dehumanization (fetishization) in fantasy of the desired person. He speculates that this is true in some degree of everyone, both men and women, with "normal" or "perverted" activities and fantasies.[7]

Thinking of sex objects as harmed objects enables us to explain some of the first three reasons why one wouldn't want to be treated as a sex object: (1) I may object to being treated only as a tennis partner, but being a tennis partner is not connected in our culture with being a harmed object; and (2) I may not think that sex is dirty and that I would be a harmed object; I may not know what your view is; but what bothers me is that this is the view embodied in our language and culture.

Awareness of the connection between sex and harm helps explain other interesting points. Women are angry about being treated as sex objects in situations or roles in which they do not intend to be regarded in that manner—for example, while serving on a committee or attending a discussion. It is not merely that a sexual role is inappropriate for the circumstances; it is thought to be a less fully human role than the one in which they intended to function.

Finally, the sex-harm connection makes clear why it is worse to treat women as sex objects than to treat men as sex objects, and why some men have had difficulty understanding women's anger about the matter. It is more difficult for heterosexual men than for women to assume the role of "harmed object" in sex; for men have the self-concept of sexual agents, not of passive objects. This is also related to my earlier point concerning the difference in the solidity of respect for men and for women; respect for women is more fragile. Despite exceptions, it is generally harder for people to degrade men, either sexually or nonsexually, than to degrade women. Men and women have grown up with different patterns of self-respect and expectations regarding the extent to which they deserve and will receive respect or degradation. The man who doesn't understand why women do not want to be treated as sex objects (because he'd sure like to be) would not think of himself as being harmed by that treatment; a woman might.[8] Pornography, probably more than any other contemporary institution, succeeds in treating men as sex objects.

Having seen that the connection between sex and harm helps explain both what is wrong with treating someone as a sex object and why it is worse to treat a woman in this way, I want to use the sex-harm connection to try to resolve a dispute about pornography and women. Brownmiller's view, remember, was that pornography is "the undiluted essence of anti-female propaganda" whose purpose is to degrade women. Some people object to Brownmiller's view by saying that, since pornography treats both men and women as sex objects for the purpose of arousing the viewer, it is neither sexist, antifemale, nor designed to degrade women; it just happens that degrading of women arouses some men. How can this dispute be resolved?

Suppose we were to rate the content of all pornography from most morally objectionable to least morally objectionable. Among the most objectionable would be the most degrading—for example, "snuff" films and movies which recommend that men rape women, molest children and puppies, and treat nonmasochists very sadistically.

Next we would find a large amount of material (probably most pornography) not quite so blatantly offensive. With this material it is relevant to use the analysis of sex objects given above. As long as sex is connected with harm done to women, it will be very difficult not to see pornography as degrading to women. We can agree with Brownmiller's opponent that pornography treats men as sex objects, too, but we maintain that this is only pseudoequality: such treatment is still more degrading to women.[9]

In addition, pornography often exemplifies the active/passive, harmer/harmed object roles in a very obvious way. Because pornography today is male-oriented and is supposed to make a profit, the content is designed to appeal to male fantasies. Judging from the content of the most popular legally

available pornography, male fantasies still run along the lines of stereotypical sex roles—and, if Stoller is right, include elements of hostility. In much pornography the women's purpose is to cater to male desires, to service the man or men. Her own pleasure is rarely emphasized for its own sake; she is merely allowed a little heavy breathing, perhaps in order to show her dependence on the great male "lover" who produces her pleasure. In addition, women are clearly made into passive objects in still photographs showing only close-ups of their genitals. Even in movies marketed to appeal to heterosexual couples, such as *Behind the Green Door*, the woman is passive and undemanding (and in this case kidnapped and hypnotized as well). Although many kinds of specialty magazines and films are gauged for different sexual tastes, very little contemporary pornography goes against traditional sex roles. There is certainly no significant attempt to replace the harmer/harmed distinction with anything more positive and healthy. In some stag movies, of course, men are treated sadistically by women; but this is an attempt to turn the tables on degradation, not a positive improvement.

What would cases toward the least objectionable end of the spectrum be like? They would be increasingly less degrading and sexist. The genuinely nonobjectionable cases would be nonsexist and nondegrading; but commercial examples do not readily spring to mind.[10] The question is: Does or could any pornography have nonsexist, nondegrading content?

II

I want to start with the easier question: Is it possible for pornography to have nonsexist, morally acceptable content? Then I will consider whether any pornography of this sort currently exists.

Imagine the following situation, which exists only rarely today: Two fairly conventional people who love each other enjoy playing tennis and bridge together, cooking good food together, and having sex together. In all these activities they are free from hang-ups, guilt, and tendencies to dominate or objectify each other. These two people like to watch tennis matches and old romantic movies on TV, like to watch Julia Child cook, like to read the bridge column in the newspaper, and like to watch pornographic movies. Imagine further that this couple is not at all uncommon in society and that nonsexist pornography is as common as this kind of nonsexist sexual relationship. This situation sounds fine and healthy to me. I see no reason to think that an interest in pornography would disappear in these circumstances. People seem to enjoy watching others experience or do (especially do well) what they enjoy experiencing, doing, or wish they could do themselves. We do not morally object to people watching tennis on TV; why would we object to these hypothetical people watching pornography?

Can we go from the situation today to the situation just imagined? In much current pornography, people are treated in morally objectionable ways. In the scene just imagined, however, pornography would be nonsexist, nondegrading, morally acceptable. The key to making the change is to break the connection between sex and harm. If Stoller is right, this task may be impossible without changing the scenarios of our sexual lives—scenarios that we have been writing since early childhood. (Stoller does not indicate whether he thinks it possible for adults to rewrite their scenarios or for social change to bring about the possibility of new scenarios in future generations.) But even if we believe that people can change their sexual scenarios, the sex-harm connection is deeply entrenched and has widespread implications. What is needed is a thorough change in people's deep-seated attitudes and feelings about sex roles in general, as well as about sex and roles in sex (sexual roles). Although I cannot even sketch a general outline of such changes here, changes in pornography should be part of a comprehensive program. Television, children's educational material, and nonpornographic movies and novels may be far better avenues for attempting to change attitudes; but one does not want to take the chance that pornography is working against one.

What can be done about pornography in particular? If one wanted to work within the current institutions, one's attempt to use pornography as a tool for the education of male pornography audiences would have to be fairly subtle at first; nonsexist pornography must become familiar enough to sell and be watched. One should realize too that any positive educational value that nonsexist pornography might have may well be as short-lived as most of the effects of pornography. But given these limitations, what could one do?

Two kinds of films must be considered. First is the short film with no plot or character development, just depicted sexual activity in which nonsexist pornography would treat men and women as equal sex partners.[11] The man would not control the circumstances in which the partners had sex or the choice of positions or acts; the woman's preference would be counted equally. There would be no suggestion of a power play or conquest on the man's part, no suggestion that "she likes it when I hurt her." Sexual intercourse would not be portrayed as primarily for the purpose of male ejaculation—his orgasm is not "the best part" of the movie. In addition, both the man and woman would express their enjoyment; the man need not be cool and detached.

The film with a plot provides even more opportunity for nonsexist education. Today's pornography often portrays the female characters as playthings even when not engaging in sexual activity. Nonsexist pornography could show women and men in roles equally valued by society, and sex equality would amount to more than possession of equally functional genitalia. Characters would customarily treat each other with respect and consideration, with no attempt to treat men or women brutally or thoughtlessly. The local Pussycat Theater showed a film written and directed by a woman (*The Passions of Carol*), which exhibited a few of the features just mentioned. The main female character in it was the editor of a magazine parody of *Viva*. The fact that some of the characters treated each other very nicely, warmly, and tenderly did not detract from the pornographic features of the movie. This did not surprise us, for even in traditional male-oriented films, lesbian scenes usually exhibit tenderness and kindness.

Plots for nonsexist films could include women in traditionally male jobs (e.g., long-distance truckdriver) or in positions usually held in respect by pornography audiences. For example, a high-ranking female Army officer, treated with respect by men and women alike, could be shown not only in various sexual encounters with other people but also carrying out her job in a humane manner.[12] Or perhaps the main character could be a female urologist. She could interact with nurses and other medical personnel, diagnose illnesses brilliantly, and treat patients with great sympathy as well as have sex with them. When the Army officer or the urologist engages in sexual activities, she will treat her partners and be treated by them in some of the considerate ways describe above.

In the circumstances we imagined at the beginning of [this part of the] paper, our nonsexist films could be appreciated in the proper spirit. Under these conditions the content of our new pornography would clearly be nonsexist and morally acceptable. But would the content of such a film be morally acceptable if shown to a typical pornography audience today? It might seem strange for us to change our moral evaluation of the content on the basis of a different audience, but an audience today is likely to see the "respected" urologist and Army officer as playthings or unusual prostitutes—even if our intention in showing the film is to counteract this view. The effect is that although the content of the film seems morally acceptable and our intention in showing it is morally flawless, women are still degraded.[13] The fact that audience attitude is so important makes one wary of giving wholehearted approval to any pornography seen today.

The fact that good intentions and content are insufficient does not imply that one's efforts toward change would be entirely in vain. Of course, I could not deny that anyone who tries to change an institution from within faces serious difficulties. This is particularly evident when one is trying to change both pornography and a whole set of related attitudes, feelings, and institutions concerning sex and sex roles. But in conjunction with other attempts to change this set of attitudes, it seems preferable to try to change pornography instead of closing one's eyes in the hope that it will go away. For I suspect that pornography is here to stay.[14]

Notes

1. (New York: Simon and Schuster, 1975), p. 394.
2. *The Report of the Commission on Obscenity and Pornography* (Washington, D.C., 1970), p. 201. This article first appeared in *Social Theory and Practice*, vol. 4 (Summer 1978), pp. 395–421. It is reprinted here, by permission of the author, as it appears in *Philosophy and Women,* edited by Sharon Bishop and Majorie Weinzweig (Belmont, Calif.: Wadsworth, 1979).
3. In order to help one determine which position one feels inclined to take, consider the following statement: It is morally objectionable to write, make,

sell, act in, use, and enjoy pornography; in addition, the content of pornography is immoral; however, pornography itself is not morally objectionable. If this statement seems extremely problematic, then one might well be satisfied with the claim that pornography is degrading because its content is.
4. Many feminists point this out. One of the most accessible references is Shulamith Firestone, *The Dialectic of Sex: The Case for the Feminist Revolution* (New York: Bantam, 1970), especially pp. 128–32.
5. In Richard Wasserstrom, ed., *Today's Moral Problems* (New York: Macmillan, 1975), pp. 152—71. Also in Robert Baker and Frederick Elliston, eds., *Philosophy and Sex* (Buffalo, N.Y.: Prometheus Books, 1975).
6. Baker, in Wasserstrom, *Today's Moral Problems*, pp. 168–169.
7. "Sexual Excitement," *Archives of General Psychiatry* 33 (1976): 899–909, especially p. 903. The extent to which Stoller sees men and women in different positions with respect to harm and hostility is not clear. He often treats men and women alike, but in *Perversion: The Erotic Form of Hatred* (New York: Pantheon, 1975), pp. 89–91, he calls attention to differences between men and women especially regarding their responses to pornography and lack of understanding by men of women's sexuality. Given that Stoller finds hostility to be an essential element in male-oriented pornography, and given that women have not responded readily to such pornography, one can speculate about the possibilities for women's sexuality: their hostility might follow a different scenario; they might not be as hostile, and so on.
8. Men seem to be developing more sensitivity to being treated as sex objects. Many homosexual men have long understood the problem. As women become more sexually aggressive, some heterosexual men I know are beginning to feel treated as sex objects. A man can feel that he is not being taken seriously if a woman looks lustfully at him while he is holding forth about the French judicial system or the failure of liberal politics. Some of his most important talents are not being properly valued.
9. I don't agree with Brownmiller that the purpose of pornography is to dehumanize women, rather it is to arouse the audience. The differences between our views can be explained, in part, by the points from which we begin. She is writing about rape; her views about pornography grow out of her views about rape. I begin by thinking of pornogra-

phy as merely depicted sexual activity, though I am well aware of the male hostility and contempt for women that it often expresses. That pornography degrades women and excites men is an illustration of this contempt.

10. Virginia Wright Wexman uses the film *Group Marriage* (Stephanie Rottman, 1973) as an example of "more enlightened erotica." Wexman also asks the following questions in an attempt to point out sexism in pornographic films:

> Does it [the film] portray rape as pleasurable to women? Does it consistently show females nude but present men fully clothed? Does it present women as childlike creatures whose sexual interests must be guided by knowing experienced men? Does it show sexually aggressive women as castrating viragos? Does it pretend that sex is exclusively the prerogative of women under twenty-five? Does it focus on the physical aspects of lovemaking rather than the emotional ones? Does it portray women as purely sexual beings? ("Sexism of X-rated Films." *Chicago Sun-Times*, 28 March 1976.)

11. If it is a lesbian or male homosexual film, no one would play a caricatured male or female role. The reader has probably noticed that I have limited my discussion to heterosexual pornography, but there are many interesting analogies to be drawn with male homosexual pornography. Very little lesbian pornography exists, though lesbian scenes are commonly found in male-oriented pornography.

12. One should note that behavior of this kind is still considered unacceptable by the military. A female officer resigned from the U.S. Navy recently rather than be court-martialed for having sex with several enlisted men whom she met in a class on interpersonal relations.

13. The content may seem morally acceptable only if one disregards such questions as, "Should a doctor have sex with her patients during office hours?" More important is the propriety of evaluating content wholly apart from the attitudes and reactions of the audience; one might not find it strange to say that one film has morally unacceptable content when shown tonight at the Pussycat Theater but acceptable content when shown tomorrow at a feminist conference.

14. [Two] "final" points must be made:

1. I have not seriously considered censorship as an alternative course of action. . . . Brownmiller . . . [is] not averse to it. But . . . other principles seem too valuable to sacrifice when other options are available. I believe that even if moral objections to pornography exist, one must preclude any simple inference from "pornography is immoral" to "pornography should be censored" because of other important values and principles such as freedom of expression and self-determination. In addition, before justifying censorship on moral grounds one would want to compare pornography to other possibly offensive material: advertising using sex and racial stereotypes, violence in TV and films, and so on.

2. In discussing the audience for nonsexist pornography, I have focused on the male audience. But there is no reason why pornography could not educate and appeal to women as well.

Questions for Analysis

1. *What is the "apparent conflict" that Garry refers to in the opening paragraph?*

2. *Briefly explain why Garry believes that the current content of pornography violates the moral principle of respect for persons.*

3. *What's the connection between losing respect for a woman and treating her as a sex object?*

4. *What does Garry mean when she says, ". . . pornography often exemplifies the active/passive, harmer/harmed object roles in a very obvious way"? How is this relevant to her argument?*

5. *Feminist Susan Brownmiller, whom Garry refers to, argues that tolerance of pornography undercuts respect for women and is a kind of group defamation, much like Nazi propaganda degrades Jews. Therefore, Brownmiller concludes, pornography should be suppressed. Do you think Garry would agree with Brownmiller's conclusion?*

6. *What does Garry believe is needed for pornography to be nonsexist, nondegrading, and morally acceptable?*

7. *Do you think that Garry's objections to current pornography are consistent with natural-law theory?*

8. *The traditional Judeo-Christian objection to pornography is that pornography involves the pursuit of pleasure for its own sake, thereby excluding the higher purposes and values to which pleasure is attached. Pornography exemplifies and encourages impersonal sexual activity, which is debasing and a violation of human dignity. Compare and contrast Garry's position with this view.*

Dissenting Opinion in *United States* v. *Roth*

Judge Jerome Frank

A man named Roth conducted a business in New York publishing books, photographs, and magazines. He used sexually explicit circulars and advertising material to solicit sales. Charges were brought against him of mailing obscene circulars and advertising and of mailing an obscene book, all in violation of the federal obscenity statute. He was convicted by a jury in the District Court for the Southern District of New York on four counts of a twenty-six-count indictment. In 1956, his conviction was affirmed by the Court of Appeals for the Second Circuit, and subsequently upheld by the U.S. Supreme Court.

What follows is the dissenting opinion in the Court of Appeals ruling, written by Judge Jerome Frank. Frank's comprehensive opinion is often regarded as a classic statement against censorship of obscenity. Although written prior to the Supreme Court's disposition of the First Amendment issue and legal definition of obscenity in United States *v.* Roth *(354 U.S. 476, 1957), Frank's viewpoint remains highly influential. It deals with a wide range of pertinent issues and continues to furnish supporting material for those who claim that censorship of pornography is unconstitutional, unwise, or immoral.*

Here Frank's opinion has been edited to less than half its original length. Most footnotes have been deleted, the remainder renumbered.

I agree with my colleagues that since ours is an inferior court, we should not hold invalid a statute which our superior has . . . often said is constitutional (albeit without any full discussion). Yet I think it not improper to set forth, as I do in the Appendix, considerations concerning the obscenity statute's validity with which, up to now, I think the Supreme Court has not dealt in any of its opinions.

I do not suggest the inevitability of the conclusion that the statute is unconstitutional. I do suggest that it is hard to avoid that conclusion, if one applies to that legislation the reasoning the Supreme Court has applied to other sorts of legislation. Perhaps I have overlooked conceivable compelling contrary arguments. If so, maybe my Appendix will evoke them.

To preclude misunderstanding of my purpose in stirring doubts about this statute, I think it well to add the following:

(a) As many of the publications mailed by defendant offend my personal taste, I would not cross a street to obtain them for nothing; I happen not to be interested in so-called "pornography," and I think defendant's motives obnoxious. But if the statute were invalid, the merit of those publications would be irrelevant. . . . So, too, as to defendant's motives: "Although the defendant may be the worst of men . . . the rights of the best of men are secure only as the rights of the vilest and most abhorrent are protected."[1]

(b) It is most doubtful (as explained in the Appendix) whether anyone can now demonstrate that children's reading or looking at obscene matter has a probable causal relation to the children's anti-social conduct. If, however, such a probable causal relation could be shown, there could be little, I think, of the validity of a statute (if so worded as to avoid undue ambiguity) which specifically prohibits the distribution by mail of obscene publications for sale to young people. But discussion of such legislation is here irrelevant, since, to repeat, the existing federal statute is not thus restricted.

(c) Congress undoubtedly has wide power to protect public morals. But the First Amendment severely limits that power in the area of free speech and free press. . . .

(e) The First Amendment, of course, does not prevent any private body or group (including any church) from instructing, or seeking to persuade, its adherents or others not to read or distribute obscene (or other) publications. That constitutional provision—safeguarding a principle indispensable in a true democracy—leaves unhampered all non-governmental means of molding public opinion about not reading literature which some think undesirable; and, in that respect, experience teaches that democratically exercised censorship by public opinion has far more potency, and is far less easily evaded, than censorship by government. The incessant struggle to influence public opinion is of the very essence of the democratic process. A basic purpose of the First Amendment is to keep that struggle alive, by not permitting the dominant public opinion of the present to become embodied in legislation which will prevent the formation of a different dominant public opinion in the future.

(f) At first glance it may seem almost frivolous to raise any question about the constitutionality of the obscenity statute at a time when many seemingly graver First Amendment problems confront the courts. But (for reasons stated in more detail in the Appendix) governmental censorship of writings, merely because they may stimulate, in the reader, sexual thoughts the legislature deems undesirable, has more serious implications than appear at first glance: We have been warned by eminent thinkers of the easy path from any apparently mild governmental control of what adult citizens may read to governmental control of adults' political and religious reading. John Milton, Thomas Jefferson, James Madison, John Stuart Mill and Alexis de Tocqueville have pointed out that any paternalistic guardianship by government of the thoughts of grown-up citizens enervates their spirit, keeps them immature, all too ready to adopt towards government officers the attitude that, in general, "Papa knows best." If the government possesses the power to censor publications which arouse sexual thoughts, regardless of whether those thoughts tend probably to transform themselves into anti-social behavior, why may not the government censor political and religious publications regardless of any causal relation to probably dangerous deeds? And even if we confine attention to official censorship of publications tending to stimulate sexual thoughts, it should be asked why, at any moment, that censorship cannot be extended to advertisements and true reports or photographs, in our daily press, which, fully as much, may stimulate such thoughts?

(g) Assuming *arguendo,* that a statute aims at an altogether desirable end, nevertheless its desirability does not render it constitutional. . . .

Appendix

In 1799, eight years after the adoption of the First Amendment, Madison, in an address to the General Assembly of Virginia,[2] said that the "truth of opinion" ought not to be subject to "imprisonment, to be inflicted by those of a different opinion"; he there also asserted that it would subvert the First Amendment to make a "distinction between the freedom and the licentiousness of the press." Previously, in 1792, he wrote that "a man has property in his opinions and free communication of them," and that a government which "violates the property which individuals have in their opinion . . . is not a pattern for the United States."[3] Jefferson's proposed Constitution for Virginia (1776) provided: "Printing presses shall be free, except so far as by commission of private injury cause may be given of private action."[4] In his Second Inaugural Address (1805), he said:

> No inference is here intended that the laws provided by the State against false and defamatory publications should not be enforced. . . . The press, confined to truth, needs no other restraint . . . ; and no other definite line can be drawn between the inestimable liberty of the press and demoralizing licentiousness. If there still be improprieties which this rule would not restrain, its supplement must be sought in the censorship of public opinion.

. . . Jefferson, in 1798, quoting the First Amendment, said it guarded "in the same sentence, and under the same words, the freedom of religion, of speech, and of the press; insomuch, that whatever violates either throws down the sanctuary which covers the others."[5] In 1814, he wrote in a letter,

> I am really mortified to be told that in the United States of America, a fact like this (the sale of a book) can become a subject of inquiry, and of criminal inquiry too, as an offense against religion; that (such) a question can be carried before the civil magistrate. Is this then our freedom of religion? And are we to have a censor whose imprimatur shall say what books may be sold and what we may buy? . . . Whose foot is to be the measure to which ours are all to be cut or stretched?[6]

Those utterances highlight this fact: Freedom to speak publicly and to publish has, as its inevitable and important correlative, the private rights to hear, to read, and to think and to feel about what one hears and reads. The First Amendment protects those private rights of hearers and readers. . . .

The question therefore arises whether the courts, in enforcing the First Amendment, should interpret it in accord with the views prevalent among those who sponsored and adopted it or in accord with subsequently developed views which would sanction legislation more restrictive of free speech and free press.

So the following becomes pertinent: Some of those who in the twentieth century endorse legislation suppressing "obscene" literature have an attitude toward freedom of expression which does not match that of the framers of the First Amendment (adopted at the end of the eighteenth century) but does stem from an attitude toward writings dealing with sex which arose decades later, in the mid-nineteenth century, and is therefore labeled—doubtless too sweepingly—"Victorian." It was a dogma of "Victorian morality" that sexual misbehavior would be encouraged if one were to "acknowledge its existence or at any rate to present it vividly enough to form a lifelike image of it in the reader's mind"; this morality rested on a "faith that you could best conquer evil by shutting your eyes to its existence,"[7] and on a kind of word magic.[8] The demands at that time for "decency" in published words did not comport with the actual sexual conduct of many of those who made those demands: "The Victorians, as a general rule, managed to conceal the 'coarser' side of their lives so thoroughly under a mask of respectability that we often fail to realize how 'coarse' it really was. . . ." Could we have recourse to the vast unwritten literature of bawdry, we should be able to form a more veracious notion of life as it (then) really was. The respectables of those days often, "with unblushing license," held "high revels" in "night houses."[9] Thanks to them, Mrs. Warren's profession flourished, but it was considered sinful to talk about it in books.[10] Such a prudish and purely verbal moral code, at odds (more or less hypocritically) with the actual conduct of its adherents, was (as we have seen) not the moral code of those who framed the First Amendment. One would suppose, then, that the courts should interpret and enforce that Amendment according to the views of those framers, not according to the later "Victorian" code. . . .

The Statute, as Judicially Interpreted, Authorizes Punishment for Inducing Mere Thoughts, and Feelings, or Desires

For a time, American courts adopted the test of obscenity contrived in 1868 by L. J. Cockburn, in *Queen* v. *Hicklin*, L.R. 3 Q.B. 360: "I think the test of obscenity is this, whether the tendency of the matter charged as obscenity is to deprave and corrupt those whose minds are open to such immoral influences, and into whose hands a publication of this sort might fall." He added that the book there in question "would suggest . . . thoughts of a most impure and libidinous character."

The test in most federal courts has changed: They do not now speak of the thoughts of "those whose minds are open to . . . immoral influences" but, instead, of the thoughts of average adult normal men and women, determining what these thoughts are, not by proof at the trial, but by the standard of "the average conscience of the time," the current "social sense of what is right."

Yet the courts still define obscenity in terms of the assumed average normal adult reader's sexual thoughts or desires or impulses, without reference to any relation between those "subjective" reactions and his subsequent conduct. The judicial opinions use such key phrases as this: "suggesting lewd thoughts and exciting sensual desires," "arouse the salacity of the reader," "allowing or implanting . . . obscene, lewd, or lascivious thoughts or desires," "arouse sexual desires." The judge's charge in the instant case reads accordingly: "It must tend to stir sexual impulses and lead to sexually impure thoughts." Thus the statute, as the courts construe it, appears to provide criminal punishment for inducing no more than thoughts, feelings, desires.

No Adequate Knowledge Is Available Concerning the Effects on the Conduct of Normal Adults of Reading or Seeing the "Obscene"

Suppose we assume, *arguendo*, that sexual thoughts or feelings, stirred by the "obscene," probably will often issue into overt conduct. Still it does not at all follow that that conduct will be antisocial. For no sane person can believe it socially harmful if sexual desires lead to normal, and not antisocial, sexual behavior since, without such behavior, the human race would soon disappear.

Doubtless, Congress could validly provide punishment for mailing any publications if there were some moderately substantial reliable data showing that reading or seeing those publications probably conduces to seriously harmful sexual con-

duct on the part of normal adult human beings. But we have no such data.

Suppose it argued that whatever excites sexual longings might *possibly* produce sexual misconduct. That cannot suffice: Notoriously, perfumes sometimes act as aphrodisiacs, yet no one will suggest that therefore Congress may constitutionally legislate punishment for mailing perfumes. It may be that among the stimuli to irregular sexual conduct, by normal men and women, may be almost anything—the odor of carnations or cheese, the sight of a cane or a candle or a shoe, the touch of silk or a gunnysack. For all anyone now knows, stimuli of that sort may be far more provocative of such misconduct than reading obscene books or seeing obscene pictures. Said John Milton, "Evil manners are as perfectly learnt, without books, a thousand other ways that cannot be stopped."

Effect of "Obscenity" on Adult Conduct

To date there exist, I think, no thoroughgoing studies by competent persons which justify the conclusion that normal adults' reading or seeing of the "obscene" probably induces antisocial conduct. Such competent studies as have been made do conclude that so complex and numerous are the causes of sexual vice that it is impossible to assert with any assurance that "obscenity" represents a ponderable causal factor in sexually deviant adult behavior. "Although the whole subject of obscenity censorship hinges upon the unproved assumption that 'obscene' literature is a significant factor in causing sexual deviation from the community standard, no report can be found of a single effort at genuine research to test this assumption by singling out as a factor for study the effect of sex literature upon sexual behavior."[11] What little competent research has been done points definitely in a direction precisely opposite to that assumption.

Alpert reports[12] that, when, in the 1920s, 409 women college graduates were asked to state in writing what things stimulated them sexually, they answered thus: 218 said men; 95 said books; 40 said drama; 29 said dancing; 18 said pictures; 9 said music. Of those who replied "that the source of their sex information came from books, not one specified a 'dirty' book as the source. Instead, the books listed were: The Bible, the dictionary, the encyclopedia, novels from Dickens to Henry James, circulars about venereal diseases, medical books, and Motley's *Rise of the Dutch Republic*." Macaulay, replying to advocates of the suppression of obscene books, said: "We find it difficult to believe that in a world so full of temptations as this, any gentleman whose life would have been virtuous if he had not read Aristophanes or Juvenal, will be vicious by reading them." Echoing Macaulay, Jimmy Walker, former mayor of New York City, remarked that he had never heard of a woman seduced by a book. New Mexico has never had an obscenity statute; there is no evidence that, in that state, sexual misconduct is proportionately greater than elsewhere.

Effect on Conduct of Young People

. . . Judge Clark[13] speaks of "the strongly held views of those with competence in the premises as to the very direct connection" of obscenity "with the development of juvenile delinquency." . . . One of the cited writings is a report, by Dr. [Marie] Jahoda and associates, entitled "The Impact of Literature: A Psychological Discussion of Some Assumptions in the Censorship Debate" (1954). I have read this report (which is a careful survey of all available studies and psychological theories). I think it expresses an attitude quite contrary to that indicated by Judge Clark. In order to avoid any possible bias in my interpretation of that report, I thought it well to ask Dr. Jahoda to write her own summary of it, which, with her permission, I shall quote.

Dr. Jahoda's summary reads as follows:

Persons who argue for increased censorship of printed matter often operate on the assumption that reading about sexual matters or about violence and brutality leads to antisocial actions, particularly to juvenile delinquency. An examination of the pertinent psychological literature has led to the following conclusions:

1. There exists no research evidence either to prove or to disprove this assumption definitively.

2. In the absence of scientific proof two lines of psychological approach to the examination of the assumption are possible: (a) a review of what is known on the causes of juvenile delinquency; and (b) a review of what is known about the effect of literature on the mind of the reader.

3. In the vast research literature on the causes of juvenile delinquency there is no evidence to justify the assumption that reading about sexual matters or about violence leads to delinquent acts. Experts on juvenile delinquency agree that it has no single cause. Most of them regard early childhood events, which precede the reading age, as a necessary condition for later delinquency. At a later age, the nature of personal relations is assumed to have much greater power in determining a delinquent career than the vicarious experiences provided by reading matter. Juvenile delinquents as a group read less, and less easily, than nondelinquents. Individual instances are reported in which so-called "good" books allegedly influenced a delinquent in the manner in which "bad" books are assumed to influence him.

Where childhood experiences and subsequent events have combined to make delinquency psychologically likely, reading could have one of two effects: It could serve a trigger function releasing the criminal act or it could provide for a substitute outlet of aggression in fantasy, dispensing with the need for criminal action. There is no empirical evidence in either direction.

4. With regard to the impact of literature on the mind of the reader, it must be pointed out that there is a vast overlap in content between all media of mass communication. The daily press, television, radio, movies, books and comics all present their share of so-called "bad" material, some with great realism as reports of actual events, some in clearly fictionalized form. It is virtually impossible to isolate the impact of one of these media on a population exposed to all of them. Some evidence suggests that the particular communications which arrest the attention of an individual are in good part a matter of choice. As a rule, people do not expose themselves to everything that is offered, but only to what agrees with their inclinations.

Children, who have often not yet crystallized their preferences and have more unspecific curiosity than many adults, are therefore perhaps more open to accidental influences from literature. This may present a danger to youngsters who are insecure or maladjusted who find in reading (of "bad" books as well as of "good" books) an escape from reality which they do not dare face. Needs which are not met in the real world are gratified in a fantasy world. It is likely, though not fully demonstrated, that excessive reading of comic books will intensify in children those qualities which drove them to the comic book world to begin with: an inability to face the world, apathy, a belief that the individual is hopelessly impotent and driven by uncontrollable forces and, hence, an acceptance of violence and brutality in the real world.

It should be noted that insofar as causal sequence is implied, insecurity and maladjustment in a child must precede this exposure to the written word in order to lead to these potential effects. Unfortunately, perhaps, the reading of Shakespeare's tragedies or of Andersen's and Grimm's fairy tales might do much the same.

Maybe someday we will have enough reliable data to show that obscene books and pictures do tend to influence children's sexual conduct adversely. Then a federal statute could be enacted which would avoid constitutional defects by authorizing punishment for using the mails or interstate shipments in the sale of such books and pictures to children.

It is, however, not at all clear that children would be ignorant, in any considerable measure, of obscenity, if no obscene publications ever came into their hands. Youngsters get a vast deal of education in sexual smut from companions of their own age. A verbatim report of conversations among young teen-age boys (from average respectable homes) will disclose their amazing proficiency in obscene language, learned from other boys. Replying to the argument of the need for censorship to protect the young, Milton said: "Who shall regulate all the . . . conversation of our youth . . . appoint what shall be discussed . . . ?" Most judges who reject that view are long past their youth and have probably forgotten the conversational ways of that period of life: "I remember when I was a little boy," said Dr. Dooley, "but I don't remember how I was a little boy."

The Obscenity Statute and the Reputable Press

Let it be assumed, for the sake of the argument, that contemplation of published matter dealing with sex has a significant impact on children's conduct. On that assumption, we cannot overlook the fact that our most reputable newspapers and periodicals carry advertisements and photographs displaying women in what decidedly are sexually alluring postures, and at times emphasizing the importance of "sex appeal." That women are there shown scantily clad increases "the mystery and allure of the bodies that are hidden," writes an eminent psychiatrist. "A leg covered by a silk stocking is much more attractive than a naked one; a bosom pushed into shape by a brassiere is more alluring than the pendant realities."[14] Either, then, the statute must be sternly applied to prevent the mailing of many reputable newspapers and periodicals containing such ads and photographs, or else we must acknowledge that they have created a cultural atmosphere for children in which, at a maximum, only the most trifling additional effect can be imputed to children's perusal of the kind of matter mailed by the defendant. . . .

Da Capo: Available Data Seem Wholly Insufficient to Show That the Obscenity Statutes Come Within Any Exception to the First Amendment

I repeat that because that statute is not restricted to obscene publications mailed for sale to minors, its validity should be tested in terms of the evil effects of adult reading of obscenity on adult conduct. With the present lack of evidence that publications probably have such effects, how can the government discharge its burden of demonstrating sufficiently that the statute is within the narrow exceptions to the scope of the First Amendment? One would think that the mere possibility of a causal relation to misconduct ought surely not be enough. . . .

If the Obscenity Statute Is Valid, Why May Congress Not Validly Provide Punishment for Mailing Books Which Will Provoke Thoughts It Considers Undesirable About Religion or Politics?

If the statute is valid, then, considering the foregoing, it would seem that its validity must rest on this ground: Congress, by statute, may constitutionally provide punishment for the mailing of books evoking mere thoughts or feelings about sex, if Congress considers them socially dangerous, even in the absence of any satisfactory evidence that those thoughts or feelings will tend to bring about socially harmful deeds. If that be correct, it is hard to understand why, similarly, Congress may not constitutionally provide punishment for such distribution of books evoking mere thoughts or feelings about religion or politics which Congress considers socially dangerous, even in the absence of any satisfactory evidence that those thoughts or feelings will tend to bring about socially dangerous deeds.

The Judicial Exception of the "Classics"

As I have said, I have no doubt the jury could reasonably find, beyond a reasonable doubt, that many of the publications mailed by defendant were obscene within the current judicial definition of the term as explained by the trial judge in his charge to the jury. But so, too, are a multitude of recognized works of art found in public libraries. Compare, for instance, the books which are exhibits in this case with Montaigne's *Essay on Some Lines of Virgil* or with Chaucer. Or consider the many nude pictures which the defendant transmitted through the mails, and then turn to the reproductions in the articles on paintings and sculptures in the *Encyclopaedia Britannica* (14th edition). Some of the latter are no less "obscene" than those which led to the defendant's conviction. Yet these Encyclopedia volumes are readily accessible to everyone, young or old, and, without let or hindrance, are frequently mailed to all parts of the country. Catalogues of famous art museums, almost equally accessible and also often mailed, contain reproductions of paintings and sculpture, by great masters, no less "obscene."

To the argument that such books (and such reproductions of famous paintings and works of sculpture) fall within the statutory ban, the courts have answered that they are "classics"—books of "literary distinction" or works which have "an accepted place in the arts," including, so this court has held, Ovid's *Art of Love* and Boccaccio's *Decameron*. There is a "curious dilemma" involved in this answer that the statute condemns "only books which are dull and without merit," that in no event will the statute be applied to the "classics," that is, books "of literary distinction."[15] The courts have not explained how they escape that dilemma, but instead seem to have gone to sleep (although rather uncomfortably) on its horns.

. . . No one can rationally justify the judge-made exception. The contention would scarcely pass as rational that the "classics will be read or seen solely by an intellectual or artistic elite; for, even ignoring the snobbish, undemocratic nature of this contention, there is no evidence that the elite has a moral fortitude (an immunity from moral corruption) superior to that of the "masses." And if the exception, to make it rational, were taken as meaning that a contemporary book is exempt if it equates in "literary distinction" with the "classics," the result would be amazing: Judges would have to serve as literary critics; jurisprudence would merge with aesthetics; authors and publishers would consult the legal digests for legal-artistic precedents; we would some day have a Legal Restatement of the Canons of Literary Taste. . . .

How Censorship Under the Statute Actually Operates

Prosecutors, as censors, actually exercise prior restraint. Fear of punishment serves as a powerful restraint on publication, and fear of punishment often means, practically, fear of prosecution. For most men dread indictment and prosecution; the publicity alone terrifies, and to defend a criminal action is expensive. If the definition of obscenity had a limited and fairly well-known scope, that fear might deter restricted sorts of publications only. But on account of the extremely vague judicial definition of the obscene, a person threatened with prosecution if he mails (or otherwise sends in interstate commerce) almost any book which deals in an unconventional, unorthodox manner with sex may well apprehend that, should the threat be carried out, he will be punished. As a result, each prosecutor becomes a literary censor (dictator) with immense unbridled power, a virtually uncontrolled discretion. A statute would be invalid which gave the Postmaster General the power, without reference to any standard, to close the mails to any publication he happened to dislike. Yet a federal prosecutor, under the federal obscenity statute, approximates that position: Within wide limits, he can (on the advice of the Postmaster General or on no one's advice) exercise such a censorship by threat without a trial, without any judicial supervision, capriciously and arbitrarily. Having no special qualifications for that task, nevertheless, he can, in large measure, determine at his will what those within his district may not read on sexual subjects. In that way, the statute brings about an actual prior restraint of free speech and free press which strikingly flouts the First Amendment. . . .

The Dangerously Infectious Nature of Governmental Censorship of Books

Governmental control of ideas or personal preferences is alien to a democracy. And the yearning to use governmental censorship of any kind is infectious. It may spread insidiously. Commencing with suppression of books as obscene, it is not unlikely to develop into official lust for the power of thought-control in the areas of religion, politics, and elsewhere. Milton observed that "licensing of books . . . necessarily pulls along with it so many other kinds of licensing." Mill noted that the "bounds of what may be called moral police" may easily extend "until it encroaches on the most unquestionably legitimate liberty of the individual." We should beware of a recrudescence of the undemocratic doctrine uttered in the seventeenth century by Berkeley, Governor of Virginia: "Thank God there are no free schools or preaching, for learning has brought disobedience into the world, and printing has divulged them. God keep us from both."

The People as Self-Guardians: Censorship by Public Opinion, Not by Government

Plato, who detested democracy, proposed to banish all poets; and his rulers were to serve as guardians of the people, telling lies for the people's good, vigorously suppressing writings these guardians thought dangerous. Governmental guardianship is repugnant to the basic tenet of our democracy: According to our ideals, our adult citizens are self-guardians, to act as their own fathers, and thus become self-dependent. When our governmental officials act towards our citizens on the thesis that "Papa knows best what's good for you," they enervate the spirit of the citizens: To treat grown men like infants is to make them infantile, dependent, immature.

So have sagacious men often insisted. Milton, in his *Areopagitica,* denounced such paternalism: "We censure them for a giddy, vicious and unguided people, in such sick and weak (a) state of faith and discretion as to be able to take down nothing but through the pipe of a licensor." "We both consider the people as our children," wrote Jefferson to

Dupont de Nemours, "but you love them as infants whom you are afraid to trust without nurses, and I as adults whom I freely leave to self-government." Tocqueville sagely remarked: "No form or combination of social policy has yet been devised to make an energetic people of a community of pusillanimous and enfeebled citizens." "Man," warned Goethe, "is easily accustomed to slavery and learns quickly to be obedient when his freedom is taken from him." Said Carl Becker, "Self-government, and the spirit of freedom that sustains it, can be maintained only if the people have sufficient intelligence and honesty to maintain them with a minimum of legal compulsion. This heavy responsibility is the price of freedom."[16] The "great art," according to Milton, "lies to discern in what the law is to bid restraint and punishment, and in what things persuasion only is to work." So, we come back, once more, to Jefferson's advice: The only completely democratic way to control publications which arouse mere thoughts or feelings is through nongovernmental censorship by public opinion.

The Seeming Paradox of the First Amendment

Here we encounter an apparent paradox: The First Amendment, judicially enforced, curbs public opinion when translated into a statute which restricts freedom of expression (except that which will probably induce undesirable conduct). The paradox is unreal: The Amendment ensures that public opinion—the "common conscience of the time"—shall not commit suicide through legislation which chokes off today the free expression of minority views which may become the majority public opinion of tomorrow.

Private Persons or Groups May Validly Try to Influence Public Opinion

The First Amendment obviously has nothing to do with the way persons or groups, not a part of government, influence public opinion as to what constitutes "decency" or "obscenity." The Catholic Church, for example, has a constitutional right to persuade or instruct its adherents not to read designated books or kinds of books.

The Fine Arts Are Within the First Amendment's Protection

"The framers of the First Amendment," writes Chafee, "must have had literature and art in mind, because our first national statement on the subject of freedom of the press, the 1774 address of the Continental Congress to the inhabitants of Quebec, declared, 'The importance of this (freedom of the press) consists, beside the advancement of truth, science, morality and *arts* in general, in its diffusion of liberal sentiments on the administration of government.' "[17] One hundred and sixty-five years later, President Franklin Roosevelt said, "The arts cannot thrive except where men are free to be themselves and to be in charge of the discipline of their own energies and ardors. The conditions for democracy and for art are one and the same. What we call liberty in politics results in freedom of the arts."[18] The converse is also true.

In our industrial era when, perforce, economic pursuits must be, increasingly, governmentally regulated, it is especially important that the realm of art—the noneconomic realm—should remain free, unregimented, the domain of free enterprise, of unhampered competition at its maximum. An individual's taste is his own private concern. *De gustibus non [est] disputandum* represents a valued democratic maxim.

Milton wrote: "For though a licenser should happen to be judicious more than the ordinary, yet his very office . . . enjoins him to let pass nothing but what is vulgarly received already." He asked, "What a fine conformity would it starch us all into? We may fall . . . into a gross conformity stupidly. . . ." In 1859 Mill, in his essay *On Liberty*, maintained that conformity in taste is not a virtue, but a vice. "The danger," he wrote, "is not the excess but the deficiency of personal impulses and preferences. By dint of not following their own nature (men) have no nature to follow. . . . Individual spontaneity is entitled to free exercise. . . . That so few men dare to be eccentric marks the chief danger of the time." Pressed by the demand for conformity, a people degenerate into "the deep slumber of a decided opinion," yield a "dull and torpid consent" to the accustomed. "Mental despotism" ensues. For "whatever crushes individuality is despotism by whatever name it be called. . . . It is not by wearing down into uniformity all that is individual in themselves, but by cultivating it, and calling it forth, within the limits imposed by the rights and interests of others, that human beings become a noble and beautiful object of contemplation; and as the works partake the character of those who do

them, by the same process human life also becomes rich, diversified, and animating. . . . In proportion to the development of his individuality, each person becomes more valuable to himself, and is therefore capable of being more valuble to others. There is a greater fullness of life about his own existence, and when there is more life in the units there is more in the mass which is composed of them."

To vest a few fallible men—prosecutors, judges, jurors—with vast powers of literary or artistic censorship, to convert them into what Mill called a "moral police," is to make them despotic arbiters of literary products. If one day they ban mediocre books as obscene, another day they may do likewise to a work of genius. Originality, not too plentiful, should be cherished, not stifled. An author's imagination may be cramped if he must write with one eye on prosecutors or juries; authors must cope with publishers who, fearful about the judgments of governmental censors, may refuse to accept the manuscripts of contemporary Shelleys or Mark Twains or Whitmans.

Some few men stubbornly fight for the right to write or publish or distribute books which the great majority at the time consider loathsome. If we jail those few, the community may appear to have suffered nothing. The appearance is deceptive. For the conviction and punishment of these few will terrify writers who are more sensitive, less eager for a fight. What, as a result, they do not write might have been major literary contributions. "Suppression," Spinoza said, "is paring down the state till it is too small to harbor men of talent."

Notes

1. Judge Cuthbert Pound dissenting in *People* v. *Gitlow*, 234 N.Y. 132, 158, 136 N.E. 317, 327.

2. Padover, *The Complete Madison* (1953), pp. 295–296.

3. Padover, *The Complete Madison* (1953), pp. 267, 268–269.

4. Padover, *The Complete Jefferson* (1943), p. 109.

5. Padover, *The Complete Jefferson* (1943), p. 130.

6. Padover, *The Complete Jefferson* (1943), p. 889.

7. Wingfield-Stratford, *Those Earnest Victorians* (1930), p. 151.

8. See Kaplan, "Obscenity as an Esthetic Category," 20 *Law and Contemporary Problems* (1955), pp. 544,

550: "In many cultures, obscenity has an important part in magical rituals. In our own, its magical character is betrayed in the puritan's supposition that words alone can work evil, and that evil will be averted if only the words are not uttered."

9. Wingfield-Stratford, *Victorians*, pp. 296–297.

10. Paradoxically, this attitude apparently tends to "create" obscenity, for the foundation of obscenity seems to be secrecy and shame: "The secret becomes shameful because of its secrecy." Kaplan, "Obscenity as an Esthetic Category," 20 *Law and Contemporary Problems* (1955), pp. 544, 556.

11. Lockhart and McClure, "Obscenity and the Courts," 20 *Law and Contemporary Problems* (1955), pp. 587, 595.

12. Alpert, "Judicial Censorship and the Press," 52 *Harvard Law Review* (1938), pp. 40, 72.

13. The majority opinion upholding Roth's conviction was delivered by Chief Judge Clark, U.S. Court of Appeals, Second Circuit. [The Editor]

14. Myerson, *Speaking of Man* (1950), p. 92.

15. *Ruth v. Goldman*, 2 Cir., 172 F.2d 788.

16. Becker, *Freedom and Responsibility in the American Way of Life* (1945), p. 42.

17. Chafee, *Government and Mass Communication* (1947), p. 53.

18. Message at dedicating exercises of the New York Museum of Modern Art, May 8, 1939.

Questions for Analysis

1. *What evidence does Frank offer for the claim "Freedom to speak publicly and to publish has, as its inevitable and important correlative, the private right to hear, to read, and to think about what one hears and reads"? Do you agree?*

2. *Do you agree that pro-censorship views can be traced to Victorian influences?*

3. *On what grounds does Frank dispute the claim that there is a connection between pornography and conduct?*

4. *Would it be accurate to say that Frank would oppose even pornography aimed at minors?*

5. *Do you think, as Frank claims, that a prohibition against the dissemination of sexual materials would logically justify a prohibition against other things considered "socially dangerous"?*

6. *Frank contends that government control of ideas or personal preferences is alien to a democracy. Contrast this view with Walter Berns's view in "Beyond the (Garbage) Pale, or Democracy, Censorship and the Arts."*

7. *Distinguish the utilitarian from the nonutilarian considerations that make up Frank's argument.*

The Moral Theory of Free Speech and Obscenity Law

David A. J. Richards

In Chapter 2 you were introduced to the social-justice theory of John Rawls. Recall that in Rawls's view, basic political rights are not, as utilitarians believe, justified by appeal to consequences, nor may they be overridden in order to further social welfare. Rawls has argued for a comprehensive theory of justice that holds that principles of justice can be discovered by consideration of which principles for regulating their basic social structures a group of people would choose if they were coming together to form a society. Rawls imposes the condition that the people are not to know what positions in society they will occupy. Such a procedure, he claims, would represent a fair choice of principles. He argues further that given the constraints of the principles of justice that would be selected, such people would further choose the protections of basic political rights, including that of free speech.

The following essay is a good illustration of how Rawls's thought, which applies primarily to economic transactions, is useful in other situations. David A. J. Richards outlines a theory of the First Amendment based on a Rawlsian conception of justice. After carefully examining the nature of pornography, Richards argues that the Supreme Court's reasoning in Paris Adult Theatre *cannot be accepted. Specifically, Richards argues that regulating obscene communications subverts the central moral purpose of the First Amendment, which, in his view, is to secure the greatest equal liberty of communication compatible with a like liberty for all. This, of course, is an application of Rawls's first principle of justice, the liberty principle.*

. . . We begin with a discussion of the moral theory underlying the First Amendment. Then, we turn to the examination of the notion of the obscene. The contours of the notion are not self-evident. In order to understand the law of obscenity, some precision must be given to this notion itself. Finally, the analysis will focus on the issue of the constitutionality of obscenity law. . . .

In interpreting and enforcing the First Amendment, courts must determine the proper standards under which their responsibility is to be discharged. On the basis of our formulation of applicable principles of justice, the constitutional notions of free speech and free press should be understood in terms of certain relevant requirements of the first principle of justice, namely, the greatest equal liberty of communication compatible with a like liberty for all. Thus, all legal prohibitions and regulations which constrain liberty of communication in a manner incompatible with this idea should be constitutionally forbidden and invalid. But how are we to understand the concrete application of the equal liberty idea?[1]

One important point is that in applying the equal liberty principle, the basic liberties must be assessed as an interrelated system. The weights of each kind of liberty may depend on the specification of other kinds of liberty. The liberties of expression constitute both a right to communicate and a right to be the object of communication. Obviously, these liberties must be adjusted to one another in such a way as to best realize the underlying values

of autonomous self-determination. The morally preferable adjustment is a liberty to communicate to any audience that is itself at liberty to choose to be or not to be an audience. Given this interpretation, the liberty to communicate and other liberties are to be assessed as a whole in the light of the principle requiring the greatest equal liberty compatible with a like liberty for all.

The crucial analytic question is whether institutions and practices governing human expression, assessed as a system,[2] violate or cohere with the idea of a system of greatest equal liberty compatible with a like liberty for all. For example, it is clear that procedural rules of order, time, and place, which regulate a reasonable pattern of communications, cohere with this idea, for they enlarge the equal liberty of communication compatible with a like liberty for all.[3] Without such rules of order, time, and place, the liberty of communication of one will be used to violate the liberty of communication of another so that the system of liberties is not the greatest *equal* liberty compatible with a like liberty for all.

Similarly, the punishment of communications that are an indispensable part of actions designed to and capable of overthrowing the constitutional order—for example, communicating military secrets to the enemy—does not violate this equal liberty of communications, for such communications would help to overthrow the system of equal liberties. The proof that such communications do advance the overthrow of the constitutional order must, however, appeal to general principles of empirical induction and inference. No special principles of inference, not admissible in deciding on the principles of justice, are admissible in the interpretation of those principles. Thus, special a priori views regarding the relation of certain communications to the decline and fall of the constitutional order, not justified on generally acceptable empirical grounds, are not morally tolerable as reasons for limiting such communications.

Attempts by the state to prohibit certain contents of communication per se are fundamentally incompatible with the moral and constitutional principle of equal liberty. Notwithstanding the outrage felt by the majority toward certain contents of communication, the equal liberty principle absolutely forbids the prohibition of such communications on the ground of such outrage alone. Otherwise, the liberty of expression, instead of the vigorous and potent defense of individual autonomy that it is, would be a pitifully meager permission allowing people to communicate only in ways to which no one has any serious objection. The interest of the few in free expression is not to be sacrificed on such grounds to the interest of the many. Conventional attitudes are not to be the procrustean measure of the exercise of human expressive and judgmental competence.

On this view, the constitutionally protected liberty of free expression is the legal embodiment of a moral principle which ensures to each person the maximum equal liberty of communication compatible with a like liberty for all. Importantly, if the First Amendment freedoms rest on a fundamental moral principle, they have no necessary justificatory relation to the liberty of equal voting rights. No doubt, both rights advance values of self-direction and autonomy, but a maximum equal liberty of self-expression is neither a necessary nor a sufficient condition of democratic voting rights or the competent exercise of those rights. Voting rights may exist and be competently exercised in a regime where expression is not in general free, but is limited to a small class of talented technicians who circulate relevant data on policy issues to the electorate. Similarly, free expression may exist in a political aristocracy or in a democracy where voting rights are not competently exercised because of illiteracy or political apathy.

The independent status of the value of free expression shows that its value is not intrinsically political but rests on deeper moral premises regarding the general exercise of autonomous expressive and judgmental capacity and the good that this affords in human life. It follows that the attempt to limit the constitutional protection of free expression to the political[4] must be rejected on moral and constitutional grounds.[5]

The foregoing account makes clear that strong moral ideas are implicit in the First Amendment and that moral analysis may clarify the proper constitutional interpretation and application of those ideas. It is significant in this connection that the account here proposed clarifies many concrete features of First Amendment adjudications,[6] for example, the propriety of reasonable regulations of time, place, and procedure,[7] the insistence that majority dislike of protected expression has no constitutional weight,[8] the basis of the clear and present danger test,[9] and the refusal to limit the First Amendment to the political.[10] It is equally clear that this account provides a framework from which the case law may be crucially assessed both as regards proper extensions of First Amendment rights, such as rights of access to the media,[11] and the criticism of anomalies in existing case law which depart from its deepest moral strains.

The Concept of the Obscene

A satisfying philosophical explication of the notion of the obscene would clarify the notion itself, its connections to related notions (such as the pornographic, the indecent, and the immoral), its uses in speech, and its relations to fundamental attitudes which explain how the notion comes to have moving appeal to conduct. Initially, we must describe some general marks of the obscene. Then, a constructive account of the notion will be proposed, and, finally, an attempt will be made to connect the account to related notions, especially the pornographic.

The Marks of the Obscene

The etymology of *obscene* is obscure. The *Oxford English Dictionary* notes that the etymology is "doubtful,"[12] while *Webster's* suggests a derivation from the Latin *ob*, meaning *to, before, against,* and the Latin *caenum*, meaning *filth*.[13] Other commentators suggest alternative derivations from the Latin *obscurus*, meaning *concealed*,[14] or a derivation as a corruption of the Latin *scena* meaning *what takes place off stage*.[15] In the latter sense, blinding Gloucester on stage in *King Lear* would have been an obscenity for a Greek playwright like Sophocles (thus, Oedipus is blinded offstage), but it was not for an Elizabethan playwright like Shakespeare, who was imbued with the bloodthirstiness of Senecan tragedy.

The standard dictionary definition of *obscene* turns on notions of what is disgusting, filthy, or offensive to decency.[16] While contemporary legal discussions emphasize the applicability of *obscene* to depictions, it is clearly significantly applied to acts themselves. Shakespeare, for example, speaks of an obscene deed,[17] and Sartre discusses obscene movements of the body.[18] In the law it is notable that the earliest English obscenity conviction was for obscene acts.[19] Judicial decisions[20] and legal and general[21] commentary emphasize the connections of the obscene to the notion of shame. It is clear that in European thought the notion of the obscene has long been connected to the scatological[22] and the sexually lascivious,[23] a connection emphasized in Anglo-American legal history.[24] This history also makes clear the significant relation of the obscene to the notion of the morally corrupting. Many of these connections were summarized in the language of the Comstock Act, which, in forbidding the mailing of obscene material in interstate commerce in the United States, speaks of "obscene, lewd, or lascivious . . . publication(s)" and included in its prohibitions contraceptives and abortifacients or anything else "for any indecent or immoral use."[25]

The most significant class of speech acts involving the notion of the obscene is that class of epithets, known as *obscenities*, which relate to excretory or sexual functions.[26] Such expressions are, at least in reasonably well-educated circles, conventionalized ways of expressing attitudes of disgust and contempt which depend for their sometimes shocking and bracing effect on the impropriety of their use.[27] In circles, like the army, where the verbal obscenities are constantly employed, their function seems quite different;[28] there they are used as a kind of manly, transgression-braving vocabulary whose use is a criterion of intimate membership in the group. Related to this is the use of obscenities among intimate friends and even as a language of love.

The verbal obscenities demonstrate the relation of the obscene not only to shock and offense, but to the anxiety-producing loss of control. On hearing or using such expressions in reasonably well-educated circles, one has the sense of a loss of control, a sudden frustration, or an explosion of pique, which may surprise the speaker as much as the listener.

In the light of these functions and marks of the verbal obscenities, one can better understand the functions of literature which employs obscene contents—for example, some works of Swift[29] and Pope.[30] By employing contents known to be offensive to the conventional proprieties, such literature can express complex communicative intentions of bitter satire and burlesque in ways related to the capacity of the verbal obscenities to express disgust and contempt.[31] Similarly, one can understand the use of the obscene in literary humor as well as in the smutty joke and obscene witticism.[32] Obviously, such effects of the obscene are in some important way tied to attitudes, the existence of which accounts for these effects.

An Explication of the Obscene

The concept of the obscene is identical with the concept of those actions, representations, works, or states which display an exercise of bodily or personal function which in certain circumstances constitutes an abuse of that function, as dictated by standards in which one has invested self-esteem, so that the supposed abuse of function is regarded as a demeaning object of self-contempt and self-disgust.[33]

On this view, the obscene is a subcategory of the objects of shame. Shame is, I believe, properly understood in terms of a fall from one's self-concept in the exercise of capacities which one desires to exercise competently. The objects of shame, thus, are explained by reference to the notions of personal competence and self-respect which are their bases. One feels ashamed because, for example, one has been cowardly, failing to exercise courageous self-control over fear when danger threatened. A characteristic mark of such failure is self-contempt or self-disgust.

The obscene identifies a special class of the possible objects of shame which are explained by reference to certain defined notions of competence in bodily or personal function. Thus, just as one explains to a child that it is an abuse and misuse of the function of a knife or fork to put either in the ear, so too one explains the proper exercise of bodily function. The use of the body is thought to have precise and sharply defined functions and ends. This idea, found widely among primitive peoples and the most ancient cultures,[34] including, significantly, ancient Judaism,[35] rigidly defines certain clear proprieties of bodily function as pure or clean. Failure to so exercise bodily function is unclean, polluting, an abomination, in short, obscene.[36]

The obscene, thus, is a conceptual residuum of very ancient ways of thinking about human conduct. Human beings are thought of as clusters of strengths or virtues and corresponding weaknesses or vices, where virtues and vices are not conceived in narrow moral terms.[37] Obscenity within this view is a kind of vice, a wasting and abuse of the natural employment of bodily or personal function. Hence, a culture's definition of the obscene will indicate those areas of bodily or personal function in which the culture centrally invests its self-esteem and in which deviance provokes the deepest anxieties. For example, incompetence with respect to excretory function typically defines the frailest members of society, infants and the senile. Where frailty and declining powers are a source of anxiety, excretory impropriety is likely to be regarded as obscene. Moreover, where the sexual function is regarded as akin to the excretory function, as it easily may be,[38] sexual behavior will come to share this condemnation.

This explication is intended to apply cross-culturally.[39] To the extent people in different cultures take different attitudes to certain bodily or personal functions, those cultures will take different views of those things that are obscene, though the cultures share the concept of the obscene as an abuse of bodily or personal function. A striking example is provided by the Tahitians, who do not take the Western view of the competent exercise of sexual function, but do take a rather stringent view of eating; thus for Tahitians, displays of coitus are not obscene, but displays of eating are.[40] For us, aside from contexts of satirical humor,[41] eating conventional food would be obscene only in extreme circumstances of gluttonous self-indulgence[42] or in circumstances where eating is associated with aphrodisiacal allure.[43]

Similarly, this explication is true over time as well. For example, English society in the eighteenth century was apparently very tolerant of obscene literature, despite the fact that obscene libel had become a common-law offense.[44] But in the nineteenth century, changing moral standards gave rise to groups like the Society for the Suppression of Vice and prosecutions for obscene libel increased rapidly.[45] Concern over the explosion of pornographic literature[46] finally received expression in English statutes.[47] In the same way, contemporary attitudes evince a shift in the application of the obscene; a growing modern usage applies the notion, for example, to violence and death and displays of violence and death (based on the idea, I believe, that these represent demeaning abuses of competences of the person),[48] but no longer applies the notion to sex or sexual displays.[49]

Significantly, this explication accounts for the application of *obscene* to acts as well as to depictions of acts. Both acts and depictions are obscene if they display certain exercises of bodily function; whether by the act itself or by depiction, our anxiety is aroused when we become aware of phenomena which threaten our self-esteem. It does not follow, of course, that obscene depictions are only of obscene acts. Normal heterosexual intercourse between a married couple is not typically viewed as obscene; but a public depiction of such intercourse would, by some people, be viewed as obscene. Nonetheless, there is little question that the obscenity of an act is a sufficient condition for the obscenity of a depiction of that act. Most cases of obscene depictions fall into this category. At one time obscenity convictions were granted for the mere sympathetic discussion of homosexuality or advocacy of birth control or abortion, apart from any pornographic representation of any kind.[50] The idea seems to have been that since homosexuality, birth control, and abortion were obscene, any favorable discussion of them was obscene. Even today, it is clear that courts are quickest to make or affirm judgments of obscenity with respect to depictions of sexual acts such as cunnilingus, fellatio, sodomy, sadomasochism, and bestiality that are regarded as obscene in themselves.[51] The view that these acts are obscene is the basis for judging their depiction to be obscene.

The connection between the obscenity of acts and depictions of acts distinguishes the obscene from the indecent. The distinctive mark of the indecent is the public exhibition of that which, while unobjectionable in private, is offensive and embarrassing when done in public.[52] The obscene, by contrast, may be and often is condemned whether or not it involves a public display.

Finally, this linkage between the act and its depiction accounts for the use of obscenities to express contempt and disgust. Since the obscene identifies a disgusting abuse of bodily function, it is wholly natural that it should be used to express disgust. It follows that if one does not find certain communicative contents obscene, one may tendentiously advocate the abandonment of speech acts using those contents to express disgust.[53]

The Obscene and the Pornographic

Pornography etymologically derives from the Greek *pornographos*, meaning *writing of harlots*, literally, writing concerning or descriptive of prostitutes in their profession.[54] Thus, the depictions of various forms of sexual intercourse on the walls of a certain building in Pompeii, intended as aphrodisiacs for the orgiastic bacchanales housed there, were literally *pornographos*.[55] Pornography in this sense is identified by its sexually explicit content, its depiction of varied forms of sexual intercourse, turgid genitalia, and so on.[56]

Pornography is neither conceptually nor factually identical with the obscene. Conceptually, the notion of sexually explicit, aphrodisiacal depictions is not the same idea as that of the abuse of a bodily or personal function. Many cultures, though sharing the fundamental concept of the obscene, do not regard pornography as obscene.[57] Individuals within our culture may find coprophagy (eating feces) obscene,[58] but do not find pornography obscene,[59] because they fail to take a certain attitude toward "proper" sexual function although they do have ideas about "proper" excretory function. For such people, viewing sex or depictions of sex as obscene is an unfortunate blending of the sexual and the excremental.[60]

If there is no necessary connection between the pornographic and the obscene, how did the connection between them arise?

One account of the sexual morality behind this connection is that of Catholic canon law which

> holds, as a basic and cardinal fact, that complete sexual activity and pleasure is licit and moral only in a naturally completed act in valid marriage. All acts which, of their psy-

chological and physical nature, are designed to be preparatory to the complete act, take their licitness and their morality from the complete act. If, therefore, they are entirely divorced from the complete act, they are distorted, warped, meaningless, and hence immoral.[61]

This view of course derives from St. Augustine's classic conception that the only proper "genital commotion"[62] is one with the voluntary aim of reproduction of the species.[63] It follows from this view that only certain rigidly defined kinds of "natural" intercourse in conventional marriage are moral; "unnatural" forms of such intercourse are forbidden; extramarital and of course homosexual intercourse are forbidden. Further, all material that will induce to "genital commotion" not within marriage is forbidden. Pornography is obscene not only in itself, because it displays intercourse not within marriage, but also because it tempts to intercourse outside marriage or to masturbation, which are independently obscene acts because they are forms of sexual conduct that violate minimum standards of proper bodily function and thus cause disgust.

While this specific Catholic view is not the universal basis for the connection of the obscene and the pornographic, this general kind of view seems always present. Sexual function of certain rigidly defined kinds is alone the correct and competent exercise of sexual function. All other forms are marked by failure, weakness, and disgust. Masturbation in particular is a moral wrong.

Clearly this general notion, premised on supposed medical as well as theological facts, was behind the extraordinary explosion in obscenity legislation in England and the United States in the 1850s, 1860s, and 1870s. This legislation rested squarely on the remarkable Victorian medical view relating masturbation and sexual excess in general to insanity.[64] Pornography, being in part masturbation fantasy, was condemned on medical as well as theological grounds, so that Anthony Comstock, the father of the Comstock Act, could point with the support of medical authority to the fact that pornography's "most deadly effects are felt by the victims in the habit of secret vices."[65]

Significantly, Victorian medical literature and pornography[66] make transparent that sexual function was construed on the model of excretory function.[67] The proper exercise of sexual function was rigidly defined in terms of one mode, marital reproductive sexuality. Within that mode, the proper function was one of regularity and moderation. Thus, doctors condemned sexual excess within marriage[68] and deprecated infertile sexual activity within marriage as "conjugal onanism."[69] This rigid and narrow conception of sexual function was obviously profoundly opposed to pornography which would expose, in the words of one prominent Victorian court, "the minds of those hitherto pure . . . to the danger of contamination and pollution from the impurity it contains."[70]

Similar views regarding the evils of masturbation are echoed in contemporary writers who condemn pornography. Thus, D. H. Lawrence emphasized the corrosive effects of autoeroticism on the capacity for the central spiritual experience, for Lawrence, of sexual mutuality between partners.[71]

Whatever the form of theological, medical, or psychological belief underlying the association of the obscene and the pornographic, some such belief always prevails, so that there is a significant correlation between judgments of obscenity and the judgments that a certain work is both sexually arousing and quite unpleasant.[72]

The Constitutionality of Obscenity Law

It should now be possible to apply the foregoing explication of the obscene and the moral analysis of the First Amendment to the issue raised in *Miller* v. *California* and *Paris Adult Theatre I* v. *Slaton*—the constitutionally permissible concept of the obscene.

Miller reaffirmed the holding of *Roth* v. *United States* that obscene expression is not protected by the First Amendment. In addition, the Court, speaking through the Chief Justice, formulated a constitutional test for obscenity. The test is threefold:

> (a) whether "the average person, applying contemporary community standards" would find that the work, taken as a whole, appeals to the prurient interest . . . ; (b) whether the work depicts or describes, in a patently offensive way, sexual conduct specifically defined by the applicable state law; and (c) whether the work, taken as a whole, lacks serious literary, artistic, political, or scientific value.[73]

This test imposes on states that wish to ban obscenity an obligation to formulate specific standards. Moreover, *Miller* limits the obscene to "representations or descriptions of ultimate sexual acts, normal or perverted, actual or simulated" or "of masturbation, excretory functions and lewd exhibition of the genitals."[74] In effect, only hard-core scatology and pornography may be banned.[75]

On the other hand, the *Miller* test permits censorship wherever the allegedly obscene work is without "serious" value.[76] Thus, a lighter burden is imposed on the prosecution than was imposed under the prior "utterly without redeeming social value" test.[77] Moreover, reliance on local standards,[78] within the bounds of the court's test, permits a variety of constitutionally permissible restrictions. Hence, a person's First Amendment rights may be restricted in one jurisdiction without appeal to a national standard.[79]

The *Miller* case involved a conviction for mailing unsolicited sexually explicit material, which is, of course, a problem of nonconsensual intrusion of offensive material. In *Paris Adult Theatre I* v. *Slaton*, however, a majority of the Court, again speaking through Chief Justice Burger, applied the *Miller* criteria for obscenity to an adult's fully informed and consensual access to obscene materials. The Court thus narrowly limited the holding of *Stanley* v. *Georgia*[80] to its facts. There the Court invalidated a state statute prohibiting the possession and private use in one's home of obscene (pornographic) materials on the grounds of infringing the constitutional right of privacy. In *Paris Adult Theatre*, and other cases decided concurrently, the Court made clear that the constitutional right of privacy as regards the use of obscene materials applies only to one's home, not to any theater, nor even to the transport of such materials in one's traveling bags for private use.[81]

Miller and *Paris Adult Theatre*, then, find obscenity, even for consenting adults, to be outside the protection of the First Amendment, but the analysis here presented suggests that the Court's decisions are wrong. An understanding of the moral function of the First Amendment compels a conclusion contrary to the Court's; there should be a presumption that obscenity, like other forms of expression, falls within the protection of the First Amendment.

To summarize, obscene communications, it has been proposed, implicate the idea of the abuse of basic bodily functions, the proper exercise of which is an object of basic self-esteem and the improper use of which is an object of shame and disgust. A sufficient, though not a necessary, condition of the obscenity of a communication is that the act depicted be obscene.

On this view, the precise application of the notion of the obscure crucially depends on beliefs and attitudes involving precise and rigid definitions of the proper exercise of bodily functions. Thus, different cultures, with different beliefs and attitudes, may regard dissimilar acts or objects as obscene. Similarly, within a culture, individuals may apply the label *obscene* to different phenomena. In the United States, for example, many people regard pornography as obscene because it reflects, for them, an improper exercise of sexual function. But others, not sharing their beliefs and attitudes, do not regard pornography as obscene,[82] though they may think that other things, like depictions of coprophagy or gratuitous violence, are obscene.

An obscenity law, then, must be understood as a political expression of broader popular attitudes toward the putative proper and improper use of the body. It is no accident that such laws have been used to forbid the transport of abortifacient and contraceptive information[83] and dissemination of sex manuals[84] and to prosecute advocacy of contraception and population control.[85] The moral attitudes behind such laws, directed against a supposed "abuse" of the body, were founded on a compound of religious, psychological, and medical beliefs basic to which was a deep fear of masturbation.[86] Masturbation, it was believed, led directly to physical debility and even death,[87] as well as crime and civil disorder.[88]

In judicial interpretation of the notion of the obscene, courts implicitly decide on and enforce popular attitudes about bodily function. Whatever may be the constitutional legitimacy of regulating obscene acts, it is impossible to see how regulating obscene communications can avoid raising the deepest First Amendment problems. Because judicial application of obscenity laws necessarily enforces a particular attitude, albeit presumably majoritarian, about the contents of communication, it seems to be obnoxious in principle to the central moral purpose of the First Amendment—to secure the greatest equal liberty of communication compatible with a like liberty for all.

Notes

1. For an interesting consideration of this general problem, see J. Feinberg, "Limits to the Free Expression of Opinion," J. Feinberg and H. Gross, *Philosophy of Law,* pp. 135–151.

2. I take the notion of a system of free expression from T. Emerson, *The System of Freedom of Expression* (1970).

3. See A. Meiklejohn, *Political Freedom* 21–28 (1960).

4. See A. Meiklejohn, *supra* note 3. Meiklejohn attempted to defend his view by interpreting the political quite broadly. A. Meiklejohn, "The First Amendment Is an Absolute," 1961 *Sup. Ct. Rev.* 245, 255–257, 262–263.

5. See Z. Chafee, Book Review, 62 *Harv. L. Rev.* 891, 896–898 (1949).

6. As an explication, this account seems to have more explanatory power than other comparable general theories of the First Amendment. Unlike Meiklejohn's theory, it accounts for the fact that free expression is not limited to politics. See Meiklejohn, *supra* note 3. It also accounts for the clear and present danger test, unlike the work of Thomas Emerson. See T. Emerson, *supra* note 2; T. Emerson, *Toward a General Theory of the First Amendment* (1966).

7. See, e.g., Cox v. Louisiana, 379 U.S. 536, 554–55 (1965); Poulos v. New Hampshire, 345 U.S. 395, 405 (1953); Kovacs v. Cooper, 336 U.S. 77 (1949).

8. See, e.g., A Book Named "John Cleland's Memoirs of a Woman of Pleasure" v. Attorney General, 383 U.S. 413, 427 (1966) (Douglas, J., concurring); Kingsley International Pictures Corp. v. Regents, 360 U.S. 684, 688–89 (1959); Roth v. United States, 354 U.S. 476, 484 (1957); Terminiello v. Chicago, 337 U.S. 1, 3–5 (1949).

9. See, e.g., Brandenburg v. Ohio, 395 U.S. 444 (1969); Dennis v. United States, 341 U.S. 494 (1951).

10. See, e.g., Roth v. United States, 354 U.S. 476, 484 (1957) (all ideas with the slightest redeeming social value have First Amendment protection); Joseph Burstyn, Inc. v. Wilson, 343 U.S. 495 (1952).

11. See J. Barron, "Access to the Press—a New First Amendment Right," 80 *Harv. L. Rev.* 1641 (1967).

12. See 7 *Oxford English Dictionary* 0.26 (1961).

13. See *Webster's Third New International Dictionary* 1557 (1965).

14. A. Kaplan, "Obscenity as an Esthetic Category," 20 *Law & Contemp. Prob.* 544, 550 (1955).

15. H. Ellis, *On Life and Sex* 175 (1962); G. Gorer, *The Danger of Equality* 218 (1966); W. Allen, "The Writer and the Frontiers of Tolerance," in *"To Deprave and Corrupt . . ."* 141, 147 (J. Chandos ed. 1962).

16. See notes 12 and 13 *supra.*

17. "O. forfend it, God, that, in a Christian climate, souls refin'd should show so heinous, black, obscene a deed!" W. Shakespeare, *Richard II*, act 4, sc. 1. The deed in question is a subject's judging his king.

18. J. P. Sartre, *Being and Nothingness* 401–402 (H. Barnes trans. 1956): cf. the notion of "the jest obscene," as used in Nitocris's condemnation of her son in Handel, *Belshazzar*, act I, sc. 4 (1744).

19. *Sir Charles Sedley's Case*, 83 Eng. Rep. 1146 (K.B. 1663). Sir Charles Sedley was here convicted "for shewing himself naked in a balcony, and throwing down bottles (pist in) vi & armis among the people in Covent Garden, contra pacem and to the scandal of the Government," *Id.* at 1146–1147. Sedley's conduct was condemned for its intrinsic obscenity as well as on the four additional grounds of indecent exposure, blasphemy, throwing missiles containing urine, and inciting to the small riot that ensued. See L. M. Alpert, "Judicial Censorship of Obscene Literature," 52 *Harv. L. Rev.* 40, 41–43 (1938). One commentary on these events states that Sedley also excreted in public. See A. Craig, *The Banned Books of England* 23–24 (1962); D. Thomas, *A Long Time Burning* 81 (1969).

20. Thus, the prurient interest test for obscenity, established in Roth v. United States, 354 U.S. 476, 487 (1957), and reaffirmed in Miller v. California, 413 U.S. 15, 24 (1973), and Paris Adult Theatre I v. Slaton, 413 U.S. 49 (1973), is defined in terms of "a shameful or morbid interest in nudity, sex, or excretion."

21. See *Model Penal Code* §207.10, Comment at 1, 10, 29–31 (Tent. Draft No. 6 1957), and commentary thereon in L. B. Schwartz, "Morals Offenses and the Model Penal Code," 63 *Col. L. Rev.* 669 (1963), reprinted in Feinberg and Gross, *Philosophy of Law* 152–161. See also Kaplan, *supra* note 14, at 556.

22. For example, Alexander Pope in his remarkable denunciations of Curl in *The Dunciad* uses "obscene" in excretory contexts. See A. Pope, *The Dunciad* 299, 300 (J. Sutherland ed. 1963) (first published 1728, 1743).

23. For example, in Cavalli's characteristically lascivious opera *La Calisto* (ca. 1650), Calisto's amorous approach to the goddess Diana is rejected with "Taci, lascia, taci/ Qual, qual delirio osceno/ l'ingeno ti confonde?" meaning, "Silence, lascivious girl!/ What, what obscene delirium/ has come over your reason?" Cavalli, *La Calisto*, act I, sc. 1.

24. For a useful general account, see Alpert, *supra* note 19. For accounts of English legal development, see D. Thomas, *supra* 19; N. St. John-Stevas, *Obscenity and the Law* (1956). For the best general account of earlier American developments, see W. B. Lockhart and R. C. McClure, "Literature, the Law of Obscenity, and the Constitution," 38 *Minn. L. Rev.* 295 (1954).

25. Comstock Act §2, ch. 258, §2, 17 Stat. 598, 599 (1873), as amended, 18 U.S.C. 1461 (1970).

26. See E. Sagarin, *The Anatomy of Dirty Words* (1962); Read, "An Obscenity Symbol," 9 *Am. Speech* 264 (1934).

27. For the force of such expressions in psychoanalysis, see S. Ferenczi, *Sex in Psychoanalysis* 132–153 (E. Jones trans. 1950); cf. Stone, "On the Principal Obscene Word of the English Language," 33 *Int'l J. Psycho-Anal.* 30 (1954).

28. See *Songs and Slang of the British Soldier* 1914–1918, at 15 (3d ed. Brophy & Partridge eds. 1931).

29. See, e.g., J. Swift, *A Tale of a Tub*, in *Gulliver's Travels and Other Writings* 245, 327–329, 334–336 (L. Landa ed. 1960); J. Swift, *A Voyage to Lilliput*, in *id.* 3, 34–35.

30. See A. Pope, *supra* note 22, at 299–300, 303–304, 306, 308–314.

31. Cf. D. Thomas, *supra* note 19, at 273–274, 313–314 (1969); S. Sontag, *Styles of Radical Will* 35–73 (1969).

32. Cf. S. Freud, *Wit and Its Relation to the Unconscious*, in *The Basic Writings of Sigmund Freud* 631, 692–697 (A. Brill trans. & ed. 1938).

33. I am indebted, for this idea of the relevance of the demeaning to the obscene, to criticisms of John Kleining.

34. See M. Douglas, *Purity and Danger* (1966).

35. See *id.* 41–57.

36. See, e.g., *Leviticus* 11–15, 17–18.

37. See Aristotle *Nicomachean Ethics* 116–251 (M. Ostwald trans. 1962).

38. See notes 66 and 67 *infra* and accompanying text.

39. Cf. Honigman, "A Cultural Theory of Obscenity," in *Sexual Behavior and Personality Characteristics* 31 (M. DeMartino ed. 1963).

40. See W. LaBarre, "Obscenity: An Anthropological Appraisal," 20 *Law and Contemp. Prob.* 533, 541–542 (1955). Geoffrey Gorer cites the Trobriand Islanders as a people who finds public eating of solid food an obscenity; G. Gorer, *supra* note 15. For a discussion of the Indian idea that eating may be polluting, see M. Douglas, *supra* note 34, at 33–34.

41. The suggestion of the reversal of the roles of eating and excretion (namely, that eating would be obscene and excretion a social occasion) is the subject of one scene of hilarious social satire in L. Bunuel's movie *Le Fantôme de la Liberté* (1974).

42. E.g., the movie *La Grande Bouffe* (1974).

43. E.g., the famous eating scene in the movie *Tom Jones* (1963).

44. Rex v. Curl, 93 Eng. Rep. 849 (K.B. 1727).

45. See N. St. John-Stevas, *supra* note 24, at 29–65.

46. For a literary analysis of some notable examples of Victorian pornography, see S. Marcus, *The Other Victorians* (1966).

47. E.g., the Customs Consolidating Act of 1853. 16 & 17 Vict., c. 107 (repealed by Customs Consolidating Act of 1876, 39 & 40 Vict., c. 36 paragraphs 42, 288); and Lord Campbell's Act of 1857, 20 & 21 Vict., c. 83 (repealed by Obscene Publications Act of 1959, 7 & 8 Eliz. 2, c. 66, paragraph 3(8)).

48. In 1948, the Supreme Court expressly declined to find that depictions of violence could be obscene, Winters v. New York, 333 U.S. 507 (1948), but this holding seems quite questionable today in view of growing modern usage. My views on the obscenity of violence and death gratefully acknowledge helpful criticisms of Joel Feinberg.

49. See note 59 *infra* and associated text.

50. See H. M. Hyde, *A History of Pornography* 3–8 (1964); N. St. John-Stevas, *supra* note 24, at 70–74, 98–103. See also notes 83, 84, and 85 *infra*.

51. Compare, e.g., Paris Adult Theatre I v. Slaton, 413 U.S. 49, 52 (Burger, C. J., emphasized the occurrence of "scenes of simulated fellatio, cunnilingus, and group sex intercourse") and Mishkin v. New York, 383 U.S. 502, 508 (1965) (depictions of flagellation, fetishism, and lesbianism held obscene), with Sunshine Book Co. v. Summerfield, 355 U.S. 372 (1958) (per curiam), rev'd 249 F.2d 114 (D.C. Cir. 1957), aff'd 128 F. Supp. 564 (D.D.C. 1955) (nudity per se not obscene). Cf. R. Kuh, *Foolish Figleaves?* 306–307 (1967) (suggesting that pictured bestiality and homosexuality are more obscene than comparable pictured heterosexuality).

52. See J. Feinberg, " 'Harmless Immoralities' and Offensive Nuisances," in *Issues in Law and Morality* 83, 87 (N. Care and T. Trelogan eds. 1973).

53. This proposal has been made with respect to sexual contents. See E. Sagarin, *supra* note 26, at 9–12, 160–174. Lenny Bruce, according to the show *The World of Lenny Bruce,* sc. 1 (1974), predicted the day when, pursuant to his view of the nonobscenity of sex, the erstwhile sexual obscenities would be used as forms of congratulation and good wishes.

54. See, e.g., *Webster's Third New International Dictionary* 1767 (1966).

55. See H. M. Hyde, *supra* note 50 at 1, 10.

56. See, e.g., M. Peckham *Art and Pornography* 46–47 (1969); A. Kinsey, *Sexual Behavior in the Human Female* 671–672 (1953); E. Kronhausen and P. Kronhausen, *Pornography and the Law* 262, 265 (1959).

57. See H. M. Hyde, *supra* note 50, at 30–58; D. Loth, *The Erotic in Literature* 41–68 (1961); M. Peckham, *supra* note 56, at 257–301: La Barre *supra* note 40, at 533–35.

58. The example of coprophagy occurs in M. de Sade, *120 Days of Sodom,* in 2 *The Complete Marquis De Sade* 215, 222 (P. Gillette trans. 1966). De Sade suggests other examples, such as eating vomit, which someone might find obscene, even if he would not find pornography obscene. *Id.* 215.

59. See R. Haney, *Comstockery in America* 58–59, 67–69, 75 (1960); D. Loth, *supra* note 57, at 208–233; L. Marcuse, *Obscene: The History of an Indignation* 307–327 (K. Gershon trans. 1965); M. Peckham, *supra* note 56, t 19–20; B. Russell, *Marriage and Morals* 93–117 (1929).

60. See H. Ellis, *supra* note 15, at 21–37; E. Kronhausen and P. Kronhausen, *supra* note 56, at 167; B. Russell, *supra* note 59, at 106–107.

61. H. Gardiner, "Moral Principles toward a Definition of the Obscene," 20 *Law & Contemp. Prob.* 560, 564 (1955).

62. This quaint phrase appears in Gardiner, *id.* 567.

63. See Augustine, *The City of God* 470–472 (M. Dods trans. 1950). St. Thomas is in accord with Augustine's view. Of the emission of semen apart from generation in marriage, he wrote, "after the sin of homicide whereby a human nature already in existence is destroyed, this type of sin appears to take next place, for by it the generation of human nature is precluded." T. Aquinas, *On the Truth of the Catholic Faith: Summa Contra Gentiles* 146 (V. Bourke trans. 1946).

64. See A. Comfort, *The Anxiety Makers* (1970); J. Haller and R. Haller, *The Physician and Sexuality in Victorian America* 199–234 (1974); S. Marcus, *supra* note 46; E. H. Hare, "Masturbational Insanity: The History of an Idea," 108 *J. Mental Science* 1, 6–9 (1962).

65. A. Comstock, *Traps for the Young* 136 (R. Bremner ed. 1967). See also *id.* 132–133, 139, 145, 169, 179, 205; A. Comstock, *Frauds Exposed* 388–389, 416, 437–438, 440–441 (1880; reprinted 1969).

66. See S. Marcus, *supra* note 46, at 24–25, 233, 243.

67. See H. Ellis, *supra* note 19, at 21–25. On the fundamental mistake involved in confusing sexual and excretory function, see W. Masters and V. Johnson, *Human Sexual Inadequacy* 10 (1970), who state:

"Seemingly, many cultures and certainly many religions have risen and fallen on their interpretation and misinterpretation of one basic physiological fact. Sexual functioning is a natural physiological process, yet it has a unique facility that no other natural physiological process, such as respiratory, bladder, or bowel function, can imitate. *Sexual responsivity can be delayed indefinitely or functionally denied for a lifetime.* No other basic physiological process can claim such malleability of physical expression."

68. A. Comfort, *supra* note 64, at 57.

69. *Id.* 155, 161.

70. The Queen v. Hicklin, L. R. 3 Q.B. 359, 372 (1868).

71. See D. H. Lawrence, *Sex, Literature, and Censorship* 64–81 (1953). For similar sentiments, see M. Mead, "Sex and Censorship in Contemporary Society," in *New World Writing*, 7, 19–21 (1953).

72. See *United States Comm'n on Obscenity and Pornography, Report of the Comm'n on Obscenity and Pornography* 210–212 (GPO ed. 1979) [hereinafter *Report*] cf. J. W. Higgins & M. B. Katzman, "Determinants in the Judgment of Obscenity," 125 *Am. J. Psychiat.* 1733 (1969).

73. 413 U.S. at 24 (quoting Roth, 354 U.S. at 489).

74. *Id.* 25. In Jenkins v. Georgia, 418 U.S. 153 (1974), the Court made clear the force of these requirements; the movie *Carnal Knowledge* could not constitutionally be found obscene, for the depictions therein are not sexually explicit within the meaning of the *Miller* tests.

75. 413 U.S. at 27–28.

76. 413 U.S. at 24–25.

77. A Book Named "John Cleland's Memoirs of a Woman of Pleasure" v. Massachusetts, 383 U.S. 413, 419 (1966).

78. 413 U.S. at 30–34.

79. The Court thus rejected the previously urged view that the standards to be applied were national, not local. E.g., Jacobellis v. Ohio, 378 U.S. 184, 192–193 (1974) (Brennan, J.).

80. 394 U.S. 557 (1969).

81. United States v. Orito, 413 U.S. 139 (1973); United States v. 12 200-Ft. Reels of Film, 413 U.S. 123 (1973).

82. See notes 57 to 60 *supra*.

83. See note 25 *supra*; 18 U.S.C. paragraph 1461 (1964), as amended, 18 U.S.C. paragraph 1461 (1970) (mail); 18 U.S.C. paragraph 1462(c), as amended, 18 U.S.C. paragraph 1462(c) (1970) (interstate commerce).

84. See, e.g., United States v. Chesman, 19 F. 497 (E.D. Mo. 1881).

85. See, e.g., United States v. Bennett, 24 F. Cas, 1093, No. 14, 571 (C.C.S.D.N.Y. 1879); Regina v. Bradlaugh, 2 Q.B.D. 569 (1977), *rev'd on other grounds*, 3 A.B.D. 607 (1878).

86. See text accompanying notes 61 to 70, *supra*.

87. Comstock, for example, noted the case of a thirteen-year-old girl, in whose bureau he "found a quantity of the most debasing and foul-worded matter. The last heard from this child was she was in a dying condition, the result of habits induced by this foul reading." A. Comstock, *Traps for the Young* 139 (R. Bremner ed. 1967).

88. Comstock cited a number of instances where, in his view, access to obscene material led to robbery, burglary, and murder. A. Comstock, *Frauds Exposed* 437–39 (1880, reprinted 1969). See also A. Comstock, *supra* note 87, at 132–33, 169, 179).

Questions for Analysis

1. Why does Richards think "Attempts by the state to prohibit certain contents of communication per se are fundamentally incompatible with the moral and constitutional principle of equal liberty"?

2. What reasons does Richards give for asserting that "strong moral ideas are implicit in the First Amendment"?

3. What, in Richards's view, are the "marks of the obscene"?

4. According to Richards, what does the precise application of the notion of the obscene depend on?

5. *What do the courts implicitly decide on and enforce in their interpretations of the notion of the obscene?*

6. *Richards concludes that the regulation of obscene communications is "obnoxious in principle to the central moral purpose of the First Amendment—to securing the greatest equal liberty of communication compatible with a like liberty for all." Precisely how does such regulation sully this central moral purpose?*

CASE PRESENTATION
Ginzburg *v.* United States *(1966)*

Ralph Ginzburg, publisher of *Eros* and other erotic magazines, was convicted under an obscenity statute for publishing or circulating obscene materials. In appealing the conviction to the U.S. Supreme Court, Ginzburg's lawyers felt they had a good chance of having the conviction overturned, for the Court had consistently overturned similar convictions (and, incidentally, has since). But their optimism went unfulfilled: In 1966 the Court upheld the conviction, and Ginzburg went to prison.

The Court held that Ginzburg had been properly convicted because the materials he sold were obscene under the *Roth* definition and because he had engaged in "pandering": He had not only published and distributed erotic materials, but had "purveyed textual or graphic matter openly advertised to appeal to the erotic interest" of his customers.

For example, Ginzburg admittedly sought out a town with a sexually suggestive name from which to mail his publications. Intercourse, Pennsylvania, was his first choice, but its post office couldn't handle the volume of mail. So he chose Middlesex, New Jersey. In advertising *Eros*, Ginzburg portrayed the magazine as a child of its times, the result of recent court decisions safeguarding freedom of expression, *the* magazine of sexual candor. And in direct-mail advertising for *Eros* and other Ginzburg publications, the publisher guaranteed customers a full refund should the magazines fail to reach them because of U.S. Post Office censorship interference.

In a dissenting opinion, Justice Hugo Black contended that the criteria employed by the Court in upholding the conviction of Ginzburg were "so vague and meaningless that they practically leave the fate of a person charged with violating censorship statutes to the unbridled discretion, whim and caprice of the judge or jury which tries him."[4] Black then elaborated on these criteria:

(a) The first element considered necessary for determining obscenity is that the dominant theme of the material taken as a whole must appeal to the prurient interest in sex. It seems quite apparent to me that human beings,

---

4. *Ginzburg v. United States,* 383 U.S. 463 (1966).

serving either as judges or jurors, could not be expected to give any sort of decision on this element which would even remotely promise any kind of uniformity in the enforcement of this law. What conclusion an individual, be he judge or juror, would reach about whether the material appeals to "prurient interest in sex" would depend largely in the long run not upon testimony of witnesses such as can be given in ordinary criminal cases where conduct is under scrutiny, but would depend to a large extent upon the judge's or juror's personality, habits, inclinations, attitudes and other individual characteristics. In one community or in one courthouse a matter would be condemned as obscene under this so-called criterion but in another community, maybe only a few miles away, or in another courthouse in the same community, the material could be given a clean bill of health. In the final analysis the submission of such an issue as this to a judge or jury amounts to practically nothing more than a request for the judge or juror to assert his own personal beliefs about whether the matter should be allowed to be legally distributed. Upon this subjective determination the law becomes certain for the first and last time.

(b) The second element for determining obscenity . . . is [supposedly] that the material must be "patently offensive because it affronts contemporary community standards relating to the description or representation of sexual matters. . . ." Nothing . . . that has been said . . . leaves me with any kind of certainty as to whether the "community standards" referred to are world-wide, nation-wide, section-wide, state-wide, country-wide, precinct-wide, or township-wide. But even if some definite areas were mentioned, who is capable of assessing "community standards" on such a subject? Could one expect the same application of standards by jurors in Mississippi as in New York City, in Vermont as in California? So here again the guilt or innocence of a defendant charged with obscenity must depend in the final analysis upon the personal judgment and attitude of particular individuals and the place where the trial is held. . . .

(c) A third element which [is supposedly] required to establish obscenity is that the material must be "utterly without redeeming social value." This element seems to me to be as uncertain, if not even more uncertain, than is the unknown substance of the Milky Way. If we are to have a free society as contemplated by the Bill of Rights, then I can find little defense for leaving the liberty of American individuals subject to the judgment of a judge or jury as to whether material that provokes thought or stimulates desire is "utterly without redeeming social value. . . ." Whether a particular treatment of a particular subject is with or without social value in this evolving, dynamic society of ours is a question upon which no uniform agreement could possibly be reached among politicians, statesmen, professors, philosophers, scientists, religious groups or any other type of group. A case-by-case assessment of social values by individual judges and jurors is, I think, a dangerous technique for government to utilize in determining whether a man stays in or out of the penitentiary.

My conclusion is that . . . no person, not even the most learned judge, much less a layman, is capable of knowing in advance of an ultimate decision in his particular case by this Court whether certain material comes within the area of "obscenity" as that term is confused by the Court today.[5]

5.   *Ginzburg* v. *United States.*

Questions for Analysis

1. Would you agree with the majority in Ginzburg that Ginzburg had engaged in "pandering"?

2. In your view, what, if anything, is morally objectionable about pandering?

3. Black claimed that a determination of obscenity on the basis of prurient interest in sex must of necessity be subjective. Do you agree?

4. Do you agree with Black's rejection of community standards as a basis for determining obscenity?

5. Is it impossible, as Black claimed, to determine what is "utterly without socially redeeming social value"? Can you cite an illustration of what you would regard a depiction utterly without socially redeeming social value?

6. The law aside, what moral judgment, if any, are you prepared to make of publishers like Ginzburg, Hugh Hefner (Playboy), and Larry Flynt (Hustler) who publish erotic materials for sale? Do you consider their publishing activities moral, immoral, or nonmoral? Explain. If immoral, do you also think that they should be prohibited from publishing these magazines?

7. Comment on the morality of buying and reading magazines like those mentioned in the preceding question. Do you think those who do are acting immorally, or is their behavior nonmoral? Explain.

8. Under what circumstances do you think individuals or institutions should (that is, are morally obliged to) limit access to erotic materials? For example, should your college bookstore refuse to carry for sale magazines like the aforementioned? Do you think it would be morally obligated to offer them if a majority of its customers wanted it to? If the bookstore did carry these publications, would how it displayed them raise a moral issue (for example, on a stand with other publications such as Time and Newsweek, as opposed to keeping them behind the counter and indicating that they are available)?

CASE PRESENTATION
From Chaplin to Disney: A Censorship Retrospective

Some defenders of the right to publish, display, distribute, and sell allegedly pornographic materials invoke the Bill of Rights. The First Amendment, they remind us, guarantees the right of free expression, both in speech and in the press. For their part, anti-pornographers claim that this right does not extend to allegedly pornographic materials. *Really obscene* books, films, and magazines, they say, should be censored. But what's *really obscene?* free-expressionists want to know. Let the censors ban so-called really obscene materials, they warn, and they will soon be passing judgment on serious works of art and political and social thought that they deem antisocial, subversive, or offensive.

Just how far *do* censors go? And what do they base their opinions on? Does the slippery-slope argument of the free-expressionists have any validity? The following instances of film censorship may throw some light on these questions:[6]

Walt Disney's nature film *The Vanishing Prairie:* Officials in some cities deleted a sequence showing the birth of a buffalo.

The "March of Time" documentary *Inside Nazi Germany* and Charlie Chaplin's satire on Hitler, *The Great Dictator:* Before World War II the Chicago censor denied licenses to these and some other films critical of life in Nazi Germany, apparently out of deference to Chicago's large German population.

Anatomy of a Murder: In 1959, the Chicago censor refused to license the film because the words *rape* and *contraceptive* were objectionable.

The Southerner and *Curley:* Memphis censors banned the first because it dealt with poverty among tenant farmers, a theme which presumably would reflect badly on the South. It banned the second because the film contained scenes of black and white children in school together.

Lost Boundaries: In 1950, Atlanta censors banned this film about a black physician and his family who "passed" for white. Reason for ban: the film's anticipated adverse effect on the "peace, morals and good order of Atlanta."

The Russian film *Professor Mamlock:* Ohio censors banned this film, which dealt with Nazi persecution of Jews, because the film probably would "stir up hatred and ill will and gain nothing." Police in Providence, Rhode Island, wouldn't permit the film to be shown there because it was "communist propaganda."

Carmen: Various state censors rejected this film for sundry reasons, among which that the girls who worked in the cigar factory smoked in public and that a kiss lasted too long.

New York censors forbade discussion in films of pregnancy, venereal disease, eugenics, birth control, abortion, illegitimacy, prostitution, miscegenation, and divorce.

Questions for Analysis

1. Which, if any, of the preceding acts of censorship do you think were morally justified? Explain.

2. Do you think the fact that censors have on occasion gone to extremes offers a compelling argument against censorship of allegedly obscene materials? If not, what other considerations would you introduce?

3. Do you think a community is morally justified in imposing its moral standards on all its members with regard to what films and publications its citizens have access to?

6.   Burton M. Leiser, Liberty, Justice, and Morals: Contemporary Value Conflicts *(New York: Macmillan, 1973), p. 163.*

4. *Would an application of the maximin principle lead to an endorsement or rejection of a rule that permitted a community to impose its moral standards on all its citizens? Explain.*

5. *What do you think Kant might say of the morality of censoring so-called obscene materials?*

6. *Do you think religious natural law provides a theoretical basis for a community's censoring allegedly pornographic materials?*

Selections for Further Reading

Boyer, Paul S. *Purity in Print.* New York: Scribner's, 1968.

Clor, Harry M. *Obscenity and Public Morality: Censorship in a Liberal Society.* Chicago: University of Chicago Press, 1969.

Comstock, Anthony. *Traps for the Young.* Cambridge, Mass.: Harvard University Press, 1967.

Emerson, Thomas I. *The System of Freedom of Expression.* New York: Random House, 1970.

———. *Toward a General Theory of the First Amendment.* New York: Random House, 1966.

Gerber, Albert. *Sex, Pornography, and the Law.* 2nd rev. ed. New York: Ballantine, 1964.

Gilmore, Donald H. *Sex, Censorship and Pornography.* San Diego: Greenleaf Classics, 1969.

Holbrook, David, ed. *The Case Against Pornography.* New York: The Library Press, 1973.

Hoyt, Olga G., and Edwin P. Hoyt. *Censorship in America.* New York: Seabury Press, 1962.

Marcuse, Ludwig. *Obscene: The History of an Indignation.* New York: Fernhill House, 1965.

Rembar, Charles. *The End of Obscenity.* New York: Simon and Schuster, 1970.

St. John-Stevas, Norman. *Obscenity and The Law.* London: Secker and Warburg, 1956.

Sharp, Donald B., ed. *Commentaries on Obscenity.* Metuchen, N.J.: Scarecrow Press, 1970.

4
ABORTION

Jane Roe was an unmarried pregnant woman who wished to have an abortion, an intentional termination of a pregnancy by inducing the loss of the fetus. But Ms. Roe lived in Texas, where statutes forbade abortion except to save the life of the mother. So she went to court to prove that the statutes were unconstitutional.

The three-judge district court ruled that Jane Roe had reason to sue, that the Texas criminal abortion statutes were void on their face, and, most important, that the right to choose whether to have children was protected by the Ninth through the Fourteenth Amendments. Since the district court denied a number of other aspects of the suit, the case went to the United States Supreme Court. On 22 January 1973, in the now famous *Roe* v. *Wade* decision, the Supreme Court affirmed the district court's judgment.[1]

Expressing the views of seven members of the Court, Justice Blackmun pointed out that the right to privacy applies to a woman's decision on whether to terminate her pregnancy, but that her right to terminate is not absolute. Her right may be limited by the state's legitimate interests in safeguarding the woman's health, in maintaining proper medical standards, and in protecting human life. Blackmun went on to point out that fetuses are not included within the definition of *person* as used in the Fourteenth Amendment. Most important, he indicated that prior to the end of the first trimester of pregnancy, the state may not interfere with or regulate an attending physician's decision, reached in consultation with the patient, that the patient's pregnancy should be terminated. After the first trimester and until the fetus is viable, the state may regulate the abortion procedure only for the health of the mother. After the fetus becomes viable, the state may prohibit all abortions except those necessary to preserve the health or life of the mother.

1. See U.S. Supreme Court Reports, *October Term 1972, lawyers' edition (Rochester, N.Y.: Lawyers' Cooperative Publishing, 1974), p. 147.*

In dissenting, Justices White and Rehnquist said that nothing in the language or history of the U.S. Constitution supported the Court's judgment, that the Court had simply manufactured a new constitutional right for pregnant women. The abortion issue, they said, should have been left with the people and the political processes they had devised to govern their affairs.

So for the time being at least, the abortion question has been resolved legally. But the issue is hardly settled. A number of anti-abortion movements have surfaced, which indicates not only that some people think abortion should be illegal, but that many believe it is wrong. Abortion, whether legal or not, still remains a most personal moral concern for those who must confront it. Obviously its legality provides options that may not have been present before, but these can make the moral dilemma that much thornier; in the past one could always rationalize away the possibility of an abortion on the basis of its illegality.

Some say an abortion is right if (1) it is therapeutic—that is, when it is necessary to preserve the physical or mental health of the woman; (2) it prevents the birth of a severely handicapped child; or (3) it ends a pregnancy resulting from some criminal act of sexual intercourse. Others say that even therapeutic abortions are immoral. Still others argue that any restrictive abortion legislation is wrong and must be liberalized to allow a woman to have an abortion on demand—that is, at the request of her and her physician, regardless or even in the absence of reasons. In order to evaluate such claims, it is helpful to know some biological background and to consider what sort of entities the unborn are and whether they have rights.

Biological Background

Since most of the controversy surrounding the abortion issue concerns precisely when a human individual or "person" is considered to exist, it is important to have some background about the development of the human fetus and familiarity with the terms that designate the various developmental stages. Conception or fertilization occurs when a female germ cell, or *ovum*, is penetrated by a male germ cell, or *spermatozoon*. The result is a single cell, containing a full genetic code of forty-six chromosomes, called the *zygote*. The zygote then journeys down the fallopian tube, which carries ova from the ovary to the uterus. This passage generally takes two or three days. During the journey the zygote begins a process of cellular division that increases its size. Occasionally, the zygote ends its journey in the fallopian tube, where it continues to develop. Because the tube is so narrow, such a pregnancy generally must be terminated by surgery.

When the multicell zygote reaches the uterus, it floats free in the intrauterine fluid and develops into what is termed a *blastocyst*, a ball of cells surrounding a fluid-filled cavity. By the end of the second week, the blastocyst implants itself in the uterine wall. From the end of the second week until the end of the eighth week, the unborn entity is termed an *embryo*. In the interim (four to five weeks), organ systems begin to develop, and the embryo takes on distinctly human external features.

The eighth week is important in the biological development and in a discussion of abortion, because it is then that brain activity generally becomes detectable. From this point until birth, the embryo is termed a *fetus*, although in common parlance *fetus* is used to designate the unborn entity at whatever stage.

Two other terms that designate events in fetal development are worth noting because they sometimes arise in abortion discussions. One is *quickening*, which refers to when the mother begins to feel the movements of the fetus. This occurs somewhere between the thirteenth and twentieth weeks. The second term is *viability*, the point at which the fetus is capable of surviving outside the womb. The fetus ordinarily reaches viability around the twenty-fourth week. Generally, then, events during pregnancy unfold as follows:

Developmental Timetable

zygote: first through third day
blastocyst: second day through second week
embryo: third week through eighth week
fetus: ninth week until birth
quickening: thirteenth week through twentieth week
viability: around twenty-fourth week

Should the unborn entity be terminated at any point in this timetable, an abortion is said to occur. Thus, *abortion simply refers to the termination of a pregnancy.*

Abortions can happen for a number of reasons. Sometimes the abortion occurs "spontaneously," because of internal biochemical factors or because of an injury to the woman. Such spontaneous abortions are ordinarily termed *miscarriages*. These generally involve no moral issues.

Abortions also can result directly from human intervention, which can occur in a variety of ways. Sometimes it happens very early, as when a woman takes a drug such as the "morning-after pill" in order to prevent the blastocyst from implanting in the uterine wall. Subsequent intervention during the first trimester (through the twelfth week) usually takes one of two forms: (1) uterine or vacuum aspiration; (2) dilation and curettage.

In *uterine or vacuum aspiration* the narrow opening of the uterus, the *cervix*, is dilated. A small tube is then inserted into the uterus, and its contents are vacuumed or emptied by suction. In *dilation and curettage* (D&C), the cervix is also widened, and the contents of the uterus are scraped out by means of a spoon-shaped surgical instrument called a curette. These two procedures can sometimes be done through the sixteenth week, but after that the fetus is generally too large to make the procedures practical.

The most common abortion technique after the sixteenth week is called *saline injection.* In this procedure the amniotic fluid (the fluid in the amnion, which is a membrane sac surrounding the fetus) is drawn out through a hollow needle and replaced by a solution of salt and water. This leads to a miscarriage.

Another but far rarer method after the sixteenth week is the *hysterotomy.* This is a surgical procedure whereby the fetus is removed from the uterus through an incision. This procedure is generally called a cesarean section and is rarely performed for an abortion.

We can list the various abortion possibilities as follows:

1. Internally induced:

   a. Spontaneous abortion: anytime

2. Externally induced:

   a. Drug such as "morning-after pill": immediately following intercourse

   b. Uterine or vacuum aspiration: through week 12

   c. Dilation and curettage: through week 12

   d. Saline injection: after week 16

   e. Hysterotomy (extremely rare): after week 16

The Moral Problem

The key moral problem of abortion is: Under what conditions, if any, is abortion morally justifiable? In answer to this question, three positions are broadly identifiable.

(1) The so-called conservative view holds that abortion is never morally justifiable, or, at most, justifiable only when the abortion is necessary to save the mother's life. This view is commonly associated with Roman Catholics, although they are certainly not the only persons who espouse it. (2) The so-called liberal view holds that abortion is always morally justifiable, regardless of the reasons or the time in fetal development. (3) The so-called intermediate or moderate views consider abortion morally acceptable up to a certain point in fetal development and/or claim that some reasons, not all, provide a sufficient justification for abortion.

While there is no consensus on the moral acceptability of abortion, there is agreement that any answer to the question depends on one's view of what sort of entities fetuses are and whether such entities have rights. These two important problems generally are referred to as the ontological and moral status of the fetus.

The Ontological Status of the Fetus

In philosophy the term *ontology* refers to the theory and nature of being and existence. When we speak of the ontological status of the fetus, we mean the kind of entity the fetus is. Determining the ontological status of fetuses bears directly on the issue of fetal rights and, subsequently, on permissible treatment of the fetus.

Actually, the problem of ontological status embraces a number of questions, such as: (1) whether the fetus is an individual organism; (2) whether the fetus is biologically a human being; (3) whether the fetus is psychologically a human being; (4) whether the fetus is a person.[2] Presumably, to affirm question (2) is to attribute more significant status to the fetus than to affirm question (1); and to affirm question (3) is to assign even greater status. To affirm question (4), that the fetus is a person, probably is to assign the most significant status to the fetus, although this, as well as the other presumptions, depends on the precise meaning of the concepts involved.

Complicating the question of the fetus's ontological status is the meaning of the expression *human life*. The concept of "human life" can be used in at least two different ways. On the one hand, it can refer to *biological* human life, that is, to a set of biological characteristics that distinguish the human species from other nonhuman species. In this sense, "human life" may be coextensive with "individual organism," as in question (1). On the other hand, "human life" may refer to *psychological* human life, that is, to life that is characterized by the properties that are distinctly human. Among these properties might be the abilities to use symbols, to think, and to imagine. Abortion discussions can easily founder when these distinctions are not made. For example, many who would agree that abortion involves the taking of human life in the biological sense would deny that it involves taking human life in the psychological sense. Moreover, they might see nothing immoral about taking life exclusively in the biological sense, although they would consider taking life in the psychological sense morally unacceptable. Thus they find nothing morally objectionable about abortion. Of course, at the root of this judgment is an assumption about the meaning of *human life*.

Intertwined with one's concept of human life is one's concept of "personhood." The concept of personhood may or may not differ from either the biological or the psychological sense of "human life." Some would argue that to be a person is simply to have the biological and/or psychological properties that make an organism human. However, others would propose additional conditions for personhood, such as consciousness, self-consciousness, rationality, even the capacities for communication and moral judgment. In this view, an entity must satisfy some or all of these criteria, even additional ones, to be a person. Still other theorists would extend the concept of personhood to include properties bestowed by human evaluation, in addition to the factual properties possessed by a person. Thus they might argue that a person must be the bearer of legal rights and social responsibilities, and must be capable of being assigned moral responsibility, of being praised or blamed.

Clearly the conditions that one believes are necessary for "person" status directly affect the ontological status of the fetus. For example, if the condition is only of an elementary biological nature, then the fetus can more easily qualify as a person than if the conditions include a list of factual properties. Further, if "personhood" must be analyzable in terms of properties bestowed by human evaluation, it becomes infinitely more difficult for the fetus to qualify as a person.

In the final analysis, the ontological status of fetuses remains an open issue. But some viewpoint ultimately underpins any position on the morality of abor-

---

2. *Tom L. Beauchamp and Le Roy Walters,* Contemporary Issues in Bioethics *(Belmont, Calif.: Dickenson, 1978), p. 188.*

tion. Whether conservative, liberal, or moderate, one must be prepared eventually to defend one's view of the ontological status of fetuses.

When Ontological Status Is Attained

Further complicating the problem of the ontological status is the question of when in fetal development the fetus gains full ontological status. Whether one claims the fetus is an individual organism, a biological human being, a psychological human being, or a full-fledged person, one must specify at what point in its biological development the fetus attains this status. It is one thing to say what status the fetus has; it is another to say *when* it has attained such status. A judgment about *when* the fetus has the status bears as directly on abortion views as does a judgment of the status itself.

We can identify a number of positions on when status is attained. An extreme conservative position would argue that the fetus has full ontological status from conception; at the time of conception the fetus must be regarded as an individual person. In direct contrast to this view is the extreme liberal position, which holds that the fetus never achieves ontological status.

Viewing these as polar positions, we can identify a cluster of moderate views that fall between them. In every instance, the moderate view tries to pinpoint full ontological status somewhere between conception and birth. For example, some would draw the line when brain activity is first present; others draw it at quickening; still others would draw the line at viability.

The Moral Status of the Fetus

The issue of moral status of the fetus is generally, but not always, discussed in terms of the fetus's rights. What rights, if any, does it have? Any position on abortion must at some point address this question, and all seriously argued positions do, at least by implication.

Various views on the moral status of the fetus are currently circulating. Each view can be associated with one or another of the views on the fetus's ontological status. For example, claiming that the fetus has full ontological status at conception, the extreme conservative view also holds that it has full moral status at the same stage. From the moment of conception on, the unborn entity enjoys the same rights we attribute to any adult human. In this view, abortion would be a case of denying the unborn the right to life. Therefore, abortion could never be undertaken without reasons sufficient to override the unborn's claim to life. In other words, only conditions that would justify the killing of an adult human— for example, self-defense—would morally justify an abortion.

Liberals similarly derive their view of moral status from their theory of ontological status. The extreme liberal view would deny the fetus any moral status. In this view, abortion is not considered comparable to killing an adult person. Indeed, abortion may be viewed as removing a mass of organic material, not unlike an appendectomy. Its removal raises no serious moral problems. A somewhat less liberal view, while granting the fetus ontological status as being biologically human, claims it is not human in any significant moral sense and thus has no significant rights.

Likewise, moderates would assign moral status to the fetus at the point that the entity attained full ontological status. If brain activity is taken as the point of ontological status, for example, then abortions conducted before that time would not raise serious moral questions; those conducted subsequent to that development would. Currently, viability seems to be an especially popular point at which to assign ontological status. And so, many moderate theorists today insist that abortion raises significant moral questions only *after* the fetus has attained viability. This view is reflected in some of the opinions delivered in the *Roe* v. *Wade* case.

It is important to note that granting the fetus moral status does not at all deny moral status to the woman. Indeed, the question of whose rights should take precedence when a conflict develops raises thorny questions, especially for conservatives and moderates. For example, while granting the fetus full moral status, some conservatives nonetheless approve of therapeutic abortions—abortions performed to save the woman's life or to correct some life-threatening condition. These are often viewed as cases of self-defense or justifiable homicide. Since self-defense and justifiable homicide commonly are considered acceptable grounds for killing an adult person, they are also taken as moral justification for killing a fetus. But other conservatives disapprove of even therapeutic abortions.

Similarly, while moderates grant the fetus moral status at some point in development, they too must arbitrate cases of conflicting rights. They must determine just what conditions are sufficient for allowing the woman's right to override the fetus's right to life. Here the whole gamut of conditions involving the pregnancy must be evaluated, including rape, incest, fetal deformity, and of course physical or psychological harm to the woman.

Moral Implications

Determining the moral status of the fetus, then, is directly related to determining when the fetus is actually a human. There is no question that even at the zygote stage, and from then on, the fetus is at least potentially human (until it becomes actually so). At whatever point it becomes actually human, we face a set of serious moral issues regarding abortion, among which are:

1. Does the fetus have a right to be carried to full term?

2. Under what circumstances, if ever, can we take an innocent human life?

3. Is any other right more important than the right to life—for example, the woman's right to privacy?

4. If the woman's life is in danger because of the pregnancy, how do we decide whose right prevails?

If, as is the case at present, we can't determine with reasonable certainty at what point the fetus becomes fully human, we're confronted with another set of problems:

1. Can we morally disregard the possibility that the fetus may be actually human (or may not)? If we do, does that imply, at best, an indifference to an important moral value? And is not such an attitude of not caring about a moral value itself morally questionable at least?

2. Can we ever act morally on a doubt—for example, a doubt about our obligation, the morally relevant facts, the morally correct means? How are we to resolve our doubt?

Pro-Life Arguments (against Abortion)

1.   *Abortion is murder.*

POINT: "You don't have to be a lawyer to know what murder means: the intentional ending of an innocent human life. Who can imagine an uglier and more outrageous act? Well, I can think of at least one: abortion. At least when you kill adults, they usually have a chance to defend themselves. But what chance does a fetus have? None. Try as you will, you can't escape the inevitable fact that abortion is murder."

COUNTERPOINT: "You make it sound like fetuses can go out and buy ice cream cones whenever they want, as well as think, imagine, wonder, hope, dream, and create. Why, a fetus isn't any more a 'human being' than cake batter is a cake. Certainly murder is a terrible thing—the murder of a full-fledged walking, talking human being, not a glob of protoplasm."

2.   *Abortion sets a dangerous precedent.*

POINT: "Everybody would agree that any action leading to a casual attitude toward life is wrong. But that's just what abortion is. And that includes therapeutic abortion. As for abortions committed in the case of severely deformed fetuses, they're no more than the first step to 'putting away' the severely handicapped, the dysfunctional, the senile, and the incurably ill in our society. No, abortion leads to a shabby attitude toward life; it opens a Pandora's box of unspeakable affronts to human dignity and worth. Remember: The Holocaust under Hitler began with the legalization of abortion. Every abortion that's demanded or performed takes us one step closer to a systematic recognition of abortion, and everything that implies."

COUNTERPOINT: "Why do you assume that the practice of abortion inevitably will lead to disrespect for life and usher in an age of nightmarish inhumanity? In fact, anthropological studies indicate that societies condoning abortion have better records on 'civil rights' and 'protections' than those that don't. You and I both know that issues dealing with the severely handicapped or incurably ill are separate and distinct questions from abortion and must be examined on their own merits. As for your Hitler reference, that has nothing to do with the question of whether abortion's right or wrong. It's outrageously irrelevant. Besides, legal abortion didn't produce the Holocaust; Hitler's madness and those who cooperated with it did. Even if your point had any merit, it really argues against *allowing* abortions, and not their morality."

3.   *Abortion involves psychological risks for the woman.*

POINT: "Let's face it: A woman and the child she's bearing are about as close as any two humans can ever get. And I don't mean just biologically, but emotionally and psychologically, too. Ask any mother—she'll tell you. For a woman to intentionally harm her unborn violates the deepest levels of her unconscious needs, impulses, and desires. And she's bound to pay a big price for this psychologically. Plenty of women already have—ask the psychologists. There's no question about it: The woman who has an abortion not only kills her unborn, she also seriously damages herself."

COUNTERPOINT: "If there was an annual award for sweeping generalizations, you'd certainly get it. You talk of 'women' as if they were all the same. Sure, lots of women, maybe even most, want to carry their unborn to term. But *lots* and *most* don't mean *all*. Who knows what lurks in the so-called unconscious mind? Maybe a woman who outwardly wants to bear children secretly doesn't. Ask the psychologists, you say. All right, ask them. And while you're at it, ask about child abuse, post- and neonatal trauma, and nervous breakdowns. What makes you think every woman is suited to be a mother? Some women discover only after giving birth that they genuinely *don't* want the child. They assumed they did largely because of environmental conditioning which, as you well illustrated, has had the effect of heaping guilt on the poor woman who might honestly admit she does not want to carry, bear, and rear children. It's time we put aside these stereotypes about women for good. And while we're at it, let's not confuse what women actually want to do with what we believe they *should* want to do."

4.   *Alternatives to abortion are available.*

POINT: "All this talk about unwanted pregnancies and bringing undesired and unloved children into the world just won't cut it. Whom are we kidding? There are countless individuals and couples who are dying to have kids but can't. If a woman doesn't want to carry a child to term, that's no reason to abort it. Just put it up for adoption at birth. As for the tragically deformed infant no one may want to adopt, there are plenty of institutions and agencies set up for those pitiful souls."

COUNTERPOINT: "Sure, there are plenty of people willing and able to adopt. But even if the child will be adopted, the woman still has to carry it for nine months. And she may be either unwilling or unable to do that. What's more, giving up your child for adoption is no emotional picnic, you know. And often it's no easier on the child. Plenty of adoptees anguish over unresolved feelings of parental rejection. As for the deformed, why make society foot the bill for someone else's responsibility? I for one don't want my hard-earned tax dollars spent caring for someone else's problems that easily could have been prevented in the first place."

5.   *The woman must be responsible for her sexual activity.*

POINT: "No woman *has* to get pregnant. You don't have to be the 'happy hooker' to know that there are plenty of readily available contraceptives. When a woman doesn't practice some form of birth control, she takes responsibility for what happens. For a woman to sacrifice an innocent human life just because she's been careless, ignorant, or indiscreet is the height of sexual and moral irresponsibility."

COUNTERPOINT: "Come now, everybody knows that there's no surefire birth control method, except abstinence. Any woman who has sex stands the same chance of getting pregnant as a driver of having an accident. Why, even if a driver drives recklessly and has a serious accident, we allow her the opportunity to repair the damage to herself and others, don't we? In fact, we help her do it! To make a woman bear a child out of some warped sense of 'person responsibility' is like turning our back on a torn and bloody motorist because 'she got what she deserved.' Such an attitude reflects more vindictiveness and punishment than commitment to the principle of personal responsibility. No matter why a woman gets pregnant, she still has the right to dispose of her pregnancy as she sees fit. Sure, she may have been irresponsible, but that's a separate issue from what she then chooses to do about the result of her indiscretion."

Pro-Choice Arguments (for Abortion)

1.   *Pregnancies are dangerous for the woman.*

POINT: "There are very few adults, if any, who haven't had a direct or indirect experience that shows how dangerous pregnancies can be to the life and health of women. Let those without such knowledge look at the record. They'll see that in some cases the woman's life is actually on the line. In other cases, the woman must endure heroic suffering and hardship during the term. In still other cases, the woman must endure lifelong health problems that are the direct result of the pregnancy. Given these possible risks, women should have the say about whether they want to run them or not."

COUNTERPOINT: "Your argument would be very persuasive if this were the nineteenth century. Where have you been for the last thirty years? Don't you realize that modern medicine has, in effect, wiped out the dangers connected with pregnancy? Sure, there remain some cases where the woman's life is in jeopardy. But even in those cases, why assume that her life must be saved at all costs? There's another human life at stake, you know. As for your long-term ill effects of pregnancy, what did you have in mind—varicose veins, hemorrhoids, and an aching back? When such 'horrors' become justification for abortion, we're really in trouble. What will be acceptable justification next—a ski trip to Aspen which, unluckily for the fetus, pops up in the seventh month?"

2. *Many unborn are unwanted or deformed.*

POINT: "Everybody knows that society has serious population, pollution, and poverty problems—not to mention crime, disease, and world hunger. These problems already are taxing our financial capacity to deal with them. One way we can begin to deal with them is to make sure every child that's brought into the world is wanted and healthy. Ignoring this, we just worsen the world's problems. Fortunately, we've got lots of ways to ensure that unwanted and unhealthy children are never born. Contraceptives are one way. But for one reason or another, some people don't play it safe, and it's usually those who can least afford to maintain children physically and emotionally. Such people need an alternative form of birth control: abortion. Abortion's especially necessary in the case of monstrously deformed fetuses. If a woman is willing and able to bear and care for the deformed or unintended child, fine. But if she isn't willing or can't, it's unfair to make the rest of us pay the price for the problem she's created and the responsibility she's shirked.

COUNTERPOINT: "You make it sound like the unloved and the deformed are responsible for every social and global problem we have; if we can just keep these 'undesirables' from being born, all our headaches will vanish. Sure, we have considerable problems, but lots of things account for them, including human mismanagement of resources, inadequate or misguided technology, nearsighted and unimaginative leadership, as well as the age-old conditions of human greed, prejudice, and downright stupidity. The idea that abortions can help improve these conditions is exactly the kind of mindless proposal that contributes to our problems. It's unfair, you say, to make society pay the price for maintaining the unwanted or deformed child. What's so unfair about it? I always thought that part of a society's function was to provide for those least able to fend for themselves. What would you suggest we do with our mental health services and facilities? Discontinue them, I guess. How about simply exterminating the mentally defective? That would really save us a bundle. And how about just executing criminals instead of incarcerating them? You shouldn't find that objectionable. After all, what could be more 'unfair' by your standard than making society pay the price for maintaining those who have flouted society's conventions?"

3. *Some pregnancies result from rape or incest.*

POINT: "There's no more heinous a crime committed against a woman than rape or incest. To oblige a woman morally to bear the child of such an outrage goes beyond adding insult to injury. It's brutally barbaric. Nothing short of the woman's free choice would morally justify going through with a rape or incest pregnancy."

COUNTERPOINT: "Agreed, rape and incest are ugly. But pregnancies resulting from them are rare. You're so concerned with not punishing the woman who has already been sexually abused. Well, by the same token, why punish the unborn by making them give up their lives? If making a woman carry to term a fetus that's resulted from rape or incest is a case of making the innocent suffer, then how much more innocent suffering is terminating the life of the fetus? Besides, nobody is asking the woman to raise a child she doesn't want or can't maintain. There are plenty of individuals and institutions who'll do that if she's unwilling or unable."

4. *Women have rights over their own bodies.*

POINT: "Women bear the full and exclusive burden of carrying a fetus to term. They must endure the physical and emotional risks, the discomfort, the disruptions of career and routine living. Given this burden, they have the right to decide whether or not they want to go through with a pregnancy. But beyond this, the unborn is a part of the woman's body, and she should have absolute say over whether or not it's going to remain in her body and be allowed to be born. To deny her that right is about as crude and basic a violation of free choice as anything imaginable."

COUNTERPOINT: "Of course women have certain rights over their own bodies. But having basic rights doesn't mean that those rights are absolute and take precedence over all others' rights. My right to free speech doesn't justify my yelling 'Fire!' in a crowded theater when, in fact, there is no fire. Nor does the woman's right over her own body mean she's justified in taking the life of the unborn. As soon as a woman gets pregnant, a relationship exists between her and the unborn. And like any other relationship, this one must involve a careful defining, assigning, and setting the priorities of rights and responsibilities. This is especially important in pregnancies because the unborn are in no position to argue for or defend their own rights. Let the woman who's so concerned about her own body make sure she doesn't get pregnant in the first place. But once she gets pregnant, her right takes a back seat to the unborn's right to life, certainly so long as the unborn's life doesn't threaten the woman's life."

Legal Considerations

We began this chapter by referring to a landmark abortion ruling. It is important to recognize that the question of whether a woman ought to have a legal right to an abortion is related to, but different from, the question of whether an abortion is ever morally justifiable.

Naturally, the morality of abortion can and does bear on the morality of restrictive abortion legislation. Thus people who believe that abortion is in and of itself morally objectionable often object to nonrestrictive legislation. And those who believe that abortion is unobjectionable often support nonrestrictive legislation. But it is also perfectly consistent to object to abortion while opposing restrictive abortion legislation because, say, such laws would abridge the individual's right to free choice. And it is perfectly consistent, and common, to argue that individual acts of abortion may be moral, even obligatory, while opposing a loosening of abortion laws because, for example, such a systematic policy may lead to abuses. In short, one can be opposed to abortion but also opposed to restrictive abortion legislation, or in favor of individual acts of abortion but against nonrestrictive legislation.

Any of the pro-life arguments can be marshaled in support of restrictive legislation, and any of the pro-choice arguments can be marshaled on behalf of nonrestrictive legislation. So one could argue that since abortion is murder, the state has a moral obligation to protect its citizens by preventing their murder; or, since abortion involves risks for women, the state has an obligation to protect its citizens from such risks. A person could also argue that the state has an obligation to relieve society's burden of caring for the unwanted or deformed unborn by making abortions possible for women; or that the state has an obligation to minimize the profound hardship a rape or incest pregnancy causes a woman by allowing her to have an abortion.

Especially relevant to the legislation question are the probable consequences of restrictive legislation, some of which can best be anticipated by considering some statistics prior to the Roe decision. By some estimates, in the early 1960s a million women obtained abortions, most of which were illegal.[3] Whatever the exact figure, before 1973 most abortions were obtained clandestinely. Poor women seemed to have been particularly vulnerable to the health-threatening conditions that often accompanied clandestine abortions, particularly those that were self-induced or performed by unqualified persons. In 1960 alone, 50 percent of the deaths in New York City associated with pregnancy and births resulted from illegal abortions.[4] It's a safe guess, then, that if abortion is returned to its pre-1973 legal status there will likely be an increase in clandestine abortions, with the poor bearing the brunt of the riskiest procedures.

In addition, physicians who believe in the morality of nontherapeutic abortions in the first trimester will presumably be forced to choose between obeying the law and following their conscience. Furthermore, restrictive legislation may create a fee system that borders on price-gouging. These concerns should at least be part of an analysis of the morality of proposed abortion legislation.

All the same, a knot of moral problems has developed since the passage of nonrestrictive legislation. For one thing, women today are often subjected to humiliating encounters with medical personnel. For example, sometimes they are asked to sign fetal "death certificates." In some cases machines are set next to them that record fetal heartbeats; abortions are performed in the same wards where other women are giving birth. Still other times women are given bags with a picture of a fetus that they are expected to return to the hospital after aborting at home.[5] At minimum, such procedures are callous and raise doubt about how well some health professionals and institutions are meeting their obligations to provide adequate care for the pregnant woman and to respect her autonomy.

3.   N. Lee, The Search for an Abortionist (Chicago: University of Chicago Press, 1969), pp. 5–6.

4.   A. F. Guttmacher, "Abortion—Yesterday, Today, Tomorrow," in The Case for Legalized Abortion, ed. A. F. Guttmacher (Berkeley, Calif.: Diablo Press, 1967), pp. 8–9.

5.   Ellen Frankfort, Vaginal Politics (New York: Quadrangle Books, 1972), pp. xxiii–xxv.

In addition, legalization of abortion has not necessarily meant an end to profiteering, inadequate facilities, or poorly trained personnel.[6] Nor does abortion reform appear to have significantly altered the plight of the poor. On the contrary, some evidence indicates that first- and second-trimester abortions are sometimes not available to institutional patients, whereas in the very same institution abortions are being performed on private patients.[7] More important, according to recent federal legislation, Medicaid payments are permitted only for medical care following termination of a pregnancy by miscarriage or by an abortion to save the life of the mother; Medicaid payments are prohibited for all abortions except those performed to save the life of the mother.[8]

Undoubtedly, then, any proposed abortion legislation will be fraught with serious moral questions about autonomy, suffering, adequate care, and social justice. Discussions of the morality of the legislation must address these issues.

6.   *S. Burth Rauzek,* The Women's Health Movement: Feminist Alternatives to Medical Control *(New York: Praeger, 1979), pp. 26–27.*

7.   *Diane Scully,* Men Who Control Women's Health: The Miseducation of Obstetrician-Gynecologists *(Boston: Houghton-Mifflin, 1980), pp. 229–30.*

8.   *The Child Health Assurance Program (CHAP) was passed by the House of Representatives on December 11, 1979, HR 4962. For a synopsis of the bill, see* Health Policy: The Legislative Agenda *(Washington, D.C.: Congressional Quarterly, Inc., 1980), p. 90.*

An Almost Absolute Value in History

John T. Noonan

Like many authors on the subject of abortion, law professor John T. Noonan locates the central issue in the ontological status of the fetus. In his essay Noonan assigns the fetus full ontological status at the moment of conception.

Noonan not only puts this view in the context of traditional Christian theology, he also tests its strength compared with the other distinctions of ontological status that are commonly made: viability, experience, quickening, attitude of parents, and social visibility. Noonan shows why he thinks each of these distinctions is unsound.

In addition to the unique problems that each of these distinctions has, Noonan believes that they share one overriding problem: They are distinctions that appear to be arbitrary. Noonan feels that if distinctions leading to moral judgments are not to appear arbitrary, they should relate to some real difference in probabilities. He argues that his position passes this test, because it recognizes the fact that 80 percent of the zygotes formed will develop into new beings. For Noonan this probability is a most compelling reason for granting the conceptus (fetus) full ontological status.

In short, conception is the decisive moment of humanization, for it is then that the fetus receives the genetic code of the parents. These arguments lead Noonan to condemn abortion, except in cases of self-defense.

From John T. Noonan, "An Almost Absolute Value in History," in Morality of Abortion: Legal and Historical Perspectives, *ed. John T. Noonan (Harvard University Press, 1970). Reprinted by permission.*

The most fundamental question involved in the long history of thought on abortion is: How do you determine the humanity of a being? To phrase the question that way is to put in comprehensive humanistic terms what the theologians either dealt with as an explicitly theological question under the heading of "ensoulment" or dealt with implicitly in their treatment of abortion. The Christian position as it originated did not depend on a narrow theological or philosophical concept. It had no relation to theories of infant baptism. It appealed to no special theory of instantaneous ensoulment. It took the world's view on ensoulment as that view changed from Aristotle to Zacchia. There was, indeed, theological influence affecting the theory of ensoulment finally adopted, and, of course, ensoulment itself was a theological concept, so that the position was always explained in theological terms. But the theological notion of ensoulment could easily be translated into humanistic language by substituting "human" for "rational soul"; the problem of knowing when a man is a man is common to theology and humanism.

If one steps outside the specific categories used by the theologians, the answer they gave can be analyzed as a refusal to discriminate among human beings on the basis of their varying potentialities. Once conceived, the being was recognized as man because he had man's potential. The criterion for humanity, thus, was simple and all-embracing: If you are conceived by human parents, you are human.

The strength of this position may be tested by a review of some of the other distinctions offered in the contemporary controversy over legalizing abortion. Perhaps the most popular distinction is in terms of viability. Before an age of so many months, the fetus is not viable, that is, it cannot be removed from the mother's womb and live apart from her. To that extent, the life of the fetus is absolutely dependent on the life of the mother. This dependence is made the basis of denying recognition to its humanity.

There are difficulties with this distinction. One is that the perfection of artificial incubation may make the fetus viable at any time: It may be removed and artificially sustained. Experiments with animals already show that such a procedure is possible. This hypothetical extreme case relates to an actual difficulty: there is considerable elasticity to the idea of viability. Mere length of life is not an exact measure. The viability of the fetus depends on the extent of its anatomical and functional development. The weight and length of the fetus are better guides to the state of its development than age, but weight and length vary. Moreover, different racial groups have different ages at which their fetuses are viable. Some evidence, for example, suggests that Negro fetuses mature more quickly than white fetuses. If viability is the norm, the standard would vary with race and with many individual circumstances.

The most important objection to this approach is that dependence is not ended by viability. The fetus is still absolutely dependent on someone's care in order to continue existence; indeed a child of one or three or even five years of age is absolutely dependent on another's care for existence; uncared for, the older fetus or the younger child will die as surely as the early fetus detached from the mother. The unsubstantial lessening in dependence at viability does not seem to signify any special acquisition of humanity.

A second distinction has been attempted in terms of experience. A being who has had experience, has lived and suffered, who possesses memories, is more human than one who has not. Humanity depends on formation by experience. The fetus is thus "unformed" in the most basic human sense.

This distinction is not serviceable for the embryo which is already experiencing and reacting. The embryo is responsive to touch after eight weeks and at least at that point is experiencing. At an earlier stage the zygote is certainly alive and responding to its environment. The distinction may also be challenged by the rare case where aphasia has erased adult memory: Has it erased humanity? More fundamentally, this distinction leaves even the older fetus or the younger child to be treated as an unformed inhuman thing. Finally, it is not clear why experience as such confers humanity. It could be argued that certain central experiences such as loving or learning are necessary to make a man human. But then human beings who have failed to love or to learn might be excluded from the class called man.

A third distinction is made by appeal to the

sentiments of adults. If a fetus dies, the grief of the parents is not the grief they would have for a living child. The fetus is an unnamed "it" till birth, and is not perceived as personality until at least the fourth month of existence, when movements in the womb manifest a vigorous presence demanding joyful recognition by the parents.

Yet feeling is notoriously an unsure guide to the humanity of others. Many groups of humans have had difficulty in feeling that persons of another tongue, color, religion, sex, are as human as they. Apart from reactions to alien groups, we mourn the loss of a ten-year-old boy more than the loss of his one-day-old brother or his 90-year-old grandfather. The difference felt and the grief expressed vary with the potentialities extinguished, or the experience wiped out; they do not seem to point to any substantial difference in the humanity of baby, boy, or grandfather.

Distinctions are also made in terms of sensation by the parents. The embryo is felt within the womb only after about the fourth month. The embryo is seen only at birth. What can be neither seen nor felt is different from what is tangible. If the fetus cannot be seen or touched at all, it cannot be perceived as man.

Yet experience shows that sight is even more untrustworthy than feeling in determining humanity. By sight, color became an appropriate index for saying who was a man, and the evil of racial discrimination was given foundation. Nor can touch provide the test; a being confined by sickness, "out of touch" with others, does not thereby seem to lose his humanity. To the extent that touch still has appeal as a criterion, it appears to be a survival of the old English idea of "quickening"— a possible mistranslation of the Latin *animatus* used in the canon law. To that extent, touch as a criterion seems to be dependent on the Aristotelian notion of ensoulment, and to fall when this notion is discarded.

Finally, a distinction is sought in social visibility. The fetus is not socially perceived as human. It cannot communicate with others. Thus, both subjectively and objectively, it is not a member of society. As moral rules are rules for the behavior of members of society to each other, they cannot be made for behavior toward what is not yet a member. Excluded from the society of men, the fetus is excluded from the humanity of men.

By force of the argument from the consequences, this distinction is to be rejected. It is more subtle than that founded on an appeal to physical sensation, but it is equally dangerous in its implications. If humanity depends on social recognition, individuals or whole groups may be dehumanized by being denied any status in their society. Such a fate is fictionally portrayed in *1984* and has actually been the lot of many men in many societies. In the Roman empire, for example, condemnation to slavery meant the practical denial of most human rights; in the Chinese Communist world, landlords have been classified as enemies of the people and so treated as nonpersons by the state. Humanity does not depend on social recognition, though often the failure of society to recognize the prisoner, the alien, the heterodox as human has led to the destruction of human beings. Anyone conceived by a man and a woman is human. Recognition of this condition by society follows a real event in the objective order, however imperfect and halting the recognition. Any attempt to limit humanity to exclude some group runs the risk of furnishing authority and precedent for excluding other groups in the name of the consciousness or perception of the controlling group in the society.

A philosopher may reject the appeal to the humanity of the fetus because he views "humanity" as a secular view of the soul and because he doubts the existence of anything real and objective which can be identified as humanity. One answer to such a philosopher is to ask how he reasons about moral questions without supposing that there is a sense in which he and the others of whom he speaks are human. Whatever group is taken as the society which determines who may be killed is thereby taken as human. A second answer is to ask if he does not believe that there is a right and wrong way of deciding moral questions. If there is such a difference, experience may be appealed to: To decide who is human on the basis of the sentiment of a given society has led to consequences which rational men would characterize as monstrous.

The rejection of the attempted distinctions based on viability and visibility, experience and feeling, may be buttressed by the following considerations: Moral judgments often rest on distinctions, but if the distinctions are not to appear arbitrary fiat, they should relate to some real difference in probabilities. There is a kind of continuity in all life, but the earlier stages of the elements of human life possess tiny probabilities of development. Consider, for example, the spermatozoa in any normal ejaculate: There are about 200,000,000 in any single ejaculate, of which one has a chance of developing into a zygote. Consider the oocytes which may become ova: There are 100,000 to 1,000,000 oocytes in a female infant, of which a maximum of 390 are ovulated. But once spermatozoon and ovum meet and the conceptus is formed, such studies as have been made show that roughly in only 20 percent of the cases will spontaneous abortion occur. In other words, the chances are about 4 out of 5 that this new being will develop. At this stage in the life of the being there is a sharp shift in probabilities, an immense jump in potentialities. To make a distinction between the rights of spermatozoa and the rights of the fertilized ovum is to respond to an enormous shift in possibilities. For about twenty days after conception, the egg may split to form twins or combine with another egg to form a chimera, but the probability of either event happening is very small.

It may be asked, What does a change in biological probabilities have to do with establishing humanity? The argument from probabilities is not aimed at establishing humanity but at establishing an objective discontinuity which may be taken into account in moral discourse. As life itself is a matter of probabilities, as most moral reasoning is an estimate of probabilities, so it seems in accord with the structure of reality and the nature of moral thought to found a moral judgment on the change in probabilities at conception. The appeal to probabilities is the most commonsensical of arguments, to a greater or smaller degree all of us base our actions on probabilities, and in morals, as in law, prudence and negligence are often measured by the account one has taken of the probabilities. If the chance is 200,000,000 to 1 that the movement in the bushes into which you shoot is a man's, I doubt if many persons would hold you careless in shooting; but if the chances are 4 out of 5 that the movement is a human being's, few would acquit you of blame. Would the argument be different if only one out of ten children conceived came to term? Of course this argument would be different. This argument is an appeal to probabilities that actually exist, not to any and all states of affairs which may be imagined.

The probabilities as they do exist do not show the humanity of the embryo in the sense of a demonstration in logic any more than the probabilities of the movement in the bush being a man demonstrate beyond all doubt that the being is a man. The appeal is a "buttressing" consideration, showing the plausibility of the standard adopted. The argument focuses on the decisional factor in any moral judgment and assumes that part of the business of a moralist is drawing lines. One evidence of the nonarbitrary character of the line drawn is the difference of probabilities on either side of it. If a spermatozoon is destroyed, one destroys a being which had a chance of far less than 1 in 200 million of developing into a reasonable being, possessed of the genetic code, a heart and other organs, and capable of pain. If a fetus is destroyed, one destroys a being already possessed of the genetic code, organs, and sensitivity to pain, and one which had an 80 percent chance of developing further into a baby, outside the womb, who, in time, would reason.

The positive argument for conception as the decisive moment of humanization is that at conception the new being receives the genetic code. It is this genetic information which determines his characteristics, which is the biological carrier of the possibility of human wisdom, which makes him a self-evolving being. A being with a human genetic code is man.

This review of current controversy over the humanity of the fetus emphasizes what a fundamental question the theologians resolved in asserting the inviolability of the fetus. To regard the fetus as possessed of equal rights with other humans was not, however, to decide every case where abortion might be employed. It did decide the case where the argument was that the fetus should be aborted for its own good. To say a being was human was to say it had a destiny to decide for itself which could not be taken from it by another man's decision. But human beings with equal rights often come in conflict with each other, and some decision must be made as to whose claims are to prevail. Cases of conflict involving the fetus are different only in two respects: the total inability of the fetus to speak for itself and the fact that the right of the fetus regularly at stake is the right to life itself.

The approach taken by the theologians to these conflicts was articulated in terms of "direct" and "indirect." Again, to look at what they were doing from outside their categories, they may be said to have been drawing lines or "balancing values." "Direct" and "indirect" are spatial metaphors: "line-drawing" is another. "To weigh" or "to balance" values is a metaphor of a more complicated mathematical sort hinting at the process which goes on in moral judgments. All the metaphors suggest that, in the moral judgments made, comparisons were necessary, that no value completely controlled. The principle of double effect was no doctrine fallen from heaven, but a method of analysis appropriate where two relative values were being compared. In Catholic moral theology, as it developed, life even of the innocent was not taken as an absolute. Judgments on acts affecting life issued from a process of weighing. In the weighing, the fetus was always given a value greater than zero, always a value separate and independent from its parents. This valuation was crucial and fundamental in all Christian thought on the subject and marked it off from any approach which considered that only the parents' interests needed to be considered.

Even with the fetus weighed as human, one interest could be weighed as equal or superior: that of the mother in her own life. The casuists between 1450 and 1895 were willing to weigh this interest as superior. Since 1895, that interest was given decisive weight only in the two special cases of the cancerous uterus and the ectopic pregnancy. In both of these cases the fetus itself had little chance of survival even if the abortion were not performed. As the balance was once struck in favor of the mother whenever her life was endangered, it could be so

struck again. The balance reached between 1895 and 1930 attempted prudentially and pastorally to forestall a multitude of exceptions for interests less than life.

The perception of the humanity of the fetus and the weighing of fetal rights against other human rights constituted the work of the moral analysts. But what spirit animated their abstract judgments? For the Christian community it was the injunction of Scripture to love your neighbor as yourself. The fetus as human was a neighbor; his life had parity with one's own. The commandment gave life to what otherwise would have been only rational calculation.

The commandment could be put in humanistic as well as theological terms: Do not injure your fellow man without reason. In these terms, once the humanity of the fetus is perceived, abortion is never right except in self-defense. When life must be taken to save life, reason alone cannot say that a mother must prefer a child's life to her own. With this exception, now of great rarity, abortion violates the rational humanist tenet of the equality of human lives.

For Christians the commandment to love had received a special imprint in that the exemplar proposed of love was the love of the Lord for his disciples. In the light given by this example, self-sacrifice carried to the point of death seemed in the extreme situations not without meaning. In the less extreme cases, preference for one's own interests to the life of another seemed to express cruelty or selfishness irreconcilable with the demands of love.

Questions for Analysis

1. *Do you agree that considering the unborn a person from the moment of conception poses fewer problems than any of the alternative views?*

2. *What problems does Noonan see in distinctions based on: (a) viability, (b) experience, (c) feelings of adults, (d) social visibility?*

3. *Explain how Noonan used "biological probabilities" to buttress his view of the unborn as a person from the moment of conception. Is his argument persuasive?*

4. *On what grounds does Noonan object to abortion?*

5. *Is it accurate to say that Noonan finds abortion always impermissible?*

In Defense of Abortion and Infanticide

Michael Tooley

In the following essay, professor of philosophy Michael Tooley focuses on the basic moral objection traditionally raised to abortion and infanticide, namely, that the unborn and newborn have a right to life. In testing this assumption, Tooley attempts to isolate the properties a thing must possess in order to have a right to life.

In Tooley's view, only if an entity is capable of having an interest in its own continued existence can it have a right to life, and only if an entity possesses at some time the concept of a continuing self is it capable of having an interest in its own continued existence. Since fetuses and infants cannot satisfy these conditions, Tooley concludes that they have no right to life—their potential for satisfying these conditions notwithstanding. Therefore, barring other objections besides the traditional one, Tooley considers both abortion and infanticide morally acceptable. In contrast, he thinks that since adult members of nonhuman species may satisfy these conditions, our treatment of them may be morally suspect.

It's important to realize that Tooley is not arguing for indiscriminate abortion and infanticide, but trying to make a case for the moral permissibility of acts of abortion and infanticide that might be considered immoral because they violate a right-to-life claim. It doesn't necessarily follow that every act of abortion and infanticide would therefore be morally permissible.

This essay deals with the question of the morality of abortion and infanticide. The fundamental ethical objection traditionally advanced against these practices rests on the contention that human fetuses and infants have a right to life. It is this claim which will be the focus of attention here. The basic issue to be discussed, then, is what properties a thing must possess in order to have a right to life. My approach will be to set out and defend a basic moral principle specifying a condition an organism must satisfy if it is to have a right to life. It will be seen that this condition is not satisfied by human fetuses and infants, and thus that they do not have a right to life. So unless there are other objections to abortion and infanticide which are sound, one is forced to conclude that these practices are morally acceptable ones.[1] In contrast, it may turn out that our treatment of adult members of some other species is morally indefensible. For it is quite possible that some nonhuman animals do possess properties that endow them with a right to life.

I. Abortion and Infanticide

What reason is there for raising the question of the morality of infanticide? One reason is that it seems very difficult to formulate a completely satisfactory pro-abortion position without coming to grips with the infanticide issue. For the problem that the liberal on abortion encounters here is that of specifying a cutoff point which is not arbitrary: at what stage in the development of a human being does it cease to be morally permissible to destroy it, and why?

It is important to be clear about the difficulty here. The problem is not, as some have thought, that since there is a continuous line of development from a zygote to a newborn baby, one cannot hold that it is seriously wrong to destroy a newborn baby without also holding that it is seriously wrong to destroy a zygote, or any intermediate stage in the development of a human being. The problem is rather that if one says that it is wrong to destroy a newborn baby but not a zygote or some intermediate stage, one should be prepared to point to a *morally relevant* difference between a newborn baby and the earlier stage in the development of a human being.

Precisely the same difficulty can, of course, be raised for a person who holds that infanticide is morally permissible, since one can ask what mor-

This article first appeared in The Problem of Abortion, *edited by Joel Feinberg (Belmont, Calif.: Wadsworth, 1984). Reprinted here by permission of the author.*

ally relevant difference there is between an adult human being and a newborn baby. What makes it morally permissible to destroy a baby, but wrong to kill an adult? So the challenge remains. But I shall argue that in the latter case there is an extremely plausible answer.

Reflecting on the morality of infanticide forces one to face up to this challenge. In the case of abortion a number of events—quickening or viability, for instance—might be taken as cutoff points, and it is easy to overlook the fact that none of these events involves any morally significant change in the developing human. In contrast, if one is going to defend infanticide, one has to get very clear about what it is that gives something a right to life.

One of the interesting ways in which the abortion issue differs from most other moral issues is that the plausible positions on abortion appear to be extreme ones. For if a human fetus has a right to life, one is inclined to say that, in general, one would be justified in killing it only to save the life of the mother, and perhaps not even in that case.[2] Such is the extreme anti-abortion position. On the other hand, if the fetus does not have a right to life, why should it be seriously wrong to destroy it? Why would one need to point to special circumstances—such as the presence of genetic disease, or a threat to the woman's health—in order to justify such action? The upshot is that there does not appear to be any room for a moderate position on abortion such as one finds, for example, in the Model Penal Code recommendations.[3]

Aside from the light it may shed on the abortion question, the issue of infanticide is both interesting and important in its own right. The theoretical interest has been mentioned above: it forces one to face up to the question of what it is that gives something a right to life. The practical importance need not be labored. Most people would prefer to raise children who do not suffer from gross deformities or from severe physical, emotional, or intellectual handicaps. If it could be shown that there is no moral objection to infanticide, the happiness of society could be significantly and justifiably increased.

The suggestion that infanticide may be morally permissible is not an idea that many people are able to consider dispassionately. Even philosophers tend to react in a way which seems primarily visceral—

offering no arguments, and dismissing infanticide out of hand.

Some philosophers have argued, however, that such a reaction is not inappropriate, on the ground that, first, moral principles must, in the final analysis, be justified by reference to our moral feelings, or intuitions, and secondly, infanticide is one practice that is judged wrong by virtually everyone's moral intuition. I believe, however, that this line of thought is unsound, and I have argued elsewhere that even if [one] grants, at least for the sake of argument, that moral intuitions are the final court of appeal regarding the acceptability of moral principles, the question of the morality of infanticide is not one that can be settled by an appeal to our intuitions concerning it.[4] If infanticide is to be rejected, an argument is needed, and I believe that the considerations advanced in this essay show that it is unlikely that such an argument is forthcoming.

II. What Sort of Being Can Possess a Right to Life?

The issues of the morality of abortion and of infanticide seem to turn primarily upon the answers to the following four questions:

(1) What properties, other than potentialities, give something a right to life?

(2) Do the corresponding potentialities also endow something with a right to life?

(3) If not, do they at least make it seriously wrong to destroy it?

(4) At what point in its development does a member of the biologically defined species *Homo sapiens* first possess those nonpotential properties that give something a right to life? The argument to be developed in the present section bears upon the answers to the first two questions.

How can one determine what properties endow a being with a right to life? An approach that I believe is very promising starts out from the observation that there appear to be two radically different sorts of reasons why an entity may lack a certain right. Compare, for example, the following two claims:

(1) A child does not have a right to smoke.

(2) A newspaper does not have a right not to be torn up.

The first claim raises a substantive moral issue. People might well disagree about it, and support their conflicting views by appealing to different moral theories. The second dispute, in contrast, seems an unlikely candidate for moral dispute. It is natural to say that newspapers just are not the sort of thing that can have any rights at all, including a right not to be torn up. So there is no need to appeal to a substantive moral theory to resolve the question whether a newspaper has a right not to be torn up.

One way of characterizing this difference, albeit one that will not especially commend itself to philosophers of a Quinean[5] bent, is to say that the second claim, unlike the first, is true in virtue of a certain *conceptual* connection, and that is why no moral theory is needed in order to see that it is true. The explanation, then, of why it is that a newspaper does not have a right not to be torn up, is that there is some property P such that, first, newspapers lack property P, and secondly, it is a conceptual truth that only things with property P can be possessors of rights.

What might property P be? A plausible answer, I believe, is set out and defended by Joel Feinberg in his paper, "The Rights of Animals and Unborn Generations."[6] It takes the form of what Feinberg refers to as the *interest principle:* ". . . the sorts of beings who *can* have rights are precisely those who have (or can have) interests."[7] And then, since "interests must be compounded somehow out of conations,"[8] it follows that things devoid of desires, such as newspapers, can have neither interests nor rights. Here, then, is one account of the difference in status between judgments such as (1) and (2) above.

Let us now consider the right to life. The interest principle tells us that an entity cannot have any rights at all, and *a fortiori*, cannot have a right to life, unless it is capable of having interests. This in itself may be a conclusion of considerable importance. Consider, for example, a fertilized human egg cell. Someday it will come to have desires and interests. As a zygote, however, it does not have desires, nor even the *capacity* for having desires. What about interests? This depends upon the

account one offers of the relationship between desires and interests. It seems to me that a zygote cannot properly be spoken of as a subject of interests. My reason is roughly this. What is in a thing's interest is a function of its present and future desires, both those it will actually have and those it could have. In the case of an entity that is not presently capable of any desires, its interest must be based entirely upon the satisfaction of future desires. Then, since the satisfaction of future desires presupposes the continued existence of the entity in question, anything which has an interest which is based upon the satisfaction of future desires must also have an interest in its own continued existence. Therefore, something which is not presently capable of having any desires at all—like a zygote—cannot have any interests at all unless it has an interest in its own continued existence. I shall argue shortly, however, that a zygote cannot have such an interest. From this it will follow that it cannot have any interests at all, and this conclusion, together with the interest principle, entails that not all members of the species *Homo sapiens* have a right to life.

The interest principle involves, then, a thesis concerning a necessary condition which something must satisfy if it is to have a right to life, and it is a thesis which has important moral implications. It implies, for example, that abortions, if performed sufficiently early, do not involve any violation of a right to life. But on the other hand, the interest principle provides no help with the question of the moral status of human organisms once they have developed to the point where they do have desires, and thus are capable of having interests. The interest principle states that they *can* have rights. It does not state whether they *do* have rights—including, in particular, a right not to be destroyed.

It is possible, however, that the interest principle does not exhaust the conceptual connections between rights and interests. It formulates only a very general connection: a thing cannot have any rights at all unless it is capable of having at least some interest. May there not be more specific connections, between particular rights and particular sorts of interests? The following line of thought lends plausibility to this suggestion. Consider animals such as cats. Some philosophers are inclined to hold that animals such as cats do not have any rights at all. But let us assume, for the purpose of the present discussion, that cats do have some rights, such as a right not to be tortured, and consider the following claim:

(3)   A cat does not have a right to a university education.

How is this statement to be regarded? In particular, is it comparable in status to the claim that children do not have a right to smoke, or, instead, to the claim that newspapers do not have a right not to be torn up? To the latter, surely. Just as a newspaper is not the sort of thing that can have any rights at all, including a right not to be destroyed, so one is inclined to say that a cat, though it may have some rights, such as a right not to be tortured, is not the sort of thing that can possibly have a right to a university education.

This intuitive judgment about the status of claims such as (3) is reinforced, moreover, if one turns to the question of the grounds of the interest principle. Consider, for example, the account offered by Feinberg, which he summarizes as follows:

> Now we can extract from our discussion of animal rights a crucial principle for tentative use in the resolution of the other riddles about the applicability of the concept of a right, namely, that the sorts of beings who *can* have rights are precisely those who have (or can have) interests. I have come to this tentative conclusion for two reasons: (1) because a right holder must be capable of being represented and it is impossible to represent a being that has no interests, and (2) because a right holder must be capable of being a beneficiary in his own person, and a being without interests is a being that is incapable of being harmed or benefited, having no good or 'sake' of its own. Thus a being without interests has no 'behalf' to act in, and no 'sake' to act for.[9]

If this justification of the interest principle is sound, it can also be employed to support principles connecting particular rights with specific sorts of interests. Just as one cannot represent a being that has no interests at all, so one cannot, in demanding a university education for a cat, be representing the cat unless one is thereby representing some interest that the cat has, and that would be served by its receiving a university education. Similarly, one cannot be acting for the sake of a cat in arguing that it should receive a university education unless the

cat has some interest that will thereby be furthered. The conclusion, therefore, is that if Feinberg's defense of the interest principle is sound, other more specific principles must also be correct. These more specific principles can be summed up, albeit somewhat vaguely, by the following *particular-interests principle:*

> It is a conceptual truth that an entity cannot have a particular right, R, unless it is at least capable of having some interest, I, which is furthered by its having right R.

Given this particular-interests principle, certain familiar facts, whose importance has not often been appreciated, become comprehensible. Compare an act of killing a normal adult human being with an act of torturing one for five minutes. Though both acts are seriously wrong, they are not equally so. Here, as in most cases, to violate an individual's right to life is more seriously wrong than to violate his right not to have pain inflicted upon him. Consider, however, the corresponding actions in the case of a newborn kitten. Most people feel that it is seriously wrong to torture a kitten for five minutes, but not to kill it painlessly. How is this difference in the moral ordering of the two types of acts, between the human case and the kitten case, to be explained? One answer is that while normal adult human beings have both a right to life and a right not to be tortured, a kitten has only the latter. But why should this be so? The particular-interests principle suggests a possible explanation. Though kittens have some interests, including, in particular, an interest in not being tortured, which derives from their capacity to feel pain, they do not have an interest in their own continued existence, and hence do not have a right not to be destroyed. This answer contains, of course, a large promissory element. One needs a defense of the view that kittens have no interest in continued existence. But the point here is simply that there is an important question about the rationale underlying the moral ordering of certain sorts of acts, and that the particular-interests principle points to a possible answer.

This fact lends further plausibility, I believe, to the particular-interests principle. What one would ultimately like to do, of course, is to set out an analysis of the concept of a right, show that the analysis is indeed satisfactory, and then show that the particular-interests principle is entailed by the analysis. Unfortunately, it will not be possible to pursue such an approach here, since formulating an acceptable analysis of the concept of a right is a far from trivial matter. What I should like to do, however, is to touch briefly upon the problem of providing such an analysis, and then to indicate the account that seems to me most satisfactory—an account which does entail the particular-interests principle.

It would be widely agreed, I believe, both that rights impose obligations, and that the obligations they impose upon others are *conditional* upon certain factors. The difficulty arises when one attempts to specify what the obligations are conditional upon. There seem to be two main views in this area. According to the one, rights impose obligations that are conditional upon the interests of the possessor of the right. To say that Sandra has a right to something is thus to say, roughly, that if it is in Sandra's interest to have that thing, then others are under an obligation not to deprive her of it. According to the second view, rights impose obligations that are conditional upon the right's not having been waived. To say that Sandra has a right to something is to say, roughly, that if Sandra has not given others permission to take the thing, then they are under an obligation not to deprive her of it.

Both views encounter serious difficulties. On the one hand, in the case of minors, and nonhuman animals, it would seem that the obligations that rights impose must be taken as conditional upon the interests of those individuals, rather than upon whether they have given one permission to do certain things. On the other, in the case of individuals who are capable of making informed and rational decisions, if that person has not given one permission to take something that belongs to him, it would seem that one is, in general, still under an obligation not to deprive him of it, even if having that thing is no longer in his interest.

As a result, it seems that a more complex account is needed of the factors upon which the obligations imposed by rights are conditional. The account which I now prefer, and which I have defended elsewhere,[10] is this:

A has a right to X

means the same as

A is such that it can be in A's interest to have X, and *either* (1) A is not capable of making an informed and rational choice whether

to grant others permission to deprive him of X, in which case, if it is in A's interest not to be deprived of X, then, by that fact alone, others are under a prima facie obligation not to deprive A of X, *or* (2) A is capable of making an informed and rational choice whether to grant others permission to deprive him of X, in which case others are under a prima facie obligation not to deprive A of X if and only if A has not granted them permission to do so.

And if this account, or something rather similar, is correct, then so is the particular-interests principle.

What I now want to do is to apply the particular-interests principle to the case of the right to life. First, however, one needs to notice that the expression "right to life" is not entirely happy, since it suggests that the right in question concerns the continued existence of a biological organism. That this is incorrect can be brought out by considering possible ways of violating an individual's right to life. Suppose, for example, that future technological developments make it possible to change completely the neural networks in a brain, and that the brain of some normal adult human being is thus completely reprogrammed, so that the organism in question winds up with memories (or rather, apparent memories), beliefs, attitudes, and personality traits totally different from those associated with it before it was subjected to reprogramming. (The pope is programmed, say, on the model of Bertrand Russell.) In such a case, however beneficial the change might be, one would surely want to say that *someone* had been destroyed, that an adult human being's right to life had been violated, even though no biological organism had been killed. This shows that the expression "right to life" is misleading, since what one is concerned about is not just the continued existence of a biological organism.

How, then, might the right in question be more accurately described? A natural suggestion is that the expression "right to life" refers to the right of a subject of experiences and other mental states to continue to exist. It might be contended, however, that this interpretation begs the question against certain possible views. For someone might hold—and surely some people in fact do—that while continuing subjects of experiences and other mental states certainly have a right to life, so do some other organisms that are only potentially such continuing subjects, such as human fetuses. A right to life, on this view, is *either* the right of a subject of experiences to continue to exist, *or* the right of something that is only potentially a continuing subject of experiences to become such an entity.

This view is, I believe, to be rejected, for at least two reasons. In the first place, this view appears to be clearly incompatible with the interest principle, as well as with the particular-interests principle. Secondly, this position entails that the destruction of potential persons is, in general, prima facie seriously wrong, and I shall argue, in the next section, that the latter view is incorrect.

Let us consider, then, the right of a subject of experiences and other mental states to continue to exist. The particular-interests principle implies that something cannot possibly have such a right unless its continued existence can be in its interest. We need to ask, then, what must be the case if the continued existence of something is to be in its interest.

It will help to focus our thinking, I believe, if we consider a crucial case, stressed by Derek Parfit. Imagine a human baby that has developed to the point of being sentient, and of having simple desires, but that is not yet capable of having any desire for continued existence. Suppose, further, that the baby will enjoy a happy life, and will be glad that it was not destroyed. Can we or can we not say that it is in the baby's interest not to be destroyed?

To approach this case, let us consider a closely related one, namely, that of a human embryo that has not developed sufficiently far to have any desires, or even any states of consciousness at all, but that will develop into an individual who will enjoy a happy life, and who will be glad that his mother did not have an abortion. Can we or can we not say that it is the embryo's interest not to be destroyed?

Why might someone be tempted to say that it is in the embryo's interest not to be destroyed? One line of thought which, I believe, tempts some people is this. Let Mary be an individual who enjoys a happy life. Then, though some philosophers have expressed serious doubts about this, it might very well be said that it was certainly in Mary's interest that a certain embryo was not destroyed several years earlier. And this claim, together with the tendency to use expressions such as "Mary before she was born" to refer to the embryo in question, may

lead one to think that it was in the embryo's interest not to be destroyed. But this way of thinking involves conceptual confusion. A subject of interests, in the relevant sense of "interest," must necessarily be a subject of conscious states, including experiences and desires. This means that in identifying Mary with the embryo, and attributing to it her interest in its earlier nondestruction, one is treating the embryo as if it were itself a subject of consciousness. But by hypothesis, the embryo being considered has not developed to the point where there is any subject of consciousness associated with it. It cannot, therefore, have any interests at all, and *a fortiori*, it cannot have any interest in its own continued existence.

Let us now return to the first case—that of a human baby that is sentient, and which has simple desires, but which is not yet capable of having more complex desires, such as a desire for its own continued existence. Given that it will develop into an individual who will lead a happy life, and who will be glad that the baby was not destroyed, does one want to say that the baby's not being destroyed is in the baby's own interest?

Again, the following line of thought may seem initially tempting. If Mary is the resulting individual, then it was in Mary's interest that the baby not have been destroyed. But the baby *is* Mary when she was young. So it must have been in the baby's interest that it not have been destroyed.

Indeed, this argument is considerably more tempting in the present case than in the former, since here there is something that is a subject of consciousness, and which it is natural to identify with Mary. I suggest, however, that when one reflects upon the case, it becomes clear that such an identification is justified only if certain further things are the case. Thus, on the one hand, suppose that Mary is able to remember quite clearly some of the experiences that the baby enjoyed. Given that sort of causal and psychological connection, it would seem perfectly reasonble to hold that Mary and the baby are one and the same subject of consciousness, and thus, that if it is in Mary's interest that the baby not have been destroyed, then this must also have been in the baby's interest. On the other hand, suppose that not only does Mary, at a much later time, not remember any of the baby's experiences, but the experiences in question are not psychologically linked, either via memory or in any other way, to mental states enjoyed by the human organism in question at *any* later time. Here it seems to me clearly incorrect to say that Mary and the baby are one and the same subject of consciousness, and therefore it cannot be correct to transfer, from Mary to the baby, Mary's interest in the baby's not having been destroyed.

Let us now return to the question of what must be the case if the continued existence of something is to be in [its] own interest. The picture that emerges from the two cases just discussed is this. In the first place, nothing at all can be in an entity's interest unless it has desires at some time or other. But more than this is required if the continued existence of the entity is to be in its own interest. One possibility, which will generally be sufficient, is that the individual have, at the time in question, a desire for its own continued existence. Yet it also seems clear that an individual's continued existence can be in its own interest even when such a desire is not present. What is needed, apparently, is that the continued existence of the individual will make possible the satisfaction of some desires existing at other times. But not just any desires existing at other times will do. Indeed, as is illustrated both by the case of the baby just discussed, and by the deprogramming/reprogramming example, it is not even sufficient that they be desires associated with the same physical organism. It is crucial that they be desires that belong to one and the same subject of consciousness.

The critical question, then, concerns the conditions under which desires existing at different times can be correctly attributed to a single, continuing subject of consciousness. This question raises a number of difficult issues which cannot be considered here. Part of the rationale underlying the view I wish to advance will be clear, however, if one considers the role played by memory in the psychological unity of an individual over time. When I remember a past experience, what I know is not merely that there was a certain experience which someone or other had, but that there was an experience that belonged to the *same* individual as the present memory beliefs, and it seems clear that this feature of one's memories is, in general, a crucial part of what it is that makes one a continuing subject of experiences, rather than merely a series of

psychologically isolated, momentary subjects of consciousness. This suggests something like the following principle:

> Desires existing at different times can belong to a single, continuing subject of consciousness only if that subject of consciousness possesses, at some time, the concept of a continuing self or mental substance.[11]

Given this principle, together with the particular-rights principle, one can set out the following argument in support of a claim concerning a necessary condition which an entity must satisfy if it is to have a right to life:

(1) The concept of a right is such that an individual cannot have a right at time *t* to continued existence unless the individual is such that it can be in its interest at time *t* that it continue to exist.

(2) The continued existence of a given subject of consciousness cannot be in that individual's interest at time *t* unless *either* that individual has a desire, at time *t*, to continue to exist as a subject of consciousness, *or* that individual can have desires at other times.

(3) An individual cannot have a desire to continue to exist as a subject of consciousness unless it possesses the concept of a continuing self or mental substance.

(4) An individual existing at one time cannot have desires at other times unless there is at least one time at which it possesses the concept of a continuing self or mental substance.

Therefore:

(5) An individual cannot have a right to continued existence unless there is at least one time at which it possesses the concept of a continuing self or mental substance.

This conclusion is obviously significant. But precisely what implications does it have with respect to the morality of abortion and infanticide? The answer will depend upon what relationship there is between, on the one hand, the behavioral and neurophysiological development of a human being, and, on the other, the development of that individual's mind. Some people believe that there is no relationship at all. They believe that a human mind, with all its mature capacities, is present in a human from conception onward, and so is there before the brain has even begun to develop, and before the individual has begun to exhibit behavior expressive of higher mental functioning. Most philosophers, however, reject this view. They believe, on the one hand, that there is, in general, a rather close relation between an individual's behavioral capacities and its mental functioning, and, on the other, that there is a very intimate relationship between the mind and the brain. As regards the latter, some philosophers hold that the mind is in fact identical with the brain. Others maintain that the mind is distinct from the brain, but causally dependent upon it. In either case, the result is a view according to which the development of the mind and the brain are necessarily closely tied to one another.

If one does adopt the view that there is a close relation between the behavioral and neurophysiological development of a human being and the development of its mind, then the above conclusion has a very important, and possibly decisive implication with respect to the morality of abortion and infanticide. For when human development, both behavioral and neurophysiological, is closely examined, it is seen to be most unlikely that human fetuses, or even newborn babies, possess any concept of a continuing self.[12] And in the light of the above conclusion, this means that such individuals do not possess a right to life.

But is it reasonable to hold that there is a close relation between human behavioral and neurophysiological development and the development of the human mind? Approached from a scientific perspective, I believe that there is excellent reason for doing so. Consider, for example, what is known about how, at later stages, human mental capacities proceed in step with brain development, or what is known about how damage to different parts of the brain can affect, in different ways, an individual's intellectual capacities.

Why, then, do some people reject the view that there is a close relationship between the development of the human mind and the behavioral and neurophysiological development of human beings? There are, I think, two main reasons. First, some philosophers believe that the scientific evidence is irrelevant, because they believe that it is possible to establish, by means of a purely metaphysical

argument, that a human mind, with its mature capacities, is present in a human from conception onward. I have argued elsewhere that the argument in question is unsound.[13]

Secondly, and more commonly, some people appeal to the idea that it is a divinely revealed truth that human beings have minds from conception onward. There are a number of points to be made about such an appeal. In the first place, the belief that a mind, or soul, is infused into a human body at conception by God is not an essential belief within many of the world religions. Secondly, even within religious traditions, such as Roman Catholicism, where that belief is a very common one, it is by no means universally accepted. Thus, for example, the well-known Catholic philosopher Joseph Donceel has argued very strongly for the claim that the correct position on the question of ensoulment is that the soul enters the body only when the human brain has undergone a sufficient process of development.[14] Thirdly, there is the question of whether it is reasonable to accept the religious outlook which is being appealed to in support of the contention that humans have minds which are capable of higher intellectual activities from conception onward. This question raises very large issues in philosophy of religion which cannot be pursued here. But it should at least be said that many contemporary philosophers who have reflected upon religious beliefs have come to the view that there is not sufficient reason even for believing in the existence of God, let alone for accepting the much more detailed religious claims which are part of a religion such as Christianity. Finally, suppose that one nonetheless decides to accept the contention that it is a divinely revealed truth that humans have, from conception onward, minds that are capable of higher mental activities, and that one appeals to this purported revelation in order to support the claim that all humans have a right to life. One needs to notice that if one then goes on to argue, not merely that abortion is morally wrong, but that there should be a law against it, one will encounter a very serious objection. For it is surely true that it is inappropriate, at least in a pluralistic society, to appeal to specific religious beliefs of a nonmoral sort—such as the belief that God infuses souls into human bodies at conception—in support of legislation that will be binding upon everyone, including those who either accept different religious beliefs, or none at all.

III. Summary and Conclusions

In this paper I have advanced three main philosophical contentions:

(1) An entity cannot have a right to life unless it is capable of having an interest in its own continued existence.

(2) An entity is not capable of having an interest in its own continued existence unless it possesses, at some time, the concept of a continuing self, or subject of experiences and other mental states.

(3) The fact that an entity will, if not destroyed, come to have properties that would give it a right to life does not in itself make it seriously wrong to destroy it.[15]

If these philosophical contentions are correct, the crucial question is a factual one: At what point does a developing human being acquire the concept of a continuing self, and at what point is it capable of having an interest in its own continued existence? I have not examined this issue in detail here, but I have suggested that careful scientific studies of human development, both behavioral and neurophysiological, strongly support the view that even newborn humans do not have the capacities in question. If this is right, then it would seem that infanticide during a time interval shortly after birth must be viewed as morally acceptable.

But where is the line to be drawn? What is the precise cutoff point? If one maintained, as some philosophers do, that an individual can possess a concept only if it is capable of expressing that concept linguistically, then it would be a relatively simple matter to determine whether a given organism possessed the concept of a continuing subject of experiences and other mental states. It is far from clear, however, that this claim about the necessary connection between the possession of concepts and the having of linguistic capabilities is correct. I would argue, for example, that one wants to ascribe mental states of a conceptual sort—such as beliefs and desires—to animals that are incapable of learning a language, and that an individual cannot have beliefs and desires unless it possesses the concepts involved in those beliefs and desires. And if that view is right—if an organism can acquire concepts without thereby acquiring a way of expressing those concepts linguistically—then the question of whether an individual possesses the concept of a continuing self may be one that requires quite subtle experimental techniques to answer.

If this view of the matter is roughly correct, there are two worries that one is left with at the level of practical moral decisions, one of which may turn out to be deeply disturbing. The lesser worry is the question just raised: Where is the line to be drawn in the case of infanticide? This is not really a troubling question since there is no serious need to know the exact point at which a human infant acquires a right to life. For in the vast majority of cases in which infanticide is desirable due to serious defects from which the baby suffers, its desirability will be apparent at birth or within a very short time thereafter. Since it seems clear that an infant at this point in its development is not capable of possessing the concept of a continuing subject of experiences and other mental states, and so is incapable of having an interest in its own continued existence, infanticide will be morally permissible in the vast majority of cases in which it is, for one reason or another, desirable. The practical moral problem can thus be satisfactorily handled by choosing some short period of time, such as a week after birth, as the interval during which infanticide will be permitted.

The troubling issue which arises out of the above reflections concerns whether adult animals belonging to species other than *Homo sapiens* may not also possess a right to life. For once one allows that an individual can possess concepts, and have beliefs and desires, without being able to express those concepts, or those beliefs and desires, linguistically, then it becomes very much an open question whether animals belonging to other species do not possess properties that give them a right to life. Indeed, I am strongly inclined to think that adult members of at least some nonhuman species do have a right to life. My reason is that, first I believe that some nonhuman animals are capable of envisaging a future for themselves, and of having desires about future states of themselves. Secondly, that anything which exercises these capacities has an interest in its own continued existence. And thirdly, that having an interest in one's own continued existence is not merely a necessary, but also a sufficient, condition for having a right to life.

The suggestion that at least some nonhuman animals have a right to life is not unfamiliar, but it is one that most of us are accustomed to dismissing very casually. The line of thought advanced here suggests that this attitude may very well turn out to be tragically mistaken. Once one reflects upon the question of the *basic* moral principles involved in the ascription of a right to life to organisms, one may find oneself driven to the conclusion that our everyday treatment of members of other species is morally indefensible, and that we are in fact murdering innocent persons.

Notes

1. My forthcoming book, *Abortion and Infanticide*, contains a detailed examination of other important objections.

2. Judith Jarvis Thomson, in her article "A Defense of Abortion," *Philosophy & Public Affairs*, vol. 1, no. 1, 1971, pp. 47–66, argues very forcefully for the view that this conclusion is incorrect. For a critical discussion of her argument, see Chapter 3 of *Abortion and Infanticide*.

3. Section 230.3 of the American Law Institute's *Model Penal Code* (Philadelphia, 1962).

4. *Abortion and Infanticide*, Chapter 10.

5. Editor's note: Followers of the Harvard philosopher Willard van Orman Quine.

6. In *Philosophy and Environmental Crisis*, edited by William T. Blackstone (Athens, Georgia, 1974), pp. 43–68.

7. Ibid., p. 51.

8. Ibid., pp. 49–50.

9. Ibid., p. 51.

10. *Abortion and Infanticide*, section 5.2.

11. For a fuller discussion, and defense of this principle, see *Abortion and Infanticide*, section 5.3.

12. For a detailed survey of the scientific evidence concerning human development, see *Abortion and Infanticide*, section 11.5.

13. *Abortion and Infanticide*, section 11.42.

14. For a brief discussion, see Joseph F. Donceel, "A Liberal Catholic's View," in *Abortion in a Changing World*, Volume I, edited by R. E. Hall, New York, 1970 [*supra*, pp. 15–20]. A more detailed philosophical discussion can be found in Donceel's "Immediate Animation and Delayed Hominization," *Theological Studies*, Volume 31, 1970, pp. 76–105.

15. Editor's note: Readers wishing to sample Tooley's arguments for this contention, which have been deleted here, are referred to Tooley's original article in *Philosophy & Public Affairs*, vol. 2, no. 1 (Fall 1972), or his forthcoming book.

Questions for Analysis

1. *How can infanticide shed light on the abortion question?*

2. *Why does Tooley consider infanticide an interesting and important question by itself?*

3. *How is the "interest principle" used in distinguishing between entities that have rights and those that don't?*

4. *What does Tooley mean by "particular-interests principle"?*

5. *Tooley states, "The particular-interests principle implies that something cannot possibly have such a right [to life] unless its continued existence can be in its interest." What, in his view, must be the case if the continued existence of something is to be in its own interest?*

6. *What response does Tooley make to the question "At what point does a developing human being acquire the concept of a continuing self, and at what point is it capable of having an interest in its own continued existence?"*

7. *Why does Tooley believe that adult members of at least some nonhuman species have a right to life?*

8. *How do you think a natural-law theorist would respond to Tooley? Do you think that an interpretation of Kant's ethics could provide any support for Tooley's analysis?*

Abortion: Law, Choice, and Morality

Daniel Callahan

Philosopher Daniel Callahan's viewpoint regarding the status of the fetus is positioned somewhere between the two extremes of Noonan and Tooley. In Callahan's view, as developed in his book Abortion: Law, Choice and Morality, *the unborn is neither just a mass of protoplasm nor a full-fledged person. As a result, Callahan believes it is equally improper to deny the fetus any moral status or to assign it full moral status.*

Essentially, Callahan believes that an abortion choice is a private choice: Individuals ought to be allowed to make their own decisions. But he quickly points out that a legal freedom to choose does not dissolve the serious moral questions that an abortion choice always raises.

The thrust of Callahan's essay, therefore, addresses the question of how a woman ought to go about making an abortion choice, if her action is to be considered moral. He isolates a number of factors to consider in any serious and responsible evaluation of an abortion choice: the biological evidence, the philosophical assumptions implied in the term human, *a philosophical theory of biological analysis, the social consequences of the different analyses of and the meaning of the word* human, *and consistency of meaning and use. He especially warns against making a personal choice easy either through intellectual ignorance or by appeal to personal convenience.*

In the last analysis, Callahan suggests that the woman who faces an abortion choice keep foremost in mind the sanctity of life and the fact that abortion always involves a violation of that sanctity. In that way she will remain sensitive to the moral gravity of an abortion decision and weigh her reasons for wanting an abortion accordingly.

The strength of pluralistic societies lies in the personal freedom they afford individuals. One is free to choose among religious, philosophical, ideological, and political creeds; or one can create one's own highly personal, idiosyncratic moral code and view of the universe. Increasingly, the individual is free to ignore the morals, manners and mores of society. The only limitations are upon those actions which seem to present clear and present dangers to the common good, and even there the range of prohibited actions is diminishing as more and more choices are left to personal and private decisions. I have contended that, apart from some regulatory laws, abortion decisions should be left, finally, up to the women themselves. Whatever one may think of the morality of abortion, it cannot be established that it poses a clear and present danger to the common good. Thus society does not have the right decisively to interpose itself between a woman and the abortion she wants. It can only intervene where it can be shown that some of its own interests are at stake *qua* society. Regulatory laws of a minimal kind therefore seem in order, since in a variety of ways already mentioned society will be affected by the number, kind, and quality of legal abortions. In short, with a few important stipulations, what I have been urging is tantamount to saying that abortion decisions should be private decisions. It is to accept, in principle, the contention of those who believe that, in a free, pluralistic society, the woman should be allowed to make her own moral choice on abortion and be allowed to implement that choice.

But pluralistic societies also lay a few traps for the unwary. It is not a large psychological step from saying that individuals should be left free to make up their own minds on some crucial moral issues (of which abortion is one) to an adoption of the view that one personal decision is as good as another, that any decision is a good one as long as it is honest or sincere, that a free decision equals a correct decision. However short the psychological step, the logical gap is very large. An absence of cant, hypocrisy and coercion may prepare the way for good personal decisions. But that is only to clean the room, and something must then be put in it. The hazard is that, once cleaned, it will be filled with capriciousness, sentimentality, a thinly disguised conformity to the reigning moral taste, or strongly felt but inadequately analyzed moral opinions. This is a particular danger in affluent pluralistic societies, heavily dominated by popular tastes, communication media and the absence of shared values. Philosophically, the view that all values are equally good and all private moral choices on a par is all but dead; but it still has a strong life at the popular level, where there is a tendency to act as if, once personal freedom is legally and socially achieved, moral questions cease to exist.

A considerable quantity of literature exists in the field of ethics concerned with such problems as subjective and objective values, the meaning and use of ethical principles and moral rules, the role of intentionality. That literature need not be reviewed here. But it is directly to the point to observe that a particular failing of the abortion-on-request literature is that it persistently scants the moral problem of how a woman, if granted the desired legal freedom to make her own decision about abortion, should go about making that decision. Up to a point, this deficiency is understandable. The immediate tactical problem has been to get the laws changed or repealed; that has been the burden of the public struggle, which has concentrated on statutes and legislators rather than on the moral contents and problems of personal decision-making. It is reasonable and legitimate to say that a woman should be left free to make the decision in the light of her own personal values; that is, I believe, the best legal solution. But it leaves totally untouched the question of how, once freedom is achieved, she ought to go about the personal business of forming a coherent, rational, sensitive moral perspective and opinion on abortion. After freedom, what then? Society may have no right to demand that a woman give it good reasons why she should have an abortion before permitting it. But this does not entail that the woman should not, as a morally responsible person, have good reasons to justify her desires or acts in her own eyes.

This is only to say that a solution of the legal problem is not the same as a solution to the moral problem. That the moral struggle is transferred from the public to the private sphere should not be taken to mean that the moral problem has been solved; only its public aspect, under a permissive law or a repeal of all laws, has been dealt with. The personal problem will remain.

Some women will be part of a religious group or ethical tradition which they freely choose and which can offer them something, possibly very much, in the way of helpful moral insight consistent with that tradition. The obvious course in that instance is for them to turn to their tradition to see what it has to offer them on the particular problem of abortion. But what of those who have no tradition to repair to or those who find their tradition wanting on this problem? One way or another, they will have to find some way of developing a set of ethical principles and moral rules to help them act responsibly, to justify their own conduct in their own eyes. To press the problem to a finer point, what ought they to think about as they try to work out their own views on abortion?

Only a few suggestions will be made here, taking the form of arguing for an ethic of personal responsibility which tries, in the process of decision-making, to make itself aware of a number of things. The biological evidence should be considered, just as the problem of methodology must be considered; the philosophical assumptions implicit in different uses of the word "human" need to be considered; a philosophical theory of biological analysis is required; the social consequences of different kinds of analyses and different meanings of the word "human" should be thought through; consistency of meaning and use should be sought to avoid *ad hoc* and arbitrary solutions.

It is my own conviction that the "developmental school" offers the most helpful and illuminating approach to the problem of the beginning of human life, avoiding, on the one hand, a too narrow genetic criterion of human life and, on the other, a too broad and socially dangerous social definition of the "human." Yet the kinds of problems which appear in any attempt to decide upon the beginning of life suggest that no one position can be either proved or disproved from biological evidence alone. It becomes a question of trying to do justice to the evidence while, at the same time, realizing that how the evidence is approached and used will be a function of one's way of looking at reality, one's moral policy, the values and rights one believes need balancing, and the type of questions one thinks need to be asked. At the very least, however, the genetic evidence for the uniqueness of zygotes and embryos (a uniqueness of a different kind than that of the uniqueness of sperm and ova), their potentiality for development into a human person, their early development of human characteristics, their genetic and organic distinctness from the organism of the mother, appear to rule out a treatment even of zygotes, much less the more developed stages of the conceptus, as mere pieces of "tissue," of no human significance or value. The "tissue" theory of the significance of the conceptus can only be made plausible by a systematic disregard of the biological evidence. Moreover, though one may conclude that a conceptus is only potential human life, in the process of continually actualizing its potential through growth and development, a respect for the sanctity of life, with its bias in favor even of undeveloped life, is enough to make the taking of such life a moral problem. There is a choice to be made and it is a moral choice. In the near future, it is likely that some kind of simple, safe abortifacient drug will be developed, which either prevents implantation or destroys the conceptus before it can develop. It will be tempting then to think that the moral dilemma has vanished, but I do not believe it will have.

It is possible to imagine a huge number of situations where a woman could, in good and sensitive conscience, choose abortion as a moral solution to her personal or social difficulties. But, at the very least, the bounds of morality are overstepped when either through a systematic intellectual negligence or a willful choosing of that moral solution most personally convenient, personal choice is deliberately made easy and problem-free. Yet it seems to me that a pressure in that direction is a growing part of the ethos of technological societies; it is easily possible to find people to reassure us that we need have no scruples about the way we act, whether the issue is war, the suppression of rebellion and revolution, discrimination against minorities or the use of technological advances. Pluralism makes possible the achieving of freer, more subtle moral thinking; but it is a possibility constantly endangered by cultural pressures which would simplify or dissolve moral doubts and anguish.

The question of abortion "indications" returns at the level of personal choice. I have contended that the advent of permissive laws should not mean a cessation of efforts to explore the problem of "indications." When a woman asks herself, as she ought, whether her reasons for wanting an abortion are sound reasons—which presumes abortion is a serious enough moral issue to warrant the need to provide oneself with good reasons for choosing it—she will be asking herself about justifiable indications. Thus, transposed from the legal to the personal level, the kinds of concerns adumbrated in the earlier chapters on indications remain fully pertinent. It was argued in those chapters that, with the possible exception of exceedingly rare instances of a direct threat to the physical life of the mother, one cannot speak of general categories of abortion indications as *necessitating* an abortion. In a number of circumstances, abortion may be a wise and justifiable solution to a distressed pregnancy. But when the language of necessity is used, the implication is that no other conceivable alternative is available. It may be granted, willingly enough, that some set of practical circumstances in some (possibly very many) concrete cases may indicate that abortion is the only feasible option open. But these cases cannot readily be determined in advance, and, for that reason, it is necessary to say that no formal indication as such (e.g., a psychiatric indication) entails a necessary, predetermined choice in favor of abortion.

The word "indication" remains the best word, suggesting that a number of given circumstances will bring the possibility or desirability of abortion to the fore. But to escalate the concept of an indication into that of a required procedure is to go too far. Abortion is *one* way to solve the problem of an unwanted or hazardous pregnancy (physically, psychologically, economically or socially), but it is rarely the only way, at least in affluent societies (I would be considerably less certain about making the same statement about poor societies). Even in the most extreme cases—rape, incest, psychosis, for instance—alternatives will usually be available and different choices open. It is not necessarily the end of every woman's chance for a happy, meaningful life to bear an illegitimate child. It is not necessarily the automatic destruction of a family to have a seriously defective child born into it. It is not necessarily the ruination of every family living in overcrowded housing to have still another child. It is not inevitable that every immature woman would become even more so if she bore a child or another child. It is not inevitable that a gravely handicapped child can hope for nothing from life. It is not inevitable that every unwanted child is doomed to misery. It is not written in the essence of things, as a fixed law of human nature, that a woman cannot come to accept, love and be a good mother to a child who was initially unwanted. Nor is it a fixed law that she could not come to cherish a grossly deformed child. Naturally, these are only generalizations. The point is only that human beings are as a rule flexible, capable of doing more than they sometimes think they can, able to surmount serious dangers and challenges, able to grow and mature, able to transform inauspicious beginnings into satisfactory conclusions. Everything in life, even in procreative and family life, is not fixed in advance; the future is never wholly unalterable.

Yet the problem of personal question-asking must be pushed a step farther. The way the questions are answered will be very much determined by a woman's way of looking at herself and at life. A woman who has decided, as a personal moral policy, that nothing should be allowed to stand in the way of her own happiness, goals and self-interest will have no trouble solving the moral problem. For her, an unwanted pregnancy will, by definition, be a pregnancy to be terminated. But only by a Pickwickian use of words could this form of reasoning be called moral. It would preclude any need to consult the opinion of others, any need to exam-

ine the validity of one's own viewpoint, any need to, for instance, ask when human life begins, any need to interrogate oneself in any way, intellectually or morally; will and desire would be king.

Assuming, however, that most women would seek a broader ethical horizon than that of their exclusively personal self-interest, what might they think about when faced with an abortion decision? A respect for the sanctity of human life should, I believe, incline them toward a general and strong bias against abortion. Abortion is an act of killing, the violent, direct destruction of potential human life, already in the process of development. That fact should not be disguised, or glossed over by euphemism and circumlocution. It is not the destruction of a human person—for at no stage of its development does the conceptus fulfill the definition of a person, which implies a developed capacity for reasoning, willing, desiring and relating to others—but it is the destruction of an important and valuable form of human life. Its value and its potentiality are not dependent upon the attitude of the woman toward it; it grows by its own biological dynamism and has a genetic and morphological potential distinct from that of the woman. It has its own distinctive and individual future. If contraception and abortion are both seen as forms of birth limitation, they are distinctly different acts; the former precludes the possibility of a conceptus being formed, while the latter stops a conceptus already in existence from developing. The bias implied by the principle of the sanctity of human life is toward the protection of all forms of human life, especially, in ordinary circumstances, the protection of the right to life. That right should be accorded even to doubtful life; its existence should not be wholly dependent upon the personal self-interest of the woman.

Yet she has her own rights as well, and her own set of responsibilities to those around her; that is why she may have to choose abortion. In extreme situations of overpopulation, she may also have a responsibility for the survival of the species or of a people. In many circumstances, then, a decision in favor of abortion—one which overrides the right to life of that potential human being she carries within—can be a responsible moral decision, worthy neither of the condemnation of others nor of self-condemnation. But the bias of the principle of the sanctity of life is against a routine, unthinking employment of abortion; it bends over backwards not to take life and gives the benefit of the doubt to life. It does not seek to diminish the range of responsibility toward life—potential or actual—but to extend it. It does not seek the narrowest definition of life, but the widest and the richest. It is mindful of individual possibility, on the one hand, and of a destructive human tendency, on the other, to exclude from the category of "the human" or deny rights to those beings whose existence is or could prove burdensome to others.

The language used to describe abortion will have an important bearing on the sensitivities and imagination of those women who must make abortion decisions. Abortion can be talked about in the language of medical technology and technique—as, say, "a therapeutic procedure involving the emptying of the uterine contents." That language is neutral, clinical, unemotional. Or abortion can be talked about in the emotive language of relieving woman from suffering, or meeting the need for freedom among women, or saving a nation from a devastating overpopulation. Both kinds of language have their place, for abortion has more than one result and meaning and abortion can legitimately be talked about in more than one way. What is objectionable is a conscious manipulation of language to incite an irrational emotional response, to allay doubts or to mislead the imagination. Particularly misleading is one commonly employed mixture of rhetorical modes by advocates of abortion on request. That is the use of a detached, clinical language to describe the actual operation itself combined with an emotive rhetoric to evoke the personal and social goods which an abortion can bring about. Thus, when every effort is made to suggest that emotion and feeling are perfectly appropriate to describe the social and personal goals of abortion, but that a clinical language only is appropriate when the actual technique and medical objective of an abortion are described, then the moral imagination is being misled.

Any human act can be described in impersonal, technological language, just as any act can be described in emotive language. What is wanted is an equity in the language. It is fair enough and to the point to say that in many circumstances abortion will save a woman's health or her family. It only becomes misleading when the act itself, as distinguished from its therapeutic goal, is talked

about in an entirely different way. For abortion is not just an "emptying of the uterine contents." It is also an act of killing; there will be no abortion unless the conceptus is killed (or its further existence made impossible, which amounts to the same thing). If it is appropriate to evoke the imagination and elicit sympathy for those women in a distressed pregnancy who could be helped by abortion, it is no less appropriate to evoke the imagination about what actually occurs in an abortion "procedure."

Imagination should also come into play at another point. It is often argued by proponents of abortion that there is no need for a woman ever to take any chances in a distressed pregnancy, particularly in the instance of an otherwise healthy woman who, if she has an abortion on one occasion, could simply get pregnant again on another, more auspicious occasion. This might be termed the "replacement theory" of abortion indications: since fetus "x" can be replaced by fetus "y," then there is no reason why a woman should have any scruples about such a replacement. This way of conceiving the choices effectively dissolves them; it becomes important only to know whether a woman can get pregnant again when she wants to. But this strategy can be employed only at the price of convincing oneself that there is no difference whatever among embryos or fetuses, that they all have exactly the same potentiality. But even the sketchiest knowledge of the genetic uniqueness of each conceptus (save in the instance of monozygotic twins), and thus the different genetic potentialities of each, should raise doubts on that point. Yet, having said that, I would not want to deny that the possibility of a further pregnancy could have an important bearing on the moral reasoning of a woman whose present pregnancy was threatening. If, out of a sense of responsibility toward her present children or her present life situation, a woman decided that an abortion was the wisest, most moral course, then the possibility that she could become pregnant later, when these responsibilities would be less pressing, would be a pertinent consideration.

The goal of these remarks is to keep alive in the consciences of women who have an abortion choice a moral tension; and it is to hope that they will be willing to bear the pain and the uncertainty of having to make a moral choice. It is the automatic, unthinking and unimaginative personal solution of abortion questions which women themselves should be extremely wary of, either for or against an abortion. A woman can, with little trouble, find both people and books to reassure her that there is no problem about abortion at all; or people and books to convince her that she would be a moral monster if she chose abortion. A woman can choose in advance the views she will listen to and thus have her predispositions confirmed. Yet a willingness to keep alive a moral tension, and to be wary of precipitous solutions, presupposes two things. First, that the woman herself wants to do what is right, realizing that what is right may not always be that which is most convenient, most easy or most immediately apt to solve a pressing problem. It is simply not the case that what one wants to do, or would like to do, or is predisposed to do is necessarily the right thing to do. A willingness seriously to entertain that moral perception—which, of course, does not in itself imply a decision for or against abortion—is one sign of moral seriousness.

Second, moral seriousness presupposes one is concerned with the protection and furthering of life. This means that, out of respect for human life, one bends over backwards not to eliminate human life, not to desensitize oneself to the meaning and value of potential life, not to seek definitions of the "human" which serve one's self-interest only. A desire to respect human life in all of its forms means, therefore, that one voluntarily imposes upon oneself a pressure against the taking of life; that one demands of oneself serious reasons for doing so, even in the case of a very early embryo; that one use not only the mind but also the imagination when a decision is being made; that one seeks not to evade the moral issues but to face them; that one

searches out the alternatives and conscientiously entertains them before turning to abortion. A bias in favor of the sanctity of human life in all of its forms would include a bias against abortion on the part of women; it would be the last rather than the first choice when unwanted pregnancies occurred. It would be an act to be avoided if at all possible.

A bias of this kind, voluntarily imposed by a woman upon herself, would not trap her; for it is also part of a respect for the dignity of life to leave the way open for an abortion when other reasonable choices are not available. For she also has duties toward herself, her family and her society. There can be good reasons for taking the life even of a very late fetus; once that also is seen and seen as a counterpoise in particular cases to the general bias against the taking of potential life, the way is open to choose abortion. The bias of the moral policy implies the need for moral rules which seek to preserve life. But, as a policy which leaves room for choice—rather than entailing a fixed set of rules—it is open to flexible interpretation when the circumstances point to the wisdom of taking exception to the normal ordering of the rules in particular cases. Yet, in that case, one is not genuinely taking exception to the rules. More accurately, one would be deciding that, for the preservation or furtherance of other values or rights—species-rights, person-rights—a choice in favor of abortion would be serving the sanctity of life. That there would be, in that case, conflict between rights, with one set of rights set aside (reluctantly) to serve another set, goes without saying. A subversion of the principle occurs when it is made out that there is no conflict and thus nothing to decide.

Questions for Analysis

1. What does Callahan mean by a "pluralistic society"?

2. When are regulatory laws justifiable? Is this a utilitarian justification?

3. Callahan says ". . . a solution of the legal problem is not the same as a solution to the moral problem." What does this mean? How does it apply to an abortion choice?

4. What is the "tissue theory" and why does Callahan reject it?

5. *Callahan claims a woman's abortion decision will very much be determined by her way of looking at herself and at life. What does he mean, and do you agree?*

6. *In Callahan's view, are there any formal indications that entail a necessary choice in favor of an abortion? How does this view relate to his cautions about abortion decisions?*

7. *What does Callahan mean by keeping alive a "moral tension" in the conscience of a woman who faces an abortion choice?*

8. *Would it be accurate to say that Callahan considers some acts of abortion morally justifiable? If so, under what conditions would such abortions be justifiable?*

A Defense of Abortion

Judith Jarvis Thomson

Philosopher Judith Jarvis Thomson wrote this essay in 1971. It has since become a classic in the literature of abortion.

What makes her treatment of the pro-choice position unique is that it begins by conceding, for the sake of argument, that the fetus is a person from the moment of conception. This concession is significant because, as Thomson points out, most opposition to abortion builds on the assumption that the fetus has person status and rights from the moment of conception.

Thomson focuses her essay on an important question: Granted that the fetus is a person from the moment of conception, does it necessarily follow that abortion is always wrong? She thinks not. Relying primarily on a series of analogies, she attacks the argument that the immorality of abortion is entailed by the premise that asserts the person status of the fetus.

Toward the end of her essay, Thomson admits that anti-abortionists might object that the immorality of abortion follows not so much from the fact that the fetus is a person as from the special relationship between the fetus and the mother. Thus, anti-abortionists claim that the fetus is a person for whom the woman has a unique kind of responsibility because she is the mother.

In responding to this claim, Thomson argues that we have no responsibility for another person unless we have assumed it. If parents do not take any birth control measures, if they do not elect an abortion, if they choose to take the child home with them from the hospital, then certainly they have a responsibility to and for the child. For they then have assumed responsibility, implicitly and explicitly, in all their actions. But if a couple has taken measures to prevent conception, this implies quite the opposite of any "special responsibility" for the unintended and unwanted fetus. Thus, in Thomson's view, the woman has no special responsibility to the fetus simply because of a biological relationship.

Ironically, as Thomson points out, many pro-choice advocates object to her argument for a couple of reasons. First, while Thomson argues that abortion is not impermissible, she does not think that it is always permissible. There may be times, for example, when carrying the child to term requires only minimal inconvenience; in such cases the woman would be required by

From Judith Jarvis Thomson, "A Defense of Abortion," Philosophy and Public Affairs, 1, no. 1 (Fall 1971). Copyright© 1971 by Princeton University Press. Reprinted by permission of Princeton University Press. Ms. Thomson acknowledges her indebtedness to James Thomson for discussion, criticism, and many helpful suggestions.

"Minimally Decent Samaritanism" to have the child. Those supporting abortion on demand object to such a limitation of choice.

Second, while Thomson, like act utilitarians, would sanction some acts of abortion, she is not arguing for the right to kill the unborn child. That is, removing a nonviable fetus from the mother's body and thereby guaranteeing its death is not the same as removing a viable fetus from the mother's body and then killing it. In Thomson's view, the former may be permissible; the latter never is. Again, some pro-choice advocates object to this limitation of choice.

Most opposition to abortion relies on the premise that the fetus is a human being, a person, from the moment of conception. The premise is argued for, but, as I think, not well. Take, for example, the most common argument. We are asked to notice that the development of a human being from conception through birth into childhood is continuous; then it is said that to draw a line, to choose a point in this development and say "before this point the thing is not a person, after this point it is a person" is to make an arbitrary choice, a choice for which in the nature of things no good reason can be given. It is concluded that the fetus is, or anyway that we had better say it is, a person from the moment of conception. But this conclusion does not follow. Similar things might be said about the development of an acorn into an oak tree, and it does not follow that acorns are oak trees, or that we had better say they are. Arguments of this form are sometimes called "slippery slope arguments"—the phrase is perhaps self-explanatory—and it is dismaying that opponents of abortion rely on them so heavily and uncritically.

I am inclined to agree, however, that the prospects for "drawing a line" in the development of the fetus look dim. I am inclined to think also that we shall probably have to agree that the fetus has already become a human person well before birth. Indeed, it comes as a surprise when one first learns how early in its life it begins to acquire human characteristics. By the tenth week, for example, it already has a face, arms and legs, fingers and toes; it has internal organs, and brain activity is detectable.[1] On the other hand, I think that the premise is false, that the fetus is not a person from the moment of conception. A newly fertilized ovum, a newly implanted clump of cells, is no more a person than an acorn is an oak tree. But I shall not discuss any of this. For it seems to me to be of great interest to ask what happens if, for the sake of argument, we allow the premise. How, precisely, are we supposed to get from there to the conclusion that abortion is morally impermissible? Opponents of abortion commonly spend most of their time establishing that the fetus is a person, and hardly any time explaining the step from there to the impermissibility of abortion. Perhaps they think the step too simple and obvious to require much comment. Or perhaps instead they are simply being economical in argument. Many of those who defend abortion rely on the premise that the fetus is not a person, but only a bit of tissue that will become a person at birth; and why pay out more arguments than you have to? Whatever the explanation, I suggest that the step they take is neither easy nor obvious, that it calls for closer examination than it is commonly given, and that when we do give it this closer examination we shall feel inclined to reject it.

I propose, then, that we grant that the fetus is a person from the moment of conception. How does the argument go from here? Something like this, I take it. Every person has a right to life. So the fetus has a right to life. No doubt the mother has a right to decide what shall happen in and to her body; everyone would grant that. But surely a person's right to life is stronger and more stringent than the mother's right to decide what happens in and to her body, and so outweighs it. So the fetus may not be killed; an abortion may not be performed.

It sounds plausible. But now let me ask you to imagine this. You wake up in the morning and find yourself back to back in bed with an unconscious violinist. A famous unconscious violinist. He has been found to have a fatal kidney ailment, and the Society of Music Lovers has canvassed all the available medical records and found that you alone have the right blood type to help. They have therefore kidnapped you, and last night the violinist's circulatory system was plugged into yours, so that your kidneys can be used to extract poisons from his blood as well as your own. The director of the hospital now tells you, "Look, we're sorry the Society of Music Lovers did this to you—we would never have permitted it if we had known. But still, they did it, and the violinist now is plugged into you. To unplug you would be to kill him. But never mind, it's only for nine months. By then he will have recovered from his ailment, and can safely be unplugged from you." Is it morally incumbent on you to accede to this situation? No doubt it would be very nice of you if you did, a great kindness. But do you *have* to accede to it? What if it were not nine months, but nine years? Or longer still? What if the director of the hospital says, "Tough luck, I agree, but you've now got to stay in bed, with the violinist plugged into you, for the rest of your life. Because remember this. All persons have a right to life, and violinists are persons. Granted you have a right to decide what happens in and to your body, but a person's right to life outweighs your right to decide what happens in and to your body. So you cannot ever be unplugged from him." I imagine you would regard this as outrageous, which suggests that something really is wrong with that plausible-sounding argument I mentioned a moment ago.

In this case, of course, you were kidnapped; you didn't volunteer for the operation that plugged the violinist into your kidneys. Can those who oppose abortion on the ground I mentioned make an exception for a pregnancy due to rape? Certainly. They can say that persons have a right to life only if they didn't come into existence because of rape; or they can say that all persons have a right to life, but that some have less of a right to life than others, in particular, that those who came into existence because of rape have less. But these statements have a rather unpleasant sound. Surely the question of whether you have a right to life at all, or how much of it you have, shouldn't turn on the question of whether or not you are the product of a rape. And in fact the people who oppose abortion on the ground I mentioned do not make this distinction, and hence do not make an exception in the case of rape.

Nor do they make an exception for a case in which the mother has to spend the nine months of her pregnancy in bed. They would agree that would be a great pity, and hard on the mother; but all the same, all persons have a right to life, the fetus is a person, and so on. I suspect, in fact, that they would not make an exception for a case in which, mirac-

ulously enough, the pregnancy went on for nine years, or even the rest of the mother's life.

Some won't even make an exception for a case in which continuation of the pregnancy is likely to shorten the mother's life; they regard abortion as impermissible even to save the mother's life. Such cases are nowadays very rare, and many opponents of abortion do not accept this extreme view. All the same, it is a good place to begin: A number of points of interest come out in respect to it.

1. Let us call the view that abortion is impermissible even to save the mother's life "the extreme view." I want to suggest first that it does not issue from the argument I mentioned earlier without the addition of some fairly powerful premises. Suppose a woman has become pregnant, and now learns that she has a cardiac condition such that she will die if she carries the baby to term. What may be done for her? The fetus, being a person, has a right to life, but as the mother is a person too, so has she a right to life. Presumably they have an equal right to life. How is it supposed to come out that an abortion may not be performed? If mother and child have an equal right to life, shouldn't we perhaps flip a coin? Or should we add to the mother's right to life her right to decide what happens in and to her body, which everybody seems to be ready to grant—the sum of her rights now outweighing the fetus' right to life?

The most familiar argument here is the following. We are told that performing the abortion would be directly killing[2] the child, whereas doing nothing would not be killing the mother, but only letting her die. Moreover, in killing the child, one would be killing an innocent person, for the child has committed no crime, and is not aiming at his mother's death. And then there are a variety of ways in which this might be continued. (1) But as directly killing an innocent person is always and absolutely impermissible, an abortion may not be performed. Or, (2) as directly killing an innocent person is murder, and murder is always and absolutely impermissible, an abortion may not be performed.[3] Or, (3) as one's duty to refrain from directly killing an innocent person is more stringent than one's duty to keep a person from dying, an abortion may not be performed. Or, (4) if one's only options are directly killing an innocent person or letting a person die, one must prefer letting the person die, and thus an abortion may not be performed.[4]

Some people seem to have thought that these are not further premises which must be added if the conclusion is to be reached, but that they follow from the very fact that an innocent person has a right to life.[5] But this seems to me to be a mistake, and perhaps the simplest way to show this is to bring out that while we must certainly grant that innocent persons have a right to life, the theses in (1) through (4) are all false. Take (2), for example. If directly killing an innocent person is murder, and thus is impermissible, then the mother's directly killing the innocent person inside her is murder, and thus is impermissible. But it cannot seriously be thought to be murder if the mother performs an abortion on herself to save her life. It cannot seriously be said that she *must* refrain, that she *must* sit passively by and wait for her death. Let us look again at the case of you and the violinist. There you are, in bed with the violinist, and the director of the hospital says to you, "It's all most distressing, and I deeply sympathize, but you see this is putting an additional strain on your kidneys, and you'll be dead within the month. But you *have* to stay where you are all the same. Because unplugging you would be directly killing an innocent violinist, and that's murder, and that's impermissible." If anything in the world is true, it is that you do not commit murder, you do not do what is impermissible, if you reach around to your back and unplug yourself from that violinist to save your life.

The main focus of attention in writings on abortion has been on what a third party may or may not do in answer to a request from a woman for an abortion. This is in a way understandable. Things being as they are, there isn't much a woman can safely do to abort herself. So the question asked is what a third party may do, and what the mother may do, if it is mentioned at all, is deduced, almost as an afterthought, from what it is concluded that third parties may do. But it seems to me that to treat the matter in this way is to refuse to grant to the mother that very status of person which is so firmly insisted on for the fetus. For we cannot simply read off what a person may do from what a third party may do. Suppose you find yourself trapped in a tiny house with a growing child. I mean a very tiny house, and a rapidly growing child—you are already up against the wall of the house and in a few minutes you'll be crushed to death. The child on the other hand won't be crushed

to death; if nothing is done to stop him from growing he'll be hurt, but in the end he'll simply burst open the house and walk out a free man. Now I could well understand it if a bystander were to say, "There's nothing we can do for you. We cannot choose between your life and his, we cannot be the ones to decide who is to live, we cannot intervene." But it cannot be concluded that you too can do nothing, that you cannot attack it to save your life. However innocent the child may be, you do not have to wait passively while it crushes you to death. Perhaps a pregnant woman is vaguely felt to have the status of house, to which we don't allow the right of self-defense. But if the woman houses the child, it should be remembered that she is a person who houses it.

I should perhaps stop to say explicitly that I am not claiming that people have a right to do anything whatever to save their lives. I think, rather, that there are drastic limits to the right of self-defense. If someone threatens you with death unless you torture someone else to death, I think you have not the right, even to save your life, to do so. But the case under consideration here is very different. In our case there are only two people involved, one whose life is threatened, and one who threatens it. Both are innocent: The one who is threatened is not threatened because of any fault, the one who threatens does not threaten because of any fault. For this reason we may feel that we bystanders cannot intervene. But the person threatened can.

In sum, a woman surely can defend her life against the threat to it posed by the unborn child, even if doing so involves its death. And this shows not merely that the theses in (1) through (4) are false; it shows also that the extreme view of abortion is false, and so we need not canvass any other possible ways of arriving at it from the argument I mentioned at the outset.

2. The extreme view could of course be weakened to say that while abortion is permissible to save the mother's life, it may not be performed by a third party, but only by the mother herself. But this cannot be right either. For what we have to keep in mind is that the mother and the unborn child are not like two tenants in a small house which has, by an unfortunate mistake, been rented to both: The mother *owns* the house. The fact that she does adds to the offensiveness of deducing that the mother can do nothing from the supposition that

third parties can do nothing. But it does more than this: It casts a bright light on the supposition that third parties can do nothing. Certainly it lets us see that a third party who says "I cannot choose between you" is fooling himself if he thinks this is impartiality. If Jones has found and fastened on a certain coat, which he needs to keep him from freezing, but which Smith also needs to keep him from freezing, then it is not impartiality that says "I cannot choose between you" when Smith owns the coat. Women have said again and again "This body is *my* body!" and they have reason to feel angry, reason to feel that it has been like shouting into the wind. Smith, after all, is hardly likely to bless us if we say to him, "Of course it's your coat, anybody would grant that it is. But no one may choose between you and Jones who is to have it."

We should really ask what it is that says "no one may choose" in the face of the fact that the body that houses the child is the mother's body. It may be simply a failure to appreciate this fact. But it may be something more interesting, namely the sense that one has a right to refuse to lay hands on people, even where it would be just and fair to do so, even where justice seems to require that somebody do so. Thus justice might call for somebody to get Smith's coat back from Jones, and yet you have a right to refuse to be the one to lay hands on Jones, a right to refuse to do physical violence to him. This, I think, must be granted. But then what should be said is not "no one may choose," but only "*I* cannot choose," and indeed not even this, but "*I* will not *act*," leaving it open that somebody else can or should, and in particular that anyone in a position of authority, with the job of securing people's rights, both can and should. So this is no difficulty. I have not been arguing that any given third party must accede to the mother's request that he perform an abortion to save her life, but only that he may.

I suppose that in some views of human life the mother's body is only on loan to her, the loan not being one which gives her any prior claim to it. One who held this view might well think it impartiality to say "I cannot choose." But I shall simply ignore this possibility. My own view is that if a human being has any just, prior claim to anything at all, he has a just, prior claim to his own body. And perhaps this needn't be argued for here anyway, since, as I mentioned, the arguments against abortion we are looking at do grant that the woman has a right to decide what happens in and to her body.

But although they do grant it, I have tried to show that they do not take seriously what is done in granting it. I suggest the same thing will reappear even more clearly when we turn away from cases in which the mother's life is at stake, and attend, as I propose we now do, to the vastly more common cases in which a woman wants an abortion for some less weighty reason than preserving her own life.

3. Where the mother's life is not at stake, the argument I mentioned at the outset seems to have a much stronger pull. "Everyone has a right to life, so the unborn person has a right to life." And isn't the child's right to life weightier than anything other than the mother's own right to life, which she might put forward as ground for an abortion?

This argument treats the right to life as if it were unproblematic. It is not, and this seems to me to be precisely the source of the mistake.

For we should now, at long last, ask what it comes to, to have a right to life. In some views having a right to life includes having a right to be given at least the bare minimum one needs for continued life. But suppose that what in fact *is* the bare minimum a man needs for continued life is something he has no right at all to be given? If I am sick unto death, and the only thing that will save my life is the touch of Henry Fonda's cool hand on my fevered brow, then all the same, I have no right to be given the touch of Henry Fonda's cool hand on my fevered brow. It would be frightfully nice of him to fly in from the West Coast to provide it. It would be less nice, though no doubt well meant, if my friends flew out to the West Coast and carried Henry Fonda back with them. But I have no right at all against anybody that he should do this for me. Or again, to return to the story I told earlier, the fact that for continued life that violinist needs the continued use of your kidneys does not establish that he has a right to be given the continued use of your kidneys. He certainly has no right against you that *you* should give him continued use of your kidneys. For nobody has any right to use your kidneys unless you give him such a right; and nobody has the right against you that you shall give him this right—if you do allow him to go on using your kidneys, this is a kindness on your part, and not something he can claim from you as his due. Nor has he any right against anybody else that *they* should give him continued use of your kidneys. Certainly he had no right against the Society of Music Lovers that they should plug him into you in the first place. And if you now start to unplug yourself, having learned that you will otherwise have to spend nine years in bed with him, there is nobody in the world who must try to prevent you, in order to see to it that he is given something he has a right to be given.

Some people are rather stricter about the right to life. In their view, it does not include the right to be given anything, but amounts to, and only to, the right not to be killed by anybody. But here a related difficulty arises. If everybody is to refrain from killing that violinist, then everybody must refrain from doing a great many different sorts of things. Everybody must refrain from slitting his throat, everybody must refrain from shooting him—and everybody must refrain from unplugging you from him. But does he have a right against everybody that they shall refrain from unplugging you from him? To refrain from doing this is to allow him to continue to use your kidneys. It could be argued that he has a right against us that *we* should allow him to continue to use your kidneys. That is, while he had no right against us that we should give him the use of your kidneys, it might be argued that he anyway has a right against us that we shall not now intervene and deprive him of the use of your kidneys. I shall come back to third-party interventions later. But certainly the violinist has no right against you that *you* shall allow him to continue to use your kidneys. As I said, if you do allow him to use them, it is a kindness on your part, and not something you owe him.

The difficulty I point to here is not peculiar to the right of life. It reappears in connection with all the other natural rights; and it is something which an adequate account of rights must deal with. For present purposes it is enough just to draw attention to it. But I would stress that I am not arguing that people do not have a right to life—quite to the contrary, it seems to me that the primary control we must place on the acceptability of an account of rights is that it should turn out in that account to be a truth that all persons have a right to life. I am arguing only that having a right to life does not guarantee having either a right to be given the use of or a right to be allowed continued use of another

person's body—even if one needs it for life itself. So the right to life will not serve the opponents of abortion in the very simple and clear way in which they seem to have thought it would.

4. There is another way to bring out the difficulty. In the most ordinary sort of case, to deprive someone of what he has a right to is to treat him unjustly. Suppose a boy and his small brother are jointly given a box of chocolates for Christmas. If the older boy takes the box and refuses to give his brother any of the chocolates, he is unjust to him, for the brother has been given a right to half of them. But suppose that, having learned that otherwise it means nine years in bed with that violinist, you unplug yourself from him. You surely are not being unjust to him, for you gave him no right to use your kidneys, and no one else can have given him any such right. But we have to notice that in unplugging yourself, you are killing him; and violinists, like everybody else, have a right to life, and thus in the view we were considering just now, the right not to be killed. So here you do what he supposedly has a right you shall not do, but you do not act unjustly to him in doing it.

The emendation which may be made at this point is this: The right to life consists not in the right not to be killed, but rather in the right not to be killed unjustly. This runs a risk of circularity, but never mind: It would enable us to square the fact that the violinist has a right to life with the fact that you do not act unjustly toward him in unplugging yourself, thereby killing him. For if you do not kill him unjustly, you do not violate his right to life, and so it is no wonder you do him no injustice.

But if this emendation is accepted, the gap in the argument against abortion stares us plainly in the face: It is by no means enough to show that the fetus is a person, and to remind us that all persons have a right to life—we need to be shown also that killing the fetus violates its right to life, i.e., that abortion is unjust killing. And is it?

I suppose we may take it as a datum that in the case of pregnancy due to rape the mother has not given the unborn person a right to the use of her body for food and shelter. Indeed, in what pregnancy should it be supposed that the mother has given the unborn person such a right? It is not as if there were unborn persons drifting about the world, to whom a woman who wants a child says "I invite you in."

But it might be argued that there are other ways one can have acquired a right to the use of another person's body than by having been invited to use it by that person. Suppose a woman voluntarily indulges in intercourse, knowing of the chance it will issue in pregnancy, and then she does become pregnant; is she not in part responsible for the presence, in fact the very existence, of the unborn person inside? No doubt she did not invite it in. But doesn't her partial responsibility for its being there itself give it a right to the use of her body?[6] If so, then her aborting it would be more like the boy's taking away the chocolates, and less like your unplugging yourself from the violinist—doing so would be depriving it of what it does have a right to, and thus would be doing it an injustice.

And then, too, it might be asked whether or not she can kill it even to save her own life: If she voluntarily called it into existence, how can she now kill it, even in self-defense?

The first thing to be said about this is that it is something new. Opponents of abortion have been so concerned to make out the independence of the fetus, in order to establish that it has a right to life, just as its mother does, that they have tended to overlook the possible support they might gain from making out that the fetus is *dependent* on the mother, in order to establish that she has a special kind of responsibility for it, a responsibility that gives it rights against her which are not possessed by any independent person—such as an ailing violinist who is a stranger to her.

On the other hand, this argument would give the unborn person a right to its mother's body only if her pregnancy resulted from a voluntary act, undertaken in full knowledge of the chance a pregnancy might result from it. It would leave out entirely the unborn person whose existence is due to rape. Pending the availability of some further argument, then, we would be left with the conclusion that unborn persons whose existence is due to rape have no right to the use of their mothers' bodies, and thus that aborting them is not depriving them of anything they have a right to and hence is not unjust killing.

And we should also notice that it is not at all plain that this argument really does go even as far as it purports to. For there are cases and cases, and the details make a difference. If the room is stuffy, and I therefore open a window to air it, and a bur-

glar climbs in, it would be absurd to say, "Ah, now he can stay, she's given him a right to the use of her house—for she is partially responsible for his presence there, having voluntarily done what enabled him to get in, in full knowledge that there are such things as burglars, and that burglars burgle." It would be still more absurd to say this if I had had bars installed outside my windows, precisely to prevent burglars from getting in, and a burglar got in only because of a defect in the bars. It remains equally absurd if we imagine it is not a burglar who climbs in, but an innocent person who blunders or falls in. Again, suppose it were like this: Peopleseeds drift about in the air like pollen, and if you open your windows, one may drift in and take root in your carpets or upholstery. You don't want children, so you fix up your windows with fine mesh screens, the very best you can buy. As can happen, however, and on very, very rare occasions does happen, one of the screens is defective; and a seed drifts in and takes root. Does the personplant who now develops have a right to the use of your house? Surely not—despite the fact that you voluntarily opened your windows, you knowingly kept carpets and upholstered furniture, and you knew that screens were sometimes defective. Someone may argue that you are responsible for its rooting, that it does have a right to your house, because after all you *could* have lived out your life with bare floors and furniture, or with sealed windows and doors. But this won't do—for by the same token anyone can avoid a pregnancy due to rape by having a hysterectomy, or anyway by never leaving home without a (reliable!) army.

It seems to me that the argument we are looking at can establish at most that there are *some* cases in which the unborn person has a right to the use of its mother's body, and therefore *some* cases in which abortion is unjust killing. There is room for much discussion and argument as to precisely which, if any. But I think we should sidestep this issue and leave it open, for at any rate the argument certainly does not establish that all abortion is unjust killing.

5. There is room for yet another argument here, however. We surely must grant that there may be cases in which it would be morally indecent to detach a person from your body at the cost of his life. Suppose you learn that what the violinist needs is not nine years of your life, but only one hour: All

you need do to save his life is spend one hour in that bed with him. Suppose also that letting him use your kidneys for that one hour would not affect your health in the slightest. Admittedly you were kidnapped. Admittedly you did not give anyone permission to plug him into you. Nevertheless it seems to me plain you *ought* to allow him to use your kidneys for that hour—it would be indecent to refuse.

Again, suppose pregnancy lasted only an hour, and constituted no threat to life or death [sic]. And suppose that a woman becomes pregnant as a result of rape. Admittedly she did not voluntarily do anything to bring about the existence of a child. Admittedly she did nothing at all which would give the unborn person a right to the use of her body. All the same it might well be said, as in the newly emended violinist story, that she *ought* to allow it to remain for that hour—that it would be indecent in her to refuse.

Now some people are inclined to use the term "right" in such a way that it follows from the fact that you ought to allow a person to use your body for the hour he needs, that he has a right to use your body for the hour he needs, even though he has not been given that right by any person or act. They may say that it follows also that if you refuse, you act unjustly toward him. This use of the term is perhaps so common that it cannot be called wrong; nevertheless it seems to me to be an unfortunate loosening of what we would do better to keep a tight rein on. Suppose that box of chocolates I mentioned earlier had not been given to both boys jointly, but was given only to the older boy. There he sits, stolidly eating his way through the box, his small brother watching enviously. Here we are likely to say "You ought not to be so mean. You ought to give your brother some of those chocolates." My own view is that it just does not follow from the truth of this that the brother has any right to any of the chocolates. If the boy refuses to give his brother any, he is greedy, stingy, callous—but not unjust. I suppose that the people I have in mind will say it does follow that the brother has a right to some of the chocolates, and thus that the boy does act unjustly if he refuses to give his brother any. But the effect of saying this is to obscure what we should keep distinct, namely the difference between the boy's refusal in this case and the boy's refusal in the earlier case, in which the box was

given to both boys jointly, and in which the small brother thus had what was from any point of view clear title to half.

A further objection to so using the term "right" that from the fact that A ought to do a thing for B, it follows that B has a right against A that A do it for him, is that it is going to make the question of whether or not a man has a right to a thing turn on how easy it is to provide him with it; and this seems not merely unfortunate, but morally unacceptable. Take the case of Henry Fonda again. I said earlier that I had no right to the touch of his cool hand on my fevered brow, even though I needed it to save my life. I said it would be frightfully nice of him to fly in from the West Coast to provide me with it, but that I had no right against him that he should do so. But suppose he isn't on the West Coast. Suppose he has only to walk across the room, place a hand briefly on my brow—and lo, my life is saved. Then surely he ought to do it, it would be indecent to refuse. Is it to be said, "Ah, well, it follows that in this case she has a right to the touch of his hand on her brow, and so it would be an unjustice in him to refuse"? So that I have a right to it when it is easy for him to provide it, though no right when it's hard? It's rather a shocking idea that anyone's rights should fade away and disappear as it gets harder and harder to accord them to him.

So my own view is that even though you ought to let the violinist use your kidneys for the one hour he needs, we should not conclude that he has a right to do so—we should say that if you refuse, you are, like the boy who owns all the chocolates and will give none away, self-centered and callous, indecent in fact, but not unjust. And similarly, that even supposing a case in which a woman pregnant due to rape ought to allow the unborn person to use her body for the hour he needs, we should not conclude that he has a right to do so; we should conclude that she is self-centered, callous, indecent, but not unjust, if she refuses. The complaints are no less grave; they are just different. However, there is no need to insist on this point. If anyone does wish to deduce "he has a right" from "you ought," then all the same he must surely grant that there are cases in which it is not morally required of you that you allow that violinist to use your kidneys, and in which he does not have a right to use them, and in which you do not do him an injustice if you refuse. And so also for mother and unborn child. Except in such cases as the unborn person has a right to demand it—and we were leaving open the possibility that there may be such cases—nobody is morally *required* to make large sacrifices, of health, of all other interests and concerns, of all other duties and commitments, for nine years, or even for nine months, in order to keep another person alive.

6. We have in fact to distinguish between the two kinds of Samaritan: the Good Samaritan and what we might call the Minimally Decent Samaritan. The story of the Good Samaritan, you will remember, goes like this:

> A certain man went down from Jerusalem to Jericho, and fell among thieves, which stripped him of his raiment, and wounded him, and departed, leaving him half dead.
>
> And by chance there came down a certain priest that way; and when he saw him, he passed by on the other side.
>
> And likewise a Levite, when he was at the place, came and looked on him, and passed by on the other side.
>
> But a certain Samaritan, as he journeyed, came where he was; and when he saw him he had compassion on him.
>
> And went to him, and bound up his wounds, pouring in oil and wine, and set him on his own beast, and brought him to an inn, and took care of him.
>
> And on the morrow, when he departed, he took out two pence, and gave them to the host, and said unto him, "Take care of him; and whatsoever thou spendest more, when I come again, I will repay thee."
>
> (Luke 10:30–35)

The Good Samaritan went out of his way, at some cost to himself, to help one in need of it. We are not told what the options were, that is, whether or not the priest and the Levite could have helped by doing less than the Good Samaritan did, but assuming they could have, then the fact they did nothing at all shows they were not even Minimally Decent Samaritans, not because they were not Samaritans, but because they were not even minimally decent.

These things are a matter of degree, of course, but there is a difference, and it comes out perhaps most clearly in the story of Kitty Genovese, who, as you will remember, was murdered while thirty-eight people watched or listened, and did nothing at all to help her. A Good Samaritan would have rushed out to give direct assistance against the murderer. Or perhaps we had better allow that it would have been a Splendid Samaritan who did this, on the ground that it would have involved a risk of death for himself. But the thirty-eight not only did not do this, they did not even trouble to pick up a phone to call the police. Minimally Decent Samaritanism would call for doing at least that, and their not having done it was monstrous.

After telling the story of the Good Samaritan, Jesus said, "Go, and do thou likewise." Perhaps he meant that we are morally required to act as the Good Samaritan did. Perhaps he was urging people to do more than is morally required of them. At all events it seems plain that it was not morally required of any of the thirty-eight that he rush out to give direct assistance at the risk of his own life, and that it is not morally required of anyone that he give long stretches of his life—nine years or nine months—to sustaining the life of a person who has no special right (we were leaving open the possibility of this) to demand it.

Indeed, with one rather striking class of exceptions, no one in any country in the world is *legally* required to do anywhere near as much as this for anyone else. The class of exceptions is obvious. My main concern here is not the state of the law in respect to abortion, but it is worth drawing attention to the fact that in no state in this country is any man compelled by law to be even a Minimally Decent Samaritan to any person; there is no law under which charges could be brought against the thirty-eight who stood by while Kitty Genovese died. By contrast, in most states in this country women are compelled by law to be not merely Minimally Decent Samaritans, but Good Samaritans to unborn persons inside them. This doesn't by itself settle anything one way or the other, because it may well be argued that there should be laws in this country—as there are in many European countries—compelling at least Minimally Decent Samaritanism.[7] But it does show that there is a gross injustice in the existing state of the law. And it shows also that the groups currently working against liberalization of abortion laws, in fact working toward having it declared unconstitutional for a state to permit abortion, had better start working for the adoption of Good Samaritan laws generally, or earn the charge that they are acting in bad faith.

I should think, myself, that Minimally Decent Samaritan laws would be one thing, Good Samaritan laws quite another, and in fact highly improper. But we are not here concerned with the law. What we should ask is not whether anybody should be compelled by law to be a Good Samaritan, but whether we must accede to a situation in which somebody is being compelled—by nature, perhaps—to be a Good Samaritan. We have, in other words, to look now at third-party interventions. I have been arguing that no person is morally required to make large sacrifices to sustain the life of another who has no right to demand them, and this even where the sacrifices do not include life itself; we are not morally required to be Good Samaritans or anyway Very Good Samaritans to one another. But what if a man cannot extricate himself from such a situation? What if he appeals to us to extricate him? It seems to me plain that there are cases in which we can, cases in which a Good Samaritan would extricate him. There you are, you were kidnapped, and nine years in bed with that violinist lie ahead of you. You have your own life to lead. You are sorry, but you simply cannot see giving up so much of your life to the sustaining of his. You cannot extricate yourself, and ask us to do so. I should have thought that—in light of his having no right to the use of your body—it was obvious that we do not have to accede to your being forced to give up so much. We can do what you ask. There is no injustice to the violinist in our doing so.

7. Following the lead of the opponents of abortion, I have throughout been speaking of the fetus merely as a person, and what I have been asking is whether or not the argument we began with, which proceeds only from the fetus' being a person, really does establish its conclusion. I have argued that it does not.

But of course there are arguments and arguments, and it may be said that I have simply fastened on the wrong one. It may be said that what is important is not merely the fact that the fetus is a person, but that it is a person for whom the woman has a special kind of responsibility issuing from the fact that she is its mother. And it might be argued that all my analogies are therefore irrelevant—for you do not have that special kind of responsibility for that violinist, Henry Fonda does not have that special kind of responsibility for me. And our attention might be drawn to the fact that men and

women both *are* compelled by law to provide support for their children.

I have in effect dealt (briefly) with this argument in section 4 above; but a (still briefer) recapitulation now may be in order. Surely we do not have any such "special responsibility" for a person unless we have assumed it, explicitly or implicitly. If a set of parents do not try to prevent pregnancy, do not obtain an abortion, but rather take it home with them, then they have assumed responsibility for it, they have given it rights, and they cannot *now* withdraw support from it at the cost of its life because they now find it difficult to go on providing for it. But if they have taken all reasonable precautions against having a child, they do not simply by virtue of their biological relationship to the child who comes into existence have a special responsibility for it. They may wish to assume responsibility for it, or they may not wish to. And I am suggesting that if assuming responsibility for it would require large sacrifices, then they may refuse. A Good Samaritan would not refuse—or anyway, a Splendid Samaritan, if the sacrifices that had to be made were enormous. But then so would a Good Samaritan assume responsibility for that violinist; so would Henry Fonda, if he is a Good Samaritan, fly in from the West Coast and assume responsibility for me.

8. My argument will be found unsatisfactory on two counts by many of those who want to regard abortion as morally permissible. First, while I do argue that abortion is not impermissible, I do not argue that it is always permissible. There may well be cases in which carrying the child to term requires only Minimally Decent Samaritanism of the mother, and this is a standard we must not fall below. I am inclined to think it a merit of my account precisely that it does *not* give a general yes or a general no. It allows for and supports our sense that, for example, a sick and desperately frightened fourteen-year-old schoolgirl, pregnant due to rape, may of *course* choose abortion, and that any law which rules this out is an insane law. And it also allows for and supports our sense that in other cases resort to abortion is even positively indecent. It would be indecent in the woman to request an abortion, and indecent in a doctor to perform it, if she is in her seventh month, and wants the abortion just to avoid the nuisance of postponing a trip abroad. The very fact that the arguments I have been drawing atten-

tion to treat all cases of abortion, or even all cases of abortion in which the mother's life is not at stake, as morally on a par ought to have made them suspect at the outset.

Secondly, while I am arguing for the permissibility of abortion in some cases, I am not arguing for the right to secure the death of the unborn child. It is easy to confuse these two things in that up to a certain point in the life of the fetus it is not able to survive outside the mother's body; hence removing it from her body guarantees its death. But they are importantly different. I have argued that you are not morally required to spend nine months in bed, sustaining the life of that violinist; but to say this is by no means to say that if, when you unplug yourself, there is a miracle and he survives, you then have a right to turn around and slit his throat. You may detach yourself even if this costs him his life; you have no right to be guaranteed his death, by some other means, if unplugging yourself does not kill him. There are some people who will feel dissatisfied by this feature of my argument. A woman may be utterly devastated by the thought of a child, a bit of herself, put out for adoption and never seen or heard of again. She may therefore want not merely that the child be detached from her, but more, that it die. Some opponents of abortion are inclined to regard this as beneath contempt—thereby showing insensitivity to what is surely a powerful source of despair. All the same, I agree that the desire for the child's death is not one which anybody may gratify, should it turn out to be possible to detach the child alive.

At this place, however, it should be remembered that we have only been pretending throughout that the fetus is a human being from the moment of conception. A very early abortion is surely not the killing of a person, and so is not dealt with by anything I have said here.

Notes

1. Daniel Callahan, *Abortion: Law, Choice and Morality* (New York, 1970), p. 373. This book gives a fascinating survey of the available information on abortion. The Jewish tradition in David M. Feldman, *Birth Control in Jewish Law* (New York, 1963), part 5; the Catholic tradition in John T. Noonan, Jr., "An Almost Absolute Value in History," in *The Morality of Abortion*, ed. John T. Noonan, Jr. (Cambridge, Mass., 1970).

2. The term "direct" in the arguments I refer to is a technical one. Roughly, what is meant by "direct killing" is either killing as an end in itself, or killing as a means to some end, for example, the end of saving someone else's life. See note 5 on this page, for an example of its use.

3. Cf. *Encyclical Letter of Pope Pius XI on Christian Marriage*, St. Paul Editions (Boston, n.d.), p. 32: "However much we may pity the mother whose health and even life is gravely imperiled in the performance of the duty allotted to her by nature, nevertheless what could ever be a sufficient reason for excusing in any way the direct murder of the innocent? This is precisely what we are dealing with here." Noonan (*The Morality of Abortion*, p. 43) reads this as follows: "What cause can ever avail to excuse in any way the direct killing of the innocent? For it is a question of that."

4. The thesis in (4) is in an interesting way weaker than those in (1), (2), and (3): They rule out abortion even in cases in which both mother *and* child will die if the abortion is not performed. By contrast, one who held the view expressed in (4) could consistently say that one needn't prefer letting two persons die to killing one.

5. Cf. the following passage from Pius XII, *Address to the Italian Catholic Society of Midwives*: "The baby in the maternal breast has the right to life immediately from God.—Hence there is no man, no human authority, no science, no medical, eugenic, social, economic or moral 'indication' which can establish or grant a valid juridical ground for a direct deliberate disposition of an innocent human life, that is a disposition which looks to its destruction either as an end or as a means to another end perhaps in itself not illicit.—The baby, still not born, is a man in the same degree and for the same reason as the mother" (quoted in Noonan, *The Morality of Abortion*, p. 45).

6. The need for a discussion of this argument was brought home to me by members of the Society for Ethical and Legal Philosophy, to whom this paper was originally presented.

7. For a discussion of the difficulties involved, and a survey of the European experience with such laws, see *The Good Samaritan and the Law*, ed. James M. Ratcliffe (New York, 1966).

Questions for Analysis

1. *Does the belief that abortion is always impermissible necessarily result from the argument that the unborn is a person from the moment of conception? If not, what additional premises are necessary?*

2. *Why does Thomson conclude that "a woman surely can defend her life against the threat to it posed by the unborn child, even if doing so involves its death"?*

3. *How does Thomson answer the claim that the fetus's right to life weighs more (in the moral sense) than anything other than the mother's own right to life?*

4. *Does Thomson feel that there may be cases in which it would be wrong for a woman to have an abortion? Explain.*

5. *Distinguish between a "Good Samaritan" and a "Minimally Decent Samaritan."*

CASE PRESENTATION
Mrs. Sherri Finkbine and the Thalidomide Tragedy

In 1962 Mrs. Sherri Finkbine, the mother of four normal children, found herself pregnant. The pregnancy was going well, except that Mrs. Finkbine was experiencing trouble sleeping. Instead of consulting her physician, she simply took some of the tranquilizers her husband had brought back from a trip to Europe, where the sedative was a widely used over-the-counter-drug.

A short time later, Mrs. Finkbine read an article concerning the great increase in the number of deformed children being born in Europe. Some of the children's limbs failed to develop, or developed only in malformed ways; some of the children were born blind and deaf, or had seriously defective internal organs. What alarmed Mrs. Finkbine was that the birth defects had been traced to the use in pregnancy of a supposedly harmless and widely used tranquilizer, whose active ingredient was thalidomide.

A visit to her physician confirmed Mrs. Finkbine's worst fears: The tranquilizer she had taken did indeed contain thalidomide. Convinced that his patient stood little chance of delivering an undeformed baby, the physician recommended termination of the pregnancy. He explained to Mrs. Finkbine that getting approval for an abortion under such conditions should prove simple. All she had to do was explain them to the three-member medical board of Phoenix. Mrs. Finkbine followed her physician's counsel, which proved correct: The board granted approval for the abortion.

Concerned about other women who might have unwittingly taken thalidomide, Mrs. Finkbine then called a local newspaper and told her story to the editor. While agreeing not to identify her, the editor ran the story bordered in black on the front page under the headline "Baby-Deforming Drug May Cost Woman Her Child Here."

The wire services picked up the story straightaway, and it wasn't long before enterprising reporters discovered and published Mrs. Finkbine's identity. In no time, Mrs. Finkbine became the object of intense anti-abortion sentiment. *L'Osservatore Romano,* the official Vatican newspaper, condemned Mrs. Finkbine and her husband as murderers. Although she received some letters of support, many were abusive. "'I hope someone takes the other four children and strangles them," one person wrote, "because it's all the same thing." Another wrote from the perspective of the fetus: "Mommy, please dear Mommy, let me live. Please please, I want to live. Let me love you, let me see the light of day, let me smell a rose, let me sing a song, let me look into your face, let me say Mommy."

In the heat of the controversy, the medical board members decided that, if challenged, their approval could not survive a court test, for Arizona statute legally sanctioned abortion only when it was required to save the mother's life. Rather than attempt to defend its judgment if asked to, it withdrew its approval.

Thwarted in her attempted to get a legal abortion in some other state, Mrs. Finkbine went to Sweden. After a rigorous investigation by a medical board there, she was given an abortion in a Swedish hospital.

Questions for Analysis

1. *Do you think Mrs. Finkbine acted rightly or wrongly in having an abortion?*

2. *What bearing, if any, do you think probable or certain deformities have on the person status of the unborn?*

3. *How would you assess this argument: "If you're willing to permit abortions for the reason operating in the Finkbine case, then it follows that you should permit the termination of the existence of similarly defective infants and adults."*

4. *Do you believe that a government has a right and perhaps even a duty to prohibit abortions in cases like Mrs. Finkbine's? Or do you believe it doesn't? Explain with reference to concepts of justice and freedom.*

5. *Which of the moral principles discussed in Chapter 2 do you think are especially relevant to cases like this one?*

CASE PRESENTATION
"CONCEIVED IN VIOLENCE, BORN IN HATE"[9]

Shortly after returning home, a twenty-seven-year-old mother was gagged, tied up, and raped by a 220-pound guard from a nearby Air Force base who had forced his way into her home. The woman received medical treatment at a hospital and from her own physician. Nevertheless, the episode had left her pregnant.

9. *Reported in Burton M. Leiser,* Liberty, Justice, and Morals: Contemporary Value Conflicts *(New York: Macmillan, 1973), p. 96.*

Not wanting the child, the woman sought an abortion. Although the state's abortion law was, at the time (1955), one of the least restrictive, no hospital in her state would permit her to have an abortion.

Unable to afford to travel abroad for a legal abortion, the woman and her husband were left with two choices: a clandestine illegal abortion or having the baby. Deeply religious and law abiding; the couple chose to carry the baby to term.

During her pregnancy, the woman admitted to hating the fetus she was carrying and to eagerly awaiting the time she would be rid of it. "Thus the child, conceived in violence and born in hatred, came into the world."[10]

10.   *Leiser,* Liberty, Justice, and Morals: Contemporary Value Conflicts, *p. 96.*

Questions for Analysis

1. *Do you think abortion should or should not be legal in cases like the preceding?*

2. *The traditional Roman Catholic position on abortion rests on the assumption that the unborn is a person from conception. Since the fetus is an innocent person, even when a pregnancy is due to rape or incest the fetus may not be held accountable and made to suffer through its death. According to Roman Catholicism, then, a* direct *abortion is never morally justifiable. (Although the fetus may never be deliberately killed, it may be allowed to die as a consequence of an action that is intended to save the life of the mother, such as the removal of a malignant uterus.) By this account, an abortion in the preceding case would be immoral. Evaluate this position.*

3. *Christian moralist Joseph Fletcher has written: "No unwanted and unintended baby should ever be born."[11] Do you think such a rule would produce the greatest social benefit?*

4. *Do you think Aristotle's principle of rational development could provide a basis for sanctioning abortion in cases like the preceding? Explain.*

5. *Do you think Rawls's maximin principle of social justice has any relevance to the abortion issue?*

11.   *Joseph Fletcher,* Situation Ethics: The New Morality *(Philadelphia: Westminster Press, 1966), p. 39.*

Selections for Further Reading

Braggin, Mary V.; Frederick Elliston; and Jane English, eds. *Feminism and Philosophy,* Section 7. Totowa, N.J.: Littlefield, Adams, 1977.

Brody, B. *Abortion and the Sanctity of Human Life.* Cambridge, Mass.: Harvard University Press, 1975.

Callahan, Daniel. *Abortion: Law, Choice, and Morality.* New York: Macmillan, 1970.

Cohen, Marshall; Thomas Nagen; and Thomas Scanlon, eds. *The Rights and Wrongs of Abortion.* Princeton, N.J.: Princeton University Press, 1974.

Denes, Magda. *In Necessity and Sorrow: Life and Death in an Abortion Hospital.* New York: Penguin Books, 1977.

Feinberg, Joel. *The Problem of Abortion*, 2nd ed. Belmont, Calif.: Wadsworth, 1974.

Finnish, J., et al. *The Rights and Wrongs of Abortion.* Princeton, N.J.: Princeton University Press, 1974.

Nicholson, Susan. *Abortion and the Roman Catholic Church.* Knoxville, Tenn.: Religious Ethics, 1978.

Noonan, John T. *The Morality of Abortion: Legal and Historical Perspectives.* Cambridge, Mass.: Harvard University Press, 1970.

Perkins, Robert L., ed. *Abortion: Pro and Con.* Cambridge: Mass.: Schenkman, 1974.

5
EUTHANASIA

The case of Karen Ann Quinlan has probably done more than any other in recent years to rivet public attention on the legal and moral aspects of euthanasia, which generally refers to the act of painlessly putting to death a person suffering from a terminal or incurable disease or condition. On the night of April 15, 1975, for reasons still unclear, Karen Ann Quinlan ceased breathing for at least two 15-minute periods. Failing to respond to mouth-to-mouth resuscitation by friends, she was taken by ambulance to Newton Memorial Hospital in New Jersey. She had a temperature of 100 degrees, her pupils were unreactive, and she did not respond even to deep pain. Physicians who examined her characterized Karen as being in a "chronic, persistent, vegetative state," and later it was judged that no form of treatment could restore her to cognitive life. Her father, Joseph Quinlan, asked to be appointed her legal guardian with the expressed purpose of discontinuing the use of the respirator by which Karen was being sustained. Eventually the Supreme Court of New Jersey granted the request. The respirator was turned off. However, as of this writing Karen Ann Quinlan remains alive but comatose. Although widely publicized, the Quinlan case is by no means the only one that has raised questions concerning euthanasia.

In fact, improvements in biomedical technology have made euthanasia an issue that more and more individuals and institutions must confront and that society must address. Respirators, artificial kidneys, intravenous feeding, new drugs—all have made it possible to sustain an individual's life artificially, that is, long after the individual has lost the capacity to sustain life independently. In cases like Quinlan's, individuals have fallen into a state of irreversible coma, what some health professionals term a vegetative state. In other instances, such as after severe accidents or with congenital brain disease, the individual's consciousness has been so dulled and the personality has so deteriorated that he or she lacks the capacity for development and growth. In still other cases, such as with terminal cancer, individuals vacillate between agonizing pain and a drug-induced stupor, with no possibility of ever again enjoying life. Not too long ago, "nature would have taken its course"; such patients would have died. Today we have the technological capacity to keep them alive artificially. Should we? Or, at least in some instances, are we justified in not doing this, even obliged not to?

As with abortion and pornography, euthanasia raises two basic moral issues that must be distinguished. The first deals with the morality of euthanasia itself; the second concerns the morality of euthanasia legislation. We will consider both issues in this chapter.

Before discussing the arguments related to these issues, we must clarify a number of concepts central to euthanasia. Among them are the meanings of *personhood* and *death*, the difference between "ordinary" and "extraordinary" treatment, the distinctions between "killing" and "allowing to die," the various meanings of *euthanasia*, and the difference between "voluntary" and "nonvoluntary" euthanasia.

Personhood

The question of personhood bears as much on euthanasia as on abortion debates. What conditions should be used as the criteria of personhood? Can an entity be considered a person merely because it possesses certain biological properties? Or should other factors be introduced, such as consciousness, self-consciousness, rationality, and the capacities for communication and moral judgment? If personhood is just an elementary biological matter, then patients like Karen Ann Quinlan can qualify as persons more easily than if personhood depends on a complex list of psychosocial factors.

In part, the significance of the personhood issue lies in the assignment of basic patient rights; once the criteria for personhood are established, those qualifying presumably enjoy the same general rights as any other patient. Conversely, for those who do not qualify and have no reasonable chance of ever qualifying, the rights issue is far less problematic. This doesn't mean that a death decision necessarily follows when an entity is determined to be a nonperson. But it does mean that whatever may be inherently objectionable about allowing or causing a *person* to die dissolves, because the entity is no longer a person. So the concept of personhood bears directly on a death decision.

Death

Related to personhood is the conceptual issue of death. To get some idea of the complexities enshrouding the concept of death, consider this episode, which is based on an actual case.[1]

A terrible auto accident has occurred. One of the cars was occupied by a husband and wife. Authorities on the scene pronounce the man dead and rush the unconscious woman to a hospital, where she spends the next seventeen days in a coma due to severe brain damage. On the morning of the eighteenth day,

1. Smith *v.* Smith, *229 Arkansas 579, 3175.W, 2d, 275, 1958.*

she dies. Some time afterward, a relative contesting the couple's estate claims that the two people died simultaneously. Did they?

Not too long ago, legal and medical experts would have said yes. But when this case went to the Supreme Court of Arkansas in 1958, the court ruled that since the woman was breathing after the accident, she was alive, even though unconscious. The court relied on the time-honored definition of death as "the cessation of life; the ceasing to exist; defined by physicians as a total stoppage of the circulation of blood and a cessation of the animal and vital functions consequent thereon, such as respiration, pulsation, etc."[2] By this definition, death occurs if and only if there is a total cessation of respiration and blood flow.

Using heart-lung functioning as a criterion for death served well enough until recent developments in biomedical technology made it questionable. One of these developments is the increasing and widespread use of devices that can sustain respiration and heartbeat indefinitely, even when there is no brain activity. If the traditional heart-lung criterion is applied in cases like the preceding, then these individuals are technically still alive. Yet to many—including relatives of the comatose and those who must treat them—such people are, for all intents and purposes, dead.

Another development that has cast doubt on the traditional definition of death is the need for still-viable organs in transplant surgery. In general, a transplant is most successful if the organs are removed immediately after death. Thus there is intense pressure on transplant teams to harvest organs as soon as possible. The moral implications of this pressure are serious, as we'll see shortly.

But these developments are only part of what makes the whole issue of defining death so nettlesome. Also relevant are three distinct categories of concerns that can be identified in any discussion of death: the philosophical, the physiological, and the methodical.

Philosophical Concerns

The philosophical level refers to one's basic concept of death, which inevitably springs from some view of what it means to be human. For example, if we believe it is the capacity to think and reason that makes one a human, we will likely associate the loss of personhood with the loss of rationality. If we consider consciousness as the defining characteristic, we will be more inclined to consider a person to have lost that status when a number of characteristics such as the capacities to remember, enjoy, worry, and will are gone. Although the absence of rational or experimental capacities would not necessarily define death, it would dispose us toward such a definition, since we are already disposed to accept the absence of personhood in the absence of those criteria. So there is interplay between our concepts of personhood and death.

Physiological Concerns

These relate to the functioning of specific body systems or organs. The traditional physiological standard for recognizing death has been irreversible loss

2.   Black's Law Dictionary, *rev. 4th ed. (St. Paul Minn.: West Publishing)*, 1968, p. 488.

of circulatory and respiratory functions. More recent physiological standards defined by the Harvard Ad Hoc Committee (1968) have focused on the central nervous system—the brain and spinal cord. Specifically, these standards are the irreversible loss of reflex activity mediated through the brain or spinal cord, electrical activity in the cerebral neocortex, and/or cerebral blood flow. Whether traditional or recent, these physiological standards can be used individually or in combination. The significance of the physiological category in death decisions is that a patient who might be declared alive by one set of criteria might be ruled dead by another. If a patient is considered dead, obviously euthanasia becomes academic; if the person is considered alive, euthanasia is a real concern.

Methodical Concerns

This category refers to specific means for determining physiological standards. The method used to determine traditional heart-lung standards has been taking the pulse or reading an electrocardiogram, or both. For the central nervous system, electroencephalographs can be used to measure electrical activity in the neocortex, and radioactive tracers can be injected into the circulatory system for detecting cerebral blood flow.

Moral Implications

What makes defining death so important in discussions of euthanasia and the general study of bioethics is the interplay between definitional and moral considerations. To illustrate, suppose an attacker has clubbed a woman into a comatose condition. She is rushed to a hospital, is determined to have suffered profound and irreversible brain damage, and is put on an artificial respirator. Efforts to identify her fail. As the team tending her debates whether to remove her from the respirator, one member, using one of the brain-death criteria, claims she is already dead. Therefore, withdrawing the respirator poses no special problems. Another member demurs. Using the heart-lung criterion, she insists that the woman is still alive and that the team has an obligation to sustain her life. What ought the team do?

One answer is, Let the law decide. But many states lack an adequate definition of death. Complicating matters, some states allow either of the two alternative definitions. And even where the law is decisive, moral problems remain about the rightness of the standard itself. Beyond this, even when the law sanctions a brain-death criterion, it does not *compel* health professionals or anyone else to implement it. So although brain-death law may legally protect health professionals, it does not obligate them to act. Health professionals, presumably in consultation with others, must still wrestle with moral decisions in cases of irreversible coma.

Then there is the phenomenon of organ transplants, which promises to become of even greater concern as technology and techniques improve. A number of interests are identifiable in such cases. First there are the interests of recipients, whose welfare depends on the availability of organs. Then there are the interests of health teams, who are obliged to provide adequate health care, which may include appropriate quality organs. There are also the interests of the donors, who may fear that their organs will be pirated prior to death or that their own health-care providers will perform less than adequately in trying to sustain their lives. Moreover, there are the obligations of health teams to guard donors against physical violations as well as the psychological threat of violations, and to guard themselves against developing a cannibalistic image. And finally, society at large must be watchful that the rights of its citizens to protection are not flouted, while at the same time ensuring that its ill citizens are not denied needed medical care and treatment, which may involve transplants.

Ordinary vs. Extraordinary Treatment

A third issue that arises in euthanasia discussions involves the concept of ordinary as opposed to extraordinary treatment, terms used to differentiate two broad categories of medical intervention. Although the terms are often applied facilely, they elude hard-and-fast definition.

Moralist Paul Ramsey, for one, has applied *ordinary* to all medicines, treatments, and surgical procedures that offer a reasonable hope of benefit to the patient but do not involve excessive pain, expense, or other inconveniences. In contrast, he has identified *extraordinary* as measures that are unusual, extremely difficult, dangerous, inordinately expensive, or that offer no reasonable hope of benefit to the patient.[3]

Such descriptions are useful and probably find widespread acceptance. But they do raise questions. An obvious one concerns the concepts used to define *ordinary* and *extraordinary*. What can be considered "reasonable hope of benefit to the patient"? What measures qualify as "unusual"? Ramsey mentions cost, but some would claim that cost has no place in a moral calculation. And then there is always the question of whether these criteria should be used individually or in combination; if in combination, what is the proper mix? Furthermore, patient idiosyncrasies inevitably influence a determination of ordinary and extraordinary in a particular case. For example, the use of antibiotics for a pneumonia patient undoubtedly qualifies as ordinary treatment. But does it remain ordinary treatment when the patient with pneumonia happens to have terminal cancer with metastasis to the brain and liver? The institutional setting can also affect evaluations of what constitutes ordinary and extraordinary: What is extraordinary treatment in a small community hospital could well be ordinary in a large teaching hospital.[4]

The significance of trying to pin down these two concepts is that euthanasia arguments often rely on them to distinguish the permissible from the impermissible act of euthanasia. Some moralists argue that health professionals should provide ordinary treatment for the moribund but not extraordinary, which may

---

3. *Paul Ramsey,* The Patient as Person *(New Haven, Conn.: Yale University Press, 1970), pp. 122–23.*

4. *See A. J. Davis and M. A. Aroskar,* Ethical Dilemmas and Nursing Practice *(New York: Appleton-Century-Crofts, 1978), p. 117.*

be withheld or never started. Others insist that health professionals initiate extraordinary measures. Indeed, the medical profession itself makes similar operational distinctions in making death decisions.

Killing vs. Allowing to Die

A fourth conceptual issue that we should try to clarify is what some consider to be the difference between killing a person and allowing a person to die. Presumably, "killing" a person refers to a definite action taken to end someone's life, as in the case of the physician who, out of mercy, injects a terminally ill patient with air or a lethal dose of a medication. Killing is an act of commission. In contrast, "allowing to die" presumably is an act of omission, whereby the steps needed to preserve someone's life simply are not taken. For example, a doctor, again out of mercy, fails to give an injection of antibiotics to a terminally ill patient who has contracted pneumonia. As a result of this omission, the patient dies.

Those making this distinction, such as the American Medical Association (AMA), say that the distinction is reasonable because in ordinary language and everyday life we distinguish between causing someone harm and permitting the harm to happen to them. If, in cases of euthanasia, the distinction is not made between killing and allowing to die, we lose the important distinction between causing someone harm and permitting that harm to happen.

Proponents also claim that the distinction acknowledges cases in which additional curative treatment would serve no purpose, and in fact would interfere with a person's natural death. It recognizes that medical science will not initiate or sustain extraordinary means to preserve the life of a dying patient when such means would obviously serve no useful purpose for the patient or the patient's family.

Finally, some argue that the distinction is important in determining causation of death, and ultimate responsibility. In instances where the patient dies following nontreatment, the proximate cause of the death is the patient's disease, not the treatment or the person who did not provide it. If we fail to differentiate between killing and allowing to die, we blur this distinction. If allowing to die is subsumed under the category of euthanasia, then the nontreatment is the cause of the death, not the disease.

Not everyone, however, agrees that the distinction is a logical one. Some argue that withholding extraordinary treatment or suspending heroic measures in terminal cases is tantamount to the intentional termination of the life of one human being by another; that is, it is an act of killing. Thus they claim that no logical distinction can be made between killing and allowing to die.

Whether or not the distinction between the two can be sustained logically is only one question raised by the killing-vs.-letting-die debate. Another is the moral relevance of such a distinction. Even if the distinction is logical, does it have any bearing on the rightness or wrongness of acts commonly termed *euthanasia*?

On the one hand, for those making the distinction, allowing a patient to die under carefully circumscribed conditions could be moral. On the other hand, they seemingly would regard the killing of a patient, even out of mercy, an immoral act. But those opposing the killing–letting die distinction would not necessarily accept the close connection between killing a dying patient and an immoral act. For them, while killing may be wrong, in some cases it may be the right thing to do. What determines the morality of killing a patient, what is of moral relevance and importance, is not the manner of causing the death but the circumstances in which the death is caused.

In summary, those distinguishing killing from allowing to die claim that the distinction is logically and morally relevant. Generally, they would condemn any act of killing a patient, while recognizing that some acts of allowing a patient to die may be moral (as, for example, in cases where life is being preserved heroically and death is imminent). In contrast are those who hold that the killing–letting die distinction is not logical, that allowing to die is in effect killing. They claim that killing a patient may be morally justifiable depending on the *circumstances* and not the *manner* in which the death is caused. The debate that surrounds the killing-vs.-allowing-to-die question is basic to the very meaning of *euthanasia,* a fifth conceptual issue that needs clarification.

Meaning of *Euthanasia:* Narrow vs. Broad Interpretations

Construing euthanasia (from the Greek, meaning "good or happy death") narrowly, some philosophers have taken it to be the equivalent of killing. Since allowing someone to die does not involve killing, allowing to die would not actually be an act of euthanasia at all. By this account, then, there are acts of allowing to die, which may be moral, and acts of euthanasia, which are always wrong.

Other philosophers interpret the meaning of *euthanasia* more broadly. For them euthanasia includes not only acts of killing but also acts of allowing to die. In other words, euthanasia can take an active or passive form. *Active* (sometimes termed *positive*) *euthanasia refers to the act of painlessly putting to death persons suffering from incurable conditions or diseases.* Injecting a lethal dosage of medication into a terminally ill patient would constitute active euthanasia. *Passive euthanasia,* in contrast, *refers to any act of allowing a patient to die.* Not providing a terminally ill patient the needed antibiotics to survive pneumonia would be an example of passive euthanasia.

It is tempting to view the debate between the narrow and the broad interpretations of *euthanasia* largely in terms of semantics. While the meaning of *euthanasia* certainly is a factor in the disagreement, the issue involves more than mere word definition.

One side, the narrow interpretation, considers killing a patient always morally wrong. Since euthanasia, by this definition, is killing a patient, euthanasia is always morally wrong. But allowing a patient to die does not involve killing a patient. Therefore, allowing a patient to die does not fall under the moral prohibition that euthanasia does; allowing a patient to die may be morally right.

The other side, the broad interpretation, considers acts of allowing patients to die acts of euthanasia, albeit passive euthanasia. They argue that if euthanasia is wrong, then so is allowing patients to die (since it is a form of euthanasia). But if allowing patients to die is not wrong, then euthanasia is not always wrong. Generally, those favoring the broad interpretation, in fact, claim that allowing patients to die is not always wrong; that euthanasia, therefore, may be morally justifiable. With the possible moral justifiability of euthanasia established, it is conceivable that acts of active euthanasia, as well as passive, may be moral. What determines their morality are the conditions under which the death is caused, and not the manner in which it is caused. It's within these broad interpretations that the most problematic cases of death decisions fall—including the Quinlan case.

Voluntary vs. Nonvoluntary Euthanasia

In addition to the preceding, there is another conceptual issue that arises in discussions of euthanasia. It concerns the difference between voluntary and nonvoluntary decisions about death.

Voluntary decisions about death refer to cases in which a competent adult patient requests or gives informed consent to a particular course of medical treatment or nontreatment. Generally speaking, informed consent exists when patients can understand what they are agreeing to and voluntarily choose it. Voluntary decisions also include cases in which persons take their own lives either directly or by refusing treatment, and cases where patients deputize others to act in their behalf. For example, a woman who is terminally ill instructs her husband and family not to permit antibiotic treatment should she contract pneumonia, or not to use artificial support systems should she lapse into a coma and be unable to speak for herself. Similarly, a man requests that he be given a lethal injection after an industrial explosion has left him with third-degree burns over most of his body and no real hope of recovery. For a decision about death to be voluntary, the individual must give explicit consent.

A nonvoluntary decision about death refers to cases in which the decision is not made by the person who is to die. Such cases would include situations where, because of age, mental impairment, or unconsciousness, patients are not competent to give informed consent to life-or-death decisions and where others make the decisions for them. For example, suppose that as a result of an automobile accident, a man suffers massive and irreparable brain damage, falls into unconsciousness, and can be maintained only by artificial means. Should he regain consciousness, he would likely be little more than a vegetable. Given this prognosis, the man's family, in consultation with his physicians, decide to suspend artificial life-sustaining means and allow him to die.

In actual situations, the difference between voluntary and nonvoluntary decisions about death is not always clear. For example, take the case of a man who has heard his mother say that she would never want to be kept alive with "machines and pumps and tubes." Now that she is, in fact, being kept alive that way, and is unable to express a life-or-death decision, the man is not sure that his mother actually would choose to be allowed to die. Similarly, a doctor might not be certain that the tormented cries of a stomach-cancer patient to be "put out of my misery" is an expression of informed consent or of profound pain and momentary despair.

The voluntary-nonvoluntary distinction is relevant to both the narrow and the broad interpretations of the meaning of *euthanasia*. Each interpretation seemingly distinguishes four kinds of death decisions, in which the voluntary-nonvoluntary distinction plays a part. Thus, the narrow interpretation recognizes cases of:

1. Voluntary euthanasia
2. Nonvoluntary euthanasia
3. Voluntary allowing to die
4. Nonvoluntary allowing to die

By this account, the first two generally are considered immoral; instances of the second two may be moral under carefully circumscribed conditions.

Recognizing no logical or morally relevant distinction between euthanasia and allowing to die, the broad interpretation allows four forms of euthanasia:

1. Voluntary active euthanasia
2. Nonvoluntary active euthanasia
3. Voluntary passive euthanasia
4. Nonvoluntary passive euthanasia

By this account, any of these types of euthanasia may be morally justifiable under carefully circumscribed conditions.

The narrow and the broad interpretations differ sharply in their moral judgment of *deliberate* acts taken to end or shorten a patient's life—that is, acts that the narrow interpretation terms voluntary or nonvoluntary euthanasia, and that the broad interpretation terms voluntary or nonvoluntary *active* euthanasia. Generally, the narrow interpretation considers such acts always morally repugnant; the broad interpretation views them as being morally justifiable under carefully circumscribed conditions.

With these complicated conceptual issues behind us, we can now turn to the arguments for and against death decisions. The most conservative death decisions involve cases of voluntary allowing to die, which we will take as circumstantially a rough equivalent to voluntary passive euthanasia. Having raised the relevant pro and con arguments, we will then see how they can be and are applied to other forms of death decisions.

Arguments for Voluntary
Allowing to Die

1.   *Individuals have the right to decide about their own lives and deaths.*

POINT: "What more basic right is there than to decide whether or not you're going to live? There is none. A person under a death sentence who's being kept alive through so-called heroic measures certainly has a fundamental right to say, 'Enough's enough. The treatment's worse than the disease. Leave me alone. Let me die!' Ironically, those who would deny the terminally ill this right do so out of a sense of high morality. Don't they realize that in denying the gravely ill and the suffering the right to release themselves from pain, they commit the arch-villainy?"

COUNTERPOINT: "The way you talk you'd swear people have absolute rights over their bodies and lives: You know as well as I that just isn't true. No individual has absolute freedom. Even 'A Patient's Bill of Rights,' which was drawn up by the American Hospital Association, recognizes this. While acknowledging that patients have the right to refuse treatment, the document also recognizes that they have this right and freedom only to the extent permitted by law. Maybe people should be allowed to die if they want to. But if so, it's not because they have an absolute right to dispose of themselves if they so choose."

2.   *The period of suffering can be shortened.*

POINT: "Have you ever been in a terminal-cancer ward? It's grim, but enlightening. Anyone who has knows how much people can suffer before they die. And not just physically. The emotional, even spiritual, agony is often worse. Today our medical hardware is so sophisticated that the period of suffering can be extended beyond the limit of human endurance. What's the point of allowing someone a few more months or days or hours of so-called life when recovery is impossible? There's no point. In fact, it's downright inhumane. When someone under such conditions asks to be allowed to die, it's far more humane to honor that request than deny it."

COUNTERPOINT: "Only a fool would discount the agony that many terminally ill patients endure. And there's no question that by letting them die on request we shorten their period of suffering. But we also shorten their lives. Can you seriously argue that the saving of pain is a greater good than the saving of life? Or that the presence of pain is a greater evil than the loss of life? I don't think so. Of course nobody likes to see a creature suffer, especially when the creature has requested a halt to the suffering. But we have to keep our priorities straight. In the last analysis, life is a greater value than freedom from pain; death is a worse evil than suffering."

3.   *People have a right to die with dignity.*

POINT: "Nobody wants to end up plugged into machines and wired to tubes. Who wants to spend his last days lying in a hospital bed wasting away to something that's hardly recognizable as a human being, let alone his former self?

Nobody. And rightly so. Why, the very prospect insults the whole concept of what it means to be a human. People are entitled to dignity, in life *and* in death. Just as we respect people's right to live with dignity, so we must respect their right to die with dignity. In the case of the terminally ill, that means people have the right to refuse life-sustaining treatment when it's obvious to them that the treatment is only eroding their dignity, destroying their self-concept and self-respect, and reducing them to some subhuman level of biological life."

COUNTERPOINT: "Listening to you, someone would swear that the super-human efforts often made to keep someone alive are not worthy of human beings. What could be more dignified, more respectful of human life, than to maintain life against all odds, against all hope? Why, in situations like those, humans live their finest hours. And that includes many patients. All of life is a struggle, and a gamble. Nobody ever knows what the outcome will be. But on we go—dogged in our determination to see things through to a meaningful resolution. Indeed, humans are noblest when they persist in the face of the inevitable. Look at our literature. Reflect on our heroes. They are not those who have capitulated, but those who have endured. No, there's nothing undignified about being hollowed out by a catastrophic disease, about writhing in pain, about wishing it would end. The indignity lies in capitulation."

Arguments against Voluntary Allowing to Die

1.   *We should not play God.*

POINT: "Our culture traditionally has recognized that only God gives life, and only God should take life away. When humans take it upon themselves to shorten their lives or have others do that by withdrawing life-sustaining appa-ratus, they play God. They usurp the divine function; they interfere with the divine plan."

COUNTERPOINT: "Well, I'm impressed! It's not every day that I meet some-body who knows the mind of God. But you obviously do. How you can be so sure about the 'divine plan,' however, quite escapes me. Did it ever occur to you that the intervention of modern medicine to keep people alive who otherwise would have long since died might itself be interfering with God's will? If there is a God and a divine plan, it seems pretty clear that God didn't intend that his creatures should live forever. Judging from history, God meant for all humans to die. Don't you think modern medicine has interfered with this plan? What could be more like 'playing God' than keeping people alive artificially? Let's face it: Nobody knows what God's plan is for allowing people to die."

2.   *We cannot be sure consent is voluntary.*

POINT: "Many of those opposed to nonvoluntary death decisions are quick to approve of voluntary ones. What they overlook is that we can't ever be sure consent is voluntary. In fact, the circumstances that surround most terminal cases make voluntary consent impossible. Take the case of terminal patients who have built up a tolerance to drugs and, as a result, are tortured by pain. Just when are we supposed to get their consent? If we get it when they're drugged, then they're not clearheaded enough for the consent to be voluntary. If we withdraw the drugs, then they'll probably be so crazed with pain that their free consent still will be in question. Since consent in such cases can't be voluntary, it can only be presumed. And to allow a death decision on the basis of presumed consent is wrong."

COUNTERPOINT: "Agreed, in the situations you set up, rational free choice is in question. But you've overlooked cases where people facing a death due to a dreadful disease make a death request *before* they're suffering pain. Maybe you'll reply that the consent of people in such situations is uninformed and anticipatory, and that patients can't bind themselves to be killed in the future. Okay, but what about cases where patients not under pain indicate a desire for ultimate euthanasia and reaffirm that request when under pain? Surely, by any realistic criteria, this would constitute voluntary consent."

3. *Diagnoses may be mistaken.*

POINT: "Doctors aren't infallible, that's for sure. The American Medical Association readily admits that far too many medical procedures and operations aren't even necessary. This doesn't mean doctors are malicious, only that they're human. They make mistakes in their diagnoses. Any instance of electing death runs the tragic risk of terminating a life unnecessarily, and for that reason it's wrong."

COUNTERPOINT: "Sure, doctors make mistakes, but not as often as you imply. In fact, in terminal cases mistaken diagnoses are as rare as the kiwi bird. But that fact probably won't satisfy you, because you claim that any risk makes a death decision wrong. Well, by the same token, every diagnosis, from the simplest to most complex, carries a chance of error and with it the possibility of needless treatment. Sometimes the treatment involves operations, and operations always involve some jeopardy for the patient. So what are we to say—that it's wrong for people to opt for procedures that expert medical opinion says they need, because there's always a chance of mistaken diagnosis? Of course not. The fact of the matter is that the correctness of a diagnosis is a separate issue from the individual's right to request and receive treatment. This applies with equal force to death decisions."

4. *There is always a chance of a cure or of some new relief from pain.*

POINT: "People easily forget how final death is. That may sound silly, but it's pertinent to death decisions. After all, people can never be recalled from the grave to benefit from a cure to the diseases that ravage them, or from a new drug to relieve the pain they suffered. Instances of such 'wonder' drugs, even of spontaneous remissions of disease, are common enough to make a death decision precipitate, and therefore wrong."

COUNTERPOINT: "First of all, it's highly unlikely that some kind of cure will benefit those who are already ravaged by a disease. Ask doctors. They'll tell you that a cure is most likely in the early stages of a disease, and most unlikely in its final stages. But the issue of death decisions pertains precisely to people in the final, tortured stages of a disease. So even if a cure is discovered, its likelihood of helping these patients is virtually nonexistent. Another thing: You fail to distinguish between cases where a cure is imminent, cases where it's remote, and those where it falls somewhere in between. To treat all terminal diseases as if they had an equal probability of being cured is unrealistic. Generally speaking, there's a time lapse between a medical discovery and the general availability of a drug. I might agree that it would be 'precipitate' and even wrong to elect death in that interim between discovery and general availability of the drug. But I don't see why it would be precipitate and wrong for a person to elect death when suffering from a terminal disease for which no cure or relief has ever been discovered, or who doesn't want to gamble but to die."

5.   *Allowing death decisions will lead to abuses.*

POINT: "Of course it's easy to think of death decisions as isolated instances of individuals electing to die. Looked at this way, those who make such decisions appear to be above moral reproach. But when individuals choose to die and are subsequently allowed to, their actions open the door for all sorts of abuses. The chief abuse is *nonvoluntary* death decisions. A terminal patient who elects to die at the very least brings individuals and society closer to accepting nonvoluntary killing, such as in cases of defective infants, old and senile people, and the hopelessly insane. Indeed, such 'private' decisions will likely set off a chain reaction that will lead to horrible abuses."

COUNTERPOINT: "The treatments of defective infants, old and senile people, and the hopelessly insane are issues separate and distinct from permitting death decisions. There is no causal connection between them and allowing death decisions, such that allowing death decisions will inevitably lead to the abuses you fear. But even if there were a connection, that wouldn't of itself demonstrate that voluntary death decisions are immoral, only that they shouldn't be legalized."

Arguments for and against Other Forms of Death Decisions

The foregoing are the arguments typically marshaled for and against voluntary allowing to die or voluntary passive euthanasia. They, or variations of them, are commonly enlisted in discussions of other forms of death decisions as well.

For example, those arguing for voluntary active euthanasia often stress the inherent freedom of individuals to do as they choose, so long as their actions do not hurt anyone else. They also contend that it is cruel and inhuman to make people suffer when they have requested to have their lives ended. In contrast, those opposing voluntary active euthanasia appeal to the sanctity of human life, arguing that the intentional termination of an innocent human life is always immoral. They also express concern about mistaken diagnoses, the possibility of cure and relief, and especially about the potentially dangerous consequences resulting from such a lessening of respect for human life.

Similarly, those supporting nonvoluntary active or passive euthanasia generally appeal to principles of humanness and human dignity. Those opposing it marshal all the arguments that we have catalogued against a voluntary death decision, while stressing how morally objectionable it is to allow people to die or to kill people without voluntary consent.

Of course, various positions are possible, and likely, within this broad outline. For example, some who support voluntary decisions might well oppose the nonvoluntary. And many who support nonvoluntary allowing to die or nonvoluntary passive euthanasia might object to nonvoluntary active euthanasia. In other words, for some moralists the key factor in determining the morality of a death decision is whether or not it is voluntary. For many, a death decision is moral if and only if it is voluntary. Others concern themselves primarily with the distinction between active and passive, not voluntary and nonvoluntary. In their view, the focus should be not on who makes the death decision, but on whether there is a morally significant difference between active and passive euthanasia, such that even if passive euthanasia is acceptable, the active form is not.

Defective Newborns

Much of the preceding discussion applies to the issue of babies born with serious birth defects, such as Tay-Sachs, a fatal degenerative disease; Down's syndrome, which manifests itself in mental retardation and various physical abnormalities; and duodenal atresia, in which the upper part of the small intestine, the duodenum, is closed off, thus preventing the passage and digestion of food. (Although duodenal atresia usually can be treated effectively through surgery, it often is accompanied by other serious birth defects.) Today physicians can tell much about the health of the fetus through a procedure called amniocentesis, whereby amniotic fluid is withdrawn from the pregnant woman for diagnostic purposes.

It's important to note that in the case of defective newborns, allowing to die includes withholding ordinary and not just extraordinary treatment. For example, ordinary nourishment may be withheld, resulting in the infant's death. Is this moral? In answering this question, it's necessary to come to grips with the central moral issue involving seriously defective infants, which involves determining the conditions, if any, under which it is morally permissible to allow defective newborns to die.

It is possible to identify three broad positions on the moral acceptability of allowing severely defective newborns to die. Underpinning each are controversial value assumptions.

The first and most permissive position is that allowing seriously defective infants to die is morally permissible when there is no significant potential for a meaningful human existence. It also sanctions such an act when the emotional or financial hardship of caring for the infant would place a grave burden on the family. Adherents of this view often argue their case on the grounds that the seriously defective newborn does not have person status, which, as we've seen in Chapter 14, is a controversial assumption.

The second position is that it is permissible only if there is no significant potential for a meaningful human existence. Clearly implied here is a quality-of-life judgment, which, of course, elicits debate.

The third position asserts that it is *never* morally permissible to allow a defective newborn to die. Stated more cautiously, it is never moral to withhold from a defective newborn any treatment that would be provided a normal one. The clear implication here is that the defective infant has full personhood and must be treated accordingly. Just as clearly, this view rejects any quality-of-life or cost factors in determining the acceptability of allowing a defective infant to die. Like the other positions, this one is fraught with debatable value judgments, and in cases of duodenal atresia it ignores that normal infants would not require corrective surgery in order to digest food.

It is quite apparent, then, that whether cases involve defective newborns or adults who are terminally ill, the central moral question concerns the acceptability of a death decision and subsequent action. But there are additional moral problems relating to death decisions in the institutional setting that are worth considering.

Death Decisions in the Institutional Setting

A basic problem related to death decisions in an institutional setting concerns the criteria for the decision. There are several aspects to this issue. One aspect deals with who makes the decision.

Who Should Decide?

Should it be the physician, the patient, the family, a member of the clergy, a board, or some combination? When patients can give informed consent—that is, can understand what they are agreeing to and voluntarily choose it—their rights to autonomy and adequate care would require their participation in the death decision. Cases in which patients are denied their own *request* that life-sustaining treatment be discontinued or that they be permitted to kill themselves raise serious moral questions. For to deny their requests contradicts the standard presumption that it is moral to let adults make for themselves decisions that affect themselves, and that not to do so is to use them as means, not ends, violating the Kantian principle of respect for individuals.

But cases in which patients are not competent to make a death decision are just as troublesome. Some moralists believe death decisions should never be made for patients who cannot themselves ask to die. Thus it would be wrong for health professionals or anyone else to permit or cause the deaths of incompetent older patients being kept alive artificially or of defective newborns. Others disagree, arguing that in such cases the decision rightfully shifts to those most knowledgeable about the patient: parents, guardians, spouses, physicians, or others.

Given the complexities involved in any death decision, it's understandable that many health professionals, especially nurses, prefer a board decision.[5] It's true that in cases of incompetent patients a collective decision (as opposed to a decision made exclusively by the physician, for example) seems most likely to ensure that the legitimate interests of all parties will be considered and that undue personal bias will not color the decision. But there's still the category of competent patients who request death and are denied, say, by a board. To repeat: How does a denial square with the presumption that it's moral, even obligatory, to permit adults who can to make for themselves decisions that affect themselves? To respond by saying, "Yes, such adults should be permitted to make a death decision, but I (the health professional, relative, board, etc.) am under no obligation to help them implement it" misses the point that "not helping" here is equivalent to "not permitting." There may be good reasons for not permitting the death decision in these cases, but one can't have it both ways: One cannot *not* permit and at the same time reasonably claim that one is honoring the individual's right to autonomy.

What Should the Criteria Be?

Under what conditions, if ever, should death decisions be made? The answer to this question inevitably will reflect perspectives on personhood, death, and ordinary vs. extraordinary treatment, as well as general views on allowing to die, euthanasia, and emphasis to be placed on informed consent. The question of who should formulate the criteria is related to this issue.

What Policies Should There Be for Implementation?

Vague physician orders are a problem in this area. Nurses can get caught between their legal obligation to follow physicians' orders, which may imply termination of treatment, and their professional obligation to provide life-preserving services. Such a dilemma can torture personnel in institutions for the elderly, whose nurses may be the patient's and family's own daily resources. Problems for nurses grow even murkier when the patient's family desires a course of action that conflicts with what some rarely present physician has ordered. Certainly physicians are under special obligations to clarify their orders, and by the same token, nurses are obliged to keep physicians informed of family wishes and of changes in the patient's condition that may warrant changes in standing orders. Furthermore, it's worth emphasizing the physician's obligation to draw on the nurse's perceptions of the terminally ill patient. Nurses, because of the daily contact with patients, often know more about the patient's condition than physicians do. This observation is especially relevant to institutions with guidelines for orders not to resuscitate. Although physicians are responsible for recording the decision, they risk considerable harm to patients if they don't consult on

5. N. K. Brown, J. T. Donovan, R. J. Bulger, and E. H. Laws, "How Do Nurses Feel about Euthanasia and Abortion?" American Journal of Nursing, *July 1971, pp. 1415–16.*

a *continuing* basis with their nurses who may be best informed about the patient's condition.

Although professional staff deal with dying, death, and death decisions more directly than administrative staff do, the bureaucratic line of authority does get involved in these issues, thereby raising additional questions. For one thing, administrators have an obligation to ensure a free flow of communication among health professionals involved in implementing a death decision. For another, administrative and professional staff must make sure their organizational clashes don't jeopardize the care of the dying. Physicians, nurses, and other health professionals tend to identify with the interests of patients. In contrast, administrators tend to view patients as managerial problems, relating specifically to the allocation of scarce hospital resources. When a patient happens to be terminally ill, these incompatible perspectives can cause problems for everyone, especially the patient. Health professionals generally seek to provide treatment tailored to the individual's needs and requests, but they can still be indifferent to the matter of when and under what conditions patients should choose death—especially since the cornerstone of their medical training and of their professional obligation is the preservation of life. Administrators, given their preoccupation with institutional efficiency and equality of services for all patients, can ignore individual needs.[6]

So although determining the moral acceptability of a death decision stands as the central moral issue, there are other questions health professionals and others must face. These pertain to decision criteria and to policies for implementing death decisions in an institutional setting. So complex are these problems that some argue an alternative setting is required, one that effectively minimizes the need for death decisions. Of all the alternative care systems for the dying, the hospice approach has received the most attention in recent years.

The Hospice Approach

Hospices are special settings devoted exclusively to care of the terminally ill. The hospice approach to care of the dying differs from conventional care in several important ways.[7] (1) It stresses comfort and care, including control of pain and symptoms and assistance at all levels to patients and their families. (2) Its nucleus is the hospice "team," which includes physicians, nurses, clergy, social workers, psychologists and psychiatrists, and various therapists and volunteers, as well as patients and family. (3) Hospice practitioners take a preventive rather than reactive approach to control of pain and symptoms. Accordingly, every attempt is made to preclude the patient's having pain, which means that in some cases drugs are administered not only when patients are already in pain but also *before*. (4) Hospices may have both inpatient and outpatient or home-care service.

6.   *A. J. Davis and M. A. Aroskar,* Ethical Dilemmas and Nursing Practice *(New York: Appleton-Century-Crofts, 1978), p. 127.*

7.   *See Jacques Thiroux,* Ethics: Theory and Practice, *2nd ed. (Encino, Calif.: Glencoe, 1980), pp. 187–189.*

(5) The hospice approach attempts to help patients' families adjust to death before, during, and—most important—after its occurrence.

Hospice supporters argue that their approach is calculated to relieve the very sources of requests and demands for mercy deaths: suffering and profound feelings of meaninglessness. Of course, there remains that category of patients who do not want even hospice treatment and who would rather die. And there are those for whom hospice treatment doesn't apply: for example, paraplegics, quadriplegics, paralytics, and others suffering from debilitating diseases. For them a mercy death might pose a viable alternative to their conditions. A case in point is Elizabeth Bouvia, the 26-year-old Riverside, California, woman who has cerebral palsy and who has waged an unsuccessful legal battle to compel a nursing home to help her end her life.

Legal Considerations

Even if we decide that some form of euthanasia is morally acceptable, another question arises: Should individuals have a legal right to euthanasia? Ought people be permitted under law to have their lives terminated?

Currently it is illegal to deliberately cause the death of another person. It is generally recognized, however, that people have a right to refuse life-sustaining treatment. In recent years numerous attempts have been made to legislate the individual's right to refuse life-sustaining treatment. By and large these efforts have been rebuffed. Some object to the proposed legislation because of inherent difficulties in trying to define phrases such as "death with dignity," "natural death," "extraordinary means," "heroic measures," and "informed consent." Others observe that such legislation is not needed, since there is already a widely recognized right to reject life-sustaining treatment. Still others express concern that legalizing such a right will lead to abuses.

In the absence of specific legislation, various documents and directives have been developed to allow people to inform others about the nature and extent of the treatment they wish to have should they become seriously ill. Such documents usually are termed *living wills*. While living wills do specify the person's wishes, and relieve others of having to make momentous life or death decisions, generally they are not legally binding. Thus there is no guarantee that the person's wishes will be implemented.

In 1977 the State of California, as part of the "Natural Death Act," created a version of a living will called "Directive to Physicians" (see Figure 1). What makes this document unique is that it guarantees those who execute it the same legal power guaranteed by an estate will. Of course, as with estate wills, the "Directive to Physicians" can be contested. But the document takes a giant step toward granting legal status to living wills.

It is important to remember that the morality of legalizing death decisions is a separate issue from the morality of euthanasia itself. While many of the arguments for and against the legalization of death decisions capitalize on the general arguments previously outlined, it is entirely possible that one could approve of individual death decisions but at the same time object to any systematic social policy permitting them. The objection could be based on a fear that such a policy would lead to abuses by physicians, families, and others, or that it would lead to more permissive legislation allowing, say, nonvoluntary or active euthanasia.

DIRECTIVE TO PHYSICIANS

Directive made this _____ day of _____(month, year).

I _____ , being of sound mind, willfully and voluntarily make known my desire that my life shall not be artificially prolonged under the circumstances set forth below, do hereby declare:

1. If at any time I should have an incurable injury, disease, or illness certified to be a terminal condition by two physicians, and where the application of life-sustaining procedures would serve only to artificially prolong the moment of my death and where my physician determines that my death is imminent whether or not life-sustaining procedures are utilized, I direct that such procedures be withheld or withdrawn, and that I be permitted to die naturally.

2. In the absence of my ability to give directions regarding the use of such life-sustaining procedures, it is my intention that this directive shall be honored by my family and physician(s) as the final expression of my legal right to refuse medical or surgical treatment and accept the consequences from such refusal.

3. If I have been diagnosed as pregnant and that diagnosis is known to my physician, this directive shall have no force or effect during the course of my pregnancy.

4. I have been diagnosed and notified at least 14 days ago as having a terminal condition by _____ , M.D., whose address is _____ , and whose telephone number is _____ .   I understand that if I have not filled in the physician's name and address, it shall be presumed that I did not have a terminal condition when I made out this directive.

5. This directive shall have no force or effect five years from the date filled in above.

6. I understand the full import of this directive and I am emotionally and mentally competent to make this directive.

Signed _____

City, County and State of Residence _____

The declarant has been personally known to me and I believe him or her to be of sound mind.

Witness _____

Witness _____

Figure 1

The Wrongfulness of Euthanasia

J. Gay-Williams

In this essay, professor of philosophy J. Gay-Williams defines euthanasia *as intentionally taking the life of a person suffering from some illness or injury from which recovery cannot reasonably be expected. While rejecting* voluntary euthanasia *as a* name *for actions that are usually designated by the phrase, Gay-Williams seems to approve of the actions themselves. He argues that euthanasia as intentional killing goes against natural law because it violates the natural inclination to preserve life. Furthermore, in Gay-Williams's view, both self-interest and possible practical effects of euthanasia provide reasons for rejecting it.*

My impression is that euthanasia—the idea, if not the practice—is slowly gaining acceptance within our society. Cynics might attribute this to an increasing tendency to devalue human life, but I do not believe this is the major factor. The acceptance is much more likely to be the result of unthinking sympathy and benevolence. Well-publicized, tragic stories like that of Karen Quinlan elicit from us deep feelings of compassion. We think to ourselves, "She and her family would be better off if she were dead." It is an easy step from this very human response to the view that if someone (and others) would be better off dead, then it must be all right to kill that person.[1] Although I respect the compassion that leads to this conclusion, I believe the conclusion is wrong. I want to show that euthanasia is wrong. It is inherently wrong, but it is also wrong judged from the standpoints of self-interest and of practical effects.

Before presenting my arguments to support this claim, it would be well to define "euthanasia." An essential aspect of euthanasia is that it involves taking a human life, either one's own or that of another. Also, the person whose life is taken must be someone who is believed to be suffering from some disease or injury from which recovery cannot reasonably be expected. Finally, the action must be deliberate and intentional. Thus, euthanasia is intentionally taking the life of a presumably hopeless person. Whether the life is one's own or that of another, the taking of it is still euthanasia.

It is important to be clear about the deliberate and intentional aspect of the killing. If a hopeless person is given an injection of the wrong drug by mistake and this causes his death, this is wrongful killing but not euthanasia. The killing cannot be the result of accident. Furthermore, if the person is given an injection of a drug that is believed to be necessary to treat his disease or better his condition and the person dies as a result, then this is neither wrongful killing nor euthanasia. The intention was to make the patient well, not kill him. Similarly, when a patient's condition is such that it is not reasonable to hope that any medical procedures or treatments will save his life, a failure to implement the procedures or treatments is not euthanasia. If the person dies, this will be as a result of his injuries or disease and not because of his failure to receive treatment.

The failure to continue treatment after it has been realized that the patient has little chance of benefitting from it has been characterized by some as "passive euthanasia." This phrase is misleading and mistaken.[2] In such cases, the person involved is not killed (the first essential aspect of euthanasia), nor is the death of the person intended by the withholding of additional treatment (the third essential aspect of euthanasia). The aim may be to spare the person additional and unjustifiable pain, to save him from the indignities of hopeless manipulations, and to avoid increasing the financial and emotional burden on his family. When I buy a pencil it is so that I can use it to write, not to contribute to an increase in the gross national product. This may be the unintended consequence of my action, but it is not the aim of my action. So it is with failing to continue the treatment of a dying person. I intend his death no more than I intend to reduce the GNP by not using medical supplies. His is an unintended dying, and so-called "passive euthanasia" is not euthanasia at all.

1. The Argument from Nature

Every human being has a natural inclination to continue living. Our reflexes and responses fit us to fight attackers, flee wild animals, and dodge out of the way of trucks. In our daily lives we exercise the caution and care necessary to protect ourselves. Our bodies are similarly structured for survival right down to the molecular level. When we are cut, our capillaries seal shut, our blood clots, and fibrogen is produced to start the process of healing the wound. When we are invaded by bacteria, antibodies are produced to fight against the alien organisms, and their remains are swept out of the body by special cells designed for clean-up work.

Euthanasia does violence to this natural goal of survival. It is literally acting against nature because all the processes of nature are bent towards the end of bodily survival. Euthanasia defeats these subtle mechanisms in a way that, in a particular case, disease and injury might not.

It is possible, but not necessary, to make an appeal to revealed religion in this connection.[3] Man as trustee of his body acts against God, its rightful possessor, when he takes his own life. He also violates the commandment to hold life sacred and never to take it without just and compelling cause. But since this appeal will persuade only those who are prepared to accept that religion has access to revealed truths, I shall not employ this line of argument.

It is enough, I believe, to recognize that the organization of the human body and our patterns of behavioral responses make the continuation of life a natural goal. By reason alone, then, we can recognize that euthanasia sets us against our own nature.[4] Furthermore, in doing so, euthanasia does violence to our dignity. Our dignity comes from seeking our ends. When one of our goals is survival, and actions are taken that eliminate that goal, then our natural dignity suffers. Unlike animals,

we are conscious through reason of our nature and our ends. Euthanasia involves acting as if this dual nature—inclination towards survival and awareness of this as an end—did not exist. Thus, euthanasia denies our basic human character and requires that we regard ourselves or others as something less than fully human.

2. The Argument from Self-Interest

The above arguments are, I believe, sufficient to show that euthanasia is inherently wrong. But there are reasons for considering it wrong when judged by standards other than reason. Because death is final and irreversible, euthanasia contains within it the possibility that we will work against our own interest if we practice it or allow it to be practiced on us.

Contemporary medicine has high standards of excellence and a proven record of accomplishment, but it does not possess perfect and complete knowledge. A mistaken diagnosis is possible, and so is a mistaken prognosis. Consequently, we may believe that we are dying of a disease when, as a matter of fact, we may not be. We may think that we have no hope of recovery when, as a matter of fact, our chances are quite good. In such circumstances, if euthanasia were permitted, we would die needlessly. Death is final and the chance of error too great to approve the practice of euthanasia.

Also, there is always the possibility that an experimental procedure or a hitherto untried technique will pull us through. We should at least keep this option open, but euthanasia closes it off. Furthermore, spontaneous remission does occur in many cases. For no apparent reason, a patient simply recovers when those all around him, including his physicians, expected him to die. Euthanasia would just guarantee their expectations and leave no room for the "miraculous" recoveries that frequently occur.

Finally, knowing that we can take our life at any time (or ask another to take it) might well incline us to give up too easily. The will to live is strong in all of us, but it can be weakened by pain and suffering and feelings of hopelessness. If during a bad time we allow ourselves to be killed, we never have a chance to reconsider. Recovery from a serious illness requires that we fight for it, and anything that weakens our determination by suggesting that there is an easy way out is ultimately against our own interest. Also, we may be inclined towards euthanasia because of our concern for others. If we see our sickness and suffering as an emotional and financial burden on our family, we may feel that to leave our life is to make their lives easier.[5] The very presence of the possibility of euthanasia may keep us from surviving when we might.

3. The Argument from Practical Effects

Doctors and nurses are, for the most part, totally committed to saving lives. A life lost is, for them, almost a personal failure, an insult to their skills and knowledge. Euthanasia as a practice might well alter this. It could have a corrupting influence so that in any case that is severe doctors and nurses might not try hard enough to save the patient. They might decide that the patient would simply be "better off dead" and take the steps necessary to make that come about. This attitude could then carry over to their dealings with patients less seriously ill. The result would be an overall decline in the quality of medical care.

Finally, euthanasia as a policy is a slippery slope. A person apparently hopelessly ill may be allowed to take his own life. Then he may be permitted to deputize others to do it for him should he no longer be able to act. The judgment of others then becomes the ruling factor. Already at this point euthanasia is not personal and voluntary, for others are acting "on behalf of" the patient as they see fit. This may well incline them to act on behalf of other patients who have not authorized them to exercise their judgment. It is only a short step, then, from voluntary euthanasia (self-inflicted or authorized), to directed euthanasia administered to a patient who has given no authorization, to involuntary euthanasia conducted as part of a social policy.[6] Recently many psychiatrists and sociologists have argued that we define as "mental illness" those forms of behavior that we disapprove of.[7] This gives us license then to lock up those who display the behavior. The category of the "hopelessly ill" provides the possibility of even worse abuse. Embedded in a social policy, it would give society or its representatives the authority to eliminate all those who might be considered too "ill" to function normally any longer. The dangers of euthanasia are too great to all to run the risk of approving it in any form. The first slippery step may well lead to a serious and harmful fall.

I hope that I have succeeded in showing why the benevolence that inclines us to give approval of euthanasia is misplaced. Euthanasia is inherently wrong because it violates the nature and dignity of human beings. But even those who are not convinced by this must be persuaded that the potential personal and social dangers inherent in euthanasia are sufficient to forbid our approving it either as a personal practice or as a public policy.

Suffering is surely a terrible thing, and we have a clear duty to comfort those in need and to ease their suffering when we can. But suffering is also a natural part of life with values for the individual and for others that we should not overlook. We may legitimately seek for others and for ourselves an easeful death, as Arthur Dyck has pointed out.[8] Euthanasia, however, is not just an easeful death. It is a wrongful death. Euthanasia is not just dying. It is killing.

Notes

1. For a sophisticated defense of this position see Philippa Foot, "Euthanasia," *Philosophy and Public Affairs*, vol. 6 (1977), pp. 85–112. Foot does not endorse the radical conclusion that euthanasia, voluntary and involuntary, is always right.

2. James Rachels rejects the distinction between active and passive euthanasia as morally irrelevant in his "Active and Passive Euthanasia," *New England Journal of Medicine*, vol. 292, pp. 78–80. But see the criticism by Foot, pp. 100–103.

3. For a defense of this view see J. V. Sullivan, "The Immorality of Euthanasia," in *Beneficent Euthanasia*, ed. Marvin Kohl (Buffalo, New York: Prometheus Books, 1975), pp. 34–44.

4. This point is made by Ray V. McIntyre in "Voluntary Euthanasia: The Ultimate Perversion," *Medical Counterpoint*, vol. 2, 26–29.

5. See McIntyre, p. 28.

6. See Sullivan, "Immorality of Euthanasia," pp. 34–44, for a fuller argument in support of this view.

7. See, for example, Thomas S. Szasz, *The Myth of Mental Illness*, rev. ed. (New York: Harper & Row, 1974).

8. Arthur Dyck, "Beneficent Euthanasia and Benemortasia," in Kohl, op. cit., pp. 117–129.

Questions for Analysis

1. Why doesn't Gay-Williams consider "passive euthanasia" an act of euthanasia? Do you agree with his distinction?

2. Would it be accurate to say that Gay-Williams applies both religious and nonreligious interpretations to argue against euthanasia? Explain.

3. State his arguments from self-interest.

4. State his arguments from practical effects. Which moral principle or type of ethical theory does this reflect?

5. What critical inquiries, if any, would you make about the author's arguments against euthanasia?

Active and Passive Euthanasia

James Rachels

The traditional view that there is an important moral difference between active and passive euthanasia is one that was endorsed by J. Gay-Williams in the preceding essay. Active euthanasia involves killing and passive euthanasia letting die, and this fact has led many physicians and philosophers to reject active euthanasia as morally wrong, even while approving of passive euthanasia.

In this essay, professor of philosophy James Rachels challenges both the use and moral significance of this distinction for several reasons. First, active euthanasia is in many cases more humane than passive. Second, the conventional doctrine leads to decisions concerning life and death on irrelevant grounds. Third, the doctrine rests on a distinction between killing and letting die that itself has no moral significance. Fourth, the most common arguments in favor of the doctrine are invalid. Therefore, in Rachels's view, the American Medical Association's policy statement endorsing the active-passive distinction is unwise.

The distinction between active and passive euthanasia is thought to be crucial for medical ethics. The idea is that it is permissible, at least in some cases, to withhold treatment and allow a patient to die, but it is never permissible to take any direct action designed to kill the patient. This doctrine seems to be accepted by most doctors, and it is endorsed in a statement adopted by the House of Delegates of the American Medical Association on December 4, 1973:

> The intentional termination of the life of one human being by another—mercy killing—is contrary to that for which the medical profession stands and is contrary to the policy of the American Medical Association.
>
> The cessation of the employment of extraordinary means to prolong the life of the body when there is irrefutable evidence that biological death is imminent is the decision of the patient and/or his immediate family. The advice and judgment of the physician should be freely available to the patient and/or his immediate family.

However, a strong case can be made against this doctrine. In what follows I will set out some of the relevant arguments, and urge doctors to reconsider their views on this matter.

From James Rachels, "Active and Passive Euthanasia," New England Journal of Medicine, *292 (January 9, 1975), 78–80. Reprinted by permission of the publisher.*

To begin with a familiar type of situation, a patient who is dying of incurable cancer of the throat is in terrible pain, which can no longer be satisfactorily alleviated. He is certain to die within a few days, even if present treatment is continued, but he does not want to go on living for those days since the pain is unbearable. So he asks the doctor for an end to it, and his family joins in the request.

Suppose the doctor agrees to withhold treatment, as the conventional doctrine says he may. The justification for his doing so is that the patient is in terrible agony, and since he is going to die anyway, it would be wrong to prolong his suffering needlessly. But now notice this. If one simply withholds treatment, it may take the patient longer to die, and so he may suffer more than he would if more direct action were taken and a lethal injection given. This fact provides strong reason for thinking that, once the initial decision not to prolong his agony has been made, active euthanasia is actually preferable to passive euthanasia, rather than the reverse. To say otherwise is to endorse the option that leads to more suffering rather than less, and is contrary to the humanitarian impulse that prompts the decision not to prolong his life in the first place.

Part of my point is that the process of being "allowed to die" can be relatively slow and painful, whereas being given a lethal injection is relatively quick and painless. Let me give a different sort of example. In the United States about one in 600 babies is born with Down's syndrome. Most of these babies are otherwise healthy—that is, with only the usual pediatric care, they will proceed to an otherwise normal infancy. Some, however, are born with congenital defects such as intestinal obstructions that require operations if they are to live. Sometimes, the patients and the doctor will decide not to operate, and let the infant die. Anthony Shaw describes what happens then:

> . . . When surgery is denied [the doctor] must try to keep the infant from suffering while natural forces sap the baby's life away. As a surgeon whose natural inclination is to use the scalpel to fight off death, standing by and watching a salvageable baby die is the most emotionally enhausting experience I know. It is easy at a conference, in a theoretical discussion, to decide that such infants should be allowed to die. It is altogether different to stand by in the nursery and watch as dehydration and infection wither a tiny being over hours and days. This is a terrible ordeal for me and the hospital staff—much more so than for the parents who never set foot in the nursery.[1]

I can understand why some people are opposed to all euthanasia, and insist that such infants must be allowed to live. I think I can also understand why other people favor destroying these babies quickly and painlessly. But why should anyone favor letting "dehydration and infection wither a tiny being over hours and days"? The doctrine that says that a baby may be allowed to dehydrate and wither, but may not be given an injection that would end its life without suffering, seems so patently cruel as to require no further refutation. The strong language is not intended to offend, but only to put the point in the clearest possible way.

My second argument is that the conventional doctrine leads to decisions concerning life and death made on irrelevant grounds.

Consider again the case of the infants with Down's syndrome who need operations for congenital defects unrelated to the syndrome to live. Sometimes, there is no operation, and the baby dies, but when there is no such defect, the baby lives on. Now, an operation such as that to remove an intestinal obstruction is not prohibitively difficult. The reason why such operations are not performed in these cases is, clearly, that the child has Down's syndrome and the parents and the doctor judge that because of that fact it is better for the child to die.

But notice that this situation is absurd, no matter what view one takes of the lives and potentials of such babies. If the life of such an infant is worth preserving, what does it matter if it needs a simple operation? Or, if one thinks it better that such a baby should not live on, what difference does it make that it happens to have an unobstructed intestinal tract? In either case, the matter of life and death is being decided on irrelevant grounds. It is the Down's syndrome, and not the intestines, that is the issue. The matter should be decided, if at all, on that basis, and not be allowed to depend on the essentially irrelevant question of whether the intestinal tract is blocked.

What makes this situation possible, of course, is the idea that when there is an intestinal blockage, one can "let the baby die," but when there is no such defect there is nothing that can be done, for one must not "kill" it. The fact that this idea leads to such results as deciding life or death on irrelevant grounds is another good reason why the doctrine should be rejected.

One reason why so many people think that there is an important moral difference between active and passive euthanasia is that they think killing someone is morally worse than letting someone die. But is it? Is killing, in itself, worse than letting die? To investigate this issue, two cases may be considered that are exactly alike except that one involves killing whereas the other involves letting someone die. Then, it can be asked whether this difference makes any difference to the moral assessments. It is important that the cases be exactly alike, except for this one difference, since otherwise one cannot be confident that it is this difference and not some other that accounts for any variation in the assessments of the two cases. So, let us consider this pair of cases:

In the first, Smith stands to gain a large inheritance if anything should happen to his six-year-old cousin. One evening while the child is taking his bath, Smith sneaks into the bathroom and drowns the child, and then arranges things so that it will look like an accident.

In the second, Jones also stands to gain if anything should happen to his six-year-old cousin. Like Smith, Jones sneaks in planning to drown the child in his bath. However, just as he enters the bathroom Jones sees the child slip and hit his head, and fall face down in the water. Jones is delighted; he stands by, ready to push the child's head back under if it is necessary, but it is not necessary. With only a little thrashing about, the child drowns all by himself, "accidentally," as Jones watches and does nothing.

Now Smith killed the child, whereas Jones "merely" let the child die. That is the only difference between them. Did either man behave better, from a moral point of view? If the difference between killing and letting die were in itself a morally important matter, one should say that Jones's behavior was less reprehensible than Smith's. But does one really want to say that? I think not. In the first place, both men acted from the same motive, personal gain, and both had exactly the same end in view when they acted. It may be inferred from

Smith's conduct that he is a bad man, although that judgment may be withdrawn or modified if certain further facts are learned about him—for example, that he is mentally deranged. But would not the very same thing be inferred about Jones from his conduct? And would not the same further considerations also be relevant to any modification of this judgment? Moreover, suppose Jones pleaded, in his own defense, "After all, I didn't do anything except just stand there and watch the child drown. I didn't kill him; I only let him die." Again, if letting die were in itself less bad than killing, this defense should have at least some weight. But it does not. Such a "defense" can only be regarded as a grotesque perversion of moral reasoning. Morally speaking, it is no defense at all.

Now, it may be pointed out, quite properly, that the cases of euthanasia with which doctors are concerned are not like this at all. They do not involve personal gain or the destruction of normal healthy children. Doctors are concerned only with cases in which the patient's life is of no further use to him, or in which the patient's life has become or will soon become a terrible burden. However, the point is the same in these cases: The bare difference between killing and letting die does not, in itself, make a moral difference. If a doctor lets a patient die, for humane reasons, he is in the same moral position as if he had given the patient a lethal injection for humane reasons. If his decision was wrong— if, for example, the patient's illness was in fact curable—the decision would be equally regrettable no matter which method was used to carry it out. And if the doctor's decision was the right one, the method used is not in itself important.

The AMA policy statement isolates the crucial issue very well: The crucial issue is "the intentional termination of the life of one human being by another." But after identifying this issue, and forbidding "mercy killing," the statement goes on to deny that the cessation of treatment is the intentional termination of a life. This is where the mistake comes in, for what is the cessation of treatment, in these circumstances, if it is not "the intentional termination of the life of one human being by another"? Of course it is exactly that, and if it were not, there would be no point to it.

Many people will find this judgment hard to accept. One reason, I think, is that it is very easy to conflate the question of whether killing is, in itself, worse than letting die, with the very different question of whether most actual cases of killing are more reprehensible than most actual cases of letting die. Most actual cases of killing are clearly terrible (think, for example, of all the murders reported in the newspapers), and one hears of such cases everyday. On the other hand, one hardly ever hears of a case of letting die, except for the actions of doctors who are motivated by humanitarian reasons. So one learns to think of killing in a much worse light than of letting die. But this does not mean that there is something about killing that makes it in itself worse than letting die, for it is not the bare difference between killing and letting die that makes the difference in these cases. Rather, the other factors—the murderer's motive of personal gain, for example, contrasted with the doctor's humanitarian motivation—account for different reactions to the different cases.

I have argued that killing is not in itself any worse than letting die; if my contention is right, it follows that active euthanasia is not any worse than passive euthanasia. What arguments can be given on the other side? The most common, I believe, is the following:

"The important difference between active and passive euthanasia is that in passive euthanasia, the doctor does not do anything to bring about the patient's death. The doctor does nothing, and the patient dies of whatever ills already afflict him. In active euthanasia, however, the doctor does something to bring about the patient's death: He kills him. The doctor who gives the patient with cancer a lethal injection has himself caused his patient's death; whereas if he merely ceases treatment, the cancer is the cause of death."

A number of points need to be made here. The first is that it is not exactly correct to say that in passive euthanasia the doctor does nothing, for he does do one thing that is very important: He lets the patient die. "Letting someone die" is certainly different, in some respects, from other types of action—mainly in that it is a kind of action that one may perform by way of not performing certain other actions. For example, one may let a patient die by way of not giving medication, just as one may insult someone by way of not shaking his hand. But for any purpose of moral assessment, it is a type of action nonetheless. The decision to let a patient die is subject to moral appraisal in the same way that

a decision to kill him would be subject to moral appraisal: It may be assessed as wise or unwise, compassionate or sadistic, right or wrong. If a doctor deliberately let a patient die who was suffering from a routinely curable illness, the doctor would certainly be to blame for what he had done, just as he would be to blame if he had needlessly killed the patient. Charges against him would then be appropriate. If so, it would be no defense at all for him to insist that he didn't "do anything." He would have done something very serious indeed, for he let his patient die.

Fixing the cause of death may be very important from a legal point of view, for it may determine whether criminal charges are brought against the doctor. But I do not think that this notion can be used to show a moral difference between active and passive euthanasia. The reason why it is considered bad to be the cause of someone's death is that death is regarded as a great evil—and so it is. However, if it has been decided that euthanasia—even passive euthanasia—is desirable in a given case, it has also been decided that in this instance death is no greater an evil than the patient's continued existence. And if this is true, the usual reason for not wanting to be the cause of someone's death simply does not apply.

Finally, doctors may think that all of this is only of academic interest—the sort of thing that philosophers may worry about but that has no practical bearing on their own work. After all, doctors must be concerned about the legal consequences of what they do, and active euthanasia is clearly forbidden by the law. But even so, doctors should also be concerned with the fact that the law is forcing upon them a moral doctrine that may well be indefensible, and has a considerable effect on their practices. Of course, most doctors are not now in the position of being coerced in this matter, for they do not regard themselves as merely going along with what the law requires. Rather, in statements such as the AMA policy statement that I have quoted, they are endorsing this doctrine as a central point of medical ethics. In that statement, active euthanasia is condemned not merely as illegal but as "contrary to that for which the medical profession stands," whereas passive euthanasia is approved. However, the preceding considerations suggest that there is really no moral difference between the two, considered in themselves (there may be important moral differences in some cases in their *consequences*, but, as I pointed out, these differences may make active euthanasia, and not passive euthanasia, the morally preferable option). So, whereas doctors may have to discriminate between active and passive euthanasia to satisfy the law, they should not do any more than that. In particular, they should not give the distinction any added authority and weight by writing it into official statements of medical ethics.

Note

1.   A. Shaw, "Doctor, Do We Have a Choice?" *The New York Times Magazine,* January 30, 1972, p. 54.

Questions for Analysis

1.   *Early in his essay, Rachels sets up a familiar situation involving a throat-cancer patient. What is the point of the example? Do you think that suspending pain-relieving drugs is what people generally understand by "withholding treatment"?*

2.   *Explain, through Rachels's own example of the infant with Down's syndrome, why he thinks the distinction between active and passive euthanasia leads to life-or-death decisions made on irrelevant grounds.*

3.   *Do you agree with Rachels that the cessation of treatment is tantamount to the intentional termination of life?*

4.   *Rachels claims that killing is not necessarily any worse than allowing a person to die. What are the implications of this claim for the morality of active euthanasia?*

5.   *Rachels believes it is inaccurate and misleading to say that a doctor who allows a patient to die does "nothing" to cause the death. Do you agree?*

Euthanasia

Philippa Foot

Professor of Philosophy Philippa Foot, as part of her general concerns in her essay, develops a distinction between active and passive euthanasia by using the notion of a "right to life." She disagrees with Rachels, who criticizes the distinction between active and passive as morally irrelevant and inhumane in application. In contrast, Foot offers cases to show the value of making and using the distinction.

The basic issue Foot considers, however, is whether one is ever morally justified in killing people for their own good. Replying, Foot examines the idea of "ordinary human life" and explores the question of when someone's life might be regarded as not worth living any longer. She doesn't believe that it's legitimate for us to decide that for someone else. In her view, everyone has a right to life in the sense she specifies; it is what a person wants that counts. Thus even if someone would be better off dead, if that person wants to live, we aren't justified in killing him or her. In short, Foot cannot support nonvoluntary active euthanasia. Furthermore, if a person both wants to live and has a right to medical treatment, then involuntary passive euthanasia isn't justified either.

Philippa Foot, "Euthanasia," from Philosophy and Public Affairs, *vol. 6, no. 2 (Winter 1977). Copyright © 1977 by Philippa Foot. Reprinted by permission of Princeton University Press.*

But what of cases involving those whose wishes we don't know—for example, patients in a comatose state? Foot argues that taking the lives of such people would infringe their rights. So she rejects nonvoluntary active euthanasia in these cases. But she does concede that there are cases in which the comatose, were they able, would not want to be kept alive artificially. This leads her to conclude that nonvoluntary passive euthanasia may be sometime morally permissible.

Although Foot does endorse both forms of voluntary euthanasia (active and passive) as morally legitimate, she doesn't believe that we have a duty to kill people who have decided their lives are no longer worth living. For Foot, the explicit consent by such people merely guarantees that we would not be infringing their right to life by following their wishes.

The widely used *Shorter Oxford English Dictionary* gives three meanings for the word "euthanasia": the first, "a quiet and easy death"; the second, "the means of procuring this"; and the third, "the action of inducing a quiet and easy death." It is a curious fact that no one of the three gives an adequate definition of the word as it is usually understood. For "euthanasia" means much more than a quiet and easy death, or the means of procuring it, or the action of inducing it. The definition specifies only the manner of the death, and if this were all that was implied, a murderer, careful to drug his victim, could claim that his act was an act of euthanasia. We find this ridiculous because we take it for granted that in euthanasia it is death itself, not just the manner of death, that must be kind to the one who dies.

To see how important it is that "euthanasia" should not be used as the dictionary definition allows it to be used, merely to signify that a death was quiet and easy, one has only to remember that Hitler's "euthanasia" program traded on this ambiguity. Under this program, planned before the War but brought into full operation by a decree of 1 September 1939, some 275,000 people were gassed in centers which were to be a model for those in which Jews were later exterminated. Anyone in a state institution could be sent to the gas chambers if it was considered that he could not be "rehabilitated" for useful work. As Dr. Leo Alexander reports, relying on the testimony of a neuropathologist who received 500 brains from one of the killing centers,

> In Germany the exterminations included the mentally defective, psychotics (particularly schizophrenics), epileptics and patients suffering from infirmities of old age and from various organic neurological disorders such as infantile paralysis, Parkinsonism, multiple sclerosis and brain tumors. . . . In truth, all those unable to work and considered nonrehabilitable were killed.[1]

These people were killed because they were "useless" and "a burden on society"; only the manner of their deaths could be thought of as relatively easy and quiet.

Let us insist, then, that when we talk about euthanasia we are talking about a death understood as a good or happy event for the one who dies. This stipulation follows etymology, but is itself not exactly in line with current usage, which would be captured by the condition that the death should *not* be an evil rather than that it *should* be a good. That this is how people talk is shown by the fact that the case of Karen Ann Quinlan and others in a state of permanent coma is often discussed under the heading of "euthanasia." Perhaps it is not too late to object to the use of the word "euthanasia" in this sense. Apart from the break with the Greek origins of the word, there are other unfortunate aspects of this extension of the term. For if we say that the death must be supposed to be a good to the subject, we can also specify that it shall be for his sake that an act of euthanasia is performed. If we say merely that death shall not be an evil to him, we cannot stipulate that benefiting him shall be the motive where euthanasia is in question. Given the importance of the question, For whose sake are we acting? It is good to have a definition of euthanasia which brings under this heading only cases of opting for death for the sake of the one who dies. Perhaps what is most important is to say either that euthanasia is to be for the good of the subject or at least that death is to be no evil to him, thus refusing to talk Hitler's language. However, in this paper it is the first condition that will be understood, with the additional proviso that by an act of euthanasia we mean one of inducing or otherwise opting for death for the sake of the one who is to die.

A few lesser points need to be cleared up. In the first place it must be said that the word "act" is not to be taken to exclude omission; we shall speak of an act of euthanasia when someone is deliberately allowed to die, for his own good, and not only when positive measures are taken to see that he does. The very general idea we want is that of a choice of action or inaction directed at another man's death and causally effective in the sense that, in conjunction with actual circumstances, it is a sufficient condition of death. Of complications such as overdetermination, it will not be necessary to speak.

A second, and definitely minor, point about the definition of an act of euthanasia concerns the question of fact versus belief. It has already been implied that one who performs an act of euthanasia thinks that death will be merciful for the subject since we have said that it is on account of this thought that the act is done. But is it enough that he acts with this thought, or must things actually be as he thinks them to be? If one man kills another, or allows him to die, thinking that he is in the last stages of a terrible disease, though in fact he could have been cured, is this an act of euthanasia or not? Nothing much seems to hang on our decision about this. The same condition has got to enter into the definition whether as an element in reality or only as an element in the agent's belief. And however we define an act of euthanasia, culpability or justifiability will be the same: if a man acts through ignorance, his ignorance may be culpable or it may not.[2]

These are relatively easy problems to solve, but one that is dauntingly difficult has been passed over in this discussion of the definition, and must now be faced. It is easy to say, as if this raised no problems, that an act of euthanasia is by definition one aiming at the *good* of the one whose death is in question, and that it is *for his sake* that his death is desired. But how is this to be explained? Presumably we are thinking of some evil already with him or to come on him if he continues to live, and death is thought of as a release from this evil. But this cannot be enough. Most people's lives contain evils such as grief or pain, but we do not therefore think that death would be a blessing to them. On the contrary, life is generally supposed to be a good

even for someone who is unusually unhappy or frustrated. How is it that one can ever wish for death for the sake of the one who is to die? This difficult question is central to the discussion of euthanasia, and we shall literally not know what we are talking about if we ask whether acts of euthanasia defined as we have defined them are ever morally permissible without first understanding better the reason for saying that life is a good, and the possibility that it is not always so.

If a man should save my life he would be my benefactor. In normal circumstances this is plainly true; but does one always benefit another in saving his life? It seems certain that he does not. Suppose, for instance, that a man were being tortured to death and was given a drug that lengthened his sufferings; this would not be a benefit but the reverse. Or suppose that in a ghetto in Nazi Germany a doctor saved the life of someone threatened by disease, but that the man once cured was transported to an extermination camp; the doctor might wish for the sake of the patient that he had died of the disease. Nor would a longer stretch of life always be a benefit to the person who was given it. Comparing Hitler's camps with those of Stalin, Dmitri Panin observes that in the latter the method of extermination was made worse by agonies that could stretch out over months.

> Death from a bullet would have been bliss compared with what many millions had to endure while dying of hunger. The kind of death to which they were condemned has nothing to equal it in treachery and sadism.[3]

These examples show that to save or prolong a man's life is not always to do him a service: it may be better for him if he dies earlier rather than later. It must therefore be agreed that while life is normally a benefit to the one who has it, this is not always so.

The judgment is often fairly easy to make—that life is or is not a good to someone—but the basis for it is very hard to find. When life is said to be a benefit or a good, on what grounds is the assertion made?

The difficulty is underestimated if it is supposed that the problem arises from the fact that one who is dead has nothing, so that the good someone gets from being alive cannot be compared with the amount he would otherwise have had. For why should this particular comparison be necessary? Surely it would be enough if one could say whether or not someone whose life was prolonged had more good than evil in the extra stretch of time. Such estimates are not always possible, but frequently they are; we say, for example, "He was very happy in those last years," or, "He had little but unhappiness then." If the balance of good and evil determined whether life was a good to someone, we would expect to find a correlation in the judgments. In fact, of course, we find nothing of the kind. First, a man who has no doubt that existence is a good to him may have no idea about the balance of happiness and unhappiness in his life, or of any other positive and negative factors that may be suggested. So the supposed criteria are not always operating where the judgment is made. And secondly, the application of the criteria gives an answer that is often wrong. Many people have more evil than good in their lives; we do not, however, conclude that we would do these people no service by rescuing them from death.

To get around this last difficulty Thomas Nagel has suggested that experience itself is a good which must be brought in to balance accounts.

> . . . life is worth living even when the bad elements of experience are plentiful, and the good ones too meager to outweigh the bad ones on their own. The additional positive weight is supplied by experience itself, rather than by any of its contents.[4]

This seems implausible because if experience itself is a good it must be so even when what we experience is wholly bad, as in being tortured to death. How should one decide how much to count for this experiencing; and why count anything at all?

Others have tried to solve the problem by arguing that it is a man's desire for life that makes us call life a good: if he wants to live, then anyone who prolongs his life does him a benefit. Yet someone may cling to life where we would say confidently that it would be better for him if he died, and he may admit it too. Speaking of those same conditions in which, as he said, a bullet would have been merciful, Panin writes,

> I should like to pass on my observations concerning the absence of suicides under the extremely severe conditions of our concentration camps. The more that life became desperate, the more a prisoner seemed determined to hold on to it.[5]

One might try to explain this by saying that hope was the ground of this wish to survive for further days and months in the camp. But there is nothing unintelligible in the idea that a man might cling to life though he knew those facts about his future which would make any charitable man wish that he might die.

The problem remains, and it is hard to know where to look for a solution. Is there a conceptual connection between *life* and *good*? Because life is not always a good we are apt to reject this idea, and to think that it must be a contingent fact that life is usually a good, as it is a contingent matter that legacies are usually a benefit, if they are. Yet it seems not to be a contingent matter that to save someone's life is ordinarily to benefit him. The problem is to find where the conceptual connection lies.

It may be good tactics to forget for a time that it is euthanasia we are discussing and to see how *life* and *good* are connected in the case of living beings other than men. Even plants have things done to them that are harmful or beneficial, and what does them good must be related in some way to their living and dying. Let us therefore consider plants and animals, and then come back to human beings. At least we shall get away from the temptation to think that the connection between life and benefit must everywhere be a matter of happiness and unhappiness or of pleasure and pain; the idea being absurd in the case of animals and impossible even to formulate for plants.

In case anyone thinks that the concept of the beneficial applies only in a secondary or analogical way to plants, he should be reminded that we speak quite straightforwardly in saying, for instance, that a certain amount of sunlight is beneficial to most plants. What is in question here is the habitat in which plants of particular species flourish, but we can also talk, in a slightly different way, of what does them good, where there is some suggestion of improvement or remedy. What has the beneficial to do with sustaining life? It is tempting to answer, "everything," thinking that a healthy condition just is the one apt to secure survival. In fact, however, what is beneficial to a plant may have to do with reproduction rather than the survival of the individual member of the species. Nevertheless there is a plain connection between the beneficial and the life-sustaining even for the individual plant; if something makes it better able to survive in conditions normal for that species, it is ipso facto good for it. We need go no further, and could go no further, in explaining why a certain environment or treatment is good for a plant than to show how it helps this plant to survive.[6]

This connection between the life-sustaining and the beneficial is reasonably unproblematic, and there is nothing fanciful or zoomorphic in speaking of benefiting or doing good to plants. A connection with its survival can make something beneficial to a plant. But this is not, of course, to say that we count life as a good to a plant. We may save its life by giving it what is beneficial; we do not benefit it by saving its life.

A more ramified concept of benefit is used in speaking of animal life. New things can be said, such as that an animal is better or worse off for something that happened, or that it was a good or bad thing for it that it did happen. And new things count as benefit. In the first place, there is comfort, which often is, but need not be, related to health. When loosening a collar which is too tight for a dog we can say, "That will be better for it." So we see that the words "better for it" have two different meanings which we mark when necessary by a difference of emphasis, saying "better *for* it" when health is involved. And secondly, an animal can be benefited by having its life saved. "Could you do anything for it?" can be answered by, "Yes, I managed to save its life." Sometimes we may understand this, just as we would for a plant, to mean that we had checked some disease. But we can also do something for an animal by scaring away its predator. If we do this, it is a good thing for the animal that we did, unless of course it immediately meets a more unpleasant end by some other means. Similarly, on the bad side, an animal may be worse off for our intervention, and this is not because it pines or suffers but simply because it gets killed.

The problem that vexes us when we think about euthanasia comes on the scene at this point. For if we can do something for an animal—can benefit it—by relieving its suffering but also by saving its life, where does the greater benefit come when only death will end pain? It seemed that life was a good in its own right; yet pain seemed to be an evil with equal status and could therefore make life not a good after all. Is it only life without pain that is a good when animals are concerned? This does not seem a crazy suggestion when we are thinking of animals, since unlike human beings they do not have suffering as part of their normal life. But it is perhaps the idea of ordinary life that matters here. We would not say that we had done anything for an animal if we had merely kept it alive, either in an unconscious state or in a condition where, though conscious, it was unable to operate in an ordinary way; and the fact is that animals in severe and continuous pain simply do not operate normally. So we do not, on the whole, have the option of doing the animal good by saving its life though the life would be a life of pain. No doubt there are borderline cases, but that is no problem. We are not trying to make new judgments possible, but rather to find the principle of the ones we do make.

When we reach human life, the problems seem even more troublesome. For now we must take quite new things into account, such as the subject's own view of his life. It is arguable that this places extra constraints on the solution: might it not be counted as a necessary condition of life's being a good to a man that he should see it as such? Is there not some difficulty about the idea that a benefit might be done to him by saving or prolonging his life even though he himself wished for death? Of course he might have a quite mistaken view of his own prospects, but let us ignore this and think only of cases where it is life as he knows it that is in question. Can we think that the prolonging of this life would be a benefit to him even though he would rather have it end than continue? It seems that this cannot be ruled out. That there is no simple incompatibility between life as a good and the wish for death is shown by the possibility that a man should wish himself dead, not for his own sake, but for the sake of someone else. And if we try to amend the thesis to say that life cannot be a good to one who wishes *for his own sake* that he should die, we find the crucial concept slipping through our fingers. As Bishop Butler pointed out long ago, not all ends are either benevolent or self-interested. Does a man wish for death for his own sake in the relevant sense if, for instance, he wishes to revenge himself on another by his death? Or what if he is proud and refuses to stomach dependence or incapacity even though there are many good things left in life for him? The truth seems to be that the wish for death is sometimes compatible with life's being a good and sometimes not, which is possible because the description "wishing for death" is one covering diverse states of mind from that of the determined suicide, pathologically depressed, to that of one who is surprised to find that the thought of a fatal accident is viewed with relief. On the one hand, a man may see his life as a burden but go about his business in a more or less ordinary way; on the other hand, the wish for death may take the form of a rejection of everything that is in life, as it does in severe depression. It seems reasonable to say that life is not a good to one permanently in the latter state, and we must return to this topic later on.

When are we to say that life is a good or a benefit to a man? The dilemma that faces us is this. If we say that life as such is a good, we find ourselves refuted by the examples given at the beginning of this discussion. We therefore incline to think that it is as bringing good things that life is a good, where it is a good. But if life is a good only because it is the condition of good things, why is it not equally an evil when it brings bad things? And how can it be a good even when it brings more evil than good?

It should be noted that the problem has here been formulated in terms of the balance of good and evil, not that of happiness and unhappiness, and that it is not to be solved by the denial (which may be reasonable enough) that unhappiness is the only evil or happiness the only good. In this paper no view has been expressed about the nature of goods other than life itself. The point is that on any view of the goods and evils that life can contain, it seems that a life with more evil than good could still itself be a good.

It may be useful to review the judgments with which our theory must square. Do we think that life can be a good to one who suffers a lot of pain? Clearly we do. What about severely handicapped people; can life be a good to them? Clearly it can be, for even if someone is almost completely paralyzed, perhaps living in an iron lung, perhaps able to move things only by means of a tube held between his lips, we do not rule him out of order if he says that some benefactor saved his life. Nor is it different with mental handicap. There are many fairly severely handicapped people—such as those with Down's Syndrome (Mongolism)—for whom a simple affectionate life is possible. What about senility?

Does this break the normal connection between life and good? Here we must surely distinguish between forms of senility. Some forms leave a life which we count someone as better off having than not having, so that a doctor who prolonged it would benefit the person concerned. With some kinds of senility this is, however, no longer true. There are some in geriatric wards who are barely conscious, though they can move a little and swallow food put into their mouths. To prolong such a state, whether in the old or in the very severely mentally handicapped, is not to do them a service or confer a benefit. But of course it need not be the reverse: only if there is suffering would one wish for the sake of the patient that he should die.

It seems, therefore, that merely being alive even without suffering is not a good, and that we must make a distinction similar to that which we made when animals were our topic. But how is the line to be drawn in the case of men? What is to count as ordinary human life in the relevant sense? If it were only the very senile or very ill who were to be said not to have this life, it might seem right to describe it in terms of *operation*. But it will be hard to find the sense in which the men described by Panin were not operating, given that they dragged themselves out to the forest to work. What is it about the life that the prisoners were living that makes us put it on the other side of the dividing line from that of some severely ill or suffering patients, and from most of the physically or mentally handicapped? It is not that they were in captivity, for life in captivity can certainly be a good. Nor is it merely the unusual nature of their life. In some ways the prisoners were living more as other men do than the patient in an iron lung.

The suggested solution to the problem is, then, that there is a certain conceptual connection between *life* and *good* in the case of human beings as in that of animals and even plants. Here, as there, however, it is not the mere state of being alive that can determine, or itself count as, a good, but rather life coming up to some standard of normality. It was argued that it is as part of ordinary life that the elements of good that a man may have are relevant to the question of whether saving his life counts as benefiting him. Ordinary human lives, even very hard lives, contain a minimum of basic goods, but when these are absent the idea of life is no longer linked to that of good. And since it is in this way that the elements of good contained in a man's life are relevant to the question of whether he is benefited if his life is preserved, there is no reason why it should be the balance of good and evil that counts.

It should be added that evils are relevant in one way when, as in the examples discussed above, they destroy the possibility of ordinary goods, but in a different way when they invade a life from which the goods are already absent for a different reason. So, for instance, the connection between *life* and *good* may be broken because consciousness has sunk to a very low level, as in extreme senility or severe brain damage. In itself this kind of life seems to be neither good nor evil, but if suffering sets in, one would hope for a speedy end.

The idea we need seems to be that of life which is ordinary human life in the following respect— that it contains a minimum of basic human goods. What is ordinary in human life—even in very hard lives—is that a man is not driven to work far beyond his capacity; that he has the support of a family or community; that he can more or less satisfy his hunger; that he has hopes for the future; that he can lie down to rest at night. Such things were denied to the men in the Vyatlag camps described by Panin; not even rest at night was allowed them when they were tormented by bed-bugs, by noise and stench, and by routines such as body-searches and bath-parades—arranged for the night time so that work norms would not be reduced. Disease too can so take over a man's life that the normal human goods disappear. When a patient is so overwhelmed by pain or nausea that he cannot eat with pleasure, if he can eat at all, and is out of the reach of even the most loving voice, he no longer has ordinary human life in the sense in which the words are used here. And we may now pick up a thread from an earlier part of the discussion by remarking that crippling depression can destroy the enjoyment of ordinary goods as effectively as external circumstances can remove them.

This, admittedly inadequate, discussion of the sense in which life is normally a good, and of the reasons why it may not be so in some particular case, completes the account of what euthanasia is here taken to be. An act of euthanasia, whether literally act or rather omission, is attributed to an agent who opts for the death of another because in his case life seems to be an evil rather than a good.

The question now to be asked is whether acts of euthanasia are ever justifiable. But there are two topics here rather than one. For it is one thing to say that some acts of euthanasia considered only in themselves and their results are morally unobjectionable, and another to say that it would be all right to legalize them. Perhaps the practice of euthanasia would allow too many abuses, and perhaps there would be too many mistakes. Moreover, the practice might have very important and highly undesirable side effects, because it is unlikely that we could change our principles about the treatment of the old and the ill without changing fundamental emotional attitudes and social relations. The topics must, therefore, be treated separately. In the next part of the discussion, nothing will be said about the social consequences and possible abuses of the practice of euthanasia, but only about acts of euthanasia considered in themselves.

What we want to know is whether acts of euthanasia, defined as we have defined them, are ever morally permissible. To be more accurate, we want to know whether it is ever sufficient justification of the choice of death for another that death can be counted a benefit rather than harm, and that this is why the choice is made.

It will be impossible to get a clear view of the area to which this topic belongs without first marking the distinct grounds on which objection may lie when one man opts for the death of another. There are two different virtues whose requirements are, in general, contrary to such actions. An unjustified act of killing, or allowing to die, is contrary to justice or to charity, or to both virtues, and the moral failings are distinct. Justice has to do with what men *owe* each other in the way of noninterference and positive service. When used in this wide sense, which has its history in the doctrine of the cardinal virtues, justice is not especially connected with, for instance, law courts but with the whole area of rights, and duties corresponding to rights. Thus murder is one form of injustice, dishonesty another, and wrongful failure to keep contracts a third; chicanery in a law court or defrauding someone of his inheritance are simply other cases of injustice. Justice as such is not directly linked to the good of another, and may require that something be rendered to him even where it will do him harm, as Hume pointed out when he remarked that a debt must be paid even to a profligate debauchee who "would rather receive harm than benefit from large possessions."[7] Charity, on the other hand is the virtue which attaches us to the good of others. An act of charity is in question only where something is not demanded by justice, but a lack of charity and of justice can be shown where a man is denied something which he both needs and has a right to; both charity and justice demand that widows and orphans are not defrauded, and the man who cheats them is neither charitable nor just.

It is easy to see that the two grounds of objection to inducing death are distinct. A murder is an act of injustice. A culpable failure to come to the aid of someone whose life is threatened is normally contrary, not to justice, but to charity. But where one man is under contract, explicit or implicit, to come to the aid of another, injustice too will be shown. Thus injustice may be involved either in an act or an omission, and the same is true of a lack of charity; charity may demand that someone be aided, but also that an unkind word not be spoken.

The distinction between charity and justice will turn out to be of the first importance when voluntary and nonvoluntary euthanasia are distinguished later on. This is because of the connection between justice and rights, and something should now be said about this. I believe it is true to say that wherever a man acts unjustly he has infringed a right, since justice has to do with whatever a man is owed, and whatever he is owed is his as a matter of right. Something should therefore be said about the different kinds of rights. The distinction commonly made is between having a right in the sense of having a liberty, and having a "claim-right" or "right of recipience."[8] The best way to understand such a distinction seems to be as follows. To say that a man has a right in the sense of a liberty is to say that no one can demand that he do not do the thing which he has a right to do. The fact that he has a right to do it consists in the fact that a certain kind of objection does not lie against his doing it. Thus a man has a right in this sense to walk down a public street or park his car in a public parking space. It does not follow that no one else may prevent him from doing so. If for some reason I want a certain man not to park in a certain place I may lawfully park there myself or get my friends to do so, thus preventing him from doing what he has a right (in the sense of a liberty) to do. It is different,

however, with a claim-right. This is the kind of right which I have in addition to a liberty when, for example, I have a private parking space; now others have duties in the way of noninterference, as in this case, or of service, as in the case where my claim-right is to goods or services promised to me. Sometimes one of these rights gives other people the duty of securing to me that to which I have a right, but at other times their duty is merely to refrain from interference. If a fall of snow blocks my private parking space, there is normally no obligation for anyone else to clear it away. Claim-rights generate duties; sometimes these duties are duties of noninterference; sometimes they are duties of service. If your right gives me the duty not to interfere with you, I have "no right" to do it; similarly, if your right gives me the duty to provide something for you, I have "no right" to refuse to do it. What *I* lack is the right which is a liberty; I am not "at liberty" to interfere with you or to refuse the service.

Where in this picture does the right to life belong? No doubt people have the right to live in the sense of a liberty, but what is important is the cluster of claim-rights brought together under the title of the right to life. The chief of these is, of course, the right to be free from interferences that threaten life. If other people aim their guns at us or try to pour poison into our drink we can, to put it mildly, demand that they desist. And then there are the services we can claim from doctors, health officers, bodyguards, and firemen; the rights that depend on contract or public arrangement. Perhaps there is no particular point in saying that the duties these people owe us belong to the right to life; we might as well say that all the services owed to anyone by tailors, dressmakers, and couturiers belong to a right called the right to be elegant. But contracts such as those understood in the patient-doctor relationship come in an important way when we are discussing the rights and wrongs of euthanasia, and are therefore mentioned here.

Do people have the right to what they need in order to survive, apart from the right conferred by special contracts into which other people have entered for the supplying of these necessities? Do people in the underdeveloped countries in which starvation is rife have the right to the food they so evidently lack? Joel Feinberg, discussing this question, suggests that they should be said to have "a claim," distinguishing this from a "valid claim," which gives a claim-right.

> The manifesto writers on the other side who seem to identify needs, or at least basic needs, with what they call "human rights," are more properly described, I think, as urging upon the world community the moral principle that *all* basic human needs ought to be recognized as *claims* (in the customary *prima facie* sense) worthy of sympathy and serious consideration right now, even though, in many cases, they cannot yet plausibly be treated as *valid* claims, that is, as grounds of any other people's duties. This way of talking avoids the anomaly of ascribing to all human beings now, even those in pre-industrial societies, such "economic and social rights" as "periodic holidays with pay."[9]

This seems reasonable, though we notice that there are some actual rights to service which are not based on anything like a contract, as for instance the right that children have to support from their parents and parents to support from their children in old age, though both sets of rights are to some extent dependent on existing social arrangements.

Let us now ask how the right to life affects the morality of acts of euthanasia. Are such acts sometimes or always ruled out by the right to life? This is certainly a possibility; for although an act of euthanasia is, by our definition, a matter of opting for death for the good of the one who is to die, there is, as we noted earlier, no direct connection between that to which a man has a right and that which is for his good. It is true that men have the right only to the kind of thing that is, in general, a good: we do not think that people have the right to garbage or polluted air. Nevertheless, a man may have the right to something which he himself would be better off without; where rights exist, it is a man's will that counts, not his or anyone else's estimate of benefit or harm. So the duties complementary to the right to life—the general duty of noninterference and the duty of service incurred by certain persons—are not affected by the quality of a man's life or by his prospects. Even if it is true that he would be, as we say, "better off dead," so long as he wants to live this does not justify us in killing him and may not justify us in deliberately allowing him to die. All of us have the duty of noninterference, and some of us may have the duty to sustain his life. Suppose, for example, that a retreating army has to leave behind wounded or exhausted soldiers in the wastes of an arid or snowbound land where the only prospect is death by starvation or at the hands of an enemy notoriously cruel. It has often been the practice to accord a merciful bullet to men in such desperate straits. But suppose that one of them demands that he should be left alive? It seems clear that his comrades have no right to kill him, though it is a quite different question as to whether they should give him a life-prolonging drug. The right to life can sometimes give a duty of positive service, but does not do so here. What it does give is the right to be left alone.

Interestingly enough, we have arrived by way of a consideration of the right to life at the distinction normally labeled "active" versus "passive" euthanasia, and often thought to be irrelevant to the moral issue.[10] Once it is seen that the right to life is a distinct ground of objection to certain acts of euthanasia, and that this right creates a duty of noninterference more widespread than the duties of care, there can be no doubt about the relevance of the distinction between passive and active euthanasia. Where everyone may have the duty to leave someone alone, it may be that no one has the duty to maintain his life, or that only some people do.

Where then do the boundaries of the "active" and "passive" lie? In some ways the words are themselves misleading, because they suggest the difference between act and omission which is not quite what we want. Certainly the act of shooting someone is the kind of thing we were talking about under the heading of "interference," and omitting to give him a drug a case of refusing care. But the act of turning off a respirator should surely be thought of as no different from the decision not to start it; if doctors had decided that a patient should be allowed to die, either course of action might follow, and both should be counted as passive rather than active euthanasia if euthanasia were in question. The point seems to be that interference in a course of treatment is not the same as other interference in a man's life, and particularly if the same body of people are responsible for the treatment and for its discontinuance. In such a case we could speak of the disconnecting of the apparatus as killing the man, or of the hospital as allowing him to die. By and large, it is the act of killing that is ruled out under the heading of noninterference, but not in every case.

Doctors commonly recognize this distinction, and the grounds on which some philosophers have denied it seem untenable. James Rachels, for instance, believes that if the difference between active and passive is relevant anywhere, it should be relevant everywhere, and he has pointed to an example in which it seems to make no difference which is done. If someone saw a child drowning in a bath it would seem just as bad to let it drown as to push its head under water.[11] If "it makes no difference" means that one act would be as iniquitous as the other, this is true. It is not that killing is *worse* than allowing to die, but that the two are contrary to distinct virtues, which gives the possibility that in some circumstances one is impermissible and the other permissible. In the circumstances invented by Rachels, both are wicked: it is contrary to justice to push the child's head under the water—something one has no right to do. To leave it to drown is not contrary to justice, but it is a particularly glaring example of lack of charity. Here it makes no practical difference because the requirements of justice and charity coincide; but in the case of the retreating army they did not: charity would have required that the wounded soldier be killed had not justice required that he be left alive.[12] In such a case it makes all the difference whether a man opts for the death of another in a positive action, or whether he allows him to die. An analogy with the right to property will make the point clear. If a man owns something, he has the right to it even when its possession does him harm, and we have no right to take it from him. But if one day it should blow away, maybe nothing requires us to get it back for him; we could not deprive him of it, but we may allow it to go. This is not to deny that it will often be an unfriendly act or one based on an arrogant judgment when we refuse to do what he wants. Nevertheless, we would be within our rights, and it might be that no moral objection of any kind would lie against our refusal.

It is important to emphasize that a man's rights may stand between us and the action we would dearly like to take for his sake. They may, of course, also prevent action which we would like to take for the sake of others, as when it might be tempting to kill one man to save several. But it is interesting that the limits of allowable interference, however

uncertain, seem stricter in the first case than the second. Perhaps there are no cases in which it would be all right to kill a man against his will *for his own sake* unless they could equally well be described as cases of allowing him to die, as in the example of turning off the respirator. However, there are circumstances, even if these are very rare, in which one man's life would justifiably be sacrificed to save others, and "killing" would be the only description of what was being done. For instance, a vehicle which had gone out of control might be steered from a path on which it would kill more than one man to a path on which it would kill one.[13] But it would not be permissible to steer a vehicle towards someone in order to kill him, against his will, for his own good. An analogy with property rights illustrates the point. One may not destroy a man's property against his will on the grounds that he would be better off without it; there are, however, circumstances in which it could be destroyed for the sake of others. If his house is liable to fall and kill him, that is his affair; it might, however, without injustice be destroyed to stop the spread of a fire.

We see then that the distinction between active and passive, important as it is elsewhere, has a special importance in the area of euthanasia. It should also be clear why James Rachels' other argument, that it is often "more humane" to kill than to allow to die, does not show that the distinction between active and passive euthanasia is morally irrelevant. It might be "more humane" in this sense to deprive a man of the property that brings evils on him, or to refuse to pay what is owed to Hume's profligate debauchee; but if we say this we must admit that an act which is "more humane" than its alternative may be morally objectionable because it infringes rights.

So far we have said very little about the right to service as opposed to the right to noninterference, though it was agreed that both might be brought under the heading of "the right to life." What about the duty to preserve life that may belong to special classes of persons such as bodyguards, firemen, or doctors? Unlike the general public, they are not within their rights if they merely refrain from interfering and do not try to sustain life. The subject's claim-rights are twofold as far as they are concerned, and passive as well as active euthanasia may be ruled out here if it is against his will. This is not to say that he has the right to any and every service needed to save or prolong his life; the rights of other people set limits to what may be demanded, both because they have the right not to be interfered with and because they may have a competing right to services. Furthermore, one must inquire just what the contract or implicit agreement amounts to in each case. Firemen and bodyguards presumably have a duty which is simply to preserve life, within the limits of justice to others and of reasonableness to themselves. With doctors it may, however, be different, since their duty relates not only to preserving life but also to the relief of suffering. It is not clear what a doctor's duties are to his patient if life can be prolonged only at the cost of suffering or suffering relieved only by measures that shorten life. George Fletcher has argued that what the doctor is under contract to do depends on what is generally done, because this is what a patient will reasonably expect.[14] This seems right. If procedures are part of normal medical practice, then it seems that the patient can demand them however much it may be against his interest to do so. Once again, it is not a matter of what is "most humane."

That the patient's right to life may set limits to permissible acts of euthanasia seems undeniable. If he does not want to die, no one has the right to practice active euthanasia on him, and passive euthanasia may also be ruled out where he has a right to the services of doctors or others.

Perhaps few will deny what has so far been said about the impermissibility of acts of euthanasia simply because we have so far spoken about the case of one who positively wants to live, and about his rights, whereas those who advocate euthanasia are usually thinking either about those who wish to die or about those whose wishes cannot be ascertained either because they cannot properly be said to have wishes or because, for one reason or another, we are unable to form a reliable estimate of what they are. The question that must now be asked is whether the latter type of case, where euthanasia though not involuntary would again be nonvoluntary, is different from the one discussed so far. Would we have the right to kill someone for his own good so long as we had no idea that he positively wished to live? And what about the life-prolonging duties of doctors in the same circumstances? This is a very difficult problem. On the one hand, it seems ridiculous to suppose that a man's right to life is something which generates duties only where he has signaled that he wants to live; as a borrower does indeed have a duty to return something lent on indefinite loan only if the lender indicates that he wants it back. On the other hand, it might be argued that there is something illogical about the idea that a right has been infringed if someone incapable of saying whether he wants it or not is deprived of something that is doing him harm rather than good. Yet on the analogy of property we would say that a right has been infringed. Only if someone had earlier told us that in such circumstances he would not want to keep the thing could we think that his right had been waived. Perhaps if we could make confident judgments about what anyone in such circumstances would wish, or what he would have wished beforehand had he considered the matter, we could agree to consider the right to life as "dormant," needing to be asserted if the normal duties were to remain. But as things are, we cannot make any such assumption; we simply do not know what most people would want, or would have wanted, us to do unless they tell us. This is certainly the case so far as active measures to end life are concerned. Possibly it is different, or will become different, in the matter of being kept alive, so general is the feeling against using sophisticated procedures on moribund patients, and so much is this dreaded by people who are old or terminally ill. Once again the distinction between active and passive euthanasia has come on the scene, but this time because most people's attitudes to the two are so different. It is just possible that we might presume, in the absence of specific evidence, that someone would not wish, beyond a certain point, to be kept alive; it is certainly not possible to assume that he would wish to be killed.

In the last paragraph we have begun to broach the topic of voluntary euthanasia, and this we must now discuss. What is to be said about the case in which there is no doubt about someone's wish to die: either he has told us beforehand that he would wish it in circumstances such as he is now in, and has shown no sign of a change of mind, or else he tells us now, being in possession of his faculties and of a steady mind. We should surely say that the objections previously urged against acts of euthanasia, which it must be remembered were all on the ground of rights, had disappeared. It does not seem that one would infringe someone's right to life in killing him with his permission and in fact at his request. Why should someone not be able to waive his right to life, or rather, as would be more likely to happen, to cancel some of the duties of noninterference that this right entails? (He is more likely to say that he should be killed by this man at this time in this manner, than to say that anyone may kill him at any time and in any way.) Similarly, someone may give permission for the destruction of his property, and request it. The important thing is that he gives a critical permission, and it seems that this is enough to cancel the duty normally associated with the right. If someone gives you permission to destroy his property, it can no longer be said that you have no right to do so, and I do not see why it should not be the case with taking a man's life. An objection might be made on the ground that only God has the right to take life, but in this paper religious as opposed to moral arguments are being left aside. Religion apart, there seems to be no case to be made out for an infringement of rights if a man who wishes to die is allowed to die or even killed. But of course it does not follow that there is no moral objection to it. Even with property, which is after all a relatively small matter, one might be wrong to destroy what one had the right to destroy. For, apart from its value to other people, it might be valuable to the man who wanted it destroyed, and charity might require us to hold our hand where justice did not.

Let us review the conclusion of this part of the argument, which has been about euthanasia and the right to life. It has been argued that from this side come stringent restrictions on the acts of euthanasia that could be morally permissible. Active nonvoluntary euthanasia is ruled out by that part of the right to life which creates the duty of noninterference, though passive nonvoluntary euthanasia is not ruled out, except where the right to life-preserving action has been created by some special condition such as a contract between a man and his doctor, and it is not always certain just what such a contract involves. Voluntary euthanasia is another matter: as the preceding paragraph suggested, no right is infringed if a man is allowed to die or even killed at his own request.

Turning now to the other objection that normally holds against inducing the death of another, that it is against charity, or benevolence, we must tell a very different story. Charity is the virtue that gives attachment to the good of others, and because life is normally a good, charity normally demands that it should be saved or prolonged. But as we so defined an act of euthanasia that it seeks a man's death for his own sake—for his good—charity will normally speak in favor of it. This is not, of course, to say that charity can require an act of euthanasia which justice forbids, but if an act of euthanasia is not contrary to justice—that is, it does not infringe rights—charity will rather be in its favor than against.

Once more the distinction between nonvoluntary and voluntary euthanasia must be considered. Could it ever be compatible with charity to seek a man's death although he wanted to live, or at least had not let us know that he wanted to die? It has been argued that in such circumstances active euthanasia would infringe his right to life, but passive euthanasia would not do so, unless he had some special right to life-preserving service from the one who allowed him to die. What would charity dictate? Obviously when a man wants to live there is a presumption that he will be benefited if his life is prolonged, and if it is so the question of euthanasia does not arise. But it is, on the other hand, possible that he wants to live where it would be better for him to die: perhaps he does not realize the desperate situation he is in, or perhaps he is afraid of dying. So, in spite of a very proper resistance to refusing to go along with a man's own wishes in the matter of life and death, someone might justifiably refuse to prolong the life even of someone who asked him to prolong it, as in the case of refusing to give the wounded soldier a drug that would keep him alive to meet a terrible end. And it is even more obvious that charity does not always dictate that life should be prolonged where a man's own wishes, hypothetical or actual, are not known.

So much for the relation of charity to nonvoluntary passive euthanasia, which was not, like nonvoluntary active euthanasia, ruled out by the right to life. Let us now ask what charity has to say about voluntary euthanasia, both active and passive. It was suggested in the discussion of justice that if of sound mind and steady desire, a man might give others the *right* to allow him to die or even to kill him, where otherwise this would be ruled out. But it was pointed out that this would not settle the question of whether the act was morally permissible, and it is this that we must now consider. Could not charity speak against what justice allowed? Indeed it might do so. For while the fact that a man wants to die suggests that his life is wretched, and while his rejection of life may itself tend to take the good out of the things he might have enjoyed, nevertheless his wish to die might here be opposed for his own sake just as it might be if suicide were in question. Perhaps there is hope that his mental condition will improve. Perhaps he is mistaken in thinking his disease incurable. Perhaps he wants to die for the sake of someone else on whom he feels he is a burden, and we are not ready to accept this sacrifice whether for ourselves or others. In such cases, and there will surely be many of them, it could not be for his own sake that we will him or allow him to die, and therefore euthanasia as defined in this paper would not be in question. But this is not to deny that there could be acts of voluntary euthanasia both passive and active against which neither justice nor charity would speak.

We have now considered the morality of euthanasia both voluntary and nonvoluntary, and active and passive. The conclusion has been that nonvoluntary active euthanasia (roughly, killing a man against his will or without his consent) is never justified; that is to say, that a man's being killed for his own good never justifies the act unless he himself has consented to it. A man's rights are infringed by such an action, and it is therefore contrary to justice. However, all the other combinations, nonvoluntary passive euthanasia, voluntary active euthanasia, and voluntary passive euthanasia, are sometimes compatible with both justice and charity. But the strong condition carried in the definition of euthanasia adopted in this paper must not be forgotten; an act of euthanasia as here understood is one whose purpose is to benefit the one who dies.

In the light of this discussion let us look at our present practices. Are they good or are they bad? And what changes might be made, thinking now not only of the morality of particular acts of euthanasia but also of the indirect effects of instituting different practices, of the abuses to which they might be subject and of the changes that might come about if euthanasia became a recognized part of the social scene.

The first thing to notice is that it is wrong to ask whether we should introduce the practice of euthanasia as if it were not something we already had. In fact we do have it. For instance, it is common, where the medical prognosis is very bad, for doctors to recommend against measures to prolong life, and particularly where a process of degeneration producing one medical emergency after another has already set in. If these doctors are not certainly within their legal rights, this is something that is apt to come as a surprise to them as to the general public. It is also obvious that euthanasia is often practiced where old people are concerned. If someone very old and soon to die is attacked by a disease that makes his life wretched, doctors do not always come in with life-prolonging drugs. Perhaps poor patients are more fortunate in this respect than rich patients, being more often left to die in peace; but it is in any case a well-recognized piece of medical practice, which is a form of euthanasia.

No doubt the case of infants with mental or physical defects will be suggested as another example of the practice of euthanasia as we already have it, since such infants are sometimes deliberately allowed to die. That they are deliberately allowed to die is certain; children with severe spina bifida malformations are not always operated on even where it is thought that without the operation they will die; and even in the case of children with Down's Syndrome who have intestinal obstructions, the relatively simple operation that would make it possible to feed them is sometimes not performed.[15] Whether this is euthanasia in our sense or only as the Nazis understood it is another matter. We must ask the crucial question, "Is it for the sake of the child himself that the doctors and parents choose his death?" In some cases the answer may really be yes, and, what is more important, it may really be true that the kind of life which is a good is not possible or likely for this child, and that there is little but suffering and frustration in store for him.[16] But this must presuppose that the medical prognosis is wretchedly bad, as it may be for some spina bifida children. With children who are born with Down's Syndrome it is, however, quite different. Most of these are able to live on for quite a time in a reasonably contented way, remaining like children all their lives but capable of affectionate relationships and able to play games and perform simple tasks. The fact is, of course, that the doctors who recommend against lifesaving procedures for handicapped infants are usually thinking not of them but rather of their parents and of other children in the family or of the "burden on society" if the children survive. So it is not for their sake but to avoid trouble to others that they are allowed to die. When brought out into the open this seems unacceptable: at least we do not easily accept the principle that adults who need special care should be counted too burdensome to be kept alive. It must in any case be insisted that if children with Down's Syndrome are deliberately allowed to die this is not a matter of euthanasia except in Hitler's sense. And for our children, since we scruple to gas them, not even the manner of their death is "quiet and easy"; when not treated for an intestinal obstruction a baby simply starves to death. Perhaps some will take this as an argument for allowing active euthanasia, in which case they will be in the company of an S.S. man stationed in the Warthgenau who sent Eichmann a memorandum telling him that "Jews in the coming winter could no longer be fed" and submitting for his consideration a proposal as to whether "it would not be the most humane solution to kill those Jews who were incapable of work through some quicker means."[17] If we say we are *unable* to look after children with handicaps, we are no more telling the truth than was the S.S. man who said that the Jews could not be fed.

Nevertheless, if it is ever right to allow deformed children to die because life will be a misery to them, or not to take measures to prolong for a little the life of a newborn baby whose life cannot extend beyond a few months of intense medical intervention, there is a genuine problem about active as opposed to passive euthanasia. There are well-known cases in which the medical staff has looked on wretchedly while an infant died slowly from starvation and dehydration because they did not feel able to give a lethal injection. According to the principles discussed in the earlier part of this paper they would indeed have had no right to give it, since an infant cannot ask that it should be done. The only possible solution—supposing that voluntary active euthanasia were to be legalized—would be to appoint guardians to act on the infant's behalf. In a different climate of opinion this might not be dangerous, but at present, when people so readily assume that the life of a handicapped baby is of no value, one would be loath to support it.

Finally, on the subject of handicapped children, another word should be said about those with severe mental defects. For them too it might sometimes be right to say that one would wish for death

for their sake. But not even severe mental handicap automatically brings a child within the scope even of a possible act of euthanasia. If the level of consciousness is low enough it could not be said that life is a good to them, any more than in the case of those suffering from extreme senility. Nevertheless, if they do not suffer it will not be an act of euthanasia by which someone opts for their death. Perhaps charity does not demand that strenuous measures are taken to keep people in this state alive, but euthanasia does not come into the matter, any more than it does when someone is, like Karen Ann Quinlan, in a state of permanent coma. Much could be said about this last case. It might even be suggested that in the case of unconsciousness this "life" is not the life to which "the right to life" refers. But that is not our topic here.

What we must consider, even if only briefly, is the possibility that euthanasia, genuine euthanasia, and not contrary to the requirements of justice or charity, should be legalized over a wider area. Here we are up against the really serious problem of abuse. Many people want, and want very badly, to be rid of their elderly relatives and even of their ailing husbands or wives. Would any safeguards ever be able to stop them describing as euthanasia what was really for their own benefit? And would it be possible to prevent the occurrence of acts which were genuinely acts of euthanasia but morally impermissible because infringing the rights of a patient who wished to live?

Perhaps the furthest we should go is to encourage patients to make their own contracts with a doctor by making it known whether they wish him to prolong their life in case of painful terminal illness or of incapacity. A document such as the Living Will seems eminently sensible, and should surely be allowed to give a doctor following the previously expressed wishes of the patient immunity from legal proceedings by relatives.[18] Legalizing active euthanasia is, however, another matter. Apart from the special repugnance doctors feel towards the idea of a lethal injection, it may be of the very greatest importance to keep a psychological barrier up against killing. Moreover, it is active euthanasia which is the most liable to abuse. Hitler would not have been able to kill 275,000 people in his "euthanasia" program if he had had to wait for them to need life-saving treatment. But there are other objections to active euthanasia, even voluntary active euthanasia. In the first place, it would be hard to devise procedures that would protect people from being persuaded into giving their consent. And secondly, the possibility of active voluntary euthanasia might change the social scene in ways that would be very bad. As things are, people do, by and large, expect to be looked after if they are old or ill. This is one of the good things that we have, but we might lose it, and be much worse off without it. It might come to be expected that someone likely to need a lot of looking after should call for the doctor and demand his own death. Something comparable could be good in an extremely poverty-stricken community where the children genuinely suffered from lack of food; but in rich societies such as ours it would surely be a spiritual disaster. Such possibilities should make us very wary of supporting large measures of euthanasia, even where moral principle applied to the individual act does not rule it out.

Notes

I would like to thank Derek Parfit and the editors of *Philosophy & Public Affairs* for their very helpful comments.

1. Leo Alexander, "Medical Science under Dictatorship," *New England Journal of Medicine*, 14 July 1949, p. 40.

2. For a discussion of culpable and nonculpable ignorance see Thomas Aquinas, *Summa Theologica*, First Part of the Second Part, Question 6, article 8, and Question 19, articles 5 and 6.

3. Dmitri Panin, *The Notebooks of Sologdin* (London, 1976), pp. 66–67.

4. Thomas Nagel, "Death," in James Rachels, ed., *Moral Problems* (New York, 1971), p. 362.

5. Panin, *Sologdin*, p. 85.

6. Yet some detail needs to be filled in to explain why we should not say that a scarecrow is beneficial to the plants it protects. Perhaps what is beneficial must either be a feature of the plant itself, such as protective prickles, or else must work on the plant directly, such as a line of trees which give it shade.

7. David Hume, *Treatise*, Book III, Part II, Section 1.

8. See, for example, D. D. Raphael, "Human Rights Old and New," in D. D. Raphael, ed., *Political Theory and the Rights of Man* (London, 1967), and Joel Feinberg, "The Nature and Value of Rights," *The Journal of Value Inquiry* 4, no. 4 (Winter 1970): 243–257. Reprinted in Samuel Gorovitz, ed., *Moral Problems in Medicine* (Englewood Cliffs, New Jersey, 1976).

9. Feinberg, "Human Rights," *Moral Problems in Medicine*, p. 465.

10. See, for example, James Rachels, "Active and Passive Euthanasia," *New England Journal of Medicine* 292, no. 2 (9 Jan. 1975): 78–80.

11. Ibid.

12. It is not, however, that justice and charity conflict. A man does not lack charity because he refrains from an act of injustice which would have been for someone's good.

13. For a discussion of such questions, see my article "The Problem of Abortion and the Doctrine of Double Effect," *Oxford Review*, no. 5 (1967); reprinted in Rachels, *Moral Problems*, and Gorovitz, *Moral Problems in Medicine*.

14. George Fletcher, "Legal Aspects of the Decision not to Prolong Life," *Journal of the American Medical Association* 203, no. 1 (1 Jan. 1968): 119–122. Reprinted in Gorovitz.

15. I have been told this by a pediatrician in a well-known medical center in the United States. It is confirmed by Anthony M. Shaw and Iris A. Shaw, "Dilemma of Informed Consent in Children," *The New England Journal of Medicine* 289, no. 17 (25 Oct. 1973): 885–890. Reprinted in Gorovitz.

16. It must be remembered, however, that many of the social miseries of spina bifida children could be avoided. Professor R. B. Zachary is surely right to insist on this. See, for example, "Ethical and Social Aspects of Spina Bifida," *The Lancet*, 3 Aug. 1968, pp. 274–276. Reprinted in Gorovitz.

17. Quoted by Hannah Arendt, *Eichmann in Jerusalem* (London 1963), p. 90.

18. Details of this document are to be found in J. A. Behnke and Sissela Bok, eds., *The Dilemmas of Euthanasia* (New York, 1975), and in A. B. Downing, ed., *Euthanasia and the Right to Life: The Case for Voluntary Euthanasia* (London, 1969).

Questions for Analysis

1. *What does Foot mean by "right to life," and how does she use this notion to distinguish between active and passive euthanasia?*

2. *Under what conditions might a person's life be regarded as no longer worth living?*

3. *Why does Foot believe it is not legitimate for us to decide when someone else's life is no longer worth living?*

4. *Which forms of euthanasia does Foot regard as legitimate, and which illegitimate? Cite her reasons.*

5. *Why does Foot believe we don't have a duty to kill a person who has decided his or her life is no longer worth living?*

A Moral Principle about Killing

Richard Brandt

The preceding writers, either explicitly or implicitly, dealt with the moral principle "It is morally wrong to kill innocent human beings." In this essay, philosopher Richard Brandt observes that this principle is really more useful in determining blame than for guiding us in making decisions. Brandt thinks a more appropriate principle can be based on the presumed obligation not to kill any human being except in justifiable self-defense—unless we have an even stronger moral obligation to do something that cannot be done without killing. In Brandt's view, that other overriding obligation is not to cause injury to another.

Brandt is distinguishing, then, between killing and causing injury, so that not every act of killing is an act of injury. After citing examples of what he believes are noninjurious killings and specifying conditions under which an act is noninjurious, Brandt argues that a person in irreversible coma is "beyond injury." If such a person has left instructions that his or her life should be ended, then, in Brandt's view, we are under a prima facie obligation to do so. In the absence of explicit instructions, we may attempt to determine what the person's wishes likely would be and carry them out. Of course, if a person has left instructions to be maintained under any circumstances, then we have an obligation to respect that preference.

Throughout the essay, Brandt uses the term prima facie *duty or obligation, which he has borrowed from the English philosopher William David Ross.* Prima facie *means "at first sight" or "on the surface." Accordingly, a* prima facie *duty is one that dictates what I should do when other relevant factors aren't considered. For example, I have a* prima facie *duty not to lie in every case in which lying is possible. Likewise, I have a* prima facie *duty to prevent the needless suffering of others. In other words, all things being equal, this is what I ought to try to do.*

In this essay, Brandt is taking issue with the commonplace view that killing a person is something that is prima facie *wrong in itself. In his view, killing is wrong* only if *and because it is an injury to someone, or if and because it runs counter to the person's known preference. In short, Brandt believes that a principle about the* prima facie *wrongness of killing derives from principles about when we are* prima facie *obligated not to injure and when we are* prima facie *obligated to respect a person's wishes.*

One of the Ten Commandments states: "Thou shalt not kill." The commandment does not supply an object for the verb, but the traditional Catholic view has been that the proper object of the verb is "innocent human beings" (except in cases of extreme necessity), where "innocent" is taken to exclude persons convicted of a capital crime or engaged in an unjust assault aimed at killing, such as members of the armed forces of a country prosecuting an unjust war. Thus construed, the prohibition is taken

This article first appeared in the book Beneficent Euthanasia, *edited by Marvin Kohl, published by Prometheus Books, Buffalo, N.Y., 1975, and is reprinted by permission.*

to extend to suicide and abortion. (There is a qual-ification: that we are not to count cases in which the death is not wanted for itself or intended as a *means* to a goal that is wanted for itself, provided that in either case the aim of the act is the avoidance of some evil greater than the death of the person.) Can this view that all killing of innocent human beings is morally wrong be defended, and if not, what alternative principle can be?

This question is one the ground rules for answering which are far from a matter of agree-ment. I should myself be content if a principle were identified that could be shown to be one that would be included in any moral system that rational and benevolent persons would support for a society in which they expected to live. Apparently others would not be so content; so in what follows I shall simply aim to make some observations that I hope will identify a principle with which the consciences of intelligent people will be comfortable. I believe the rough principle I will suggest is also one that would belong to the moral system rational and benevolent people would want for their society.

Let us begin by reflecting on what it is to kill. The first thing to notice is that *kill* is a biological term. For example, a weed may be killed by being sprayed with a chemical. The verb *kill* involves essentially the broad notion of death—the change from the state of being biologically alive to the state of being dead. It is beyond my powers to give any general characterization of this transition, and it may be impossible to give one. If there is one, it is one that human beings, flies, and ferns all share; and to kill is in some sense to bring that transition about. The next thing to notice is that at least human beings do not live forever, and hence killing a human being at a given time must be construed as *advanc-ing the date* of its death, or as *shortening its life*. Thus it may be brought about that the termination of the life of a person occurs at the time *t* instead of at the time *t + k*. Killing is thus shortening the span of organic life of something.

There is a third thing to notice about *kill*. It is a term of causal agency and has roots in the legal tradition. As such, it involves complications. For instance, suppose I push a boulder down a moun-tainside, aiming it at a person X and it indeed strikes X, and he is dead after impact and not before (and not from a coincidental heart attack); in that case we would say that I killed X. On the other hand,

suppose I tell Y that X is in bed with Y's wife, and Y hurries to the scene, discovers them, and shoots X to death; in that case, although the unfolding of events from my action may be as much a matter of causal law as the path of the boulder, we should *not* say that I killed X. Fortunately, for the purpose of principles of the morally right, we can sidestep such complications. For suppose I am choosing whether to do *A* or *B* (where one or the other of these "acts" may be construed as essentially *inac-*tion—for example, *not* doing what I know is the one thing that will *prevent* someone's death); then it is enough if I know, or have reason to think it highly probable, that were I to do *A*, a state of the world including the death of some person or per-sons would ensue, whereas were I to do *B*, a state of the world of some specified different sort would ensue. If a moral principle will tell me in this case whether I am to do *A* or *B*, that is all I need. It could be that a moral principle would tell me that I am absolutely never to perform any action *A*, such that were I to do it the death of some innocent human being would ensue, provided there is some alter-native action I might perform, such that were I to do it no such death would ensue.

It is helpful, I think, to reformulate the tradi-tional Catholic view in a way that preserves the spirit and intent of that view (although some phi-losophers would disagree with this assessment) and at the same time avoids some conceptions that are both vague and more appropriate to a principle about when a person is morally blameworthy for doing something than to a principle about what a person ought morally to do. The terminology I use goes back, in philosophical literature, to a phrase introduced by W. D. Ross, but the conception is quite familiar. The alternative proposal is that there is a *strong prima facie obligation* not to kill any human being except in justifiable self-defense; in the sense (of prima facie) that it is morally *wrong* to kill any human being except in justifiable self-defense *unless* there is an even stronger prima facie moral obli-gation to do something that cannot be done with-out killing. (The term *innocent* can now be omitted, since if a person is not innocent, there may be a stronger moral obligation that can only be dis-charged by killing him; and this change is to the good since it is not obvious that we have no prima facie obligation to avoid killing people even if they are not innocent.) This formulation has the result that sometimes, to decide what is morally right, we have to compare the stringencies of conflicting moral obligations—and that is an elusive business; but the other formulation either conceals the same problem by putting it in another place, or else leads to objectionable implications. (Consider one implication of the traditional formulation for a party of spelunkers in a cave by the oceanside. It is found that a rising tide is bringing water into the cave and all will be drowned unless they escape at once. Unfortunately, the first man to try to squeeze through the exit is fat and gets wedged inextricably in the opening, with his head inside the cave. Somebody in the party has a stick of dynamite. Either they blast the fat man out, killing him, or all of them, including him, will drown. The traditional formulation leads to the conclusion that all must drown.)

Let us then consider the principle: "There is a strong prima facie moral obligation not to kill any human being except in justifiable self-defense." I do not believe we want to accept this principle without further qualification; indeed, its status seems not to be that of a basic principle at all, but derivative from some more-basic principles. W. D. Ross listed what he thought were the main basic prima facie moral obligations; it is noteworthy that he listed a prima facie duty not to *cause injury*, but he did not include an obligation not to kill. Presumably this was no oversight. He might have thought that killing a human being is always an injury, so that the additional listing of an obligation not to kill would be redundant; but he might also have thought that killing is sometimes *not* an injury and that it is prima facie obligatory not to kill only when, and because, so doing would injure a sentient being.

What might be a noninjurious killing? If I come upon a cat that has been mangled but not quite killed by several dogs and is writhing in pain, and I pull myself together and put it out of its misery, I have killed the cat but surely not *injured* it. I do not injure something by relieving its pain. If someone is being tortured and roasted to death and I know he wishes nothing more than a merciful termination of life, I have not injured him if I shoot him; I have done him a favor. In general, it seems I have not injured a person if I treat him in a way in which he would want me to treat him if he were fully rational, or in a way to which he would be

indifferent if he were fully rational. (I do not think that terminating the life of a human fetus in the third month is an injury; I admit this view requires discussion.[1])

Consider another type of killing that is not an injury. Consider the case of a human being who has become unconscious and will not, it is known, regain consciousness. He is in a hospital and is being kept alive only through expensive supportive measures. Is there a strong prima facie moral obligation not to withdraw these measures and not to take positive steps to terminate his life? It seems obvious that if he is on the only kidney machine and its use could *save* the life of another person, who could lead a normal life after temporary use, it would be wrong not to take him off. Is there an obligation to continue, or not to terminate, if there is no countering obligation? I would think not, with an exception to be mentioned; and this coincides with the fact that he is *beyond* injury. There is also not an obligation *not* to preserve his life, say, in order to have his organs available for use when they are needed.

There seems, however, to be another morally relevant consideration in such a case—knowledge of the patient's own wishes when he was conscious and in possession of his faculties. Suppose he had feared such an eventuality and prepared a sworn statement requesting his doctor to terminate his life at once in such circumstances. Now, if it is morally obligatory to some degree to carry out a person's wishes for disposal of his body and possessions after his death, it would seem to be equally morally obligatory to respect his wishes in case he becomes a "vegetable." In the event of the existence of such a document, I would think that if he can no longer be injured we are free to withdraw life-sustaining measures and also to take positive steps to terminate life—and are even morally bound, prima facie, to do so. (If, however, the patient had prepared a document directing that his body be preserved alive as long as possible in such circumstances, then there would be a prima facie obligation *not* to cease life-sustaining measures and not to terminate. It would seem obvious, however, that such an obligation would fall far short of giving the patient the right to continued use of a kidney machine when its use by another could save that person's life.) Some persons would not hesitate to discontinue life-sustaining procedures in such a situation, but would balk at more positive measures. But the hesitation to use more positive procedures, which veterinarians employ frequently with animals, is surely nothing but squeamishness; if a person is in the state described, there can be no injury to him in positive termination more than or less than that in allowing him to wither by withdrawing life-supportive procedures.

If I am right in my analysis of this case, we must phrase our basic principle about killing in such a way as to take into account (1) whether the killing would be an injury and (2) the person's own wishes and directives. And perhaps, more important, any moral principle about killing must be viewed simply as an implicate of more basic principles about these matters.

Let us look for corroboration of this proposal to how we feel about another type of case, one in which termination would be of positive benefit to the agent. Let us suppose that a patient has a terminal illness and is in severe pain, subject only to brief remissions, with no prospect of any event that could make his life good, either in the short or long term. It might seem that here, with the patient in severe pain, at least life-supportive measures should be discontinued, or positive termination adopted. But I do not think we would accept this inference, for in this situation the patient, let us suppose, has his preferences and is able to express them. The patient may have strong religious convictions and prefer to go on living despite the pain; if so, surely there is a prima facie moral obligation not positively to terminate his life. Even if, as seemingly in this case, the situation is one in which it would be *rational* for the agent, from the point of view of his own welfare, to direct the termination of his life,[2] it seems that if he (irrationally) does the opposite, there is a prima facie moral obligation not to terminate and some prima facie obligation to sustain it. Evidently a person's own expressed wishes have moral force. (I believe, however, that we think a person's expressed wishes have *less* moral force when we think the wishes are irrational.)

What is the effect, in this case, if the patient himself expresses a preference for termination and would, if he were given the means, terminate his own existence? Is there a prima facie obligation to sustain his life—and pain—against his will? Surely not. Or is there an obligation *not* to take positive measures to terminate his life immediately, thereby saving the patient much discomfort? Again, surely not. What possible reason could be offered to justify the claim that the answer is affirmative, beyond theological ones about God's will and our being bound to stay alive at His pleasure? The only argument I can think of is that there is some consideration of public policy, to the effect that a recognition of such moral permission might lead to abuses or to some other detriment to society in the long run. Such an argument does seem weak.

It might be questioned whether a patient's request should be honored, if made at a time when he is in pain, on the grounds that it is not rational. (The physician may be in a position to see, however, that the patient is quite right about his prospects and that his personal welfare would be maximized by termination.) It might also be questioned whether a patient's formal declaration, written earlier, requesting termination if he were ever in his present circumstances should be honored, on the grounds that at the earlier time he did not know what it would be like to be in his present situation. It would seem odd, however, if *no* circumstances are identifiable in which a patient's request for termination is deemed to have moral force, when his request *not* to terminate is thought morally weighty in the same circumstances even when this request is clearly irrational. I think we may ignore such arguments and hold that, in a situation in which it is rational for a person to choose termination of his life, his expressed wish is morally definitive and removes both the obligation to sustain life and the obligation not to terminate.

Indeed, there is a question whether or not in these circumstances a physician has not a moral obligation at least to withdraw life-supporting measures, and perhaps positively to terminate life. At least there seems to be a general moral obligation to render assistance when a person is in need, when it can be given at small cost to oneself, and when it is requested. The obligation is the stronger when one happens to be the only person in a position to receive such a request or to know about the situation. Furthermore, the physician has acquired a special obligation if there has been a long-standing personal relationship with the patient—just as a friend or relative has special obligations. But since we are discussing not the possible obligation to terminate but the obligation *not* to terminate, I shall not pursue this issue.

The patient's own expression of preference or consent, then, seems to be weighty. But suppose he is unable to express his preference; suppose that his terminal disease not only causes him great pain but has attacked his brain in such a way that he is incapable of thought and of rational speech. May the physician, then, after consultation, take matters into his own hands? We often think we know what is best for another, but we think one person should not make decisions for another. Just as we must respect the decision of a person who has decided after careful reflection that he wants to commit suicide, so we must not take the liberty of deciding to bring another's life to a close contrary to his wishes. So what may be done? Must a person suffer simply because he cannot express consent? There is evidence that can be gathered about what conclusions a person would draw if he were in a state to draw and express them. The patient's friends will have some recollection of things he has said in the past, of his values and general ethical views. Just as we can have good reason to think, for example, that he would vote Democratic if voting for president in a certain year, so we can have good reason to think he would take a certain stand about the termination of his own life in various circumstances. We can know of some persons who because of their religious views would want to keep on living until natural processes bring their lives to a close. About others we can know that they decidedly would not take this view. We can also know what would be the *rational* choice for them to make, and our knowledge of this can be *evidence* about what they would request if they were able. There are, of course, practical complications in the mechanics of a review board of some kind making a determination of this sort, but they are hardly insurmountable.

I wish to consider one other type of case, that of a person who, say, has had a stroke and is leading, and for some time can continue to lead, a life that is comfortable but one on a very low level, *and* who has antecedently requested that his life be terminated if he comes, incurably, into such a situation. May he then be terminated? In this case, unlike the others, there are probably ongoing pleasant experiences, perhaps on the level of some animals, that seem to be a good thing. One can hardly say that *injury* is being done such a person by keeping him alive; and one might say that some slight injury

is being done him by terminating his existence. There is a real problem here. Can the (slight) goodness of these experiences stand against the weight of an earlier firm declaration requesting that life be terminated in a situation of hopeless senility? There is no *injury* in keeping the person alive despite his request, but there seems something *indecent* about keeping a mind alive after a severe stroke, when we know quite well that, could he have anticipated it, his own action would have been to terminate his life. I think that the person's own request should be honored; it should be if a person's expressed preferences have as much moral weight as I think they should have.

What general conclusions are warranted by the preceding discussion? I shall emphasize two. First, there is a prima facie obligation *not* to terminate a person's existence when this would injure him (except in cases of self-defense or of senility of a person whose known wish is to be terminated in such a condition) *or* if he wishes not to be terminated. Second, there is *not* a prima facie obligation not to terminate when there would be *no* injury, or when there would be a positive benefit (release from pain) in so doing, provided the patient has not declared himself otherwise or there is evidence that his wishes are to that effect. Obviously there are two things that are decisive for the morality of terminating a person's life: whether so doing would be an *injury* and whether it conforms to what is known of his *preferences*.

I remarked at the outset that I would be content with some moral principles if it could be made out that rational persons would want those principles incorporated in the consciences of a group among whom they were to live. It is obvious why rational persons would want these principles. They would want injury avoided both because they would not wish others to injure them and because, if they are benevolent, they would not wish others injured. Moreover, they would want weight given to a person's own known preferences. Rational people do want the decision about the termination of their lives, where that is possible; for they would be uncomfortable if they thought it possible that others would be free to terminate their lives without consent. The threat of serious illness is bad enough without that prospect. On the other hand, this discomfort would be removed if they knew that termination would not be undertaken on their behalf without their explicit consent, except after a careful inquiry had been made, both into whether termination would constitute an injury and whether they would request termination under the circumstances if they were in a position to do so.

If I am right in all this, then it appears that killing a person is not something that is just prima facie wrong *in itself*; it is wrong roughly only if and because it is an *injury* of someone, or if and because it is contrary to the *known preferences* of someone. It would seem that a principle about the prima facie wrongness of killing is *derivative* from principles about when we are prima facie obligated not to injure and when we are prima facie obligated to respect a person's wishes, at least about what hap-

pens to his own body. I do not, however, have any suggestions for a general statement of principles of this latter sort.

Notes

1. See my "The Morality of Abortion" in *The Monist*, 56 (1972), pp. 503–26; and, in revised form, in *Abortion: Pro and Con*, ed. R. L. Perkins (General Learning Press, 1975).
2. See my "The Morality and Rationality of Suicide," in James Rachels, ed., *Moral Problems* (Harper & Row, 1975); and, in revised form, in E. S. Shneidman, ed., *Suicidology: Current Developments* (Grune & Stratton, 1976).

Questions for Analysis

1. Under what conditions, according to Brandt, can one person be said to injure another?

2. Give an example of killing that causes injury, and of killing that doesn't.

3. How do we determine what a comatose person's wishes are, if the person has left no directions about terminating his or her life?

4. According to Brandt, under what conditions are we prima facie *obliged not to* terminate a person's existence? Under what conditions is there no such prima facie *obligation?*

5. Explain the significance (with respect to mercy deaths) of Brandt's deriving a principle about the prima facie *wrongness of killing from principles about when we are* prima facie *obligated not to injure and when we are* prima facie *obligated to respect a person's wishes.*

6. As an expression of duty ethics, would you say that Brandt's analysis is consistent or inconsistent with a Kantian view of the morality of euthanasia? (In order to answer this question, you of course should first try to apply Kant's ethics to the problem of euthanasia. Under what conditions, if ever, do you think Kant would approve of a mercy death?)

CASE PRESENTATION
Earle N. Spring

Seventy-eight-year-old Earle N. Spring was suffering from end-stage kidney disease, which required him to undergo hemodialysis three days a week, five hours a day. He was also suffering from chronic organic brain syndrome, or senility, which left him completely confined and disoriented, and thus mentally incom-

petent. Physicians considered both the kidney disease and the senility permanent and irreversible, and saw no prospect of a medical breakthrough that would
provide a cure for either disease. Without the dialysis treatment, Spring would
die; with it, he might survive for months or years.

In 1979, Spring's wife and son, who had been appointed temporary guardian
of his father, petitioned a probate court for legal authorization to discontinue
Spring's life-sustaining medical treatment. The court appointed a guardian for
Spring to look into the matter. Although the guardian opposed the cessation of
treatment, the judge authorized it. In response, the guardian appealed the judgment to the Massachusetts Appeals Court, which upheld the judgment of the
lower court. Undaunted, the court-appointed guardian made other legal moves.
But before any final legal resolution, Earle Spring died in April 1980.

Questions for Analysis

1. *The Massachusetts Appeals Court based its decision on the presumption that if
Spring were competent, he would wish to discontinue dialysis treatments (the
court felt there was enough circumstantial evidence to warrant this presumption).
What moral principle does this ruling implicitly recognize? With which ethical
theory would you especially associate this principle?*

2. *The appeals court based its presumption about Spring's wishes on many factors,
but especially on the fact that Spring's family and attending physician were at
one regarding the suspension of treatment. Do you think the views of those who
best know an incompetent, incurably ill patient such as Spring should be given
paramount consideration in determining a course of treatment or nontreatment?*

3. *Suppose the appeals court had overturned the lower court's decision, thereby
upholding the court-appointed guardian's request that treatment be continued.
Do you think Spring's family would have been morally justified in "taking matters
into their own hands," that is, discontinuing Spring's hemodialysis treatment?
Or do you think even if they had thought that such an action would have been
respecting Spring's autonomous will, their overriding obligation would have been
to obey the court's judgment?*

4. *Do you think the court should decide when the use of life-sustaining treatment
should be discontinued? Or do you think other parties should—for example, the
patient, if competent; the patient's family or physician; or a hospital ethics committee, when the patient is incompetent or even competent?*

CASE PRESENTATION
Baby Jane Doe

In October 1983, Baby Jane Doe, as the infant was called by the court to protect
her anonymity, was born with a protruding spinal cord (spina bifida) and a host

of other congenital defects. Surgery could be performed to prolong her life, but the prognosis was grim. According to best medical opinion, the child would be severely mentally retarded, bedridden, and suffer considerable pain during her life which, in all likelihood, wouldn't reach beyond twenty-five years. Faced with so tragic a prospect and after agonized consultations with medical experts and religious counselors, Mr. and Mrs. A (as the parents were designated in court documents) decided not to authorize permission for the surgery.

A right-to-life activist lawyer sought to force the surgery, but two New York appeals courts and a state children's agency declined to override the parents. The U.S. Justice Department then sued to obtain the records from the University Hospital in Stony Brook, New York, to determine whether it had violated a federal law that forbids discrimination against the handicapped.[8] Appearing on the *Face the Nation* television program of November 6, 1983, U.S. Surgeon General Dr. C. Everett Koop expressed the view that the government has a moral obligation to intercede on behalf of such infants in order to protect their basic right to life. He implied further that denying Baby Jane Doe the needed corrective surgery was tantamount to saying that as a society we value certain kinds of life more than others. This, in his view, was a most dangerous practice to establish.

Two weeks later, Federal District Judge Leonard Wexler threw out the Justice Department's unprecedented suit. Wexler found no discrimination, only a great deal of caring. The hospital had always been willing to do the surgery, the judge said, and had failed to do so, not because the baby was handicapped, but because her parents had refused to consent to such procedures. Wexler concluded that the parents' decision was a reasonable one based on genuine concern for the best interests of the child.

The day after the ruling, the Justice Department announced an appeal. On January 9, 1984, federal regulations were issued preventing federally funded hospitals from withholding treatment in such cases.

Questions for Analysis

1. *Do you think this is a case of discrimination against the handicapped?*

2. *In a similar case ten years earlier, the Supreme Court of Maine ordered, against parental wishes, that an operation be performed on a grotesquely deformed infant in order to save its life. In defending his ruling, Judge David G. Roberts said: "At the moment of live birth, there does exist a human being entitled to the fullest protection of the law. The most basic right enjoyed by every human being is the right to life itself."[9] Do you agree with Judge Roberts?*

3. *Some would argue that the view shared by the U.S. Justice Department and Judge Roberts is cruel and inhumane—that they, in effect, sentence infants like*

8.   *Early in the Reagan Administration a twenty-four-hour "hotline" had been set up to receive calls from anyone who, among other things, thought that the civil rights of infants like Baby Jane Doe were being violated.*

9.   *Richard A. McCormick, "To Save or Let Die: The Dilemma of Modern Medicine,"* Journal of the American Medical Association, July 1974, p. 172.

Baby Jane and their families to lives of profound pain, suffering, humiliation, frustration, and unhappiness. They might further charge that these officials are callously insensitive to the feelings and capabilities of the parents. What is your view of such criticisms?

4. *Which ethical principles do you think are of utmost concern in cases like Baby Jane Doe?*

5. *Some people claim that it is morally permissible to allow a seriously and irreversibly defective newborn like Baby Jane to die if and only if there is no significant potential for a meaningful human existence. There comes a point, they say, when an individual life precludes satisfying any human potential, such as establishing meaningful human relationships. Implicit in this argument is that the quality of life not only is morally significant in cases like these but may rank as a higher moral value than mere survival. Do you agree? Or would you say that the sanctity of life, regardless of a particular life's quality or lack of potential for development, is the supreme moral value?*

6. *If society through its government and judicial system intercedes to preserve the lives of infants like Baby Jane Doe, do you think it then bears the chief responsibility for maintenance costs?*

Selections for Further Reading

Behnke, John A., and Sissela Bok. *The Dilemmas of Euthanasia.* New York: Doubleday, Anchor, 1975.

Caughill, R. E., ed. *The Dying Patient: A Supportive Approach.* Boston: Little, Brown, 1976.

Cooper, I. S. *Hard to Leave When the Music's Playing.* New York: Norton, 1977.

Grisez, Germain, and Joseph Boyle. *Life and Death with Liberty and Justice.* Notre Dame, Ind.: University of Notre Dame Press, 1979.

Kluge, Eike-Henner. *The Practice of Death.* New Haven: Yale University Press, 1975.

Kohl, Marvin, ed. *Beneficent Euthanasia.* Buffalo, N.Y.: Prometheus Press, 1975.

Kübler-Ross, Elisabeth. *On Death and Dying.* New York: Macmillan, 1969.

———. *Questions and Answers on Death and Dying.* New York: Macmillan, 1974.

Maguire, Daniel C. *Death by Choice.* Garden City, N.Y.: Doubleday, 1974.

Russell, O. Ruth. *Freedom to Die: Moral and Legal Aspects of Euthanasia.* New York: Human Sciences Press, 1975; Dell, 1976.

Steinbock, Bonnie, ed. *To Live and to Die: When, Why, and How.* New York: Springer, 1974.

6
CAPITAL PUNISHMENT

Late on the night of October 4, 1983, in Huntsville, Texas, convicted killer J. D. Autry was taken from his death-row cell in the penitentiary and strapped to a wheeled cot. Intravenous tubes were connected to both arms, ready to administer a dose of poison.

Outside, a crowd shouted "Kill him, kill him, kill him!" whenever television lights were turned on.

In Washington, Supreme Court Justice Byron White waited for a last-minute application for a stay of execution. The application, written on three sheets of a yellow pad, made a new argument related to another case due to be heard by the Court. Shortly after midnight White granted the stay. The intravenous tubes were disconnected, the straps unbuckled. Autry was returned to his cell. Only in March of 1984 was the execution carried out.

Who of the twelve hundred Americans on death row will be executed next? The answer is uncertain, because none of the cases has exhausted its appeals. An added complication is that as of now, the U.S. Supreme Court has not ruled comprehensively on whether capital punishment by its very nature is cruel and unusual punishment and thus violates the Eighth Amendment to the Constitution. However, in the case of *Furman* v. *Georgia* (1972), the Court did rule that capital punishment *as currently administered* was cruel and unusual punishment. In *Furman* v. *Georgia*, the Court actually was ruling on the constitutionality of the death penalty as imposed in three cases, one of murder, two of rape. Since nothing seemed atypical about those cases, the Court's ruling was taken to mean that the death penalty as currently administered violated the Eighth Amendment and, therefore, was unconstitutional. However, all this changed with the executions between 1977 and 1979 of Gary Gilmore by firing squad, John Spenkelink by electrocution, and Jesse Walter Bishop by gas.

The death penalty is a form of punishment. Consequently, one's view of the morality of the death penalty usually is influenced by one's view of punishment generally. So the specific moral question under discussion in this chapter is: Is capital punishment ever a justifiable form of punishment?

The Nature and Definition of Punishment

Generally, philosophers discuss punishment in terms of five elements. For something to be punishment it must (1) involve pain, (2) be administered for an offense against a law or rule, (3) be administered to someone who has been judged guilty of an offense, (4) be imposed by someone other than the offender, and (5) be imposed by rightful authority. Whether a punishment is commensurate with an offense, whether it is fair and equitable—these are very important moral and legal questions. But they must be distinguished from the question of what punishment is.

1. *Punishment must involve pain, harm, or some other consequence normally considered unpleasant.* For example, if a convicted robber was sentenced to "five-to-twenty" in a Beverly Hills country club, this would not be considered punishment, since ordinarily it would not involve pain or other unpleasant consequences (unless the robber had to pick up the tab). If he were sentenced to have his hands cut off, this could constitute punishment, though draconian by many people's standards.

2. *The punishment must be administered for an offense against a law or rule.* While punishment involves pain, obviously not all pain involves punishment. If a robber breaks into your house and steals your stereo, he is not "punishing" you, even though his action satisfies element (1). Although it caused you pain, his action is not taken to punish an offense against a law or rule. However, should the robber subsequently be sent to prison for the crime, then *that* action would be administered for breaking a law and thus satisfy element (2).

3. *The punishment must be administered to someone who has been judged guilty of an offense.* Suppose the robber is apprehended and imprisoned, although never judged guilty of the robbery. This would not be considered punishment. However, if he is imprisoned after his conviction for stealing your stereo, then he is being punished.

4. *The punishment must be imposed by someone other than the offender.* It is true that people sometimes speak of "punishing themselves" for a transgression. This, however, is not punishment in the strict sense, but a self-imposed act of atonement. Suffering from a twinge of conscience as he listens to the latest Willie Nelson album on your stereo, the robber decides to "punish" himself by listening to Robert Goulet, whom he detests, for two hours each day for a year. Properly speaking, this would not be punishment, although it might qualify as masochism.

5. *The punishment must be imposed by rightful authority.* In a strictly legal sense, "rightful authority" would be that constituted by a legal system against whom the offense is committed. In the case of the robber, "rightful authority" likely would be a court judge and jury. In a less legal sense, the authority might be a parent, a teacher, or some official who has a right to harm a person in a particular way for having done something or failed to do something.

These five elements, then, generally constitute the nature of punishment. Combining them produces a useful definition of punishment. Thus a punishment is harm inflicted by a rightful authority on a person who has been judged to have violated a law or rule.[1]

The Moral Acceptability of Punishment

Is punishment ever morally acceptable? This may seem a foolish question to ask, since it is hard to imagine society functioning without an established legal system of punishment. In fact, philosophers generally agree that punishment is morally acceptable. They, like most others, view punishment as a part of rule and law necessary to minimize the occurrence of forbidden acts. In short, law without punishment is toothless.

Still, there are people who do not share this view. They argue that society should be restructured so that a legal system of punishment is unnecessary. Just how this can or should be done remains problematic. The method most often proposed involves some form of therapeutic treatment or behavior modification for antisocial behavior, rather than a traditional form of punishment. Among the most morally controversial procedures for modifying undesirable social behavior are those associated with some startling advances in biomedicine. Such cases rarely can be resolved by a simple appeal to the individual's right to obtain appropriate treatment on request, and are even less likely to be resolved by an appeal to society's right to order such treatment.

Consider one case provided by a leading research scientist in the field, Dr. J. R. Delgado. A number of years ago, Delgado recalls, an attractive twenty-four-year-old woman of average intelligence and education and a long record of arrests for disorderly conduct approached him and his associates. The patient explained that she had been repeatedly involved in bar brawls in which she would entice men to fight over her. Having spent a number of years in jail and mental institutions, the woman expressed a strong desire but inability to change her behavior. Because past psychological therapy had proved ineffective, both she and her mother urgently requested that some sort of brain surgery be performed to control her antisocial and destructive behavior. As Delgado said: "They asked specifically that electrodes be implanted to orient a possible electrocoagulation of a limited cerebral area; and if that wasn't possible, they wanted a lobotomy."[2]

---

1. *See Burton M. Leiser,* Liberty, Justice, and Morals *(New York: Macmillan, 1973), pp. 195–97.*

2. *J. R. Delgado,* Physical Control of the Mind: Toward a Psycho-Civilized Society *(New York: Harper & Row, 1969), p. 85.*

At that time, medical knowledge could not determine whether such procedures could help resolve the woman's problem, so the physicians rejected surgical intervention. When Delgado and his colleagues explained their decision to the woman and her mother, the two reacted with disappointment and anxiety: "What is the future? Only jail or the hospital?"[3]

What is the future, indeed? The day could very well come when such therapeutic treatment renders traditional kinds of punishment obsolete, perhaps barbaric. But even then, pressing moral questions will remain concerning society's right to alter an individual's personality against his or her will. For now, most agree that punishment is a morally acceptable practice. What they do not agree on, however, is the aim of punishment.

Aims of Punishment

The aims of punishment can be divided into two categories: (1) in terms of giving people what they deserve, or (2) in terms of its desirable consequences. The first category includes retributive theories of punishment; the second includes preventive, deterrent, and reformative theories.

Retribution

The term *retribution* refers to punishment given in return for some wrong done. This view of punishment holds that we should punish people simply because they deserve it. Traditionally, retributive theorists have considered punishment a principle of justice, whereby offenders are made to suffer in kind for the harm they have caused others. Arguments in favor of capital punishment commonly make this point.

But another version of retribution associates punishment not with revenge, but with respect for persons, both noncriminals and criminals. Proponents of this theory argue that the robber, for example, like everyone else in society, ought to live under the same limitations of freedom. When the robber steals your stereo, he is taking unfair advantage of you, disrupting the balance of equal limitations. When the state subsequently punishes him, the punishment is viewed as an attempt to restore this disrupted balance, to reaffirm society's commitment to fair treatment for all. This version of retribution focuses on the noncriminal generally and the victim in particular, claiming that respect for the parties who abide by society's limitations requires punishment of those who flout those limitations.

The other side of the respect-retribution theory concerns respect for the offender. Proponents of retribution sometimes argue that failure to punish is tantamount to treating offenders with disrespect because it denies them autonomy and responsibility for their actions. Showing respect entails giving people what they deserve, whether that be reward or punishment. To deny praise to a deserving person is disrespectful. By the same token, to deny punishment to a

3. *Ibid.*

deserving person is equally disrespectful. Both views of respect-retribution can be used in defense of capital punishment.

Prevention

The prevention view of punishment holds that we should punish to ensure that offenders do not repeat their offense and so further injure society. Thus robbers should be punished, perhaps imprisoned, so that they will not steal anything else. Prevention is one of the most common justifications for capital punishment.

Deterrence

The deterrence view holds that we should punish in order to discourage others from committing similar offenses. Like the prevention theory, it aims to minimize the crime rate. Thus when other potential thieves see that the robber has been punished for the crime, they will be less likely to steal. Deterrence is perhaps the most common argument made on behalf of capital punishment, and thus is the one that those against capital punishment often focus on. For the moment, we will simply observe that if a punishment is to function effectively as a deterrent, it must be severe enough to be undesirable and, just as important, it must be known and certain. Thus, potential offenders must be aware of the kind and severity of the punishment that awaits them, and they must be convinced that they will receive it if they commit the offense.

Reform

The reform theory holds that one should punish in order to induce people to conform to standards of behavior they have tended to ignore or violate. The idea here is that people will emerge from punishment better than they were before, insofar as they will be less likely to breach conventional standards of behavior.

Although rehabilitation often accompanies reform, the aims of each are different. Rehabilitation aims not to punish but to offer the offenders opportunities to find a useful place in society on release from prison. Modern penal institutions attempt to accomplish this by providing various recreational, educational, and vocational services for prisoners.

It's important to keep in mind that the aforementioned aims of punishment are not mutually exclusive. It's possible for more than one purpose of punishment to be morally legitimate. In fact, perhaps all four, in varying degrees, might be called for.

Retentionist and *Abolitionist* Defined

Having briefly examined some aspects of punishment, including its nature and definition, its moral acceptability, and its aims, let us now turn to the particular form of punishment that is the topic of this chapter: capital punishment. The central moral question that concerns us is: Is capital punishment ever a justifiable form of punishment?

Those who support retaining or reinstituting capital punishment can be termed *retentionists*. Retentionists are not agreed that all the arguments supporting capital punishment are acceptable or on the conditions under which capital punishment should be imposed. But they do agree that capital punishment is at least sometimes morally justifiable. Those who oppose capital punishment are commonly termed *abolitionists*. Like retentionists, abolitionists disagree among themselves about which arguments against capital punishment are acceptable. But all abolitionists share the belief that capital punishment is never morally justifiable.

One common argument enlisted by both retentionists and abolitionists concerns capital punishment as a deterrent. As we'll see, retentionists sometimes claim that capital punishment deters potential murderers, and therefore should be kept. For their part, some abolitionists claim that capital punishment does not serve as a deterrent, and offer this—usually with other reasons—for abolishing the death penalty. Because the deterrent argument figures so prominently in capital punishment debates, we should inspect it before beginning this chapter's dialogues.

Capital Punishment as Deterrent

Does capital punishment succeed in deterring potential murderers? At first glance, the answer seems to be a resounding yes. After all, virtually everyone seems deterred from lawbreaking by relatively mild intimidation—for example, being towed away for illegal parking or losing one's driver's license for recklessness. How much more, common sense suggests, must potential murderers be intimidated by the threat of their own death at the executioner's hand. In this instance, however, common sense misleads by failing to recognize that murderers differ from the rest of us in important respects.

First, there's the large category of murderers who kill in a fit of rage or passion. A barroom brawl escalates and one man kills another; in a gang fight a member of one group kills a member of another, perhaps to save face or avenge a harm; in a family quarrel a person kills a relative when things get out of hand. The list goes on and on. Such murders, of which there are many, are committed not with forethought of the consequences, but in a moment of white-hot anger. Hence not even the death penalty is likely to deter these murderers. (In fact, in instances of gang killings it might have the opposite effect: In risking their own lives at the hands of the state, killers might feel they're proving their mettle or giving ultimate evidence of gang loyalty.)

Then there's the category of so-called professional criminals, those who deliberately calculate when, where, and how to commit crimes. It's not at all clear that this type of criminal is deterred by the death penalty. In fact, if professional criminals perceive the likely punishment for nonhomicidal crimes (e.g., robbery, burglary, rape, and so forth) as overly severe, they might be encouraged to kill their victims and witnesses rather than risk getting caught: Killing these people greatly increases the criminals' chances of getting away with their crimes, and so they may not in the least be deterred by the threat of the death penalty.

Besides these kinds of potential murderers are those who seemingly have a death wish. The annals of psychiatry are replete with cases of people so emotionally disturbed that they kill in order to win the death penalty to end their tortured existence. In effect, their murderous acts are expressions of suicidal impulses. Since they lack the nerve to kill themselves, they want someone else to do it for them—in this case, the state.

But what about cases of so-called normal, nonsuicidal persons who carefully weigh the risks before killing? Are these potential murderers deterred by the death penalty? Even here, the deterrent effect of capital punishment is by no means obvious or certain. What's required is a determination of how many, if any, calculating potential murderers (a small class to begin with) who are not deterred by the threat of life imprisonment would be deterred by the threat of death. Even if such a determination is possible, it's not obvious or certain that there would be any such people at all, or much more than a small number annually.

A further complication in assessing the death penalty as deterrent relates not to factual questions such as the preceding, but to the moral and legal costs of deterrence. Some claim there's a basic incompatibility between the deterrent efficacy of the death penalty and due process, which refers to a constitutionally guaranteed, specific, systematic procedure of appeal. The death penalty can be deterrent, the argument goes, only if due process is sacrificed. Conversely, due process can govern the inflicting of capital punishment but at the cost of deterrence. When human life is at issue—as of course it is in capital punishment cases—the courts have been understandably scrupulous in reviewing cases for error and ensuring that basic rights have been respected. The consequences of this process of rigorous judicial review are quite apparent: increasing delays of execution, an ever-increasing percentage of those convicted who are never executed, and large numbers of convictions overturned. When fully exercised, the right of appeal can lead to costly, protracted litigation, in which a criminal's fate may hinge as much on the quality of legal representation as on any other factor. Given the delay between murder and the death penalty, and the uncertainty that a death sentence will ever be carried out, one wonders about the death penalty's deterrent effect. On the other hand, to ensure swiftness and certainty mocks one of the most cherished ideals of our system of justice: due process.

Currently, the consensus among social scientists is that no statistical studies on the deterrent effect of capital punishment yield a conclusive answer. We simply don't know whether the threat of death deters people from killing. Given this picture, some argue that since there is a moral presumption against the taking of life, the burden of proving capital punishment is a deterrent should fall on those who advocate the taking of life in the form of capital punishment. But by the same token, one could contend that abolitionists should bear the burden of proof: Since we don't know for sure whether the death penalty is a deterrent, we should give the benefit of doubt to the lives of potential victims of murderers rather than to the murderers. This tack is especially forceful when applied to measures intended to reserve the death penalty for the intentional killings of law-enforcement agents and others who need special protection, which they might get from the threat of the death penalty.

Abolitionist Arguments
(against Capital Punishment)

1.   *Every life has dignity and worth, even that of a convicted murderer.*

POINT: "I'm sure you'll agree that every individual has inherent dignity and worth. While the taking of human life is sometimes morally permissible—for example, in self-defense—it's always a very serious matter and should not be permitted in the absence of weighty overriding reasons. The death penalty is cruel and inhumane. Since retentionists haven't marshaled substantial reasons in its defense, it must be judged morally unacceptable and should be prohibited.

"I expect you'll consider my absolute prohibition against capital punishment improbable since what I'm saying is that even when the end in question is the net saving of human lives, capital punishment is still absolutely impermissible morally. But I suggest that you look at your own presumably 'absolutist' view of torturing to death as a possible punishment. Suppose, for example, we had good reason to believe that by reinstituting death by torture for murder, we could save 100 percent of victims' lives a year. I think that you and almost everyone would reject such a penalty. No matter its positive social effect, you'd probably agree torture simply is not an eligible instrument of social policy in a civilized nation. Well, I feel the same way about the gallows or the electric chair, or any other form of capital punishment. In short, executing people, no matter how heinous their offenses, is an insult to the highest principle of morality and civilization: the sanctity of life."

COUNTERPOINT: "I share your reverence for life. I also agree that there are times when the taking of a human life is morally permissible. Where we part company is on whether the infliction of the death penalty can be one of the morally permissible occasions for taking life. If retentionists had not made a compelling case for the death penalty, I'd agree with you that the death penalty is cruel and inhuman. But, as I'll try to show later, I think we have.

"But let me just ask you to think about the notion of 'cruel and inhuman.' On what grounds do you say with such conviction that inflicting the death penalty is cruel and inhuman, but presumably that life imprisonment is not, or at least is less so? It's conceivable, isn't it, that a young killer facing a life sentence for murder with no chance of parole and all the indignities associated with prison life might consider this sentence more cruel than just being put to death? What are we to say of this? That the person is simply misinformed or demented? It seems to me that respecting the dignity and worth of a human being begins with respect for the person's autonomous will as a rational being. To call the death penalty cruel and inhuman, in effect, denies the party most affected by the punishment any voice in deciding which of two sentences—life imprisonment without possibility of parole, or death—is worse from his or her viewpoint. Of course, you'd probably say that a convicted murderer should not be given the choice, that society should determine what passes for cruel or inhuman punishment. But how is denying the convicted murderer a say consistent with honoring the dignity and worth of human beings? To me, *that* seems like a most cruel and inhuman way of treating people. In short, I think you're operating from a rather fuzzy concept of 'cruel and inhuman,' which you're treating as so clearly defined as to make capital punishment morally impermissible."

2. *Capital punishment does not deter crime.*

POINT: "A comparative analysis of states that have capital punishment and those that don't indicates that the murder rate in capital-punishment states frequently is no lower than in those states that don't have capital punishment. In some cases, it's higher. It's obvious, therefore, that capital punishment simply doesn't deter crime. And since capital punishment does not function as an effective deterrent to crime, it should be abolished."

COUNTERPOINT: "A statistical correlation does not establish a causal connection. Many things influence the commission of crimes, including economic, political, sociological, and psychological factors. A high crime rate in a non-capital-punishment state may be accounted for in a variety of ways, none of which bears on the absence of capital punishment. Conversely, a low crime rate in a non-capital-punishment state doesn't in itself disprove the deterrent value of capital punishment."

3. *Capital punishment is implemented with a class bias.*

POINT: "Statistics indicate that the poor, the underprivileged, and members of minority groups are executed proportionately in far greater numbers than the rich, the influential, and white people. Thus, capital punishment actually serves to oppress the most disadvantaged in our society. This is patently unfair and must be stopped."

COUNTERPOINT: "Your point is irrelevant because it addresses the inequity of the penalty's *distribution*, not whether it's a justifiable form of punishment. If the rich, white, or influential escape capital punishment for crimes that other people are executed for, then the problem lies with our judicial system, not with the punishment. Of course it's unfair that comparable crimes don't get the same penalties, no matter who the offender is. But let's remedy the system that allows this injustice, and not throw out the penalty."

4. *The innocent may die.*

POINT: "It's no secret that innocent people are often convicted of crimes. This is always tragic. Such a deplorable occurrence is reversible with every kind of punishment except capital punishment. We can't call the innocent back from their graves to make our apologies and offer reparation. Even if only one innocent person is executed, that's inexcusable. The very existence of capital punishment allows for such a heinous possibility, and therefore it should be abolished."

COUNTERPOINT: "Actually, very few innocent people are ever executed. True, the execution of even one innocent person is tragic and diminishes all of us and our system of justice. But no institution is perfect, certainly not the judicial system. Laws and the institutions that enforce them are made by humans, and the human factor always spells potential error. This doesn't mean we shouldn't minimize the possibility that someone will be executed for something he or she didn't do. Of course we should, and the death penalty ought never be given casually. But at the same time, we must recognize the fallibility of people and their institutions, and consequently view the rare execution of an innocent person in that sobering light."

5. *Retribution is uncivilized.*

POINT: "Putting someone to death can't bring back the victim or in any meaningful way repay the victim's loved ones. So what's the function of capital punishment? Clearly, it is to satisfy the primitive and apparently irrepressible urge for revenge. Such a motive isn't worthy of a society that considers itself civilized."

COUNTERPOINT: "Your argument focuses on only one aspect of retributive justice. Even if the desire for revenge is an unwholesome basis for punishment, one can still make a case for respect-retribution. Furthermore, your argument assumes that capital punishment can be only retributive. But punishment can have aims other than that—for example, deterrence."

6. *Capital punishment precludes reform.*

POINT: "When people are put to death, the chance that they can be restored to a useful place in society dies with them. How tragic that society should compound one heinous deed by committing another. The fact is, society bears as much responsibility for crime as criminals do. After all, societal influences help shape individuals into the criminals they subsequently become."

COUNTERPOINT: "Why assume that the sole or at least primary function of punishment is reform? And I categorically reject that societal influence can be so strong that people lose their sense of right and wrong, or have their will so constrained they cannot help committing heinous crimes. Such a degree of societal influence over individuals has never been established. In fact, many individuals who function as admirable citizens have been exposed to more sinister environmental influences than those who commit murder. Finally, your argument confuses social responsibility with personal responsibility. Where personal responsibility is involved, one can rightly assign blame. But to speak of 'social responsibility' is to blame everyone and no one. Pushed far enough, the concept of social responsibility ends up holding no one personally responsible for anything."

7. *Capital punishment injures the judicial system.*

POINT: "Capital punishment actually has the effect of making judges and juries soft on crime. It makes a mockery of the judicial system. Where capital punishment has been a mandatory sentence, judges and juries have been known to strain the evidence to acquit rather than sentence to death. And to make matters worse, cases of capital punishment inevitably involve years of costly appeals. This not only delays justice but subjects the people who are directly and indirectly involved to cruel and inhuman punishment."

COUNTERPOINT: "If judges and juries would rather acquit a guilty party than sentence the person to death, then the trouble lies not with capital punishment but with judges and juries. The same applies to the duration of capital-offense cases: The trouble isn't with capital punishment but with the judicial system. Yes, make the system more responsive, efficient, and accountable. But don't throw out capital punishment. That would be like throwing the baby out with the bathwater."

Retentionist Arguments (for Capital Punishment)

1. *Capital punishment is the only prevention against certain crimes.*

POINT: "Certain major crimes cannot be deterred in any way other than by capital punishment. Take, for example, the case of political revolutionaries or terrorists. These people won't be deterred from violent acts by threats of life imprisonment, because in their view they'll eventually gain freedom, even acclaim when their cause succeeds. Then there are those who are prone to violence, unreformable individuals whose very existence constitutes a potential threat to society. The only way society can protect itself from the possibility that such people will strike again is to execute them."

COUNTERPOINT: "Your argument assumes that those bent on murder or revolution will be deterred by capital punishment. But there's no evidence for this. In fact, it's more sensible to believe that the fanatical mind is indifferent to any potential punishment, no matter how severe. As for the unreformable, since society has never unflinchingly committed itself to a concept of punishment as rehabilitation, we have no way of knowing who, if anyone, is unreformable. This aside, protecting ourselves through executing people seems to be treating the symptoms, not the disease. The root causes of crime are social: poverty, prejudice, sickness, despair. Thinking that we're protecting ourselves through capital punishment is an illusion. The real way to protect ourselves is to root out the conditions that breed crime."

2. *Capital punishment balances the scales of justice.*

POINT: "When someone wantonly takes another's life, that person upsets the balance of equal limitations under which everyone in society ought to live. This disruption must be balanced. The only way to do this is to impose a punishment equal to the offense that upset the balance. Let the punishment fit the crime. Thus those who murder forfeit their own claim to life. The state has the right and the duty to execute them."

COUNTERPOINT: "Why do you take for granted the retributive view of punishment? Surely that theory is at least questionable. Just what is this 'balance of equal limitations' you talk about? The fact is that for no other crime except a capital offense is there a one-to-one correspondence between the crime and the punishment. Thieves aren't punished by having something stolen from them; blackmailers aren't punished by being blackmailed; muggers aren't punished by being mugged. Why should murderers necessarily be punished by being executed? It's true that, generally, punishment is given according to the crime committed. The robber is punished differently from the drunken driver, and the murderer should be punished differently from the robber. But 'difference' doesn't necessarily entail capital punishment for the murderer."

3. *Capital punishment deters crime.*

POINT: "When potential murderers realize they may have to pay for their crimes with their lives, they'll think twice before killing. There's no telling how many potential murderers have been deterred from murdering because of capital punishment. It's just common sense that people will think more seriously about committing a murder if they know they can lose their own lives as a result."

COUNTERPOINT: "The statistics on this point are inconclusive. We just don't know for sure that capital punishment does or doesn't deter crime. Until we know for sure, your assumption is unsupported."

4. *Capital punishment is an economical way to punish offenders.*

POINT: "There's no conclusive evidence that murderers can be reformed. That means society is faced with having to foot the bill for their incarceration. But is this fair? Why should innocent people be made to pay for the care of those who have wantonly violated society's conventions when there's no evidence that such care will reform them?"

COUNTERPOINT: "That is a crass disregard for the value of human life. How can you seriously measure the worth of a life, even a criminal's, in dollars and cents? Surely such considerations are beneath the dignity of a society that considers itself civilized. Destroying a human life, even a murderer's, because it's the most economical thing to do is an outrage."

Gregg v. *Georgia* (1976)[4]

Troy Gregg was charged with committing armed robbery and murder. In accordance with Georgia procedure in capital cases, the trial had two stages: a guilt stage and a penalty stage.

In the guilt stage, the jury found Gregg guilty of two counts of armed robbery and two counts of murder. At the penalty stage, which took place before the same jury, the trial judge instructed the jury that it could recommend either a death sentence or a life prison sentence on each count. The jury returned verdicts of death on each count.

On appeal, the Supreme Court of Georgia affirmed the convictions and the imposition of the death sentence for murder, but it vacated the death sentence imposed for armed robbery on grounds that the death penalty had rarely been imposed in Georgia for that offense.

4.   *Gregg* v. *Georgia*, U.S. Supreme Court, 238 U.S. (1976).

Eventually, the U.S. Supreme Court heard the case of Gregg v. Georgia. *The issue before the Court was whether capital punishment violated the Eighth Amendment's prohibition of cruel and unusual punishment. The majority of the Court held that it did not because: (1) capital punishment accords with contemporary standards of decency, (2) capital punishment may serve some deterrent or retributive purpose that is not degrading to human dignity, and (3) in the case of the Georgia law under review, capital punishment is no longer arbitrarily applied. (In* Furman v. Georgia, *1972, the court had ruled that the death penalty was unconstitutional as then administered, but did not comprehensively rule that it was unconstitutional by its very nature.)*

Dissenting, Justice Thurgood Marshall objected to the majority's decision on the grounds that: (1) capital punishment is not necessary for deterrence, (2) a retributive purpose for capital punishment is not consistent with human dignity, and (3) contemporary standards for decency with respect to capital punishment are not based on informed opinion. The following are excerpts from the majority and the dissenting views.

Majority Opinion (Written by Justice Potter Stewart)

We address initially the basic contention that the punishment of death for the crime of murder is, under all circumstances, "cruel and unusual" in violation of the Eighth and Fourteenth Amendments of the Constitution.

The Court on a number of occasions has both assumed and asserted the constitutionality of capital punishments. In several cases that assumption provided a necessary foundation for the decision, as the Court was asked to decide whether a particular method of carrying out a capital sentence would be allowed to stand under the Eighth Amendment. But until Furman v. Georgia, 408 U.S. 238 (1972), the Court never confronted squarely the fundamental claim that the punishment of death always, regardless of the enormity of the offense or the procedure followed in imposing the sentence, is cruel and unusual punishment in violation of the Constitution.

Although the issue was presented and addressed in Furman, it was not resolved by the Court. Four Justices would have held that capital punishment is not constitutional per se; two Justices would have reached the opposite conclusion; and three Justices, while agreeing that the statutes then before the Court were invalid as applied, left open the question whether such punishment may ever be imposed. We now hold that the punishment of death does not invariably violate the Constitution.

It is clear from the foregoing precedents that the Eighth Amendment has not been regarded as a static concept. As Chief Justice Warren said, in an oftquoted phrase, "[the] amendment must draw its meaning from the evolving standards of decency that mark the progress of a maturing society." Thus, an assessment of contemporary values concerning the infliction of a challenged sanction is relevant to the application of the Eighth Amendment. As we develop below more fully, this assessment does not call for a subjective judgment. It requires, rather, that we look to objective indicia that reflect the public attitude toward a given sanction.

But our cases also make clear that public perceptions of standards of decency with respect to criminal sanctions are not conclusive. A penalty also must accord with "the dignity of man," which is the "basic concept underlying the Eighth Amendment." This means, at least, that the punishment not be "excessive." When a form of punishment in the abstract (in this case, whether capital punishment may ever be imposed as a sanction for murder) rather than in the particular (the propriety of death as a penalty to be applied to a specific defendant for a specific crime) is under consideration, the inquiry into "excessiveness" has two aspects. First, the punishment must not involve the unnecessary and wanton infliction of pain. Second, the punishment must not be grossly out of proportion to the severity of the crime.

Of course, the requirements of the Eighth Amendment must be applied with an awareness of the limited role to be played by the courts. This does not mean that judges have no role to play, for the Eighth Amendment is a restraint upon the exercise of legislative power.

But, while we have an obligation to insure that constitutional bounds are not overreached, we may not act as judges as we might as legislators.

Therefore, in assessing a punishment by a democratically elected legislature against the constitutional measure, we presume its validity. We may not require the legislature to select the least severe penalty possible so long as the penalty selected is not cruelly inhumane or disproportionate to the crime involved. And a heavy burden rests on those who would attack the judgment of the representatives of the people.

This is true in part because the constitutional test is intertwined with an assessment of contemporary standards and legislative judgment weighs heavily in ascertaining such standards.

The deference we owe to the decisions of the state legislatures under our Federal system is enhanced where the specification of punishment is concerned, for "these are peculiarly questions of legislative policy." A decision that a given punishment is impermissible under the Eighth Amendment cannot be reversed short of a constitutional amendment. The ability of the people to express their preference through the normal democratic process, as well as through ballot referenda, is shut off. Revisions cannot be made in the light of further experience. We now consider specifically whether the sentence of death for the crime of murder is a per se violation of the Eighth and Fourteenth Amendments to the Constitution.

We note first that history and precedent strongly support a negative answer to this question.

The imposition of the death penalty for the crime of murder has a long history of acceptance both in the United States and in England. The common-law rule imposed a mandatory death sentence on all convicted murderers. And the penalty continued to be used into the 20th century by most American states, although the breadth of the common-law rule was diminished, initially by narrowing the class of murders to be punished by death and subsequently by widespread adoption of laws expressly granting judges the discretion to recommend mercy.

It is apparent from the text of the Constitution itself that the existence of capital punishment was accepted by the framers. At the time the Eighth Amendment was ratified, capital punishment was a common sanction in every state. Indeed, the first Congress of the United States enacted legislation providing death as the penalty for specified crimes.

For nearly two centuries, this Court, repeatedly and often expressly, has recognized that capital punishment is not invalid per se.

Four years ago, the petitioners in Furman and its companion cases predicated their argument primarily upon the asserted proposition that standards of decency had evolved to the point where capital punishment no longer could be tolerated. The petitioners in those cases said, in effect, that the evolutionary process had come to an end, and that standards of decency required that the Eighth amendment be construed finally as prohibiting capital punishment for any crime regardless of its depravity and impact on society.

The petitioners in the capital cases before the Court today renew the "standards of decency" argument, but developments during the four years since Furman have undercut substantially the assumptions upon which their argument rested. Despite the continuing debate, dating back to the 19th century, over the morality and utility of capital punishment, it is now evident that a large proportion of American society continues to regard it as an appropriate and necessary sanction.

The most marked indication of society's endorsement of the death penalty for murder is the legislative response to Furman. The legislatures of at least 35 states have enacted new statutes that provide for the death penalty for at least some crimes that result in the death of another person. And the Congress of the United States, in 1974, enacted a statute providing the death penalty for aircraft piracy that results in death.

As we have seen, however, the Eighth Amendment demands more than that a challenged punishment be acceptable to contemporary society. The Court also must ask whether it comports with the basic concept of human dignity at the core of the amendment. Although we cannot "invalidate a category of penalties because we deem less severe penalties adequate to serve the ends of penology," the sanction imposed cannot be so totally without penological justification that it results in the gratuitous infliction of suffering.

The death penalty is said to serve two principal social purposes: retribution and deterrence of capital crimes by prospective offenders.

In part, capital punishment is an expression of society's moral outrage at particularly offensive conduct. This function may be unappealing to many, but it is essential in an ordered society that asks its citizens to rely on legal processes rather than self-help to vindicate their wrongs.

Statistical attempts to evaluate the worth of the death penalty as a deterrent to crimes by potential offenders have occasioned a great deal of debate. The results simply have been inconclusive.

Although some of the studies suggest that the death penalty may not function as a significantly greater deterrent than lesser penalties, there is no convincing empirical evidence either supporting or refuting this view. We may nevertheless assume safely that there are murderers, such as those who act in passion, for whom the threat of death has little or no deterrent effect. But for many others, the death penalty undoubtedly is a significant deterrent. There are carefully contemplated murders, such as murder for hire, where the possible penalty of death may well enter into the cold calculus that precedes the decision to act. And there are some categories of murder, such as murder by a life prisoner, where other sanctions may not be adequate.

In sum, we cannot say that the judgment of the Georgia Legislature that capital punishment may be necessary in some cases is clearly wrong. Considerations of federalism, as well as respect for the ability of a legislature to evaluate, in terms of its particular state, the moral consensus concerning the death penalty and its social utility as a sanction, require us to conclude, in the absence of more convincing evidence, that the infliction of death as a punishment for murder is not without justification and thus is not unconstitutionally severe.

Finally, we must consider whether the punishment of death is disproportionate in relation to the crime for which it is imposed. There is no question that death as a punishment is unique in its severity and irrevocability. When a defendant's life is at stake, the Court has been particularly sensitive to insure that every safeguard is observed.

But we are concerned here only with the imposition of capital punishment for the crime of murder, and when a life has been taken deliberately by the offender, we cannot say that the punishment is invariably disproportionate to the crime. It is an extreme sanction, suitable to the most extreme of crimes.

We hold that the death penalty is not a form of punishment that may never be imposed, regardless of the circumstances of the offense, regardless of the character of the offender, and regardless of the procedure followed in reaching the decision to impose it.

We now consider whether Georgia may impose the death penalty on the petitioner in this case.

The basic concern of Furman centered on those defendants who were being condemned to death capriciously and arbitrarily. Under the procedures before the Court in that case, sentencing authorities were not directed to give attention to the nature or circumstances of the crime committed or to the character or record of the defendant. Left unguided, juries imposed the death sentence in a way that could only be called freakish. The new Georgia sentencing procedures, by contrast, focus the jury's attention on the particularized characteristics of the individual defendant. While the jury is permitted to consider any aggravating or mitigating circumstances, it must find and identify at least one statutory aggravating factor before it may impose a penalty of death. In this way the jury's discretion is channeled. No longer can a jury wantonly and freakishly impose the death sentence; it is always circumscribed by the legislative guidelines. In addition, the review function of the Supreme Court of Georgia affords additional assurance that the concerns that prompted our decision in Furman are not present to any significant degree in the Georgia procedure applied here.

For the reasons expressed in this opinion, we hold that the statutory system under which Gregg was sentenced to death does not violate the Constitution. Accordingly, the judgment of the Georgia Supreme Court is affirmed.

It is so ordered.

Mr. Justice Brennan, Dissenting

This Court inescapably has the duty, as the ultimate arbiter of the meaning of our Constitution, to say whether, when individuals condemned to death stand before our bar, "moral concepts" require us to hold that the law has progressed to the point where we should declare that the punishment of death, like punishments on the rack, the screw and the wheel, is no longer morally tolerable in our civilized society. My opinion in Furman v. Georgia concluded that our civilization and the law had progressed to this point and therefore the punishment of death, for whatever crime and under all circumstances, is "cruel and unusual" in violation of the Eighth and Fourteenth Amendments of the Constitution. I shall not again canvass the reasons that led to that conclusion. I emphasize only that foremost among the "moral concepts" recognized in our cases and inherent in the clause is the primary moral principle that the state, even as it punishes, must treat its citizens in a manner consistent with their intrinsic worth as human beings—a punishment must not be so severe as to be degrading to human dignity. A judicial determination whether the punishment of death comports with human dignity is therefore not only permitted but compelled by the clause.

Death is not only an unusually severe punishment, unusual in its pain, in its finality, and in its enormity, but it serves no penal purpose more effectively than a less severe punishment; therefore the principle inherent in the clause that prohibits pointless infliction of excessive punishment when less severe punishment can adequately achieve the same purposes invalidates the punishment.

Mr. Justice Marshall, Dissenting

My sole purposes here are to consider the suggestion that my conclusion in Furman has been undercut by developments since then, and briefly to evaluate the basis for my brethren's holding that the extinction of life is a permissible form of punishment under the cruel and unusual punishments clause.

In Furman I concluded that the death penalty is constitutionally invalid for two reasons. First, the death penalty is excessive. And second, the American people, fully informed as to the purposes of the death penalty and its liabilities, would in my view reject it as morally unacceptable.

Since the decision in Furman, the legislatures of 35 states have enacted new statutes, authorizing the imposition of the death sentence for certain

crimes, and Congress has enacted a law providing the death penalty for air piracy resulting in death. I would be less than candid if I did not acknowledge that these developments have a significant bearing on a realistic assessment of the moral acceptability of the death penalty to the American people. But if the constitutionality of the death penalty turns, as I have urged, on the opinion of an informed citizenry, then even the enactment of new death statutes cannot be viewed as conclusive. In Furman, I observed that the American people are largely unaware of the information critical to a judgment on the morality of the death penalty, and concluded that if they were better informed they would consider it shocking, unjust, and unacceptable.

Even assuming, however, that the post-Furman enactment of statutes authorizing the death penalty renders the prediction of the views of an informed citizenry an uncertain basis for a constitutional decision, the enactment of those statutes has no bearing whatsoever on the conclusion that the death penalty is unconstitutional because it is excessive. An excessive penalty is invalid under the cruel and unusual punishments clause "even though popular sentiment may favor" it. The inquiry here, then, is simply whether the death penalty is necessary to accomplish the legitimate legislative purposes in punishment, or whether a less severe penalty—life imprisonment—would do as well.

The two purposes that sustain the death penalty as nonexcessive in the Court's view are general deterrence and retribution.

The Solicitor General in his amicus brief in these cases relies heavily on a study by Isaac Ehrlich, reported a year after Furman, to support the contention that the death penalty does deter murder.

The Ehrlich study, in short, is of little, if any, assistance in assessing the deterrent impact of the death penalty. The evidence I reviewed in Furman remains convincing, in my view, that "capital punishment is not necessary as a deterrent to crime in our society." The justification for the death penalty must be found elsewhere.

The other principal purpose said to be served by the death penalty is retribution. The notion that retribution can serve as a moral justification for the sanction of death finds credence in the opinion of my brothers Stewart, Powell, and Stevens, and that of my brother White in Roberts vs. Louisiana. It is this notion that I find to be the most disturbing aspect of today's unfortunate decision.

The foregoing contentions—that society's expression of moral outrage through the imposition of the death penalty pre-empts the citizenry from taking the law into its own hands and reinforces moral values—are not retributive in the purest sense. They are essentially utilitarian in that they portray the death penalty as valuable because of its beneficial results. These justifications for the death penalty are inadequate because the penalty is, quite clearly I think, not necessary to the accomplishment of those results.

There remains for consideration, however, what might be termed the purely retributive justification for the death penalty—that the death penalty is appropriate, not because of its beneficial effect on society, but because the taking of the murderer's life is itself morally good. Some of the language of the plurality's opinion appears positively to embrace this notion of retribution for its own sake as a justification for capital punishment.

The mere fact that the community demands the murderer's life in return for the evil he has done cannot sustain the death penalty, for as the plurality reminds us, "the Eighth Amendment demands more than that a challenged punishment be acceptable to contemporary society." To be sustained under the Eighth Amendment, the death penalty must "[comport] with the basic concept of human dignity at the core of the amendment"; the objective in imposing it must be "[consistent] with our respect for the dignity of other men." Under these standards, the taking of life "because the wrongdoer deserves it" surely must fall, for such a punishment has as its very basis the total denial of the wrongdoer's dignity and worth.

The death penalty, unnecessary to promote the goal of deterrence or to further any legitimate notion of retribution, is an excessive penalty forbidden by the Eighth and Fourteenth Amendments. I respectfully dissent from the Court's judgment upholding the sentences of death imposed upon the petitioners in these cases.

Questions for Analysis

1. *Writing the majority view, Justices Stewart, Powell, and Stevens explained: "The instinct for retribution is part of the nature of man, and channeling that instinct in the administration of criminal justice serves an important purpose in promoting the stability of a society governed by law. When people begin to believe that organized society is unwilling or unable to impose upon criminal offenders the punishment they 'deserve,' then there are sown the seeds of anarchy—of self help, vigilante justice, and lynch law." Do you think that is essentially a retributivist or utilitarian argument? In dissenting, Justice Marshall called the majority statement "wholly inadequate to justify the death penalty." With whom would you agree—the majority or Marshall?*

2. *Here's another quotation from the majority view: "[The] decision that capital punishment may be the appropriate sanction in extreme cases is an expression of the community's belief that certain crimes are themselves so grievous an affront to humanity that the only adequate response may be the penalty of death. . . . The truth is that some crimes are so outrageous that society insists on adequate punishment, because the wrong-doer deserves it, irrespective of whether it is a deterrent or not." Do you think this notion of retribution for its own sake is consistent with the basic concept of human dignity and worth which is at the base of the Eighth Amendment?*

The Death Sentence

Sidney Hook

In this essay, professor of philosophy Sidney Hook suggests that much of the debate about capital punishment suffers from vindictiveness and sentimentality. For example, abolitionists often argue that capital punishment is no more than an act of revenge, that it is the ultimate inhumanity. Hook is no more sympathetic, however, to the thrust of retentionist arguments. He points out that capital punishment has never been established as a deterrent to crime. Furthermore, he rejects as question-begging the retentionist argument that capital punishment is justified because it fulfills a community need, or that it is the only appropriate punishment for certain unspeakable offenses.

So where does Hook stand on the issue? Despite his feelings that no valid case for capital punishment has thus far been made, Hook is not categorically opposed to it. Indeed, he cites two conditions under which he believes capital punishment is justified. The first is in cases where criminals facing a life-imprisonment sentence request it. The second involves cases of convicted murderers who murder again. Hook regards the abolitionist objections to these exceptions as expressions of sentimentalism, even cruelty.

Is there anything new that can be said for or against capital punishment? Anyone familiar with the subject knows that unless extraneous issues are introduced, a large measure of agreement about it can be, and has been, won. For example, during the last 150 years the death penalty for criminal offenses has been abolished, or remains unenforced, in many countries; just as important, the number of crimes punishable by death has been sharply reduced in all countries. But while the progress has been encouraging, it still seems to me that greater clarity on the issues involved is desirable. Much of the continuing polemic still suffers from one or the other of the twin evils of vindictiveness and sentimentality.

Sentimentality, together with a great deal of confusion about determinism, is found in Clarence Darrow's speeches and writings on the subject. Darrow was an attractive and likeable human being but a very confused thinker. He argued against capital punishment on the ground that the murderer was always a victim of heredity and environment—and therefore it was unjust to execute him. ("Back of every murder and back of every human

act are sufficient causes that move the human machine beyond their control.") The crucifiers and the crucified, the lynch mob and its prey are equally moved by causes beyond their control and the relevant differences between them are therewith ignored. Although Darrow passionately asserted that no one knows what justice is and that no one can measure it, he nonetheless was passionately convinced that capital punishment was unjust.

It should be clear that if Darrow's argument were valid, it would be an argument not only against capital punishment but against all punishment. Very few of us would be prepared to accept this. But the argument is absurd. Even if we are all victims of our heredity and environment, it is still possible to alter the environment by meting out capital punishment to deter crimes of murder. If no one can help doing what he does, if no one is responsible for his actions, then surely this holds just as much for those who advocate and administer capital punishment as for the criminal. The denunciation of capital punishment as unjust, therefore, would be senseless. The question of universal determinism is irrelevant. If capital punishment actually were a

From Sidney Hook, "The Death Sentence," The New Leader, vol. 44 (April 3, 1961). Copyright © The American Labor Conference on International Affairs, Inc. Reprinted, with three paragraphs added, by permission of the publisher. Cf. the original version which appeared in The New York Law Forum (August 1961), pp. 278–83, as an address before the New York State District Attorneys' Association.

deterrent to murder, and there existed no other more effective deterrent, and none as effective but more humane, a case could be made for it.

Nor am I impressed with the argument against capital punishment on the ground of its inhumanity. Of course it is inhumane. So is murder. If it could be shown that the inhumanity of murder can be decreased in no other way than by the inhumanity of capital punishment acting as a deterrent, this would be a valid argument for such punishment.

I have stressed the hypothetical character of these arguments because it makes apparent how crucially the wisdom of our policy depends upon the alleged facts. Does capital punishment serve as the most effective deterrent we have against murder? Most people who favor its retention believe that it does. But any sober examination of the facts will show that this has never been established. It seems plausible, but not everything which is plausible or intuitively credible is true.

The experience of countries and states which have abolished capital punishment shows that there has been no perceptible increase of murders after abolition—although it would be illegitimate to infer from this that the fear of capital punishment never deterred anybody. The fact that "the state with the very lowest murder rate is Maine, which abolished capital punishment in 1870" may be explained by the hypothesis that fishermen, like fish, tend to be cold-blooded, or by some less fanciful hypothesis. The relevant question is: What objective evidence exists which would justify the conclusion that if Maine had not abolished capital punishment, its death rate would have been higher? The answer is: No evidence exists.

The opinion of many jurists and law enforcement officers from Cesare Beccaria (the eighteenth-century Italian criminologist) to the present is that swift and certain punishment of some degree of severity is a more effective deterrent of murder than the punishment of maximum severity when it is slow and uncertain. Although this opinion requires substantiation, too, it carries the weight which we normally extend to pronouncements by individuals who report on their life experience. And in the absence of convincing evidence that capital punishment is a more effective and/or humane form of punishment for murder than any other punishment, there remains no other reasonable ground for retaining it.

This is contested by those who speak of the necessity for capital punishment as an expression of the "community need of justice," or as the fulfillment of "an instinctive urge to punish injustice." Such views lie at the basis of some forms of the retributive theory. It has been alleged that the retributive theory is nothing more than a desire for revenge, but it is a great and arrogant error to assume that all who hold it are vindictive. The theory has been defended by secular saints like G. E. Moore and Immanuel Kant, whose dispassionate interest in justice cannot reasonably be challenged. Even if one accepted the retributive theory or believed in the desirability of meeting the community need of justice, it doesn't in the least follow that this justifies capital punishment. Other forms of punishment may be retributive, too.

I suppose that what one means by community need or feeling and the necessity of regarding it is that not only must justice be done, it must be seen to be done. A requirement of good law is that it must be consonant with the feeling of the community, something which is sometimes called "the living law." Otherwise it is unenforceable and brings the whole system of law into disrepute. Meeting community feeling is a necessary condition for good law, but not a sufficient condition for good law. This is what Justice Holmes meant when he wrote in *The Common Law* that "The first requirement of a sound body of law is that it should correspond with the actual feelings and demands of the community, whether right or wrong." But I think he would admit that sound law is sounder still if in addition to being enforceable it is also just. Our moral obligation as citizens is to build a community feeling and demand which is right rather than wrong.

Those who wish to retain capital punishment on the ground that it fulfills a community need or feeling must believe either that community feeling *per se* is always justified, or that to disregard it in any particular situation is inexpedient because of the consequences, *viz.*, increase in murder. In either case they beg the question—in the first case, the question of justice, and in the second, the question of deterrence.

One thing is incontestable. From the standpoint of those who base the argument for retention of capital punishment on the necessity of satisfying community needs there could be no justification whatsoever for any *mandatory* death sentence. For a mandatory death sentence attempts to determine in advance what the community need and feeling will be, and closes the door to fresh inquiry about the justice as well as the deterrent consequences of any proposed punishment.

Community need and feeling are notoriously fickle. When a verdict of guilty necessarily entails a death sentence, the jury may not feel the sentence warranted and may bring in a verdict of not guilty even when some punishment seems to be legally and morally justified. Even when the death sentence is not mandatory, there is an argument, not decisive but still significant, against any death sentence. This is its incorrigibility. Our judgment of a convicted man's guilt may change. If he has been executed in the meantime, we can only do him "posthumous justice." But can justice ever really be posthumous to the victim? Rarely has evidence, even when it is beyond reasonable doubt, the same finality about its probative force as the awful finality of death. The weight of this argument against capital punishment is all the stronger if community need and feeling are taken as the prime criteria of what is just or fitting.

What about heinous political offenses? Usually when arguments fail to sustain the demand for capital punishment in ordinary murder cases, the names of Adolf Hitler, Adolf Eichmann, Joseph Stalin and Ilse Koch are introduced and flaunted before the audience to inflame their feelings. Certain distinctions are in order here. Justice, of course, requires severe punishment. But why is it assumed that capital punishment is, in these cases, the severest and most just of sentences? How can any equation be drawn between the punishment of one man and the sufferings of his numerous victims? After all, we cannot kill Eichmann six million times or Stalin twelve million times (a conservative estimate of the number of people who died by their order).

If we wish to keep alive the memory of political infamy, if we wish to use it as a political lesson to prevent its recurrence, it may be educationally far more effective to keep men like Eichmann in existence. Few people think of the dead. By the same token, it may be necessary to execute a politically monstrous figure to prevent him from becoming the object of allegiance of a restoration movement. Eichmann does not have to be executed. He is more useful alive if we wish to keep before mankind the enormity of his offense. But if Hitler had been taken alive, his death would have been required as a matter of political necessity, to prevent him from becoming a living symbol or rallying cry of Nazi diehards and irreconcilables.

There is an enormous amount of historical evidence which shows that certain political tyrants, after they lose power, become the focus of restoration movements that are a chronic source of bloodshed and civil strife. No matter how infamous a tyrant's actions, there is usually some group which has profited by it, resents being deprived of its privileges, and schemes for a return to power. In difficult situations, the dethroned tyrant also becomes a symbol of legitimacy around which discontented elements rally who might otherwise have waited for the normal processes of government to relieve their lot. A *mystique* develops around the tyrant, appeals are made to the "good old days," when his bread and circuses were used to distract attention from the myriads of his tortured victims, plots seethe around him until they boil over into violence and bloodshed again. I did not approve of the way Mussolini was killed. Even he deserved due process. But I have no doubt whatsoever that had he been sentenced merely to life imprisonment, the Fascist movement in Italy today would be a much more formidable movement, and that sooner or later, many lives would have been lost in consequence of the actions of Fascist legitimists.

Where matters of ordinary crime are concerned these political considerations are irrelevant. I conclude, therefore, that no valid case has so far been made for the retention of capital punishment, that the argument from deterrence is inconclusive and inconsistent (in the sense that we do not do other things to reinforce its deterrent effect if we believe it has such an effect), and that the argument from community feeling is invalid.

However, since I am not a fanatic or absolutist, I do not wish to go on record as being categorically opposed to the death sentence in all circumstances. I should like to recognize two exceptions. A defendant convicted of murder and sentenced to life should be permitted to choose the death sentence instead. Not so long ago a defendant sentenced to life imprisonment made this request and was rebuked by the judge for his impertinence. I can see no valid grounds for denying such a request out of hand. It may sometimes be denied, particularly if a way can be found to make the defendant labor for the benefit of the dependents of his victim, as is done in some European countries. Unless such considerations are present, I do not see on what reasonable ground the request can be denied, particularly by those who believe in capital punishment. Once they argue that life imprisonment is either a more effective deterrent or more justly punitive, they have abandoned their position.

In passing, I should state that I am in favor of permitting *any* criminal defendant, sentenced to life imprisonment, the right to choose death. I can understand why certain jurists, who believe that the defendant wants thereby to cheat the state out of its mode of punishment, should be indignant at the idea. They are usually the ones who believe that even the attempt at suicide should be deemed a crime—in effect saying to the unfortunate person that if he doesn't succeed in his act of suicide, the state will punish him for it. But I am baffled to understand why the absolute abolitionist, dripping with treacly humanitarianism, should oppose this proposal. I have heard some people actually oppose capital punishment in certain cases on the ground that: "Death is too good for the vile wretch! Let him live and suffer to the end of his days." But the absolute abolitionist should be the last person in the world to oppose the wish of the lifer, who regards this form of punishment as torture worse than death, to leave our world.

My second class of exceptions consists of those who having been sentenced once to prison for premeditated murder, murder again. In these particular cases we have evidence that imprisonment is not a sufficient deterrent for the individual in question. If the evidence shows that the prisoner is so psychologically constituted that, without being insane, the fact that he can kill again with impunity may lead to further murderous behavior, the court should have the discretionary power to pass the death sentence if the criminal is found guilty of a second murder.

In saying that the death sentence should be *discretionary* in cases where a man has killed more than once, I am *not* saying that a murderer who murders again is more deserving of death than the murderer who murders once. Bluebeard was not twelve times more deserving of death when he was finally caught. I am saying simply this: that in a sub-class of murderers, i.e., those who murder several times, there may be a special group of sane murderers who, knowing that they will not be executed, will not hesitate to kill again and again. For *them* the argument from deterrence is obviously valid. Those who say that there must be no exceptions to the abolition of capital punishment cannot rule out the existence of such cases on *a priori* grounds. If they admit that there is a reasonable probability that such murderers will murder again or attempt to murder again, a probability which usually grows with the number of repeated murders, and still insist they would *never* approve of capital punishment, I would conclude that they are indifferent to the lives of the human beings doomed, on their position, to be victims. What fancies itself as a humanitarian attitude is sometimes an expression of sentimentalism. The reverse coin of sentimentalism is often cruelty.

Our charity for all human beings must not deprive us of our common sense. Nor should our charity be less for the future or potential victims of the murderer than for the murderer himself. There are crimes in this world which are, like acts of nature, beyond the power of men to anticipate or control. But not all or most crimes are of this character. So long as human beings are responsible and educable, they will respond to praise and blame and punishment. It is hard to imagine it, but even Hitler and Stalin were once infants. Once you *can* imagine them as infants, however, it is hard to believe that they were already monsters in their cradles. Every confirmed criminal was once an amateur. The existence of confirmed criminals testifies to the defects of our education—where they can be reformed—and of our penology—where they cannot. That is why we are under the moral obligation to be intelligent about crime and punishment. Intelligence should teach us that the best educational and penological system is the one which prevents crimes rather than punishes them; the next best is one which punishes crime in such a way as to prevent it from happening again.

Questions for Analysis

1. *Why does Hook say that if Darrow's argument were valid, it would be an argument not against capital punishment but against all punishment?*

2.   *Why is Hook not impressed by the claim that capital punishment is inhumane? Do you agree with him?*

3.   *Why does Hook feel that those who justify capital punishment by appeal to community feeling beg the question? Do you accept his argument?*

4.   *How does Hook respond to the retentionist claim that capital punishment is justified for politically heinous offenses?*

5.   *Do you agree that a "lifer's" request for capital punishment ought to be honored? Is Hook's justification for his position utilitarian or nonutilitarian? Explain.*

6.   *Why does Hook believe capital punishment is justified when a convicted murderer murders again? Is his defense utilitarian? Explain.*

7.   *Do you agree with Hook that what are called "humanitarian" objections to his two exceptions are really expressions of sentimentalism, even cruelty?*

8.   *Do you think that Rawls's maximim principle could be used to justify Hook's two exceptions?*

On Deterrence and the Death Penalty

Ernest Van Den Haag

Professor of social philosophy Ernest Van Den Haag begins his essay by conceding that capital punishment cannot be defended on grounds of rehabilitation or protection of society from unrehabilitated offenders. But he does believe that the ultimate punishment can be justified on grounds of deterrence.

To make his point, Van Den Haag at some length provides a psychological basis for deterrence. He associates deterrence with human responses to danger. Law functions to change social dangers into individual ones: Legal threats are designed to deter individuals from actions that threaten society. Most of us, Van Den Haag argues, transfer these external penalty dangers into internal ones; that is, we each develop a conscience that threatens us if we do wrong. But this conscience is and needs to be reinforced by external authority, which imposes penalties for antisocial behavior.

Van Den Haag then critically examines the reason punishment has fallen into disrepute as a deterrent to crime: the claim that slums, ghettos, and personality disorders are the real causes of crime. He dismisses these as spurious explanations, and insists that only punishment can deter crime. In Van Den Haag's view, whether individuals will commit crimes depends exclusively on whether they perceive the penalty risks as worth it.

While he concedes that the death penalty cannot be proved to deter crime, Van Den Haag observes that this in no way means capital punishment lacks a deterrent value. Indeed, it is this very uncertainty about its deterrence that impels Van Den Haag to argue for its retention. In the last analysis, he believes that retaining capital punishment leads to a net gain for society, notwithstanding the occasional abuse of it. In arguing for capital punishment, then, Van Den Haag takes a utilitarian viewpoint.

Reprinted by special permission of the Journal of Criminal Law, Criminology, and Police Science, © *1969 by Northwestern University School of Law, Vol. 60, No. 2.*

I

If rehabilitation and the protection of society from unrehabilitated offenders were the only purposes of legal punishment, the death penalty could be abolished: It cannot attain the first end, and is not needed for the second. No case for the death penalty can be made unless "doing justice" or "deterring others" is among our penal aims.[1] Each of these purposes can justify capital punishment by itself; opponents, therefore, must show that neither actually does, while proponents can rest their case on either.

Although the argument from justice is intellectually more interesting, and, in my view, decisive enough, utilitarian arguments have more appeal: The claim that capital punishment is useless because it does not deter others is most persuasive. I shall, therefore, focus on this claim. Lest the argument be thought to be unduly narrow, I shall show, nonetheless, that some claims of injustice rest on premises which the claimants reject when arguments for capital punishment are derived therefrom; while other claims of injustice have no independent standing: Their weight depends on the weight given to deterrence.

II

Capital punishment is regarded as unjust because it may lead to the execution of innocents, or because the guilty poor (or disadvantaged) are more likely to be executed than the guilty rich.

Regardless of merit, these claims are relevant only if "doing justice" is one purpose of punishment. Unless one regards it as good, or, at least, better, that the guilty be punished rather than the innocent, and that the equally guilty be punished equally,[2] unless, that is, one wants penalties to be just, one cannot object to them because they are not. However, if one does include justice among the purposes of punishment, it becomes possible to justify any one punishment—even death—on grounds of justice. Yet, those who object to the death penalty because of its alleged injustice usually deny not only the merits, or the sufficiency, of specific arguments based on justice, but the propriety of justice as an argument: They exclude "doing justice" as a purpose of legal punishment. If justice is not a purpose of penalties, injustice cannot be an objection to the death penalty, or to any other;

if it is, justice cannot be ruled out as an argument for any penalty.

Consider the claim of injustice on its merits now. A convicted man may be found to have been innocent; if he was executed, the penalty cannot be reversed. Except for fines, penalties never can be reversed. Time spent in prison cannot be returned. However, a prison sentence may be remitted once the prisoner serving it is found innocent; and he can be compensated for the time served (although compensation ordinarily cannot repair the harm). Thus, though (nearly) all penalties are irreversible, the death penalty, unlike others, is irrevocable as well.

Despite all precautions, errors will occur in judicial proceedings: The innocent may be found guilty,[3] or the guilty rich may more easily escape conviction, or receive lesser penalties than the guilty poor. However, these injustices do not reside in the penalties inflicted but in their maldistribution. It is not the penalty—whether death or prison—which is unjust when inflicted on the innocent, but its imposition on the innocent. Inequity between poor and rich also involves distribution, not the penalty distributed.[4] Thus injustice is not an objection to the death penalty but to the distributive process—the trial. Trials are more likely to be fair when life is at stake—the death penalty is probably less often unjustly inflicted than others. It requires special consideration not because it is more, or more often, unjust than other penalties, but because it is always irrevocable.

Can any amount of deterrence justify the possibility of irrevocable injustice? Surely injustice is unjustifiable in each actual individual case; it must be objected to whenever it occurs. But we are concerned here with the process that may produce injustice, and with the penalty that would make it irrevocable—not with the actual individual cases produced, but with the general rules which may produce them. To consider objections to a general rule (the provision of any penalties by law) we must compare the likely net result of alternative rules and select the rule (or penalty) likely to produce the least injustice. For however one defines justice, to support it cannot mean less than to favor the least injustice. If the death of innocents because of judicial error is unjust, so is the death of innocents by murder. If some murders could be avoided by a penalty conceivably more deterrent than others—

such as the death penalty—then the question becomes: Which penalty will minimize the number of innocents killed (by crime and by punishment)? It follows that the irrevocable injustice sometimes inflicted by the death penalty would not significantly militate against it, if capital punishment deters enough murders to reduce the total number of innocents killed so that fewer are lost than would be lost without it.

In general, the possibility of injustice argues against penalization of any kind only if the expected usefulness of penalization is less important than the probable harm (particularly to innocents) and the probable inequities. The possibility of injustice argues against the death penalty only inasmuch as the added usefulness (deterrence) expected from irrevocability is thought less important than the added harm. (Were my argument specifically concerned with justice, I could compare the injustice inflicted by the courts with the injustice—outside the courts—avoided by the judicial process. *I.e.,* "important" here may be used to include everything to which importance is attached.)

We must briefly examine now the general use and effectiveness of deterrence to decide whether the death penalty could add enough deterrence to be warranted.

III

Does any punishment "deter others" at all? Doubts have been thrown on this effect because it is thought to depend on the incorrect rationalistic psychology of some of its 18th- and 19th-century proponents. Actually deterrence does not depend on rational calculation, on rationality or even on capacity for it; nor do arguments for it depend on rationalistic psychology. Deterrence depends on the likelihood and on the regularity—not on the rationality—of human responses to danger; and further on the possibility of reinforcing internal controls by vicarious external experiences.

Responsiveness to danger is generally found in human behavior; the danger can, but need not, come from the law or from society; nor need it be explicitly verbalized. Unless intent on suicide, people do not jump from high mountain cliffs, however tempted to fly through the air; and they take precautions against falling. The mere risk of injury often restrains us from doing what is otherwise attractive; we refrain even when we have no direct experience, and usually without explicit computation of probabilities, let alone conscious weighing of expected pleasure against possible pain. One abstains from dangerous acts because of vague, inchoate, habitual and, above all, preconscious fears. Risks and rewards are more often felt than calculated; one abstains without accounting to oneself, because "it isn't done," or because one literally does not conceive of the action one refrains from. Animals as well refrain from painful or injurious experiences presumably without calculation; and the threat of punishment can be used to regulate their conduct.

Unlike natural dangers, legal threats are constructed deliberately by legislators to restrain actions which may impair the social order. Thus legislation transforms social into individual dangers. Most people further transform external into internal danger: They acquire a sense of moral obligation, a conscience, which threatens them, should they do what is wrong. Arising originally from the external authority of rulers and rules, conscience is internalized and becomes independent of external forces. However, conscience is constantly reinforced in those whom it controls by the coercive imposition of external authority on recalcitrants and on those who have not acquired it. Most people refrain from offenses because they feel an obligation to behave lawfully. But this obligation would scarcely be felt if those who do not feel or follow it were not to suffer punishment.

Although the legislators may calculate their threats and the responses to be produced, the effectiveness of the threats neither requires nor depends on calculations by those responding. The predictor (or producer) of effects must calculate; those whose responses are predicted (or produced) need not. Hence, although legislation (and legislators) should be rational, subjects, to be deterred as intended, need not be: They need only be responsive.

Punishments deter those who have not violated the law for the same reasons—and in the same degrees (apart from internalization: moral obligation) as do natural dangers. Often natural dangers—all dangers not deliberately created by legislation (*e.g.,* injury of the criminal inflicted by the crime victim) are insufficient. Thus, the fear of injury (natural danger) does not suffice to control city traffic; it must be reinforced by the legal punishment meted out to those who violate the rules. These punishments keep most people observing the regulations. However, where (in the absence of natural danger) the threatened punishment is so light that the advantage of violating rules tends to exceed the disadvantage of being punished (divided by the risk), the rule is violated (*i.e.*, parking fines are too light). In this case the feeling of obligation tends to vanish as well. Elsewhere punishment deters.

To be sure, not everybody responds to threatened punishment. Non-responsive persons may be (a) self-destructive or (b) incapable of responding to threats, or even of grasping them. Increases in the size, or certainty, of penalties would not affect these two groups. A third group (c) might respond to more certain or more severe penalties.[5] If the punishment threatened for burglary, robbery, or rape were a $5 fine in North Carolina, and 5 years in prison in South Carolina, I have no doubt that the North Carolina treasury would become quite opulent until vigilante justice would provide the deterrence not provided by law. Whether to increase penalties (or improve enforcement) depends on the importance of the rule to society, the size and likely reaction of the group that did not respond before, and the acceptance of the added punishment and enforcement required to deter it. Observation would have to locate the points—likely to differ in different times and places—at which diminishing, zero, and negative returns set in. There is no reason to believe that all present and future offenders belong to the *a priori* non-responsive groups, or that all penalties have reached the point of diminishing, let alone zero returns.

IV

Even though its effectiveness seems obvious, punishment as a deterrent has fallen into disrepute. Some ideas which help explain this progressive heedlessness were uttered by Lester Pearson, then Prime Minister of Canada, when, in opposing the death penalty, he proposed that instead "the state seek to eradicate the causes of crime—slums, ghettos and personality disorders."[6]

"Slums, ghettos, and personality disorders" have not been shown, singly or collectively, to be "the causes" of crime.

(1) The crime rate in the slums is indeed higher than elsewhere; but so is the death rate in hospitals. Slums are no more "causes" of crime than hospitals are of death; they are locations of crime, as hospitals are of death. Slums and hospitals attract people selectively; neither is the "cause" of the condition (disease in hospitals, poverty in slums) that leads to the selective attraction.

As for poverty which draws people into slums, and, sometimes, into crime, any relative disadvantage may lead to ambition, frustration, resentment and, if insufficiently restrained, to crime. Not all relative disadvantages can be eliminated; indeed very few can be, and their elimination increases the resentment generated by the remaining ones; not even relative poverty can be removed altogether. (Absolute poverty—whatever that may be—hardly affects crime.) However, though contributory, relative disadvantages are not a necessary or sufficient cause of crime: Most poor people do not commit crimes, and some rich people do. Hence, "eradication of poverty" would, at most, remove one (doubtful) cause of crime.

In the United States, the decline of poverty has not been associated with a reduction of crime. Poverty measured in dollars of constant purchasing power, according to present government standards and statistics, was the condition of ½ of all our families in 1920; of ⅓ in 1962; and of less than ⅙ in 1966. In 1967, 5.3 million families out of 49.8 million were poor—⅑ of all families in the United States. If crime has been reduced in a similar manner, it is a well-kept secret.

Those who regard poverty as a cause of crime often draw a wrong inference from a true proposition: The rich will not commit certain crimes—Rockefeller never riots; nor does he steal. (He mugs, but only on T.V.) Yet while wealth may be the cause of not committing (certain) crimes, it does not follow that poverty (absence of wealth) is the cause of committing them. Water extinguishes or prevents fire; but its absence is not the cause of fire. Thus, if poverty could be abolished, if everybody had all "necessities" (I don't pretend to know what this would mean), crime would remain, for, in the words of Aristotle, "the greatest crimes are committed not for the sake of basic necessities but for the sake of superfluities." Superfluities cannot be provided by the government; they would be what the government does not provide.

(2) Negro ghettos have a high, Chinese ghettos have a low crime rate. Ethnic separation, voluntary or forced, obviously has little to do with crime; I can think of no reason why it should.[7]

(3) I cannot see how the state could "eradicate" personality disorders even if all causes and cures were known and available. (They are not.) Further, the known incidence of personality disorders within the prison population does not exceed the known incidence outside—though our knowledge of both is tenuous. Nor are personality disorders necessary or sufficient causes for criminal offenses, unless these be identified by means of (moral, not clinical) definition with personality disorders. In this case, Mr. Pearson would have proposed to "eradicate" crime by eradicating crime—certainly a sound, but not a helpful idea.

Mr. Pearson's views are part as well of the mental furniture of the former U.S. Attorney General Ramsey Clark, who told a congressional committee that ". . . only the elimination of the causes of crime can make a significant and lasting difference in the incidence of crime." Uncharitably interpreted, Mr. Clark revealed that only the elimination of causes eliminates effects—a sleazy cliché and wrong to boot. Given the benefit of the doubt, Mr. Clark probably meant that the causes of crime are social; and that therefore crime can be reduced "only" by non-penal (social) measures.

This view suggests a fireman who declines fire-fighting apparatus by pointing out that "in the long run only the elimination of the causes" of fire "can make a significant and lasting difference in the incidence" of fire, and that fire-fighting equipment does not eliminate "the causes"—except that such a fireman would probably not rise to fire chief. Actually, whether fires are checked depends on equipment and on the efforts of the firemen using it no less than on the presence of "the causes": inflammable materials. So with crimes. Laws, courts and police actions are no less important in restraining them than "the causes" are in impelling them. If firemen (or attorneys general) pass the buck and refuse to use the means available, we may all be burned while waiting for "the long run" and "the elimination of the causes."

Whether any activity—be it lawful or unlawful—takes place depends on whether the desire for it, or for whatever is to be secured by it, is stronger than the desire to avoid the costs involved. Accord-ingly people work, attend college, commit crimes, go to the movies—or refrain from any of these activities. Attendance at a theatre may be high because the show is entertaining and because the price of admission is low. Obviously the attendance depends on both—on the combination of expected gratification and cost. The wish, motive or impulse for doing anything—the experienced, or expected, gratification—is the cause of doing it; the wish to avoid the cost is the cause of not doing it. One is no more and no less "cause" than the other. (Common speech supports this use of "cause" no less than logic: "Why did you go to Jamaica?" "*Because* it is such a beautiful place." "Why didn't you go to Jamaica?" "*Because* it is too expensive."—"Why do you buy this?" "*Because* it is so cheap." "Why don't you buy that?" "*Because* it is too expensive.") Penalties (costs) are causes of lawfulness, or (if too low or uncertain) of unlawfulness, of crime. People do commit crimes because, given their conditions, the desire for the satisfaction sought prevails. They refrain if the desire to avoid the cost prevails. Given the desire, low cost (penalty) causes the action, and high cost restraint. Given the cost, desire becomes the causal variable. Neither is intrinsically more causal than the other. The crime rate increases if the cost is reduced or the desire raised. It can be decreased by raising the cost or by reducing the desire.

The cost of crime is more easily and swiftly changed than the conditions producing the inclination to it. Further, the costs are very largely within the power of the government to change, whereas the conditions producing propensity to crime are often only indirectly affected by government action, and some are altogether beyond the control of the government. Our unilateral emphasis on these conditions and our undue neglect of costs may contribute to an unnecessarily high crime rate.

V

The foregoing suggests the question posed by the death penalty: Is the deterrence added (return) sufficiently above zero to warrant irrevocability (or other, less clear, disadvantages)? The question is not only whether the penalty deters, but whether it deters more than alternatives and whether the difference exceeds the cost of irrevocability. (I shall assume that the alternative is actual life imprisonment so as to exclude the complication produced by the release of the unrehabilitated.)

In some fairly infrequent but important circumstances the death penalty is the only possible deterrent. Thus, in case of acute *coups d'état,* or of acute substantial attempts to overthrow the government, prospective rebels would altogether discount the threat of any prison sentence. They would not be deterred because they believe the swift victory of the revolution will invalidate a prison sentence and turn it into an advantage. Execution would be the only deterrent because, unlike prison sentences, it cannot be revoked by victorious rebels. The same reasoning applies to deterring spies or traitors in wartime. Finally, men who, by virtue of past acts, are already serving, or are threatened, by a life sentence could be deterred from further offenses only by the threat of the death penalty.[8]

What about criminals who do not fall into any of these (often ignored) classes? Prof. Thorsten Sellin has made a careful study of the available statistics: He concluded that they do not yield evidence for the deterring effect of the death penalty.[9] Somewhat surprisingly, Prof. Sellin seems to think that this lack of evidence for deterrence is evidence for the lack of deterrence. It is not. It means that deterrence has not been demonstrated statistically—not that non-deterrence has been.

It is entirely possible, indeed likely (as Prof. Sellin appears willing to concede), that the statistics used, though the best available, are nonetheless too slender a reed to rest conclusions on. They indicate that the homicide rate does not vary greatly between similar areas with or without the death penalty, and in the same area before and after abolition. However, the similar areas are not similar enough; the periods are not long enough; many social differences and changes, other than the abolition of the death penalty, may account for the variation (or lack of it) in homicide rates with and without, before and after abolition; some of these social differences and changes are likely to have affected homicide rates. I am unaware of any statistical analysis which adjusts for such changes and differences. And logically, it is quite consistent with the postulated deterrent effect of capital punishment that there be less homicide after abolition: With retention there might have been still less.

Homicide rates do not depend exclusively on penalties any more than do other crime rates. A number of conditions which influence the propensity to crime, demographic, economic or generally social changes or differences—even such matters as changes of the divorce laws or of the cotton price—may influence the homicide rate. Therefore variation or constancy cannot be attributed to variations or constancy of the penalties, unless we know that no other factor influencing the homicide rate has changed. Usually we don't. To believe the death penalty deterrent does not require one to believe that the death penalty, or any other, is the only or the decisive causal variable; this would be as absurd as the converse mistake that "social causes" are the only or always the decisive factor. To favor capital punishment, the efficacy of neither variable need be denied. It is enough to affirm that the severity of the penalty may influence some potential criminals, and that the added severity of the death penalty adds to deterrence, or may do so. It is quite possible that such a deterrent effect may be offset (or intensified) by nonpenal factors which affect propensity; its presence or absence therefore may be hard, and perhaps impossible to demonstrate.

Contrary to what Prof. Sellin *et al.* seem to presume, I doubt that offenders are aware of the absence or presence of the death penalty state by state or period by period. Such unawareness argues against the assumption of a calculating murderer. However, unawareness does not argue against the death penalty if by deterrence we mean a preconscious, general response to a severe, but not necessarily specifically and explicitly apprehended, or calculated threat. A constant homicide rate, despite abolition, may occur because of unawareness and not because of lack of deterrence: People remain deterred for a lengthy interval by the severity of the penalty in the past, or by the severity of penalties used in similar circumstances nearby.

I do not argue for a version of deterrence which would require me to believe that an individual shuns murder while in North Dakota, because of the death penalty, and merrily goes to it in South Dakota since it has been abolished there; or that he will start the murderous career from which he had hitherto refrained, after abolition. I hold that the generalized threat of the death penalty may be a deterrent, and the more so, the more generally applied. Deterrence will not cease in the particular areas of abolition or at the particular times of abolition.

Rather, general deterrence will be somewhat weakened, through local (partial) abolition. Even such weakening will be hard to detect owing to changes in many offsetting, or reinforcing, factors.

For all of these reasons, I doubt that the presence or absence of a deterrent effect of the death penalty is likely to be demonstrable by statistical means. The statistics presented by Prof. Sellin *et al.* show only that there is no statistical proof for the deterrent effect of the death penalty. But they do not show that there is no deterrent effect. Not to demonstrate presence of the effect is not the same as to demonstrate its absence; certainly not when there are plausible explanations for the non-demonstrability of the effect.

It is on our uncertainty that the case for deterrence must rest.[10]

VI

If we do not know whether the death penalty will deter others, we are confronted with two uncertainties. If we impose the death penalty, and achieve no deterrent effect thereby, the life of a convicted murderer has been expended in vain (from a deterrent viewpoint). There is a net loss. If we impose the death sentence and thereby deter some future murderers, we spared the lives of some future victims (the prospective murderers gain too; they are spared punishment because they were deterred). In this case, the death penalty has led to a net gain, unless the life of a convicted murderer is valued more highly than that of the unknown victim, or victims (and the non-imprisonment of the deterred non-murderer).

The calculation can be turned around, of course. The absence of the death penalty may harm no one and therefore produce a gain—the life of the convicted murderer. Or it may kill future victims of murderers who could have been deterred, and thus produce a loss—their life.

To be sure, we must risk something certain—the death (or life) of the convicted man, for something uncertain—the death (or life) of the victims of murderers who may be deterred. This is in the nature of uncertainty—when we invest, or gamble, we risk the money we have for an uncertain gain. Many human actions, most commitments—including marriage and crime—share this characteristic with the deterrent purpose of any penal-

ization, and with its rehabilitative purpose (and even with the protective).

More proof is demanded for the deterrent effect of the death penalty than is demanded for the deterrent effect of other penalties. This is not justified by the absence of other utilitarian purposes such as protection and rehabilitation; they involve no less uncertainty than deterrence.[11]

Irrevocability may support a demand for some reason to expect more deterrence than revocable penalties might produce, but not a demand for more proof of deterrence, as has been pointed out above. The reason for expecting more deterrence lies in the greater severity, the terrifying effect inherent in finality. Since it seems more important to spare victims than to spare murderers, the burden of proving that the greater severity inherent in irrevocability adds nothing to deterrence lies on those who oppose capital punishment. Proponents of the death penalty need show only that there is no more uncertainty about it than about greater severity in general.

The demand that the death penalty be proved more deterrent than alternatives can not be satisfied any more than the demand that six years in prison be proved to be more deterrent than three. But the uncertainty which confronts us favors the death penalty as long as by imposing it we might save future victims of murder. This effect is as plausible as the general idea that penalties have deter-effects which increase with their severity. Though we have no proof of the positive deterrence of the penalty, we also have no proof of zero or negative effectiveness. I believe we have no right to risk additional future victims of murder for the sake of sparing convicted murderers; on the contrary, our moral obligation is to risk the possible ineffectiveness of executions. However rationalized, the opposite view appears to be motivated by the simple fact that executions are more subjected to social control than murder. However, this applies to all penalties and does not argue for the abolition of any.

Notes

1. Social solidarity of "community feeling" (here to be ignored) might be dealt with as a form of deterrence.

2. Certainly a major meaning of *suum cuique tribue.*

3. I am not concerned here with the converse injustice, *which I regard as no less grave.*

4. Such inequity, though likely, has not been demonstrated. Note that, since there are more poor than rich, there are likely to be more guilty poor; and, if poverty contributes to crime, the proportion of the poor who are criminals also should be higher than of the rich.

5. I neglect those motivated by civil disobedience or, generally, moral or political passion. Deterring them depends less on penalties than on the moral support they receive, though penalties play a role. I also neglect those who may belong to all three groups listed, some successively, some even simultaneously, such as drug addicts. Finally, I must altogether omit the far-from-negligible role that problems of apprehension and conviction play in deterrence—beyond saying that, by reducing the government's ability to apprehend and convict, courts are able to reduce the risks of offenders.

6. I quote from the *New York Times* (November 24, 1967, p. 22). The actual psychological and other factors which bear on the disrepute—as distinguished from the rationalizations—cannot be examined here.

7. Mixed areas, incidentally, have higher crime rates than segregated ones (see, e.g., R. Ross and E. van den Haag, *The Fabric of Society* (New York: Harcourt, Brace & Co., 1957), pp. 102–4. Because slums are bad (morally) and crime is, many people seem to reason that "slums spawn crime"—which confuses some sort of moral with a causal relation.

8. Cautious revolutionaries, uncertain of final victory, might be impressed by prison sentences—but not in the acute stage, when faith in victory is high. And one can increase even the severity of a life sentence in prison. Finally, harsh punishment of rebels can intensify rebellious impulses. These points, though they qualify it, hardly impair the force of the argument.

9. Sellin considered mainly homicide statistics. His work may be found in his *Capital Punishment* (New York: Harper & Row, 1967); or, most conveniently, in H. A. Bedau, *The Death Penalty in America* (Garden City, N.Y.: Doubleday & Co., 1964), which also offers other material, mainly against the death penalty.

10. In view of the strong emotions aroused (itself an indication of effectiveness to me: Might not murderers be as upset over the death penalty as those who wish to spare them?) and because I believe penalties must reflect community feeling to be effective, I oppose mandatory death sentences and favor optional, and perhaps binding, recommendations by juries after their finding of guilt. The opposite course risks the non-conviction of guilty defendants by juries who do not want to see them executed.

11. Rehabilitation or protection are of minor importance in our actual penal system (though not in our theory). We confine many people who do not need rehabilitation and against whom we do not need protection (e.g., the exasperated husband who killed his wife); we release many unrehabilitated offenders against whom protection is needed. Certainly rehabilitation and protection are not, and deterrence is, the main actual function of legal punishment if we disregard non-utilitarian ones.

Questions for Analysis

1. *Van Den Haag claims that injustice is an objection not to the death penalty but to the distributive process. What does he mean? Is his distinction between penalty and distribution germane?*

2. *What does deterrence depend on, in Van Den Haag's view?*

3. *How does punishment differ from natural dangers?*

4. *What kinds of people do not respond to threatened punishment? Would you be persuaded by the anti-capital-punishment argument that insists the death penalty simply does not deter certain people?*

5. *What determines whether penalties ought to be increased? Explain how this is a utilitarian argument.*

6. *Does Van Den Haag convince you that slums and ghettos are "no more 'causes' of crimes than hospitals are of death"?*

7. *In Van Den Haag's view, what is the sole determinant of whether people will or will not commit crimes? Do you agree?*

8. *Why does Van Den Haag not believe that the presence or absence of a deterrent effect of the death penalty is likely to be proved statistically? Does this weaken, strengthen, or have no effect on his own retentionist position?*

9. *Explain why Van Den Haag believes there is more to be gained by retaining the death penalty than by abolishing it.*

The Death Penalty as a Deterrent: Argument and Evidence

Hugo Adam Bedau

The following article was written by a leading abolitionist, philosophy professor Hugo Adam Bedau. Bedau applies the scalpel of logical analysis to the contentions made by Van Den Haag in the preceding essay.

Bedau isolates five main points made by Van Den Haag, and then critically analyzes each of them. First, Bedau objects to Van Den Haag's claim that the utilitarian abolitionist considers capital punishment useless because it does not deter crime. Bedau says that Van Den Haag's point founders on the concept of "deterrence," which is "too ill-formulated to be of any serious use." Second, Bedau rejects Van Den Haag's claim that the death penalty is the only way to deter certain classes of criminals.

Third, Bedau spends considerable time critically analyzing Van Den Haag's contention that no statistical case can be made for capital punishment as a nondeterrent. Bedau points out that the issue of abolishing the death penalty is not whether the death penalty is a deterrent but whether it is a superior deterrent to life imprisonment. There is no evidence, in Bedau's view, that points to the superiority of the death penalty as a deterrent. Indeed, he suggests, there is evidence that capital punishment is not *a superior deterrent to life imprisonment.*

Fourth, therefore, Bedau rejects the claim that the death penalty should be favored to life imprisonment because it may add to deterrence. And fifth, he likewise rejects the contention that abolitionists must prove that capital punishment does not add to deterrence.

Apart from further advancing the debate on capital punishment, Bedau's essay well illustrates the rigorous analysis that philosophers apply to moral questions and positions on them.

Professor Van Den Haag's recent article, "On Deterrence and the Death Penalty,"[1] raises a number of points of that mixed (i.e., empirical-and-conceptual-and-normative) character which typifies most actual reasoning in social and political controversy but which (except when its purely formal aspects are in question) tends to be ignored by philosophers. I pass by any number of tempting points in his critique in order to focus in detail only on those which affect his account of what he says is

From Hugo Adam Bedau, "The Death Penalty as a Deterrent: Argument and Evidence," Ethics 80 (1970), *205–217. Copyright* ©*1970 by The University of Chicago Press. Reprinted by permission of the publisher and the author.*

the major topic, namely, the argument for retaining or abolishing the death penalty as that issue turns on the question of *deterrence.*

On this topic, Van Den Haag's main contentions seem to be these five: (I) Abolitionists of a utilitarian persuasion "claim that capital punishment is useless because it does not deter others" (p. 280, col. 1). (II) There are some classes of criminals and some circumstances in which "the death penalty is the only possible deterrent" (p. 284, col. 2). (III) As things currently stand, "deterrence [namely of criminal homicide by the death penalty] has not been demonstrated statistically"; but it is mistaken to think that "non-deterrence" has been demonstrated statistically (p. 285, col. 1). (IV) The death penalty is to be favored over imprisonment, because "the added severity of the death penalty adds to deterrence, or may do so" (p. 285, col. 2; cf. p. 286, col. 1). (V) "Since it seems more important to spare victims than to spare murderers, the burden of proving that the greater severity inherent in irrevocability adds nothing to deterrence lies on those who oppose capital punishment" (p. 287, col. 1).

Succinctly, I shall argue as follows: (I) is not reasonably attributable to abolitionists, and in any case it is false; (II) is misleading and, in the interesting cases, is empirically insignificant; (III), which is the heart of the dispute, is correct in what it affirms but wrong and utterly misleading in what it denies; (IV) is unempirical and one-sided as well; and (V) is a muddle and a dodge.

The reasons for pursuing in some detail what at first might appear to be mere polemical controversy is not that Professor Van Den Haag's essay is so persuasive or likely to be of unusual influence. The reason is that the issues he raises, even though they are familiar, have not been nearly adequately discussed, despite a dozen state, congressional, and foreign government investigations into capital punishment in recent years. In Massachusetts, for example, several persons under sentence of death have been granted stays of execution pending the final report of a special legislative commission to investigate the death penalty. The exclusive mandate of this commission is to study the question of deterrence.[2] Its provisional conclusions, published late in 1968, though not in the vein of Van Den Haag's views, are liable to the kind of criticism he makes. This suggests that his reasoning may be

representative of many who have tried to understand the arguments and research studies brought forward by those who would abolish the death penalty, and therefore that his errors are worth exposure and correction once and for all.

I

The claim Van Den Haag professes to find "most persuasive," namely, "capital punishment is useless because it does not deter others," is strange, and it is strange that he finds it so persuasive. Anyone who would make this claim must assume that only deterrent efficacy is relevant to assessing the utility of a punishment. In a footnote, Van Den Haag implicitly concedes that deterrence may not be the only utilitarian consideration, when he asserts that whatever our penal "theory" may tell us, "deterrence is . . . the *main actual* function of legal punishment if we disregard non-utilitarian ones" (italics added). But he does not pursue this qualification. Now we may concede that if by "function" we mean intended or professed function, deterrence is the main function of punishment. But what is deterrence? Not what Van Den Haag says it is, namely, "a preconscious, general response to a severe but not necessarily specifically and explicitly apprehended or calculated threat" (pp. 285–86). How can we count as evidence of deterrence, as we may under this rubric of "general response," the desire of persons to avoid capture and punishment for the crimes they commit? Some criminologists have thought this is precisely what severe punishments tend to accomplish; if so, then they accomplish this effect only if they have failed as a deterrent. Van Den Haag's conception of deterrence is too ill-formulated to be of any serious use, since it does not discriminate between fundamentally different types of "general response" to the threat of punishment.

Let us say (definition 1) that a given punishment (P) is a *deterrent* for a given person (A) with respect to a given crime (C) at a given time (*t*) if and only if A does not commit C at *t* because he believes he runs some risk of P if he commits C, and A prefers, *ceteris paribus*, not to suffer P for committing C. This definition does not presuppose that P really is the punishment for C (a person could be deterred through a mistaken belief); it does not presuppose that A runs a high risk of incurring P (the degree of risk could be zero); or that A consciously thinks of P prior to t (it is left open as to the sort of theory needed to account for the operation of A's beliefs and preferences on his conduct). Nor does it presuppose that anyone ever suffers P (P could be a "perfect" deterrent), or that only P could have deterred A from C (some sanction less severe than P might have worked as well); and, finally, it does not presuppose that because P deters A at t from C, therefore P would deter A at any other time or anyone else at t. The definition insures that we cannot argue from the absence of instances of C to the conclusion that P has succeeded as a deterrent: The definition contains conditions (and, moreover, contains them intentionally) which prevent this. But the definition does allow us to argue from occurrences of C to the conclusion that P has failed on each such occasion as a deterrent.

Definition 1 suggests a general functional analogue appropriate to express scientific measurements of *differential deterrent efficacy* of a given punishment for a given crime with respect to a given population (definition 2). Let us say that a given Punishment, P, deters a given population, H, from a crime, C, to the degree, D, that the members of H do not commit C because they believe that they run some risk of P if they commit C and, *ceteris paribus*, they prefer not to suffer P for committing C. If $D = 0$, then P has completely failed as a deterrent, whereas if $D = 1$, P has proved to be a perfect deterrent. Given this definition and the appropriate empirical results for various values of P, C, and H, it should be possible to establish on inductive grounds the relative effectiveness of a given punishment as a deterrent.

Definition 2 in turn leads to the following corollary for assertions of relative superior deterrent efficacy of one punishment over another. A given Punishment, P_1, is a superior deterrent to another punishment, P_2, with respect to some crime, C, and some population, H, if and only if: If the members of H, believing that they are liable to P_1 upon committing C, commit C to the degree D_1; whereas if the members of H believe that they are liable to P_2 upon committing C, they commit C to the degree D_2, and $D_1 > D_2$. This formulation plainly allows that P_1 may be a more effective deterrent than P_2 for C_1 and yet less effective as a deterrent than P_2 for a different crime C_2 (with H constant), and so forth, for other possibilities. When speaking about deterrence in the sections which follow, I shall presuppose these definitions and this corollary. For the present, it is sufficient to notice that they have, at least, the virtue of eliminating the vagueness in Van Den Haag's definition complained of earlier.

Even if we analyze the notion of deterrence to accommodate the above improvements, we are left with the central objection to Van Den Haag's claim. Neither classic nor contemporary utilitarians have argued for or against the death penalty *solely* on the ground of deterrence, nor would their ethical theory entitle them to do so. One measure of the non-deterrent utility of the death penalty derives from its elimination (through death of a known criminal) of future possible crimes from that source; another arises from the elimination of the criminal's probable adverse influence upon others to emulate his ways; another lies in the generally lower budgetary outlays of tax moneys needed to finance a system of capital punishment as opposed to long-term imprisonment. There are still further consequences apart from deterrence which the scrupulous utilitarian must weigh, along with the three I have mentioned. Therefore, it is incorrect, because insufficient, to think that if it could be demonstrated that the death penalty is not a deterrent then we would be entitled to infer, on utilitarian assumptions, that "the death penalty is useless" and therefore ought to be abolished. The problem for the utilitarian is to make commensurable such diverse social utilities as those measured by deterrent efficacy, administrative costs, etc., and then to determine which penal policy in fact maximizes utility. Finally, inspection of sample arguments actually used by abolitionists[3] will show that Van Den Haag has attacked a straw man: There are few if any contemporary abolitionists (and Van Den Haag names none) who argue solely from professional utilitarian assumptions, and it is doubtful whether there are any nonutilitarians who would abolish the death penalty solely on grounds of its deterrent inefficacy.

II

Governments faced by incipient rebellion or threatened by a coup d'état may well conclude, as Van Den Haag insists they should, that rebels (as well as traitors and spies) can be deterred, if at all, by the threat of death, since "swift victory" of the revolution "will invalidate [the deterrent efficacy] of a prison sentence" (pp. 284–85).[4] This does not yet tell us how important it is that such deterrence be provided, any more than the fact that a threat of expulsion is the severest deterrent available to university authorities tells them whether they ought to insist on expelling campus rebels. Also, such severe penalties might have the opposite effect of inducing martyrdom, of provoking attempts to overthrow the government to secure a kind of political sainthood. This possibility Van Den Haag recognizes, but claims in a footnote that it "hardly impair[s] the force of the argument" (p. 288). Well, from a logical point of view it impairs it considerably; from an empirical point of view, since we are wholly without any reliable facts or hypotheses on politics in such extreme situations, the entire controversy remains quite speculative.

The one important class of criminals deterrable, if at all, by the death penalty consists, according to Van Den Haag, of those already under "life" sentence or guilty of a crime punishable by "life." In a trivial sense, he is correct; a person already suffering a given punishment, P, for a given crime, C_1, could not be expected to be deterred by anticipating the reinfliction of P were he to commit C_2. For if the anticipation of P did not deter him from committing C_1, how could the anticipation of P deter him from committing C_2, given that he is already experiencing P? This generalization seems to apply whenever P = "life" imprisonment. Actually, the truth is a bit more complex, because in practice (as Van Den Haag concedes, again in a footnote) so-called "life" imprisonment always has its aggravations (e.g., solitary confinement) and its mitigations (parole eligibility). These make it logically possible to deter a person already convicted of criminal homicide and serving "life" imprisonment from committing another such crime. I admit that the aggravations available are not in practice likely to provide much added deterrent effect; but exactly how likely or unlikely this effect is remains a matter for empirical investigation, not idle guesswork. Van Den Haag's seeming truism, therefore, relies for its plausibility on the false assumption that "life" imprisonment is a uniform punishment not open to further deterrence-relevant aggravations and mitigations.

Empirically, the objection to his point is that persons already serving a "life" sentence do not in general constitute a source of genuine alarm to cus-

todial personnel. Being already incarcerated and integrated into the reward structure of prison life, they do not seem to need the deterrent controls allegedly necessary for other prisoners and the general public.[5] There are exceptions to this generalization, but there is no known way of identifying them in advance, their number has proved to be not large, and it would be irrational, therefore, to design a penal policy (as several states have)[6] which invokes the death penalty in the professed hope of deterring such convicted offenders from further criminal homicide. Van Den Haag cites no evidence that such policies accomplish their alleged purpose, and I know of none. As for the real question which Van Den Haag's argument raises— is there any class of actual or potential criminals for which the death penalty exerts a marginally superior deterrent effect over every less severe alternative?—we have no evidence at all, one way or the other. Until this proposition, or some corollary, is actually tested and confirmed, there is no reason to indulge Van Den Haag in his speculations.

III

It is not clear why Van Den Haag is so anxious to discuss whether there is evidence that the death penalty is a deterrent, or whether—as he thinks— there is no evidence that it is not a deterrent. For the issue over abolishing the death penalty, as all serious students of the subject have known for decades, is not whether (1) *the death penalty is a deterrent*, but whether (2) *the death penalty is a superior deterrent to "life" imprisonment*, and consequently the evidential dispute is also not over (1) but only over (2). As I have argued elsewhere,[7] abolitionists have reason to contest (1) only if they are against *all* punitive alternatives to the death penalty; since few abolitionists (and none cited by Van Den Haag) take this extreme view, it may be ignored here. We should notice in passing, however, that if it were demonstrated that (1) were false, there would be no need for abolitionists to go on to marshal evidence against (2), since the truth of (1) is a presupposition of the truth of (2). Now it is true that some abolitionists may be faulted for writing as if the falsity of (1) followed from the falsity of (2), but this is not a complaint Van Den Haag makes nor is it an error vital to the abolitionist argument against the death penalty. Similar considerations inveigh against certain pro-death-penalty arguments. Proponents must do more than establish (1), they must also provide evidence in favor of (2); and they cannot infer from evidence which establishes (1) that (2) is true or even probable (unless, of course, that evidence would establish [2] independently). These considerations show us how important it is to distinguish (1) and (2) and the questions of evidence which each raises. Van Den Haag never directly discusses (2), except when he observes in passing that "the question is not only whether the death penalty deters but whether it deters more than alternatives" (p. 284, col. 2). But since he explicitly argues only over the evidential status of (1), it is unclear whether he wishes to ignore (2) or whether he thinks that his arguments regarding (1) also have consequences for the evidential status of (2). Perhaps Van Den Haag thinks that if there is no evidence disconfirming (1), then there can be no evidence disconfirming (2); or perhaps he thinks that none of the evidence disconfirming (2) also disconfirms (1). (If he thinks either, he is wrong.) Or perhaps he is careless, conceding on the one hand that (2) is important to the issue of abolition of the death penalty, only to slide back into a discussion exclusively about (1).

He writes as if his chief contentions were these two: We must not confuse (a) the assertion that there is no evidence that not-(1) (i.e., evidence that [1] is false); and abolitionists have asserted (b) whereas all they are entitled to assert is (a).[8] I wish to proceed on the assumption that since (1) is not chiefly at issue, neither is (a) nor (b) (though I grant, as anyone must, that the distinction between [a] and [b] is legitimate and important). What is chiefly at issue, even though Van Den Haag's discussion obscures the point, is whether abolitionists must content themselves with asserting that there is no evidence against (2), or whether they may go further and assert that there is evidence that not-(2) (i.e., evidence that [2] is false). I shall argue that abolitionists may make the stronger (latter) assertion.

In order to see the issue fairly, it is necessary to see how (2) has so far been submitted to empirical tests. First of all, the issue has been confined to the death penalty for criminal homicide; consequently, it is not (2) but a subsidiary proposition which critics of the death penalty have tested, namely, (2a) *the death penalty is a superior deterrent to "life" imprisonment for the crime of criminal homicide.* The falsification of (2a) does not entail the falsity of (2); the death penalty could still be a superior deterrent

to "life" imprisonment for the crime of burglary, etc. However, the disconfirmation of (2a) is obviously a partial disconfirmation of (2). Second, (2a) has not been tested directly but only indirectly. No one has devised a way to count or estimate directly the number of persons in a given population who have been deterred from criminal homicide by the fear of the penalty. The difficulties in doing so are plain enough. For instance, it would be possible to infer from the countable numbers who have not been deterred (because they did commit a given crime) that everyone else in the population was deterred, but only on the assumption that the only reason why a person did not commit a given crime is because he was deterred. Unfortunately for this argument (though happily enough otherwise) this assumption is almost certainly false. Other ways in which one might devise to test (2a) directly have proved equally unfeasible. Yet it would be absurd to insist that there can be no *evidence* for or against (2a) unless it is *direct* evidence for or against it. Because Van Den Haag nowhere indicated what he thinks would count as evidence, direct or indirect, for or against (1), much less (2), his insistence upon the distinction between (a) and (b) and his rebuke to abolitionists is in danger of implicitly relying upon just this absurdity.

How, then, has the indirect argument over (2a) proceeded? During the past generation, at least six different hypotheses have been formulated, as corollaries of (2a), as follows:[9]

i. death-penalty jurisdictions should have a lower annual rate of criminal homicide than abolition jurisdictions;

ii. jurisdictions which abolished the death penalty should show an increased annual rate of criminal homicide after abolition;

iii. jurisdictions which reintroduced the death penalty should show a decreased annual rate of criminal homicide after reintroduction;

iv. given two contiguous jurisdictions differing chiefly in that one has the death penalty and the other does not, the latter should show a higher annual rate of criminal homicide;

v. police officers on duty should suffer a higher annual rate of criminal assault and homicide in abolition jurisdictions than in death-penalty jurisdictions;

vi. prisoners and prison personnel should suffer a higher annual rate of criminal assault and homicide from life-term prisoners in abolition jurisdictions than in death-penalty jurisdictions.

It could be objected to these six hypotheses that they are, as a set, insufficient to settle the question posed by (2a) no matter what the evidence for them may be (i.e., that falsity of [i]–[vi] does not entail the falsity of [2]). Or it could be argued that each of (i)–(vi) has been inadequately tested or insufficiently (dis)confirmed so as to establish any (dis)confirmation of (2a), even though it is conceded that if these hypotheses were highly (dis)confirmed they would (dis)confirm (2a). Van Den Haag's line of attack is not entirely clear as between these two alternatives. It looks as if he ought to take the former line of criticism in its most extreme version. How else could he argue his chief point, that the research used by abolitionists has so far failed to produce *any* evidence against (1)—we may take him to mean (2) or (2a). Only if (i)–(vi) were *irrelevant* to (2a) could it be fairly concluded from the evidential disconfirmation of (i)–(vi) that there is still no disconfirmation of (2a). And this is Van Den Haag's central contention. The other ways to construe Van Den Haag's reasoning are simply too preposterous to be considered: He cannot think that the evidence is indifferent to or *confirms* (i)–(vi); nor can he think that there has been no *attempt* at all to disconfirm (2a); nor can he think that the evidence which disconfirms (i)–(vi) is not therewith also evidence which confirms the negations of (i)–(vi). If any of these three was true, it would be a good reason for saying that there is "no evidence" against (2a); but each is patently false. If one inspects (i)–(vi) and (2a), it is difficult to see how one could argue that (dis)confirmation of the former does not constitute (dis)confirmation of the latter, even if it might be argued that verification of the former does not constitute verification of the latter. I think, therefore, that there is nothing to be gained by pursuing further this first line of attack.

Elsewhere, it looks as though Van Den Haag takes the other alternative of criticism, albeit rather crudely, as when he argues (against [iv], I suppose, since he nowhere formulated [i]–[vi]) that "the similar areas are not similar enough" (p. 285, col. 1). As to why, for example, the rates of criminal homicide in Michigan and in Illinois from 1920 to 1960

are not relevant because the states aren't "similar enough," he does not try to explain. But his criticism does strictly concede that if the jurisdictions *were* "similar enough," then it would be logically possible to argue from the evidence against (iv) to the disconfirmation of (2a). And this seems to be in keeping with the nature of the case; it is this second line of attack which needs closer examination.

Van Den Haag's own position and objections apart, what is likely to strike the neutral observer who studies the ways in which (i)–(vi) have been tested and declared disconfirmed is that their disconfirmation, and, a fortiori, the disconfirmation of (2a), is imperfect for two related reasons. First, all the tests rely upon *unproved empirical assumptions;* second, it is not known whether there is any *statistical significance* to the results of the tests. It is important to make these concessions, and abolitionists and other disbelievers in the deterrent efficacy of the death penalty have not always done so.

It is not possible here to review all the evidence and to reach a judgment on the empirical status of (i)–(vi). But it is possible and desirable to illustrate how the two qualifications cited above must be understood, and then to assess their effect on the empirical status of (2a). The absence of statistical significance may be illustrated by reference to hypothesis (v). According to the published studies, the annual rate of assaults upon on-duty policemen in abolition jurisdictions is lower than in death-penalty jurisdictions (i.e., a rate of 1.2 attacks per 100,000 population in the former as opposed to 1.3 per 100,000 in the latter). But is this difference statistically significant or not? The studies do not answer this question because the data were not submitted to tests of statistical significance. Nor is there any way, to my knowledge, that these data could be subjected to any such tests. This is, of course, no reason to suppose that the evidence is really not evidence after all, or that though it is evidence against (i) it is not evidence against (2a). Statistical significance is, after all, only a measure of the strength of evidence, not a *sine qua non* of evidential status.

The qualification concerning unproved assumptions is more important, and is worth examining somewhat more fully (though, again, only illustratively). Consider hypothesis (i). Are we entitled to infer that (i) is disconfirmed because in fact a study of the annual homicide rates (as measured by vital statistics showing cause of death) unquestionably indicates that the rate in all abolition states is consistently lower than in all death-penalty states? To make this inference we must assume that (A_1) homicides as measured by vital statistics are in a generally constant ratio to criminal homicides, (A_2) the years for which the evidence has been gathered are representative and not atypical, (A_3) however much fluctuations in the homicide rate owe to other factors, there is a nonnegligible proportion which is a function of the penalty, and (A_4) the deterrent effect of a penalty is not significantly weakened by its infrequent imposition. (There are, of course, other assumptions, but these are central and sufficiently representative here.) Assumption A_1 is effectively unmeasurable because the concept of a criminal homicide is the concept of a homicide which *deserves* to be criminally prosecuted.[10] Nevertheless, A_1 has been accepted by criminologists for over a generation. A_2 is confirmable, on the other hand, and bit by bit, a year at a time, seems to be being confirmed. Assumption A_3 is rather more interesting. To the degree to which it is admitted or insisted that other factors than the severity of the penalty affect the volume of homicide, to that degree A_3 becomes increasingly dubious; but at the same time testing (2a) by (i) becomes increasingly unimportant. The urgency of testing (2a) rests upon the assumption that it is the deterrent efficacy of penalties which is the chief factor in the volume of crimes, and it is absurd to hold that assumption and at the same time doubt A_3. On the other hand, A_4 is almost certainly false (and has been believed so by Bentham and other social theorists for nearly two hundred years). The falsity of A_4, however, is not of fatal harm to the disconfirmation of (i) because it is not known how frequently or infrequently a severe penalty such as death or life imprisonment needs to be imposed in order to maximize its deterrent efficacy. Such information as we do have on this point leads one to doubt that for the general population the frequency with which the death sentence is imposed makes any significant difference to the volume of criminal homicide.[11]

I suggest that these four assumptions and the way in which they bear upon interpretation and evaluation of the evidence against (i), and therefore the disconfirmation of (2a), are typical of what one finds as one examines the work of criminologists

as it relates to the rest of these corollaries of (2a). Is it reasonable, in the light of these considerations, to infer that we have no evidence against (i)–(vi), or that although we do have evidence against (i)–(vi), we have none against (2a)? I do not think so. Short of unidentified and probably unobtainable "crucial experiments," we shall never be able to marshal evidence for (2a) or for (i)–(vi) except by means of certain additional assumptions such as A_1–A_4. To reason otherwise is to rely on nothing more than the fact that it is logically possible to grant the evidence against (i)–(vi) and yet deny that (2a) is false; or it is to insist that the assumptions which the inference relies upon are not plausible assumptions at all (or though plausible are themselves false or disconfirmed) and that no other assumptions can be brought forward which will both be immune to objections and still preserve the linkage between the evidence and the corollaries and (2a). The danger now is that one will repudiate assumptions such as A_1–A_4 in order to guarantee the failure of efforts to disconfirm (2a) via disconfirmation of (i)–(vi); or else that one will place the standards of evidence too high before one accepts the disconfirmation. In either case one has begun to engage in the familiar but discreditable practice of "protecting the hypothesis" by making it, in effect, immune to any kind of disconfirmation.

On my view things stand in this way. An empirical proposition not directly testable, (2), has a significant corollary, (2a), which in turn suggests a number of corollaries, (i)–(vi), each of which is testable with varying degrees of indirectness. Each of (i)–(vi) has been tested. To accept the results as evidence disconfirming (i)–(vi) and as therefore disconfirming (2a), it is necessary to make certain assumptions, of which A_1–A_4 are typical. These assumptions in turn are not all testable, much less directly tested; some of them, in their most plausible formulation, may even be false (but not in that formulation necessary to the inference, however). Since this structure of indirect testing, corollary hypotheses, unproved assumptions, is typical of the circumstances which face us when we wish to consider the evidence for or against any complex empirical hypothesis such as (2), I conclude that while (2) has by no means been disproved (whatever that might mean), it is equally clear that (2) has been disconfirmed, rather than confirmed or left untouched by the inductive arguments we have surveyed.

I have attempted to review and appraise the chief "statistical" arguments (as Van Den Haag calls them) marshaled during the past fifteen years or so in this country by those critical of the death penalty. But in order to assess these arguments more adequately, it is helpful to keep in mind two other considerations. First, most of the criminologists skeptical of (1) are led to this attitude not by the route we have examined—the argument against (2)—but by a general theory of the causation of crimes of personal violence. Given their confidence in that theory, and the evidence for it, they tend not to credit seriously the idea that the death penalty deters (very much), much less the idea that it is a superior deterrent to a severe alternative such as "life" imprisonment (which may not deter very much, either). The interested reader should consult in particular Professor Marvin Wolfgang's monograph, *Patterns of Criminal Homicide* (1958). Second, very little of the empirical research purporting to establish the presence or absence of deterrent efficacy of a given punishment is entirely reliable because almost no effort has been made to isolate the relevant variables. Surely, it is platitudinously true that *some* persons in *some* situations considering *some* crimes can be deterred from committing them by *some* penalties. To go beyond this, however, and supplant these variables with a series of well-confirmed functional hypotheses about the deterrent effect of current legal sanctions is not possible today.

Even if one cannot argue, as Van Den Haag does, that there is no evidence against the claim that the death penalty is a better deterrent than life imprisonment, this does not yet tell us how good this evidence is, how reliable it is, how extensive, and how probative. Van Den Haag could, after all, give up his extreme initial position and retreat to the concession that although there is evidence against the superior deterrent efficacy of the death penalty, still, the evidence is not very good, indeed, not good enough to make reasonable the policy of abolishing the death penalty. Again, it is not possible to undertake to settle this question short of a close examination of each of the empirical studies which confirm (i)–(vi). The reply, so far as there is one, short of further empirical studies (which undoubtedly are desirable—I should not want to obscure that), is twofold: The evidence, such as it is, for (i)–(vi) is uniformly confirmatory in all cases; and the argument of Section IV which follows.

IV

Van Den Haag's "argument" rests considerable weight on the claims that "the added severity of the death penalty adds to deterrence, or may do so"; and that "the generalized threat of the death penalty may be a deterrent, and the more so, the more generally applied." These claims are open to criticism on at least three grounds.

First, as the modal auxiliaries signal, Van Den Haag has not really committed himself to any affirmative empirical claim, but only to a truism. It is always logically possible, no matter what the evidence, that a given penalty which is *ex hypothesi* more severe than an alternative, may be a better deterrent under some conditions not often realized, and be proven so by evidence not ever detectable. For this reason, there is no possible way to prove that Van Den Haag's claims are false, no possible preponderance of evidence against his conclusions which must, logically, force him to give them up. One would have hoped those who believe in the deterrent superiority of the death penalty could, at this late date, offer their critics something more persuasive than logical possibilities. As it is, Van Den Haag's appeal to possible evidence comes perilously close to an argument from ignorance: The possible evidence we might gather is used to offset the actual evidence we have gathered.

Second, Van Den Haag rightly regards his conclusion above as merely an instance of the general principle that, *ceteris paribus*, "the Greater the Severity the Greater the Deterrence," a "plausible" idea, as he says (p. 287). Yet the advantage on behalf of the death penalty produced by this principle is a function entirely of the evidence for the principle itself. But we are offered no evidence at all to make this plausible principle into a confirmed hypothesis of contemporary criminological theory of special relevance to crimes of personal violence. Until we see evidence concerning specific crimes, specific penalties, specific criminal populations, which show that in general the Greater the Severity the Greater the Deterrence, we run the risk of stupefying ourselves by the merely plausible. Besides, without any evidence for this principle we will find ourselves at a complete standoff with the abolitionist (who, of course, can play the same game), because he has his own equally plausible first principle: The Greater the Severity of Punishment the Greater the Brutality Provoked throughout Society. When at last, exhausted and frustrated by mere plausibilities, we once again turn to study the evidence, we will find that the current literature on deterrence in criminology does not encourage us to believe in Van Den Haag's principle.[12]

Third, Van Den Haag has not given any reason why, in the quest for deterrent efficacy, one should fasten (as he does) on the severity of the punishments in question, rather than (as Bentham long ago counseled) on the relevant factors, notably the ease and speed and reliability with which the punishment can be inflicted. Van Den Haag cannot hope to convince anyone who has studied the matter that the death penalty and "life" imprisonment differ only in their severity, and that in all other respects affecting deterrent efficacy they are equivalent; and if he believes this himself it would be interesting to have seen his evidence for it. The only thing to be said in favor of fastening exclusively upon the question of severity in the appraisal of punishments for their relative deterrent efficacy is that augmenting the severity of a punishment in and of itself usually imposes little if any added direct cost to operate the penal system; it even may be cheaper. This is bound to please the harried taxpayer, and at the same time gratify the demand on government to "do something" about crime. Beyond that, emphasizing the severity of punishments as the main (or indeed the sole) variable relevant to deterrent efficacy is unbelievably superficial.

V

Van Den Haag's final point concerning where the burden of proof lies is based, he admits, on playing off a certainty (the death of the persons executed) against a risk (that innocent persons, otherwise the would-be victims of those deterrable only by the death penalty, would be killed).[13] This is not as analogous as he seems to think it is to the general nature of gambling, investment, and other risk-taking enterprises. In none of them do we deliberately cause anything to be killed, as we do, for instance, when we weed out carrot seedlings

to enable those remaining to grow larger (a eugenic analogy, by the way, which might be more useful to Van Den Haag's purpose). In none, that is, do we venture a sacrifice in the hope of a future net gain; we only *risk* a present loss in that hope. Moreover, in gambling ventures we recoup what we risked if we win, whereas in executions we must lose something (the lives of persons executed) no matter if we lose or win (the lives of innocents protected). Van Den Haag's attempt to locate the burden of proof by appeal to principles of gambling is a failure.

Far more significantly, Van Den Haag frames the issue in such a way that the abolitionist has no chance of discharging the burden of proof once he accepts it. For what evidence could be marshaled to prove what Van Den Haag wants proved, namely, that "the greater severity inherent in irrevocability [of the death penalty] . . . adds nothing to deterrence"? The evidence alluded to at the end of Section IV does tend to show that this generalization (the negation of Van Den Haag's own principle) is indeed true, but it does not prove it. I conclude, therefore, that either Van Den Haag is wrong in his argument which shows the locus of burden of proof to lie on the abolitionist, or one must accept less than proof in order to discharge this burden (in which case, the very argument Van Den Haag advances shows that the burden of proof now lies on those who would retain the death penalty).

"Burden of proof" in areas outside judicial precincts where evidentiary questions are at stake tends to be a rhetorical phrase and nothing more. Anyone interested in the truth of a matter will not defer gathering evidence pending a determination of where the burden of proof lies. For those who do think there is a question of burden of proof, as Van Den Haag does, they should consider this: Advocacy of the death penalty is advocacy of a rule of penal law which empowers the state to deliberately take human life and in general to threaten the public with the taking of life. *Ceteris paribus*, one would think anyone favoring such a rule would be ready to offer considerable evidence for its necessity and efficacy. Surely, some showing of necessity, some evidentiary proof, is to be expected to satisfy the skeptical. Exactly when and in what circumstances have the apologists for capital punishment offered evidence to support their contentions? Where is that evidence recorded for us to inspect, comparable to the evidence cited in Section III against the superior deterrent efficacy of the death penalty? Van Den Haag conspicuously cited no such evidence and so it is with all other proponents of the death penalty. The insistence that the burden of proof lies on abolitionists, therefore, is nothing but the rhetorical demand of every defender of the status quo who insists upon evidence from those who would effect change, while reserving throughout the right to dictate criteria and standards of proof and refusing to offer evidence for his own view.[14]

I should have thought that the death penalty was a sufficiently momentous matter and of sufficient controversy that the admittedly imperfect evidence assembled over the past generation by those friendly to abolition would have been countered by evidence tending to support the opposite, retentionist, position. It remains a somewhat sad curiosity that nothing of the sort has happened; no one has ever published research tending to show, however inconclusively, that the death penalty after all is a deterrent, and a superior deterrent to "life" imprisonment. Among scholars at least, if not among legislators and other politicians, the perennial appeal to burden of proof really ought to give way to offering of proof by those interested enough to argue the issue.

TUFTS UNIVERSITY

Notes

1. *Ethics* 78 (July 1968):280–88. Van Den Haag later published a "revised version" under the same title in *Journal of Criminal Law, Criminology and Police Science* 60 (1969):141–47. I am grateful to Professor Van Den Haag for providing me with a reprint of each version. I should add that his revisions in the later version were minimal, especially in his Section V which is mainly what I shall criticize. All page references in the text are to the version published in *Ethics*.

2. See Massachusetts Laws, chap. 150, Resolves of 1967; "Interim Report of the Special Commission Established to Make an Investigation and Study Relative to the Effectiveness of Capital Punishment as a Deterrent to Crime," mimeographed (Boston: Clerk, Great and General Court, State House, 1968).

3. See the several essays reprinted in Bedau, ed., *The Death Penalty in America*, rev. ed. (New York, 1967),

chap. 4 and the articles cited therein at pp. 166–70.

4. The same argument has been advanced earlier by Sidney Hook (see the *New York Law Forum* [1961], pp. 278–83, and the revised version of this argument published in Bedau, pp. 150–51).

5. See, e.g., Thorsten Sellin, "Prison Homicides," in *Capital Punishment*, ed. Sellin (New York, 1967), pp. 154–60.

6. Rhode Island (1852), North Dakota (1915), New York (1965), Vermont (1965), and New Mexico (1969), have all qualified their abolition of the death penalty in this way; for further details, see Bedau, p. 12.

7. Bedau, pp. 260–61.

8. Van Den Haag accuses Professor Thorsten Sellin, a criminologist "who has made a careful study of the available statistics," of seeming to "think that this lack of evidence for deterrence is evidence for the lack of deterrence" (p. 285, col. 1), that is, of thinking that (*a*) is (*b*)! In none of Sellin's writings which I have studied (see, for a partial listing, note 9, below) do I see any evidence that Sellin "thinks" the one "is" the other. What will be found is a certain vacillation in his various published writings, which span the years from 1953 to 1967, between the two ways of putting his conclusions. His most recent statement is unqualifiedly in the (*b*) form (see his *Capital Punishment*, p. 138). Since Van Den Haag also cited my *Death Penalty in America* (though not in this connection), I might add that there I did distinguish between (*a*) and (*b*) but did not insist, as I do now, that the argument entitles abolitionists to assert (*b*) (see Bedau, pp. 264–65). It is perhaps worth noting here some other writers, all criminologists, who have recently stated the same or a stronger conclusion. "Capital punishment does not act as an effective deterrent to murder" (William J. Chambliss, "Types of Deviance and the Effectiveness of Legal Sanctions," *Wisconsin Law Review* [1967], p. 706); "The capital punishment controversy has produced the most reliable information on the general deterrent effect of a criminal sanction. It now seems established and accepted that . . . the death penalty makes no difference to the homicide rate" (Norval Morris and Frank Zimring, "Deterrence and Corrections," *Annals* 381 [January 1969]:143); "the evidence indicates that it [namely, the death penalty for murder] has no discernible effects in the United States" (Walter C. Reckless, "The Use of the Death Penalty," *Crime and Delinquency* 15 [January 1969]:52); "Capital punishment is ineffective in deterring murder" (Eugene Doleschal, "The Deterrent Effect

of Legal Punishment," *Information Review on Crime and Delinquency* 1 [June 1969]:7).

9. The relevant research, regarding each of the six hypotheses in the text, is as follows: (i) Karl Schuessler, "The Deterrent Influence of the Death Penalty," *Annals* 284 (November 1952):57; Walter C. Reckless, "The Use of the Death Penalty—a Factual Statement," *Crime and Delinquency* 15 (1969):52, table 9. (ii) Thorsten Sellin, *The Death Penalty* (Philadelphia: American Law Institute, 1959), pp. 19–24, reprinted in Bedau, pp. 274–84; updated in Sellin, *Capital Punishment*, 135–38. (iii) Sellin, *The Death Penalty*, pp. 34–38, reprinted in Bedau, pp. 339–43. (iv) See works cited in (iii), above. (v) Canada, *Minutes and Proceedings of Evidence*, Joint Committee of the Senate and House of Commons on Capital Punishment and Corporal Punishment and Lotteries (1955), appendix F, pt. 1, pp. 718–28; "The Death Penalty and Police Safety," reprinted in Bedau, pp. 284–301, and in Sellin, *Capital Punishment*, pp. 138–54, with postscript (1967); Canada, "The State Police and the Death Penalty," pp. 729–35, reprinted in Bedau, pp. 301–15. (vi) *Massachusetts, Report and Recommendations of the Special Commission . . . [on] the Death Penalty . . .* (1958), pp. 21–22, reprinted in Bedau, p. 400; Thorsten Sellin, "Prison Homicides," in Sellin, *Capital Punishment*, pp. 154–60.

10. See, for discussion surrounding this point, Bedau, pp. 56–74.

11. See Robert H. Dann, *The Deterrent Effect of Capital Punishment* (Philadelphia, 1935); Leonard H. Savitz, "A Study in Capital Punishment," *Journal of Criminal Law, Criminology and Police Science* 49 (1958):338–41, reprinted in Bedau, pp. 315–32; William F. Graves, "A Doctor Looks at Capital Punishment," *Medical Arts and Sciences* 10 (1956):137–41, reprinted in Bedau, pp. 322–32, with addenda (1964).

12. See, for a general review, Eugene Doleschal, "The Deterrent Effect of Legal Punishment: A Review of the Literature," *Information Review on Crime and Delinquency* 1 (June 1969):1–17, and the many research studies cited therein, especially the survey by Norval Morris and Frank Zimring, "Deterrence and Corrections," *Annals* 381 (January 1969):137–46; also Gordon Hawkins, "Punishment and Deterrence," *Wisconsin Law Review* (1969), pp. 550–65.

13. The same objection has been raised earlier by Joel Feinberg (see his review of Bedau in *Ethics* 76 [October 1965]:63).

14. For a general discussion which is not inconsistent with the position I have taken, and which illuminates the logicorhetorical character of the appeal to burden of proof in philosophical argument, see Robert Brown, "The Burden of Proof," *American Philosophical Quarterly* 7 (1970):74–82.

Questions for Analysis

1. Explain why Bedau believes that Van Den Haag's definition of deterrence is "too ill-formulated to be of any serious use." Do you agree?

2. On what grounds does Bedau dismiss Van Den Haag's contention that the death penalty is the only possible deterrent for some classes of criminals?

3. Why does Bedau feel it is so important to distinguish (1) the death penalty as a deterrent from (2) the death penalty as a superior deterrent to life imprisonment? Does the falsity of (1) necessarily follow from the falsity of (2)? Does the establishment of (1) thereby establish (2)?

4. What hypotheses have been formulated to test the proposition that the death penalty is a superior deterrent to life imprisonment for the crime of criminal homicide? What have been the results? What are Van Den Haag's objections to these tests, and how does Bedau respond to the objections? Do you feel that Bedau has adequately met the objections?

5. Regarding the same hypotheses, Bedau concedes that their disconfirmation is imperfect for two related reasons. What are those reasons? Does Bedau go on to turn these concessions to his own advantage? If so, how?

6. *Why does Bedau reject Van Den Haag's argument that the severity of the death penalty may add to deterrence?*

7. *How does Bedau respond to Van Den Haag's claim that abolitionists must prove that capital punishment adds nothing to deterrence?*

CASE PRESENTATION
J. D. Autry: Death in Texas

High on booze, pot, and pills, James David (J. D.) Autry and his companion John Alton Sandifer had been bumping around Port Arthur, Texas, in a borrowed pickup one warm Sunday night in April 1980, when they stopped at a convenience store for more beer. What then happened is unclear. But a jury concluded, and a succession of appellate courts affirmed, that there had been a drunken attempt at a robbery and that Autry had shot the cashier between the eyes when she resisted. Then, fleeing the store, Autry had run into two men, both of whom he shot. One was killed, and the other was crippled for life in mind and body. Autry's net profit for the bloodshed was a $2.70 six-pack.

Before the year was out, Autry was convicted of capital murder and delivered in chains to death row—protesting his innocence all the way.

A half hour before his scheduled death by lethal injection in October 1983, Autry was plucked off the gurney. Supreme Court Justice Byron White had granted a last-minute reprieve, a chance to re-examine and reargue the question of whether a killer should die. The reprieve meant that not only Autry but all death-row inmates in Texas and California, who account for about one-quarter of the nation's condemned population, might not even be considered for execution until the spring of 1984.

In the following months the Supreme Court heard arguments in a case from California that posed the question of a condemned prisoner's being entitled to a judicial review of his or her sentence to determine whether it is "proportional"; that is, whether like crimes typically warrant the death penalty. In the 1976 decisions that restored the death penalty, the Court noted with approval that both the Georgia and Florida courts made proportionality reviews to make sure the penalty wouldn't be imposed arbitrarily. Since then, the Court has struck down as "disproportional" death sentences for rapists and defendants who neither killed nor attempted to kill the victim. At the same time, it has upheld state statutes like that in Texas which make no mention of comparative sentence review. The Court decided that the absence of a proportionality review is not grounds to stay an execution. Shortly thereafter, on the morning of March 14, 1984, J. D. Autry was executed by lethal injection.

Questions for Analysis

1. *Do you think states should have proportionality reviews to ensure that the death penalty is not imposed arbitrarily? Do you think justice requires this?*

2. *Critics say proportionality-review systems don't work. They point out that the state courts have failed to set standards for real comparisons, collect complete information on the sentences of all killers, and provide other judges with guidance. Discuss the implications of these charges with regard to the equitable administration of the death penalty.*

3. *Do you think proportionality is relevant to whether the death penalty is ever morally permissible? Explain.*

4. *Some say the Autry case is just another example of delay that results in a denial of justice. Both retentionists and abolitionists view such delays as support for their positions. For example, retentionists argue that the obvious difficulties in carrying out the death penalty undermine confidence in the legal system. For their part, abolitionists claim that the very tortuousness of the appeals process demonstrates there is no way to make capital punishment work. On various occasions the Supreme Court has expressed its own concern with the delays. Justice William Rehnquist charged in 1981 that his colleagues were making a mockery of the criminal-justice system by countenancing extended appeals. In 1983 Justice Lewis F. Powell, Jr., told a group of federal judges that unless the judiciary can find a more efficient way to handle death cases, capital punishment should be abolished. And in granting Autry his last-minute stay, Justice White called for a change in the law to limit repetitive appeals. Despite the high court's impatience, it is obliged to keep reviewing death-penalty cases. Do you think that delays do, in fact, result in a denial of justice? Explain. Do they make stronger the retentionist or the abolitionist position?*

CASE PRESENTATION
Paul Crump: Death Despite Rehabilitation?[5]

When Warden Jack Johnson met Paul Crump in 1955, Crump was, according to Johnson, "choked up with hatred." "He was animalistic and belligerent," the warden said. "Self-preservation was the only law he knew." A jury had agreed, for it had sentenced Crump to death for a vicious murder.

Before Johnson's arrival at the "scandal-ridden, riot-scarred" Illinois prison, the institution had been an "abomination." Overcrowded and understaffed, it

5. *See Ronald Bailey, "Facing Death: A New Life Perhaps Too Late," Life, July 27, 1962, pp. 28–29, or Tom L. Beauchamp, William T. Blackstone, Joel Feinberg,* Philosophy and the Human Condition, *Englewood Cliffs, N.J.: Prentice-Hall, 1980, pp. 324–327.*

was an ugly throwback to a bygone era. Guards not only wore guns but armed themselves with brass knuckles, blackjacks, and miniature baseball bats. On death row, prisoners were locked up in four-by-eight-foot cells. Handcuffed and dragging leg irons, they exercised for two hours a day in the cellblock corridor. Slumbred Crump described coming to jail as being "transplanted from one jail to another." "If I hadn't been an animal," he said, "I wouldn't have survived."

Johnson immediately instituted a series of reforms. He de-emphasized punishment, disarmed the guards, ended the death-row lockup, and tried, as he put it, "a few simple words of love." Taking personal charge of death row, Johnson made daily visits there. He installed two telephones outside the tier and invited inmates to call him whenever they felt like talking. Johnson then started bringing in the men in groups of three or four for discussions with the new prison sociologists and psychologists. Eventually, Johnson created a new climate, one in which Paul Crump had a chance to change and grow.

Responding to the warden's reforms, Crump started work on his autobiographical novel, *Burn, Killer, Burn.* Limited by his ninth-grade education, Crump enlisted the aid of the assistant warden, who gave him an informal course in analytic reading. With his newly acquired skills and his awakened intellect, Crump read poetry, fiction, philosophy—virtually everything he could obtain. "I read and read and read," he said, "and some old distortions were swept away. I had thought that anything good that happened to me was all gravy, just accident. I started seeing that things don't happen by accident but because of the good will of people and their belief in the basic goodness of man."

When Johnson obtained a typewriter for him, Crump proceeded to crank out short stories, articles, and poems, which were published in small magazines. He started a second novel and began corresponding with interested and sympathetic people around the world.

Crump also began to take an interest in the problems of his fellow prisoners. Johnson made Crump "barn boss," or head of the convalescent tier for the new jail hospital. As barn boss, Crump, in the words of one guard, was "mother, father, priest, and social worker" for some fifty prisoners. An array of men came to Crump's tier: epileptics, diabetics, heart patients, old men suffering from DTs, drug addicts in withdrawal. Johnson also sent him problem prisoners and inmates needing special protection: teenagers, former policemen, potential suicides. Ministering to his charges at all hours of the day and night, Crump soon grew legendary. On various occasions, he bathed senile men unable to bathe themselves; he set aside a corner of the cellblock so that an orthodox Jew could worship in privacy; he broke up fights and prevented guards from getting hurt. Learning that the cousin of one of the guards was born with a heart defect and desperately needed blood, Crump collected the signatures of fifty men who promised to donate blood.

The rehabilitation of Paul Crump occurred over a period of seven years. If Crump underwent a dramatic change, so did Warden Jack Johnson. When he came to the prison, Johnson was ambivalent about capital punishment. But Crump turned Johnson into a vigorous opponent of capital punishment. "Paul Crump is completely rehabilitated," Johnson said, just prior to the State of Illinois's final decision on whether Crump would be executed. "Should society demand Paul's life at this point, it would be capital vengeance, not punishment. If it were humanly possible, I would put Paul back on the street tomorrow. I have no fear of any antisocial behavior on his part. I would stake my life on it. And I would trust him with my life."

On August 1, 1962, Illinois Governor Otto Kerner commuted Crump's death sentence to 199 years imprisonment without possibility of parole.

Questions for Analysis

1. *Do you think the governor's decision was proper?*

2. *How strong an argument do you think the Paul Crump case makes for the abolition of capital punishment?*

3. *Do you think it would have been morally justifiable to execute Crump despite his apparent rehabilitation? Explain.*

4. *What moral principle or principles do you think underlay Johnson's rehabilitation efforts?*

5. *Assuming Crump had been rehabilitated, do you think the governor should have been more lenient—perhaps commuting Crump's death sentence to, say, twenty additional years in prison? Explain by appeal to concepts of punishment.*

Selections for Further Reading

Adenaes, Johannes. *Punishment and Deterrence.* Ann Arbor: University of Michigan Press, 1974.

Bedau, Hugo Adam. *The Death Penalty in America.* New York: Oxford University Press, 1982.

Bedau, Hugo Adam, and C. M. Pierce, eds. *Capital Punishment in the United States.* New York: AMS Press, 1976.

Berns, Walter. *For Capital Punishment.* New York: Basic Books, 1979.

Black, Charles Jr. *Capital Punishment: The Inevitability of Caprice and Mistake.* New York: W. W. Norton, 1974.

Camus, Albert. *Reflections on the Guillotine: An Essay on Capital Punishment,* Richard Howard, trans. Michigan City, Ind.: Fridtjog-Karla Press, 1959.

Ezorsky, Gertrude, ed. *Philosophical Perspectives on Punishment.* Albany, N.Y.: State University of New York Press, 1972.

Feinberg, Joel, and Hyman Gross. *Philosophy of Law.* Belmont, Calif.: Wadsworth, 1980.

Goldinger, Milton, ed. *Punishment and Human Rights.* Cambridge, Mass.: Schenkman, 1974.

McCafferty, Jeffrie G. *Retribution, Justice, and Therapy.* Boston: D. Reidel, 1979.

Van Den Haag, Ernest. *Punishing Criminals.* New York: Basic Books, 1975.

7
JOB DISCRIMINATION

On December 10, 1970, the Equal Employment Opportunity Commission (EEOC) petitioned the Federal Communication Commission not to back a request by American Telephone and Telegraph (AT&T) for a rate increase on the grounds that AT&T was engaging in pervasive, systemwide, and blatantly unlawful discrimination against women, blacks, Spanish-surnamed Americans, and other minorities. After nearly two years of negotiation with the EEOC, AT&T finally reached an agreement with the government on December 28, 1972, whereby it agreed, among other things, not to discriminate in the future, and to set up goals and timetables for hiring women and minorities into all nonmanagement job classifications where they were underrepresented. For its part, the EEOC agreed to drop all outstanding equal-employment actions against AT&T.

Three years later, on December 8, 1975, AT&T was sued by Dan McAleer, an AT&T service representative. McAleer claimed he had lost out on a promotion to a less qualified female employee as a result of AT&T's implementation of its agreement with the EEOC. McAleer had worked for AT&T for five years and had scored thirty-four out of thirty-five on the company's performance rating. Sharon Hullery, the woman who beat out McAleer for the promotion, had worked at AT&T for less than five years and had scored thirty points.

On June 9, 1976, the U.S. District Court in Washington, D.C., ruled that AT&T owed McAleer monetary compensation, but not the promotion. AT&T owed McAleer the money, said the court, because he was an innocent victim of an agreement intended to remedy the company's wrongdoing. But the court didn't think AT&T owed McAleer the promotion because that, in the court's view, might help perpetuate and prolong the effects of the discrimination that the AT&T–EEOC agreement was designed to eliminate.

On January 18, 1979, the agreement between AT&T and the EEOC expired. AT&T had reached 99.7 percent of the female-hiring goals it had set up in 1973.

In recent years, laws have been passed and programs formulated to ensure fair and equal treatment of all people in employment practices. Nevertheless, unequal practices still exist. To help remedy these, the federal government in the early 1970s instituted an affirmative-action program.

Before affirmative action, many institutions already followed nondiscriminatory as well as merit-hiring employment practices to equalize employment opportunities. In proposing affirmative action, the government recognized the worth of such endeavors, but said that it did not think they were enough. Affirmative action, therefore, refers to positive measures beyond neutral nondiscriminatory and merit-hiring employment practices. It is an aggressive program intended to identify and remedy unfair discrimination practiced against many people who are qualified for jobs.

Among the most controversial aspects of affirmative action are its preferential and quota-hiring systems. *Preferential hiring* is an employment practice designed to give special consideration to people from groups that traditionally have been victimized by racism, sexism, or other forms of discrimination. *Quota hiring* is the policy of hiring and employing people in direct proportion to their numbers in society or in the community. According to affirmative-action guidelines, preferential and quota hiring go hand in glove; thus, for simplicity, we will refer to both by the phrase *preferential treatment*. Courts are increasingly requiring companies and unions to provide apprentice and reapprentice training to hire, promote, and train minorities and women in specified numerical ratios, in specified job categories, until specified remedial goals are reached. But critics charge that at least in some instances, implementing affirmative-action guidelines has led to *reverse discrimination—that is, the unfair treatment of a majority member (usually a white male)*. Presumably this was the basis for McAleer's complaint. Was he treated unfairly? Was AT&T's action moral? Would it have been fairer had the employees' names been thrown into a hat from which one was drawn? Obviously such preferential programs raise questions of social justice.

Undoubtedly some will wonder: Why not focus directly on the morality of sexism? By *sexism* we mean the unfair treatment of a person exclusively on the basis of sex. Perhaps we should focus on it, but consider that in all our discussions so far we have made reasonable cases for at least two sides of an issue. True, perhaps one side was more flawed than another, but in all cases reasonable people could disagree. But the fact is that few seriously argue anymore that sexism, as defined, is moral. So if we focused on sexism we would be inviting a most lopsided discussion. This would be unfortunate in the light of so many aspects of sexism that genuinely deserve moral debate. One of these aspects involves such proposed remedies as preferential treatment.

Another reason for not considering sexism exclusively is that this chapter, as well as the next, naturally raises questions of social justice. Many discussions of social justice founder because they remain abstract, content to theorize while scrupulously avoiding practice. For example, it is easy and safe to argue that a government must remedy racial injustice. It is far more controversial to argue that a government must implement forced busing to do so. The same applies to sexism. Most would agree that the government has an obligation to correct the social injustice of sexism, but how?

It is one thing to recognize, deplore, and want to correct any injustice. It is entirely another thing to remedy the injustice fairly. Sadly, too many discussions of social justice ignore means entirely, often offering the defense that the means vary from situation to situation. Undoubtedly. But the debate flying around so many social justice questions today concerns proposed means. We should learn to examine every situation's means and also the common but agonizing predicament of applauding the intention and even the probable consequences of an action, but deploring the action itself. For many people, preferential treatment is just such a problem.

Job Discrimination: Its Nature and Forms

To discriminate in employment is to make an adverse decision against employees based on their membership in a certain class.[1] Included in the preceding definition of discrimination in employment are three basic elements: (1) The decision is against employees solely because of their membership in a certain group. (2) The decision is based on the assumption that the group is in some way inferior to some other group, and thus deserving of unequal treatment. (3) The decision in some way harms those it's aimed at. Since, traditionally, most of the discrimination in the American workplace has been aimed at women and minorities such as blacks and Hispanics, the following discussion will focus on these groups.

On-the-job discrimination can be intentional or unintentional, practiced by a single individual or individuals in a company or by the institution itself. "Intentional" here means knowingly or consciously; "unintentional" means unthinkingly or not consciously. "Institution" refers to the business, company, corporation, profession, or even the system within which the discrimination operates. These distinctions provide a basis for identifying four forms of discrimination: (1) intentional individual, (2) unintentional individual, (3) intentional institutional, and (4) unintentional institutional.

1. *Intentional individual* discrimination is an isolated act of discrimination *knowingly* performed by some individual out of personal prejudice. Example: A male personnel director routinely passes over females for supervisory jobs because he believes and knowingly acts on the belief that "lady bosses mean trouble."

2. *Unintentional individual* discrimination is an isolated act of discrimination performed by some individual who *unthinkingly* or *unconsciously* adopts traditional practices and stereotypes. Example: If the male in the preceding case acted without being aware of the bias underlying his decisions, his action would fall into this category.

3. *Intentional institutional* discrimination is an act of discrimination that is part of the reactive behavior of a company or profession which knowingly dis-

---

1. *Manuel G. Velasquez,* Business Ethics: Concepts and Cases *(Englewood Cliffs, N.J.: Prentice-Hall, 1982), p. 266.*

criminates out of the personal prejudices of its members. Example: The male personnel director passes over women for supervisory jobs because "the boys in the company don't like to take orders from females."

4. *Unintentional institutional* discrimination is an act of discrimination that is part of the routine behavior of a company or profession that has unknowingly incorporated sexually or racially prejudicial practices into its operating procedures. Example: An engineering firm routinely avoids hiring women because of the stereotypical assumption that women don't make good engineers or that its clients won't do business with women.

In recent years, discussions of discrimination have focused on institutional forms of discrimination, with special emphasis on the unintentional institutional. In fact, it's been this kind of discrimination that some believe only affirmative-action programs can root out. Others consider programs like this inherently unjust or counterproductive. They say that workplace discrimination can be corrected through strict enforcement of anti-discrimination law without resorting to preferential-treatment programs. The force of these positions depends, in part, on whether the body of anti-discriminatory legislation that has developed over the past twenty years has, in fact, tended to reduce discrimination in the workplace. If it has, then it would lend weight to the anti-affirmative-action positions. If it hasn't, then the pro-affirmative-action position would be strengthened. So before inspecting the two positions, let's briefly examine the relative positions of whites and minorities and of males and females in the American workplace to see if they say anything about ongoing discrimination.

Evidence of Discrimination

Determining the presence of discrimination isn't easy, because many factors could possibly account for the relative positions of various groups in the work world. But generally speaking, there are reasonable grounds for thinking that an institution is practicing discrimination (intentional or unintentional) when (1) statistics indicate that members of a group are being treated unequally in comparison with other groups, and (2) endemic attitudes, and formal and informal practices and policies, seem to account for the skewed statistics.

Statistical Evidence

Overwhelming statistical evidence points to the fact that a disproportionate number of women and minority members hold the less desirable jobs and get paid less than their white male counterparts. For example, at all occupational levels, women make less money than men—even for the same work—despite legislation forbidding discrimination on the basis of sex. While some think the income gap between men and women is closing, it isn't. According to Labor Department statistics from 1979, women's earnings in 1977 were 58.9 percent of men's. That's a drop of more than 5 percent from what it was in 1955, when women's earnings were 64 percent of men's.[2] Most important, the differences are apparently not just after a period of time on the job, but frequently begin as soon as men and women leave school. In 1976, for example, the average starting salary offered to women college graduates majoring in marketing was $9,768, while their male counterparts were offered $10,236. Similarly, women graduates majoring in humanities were offered $8,916, while men were offered $9,792. Women social science graduates were offered $9,240, while men were offered $10,392.[3] Comparative figures concerning the incomes of whites vs. minorities' turn up similar disparities.

Another body of statistics points to unequal distribution of positions. As of 1977, the most desirable occupations (in management and administration, professions and technical jobs, sales, and crafts) were dominated by whites, while the less desirable (e.g., service and farm work) were dominated by blacks, Hispanics, and other ethnic minorities. Women predominated in the poorest-paying jobs in America: librarians, nurses, elementary teachers, sales clerks, secretaries, bank tellers, waitresses; and men in the best-paying ones: lawyers, doctors, sales representatives, insurance agents, and so on.[4] Before saying the disparities can be accounted for by educational levels, consider that, in 1977, a white head of household with one to three years of *high school* earned more than a black head of household with one to three years of *college*, and that the typical male full-time worker with no more than a grammar-school education earned nearly as much as a female full-time worker with a college degree.[5] These and other statistical studies—far too many to report here—indicate that, on the basis of median income and proportional representation in the highest-paying occupations or in the lowest, women and minorities simply aren't treated as equal to white males.

Attitudinal Evidence

Although some would disagree, the statistics alone don't establish discrimination, for one could always argue that other things account for these disparities. But there are indications of widespread attitudes and formal and informal institutional practices and policies which, taken collectively, point to discrimination as the cause of these statistical disparities.

For example, in a questionnaire submitted to 5,000 of its subscribers in 1974, the *Harvard Business Review* found a double standard with regard to managerial expectations of men and women. In sum, managers expect male employees to put job before family when conflicting obligations arise, but they expect females to sacrifice their career to family responsibilities. Also, when personal conduct threatens an employee's job, managers go to greater lengths to retain a valuable

2.   *U.S. Department of Labor,* The Earnings Gap between Women and Men *(Washington, D.C.: U.S. Government Printing Office, 1979), p. 6. These and the following statistics as reported in Velasquez,* Business Ethics.

3.   *Ibid., p. 17.*

4.   *U.S. Bureau of the Census,* Statistical Abstract of the U.S. 1980, *101st ed. (Washington, D.C.: U.S. Government Printing Office, 1980), pp. 418–20.*

5.   *U.S. Bureau of the Census,* Statistical Abstract of the U.S. 1978, *99th ed. (Washington, D.C.: U.S. Government Printing Office, 1978), p. 457.*

male employee than an equally qualified female. The survey also turned up anti-female bias: In employee selection and promotion and in career-development decisions, managers clearly favor males.[6]

Another study has found that men prefer male supervisors and feel uncomfortable with female supervisors.[7] And over the years, various reports indicate that myths, stereotypes, and false preconceptions victimize women and minorities.

Then there's the commonplace practice in many trades and industries of filling positions by word-of-mouth recruitment policies. In jobs dominated by white males, the word of a job vacancy tends to reach other white males. Furthermore, on several occasions the EEOC has found that interviewers for non-white-collar positions have biased attitudes that lead them to treat the applications of minorities and women systematically differently from those of white males. The EEOC considers these practices so flagrant and typical that it deems strict word-of-mouth recruitment policies prima facie evidence of discrimination. And according to some, the practice is as common in professional white-collar hiring.[8]

Taken together, the statistics, personal and institutional attitudes, assumptions, and practices provide powerful evidence of intractable discrimination against women and minorities in the American workplace. Recognizing the existence of such discrimination and believing that, for a variety of reasons, it's wrong, we have as a nation passed laws expressly forbidding discrimination in recruitment, screening, promotion, compensation, and firing practices. In short, specific laws have been enacted to ensure equal opportunity in employment. The aim of these policies is to prevent further discrimination, and they probably have prevented egregious instances of discrimination. But the evidence indicates that they have not had the effect of providing equal opportunity to women and minorities as groups. Furthermore, anti-discrimination laws do not address the present-day effects of past discrimination. They ignore, for example, the fact that because of past discrimination women and minorities in general lack the skills of white males and are disproportionately underrepresented in the more prestigious and better-paying jobs. In order to remedy the effects of past discrimination and seeing no other way to counteract apparently visceral racism and sexism, many people today call for specific affirmative-action programs.

Affirmative Action: Preferential Treatment

As amended by the Equal Employment Opportunity Act of 1972, the Civil Rights Act of 1964 requires businesses that have substantial dealings with the

6.   Benson Rosen and Thomas H. Jerdee, "Sex Stereotyping in the Executive Suite," Harvard Business Review, May-June 1974, pp. 45–58.

7.   Bernard M. Bass, Judith Krusell, Ralph A. Alexander, "Male Managers' Attitudes Toward Working Women," American Behavioral Scientist, November 1977, p. 223.

8.   See Gertrude Ezorsky, "The Fight Over University Women," New York Review of Books, May 16, 1974, pp. 32–39.

federal government to undertake affirmative-action programs. *Affirmative-action programs are plans designed to correct imbalances in employment that exist directly as a result of past discrimination.* Even though these acts do not technically require companies to undertake affirmative-action programs, in recent years courts have responded to acts of job discrimination by ordering the offending firms to implement such programs to combat the effects of past discrimination. In effect, then, all business institutions must adopt affirmative-action programs either in theory or in fact. They must be able to prove that they have not been practicing institutional sexism or racism, and if they cannot prove this, they must undertake programs to ensure against racism or sexism.

What do affirmative-action programs involve? The EEOC lists general guidelines as steps to affirmative action. Under these steps, firms must issue a written equal-employment policy and an affirmative-action commitment. They must appoint a top official with responsibility and authority to direct and implement their program and to publicize their policy and affirmative-action commitment. In addition, firms must survey current female and minority employment by department and job classification. Where underrepresentation of these groups is evident, firms must develop goals and timetables to improve in each area of underrepresentation. They then must develop specific programs to achieve these goals, establish an internal audit system to monitor them, and evaluate progress in each aspect of the program. Finally, companies must develop supportive in-house and community programs to combat discrimination.

In implementing such programs, some companies have adopted a policy of preferential treatment for women and minorities. *Preferential treatment refers to the practice of giving individuals favored consideration in hiring or promotions for other than job-related reasons* (such as the person is female or black). Those espousing preferential treatment argue that such a policy is the only way to remedy traditional sexism and racism, or at least that it is the most expeditious and fairest way to do it. In some instances preferential treatment for women and minorities takes the form of a quota system, that is, *an employment policy of representing women and minorities in the firm in direct proportion to their numbers in society or in the community at large.* Thus a firm operating in a community which has a 20 percent black population might try to ensure that 20 percent of its work force be black.[9]

To unravel some of the complex moral issues affirmative-action programs can raise, let's look at a specific instance of quota hiring. Suppose an equally qualified man and woman are applying for a job. The employer, conscious of affirmative-action guidelines and realizing that the company has historically discriminated against women in its employment policies, adopts a quota-hiring system. Since males are already disproportionately well represented and females underrepresented, the quota system gives the female applicant a decided advantage. As a result, the employer hires the female. Is this action moral? Are affirmative-action programs that operate in the preferential way moral?

---

9. *Some institutions simply reserve a number of places for women and minority members. The University of California at Davis, for example, had such a policy in its medical school when it denied Alan Bakke admission. Bakke appealed to the Supreme Court, which—in a 5–4 decision—found in his favor. He was presumably more qualified than some minority students who had been admitted.*

Many people argue that affirmative-action programs are inherently discriminatory and therefore unjust. In this context, *discriminatory* should be understood to refer to policies that favor individuals on non-job-related grounds (for example, on the basis of sex, color, or ethnic heritage). It has been argued that quota hiring is unjust because it involves giving preferential treatment to women and minorities over equally qualified white males, a practice that is clearly discriminatory, albeit in reverse.

Those in favor of affirmative action, however, generally attempt to rebut this objection by appealing to principles of *compensatory justice. Since women and minorities clearly continue to be victimized directly and indirectly by traditional discrimination in the workplace, they are entitled to some compensation.* This is the basis for preferential treatment. The soundness of this contention seems to rely on at least two factors: (1) that affirmative-action programs involving preferential treatment will in fact provide adequate compensation, and (2) that they will provide compensation more fairly than any other alternative.[10] Since the justice and the morality of affirmative-action programs depend to a large degree on these assumptions, we should examine them.

The question that comes to mind in regard to the first assumption is: adequate compensation for whom? The answer seems obvious: for women and minorities. But does this mean *individual* women and minority-group members, or women and minorities taken *collectively*? University of Tampa Professor Herman J. Saatkamp, Jr., has demonstrated that this question, far from being merely a technical one, bears directly on the morality of affirmative-action programs and how they are implemented.[11]

Saatkamp points out that the question of the conflict between individual and collective merit typifies the debate between government agencies and business over employment policies. On the one hand, business is ordinarily concerned with the individual merit and deserts of its employees. On the other hand, government agencies primarily focus on the relative status of groups within the population at large. To put the conflict in perspective, employment policies based solely on individual merit would try to ensure that only those individuals who could prove they deserved compensation would benefit and only those proved to be the source of discrimination would suffer. Of course, such a focus places an almost unbearable burden on the resources of an individual to provide sufficient, precise data to document employment discrimination, which is commonly acknowledged to exist at times in subtle, perhaps even imperceptible, forms at various organizational levels. Indeed, social policies recognize this difficulty by focusing on discrimination on an aggregate level. Individuals, then, need not prove they themselves were discriminated against, only that they are members of groups that have traditionally suffered because of discrimination.

Taking the collective approach to remedying job discrimination is not without its own disadvantages.

10.   *Albert W. Flores, "Reverse Discrimination: Towards a Just Society," in* Business & Professional Ethics, *a quarterly newsletter/report (Troy, N.Y.: Center for the Study of the Human Dimensions of Science & Technology, Rensselaer Polytechnic Institute, Jan. 1978), p. 4.*

11.   *Ibid., pp. 5–6.*

1. Policies based on collective merit tend to pit one social group against another. White males face off against all nonwhite males; women find themselves jockeying with other disadvantaged groups for priority employment status; black females can end up competing with Hispanic males for preferred treatment. This factionalizing aspect of policies based on collective merit can prove detrimental to society.

2. Policies based on collective merit victimize some individuals. The individual white male who loses out on a job because of preferential treatment given a woman or a minority-group member is penalized.

3. In some cases the women and minority members selected under preferential treatment are, in fact, less deserving of compensation than those women and minorities who are not selected. In short, those most in need may not benefit at all when preference by group membership is divorced from individual need.

4. Some members of majority groups may be just as deserving or more deserving of compensation than some women or members of minority groups. Many white males, for example, are more seriously limited in seeking employment than some women and minority-group members are.

5. Policies based on collective merit can be prohibitively expensive for business. In order to enforce such programs, businesses must hire people to collect data, process forms, deal with government agencies, and handle legal procedures. From business's viewpoint, this additional time, energy, and expense could have been channeled into more commercially productive directions.

In sum, those who argue that affirmative-action programs will provide adequate compensation for the victims of discrimination must grapple with the problems of determining the focus of the compensation: on the individual or on the group. While both focuses have merit, neither is without disadvantages. Furthermore, it seems neither approach can be implemented without first resolving a complex chain of moral concerns.

But even if we assume that affirmative-action programs will provide adequate compensation, it is still difficult to demonstrate the validity of the second assumption of those who endorse affirmative action by appealing to principles of compensatory justice: that such programs will provide compensation more fairly than any other alternative. By nature, affirmative-action programs provide compensation at the expense of the white males' right to fair and equal employment treatment. In other words, affirmative-action programs in the form of preferential treatment or quota systems undermine the fundamental principle of just employment practice: that a person should be hired or promoted only on job-related grounds. Apparently, then, it is an awesome undertaking to defend the proposition that affirmative action will provide compensation more fairly than any other alternative when such a proposition makes a non-job-related factor (membership in a group) a relevant employment criterion.

Although it would appear that reverse discrimination may not be justified on grounds of compensation, we should not conclude that it cannot be justified. In fact, some people contend that a more careful examination of the principles of justice suggests an alternative defense. As we have mentioned, those who argue against affirmative-action programs do so because such programs allegedly involve unequal treatment and are therefore unjust. The clear assumption here is that whatever involves unequal treatment is in and of itself unjust. But, as Professor Albert W. Flores points out, while justice would demand that equals receive equal treatment, it is likewise true that unequals should receive treatment appropriate to their differences. Hence, he concludes that "unfair or differential treatment may be required by the principles of justice."[12] In other words, unequal treatment is unfair in the absence of any characteristic difference between applicants which, from the viewpoint of justice, would constitute relevant differences. Following this line of reasoning, we must wonder whether being a female or a minority member would constitute a "relevant difference" that would justify unequal treatment.

To illustrate, let's ask how one could justify giving preferential consideration to a female job applicant over an equally qualified white male. Flores contends that while sex may be irrelevant to the job, it may be a relevant consideration as to who should be selected. In effect, he distinguishes between criteria relevant to a job and those relevant to candidate selection. He clearly bases this distinction on a concept of business's social responsibilities. As has been amply demonstrated elsewhere, business does not exist in a commercial vacuum. It is part of a social system and, as such, has obligations that relate to the welfare and integrity of society at large. Thus Flores argues that when a firm must decide between two equally qualified applicants, say a white male and a female, it is altogether justified in introducing as a selection criterion some concept of social justice, which in this case takes cognizance of a fair distribution of society's resources and scarcities among competing groups. From the viewpoint of justice, business may be correct in hiring the qualified female or minority member. Notice, however, that this contention is based primarily not on principles of compensatory justice but on a careful examination of the nature of justice.

The moral issues that affirmative-action programs raise in regard to justice are profound and complex. In this brief overview, we have been able to raise only a few, but these demonstrate that the morality of preferential treatment through affirmative action cuts to our basic assumptions about the nature of human beings and the principles of justice. Any moral resolution of the problem of reverse discrimination in the workplace will not only reflect these assumptions but must justify them.

Arguments against Reverse Discrimination

1. *Reverse discrimination is unequal treatment.*

POINT: "By definition, reverse discrimination means that one sex or race will receive preferential treatment over the other solely for biological reasons. This is inherently unfair because it means unequal treatment. Equality can exist only

12. *Ibid., p. 4.*

where all individuals are treated the same, where they are rewarded or punished to the same degree for the same behavior, regardless of their sex or race. But reverse discrimination precludes this. That's why it's wrong."

COUNTERPOINT: "If your argument was directed at sexism and racism, I'd totally agree with you. Both practices are morally repugnant. But reverse discrimination is different in purpose. First, unlike sexism or racism, reverse discrimination is designed to provide equal opportunity for all, not to ensure unequal opportunity. Second, reverse discrimination is a case not so much of preferring people because of sex or race, but of trying to compensate certain classes of people for the wrongs they've suffered."

2. *Reverse discrimination injures white males.*

POINT: "Surely two of the basic aspects of one's self-concept are the sexual and the racial. In individuals who have what psychologists call a "healthy self-concept," you will inevitably find a healthy sense of sexual and racial self-identity. Conversely, where self-image is damaged, you will likely find serious identity problems. When people have poor self-concepts, they experience anxiety and frustration and cannot attain happiness; indeed, they can hardly pursue happiness. By making individuals feel inferior, inadequate, or incomplete because of their sex or race, we do them incalculable harm by violating their right to a positive self-image. This, I think, is one of the most potent arguments against sexism and racism. But it also applies to reverse discrimination. After all, doesn't the white male have a right to a positive self-image, which reverse discrimination can only undermine?"

COUNTERPOINT: "Why do you focus exclusively on the white male? Considered from the viewpoint of women and minorities, reverse discrimination could have a quite positive effect on self-image. It could help restore to those people the dignity and sense of self-worth that years of sexism and racism have repressed. I doubt very seriously that the occasional white male who may lose an opportunity because of reverse discrimination will be irreparably damaged. After all, he is a member of a class that for centuries has held a preferred position in this society and, consequently, he has considerable resources to draw on when 'wronged.'"

3. *Reverse discrimination wastes the best human resources.*

POINT: "A most insidious part of reverse discrimination is that it wastes human resources. Just think of all the qualified individuals who will not be admitted to medical, dental, or law schools, or given entry into other areas where our nation and the world could use all the human power they can muster. In business, the picture is even bleaker. Under pressure to satisfy government standards, employers sometimes must overlook the one best qualified for a job—who just happens to be a white male. This is fair to neither the employer, the white male, nor society in general."

COUNTERPOINT: "There is no necessary connection between reverse discrimination and the waste of human resources. If anything, reverse discrimination, by enlarging the selection pool, should maximize our chances of securing the most competent people in all human endeavors. I don't doubt that there have been abuses in the administration of affirmative-action programs. But I think it's important to distinguish between the unqualified and the minimally qualified. I agree that nothing would justify employing an unqualified person, no matter the sex or color. But if a person is minimally qualified to do a job, then I don't see any reason other factors can't be introduced. Indeed, they already are: Institutions often consider regional 'qualifications'; businesses and schools have been known to consider 'who you know.' The point is that in the scramble for opportunities, the spoils don't always go to the person who on paper is 'best qualified.' So why not introduce sex and race as two considerations among many in evaluating a candidate?"

Arguments for Reverse Discrimination

1. *Compensatory justice demands reverse discrimination.*

POINT: "As groups, women and minorities traditionally have been discriminated against, often viciously. As individuals and as a nation, we can't ignore the sins of our fathers and mothers. In fact, we have an obligation to do something to help repair the wrongs of the past. Giving women and minorities preferential treatment in things like employment is one sound way to do this."

COUNTERPOINT: "If the living were made to pay for the sins of the dead, we'd be spending all our time making restitution. What's more, we wouldn't even be compensating those who rightly deserved it. So to the people who say, 'You must pay for the past,' I say, 'Why?' I didn't do the wrong; why should I be held accountable for it? And why should I be held accountable to someone who wasn't even the party wronged? What you're proposing will result in the ludicrous situation of an innocent individual being made to compensate someone who wasn't even wronged!"

2. *Reverse discrimination defuses the bomb of social unrest.*

POINT: "Conditions in our society today are volatile. Blacks are pitted against whites, females against males. At the root of class tensions is the fact that women and minorities don't share in the economic bounty of this land to the same degree as white males. Furthermore, women and minorities perceive white males and the establishment they man—no pun intended—as bent on preserving the white male's preferred social and economic position. Whether or not this perception is accurate is irrelevant. One thing's for sure: Women and minorities do, in fact, see it that way. Moreover, the economic gap between white males and others is widening, which can only deepen this perception and increase the chances of serious social unrest, even class warfare. The way to defuse this social bomb is through reverse discrimination. At least in that way, the white male establishment will have gone on record as recognizing and being sympathetic to the plight of the disenfranchised. Also, of course, by introducing women and minorities into the economic mainstream, reverse discrimination will thereby give them a vested interest in the system. This, in turn, will have the effect of getting women and minorities to work constructively within the system and not destructively outside it."

COUNTERPOINT: "I'm not sure I accept the ominous picture you draw of the relations between the sexes and races, but I'll concede it. Still, I doubt that reverse discrimination is going to bring us all together. Indeed, have you contemplated the impact reverse discrimination will have on white males who perceive it as reverse sexism and racism? Already several white males have gone to court crying 'Foul!' And more probably will. How can this be good for society? How can it draw us closer together? If anything, I think it's forcing people to take sides. And no wonder: Can any program that attempts to fight injustice with injustice possibly succeed?"

3.   *Reverse discrimination is the only way to eradicate sexism and racism.*

POINT: "If there were any other way to root out sexism and racism in our society, I'd favor it over reverse discrimination. But there isn't. While neither sexism nor racism may be as flagrant as it used to be, each is still virulent in our society. In fact, some would say they are more pernicious today because they're more subtle. Sure, I'd like to count on the good graces of the white male power elite to rid us of these inequities. But there's nothing to suggest that the white male will, in fact, do that. Quite the opposite. Until the passage of various civil rights acts and the Equal Employment Opportunity Act, very little had been done. The lesson of history is clear: Until people are forced to change, they won't; until people are forced to play fair, they will not relinquish their preferred positions."

COUNTERPOINT: "It's funny you mention the Civil Rights Act and the Equal Employment Opportunity Act. Out of these grew the Equal Employment Opportunity Commission and affirmative-action programs, which I believe represent a viable alternative to reverse discrimination. The fact is that already numerous cases of sexism and racism have been argued successfully before the EEOC. Already millions of dollars have been awarded in reparations. All of which leads me to believe that reverse discrimination isn't the way to eradicate sexism and racism. Strict, vigorous, uncompromising enforcement of the law is. If change isn't happening fast enough for some people, then the problem lies with how we're implementing the law, and we should do something about that."

The Justification of Reverse Discrimination

Tom L. Beauchamp

> *In this essay, philosophy professor Tom L. Beauchamp argues that reverse discrimination can be morally justified. But Beauchamp does not defend reverse discrimination on grounds of compensation owed for past wrongs. On the contrary, he holds that reverse discrimination is*

justified in order to eliminate present discriminatory practices. Clearly, then, Beauchamp must demonstrate that discrimination exists and that it can be eradicated only through methods of reverse discrimination.

Beauchamp approaches his task first by showing that reverse discrimination is compatible with principles of justice and utility. He then turns away from moral considerations to strictly factual ones. The principal factual matter is whether seriously discriminatory conditions exist in our society. To establish this, Beauchamp offers an array of statistical and linguistic evidence. Not only does discrimination exist, Beauchamp claims, it is intractable. Moreover, reverse discrimination is the only way it can be rooted out.

In recent years government policies intended to ensure fairer employment and educational opportunities for women and minority groups have engendered alarm. Although I shall in this paper argue in support of enlightened versions of these policies, I nonetheless think there is much to be said for the opposition arguments. In general I would argue that the world of business is now overregulated by the federal government, and I therefore hesitate to support an extension of the regulative arm of government into the arena of hiring and firing. Moreover, policies that would eventuate in reverse discrimination in present North American society have a heavy presumption against them, for both justice-regarding and utilitarian reasons: The introduction of such preferential treatment on a large scale could well produce a series of injustices, economic advantages to some who do not deserve them, protracted court battles, jockeying for favored position by other minorities, congressional lobbying by power groups, a lowering of admission and work standards in vital institutions, reduced social and economic efficiency, increased racial hostility, and continued suspicion that well-placed women and minority-group members received their positions purely on the basis of quotas. Conjointly these reasons constitute a powerful case against the enactment of policies productive of reverse discrimination in hiring.

I find these reasons against allowing reverse discrimination to occur both thoughtful and tempting, and I want to concede from the outset that policies of reverse discrimination can create serious and perhaps even tragic injustices. One must be careful, however, not to draw an overzealous conclusion from this admission. Those who argue that reverse discrimination creates injustices often say that, because of the injustice, such policies are *unjust*. I think by this use of "unjust" they generally mean "not justified" (rather than "not sanctioned by jus-

tice"). But a policy can create and even perpetuate injustices, as violations of the principle of formal equality, and yet be justified by other reasons. It would be an injustice in this sense to fire either one of two assistant professors with exactly similar professional credentials, while retaining the other of the two; yet the financial condition of the university or compensation owed the person retained might provide compelling reasons which justify the action. The first reason supporting the dismissal is utilitarian in character, and the other derives from the principle of compensatory justice. This shows both that there can be conflicts between different justice-regarding reasons and also that violations of the principle of formal equality are not in themselves sufficient to render an action unjustifiable.

A proper conclusion, then—and one which I accept—is that all discrimination, including reverse discrimination, is prima facie immoral, because a basic principle of justice creates a prima facie duty to abstain from such treatment of persons. But no absolute duty is created come what may, for we might have conflicting duties of sufficient weight to justify such injustices. The latter is the larger thesis I wish to defend: Considerations of compensatory justice and utility are conjointly of sufficient weight in contemporary society to neutralize and overcome the quite proper presumption of immorality in the case of some policies productive of reverse discrimination.

I

It is difficult to avoid accepting two important claims: (a) that the law ought never to sanction any discriminatory practices (whether plain old unadorned discrimination or reverse discrimination), and (b) that such practices can be eradicated by bringing the full weight of the law down on those who engage in discriminatory practices. The first claim is a moral one, the second a factual one. I contend in this section that it is unrealistic to believe, as *b* suggests, that in contemporary society discriminatory practices *can* be eradicated by legal measures which do not permit reverse discrimination. And because they cannot be eradicated, I think we ought to relax our otherwise unimpeachably sound reservations (as recorded in *a* and discussed in the first section) against allowing any discriminatory practices whatever.

My argument is motivated by the belief that racial, sexual, and no doubt other forms of discrimination are not antique relics but are living patterns which continue to warp selection and ranking procedures. In my view the difference between the present and the past is that discriminatory treatment is today less widespread and considerably less blatant. But its reduction has produced apathy; its subtleness has made it less visible and considerably more difficult to detect. Largely because of the reduced visibility of racism and sexism, I suggest, reverse discrimination now strikes us as all too harsh and unfair. After all, quotas and preferential treatment have no appeal if one assumes a just, primarily non-discriminatory society. Since the presence or absence of seriously discriminatory conditions in our society is a factual matter, empirical evidence must be adduced to show that the set of discriminatory attitudes and selection procedures I have alleged to exist do in fact exist. The data I shall mention derive primarily from historical, linguistic, sociological, and legal sources.

Statistical Evidence

Statistical imbalances in employment and admission are often discounted because so many variables can be hypothesized to explain why, for non-discriminatory reasons, an imbalance exists. We can all think of plausible non-discriminatory reasons why 22% of Harvard's graduate students in 1969 were women but its tenured Arts and Sciences Faculty in the Graduate School consisted of 411 males and 0 females.[1] But sometimes we are able to discover evidence which supports the claim that skewed statistics are the result of discrimination. Quantities of such discriminatory findings, in turn, raise serious questions about the real reasons for suspicious statistics in those cases where we have *not* been able to determine these reasons—perhaps because they are so subtle and unnoticed.

I shall discuss each factor in turn: (a) statistics which constitute prima facie but indecisive evidence of discrimination; (b) findings concerning discriminatory reasons for some of these statistics; and (c) cases where the discrimination is probably undetectable because of its subtleness, and yet the statistical evidence is overwhelming.

a. A massive body of statistics constituting prima facie evidence of discrimination has been assembled in recent years. Here is a tiny but diverse fragment of some of these statistical findings.[2] (1) Women college teachers with identical credentials in terms of publications and experience are promoted at almost exactly one-half the rate of their male counterparts. (2) In the United States women graduates of medical schools in 1965 stood at 7%, as compared with 36% in Germany. The gap in the number of women physicians was similar. (3) Of 3,000 leading law firms surveyed in 1957 only 32 reported a woman partner, and even these women were paid much less (increasingly so for every year of employment) than their male counterparts. (4) 40% of the white-collar positions in the United States are presently held by women, but only 10% of the management positions are held by women, and their pay again is significantly less (70% of clerical workers are women). (5) 8,000 workers were employed in May 1967 in the construction of BART (Bay Area Rapid Transit), but not a single electrician, ironworker, or plumber was black. (6) In the population as a whole in the United States, 3 out of 7 employees hold white-collar positions, but only 1 out of 7 blacks holds such a position, and these latter jobs are clustered in professions which have the fewest jobs to offer in top-paying positions. (7) In the well-known A. T. & T. case, this massive conglomerate signed a settlement giving tens of millions of dollars to women and minority employees. A. T. & T. capitulated to this settlement based on impressive statistics indicating discriminatory treatment.

b. I concede that such statistics are far from decisive indicators of discrimination. But when further evidence concerning the reasons for the statistics is uncovered, they are put in a perspective affording them greater power—clinching power in my view. Consider (3)—the statistics on the lack of women lawyers. A survey of Harvard Law School alumnae in 1970 provided evidence about male lawyers' attitudes.[3] It showed that businesses and legal firms do not generally expect the women they hire to become lawyers, that they believe women cannot become good litigators, and that they believe only limited numbers of women should be hired since clients generally prefer male lawyers. Surveys of women applicants for legal positions indicate they are frequently either told that a woman will not be hired, or are warned that "senior partners" will likely object, or are told that women will be hired to do only probate, trust, and estate work. (Other statistics confirm that these are the sorts of tasks dominantly given to women.) Consider also (5)—a particular but typical case of hiring in non-white-collar positions. Innumerable studies have shown that most of these positions are filled by word-of-mouth recruitment policies conducted by all-white interviewers (usually all-male as well). In a number of decisions of the Equal Employment Opportunity Commission, it has been shown that the interviewers have racially biased attitudes and that the applications of blacks and women are systematically handled in unusual ways, such as never even being filed. So serious and consistent have such violations been that the EEOC has publicly stated its belief that word-of-mouth recruitment policies without demonstrable supplementary and simultaneous recruitment in minority group communities is in itself a "prima facie violation of Title VII."[4] Gertrude Ezorsky has argued, convincingly I believe, that this pattern of "special ties" is no less present in professional white-collar hiring, which is neither less discriminatory nor more sensitive to hiring strictly on the basis of merit.[5]

c. Consider, finally, (1)—statistics pertaining to the treatment of women college teachers. The Carnegie Commission and others have assembled statistical evidence to show that in even the most favorable construal of relevant variables, women teachers have been discriminated against in hiring, tenuring, and ranking. But instead of summarizing this mountain of material, I wish here to take a particular case in order to illustrate the difficulty in determining, on the basis of statistics and similar empirical data, whether discrimination is occurring even where courts have been forced to find satisfactory evidence of discrimination. In December 1974 a decision was reached by the Commission against Discrimination of the Executive Department of the State of Massachusetts regarding a case at Smith College where the two complainants were women

who were denied tenure and dismissed by the English Department.[6] The women claimed sex discrimination and based their case on the following: (1) Women at the full professor level in the college declined from 54% in 1958 to 21% in 1972, and in the English department from 57% in 1960 to 11% in 1972. These statistics compare unfavorably at all levels with Mt. Holyoke's, a comparable institution (since both have an all-female student body and are located in western Massachusetts). (2) Thirteen of the department's fifteen associate and full professorships at Smith belonged to men. (3) The two tenured women had obtained tenure under "distinctly peculiar experiences," including a stipulation that one be only part-time and that the other not be promoted when given tenure. (4) The department's faculty members conceded that tenure standards were applied subjectively, were vague, and lacked the kind of precision which would avoid discriminatory application. (5) The women denied tenure were at no time given advance warning that their work was deficient. Rather, they were given favorable evaluations of their teaching and were encouraged to believe they would receive tenure. (6) Some stated reasons for the dismissals were later demonstrated to be rationalizations, and one letter from a senior member to the tenure and promotion committee contradicted his own appraisal of teaching ability filed with the department. (7) The court accepted expert testimony that any deficiencies in the women candidates were also found in male candidates promoted and given tenure during this same period, and that the women's positive credentials were at least as good as the men's.

The commissioner's opinion found that "the Complainants properly used statistics to demonstrate that the Respondents' practices operate with a discriminatory effect." Citing *Parham* v. *Southwestern Bell Telephone Co.*,[7] the commissioner argued that "in such cases extreme statistics may establish discrimination as a matter of law, without additional supportive evidence." But in this case the commissioner found abundant additional evidence in the form of "the historical absence of women," "word-of-mouth recruitment policies" which operate discriminatorily, and a number of "subtle and not so subtle, societal patterns" existing at Smith.[8] On December 30, 1974, the commissioner ordered the two women reinstated with tenure and ordered the department to submit an affirmative action program within 60 days.

This case is interesting because there is little in the way of clinching proof that the members of the English Department actually held discriminatory attitudes. Yet so consistent a pattern of *apparently* discriminatory treatment must be regarded, according to this decision, as *de facto* discrimination. The commissioner's ruling and other laws are quite explicit that "intent or lack thereof is of no consequence." If a procedure constitutes discriminatory treatment, then the parties discriminated against must be recompensed. Here we have a case where irresistible statistics and other sociological evidence of "social exclusion" and "subtle societal patterns" provide convincing evidence that strong, court-backed measures must be taken because nothing short of such measures is sufficiently strong to overcome the discriminatory pattern, as the Respondents' testimony in the case verifies.[9]

Some understanding of the attitudes underlying the statistical evidence thus far surveyed can be gained by consideration of some linguistic evidence now to be mentioned. It further supports the charge of widespread discrimination in the case of women and of the difficulty in changing discriminatory attitudes.

Linguistic Evidence

Robert Baker has assembled some impressive linguistic evidence which indicates that our language is male-slanted, perhaps male chauvinistic, and that language about women relates something of fundamental importance concerning the males' most fundamental conceptions of women.[10] Baker argues that as the term "boy" once expressed a paternalistic and dominating attitude toward blacks (and was replaced in our conceptual structure because of this denigrating association), so are there other English terms which serve similar functions in regard to women (but are not replaced because not considered by men as in need of replacement). Baker assembles evidence both from the language itself and from surveys of users of the language to show the following.

The term "woman" is broadly substitutable for and frequently interchanged in English sentences such as "Who is that _____ over there?" by terms such as those in the following divisions:

A. *Neutral Categories*	B. *Animal Categories*	C. *Plaything Categories*
lady	chick	babe
gal	bird	doll
girl	fox	cuddly thing
broad	vixen	
(sister)	filly	
	bitch	

D. *Gender Categories*	E. *Sexual Categories*
skirt	snatch
hem	cunt
	ass
	twat
	piece
	lay
	pussy

Baker notes that (1) while there are differences in the frequency of usage, all of these terms are standard enough to be recognizable at least by most male users of the language; (2) women do not typically identify themselves in sexual categories; and (3) typically only males use the nonneutral categories (B–E). He takes this to be evidence—and I agree—that the male conception of women differs significantly from the female conception and that the categories used by the male in classifying women are "prima facie denigrating." He then argues that it is clearly and not merely prima facie denigrating when categories such as C and E are used, as they are either derived from playboy male images or are outright vulgarities. Baker argues that it is most likely that B and D are similarly used in denigrating ways. His arguments center on the metaphorical associations of these terms, but the evidence cannot be further pursued here.

Although Baker does not remark that women do not have a similar language for men, it seems to me important to notice this fact. Generally, any negative categories used by women to refer to men are as frequently or more frequently used by men to apply to women. This asymmetrical relation does not hold, of course, for the language used by whites and blacks for denigrating reference. This fact perhaps says something about how blacks have caught on to the impact of the language as a tool of denigrating identification in a way women have yet to do, at least in equal numbers. It may also say something about the image of submissiveness which many women still bear about themselves—an image blacks are no longer willing to accept.

Baker concludes from his linguistic studies that "sexual discrimination permeates our conceptual structure. Such discrimination is clearly inimical to any movement toward sexual egalitarianism and virtually defeats its purpose at the outset."[11] His conclusion may somewhat overreach his premises, but when combined with the corroborating statistical evidence previously adduced, it seems apt. Linguistic dispositions lead us to categorize persons and events in discriminatory ways which are sometimes glaringly obvious to the categorized but accepted as "objective" by the categorizer. My contention, derived from Baker's and to be supported as we proceed, is that cautious, good faith movements toward egalitarianism such as affirmative action guidelines *cannot* succeed short of fundamental conceptual and ethical revisions. And since the probability of such revisions approximates zero (because discriminatory attitudes are covertly embedded in language and cultural habit), radical expedients are required to bring about the desired egalitarian results, expedients which may result in reverse discrimination.

Conclusions

Irving Thalberg has argued, correctly I believe, that the gravest contemporary problems with racism stem from its "protectively camouflaged" status, which he calls "visceral." Thalberg skillfully points to a number of attitudes held by those whites normally classified as unprejudiced which indicate that racism still colors their conception of social facts.[12] My alliance with such a position ought to be obvious by now. But my overall intentions and conclusions are somewhat different. I hold that because of the peculiarly concealed nature of the protective camouflage under which sexism and racism have so long thrived, it is not a reasonable expectation that the lightweight programs now administered under the heading of affirmative action will succeed in overturning discriminatory treatment. I turn now directly to this topic.

II

The rawest nerve of the social and political controversy concerning reverse discrimination is exposed by the following question: What government policies are permissible and required in order to bring about a society where equal treatment of persons is the rule rather than the exception? Fair-minded opponents of any government policy which might produce reverse discrimination—Carl Cohen and William Blackstone, for example—seem to me to oppose them largely because and perhaps only because of their *factual belief* that present government policies not causing reverse discrimination will, if seriously and sincerely pursued, prove sufficient to achieve the goal of equal consideration of persons.

Once again a significant factual disagreement has emerged: What means are not only fair but also sufficient? I must again support my contentions by adducing factual data to show that my pessimism is sustained by the weight of the evidence. The evidence cited here comes from government data concerning affirmative action programs. I shall discuss the affirmative action program in order to show that on the basis of present government guidelines (which, to my knowledge, are the best either in law or proposed as law by those who oppose reverse discrimination), discriminatory business as usual will surely prevail.

Affirmative Action

I begin with a sample of the affirmative action guidelines, as understood by those who administer them. I use the example of HEW guidelines for educational institutions receiving federal financial aid. These guidelines are not radically different from those directed at hiring practices throughout the world of business. Specifically, these guidelines cover three areas: admission, treatment of students, and employment. A sample of the sorts of requirements universities are under includes: (1) They may not advertise vacant positions as open only to or preferentially to a particular race or sex, except where sex is a legitimate occupational requirement. (2) The university sets standards and criteria for employment, but if these effectively work to exclude women or minorities as a class, the university must justify the job requirements. (3) An institution may not set different standards for admission for one sex, race, etc. (4) There must be active recruitment where there is an underrepresentation of women and minorities, as gauged by the availability of qualified members of these classes.

However, the relevant government officials have from time to time made it clear that (1) quotas are unacceptable, either for admission or employment, though target goals and timetables intended to correct deficiencies are acceptable and to be encouraged. (2) A university is never under any obligation to dilute legitimate standards, and hence there is no conflict with merit hiring. (3) Reserving positions for members of a minority group (and presumably for the female sex) is "an outrageous and illegal form of reverse bias" (as one former director of the program wrote).[13] By affirmative action requirements I mean this latter interpretation and nothing stronger (though I have given only a sample set of qualifications, of course).

The question I am currently asking is whether these guidelines, assuming they will be vigorously pursued, can reasonably be expected to bring about their goal, which is the social circumstance of non-discriminatory treatment of persons. If they *are* strong enough, then Cohen, Blackstone, and others are right: Reverse discrimination is not under such circumstances justified. Unfortunately the statistical and linguistic evidence previously adduced indicates otherwise. The *Smith College* case is paradigmatic of the concealed yet serious discrimination which occurs through the network of subtle distortions, old-boy procedures, and prejudices we have accumulated. Only when the statistics become egregiously out of proportion is action taken or a finding of mistreatment possible. And that is one reason why it seems unlikely that substantial progress can be made, in any realistic sense of "can," by current government measures not productive of reverse discrimination. According to Peter Holmes, once the Director of HEW's Office for Civil Rights and in charge of interpreting affirmative action guidelines: "It has been our policy that it is the institutions' responsibility to determine non-discriminatory qualifications in the first instance, and that such qualifications, in conjunction with other affirmative action steps, should yield results."[14] This is the received HEW view, but the last sentence contains an ambiguous use of the word "should." If the "should" in this statement is a moral "should," none will disagree. But if it is an empirical, predictive "should," as I take Mr. Holmes to intend, we are back to the core of the difficulty. I now turn to a consideration of how deficient such affirmative action steps have proven to be.

Government Data

The January 1975 Report of the United States Commission on Civil Rights contains a section on "compliance reviews" of various universities. These are government assessments of university compliance with Executive Orders pertaining to affirmative action plans. The report contains a stern indictment of the Higher Education Division (HED) of HEW—the division in charge of overseeing all HEW civil rights enforcement activities in the area of higher education. It concludes that "HED has, in large part, failed to follow the procedures required of compliance agencies under the Executive order regulations."[15] But more interesting than this mere failure to enforce the law is the report's discussion of how very difficult it is to obtain compliance even when there is a routine attempt to enforce the law. The Commission reviewed four major campuses in the United States (Harvard, University of Michigan, University of Washington, Berkeley). They concluded that there is a pattern of inadequate compliance reviews, inordinate delays, and inexcusable failures to take enforcement action where there were clear violations of the Executive order regulations.[16]

Consider the example of the "case history of compliance contacts" at the University of California at Berkeley. According to HED's own staff a "conciliation agreement" with this university "is now being used as a model for compliance activities with other campuses." When the Office for Civil Rights of HEW determined to investigate Berkeley (April 1971), after several complaints, including a class action sex discrimination complaint, the university refused to permit access to its personnel files and refused to permit the interviewing of faculty members without an administrator present. Both refusals are, as the report points out, "direct violations of the Executive order's equal opportunity clause," under which Berkeley held contracts. Despite this clear violation of the law, no enforcement action was taken. A year and one-half later, after negotiations and more complaints, the university was instructed to develop a written affirmative action plan to correct "documented deficiencies" of "pervasive discrimination." The plan was to include target goals and timetables wherever job underutilization had been identified.[17]

In January 1973 the university, in a letter from Chancellor Albert H. Bowker, submitted a draft affirmative action plan which was judged "totally unacceptable." Throughout 1973 Berkeley received "extensive technical assistance" from the government to aid it in developing a better plan. No such plan emerged, and OCR at the end of the year began to question "the university's commitment to comply with the executive order." The university submitted other unacceptable plans, and finally in March 1974 "a conciliation agreement was reached." However, "the document suffered from such extreme vagueness that, as of August 1974, the university and OCR were in substantial disagreement on the meaning of a number of its provisions," and "the agreement specifically violated OFCC regulations in a number of ways." These violations are extensive and serious, and the report characterizes one part as "outrageous." Four years after this "model" compliance case began, it was unresolved and no enforcement proceedings had been taken against the university. The report concludes: "In its Title VI reviews of colleges and universities, HEW routinely finds noncompliance, but it almost never imposes sanctions; instead HEW responds by making vague recommendations. Moreover, HEW does not routinely require the submission of progress reports or conduct sufficient followup to determine if its recommendations have been followed."

III

No one could be happy about the conclusions I have reached or about the depressing and disturbing facts on which they are based. But I do take it to be a *factual* and not an *evaluative* conclusion both (1) that the camouflaged attitudes I have discussed exist and affect the social position of minority groups and women and (2) that they will in all likelihood continue to have this influence. It is, of course, an evaluative conclusion that we are morally permitted and even required to remedy this situation by the imposition of quotas, target goals, and timetables. But anyone who accepts my *interpretation* of the facts bears a heavy burden of moral argument to show that we ought not to use such means to that end upon which I take it we all agree, viz., the equal consideration of persons irrespective of race, sex, religion, or nationality.

By way of conclusion, it is important to set my arguments in the framework of a distinction between real reverse discrimination and merely apparent reverse discrimination. My evidence demonstrates present, ongoing barriers to the removal of discriminatory practices. My contentions set the stage for showing that *because* of the existence of what Thalberg calls "visceral racism," and because of visceral sexism as well, there will be many occasions on which we can only avoid inevitable discrimination by policies productive of reverse discrimination. Sometimes, however, persons will be hired or admitted—on a quota basis, for example—who appear to be displacing better applicants, but the appearance is the result of visceral discriminatory perceptions of the person's qualifications. In this case there will certainly appear to the visceral racist or sexist to be reverse discrimination, and this impression will be reinforced by knowledge that quotas were used; yet the allegation of reverse discrimination will be a mistaken one. On other occasions there will be genuine reverse discrimination, and on many occasions it will be impossible to determine whether or not this consequence is occurring. The evidence I have adduced is, of course, intended to support the contention that real and not merely apparent reverse discrimination is justified. But it is justified only as a means to the end of ensuring genuinely nondiscriminatory treatment of all persons.

Notes

1. From "Statement of Dr. Bernice Sandler," *Discrimination Against Women: Congressional Hearings on Equal Rights in Education and Employment,* ed. Catharine R. Stimpson (New York: R. R. Bowker Company, 1973), pp. 61, 415. Hereafter *Discrimination Against Women.*

2. All of the statistics and quotations cited are taken from the compilations of data in the following sources: (1) Kenneth M. Davidson, Ruth B. Ginsburg, and Herma H. Kay, eds., *Sex-Based Discrimination: Text, Cases, and Materials* (Minneapolis: West Publishing Company, 1974), esp. Ch. 3. Hereafter *Sex-Based Discrimination.* (2) *Discrimination Against Women,* esp. pp. 397–441 and 449–502. (3) Alfred W. Blumrosen, *Black Employment and the Law* (New Brunswick, N.J.: Rutgers University Press, 1971), esp. pp. 107, 122f. (4) *The Federal Civil Rights Enforcement Effort—1971,* A Report of the United States Commission on Civil Rights.

3. *Discrimination Against Women,* pp. 505f.

4. *Sex-Based Discrimination,* p. 516.

5. "The Fight Over University Women," *The New York Review of Books,* May 16, 1974, pp. 32–39.

6. *Maurianne Adams and Mary Schroeder* v. *Smith College*, Massachusetts Commission Against Discrimination, Nos. 72-S-53, 72-S-54 (December 30, 1974). Hereafter *The Smith College Case.*

7. 433 F.2d 421, 426 (8 Cir. 1970).

8. *The Smith College Case*, pp. 23, 26.

9. *Ibid.*, pp. 26f.

10. Robert Baker, "'Pricks' and 'Chicks': A Plea for Persons," in Richard Wasserstrom, ed., *Today's Moral Problems* (New York: Macmillan Publishing Company, 1975), pp. 152–170.

11. *Ibid.*, p. 170.

12. "Visceral Racism," *The Monist*, 56 (1972), 43–63, and reprinted in Wasserstrom.

13. J. Stanley Pottinger, "Race, Sex, and Jobs: The Drive Towards Equality," *Change Magazine*, 4 (Oct. 1972), 24–29.

14. Peter E. Holmes, "HEW Guidelines and 'Affirmative Action,'" *The Washington Post*, Feb. 15, 1975.

15. *The Federal Civil Rights Enforcement Effort—1974*, 3:276.

16. *Ibid.*, p. 281.

17. *Ibid.*, all subsequent references are from pp. 281–286.

Questions for Analysis

1. What obligations, if any, does Beauchamp draw from claims of compensatory justice?

2. Why does Beauchamp construe reverse discrimination as primarily a factual matter?

3. When Beauchamp says reverse discrimination is compatible with principles of justice, does he mean that no injustice results from reverse discrimination or that these injustices can be justified? Explain the difference, and why the latter claim is a utilitarian one.

4. What are the two minimal principles of justice Beauchamp uses to support the claim that reverse discrimination is compatible with justice? Compare and contrast these principles with Rawls's equality and difference principles.

5. Beauchamp says: ". . . all discrimination, including reverse discrimination, is prima facie immoral." Explain why this admission is not inconsistent with his claim that reverse discrimination can be morally justified.

6. What statistical and linguistic evidence does Beauchamp provide to prove that discrimination still exists?

7. Do you think Beauchamp has established that reverse discrimination is the only way to eradicate intractable discrimination?

A Defense of Programs of Preferential Treatment

Richard Wasserstrom

> In this essay, philosophy professor Richard Wasserstrom provides a limited defense of quota hiring by attacking two of the opposition's major arguments. First, opponents of preferential treatment often charge proponents with "intellectual inconsistency." They argue that those now supporting

From Richard Wasserstrom, *"A Defense of Programs of Preferential Treatment,"* Phi Kappa Phi Journal, *LVIII (Winter 1978)*; originally Part II of *"Racism, Sexism, and Preferential Treatment: An Approach to the Topics,"* 24 U.C.L.A. Law Review, 581 (1977). *Reprinted by permission of the author.*

preferential treatment opposed it in the past. But Wasserstrom feels that social realities in respect
to the distribution of resources and opportunities make present preferential-treatment programs
enormously different from quotas of the past.

The second argument commonly raised against preferential-treatment programs is that such
programs, by introducing sex and race, compromise what really should matter: individual
qualifications. Wasserstrom counters this charge on both an operational and a theoretical level. He
feels that to be decisive, this argument must appeal, not to efficiency, but to desert: Those who are
most qualified deserve to receive the benefits. But Wasserstrom sees no necessary connection
between qualifications and desert.

Many justifications of programs of preferential treatment depend upon the claim that in one respect or another such programs have good consequences or that they are effective means by which to bring about some desirable end, e.g., an integrated, equalitarian society. I mean by "programs of preferential treatment" to refer to programs such as those at issue in the *Bakke* case—programs which set aside a certain number of places (for example, in a law school) as to which members of minority groups (for example, persons who are non-white or female) who possess certain minimum qualifications (in terms of grades and test scores) may be preferred for admission to those places over some members of the majority group who possess higher qualifications (in terms of grades and test scores).

Many criticisms of programs of preferential treatment claim that such programs, even if effective, are unjustifiable because they are in some important sense unfair or unjust. In this paper I present a limited defense of such programs by showing that two of the chief arguments offered for the unfairness or injustice of these programs do not work in the way or to the degree supposed by critics of these programs.

The first argument is this. Opponents of preferential treatment programs sometimes assert that proponents of these programs are guilty of intellectual inconsistency, if not racism or sexism. For, as is now readily acknowledged, at times past employers, universities, and many other social institutions did have racial or sexual quotas (when they did not practice overt racial or sexual exclusion), and many of those who were most concerned to bring about the eradication of those racial quotas are now untroubled by the new programs which reinstitute them. And this, it is claimed, is inconsistent. If it was wrong to take race or sex into account when blacks and women were the objects of racial and sexual policies and practices of exclusion, then it is wrong to take race or sex into account

when the objects of the policies have their race or sex reversed. Simple considerations of intellectual consistency—of what it means to give racism or sexism as a reason for condemning these social policies and practices—require that what was a good reason then is still a good reason now.

The problem with this argument is that despite appearances, there is no inconsistency involved in holding both views. Even if contemporary preferential treatment programs which contain quotas are wrong, they are not wrong for the reasons that made quotas against blacks and women pernicious. The reason why is that the social realities do make an enormous difference. The fundamental evil of programs that discriminated against blacks or women was that these programs were a part of a larger social universe which systematically maintained a network of institutions which unjustifiably concentrated power, authority, and goods in the hands of white male individuals, and which systematically consigned blacks and women to subordinate positions in the society.

Whatever may be wrong with today's affirmative action programs and quota systems, it should be clear that the evil, if any, is just not the same. Racial and sexual minorities do not constitute the dominant social group. Nor is the conception of who is a fully developed member of the moral and social community one of an individual who is either female or black. Quotas which prefer women or blacks do not add to an already relatively overabundant supply of resources and opportunities at the disposal of members of these groups in the way in which the quotas of the past did maintain and augment the overabundant supply of resources and opportunities already available to white males.

The same point can be made in a somewhat different way. Sometimes people say that what was wrong, for example, with the system of racial discrimination in the South was that it took an irrelevant characteristic, namely race, and used it systematically to allocate social benefits and burdens of various sorts. The defect was the irrelevance of the characteristic used—race—for that meant that individuals ended up being treated in a manner that was arbitrary and capricious.

I do not think that was the central flaw at all. Take, for instance, the most hideous of the practices, human slavery. The primary thing that was wrong with the institution was not that the particular individuals who were assigned the place of slaves were assigned there arbitrarily because the assignment was made in virtue of an irrelevant characteristic, their race. Rather, it seems to me that the primary thing that was and is wrong with slavery is the practice itself—the fact of some individuals being able to own other individuals and all that goes with that practice. It would not matter by what criterion individuals were assigned; human slavery would still be wrong. And the same can be said for most if not all of the other discrete practices and institutions which comprised the system of racial discrimination even after human slavery was abolished. The practices were unjustifiable—they were oppressive—and they would have been so no matter how the assignment of victims had been made. What made it worse, still, was that the institutions and the supporting ideology all interlocked to create a system of human oppression whose effects on those living under it were as devastating as they were unjustifiable.

Again, if there is anything wrong with the programs of preferential treatment that have begun to flourish within the past ten years, it should be evident that the social realities in respect to the distribution of resources and opportunities make the difference. Apart from everything else, there is simply no way in which all of these programs taken together could plausibly be viewed as capable of relegating white males to the kind of genuinely oppressive status characteristically bestowed upon women and blacks by the dominant social institutions and ideology.

The second objection is that preferential treatment programs are wrong because they take race or sex into account rather than the only thing that does matter—that is, an individual's qualification. What all such programs have in common and what makes them all objectionable, so this argument goes, is that they ignore the persons who are more qualified by bestowing a preference on those who are less qualified in virtue of their being black or female.

There are, I think, a number of things wrong with this objection based on qualifications, and not the least of them is that we do not live in a society in which there is even the serious pretense of a qualification requirement for many jobs of substantial power and authority. Would anyone claim, for example, that the persons who comprise the judiciary are there because they are the most qualified lawyers or the most qualified persons to be judges? Would anyone claim that Henry Ford II is the head of the Ford Motor Company because he is the most qualified person for the job? Part of what is wrong with even talking about qualifications and merit is that the argument derives some of its force from the erroneous notion that we would have a meritocracy were it not for programs of preferential treatment. In fact, the higher one goes in terms of prestige, power and the like, the less qualifications seem ever to be decisive. It is only for certain jobs and certain places that qualifications are used to do more than establish the possession of certain minimum competencies.

But difficulties such as these to one side, there are theoretical difficulties as well which cut much more deeply into the argument about qualifications. To begin with, it is important to see that there is a serious inconsistency present if the person who favors "pure qualifications" does so on the ground that the most qualified ought to be selected because this promotes maximum efficiency. Let us suppose that the argument is that if we have the most qualified performing the relevant tasks we will get those tasks done in the most economical and efficient manner. There is nothing wrong in principle with arguments based upon the good consequences that will flow from maintaining a social practice in a certain way. But it is inconsistent for the opponent of preferential treatment to attach much weight to qualifications on this ground, because it was an analogous appeal to the good consequences that the opponent of preferential treatment thought was wrong in the first place. That is to say, if the chief thing to be said in favor of strict qualifications and preferring the most qualified is that it is the most efficient way of getting things done, then we are right back to an assessment of the different consequences that will flow from different programs, and we are far removed from the considerations of justice or fairness that were thought to weigh so heavily against these programs.

It is important to note, too, that qualifications—at least in the educational context—are often not connected at all closely with any plausible conception of social effectiveness. To admit the most qualified students to law school, for example—given the way qualifications are now determined—is primarily to admit those who have the greatest chance of scoring the highest grades at law school. This says little about efficiency except perhaps that these students are the easiest for the faculty to teach. However, since we know so little about what constitutes being a good, or even successful lawyer, and even less about the correlation between being a very good law student and being a very good lawyer, we can hardly claim very confidently that the legal system will operate more efficiently if we admit only the most qualified students to law school.

To be at all decisive, the argument for qualifications must be that those who are the most qualified deserve to receive the benefits (the job, the place in law school, etc.) because they are the most qualified. The introduction of the concept of desert now makes it an objection as to justice or fairness of the sort promised by the original criticism of the programs. But now the problem is that there is no reason to think that there is any strong sense of "desert" in which it is correct that the most qualified deserve anything.

Let us consider more closely one case, that of preferential treatment in respect to admission to college or graduate school. There is a logical gap in the inference from the claim that a person is most qualified to perform a task, e.g., to be a good student, to the conclusion that he or she deserves to be admitted as a student. Of course, those who deserve to be admitted should be admitted. But why do the most qualified deserve anything? There is simply no necessary connection between academic merit (in the sense of being most qualified) and deserving to be a member of a student body. Suppose, for instance, that there is only one tennis court in the community. Is it clear that the two best tennis players ought to be the ones permitted to use it? Why not those who were there first? Or those who will enjoy playing the most? Or those who are the worst and, therefore, need the greatest opportunity to practice? Or those who have the chance to play least frequently?

We might, of course, have a rule that says that the best tennis players get to use the court before the others. Under such a rule the best players would deserve the court more than the poorer ones. But

that is just to push the inquiry back one stage. Is there any reason to think that we ought to have a rule giving good tennis players such a preference? Indeed, the arguments that might be given for or against such a rule are many and varied. And few if any of the arguments that might support the rule would depend upon a connection between ability and desert.

Someone might reply, however, that the most able students deserve to be admitted to the university because all of their earlier schooling was a kind of competition, with university admission being the prize awarded to the winners. They deserve to be admitted because that is what the rule of the competition provides. In addition, it might be argued, it would be unfair now to exclude them in favor of others, given the reasonable expectations they developed about the way in which their industry and performance would be rewarded. Minority-admission programs, which inevitably prefer some who are less qualified over some who are more qualified, all possess this flaw.

There are several problems with this argument. The most substantial of them is that it is an empirically implausible picture of our social world. Most of what are regarded as the decisive characteristics for higher education have a great deal to do with things over which the individual has neither control nor responsibility: such things as home environment, socioeconomic class of parents, and, of course, the quality of the primary and secondary schools attended. Since individuals do not deserve having had any of these things vis-à-vis other individuals, they do not, for the most part, deserve their qualifications. And since they do not deserve their abilities they do not in any strong sense deserve to be admitted because of their abilities.

To be sure, if there has been a rule which connects, say, performance at high school with admission to college, then there is a weak sense in which those who do well at high school deserve, for that reason alone, to be admitted to college. In addition, if persons have built up or relied upon their reasonable expectations concerning performance and admission, they have a claim to be admitted on this ground as well. But it is certainly not obvious that these claims of desert are any stronger or more compelling than the competing claims based upon the needs of or advantages to women or blacks from programs of preferential treatment. And as I have indicated, all rule-based claims of desert are very weak unless and until the rule which creates the claim is itself shown to be a justified one. Unless one has a strong preference for the status quo, and unless one can defend that preference, the practice within a system of allocating places in a certain way does not go very far at all in showing that this is the right or the just way to allocate those places in the future.

A proponent of programs of preferential treatment is not at all committed to the view that qualifications ought to be wholly irrelevant He or she can agree that, given the existing structure of any institution, there is probably some minimal set of qualifications without which one cannot participate meaningfully within the institution. In addition, it can be granted that the qualifications of those involved will affect the way the institution works and the way it affects others in the society. And the consequences will vary depending upon the particular institution. But all of this only establishes that qualifications, in this sense, are relevant, not that they are decisive. This is wholly consistent with the claim that race or sex should today also be relevant when it comes to matters such as admission to college or law school. And that is all that any preferential treatment program — even one with the kind of quota used in the *Bakke* case—has ever tried to do.

I have not attempted to establish that programs of preferential treatment are right and desirable. There are empirical issues concerning the consequences of these programs that I have not discussed, and certainly not settled. Nor, for that matter, have I considered the argument that justice may permit, if not require, these programs as a way to provide compensation or reparation for injuries suffered in the recent as well as distant past, or as a way to remove benefits that are undeservedly enjoyed by those of the dominant group. What I have tried to do is show that it is wrong to think that programs of preferential treatment are objectionable in the centrally important sense in which many past and present discriminatory features of our society have been and are racist and sexist. The social realities as to power and opportunity do make a fundamental difference. It is also wrong to think that programs of preferential treatment could, therefore, plausibly rest both on the view that such programs are not unfair to white males (except in the weak, rule-dependent sense described above) and on the view that it is unfair to continue the present set of unjust—often racist and sexist—institutions that comprise the social reality. And the case for these programs could rest as well on the proposition that, given the distribution of power and influence in the United States today, such programs may reasonably be viewed as potentially valuable, effective means by which to achieve admirable and significant social ideals of equality and integration.

Questions for Analysis

1. What does it mean to claim that proponents of preferential treatment are guilty of "intellectual inconsistency"?

2. Do you think that Wasserstrom convincingly refutes this charge? Would Kant accept his rationale?

3. What moral principle (or principles) underlies Wasserstrom's objection to slavery?

4. How does Wasserstrom respond to the charge that preferential-treatment programs comprise the only thing that really matters: individual qualifications?

5. Describe the inconsistency present for the person who favors "pure qualifications" on grounds of maximum efficiency.

6. Do you agree that there is no necessary connection between qualifications and desert?

7. Do you think Wasserstrom's tennis analogy is a sound one?

8. *Would it be accurate to say that Wasserstrom unequivocally supports preferential-treatment programs? Explain.*

Reverse Discrimination and Compensatory Justice

William T. Blackstone

In this essay, philosophy professor William T. Blackstone is concerned with a single question: Is reverse discrimination ever justified on grounds of repairing past wrongs done to women and minorities? Blackstone thinks not. In his view, reverse discrimination cannot be so justified either morally or legally.

Blackstone builds his case primarily on a utilitarian foundation. He believes that more harm than good would result from a systematic policy of reverse discrimination. (Curiously, as he points out, reverse discrimination often is justified on an appeal to utility.) Since reverse discrimination is not justified on utilitarian or justice-regarding grounds, Blackstone concludes that compensation through reverse discrimination is not justifiable. Indeed, he argues that affirmative-action programs, despite how they have sometimes been implemented, not only oppose reverse discrimination but forbid it.

Is reverse discrimination justified as a policy of compensation or of preferential treatment for women and racial minorities? That is, given the fact that women and racial minorities have been invidiously discriminated against in the past on the basis of the irrelevant characteristics of race and sex—are we now justified in discriminating in their favor on the basis of the same characteristics? This is a central ethical and legal question today, and it is one which is quite unresolved. Philosophers, jurists, legal scholars, and the man-in-the-street line up on both sides of this issue. These differences are plainly reflected (in the Supreme Court's majority opinion and Justice Douglas's dissent) in *DeFunis* v. *Odegaard*.[1] . . .

I will argue that reverse discrimination is improper on both moral and constitutional grounds, though I focus more on moral grounds. However, I do this with considerable ambivalence, even "existential guilt." Several reasons lie behind that ambivalence. First, there are moral and constitutional arguments on both sides. The ethical waters are very muddy and I simply argue that the balance

of the arguments are against a policy of reverse discrimination.[2] My ambivalence is further due not only to the fact that traditional racism is still a much larger problem than that of reverse discrimination but also because I am sympathetic to the *goals* of those who strongly believe that reverse discrimination as a policy is the means to overcome the debilitating effects of past injustice. Compensation and remedy are most definitely required both by the facts and by our value commitments. But I do not think that reverse discrimination is the proper means of remedy or compensation. . . .

I

Let us now turn to the possibility of a utilitarian justification of reverse discrimination and to the possible conflict of justice-regarding reasons and those of social utility on this issue. The category of morally relevant reasons is broader, in my opinion, than reasons related to the norm of justice. It is broader than those related to the norm of utility. Also it seems to me that the norms of justice and

Reprinted from Social Justice and Preferential Treatment *by permission of The University of Georgia Press.* © *1977 by The University of Georgia Press.*

utility are not reducible one to the other. We cannot argue these points of ethical theory here. But, if these assumptions are correct, then it is at least possible to morally justify injustice or invidious discrimination in some contexts. A case would have to be made that such injustice, though regrettable, will produce the best consequences for society and that this fact is an overriding or weightier moral reason than the temporary injustice. Some arguments for reverse discrimination have taken this line. Professor Thomas Nagel argues that such discrimination is justifiable as long as it is "clearly contributing to the eradication of great social evils."[3] . . .

Another example of what I would call a utilitarian argument for reverse discrimination was recently set forth by Congressman Andrew Young of Georgia. Speaking specifically of reverse discrimination in the context of education, he stated: "While that may give minorities a little edge in some instances, and you may run into the danger of what we now commonly call reverse discrimination, I think the educational system needs this. Society needs this as much as the people we are trying to help . . . a society working toward affirmative action and inclusiveness is going to be a stronger and more relevant society than one that accepts the limited concepts of objectivity. . . . I would admit that it is perhaps an individual injustice. But it might be necessary in order to overcome an historic group injustice or series of group injustices."[4] Congressman Young's basic justifying grounds for reverse discrimination, which he recognizes as individual injustice, are the results which he thinks it will produce: a stronger and more relevant education system and society, and one which is more just overall. His argument may involve pitting some justice-regarding reasons (the right of women and racial minorities to be compensated for past injustices) against others (the right of the majority to the uniform application of the same standards of merit to all). But a major thrust of his argument also seems to be utilitarian.

Just as there are justice-regarding arguments on both sides of the issue of reverse discrimination, so also there are utilitarian arguments on both sides. In a nutshell, the utilitarian argument in favor runs like this: Our society contains large groups of persons who suffer from past institutionalized injustice. As a result, the possibilities of social discord and disorder are high indeed. If short-term reverse discrimination were to be effective in overcoming the effects of past institutionalized injustice and if this policy could alleviate the causes of disorder and bring a higher quality of life to millions of persons, then society as a whole would benefit.

There are moments in which I am nearly convinced by this argument, but the conclusion that such a policy would have negative utility on the whole wins out. For although reverse discrimination might appear to have the effect of getting more persons who have been disadvantaged by past inequities into the mainstream quicker, that is, into jobs, schools, and practices from which they have been excluded, the cost would be invidious discrimination against majority group members of society. I do not think that majority members of society would find this acceptable, i.e., the disadvantaging of themselves for past inequities which they did not control and for which they are not responsible. If such policies were put into effect by government, I would predict wholesale rejection or noncooperation, the result of which would be negative not only for those who have suffered past inequities but also for the justice-regarding institutions of society. Claims and counter-claims would obviously be raised by other ethnic or racial minorities—by Chinese, Chicanos, American Indians, Puerto Ricans—and by orphans, illegitimate children, ghetto residents, and so on. Literally thousands of types or groups could, on similar grounds as blacks or women, claim that reverse discrimination is justified on their behalf. What would happen if government attempted policies of reverse discrimination for all such groups? It would mean the arbitrary exclusion or discrimination against all others relative to a given purpose and a given group. Such a policy would itself create an injustice for which those newly excluded persons could then, themselves, properly claim the need for reverse discrimination to offset the injustice to them. The circle is plainly a vicious one. Such policies are simply self-destructive. In place of the ideal of equality and distributive justice based on relevant criteria, we would be left with the special pleading of self-interested power groups, groups who gear criteria for the distribution of goods, services, and opportunities to their special needs and situations, primarily. Such policies would be those of special privilege, not the appeal to objective criteria which apply *and unflinching implementation of these means will satisfy the obligation to eradicate discrimination?*

9. *Explain the following statement: "Kant would agree with Blackstone's conclusion about reverse discrimination, but he would question the moral legitimacy of at least some of Blackstone's premises."*

...rse Discrimination as Unjustified

...ewton

Professor of philosophy Lisa Newton delivered a version of the following essay at a meeting of the Society for Women in Philosophy in 1972. She argues that reverse discrimination cannot be justified by an appeal to the ideal of equality. Indeed, according to Newton, reverse discrimination does not advance but actually undermines equality because it violates the concept of equal justice under law for all citizens.

Specifically, Newton attacks the defense for reverse discrimination on grounds of equality. She contends that no violation of justice can be justified by an appeal to the ideal of equality, for the idea of equality is logically dependent on the notion of justice.

In addition to this theoretical objection to reverse discrimination, Newton opposes it because she believe it raises insoluble problems. Among them are: determining what groups have been sufficiently discriminated against in the past to deserve preferred treatment in the present, and determining the degree of reverse discrimination that will be compensatory. Newton concludes that reverse discrimination destroys justice, law, equality, and citizenship itself.

...heard it argued that "simple justice" requires ...e favor women and blacks in employment ...lucational opportunities, since women and ...were "unjustly" excluded from such oppor-...s for so many years in the not so distant past. ...strange argument, an example of a possible ...ation of a true proposition advanced to dis-...e proposition itself, like an octopus absent-...dly slicing off his head with a stray tentacle. ...confusion underlies this argument, a con-...fundamentally relevant to our understand-...the notion of the rule of law.

...vo senses of justice and equality are involved ...confusion. The root notion of justice, pro-...r of the other, is the one that Aristotle ...achean Ethics 5. 6; Politics 1.2; 3.1) assumes to ...foundation and proper virtue of the political ...ation. It is the conclusion which free men

establish among themselves when they "share a common life in order that their association bring them self-sufficiency"—the regulation of their relationship by law, and the establishment, by law, of equality before the law. Rule of law is the name and pattern of this justice; its equality stands against the inequalities—of wealth, talent, etc.—otherwise obtaining among its participants, who by virtue of that equality are called "citizens." It is an achievement—complete, or, more frequently, partial—of certain people in certain concrete situations. It is fragile and easily disrupted by powerful individuals who discover that the blind equality of rule of law is inconvenient for their interests. Despite its obvious instability, Aristotle assumed that the establishment of justice in this sense, the creation of citizenship, was a permanent possibility for men and that the resultant association of citizens was

to all.[5] They would lead to social chaos, not social justice.

Furthermore, in cases in which reverse discrimination results in a lowering of quality, the consequences for society, indeed for minority victims of injustice for which reverse discrimination is designed to help, may be quite bad. It is no easy matter to calculate this, but the recent report sponsored by the Carnegie Commission on Higher Education points to such deleterious consequences.[6] If the quality of instruction in higher education, for example, is lowered through a policy of primary attention to race or sex as opposed to ability and training, everyone—including victims of past injustice—suffers. Even if such policies are clearly seen as temporary with quite definite deadlines for termination, I am skeptical about their utilitarian value. . . .

II

The inappropriateness of reverse discrimination, both on utilitarian and justice-regarding grounds, in no way means that compensation for past injustices is inappropriate. It does not mean that those who have suffered past injustices and who have been disadvantaged by them are not entitled to compensation or that they have no moral right to remedy. It may be difficult in different contexts to translate that moral right to remedy into practice or into legislation. When has a disadvantaged person or group been compensated enough? What sort of allocation of resources will compensate without creating additional inequities or deleterious consequences? There is no easy answer to these questions. Decisions must be made in particular contexts. Furthermore, it may be the case that the effects of past injustices are so severe (poverty, malnutrition, and the denial of educational opportunities) that genuine compensation—the balancing of the scales—is impossible. The effects of malnutrition or the lack of education are often nonreversible (and would be so even under a policy of reverse discrimination). This is one of the tragedies of injustice. But if reverse discrimination is inappropriate as a means of compensation and if (as I have argued) it is unjust to make persons who are not responsible for the suffering and disadvantaging of others to suffer for those past injuries, then

other means must be employed unless overriding moral considerations of another type (utilitarian) can be clearly demonstrated. That compensation must take a form which is consistent with our constitutional principles and with reasonable principles of justice. Now it seems to me that the Federal Government's Equal Opportunity and Affirmative Action programs are consistent with these principles, that they are not only not committed to reverse discrimination but rather absolutely forbid it.[7] However, it also seems to me that some officials authorized or required to implement these compensatory efforts have resorted to reverse discrimination and hence have violated the basic principles of justice embodied in these programs. I now want to argue both of these points: first, that these federal programs reject reverse discrimination in their basic principles; secondly, that some implementers of these programs have violated their own principles.

Obviously our country has not always been committed constitutionally to equality. We need no review of our social and political heritage to document this. But with the Fourteenth Amendment, equality as a principle was given constitutional status. Subsequently, social, political, and legal practices changed radically and they will continue to do so. The Fourteenth Amendment declares that states are forbidden to deny any person life, liberty, or property without due process of law or to deny to any person the equal protection of the laws. In my opinion the principles of the Equal Opportunity and Affirmative Action Programs reflect faithfully this constitutional commitment. I am more familiar with those programs as reflected in universities. In this context they require that employers "recruit, hire, train, and promote persons in all job classifications without regard to race, color, religion, sex or national origin, except where sex is a bona fide occupational qualification."[8] They state explicitly that "goals may not be rigid and inflexible quotas which must be met, but must be targets reasonably attainable by means of good faith effort."[9] They require the active recruitment of women and racial minorities where they are "underutilized," this being defined as a context in which there are "fewer minorities or women in a particular job classification than would reasonably be expected by their availability."[10] This is sometimes difficult to determine; but some relevant facts do exist and hence the meaning of a "good faith" effort is not

...sa H. Newton, "Reverse Discrimination as Unjustified," Ethics 83 (1973): 308–12. Copyright © 1973 by The University of ... Press. Reprinted by permission of the publisher and the author.

entirely fluid. In any event the Affirmative Action Program in universities requires that "goals, time-tables and affirmative action commitment, must be designed to correct any identifiable deficiencies," with separate goals and timetables for minorities and women.[11] It recognizes that there has been blatant discrimination against women and racial minorities in universities and elsewhere, and it assumes that there are "identifiable deficiencies." But it does not require that blacks be employed because they are black or women employed because they are women; that is, it does not require reverse discrimination with rigid quotas to correct the past. It requires a good faith effort in the present based on data on the availability of qualified women and racial minorities in various disciplines and other relevant facts. (Similar requirements hold, of course, for non-academic employment at colleges and universities.) It does not mandate the hiring of the unqualified or a lowering of standards; it mandates only equality of opportunity for all which, given the history of discrimination against women and racial minorities, requires affirmative action in recruitment.

Now if this affirmative action in recruitment, which is not only consistent with but required by our commitment to equality and social justice, is translated into rigid quotas and reverse discrimination by those who implement equal opportunity and affirmative action programs in the effort to get results immediately—and there is no doubt in my mind that this has occurred—then such action violates the principles of these programs.

This violation—this inconsistency of principle and practice—occurs, it seems to me, when employers hire with *priority emphasis* on race, sex, or minority-group status. This move effectively eliminates others from the competition. It is like pretending that everyone is in the game from the beginning while all the while certain persons are systematically excluded. This is exactly what happened recently when a judge declared that a certain quota or number of women were to be employed by a given agency regardless of their qualifications for the job,[12] when some public school officials fired a white coach in order to hire a black one,[13] when a DeFunis is excluded from law school on racial grounds, and when colleges or universities announce that normal academic openings will give preference to female candidates or those from racial minorities.

If reverse discrimination is prohibited by our constitutional and ethical commitments, what means of remedy and compensation are available? Obviously, those means which are consistent with those commitments. Our commitments assure the right to remedy to those who have been treated unjustly, but our government has not done enough to bring this right to meaningful fruition in practice. Sound progress has been made in recent years, especially since the Equal Employment Opportunity Act of 1972 and the establishment of the Equal Employment Opportunities Commission. This Act and other laws have extended anti-discrimination protection to over 60% of the population.[14] The Commission is now authorized to enforce anti-discrimination orders in court and, according to one report, it has negotiated out-of-court settlements which brought 44,000 minority workers over 46 million dollars in back pay.[15] Undoubtedly this merely scratches the surface. But now the framework exists for translating the right to remedy into practice, not just for sloughing off race and sex as irrelevant criteria of differential treatment but other irrelevant criteria as well—age, religion, the size of hips (I am thinking of airline stewardesses), the length of nose, and so on.

Adequate remedy to overcome the sins of the past, not to speak of the present, would require the expenditure of vast sums for compensatory programs for those disadvantaged by past injustice in order to assure equal access. Such programs should be racially and sexually neutral, benefiting the disadvantaged of *whatever sex or race.* Such neutral compensatory programs would have a high proportion of blacks and other minorities as recipients, for they as members of these groups suffer more from the injustices of the past. But the basis of the compensation would be that fact, not sex or race. Neutral compensatory policies have definite theoretical and practical advantages in contrast to policies of reverse discrimination: Theoretical advantages, in that they are consistent with our basic constitutional and ethical commitments whereas reverse discrimination is not; practical advantages, in that their consistency, indeed their requirement by our constitutional and ethical commitments, means that they can marshal united

support in overcoming inequalities whereas reverse discrimination, in my opinion, can not.

Notes

1. 94 S. Ct. 1704 (1974).

2. I hasten to add a qualification—more ambivalence!—resulting from discussion with Tom Beauchamp of Georgetown University. In cases of extreme recalcitrance to equal employment by certain institutions or businesses some quota requirements (reverse discrimination) may be justified. I regard this as distinct from a general policy of reverse discrimination.

3. "Equal Treatment and Compensatory Discrimination," *Philosophy and Public Affairs,* 2 (Summer 1974).

4. *Atlanta Journal and Constitution,* Sept. 22, 1974, p. 20-A.

5. For similar arguments see Lisa Newton, "Reverse Discrimination as Unjustified," *Ethics,* 83 (1973).

6. Richard A. Lester, *Antibias Regulation of Universities* (New York, 1974); discussed in *Newsweek,* July 15, 1974, p. 78.

7. See The Civil Rights Act of 1964, especially Title VII (which created the Equal Employment Opportunity Commission), amended by The Equal

Employment Opportunity Act of
ABC's of The Equal Employment Op
pared by the Editorial Staff of Th
National Affairs, Inc., 1972. Affir
Programs came into existence wi
Order 11246. Requirements for a
are found in the rules and regula
60-2, Order #4 (Affirmative Acti
erally known as Executive Order
Order #4 41-CFT 60-2 B. For dis
Brownstein, "Affirmative Action
Equal Employment Opportunities C
ing Law Institute, New York Cit
73–111.

8. See Brownstein, "Affirmative A(
and, for example, *The University*
tive Action Plan, Athens, Ga., 19
133, 67.

9. Brownstein and *The University o*
Action Plan, Athens, Ga., 1973–

10. *Ibid.,* p. 69.

11. *Ibid.,* p. 71.

12. See the *Atlanta Journal and Const*
1974, p. 26-D.

13. See *Atlanta Constitution,* June 7,

14. *Newsweek,* June 17, 1974, p. 75.

15. *Ibid.,* p. 75.

Questions for Analysis

1. *Why does Blackstone argue his case with a certain amount of "existential guilt"?*

2. *State the utilitarian argument for reverse discrimination.*

3. *Would it be accurate to say that Blackstone rejects utility as a legitimate standard for determining the morality of reverse discrimination?*

4. *Consider this proposition: "Blackstone is opposed to compensating those who have suffered past injustices." Is this statement true or false? Explain.*

5. *What are some of the problems that compensation raises?*

6. *Some people would claim that it is wrong to hold people today responsible for the wrongs of their ancestors and that it is equally as wrong to compensate people today for the wrongs their ancestors may have experienced. Do you agree? Explain your answers by appeal to some concept of justice.*

7. *What reasons does Blackstone offer for saying that affirmative-action programs actually forbid reverse discrimination? Do you think his argument is persuasive? What objections to his interpretations might you raise?*

8. *Granted that reverse discrimination is prohibited by our constitution and ethical commitments, what means of redress are available? Do you agree that a vigorous*

Re

Lis

I ha\
that
and
blac
tuni
It is
imp
pute
min
A fa
fusic
ing c

in th
geni
(Nicc
be th
assoc

From
Chica

the natural home of the species. At levels below the political association, this rule-governed equality is easily found; it is exemplified by any group of children agreeing together to play a game. At the level of the political association, the attainment of this justice is more difficult, simply because the stakes are so much higher for each participant. The equality of citizenship is not something that happens of its own accord, and without the expenditure of a fair amount of effort it will collapse into the rule of a powerful few over an apathetic many. But at least it has been achieved, at some times in some places; it is always worth trying to achieve, and eminently worth trying to maintain, wherever and to whatever degree it has been brought into being.

Aristotle's parochialism is notorious; he really did not imagine that persons other than Greeks could associate freely in justice, and the only form of association he had in mind was the Greek *polis.* With the decline of the *polis* and the shift in the center of political thought, his notion of justice underwent a sea change. To be exact, it ceased to represent a political type and became a moral ideal: the ideal of equality as we know it. This ideal demands that all men be included in citizenship— that one Law govern all equally, that all men regard all other men as fellow citizens, with the same guarantees, rights, and protections. Briefly, it demands that the circle of citizenship achieved by any group be extended to include the entire human race. Properly understood, its effect on our associations can be excellent: It congratulates us on our achievement of rule of law as a process of government but refuses to let us remain complacent until we have expanded the associations to include others within the ambit of the rules, as often and as far as possible. While one man is a slave, none of us may feel truly free. We are constantly prodded by this ideal to look for possible unjustifiable discrimination, for inequalities not absolutely required for the functioning of the society and advantageous to all. And after twenty centuries of pressure, not at all constant, from this ideal, it might be said that some progress has been made. To take the cases in point for this problem, we are now prepared to assert, as Aristotle would never have been, the equality of sexes and of persons of different colors. The ambit of American citizenship, once restricted to white males of property, has been extended to

include all adult free men, then all adult males including ex-slaves, then all women. The process of acquisition of full citizenship was for these groups a sporadic trail of half-measures, even now not complete; the steps on the road to full equality are marked by legislation and judicial decisions which are only recently concluded and still often not enforced. But the fact that we can now discuss the possibility of favoring such groups in hiring shows that over the area that concerns us, at least, full equality is presupposed as a basis for discussion. To that extent, they are full citizens, fully protected by the law of the land.

It is important for my argument that the moral ideal of equality be recognized as logically distinct from the condition (or virtue) of justice in the political sense. Justice in this sense exists *among* a citizenry, irrespective of the number of the populace included in that citizenry. Further, the moral ideal is parasitic upon the political virtue, for "equality" is unspecified—it means nothing until we are told in what respect that equality is to be realized. In a political context, "equality" is specified as "equal rights"—equal access to the public realm, public goods and offices, equal treatment under the law— in brief, the equality of citizenship. If citizenship is not a possibility, political equality is unintelligible. The ideal emerges as a generalization of the real condition and refers back to that condition for its content.

Now, if justice (Aristotle's justice in the political sense) is equal treatment under law for all citizens, what is injustice? Clearly, injustice is the violation of that equality, discrimination for or against a group of citizens, favoring them with special immunities and privileges or depriving them of those guaranteed to the others. When the southern employer refuses to hire blacks in white-collar jobs, when Wall Street will only hire women as secretaries with new titles, when Mississippi high schools routinely flunk all the black boys above ninth grade, we have examples of injustice, and we work to restore the equality of the public realm by ensuring that equal opportunity will be provided in such cases in the future. But of course, when the employers and the schools *favor* women and blacks, the same injustice is done. Just as the previous discrimination did, this reverse discrimination violates the public equality which defines citizenship and destroys the rule of law for the areas in which these favors are granted. To the extent that we adopt a program of discrimination, reverse or otherwise, justice in the political sense is destroyed, and none of us, specifically affected or not, is a citizen, a bearer of rights—we are all petitioners for favors. And to the same extent, the ideal of equality is undermined, for it has content only where justice obtains, and by destroying justice we render the ideal meaningless. It is, then, an ironic paradox, if not a contradiction in terms, to assert that the ideal of equality justifies the violation of justice; it is as if one should argue, with William Buckley, that an ideal of humanity can justify the destruction of the human race.

Logically, the conclusion is simple enough: All discrimination is wrong prima facie because it violates justice, and that goes for reverse discrimination too. No violation of justice among the citizens may be justified (may overcome the prima facie objection) by appeal to the ideal of equality, for that ideal is logically dependent upon the notion of justice. Reverse discrimination, then, which attempts no other justification than an appeal to equality, is wrong. But let us try to make the conclusion more plausible by suggesting some of the implications of the suggested practice of reverse discrimination in employment and education. My argument will be that the problems raised there are insoluble, not only in practice but in principle.

We may argue, if we like, about what "discrimination" consists of. Do I discriminate against blacks if I admit none to my school when none of the black applicants are qualified by the tests I always give? How far must I go to root out cultural bias from my application forms and tests before I can say that I have not discriminated against those of different cultures? Can I assume that women are not strong enough to be roughnecks on my oil rigs, or must I test them individually? But this controversy, the most popular and well-argued aspect of the issue, is not as fatal as two others which cannot be avoided: If we are regarding the blacks as a "minority" victimized by discrimination, what is a "minority"? And for any group—blacks, women, whatever—that has been discriminated against, what amount of reverse discrimination wipes out the initial discrimination? Let us grant as true that women and blacks were discriminated against, even where laws forbade such discrimination, and grant for the sake of argument that a history of discrimination must

be wiped out by reverse discrimination. What follows?

First, are there other groups which have been discriminated against? For they should have the same right of restitution. What about American Indians, Chicanos, Appalachian Mountain whites, Puerto Ricans, Jews, Cajuns, and Orientals? And if these are to be included, the principle according to which we specify a "minority" is simply the criterion of "ethnic (sub) group," and we're stuck with every hyphenated American in the lower middle class clamoring for special privileges for *his* group— and with equal justification. For be it noted, when we run down the Harvard roster, we find not only a scarcity of blacks (in comparison with the proportion in the population) but an even more striking scarcity of those second-, third-, and fourth-generation ethnics who make up the loudest voice of Middle America. Shouldn't they demand *their* share? And eventually, the WASPs will have to form their own lobby; for they too are a minority. The point is simply this: There is no "majority" in America who will not mind giving up just a bit of their rights to make room for a favored minority. There are only other minorities, each of which is discriminated against by the favoring. The initial injustice is then repeated dozens of times, and if each minority is granted the same right of restitution as the others, an entire area of rule governance is dissolved into a pushing and shoving match between self-interested groups. Each works to catch the public eye and political popularity by whatever means of advertising and power politics lend themselves to the effort, to capitalize as much as possible on temporary popularity until the restless mob picks another group to feel sorry for. Hardly an edifying spectacle, and in the long run no one can benefit: The pie is no larger—it's just that instead of setting up and enforcing rules for getting a piece, we've turned the contest into a free-for-all, requiring much more effort for no larger a reward. It would be in the interests of all the participants to reestablish an objective rule to govern the process, carefully enforced and the same for all.

Second, supposing that we do manage to agree in general that women and blacks (and all the others) have some right of restitution, some right to a privileged place in the structure of opportunities for a while, how will we know when that while is up? How much privilege is enough? When will the guilt be gone, the price paid, the balance restored? What recompense is right for centuries of exclusion? What criterion tells us when we are done? Our experience with the Civil Rights movement shows us that agreement on these terms cannot be presupposed: A process that appears to some to be going at a mad gallop into a black takeover appears to the rest of us to be at a standstill. Should a practice of reverse discrimination be adopted, we may safely predict that just as some of us begin to see "a satisfactory start toward righting the balance," others of us will see that we "have already gone too far in the other direction" and will suggest that the discrimination ought to be reversed again. And such disagreement is inevitable, for the point is that we could not *possibly* have any criteria for evaluating the kind of recompense we have in mind. The context presumed by any discussion of restitution is the context of the rule of law: Law sets the rights of men and simultaneously sets the method for remedying the violation of those rights. You may exact suffering from others and/or damage payments for yourself if and only if the others have violated your rights; the suffering you have endured is not sufficient reason for them to suffer. And remedial rights exist only where there is law: Primary human rights are useful guides to legislation but cannot stand as reasons for awarding remedies for injuries sus-

tained. But then, the context presupposed by any discussion of restitution is the context of preexistent full citizenship. No remedial rights could exist for the excluded; neither in law nor in logic does there exist a right to *sue* for a standing to sue.

From these two considerations, then, the difficulties with reverse discrimination become evident. Restitution for a disadvantaged group whose rights under the law have been violated is possible by legal means, but restitution for a disadvantaged group whose grievance is that there was no law to protect them simply is not. First, outside of the area of justice defined by the law, no sense can be made of "the group's rights," for no law recognizes that group or the individuals in it, qua members, as bearers of rights (hence *any* group can constitute itself as a disadvantaged minority in some sense and demand similar restitution). Second, outside of the area of protection of law, no sense can be made of the violation of rights (hence the amount of the recompense cannot be decided by any objective criterion). For both reasons, the practice of reverse discrimination undermines the foundation of the very ideal in whose name it is advocated; it destroys justice, law, equality, and citizenship itself, and replaces them with power struggles and popularity contests.

Questions for Analysis

1. What is the "fatal confusion" underlying the argument that "simple justice" requires preferential treatment?

2. Can you describe how justice under Aristotle moved from a "political type" to a "moral ideal"?

3. Why is it important for Newton's argument that she distinguish the moral ideal of equality from the condition of justice in the political sense?

4. Central to Newton's argument is her definition of justice and her assumptions about the relationship between justice and equality. Do you agree with her? Would you say her views are essentially Kantian?

5. Do you think Rawls would agree with Newton's analysis? Explain.

6. Would you agree that in part Newton objects to reverse discrimination on utilitarian grounds? Explain.

7. Do you agree that the problems Newton says surround reverse discrimination really are "insoluble"?

CASE PRESENTATION
Brian Weber

From its beginning in 1958, the Kaiser Aluminum plant in Grammercy, Louisiana, had very few black workers. By 1965, Kaiser had hired only 4.7 percent blacks, although 39 percent of the local work force were black. As of 1970, none of Kaiser's fifty professional employees was black; of 132 supervisors, one was black; of 146 skilled craft workers, none was black. In the fifteen years between 1958 and 1973, Kaiser had allowed several whites with no prior craft experience to transfer into skilled craft positions, whereas blacks were required to have at least five years' prior craft experience before being permitted to transfer. But getting this experience was difficult, since blacks were largely excluded from craft unions. As a result, only 2 percent of Grammercy's skilled craft workers were black.

A federal review in 1975 found things at Grammercy basically unchanged. 2.2 percent of its 290 craft workers and 7 percent of its professional employees were black. No blacks were among its eleven draftsmen. Although the percentage of blacks in Grammercy's overall work force had increased to 13.3, the local labor force remained constant at 39 percent black. Only the lowest-paying category of workers, so-called unskilled workers, included a large proportion of blacks, 35.5 percent, a proportion brought about by Kaiser's implementing a 1968 policy of hiring one black unskilled worker for every white unskilled worker.

As an upshot of these racial disparities in the allocation of jobs, federal agencies started pressuring Kaiser to employ more blacks in its better-paying skilled craft position. At the same time, the United Steelworkers Union was pressing Kaiser to institute programs for training its own workers in the crafts, instead of hiring all craft workers from outside the company. In response to both pressures, Kaiser set up a training program intended to qualify its own white and black workers for agreed-to craft positions. Under the program, Kaiser would pay for the training of its own workers who would be selected for the program on the basis of seniority. One-half of the training slots would be set aside for blacks until the percentage of black skilled craft workers at Grammercy approximated the percentage of blacks in the local labor force. Openings in the programs would be filled by alternating between the most senior qualified white employee and the most senior qualified black employee.

Thirteen workers—seven blacks and six whites—were selected during the first year of the program. Brian Weber, a young, white, semiskilled worker at Grammercy, was not among those selected, although he'd applied. Upon investigation, Weber discovered that he, in fact, had several months' more seniority than two of the blacks who had been admitted into the training program. Indeed, forty-three other white workers who had applied for the program and had been rejected had even more seniority than Weber. The conclusion was unmistakable:

Junior black employees were receiving training in preference to more senior white employees. Weber didn't think this was fair, especially since none of the blacks admitted to the program had themselves been discriminated against by Kaiser during their prior employment.

Weber decided to sue Kaiser. The case was eventually heard by the U.S. Supreme Court, which ruled that Kaiser's affirmative-action program didn't violate the Civil Rights Act of 1964.

Questions for Analysis

1. *Do you think Kaiser's preferential treatment program was fair? Explain in terms of ethical principles and concepts of justice.*

2. *Do you think Weber was treated unfairly, as he claimed? Defend your response on the basis of the moral principles you think are involved.*

3. *Companies frequently use seniority as the sole or primary basis of promotions or, as in Kaiser's case, for admission into training programs. Do you think this is fair? (Seniority generally refers to longevity on a job or with a company.)*

CASE PRESENTATION
First Hired, First Fired?

Marvin Alcott knew it was foolish. But as a personnel director faced with a sticky decision, he couldn't help wishing that Frank Stimson were anything but a white male.

Things had been going so well with the firm's pilot program for training the hard-core unemployed for positions as assistant machinists. Just a month before, Alcott had placed sixteen workers in the program, one of whom—indeed the first—was Frank Stimson. Having been out of work for the better part of a year and having no specific skills, Stimson had easily met the program's minimal qualifications for training.

A number of things about Stimson had impressed Alcott. It seemed that since returning from his two-year stint in Vietnam, Stimson had found nothing but tough employment sledding. In fact, as Stimson told it, if it hadn't been for the meager income his wife earned waitressing, he would have had to apply for welfare, something he strongly objected to on principle. As Stimson had said in the interview, "I was brought up to believe that you should carry your own weight. Anything less was being a leech, if you know what I mean." Then Stimson had explained how he didn't think it was right to expect society to bear the burden of what he termed a "misspent youth." Stimson had put it quite graphically:

"Why should I expect others to pay for my screw-ups?" Predictably enough, when Alcott informed Stimson that he was the first trainee to be selected, Stimson was elated and expressed every desire to seize this opportunity to make something of himself.

Alcott chuckled on the first day of training when Stimson showed up for work a half-hour before the prescribed time. He appreciated Stimson's enthusiasm, especially since it contrasted sharply with the apparent indifference of some of the other trainees.

After the first week of training, several instructors went out of their way to compliment Alcott on his selection of Stimson, while at the same time indicating that they'd had to admonish several other employees for being tardy, nonchalant, and generally uninterested in the opportunity the program was providing them.

It's little wonder, then, that Marvin Alcott considered Frank Stimson his top job trainee. This is precisely what made the decision he faced so painful.

It seems that when the firm launched the program, it did so with the government's implicit promise to fund sixteen positions. When the grant was actually issued, it covered only fifteen trainees. Alcott was faced with having to drop one.

Being a thoughtful, sensitive, and fair man, Alcott was trying to determine the most equitable way to manage the cut. One possibility was a lottery. He'd simply put the names of the candidates into a hat and draw one to be dropped. He had also considered making the drop on the basis of apparent job potential. But whatever method he contemplated, Alcott was haunted by the fact that Stimson was a white male. The other fifteen trainees were women and members of minority groups, and Alcott was keenly aware of affirmative-action guidelines that prescribed benefits for members of traditionally disadvantaged groups. In short, there was a real question in his mind whether he'd endanger the entire program should he decide to drop one of the fifteen disadvantaged members.

Above all else, Alcott wanted to be fair. There was no doubt in his mind that from what he and other company officials had observed, Stimson was the most promising trainee in the program. At the same time, he felt the press of fairness to members of groups traditionally discriminated against, which left him questioning the fairness of perhaps the most obvious solution: Drop the last selected.

Questions for Analysis

1. *What should Alcott do?*

2. *What moral directions do the ethical theories provide?*

3. *In the event that Alcott decides to drop Stimson, does he have an obligation to make a case to the firm for underwriting Stimson's training? Do you think the firm has a moral obligation to do this, or at least compensate Stimson in some way?*

Selections for Further Reading

Bittker, Boris. *The Case for Black Reparations.* New York: Random House, 1973.

Blackstone, William, and Robert Heslep. *Social Justice and Preferential Treatment.* Athens: University of Georgia Press, 1977.

Braggin, Mary; Frederick Elliston; and Jane English, eds. *Feminism and Philosophy,* Section 4. Totowa, N.J.: Littlefield, Adams, 1977.

Cohen, Marshall; Thomas Nagel; and Thomas Scanlon, eds. *Equality and Preferential Treatment.* Princeton, N.J.: Princeton University Press, 1976.

DeCrow, Karen. *Sexist Justice.* New York: Vintage, 1975.

Farley, J. *Affirmative Action and the Woman Worker.* New York: AMACOM, 1979.

Glazer, N. *Affirmative Discrimination: Ethnic Inequality and Public Policy.* New York: Basic Books, 1976.

Gross, Barry R., ed. *Reverse Discrimination.* Buffalo, N.Y.: Prometheus Press, 1977.

Livingston, John. *Fair Game.* San Francisco: W. H. Freeman, 1979.

Mill, John Stuart. *Essays on Sex Equality,* A. C. Rossi., ed. Chicago: University of Chicago Press, 1970.

8

WORLD HUNGER AND ECONOMIC JUSTICE

There is no question that much of the world population literally is starving to death. Recent figures estimate that at least 10,000 people die of starvation every day, that as many as 2 billion more are malnourished, that annually 14,000 children in India alone go blind because of insufficient protein. In short, two-thirds of the world's population is caught in a seemingly irreversible cycle of hunger-sickness-death.

We in the other one-third, in the West, are lucky. Rarely, if ever, do any of us directly experience the harsh fate of the world's starving masses. Fortunate to have been born in a land of plenty, we seldom realize that we feed our house pets each day enough protein to meet the daily nutritional needs of hundreds of thousands of people, that we throw away in one week more food than countless people will see in a year. Even for many who are aware of massive world starvation, the problem remains remote, even abstract. But to those facing starvation, the problem is not only real, immediate, and paramount, it also appears to have no resolution, except in death.

Given the disparity between those who have and those who have not, a moral question of considerable importance emerges: Do the affluent nations of the world have any moral obligation to help the world's starving masses? If we answer yes, then precisely how should these nations go about sharing their wealth? Stated in more global terms: How should the world's goods be distributed? This last question makes explicit the issue of economic justice, which is implied in the issue of moral obligation and world hunger.

In this chapter, then, we confront two questions of considerable moral importance. The first is whether the affluent nations have an obligation to help the starving nations; the second concerns the fairest distribution of the world's wealth. While these questions are distinct, they are not easily separated. Indeed, as we will see, many of the arguments for an obligation to help are rooted in a concept of economic justice. For this reason, we will consider first the issue of economic justice, then relate it to the problem of moral obligation and world hunger.

Initial Considerations

A number of moral problems cluster around the issues of world hunger and economic justice. Two in particular deserve careful study: the rights to property and liberty, and the causes of world hunger. Additional issues relate to the nature and form of proposed aid, including who will receive it and who should provide it.

Liberty and Property Rights

The belief in a body of rights that belong to all human beings is commonplace in our society and elsewhere. These "human" or "natural" rights are to be distinguished from rights derived from special agreements or restricted to particular groups of people. Whether we ascribe the universal character of these natural rights to God or human nature, or to the logical extension of our beliefs about human beings, there is no question that we talk of some rights as basic and universal.

The British philosopher John Locke (1632–1704) is generally credited with developing the idea that human beings have a natural right to liberty and a natural right to private property. Locke never used his theory of natural rights to argue for free markets (an economic system in which privately owned firms make their own decisions about what they will produce and how they will produce it, and exchange their goods with other firms and consumers at the most advantageous prices they can get), but a number of twentieth-century authors have. In general, they claim that given their natural rights to liberty and property, individuals must be left free to exchange their labor and property as they voluntarily choose. The free-market theorists argue further that only an economy of free private enterprise exchange allows for such voluntary transfers. In short, the existence of Lockean rights to liberty and property presumably implies that societies should include private-property institutions and free markets.

In a pure free-market system, no constraints would exist on the property you or I could own, on what we could choose to do with it, or on the voluntary exchanges we could make. But of course there are no pure free-market systems. Some things may not be owned—for example, slaves. Some things may not be done with property, such as polluting the environment. And some exchanges are not permitted, such as having young children do labor. But apart from such specific constraints, we are free to dispose of our own property as we choose and make exchanges voluntarily, and we typically view and defend these rights as a logical extension of the natural rights to liberty and private property.

In practice, then, the so-called natural rights to liberty and property serve as a basis for claiming that we can do with our holdings whatever we want that is not proscribed by law. If I choose to squander my wealth while others need it to survive, presumably I am free to do that. But am I, or better: Should I be? Is the property right so extensive? Many think not. They argue that my right to my holdings is limited by the satisfaction of the basic needs of other people. Yes, they say, I may do with my wealth whatever I choose, but only after the basic needs of others have been satisfied. But what "others" are intended? Relatives, friends, neighbors, fellow citizens, distant peoples, future generations? There's no easy answer to this question.

Related to our property rights is how we obtained our holdings. Many argue that if property rights exist, they apply only to what an owner has acquired legally and morally. Suppose a particular man is made wealthy by inheriting a fortune, much of which was amassed in the distant past through others' dishonesty and ruthless exploitation. While the man himself may be virtuous as a monk, his

same question may be asked about a nation's wealth acquired through years of dubious moral conduct. Does the nation, therefore, have no claim to its wealth, or no right to determine how it shall spend its riches? Indeed, how can we separate "clean" from "dirty" money in the first place?

Clearly the issue of how far property rights extend bears on the question of world hunger. For if I have an absolute right to dispose of my property however I choose—no matter the genesis of the holding—then seemingly I have no obligation to help the starving masses. But if that right is subordinate to the claims of those seeking to maintain themselves, then I could have an obligation to help. At issue here is the whole notion of Lockean rights—whether in fact such rights exist, and if so, what priority they warrant relative to other rights.

Criticisms of the Lockean natural rights to liberty and property, and by implication of the free-market defense based on it, have focused on several salient weaknesses, two of which concern us here. The first one relates to the assumption that individuals do, in fact, have natural rights. Do they? Critics claim that this assumption is unproven. Locke himself merely asserted that reason teaches all humankind who will consult it that the natural rights he recognizes do exist. Presumably they are self-evident; rational human beings supposedly can intuit that the rights to liberty and property exist. The problem is that plenty of rational humans have tried to intuit the existence of these rights and have failed.

The second criticism of Lockean natural rights concerns the conflict between these and other rights. Let's suppose for argument's sake that humans do have natural rights to liberty and property. Even so, it doesn't follow that these rights override all other rights.

Recall our earlier distinction between *negative* (freedom from) and *positive* (freedom to) freedoms (Chapter 1). A similar distinction can be made between rights in general. The rights to liberty and property are negative rights, which means they are solely defined in terms of the duties others have not to interfere in the activities of the person who holds these rights. But negative rights can conflict with positive rights, which impose on some party (it's not always clear whom) *positive duties* to provide the holder of the right with whatever he or she needs to freely pursue his or her interests. Thus the negative rights to liberty and property can easily conflict with someone else's positive right to food, medical care, housing, education, clean air, and so forth. Why must we believe that the negative rights of liberty and property override such positive rights? Some say we in fact shouldn't make such a glib assumption, and others go so far as to assert that positive rights like the aforementioned take precedence. In any event, it should be clear that a crucial question in discussions about feeding and caring for the world's needy is the nature and extent of liberty and property rights.

Causes of World Hunger

As indicated, the chief question that concerns us in this chapter is: Given the wide disparity between the living standards of the developed industrial countries and those of the underdeveloped agricultural or single-resource countries, should rich countries sacrifice some of their wealth for the benefit of the poorer ones? In answering this question, one crucial ethical variable is *responsibility*. Who is responsible for the famine and malnutrition in underdeveloped countries?

Some argue that since overpopulation is the cause of scarcity and people living in poor countries have failed to keep their populations under control, they themselves are primarily responsible for their plight. The key assumption here, and the one which many question, is that overpopulation is the sole cause of the scarcity leading to starvation.

Onora O'Neill, for one, has argued that the international business activities of many corporations have contributed at least partially to the grim conditions of some peoples. She points particularly to foreign-investment activities and commodity-pricing policies.

Regarding foreign investments, O'Neill hypothesizes a case in which a group of investors form a company that invests abroad, perhaps in a plantation or a mine. The investors so manage their affairs that a high level of profits goes back to their homeland, while laborers' wages are so minimal that the laborers' survival rate is reduced—in other words, their life expectancy is lower than it might have been had the company not invested there. It's true that in such a case the investors and company management don't act alone, are not the immediate causes of deaths, don't know in advance who will die, and don't intend the deaths. But they surely can't claim to be "uninvolved" the way a company with no investments there can. Indeed, they are helping set policies that determine the living standards, which in turn determine the survival rate. When people die because of the lowered standard of living established by a firm that dominates a local economy (either by limiting workers to employment on their terms or by reducing the prospects for employment through damaging traditional economic structures), and when these firms could either pay workers more or stay out of the area altogether, they seem to be directly responsible for the suffering and deaths that result.

Furthermore, even when a company investing in an underdeveloped country sets high wages and benefits, and raises the life expectancy of its workers, it often succeeds in combining these payments with high profitability only by achieving a tax-exempt status. This means the company is being subsidized by the general tax revenue of the underdeveloped economy. The company makes no contribution to the country's infrastructure—that is, to the roads, harbors, and airports that benefit it. "In this way," O'Neill writes, "many underdeveloped economies have come to include developed enclaves whose development is achieved in part at the expense of the poorer majority. In such cases, government and company policy combine to produce a high-wage sector at the expense of a low-wage sector; in consequence, some of the persons in the low-wage sector, who would not otherwise have died, may die. Those persons, whoever they may be, are killed and not merely allowed to die."[1] O'Neill concedes that such killings may be justifiable, perhaps if they are outnumbered by lives saved through having a developed society. Nonetheless, they are killings.

Then there are commodity-pricing cases. It's no secret that underdeveloped countries often depend largely on the price level of a few commodities. As a result, a precipitous drop in the world price of, say, coffee or sugar or cocoa could lower survival rates in these countries. Such drops sometimes result from factors beyond human control. But often they result from the action of investors, brokers, or government agencies. In such cases, these people or agencies are choosing policies that will kill some people, albeit not single-handedly, instantaneously, with forethought or intention.

Given the economic interdependence of countries, deaths can also result from dramatic *rises* in the prices of various commodities. Sharp increases in the international prices of essential foodstuffs such as wheat and other grains will be reflected in higher death rates among the world's poorest groups. Living on subsistence level diets to begin with, they simply lack the income to pay proportionately more for food. Where these price increases result directly from human agency, the people involved are responsible for the resulting starvation and deaths—deaths which, again, seem more properly termed killings. As before, some of these may be justifiable killings—for example, if the lives saved as a result of the pricing outnumbered those lost. Even so, they are killings.

The preceding analysis bears directly on the question of whether the rich nations have a moral obligation to help the poor ones. If, for example, one holds that those living in underdeveloped countries are themselves primarily responsible for their plight because they have failed to keep their populations under control, one has a basis, though it's not sufficient, for concluding: (1) those living in industrial countries are under no obligation to provide food, and possibly (2) it would be wrong to do so, inasmuch as such aid might encourage further overpopulation, which would put the world's resources at risk. (I have termed the bases insufficient because the assumption about overpopulation and who is responsible for it does not necessarily commit one to either of the two conclusions; one could still argue that no matter who's responsible, one is morally obliged to prevent or ease pain and suffering where one can with minor or insignificant sacrifice.)

But if variables other than overpopulation cause malnutrition and starvation, then a basis emerges for an obligation to help. Thus if through their international activities corporations are at least partially responsible for the dire conditions in certain underdeveloped countries, and since the economic chains linking U.S. multinational firms and the foreign policy of the U.S. government extend to U.S.

1.   Onora O'Neill, "Lifeboat Earth," *in* Ethical Theory and Business, *eds. Tom L. Beauchamp and Norman E. Bowie (Englewood Cliffs, N.J.: Prentice-Hall, 1979), p. 110.*

2.   *O'Neill, "Lifeboat Earth," p. 111.*

citizens, almost all of us are responsible for the deaths of famine victims. From which we might conclude: Our duty is to redirect the policy of the U.S. government and the multinational corporations.

Aid-Related Issues

What will happen if the affluent nations continue to feed the destitute nations? Many claim that the long-term results will spell catastrophe. These Neo-Malthusians,[3] as they are sometimes called, predict food relief will only swell the populations of nations already bursting with more people than they can support. By this account, food relief will increase the net suffering and deprivation not only of recipients but of donors as well. Not everyone agrees, however. Many claim that such dire forecasts are exaggerated. More important, as we've noted, they say such a horrifying outcome could result only if food relief is not coupled with developmental assistance aimed at improving productivity through modernizing agriculture.

All this raises a second issue concerning aid: If the rich nations have an obligation to help the poor ones, just what sort of help are they obliged to provide? It is possible to identify at least three kinds of aid that affluent nations such as the United States give to poor nations: (1) developmental assistance, to help underdeveloped countries educationally and technologically to accumulate capital and raise their standards of living; (2) emergency famine or disaster relief, given in the wake of natural disasters such as drought, flood, and earthquake; (3) relief for countries suffering chronic famine because their birth rate far exceeds their actual or potential productivity. If rich nations are obliged to help, just which, if any, kinds of aid are they obliged to provide?

Some would argue that affluent nations should give only emergency aid; others that they should give only emergency and developmental aid; still others that they should give all three. One common position among Neo-Malthusians is that rich nations should not provide any aid in the third category.

The issue of which kind of aid is to be given is clearly inseparable from the question of who should receive the aid. Perhaps we should dole out aid by *triage* (French for "sorting"), a method of allocating resources used first during World War I. Wounded soldiers were separated into three categories and allocated scarce medical resources on that basis. Those with superficial injuries were given immediate emergency attention; those with serious wounds who could be helped to survive were given the lion's share of intensive care; those beyond hope were allowed to die. Applied to the starving nations of the world, the method of triage might roughly classify the nations as: (1) those with slight food problems who will survive even without aid; (2) those with serious food problems who can benefit from help because they are ready to take steps to control their populations and increase their productivity; (3) those whose problems cannot be solved because they are not prepared to take any measures to help themselves. Given these

---

3.   *Named after the English economist John Malthus (1766–1834), who argued that population tends to increase faster than the means of subsistence, unless checked by such factors as war and famine.*

classifications, some would say, "Yes, affluent nations have an obligation to provide help, but only to those nations falling into categories 1 and 2." Indeed, they might and sometimes do argue that rich nations have an obligation *not* to help nations in category 3. Opposed to these positions are those who say the worst-off nations should receive immediate and massive aid. Such appears to be the United States' position. Of course, the question of who, if anyone, ought to receive help grows ever murkier as resources dwindle.

Finally, if there is an obligation to help, whose obligation is it? Is it the obligation of an individual, you and me personally? A nation, such as the United States? A group of nations, perhaps through an international organization such as the United Nations? Our discussion here of world hunger and economic justice focuses on possible obligations that richer nations have to poorer ones. But it is also perfectly reasonable to ask: Can a nation have obligations? Is it sensible to attribute rights, duties, and obligations to some disembodied entity called a nation? And if it is, to whom do nations have responsibilities and against whom do they have claims—other nations, individuals, a combination?

These are only some of the questions that make world hunger and economic justice extraordinarily complex issues. They are questions that can be investigated thoroughly only in a study of social philosophy. Given the narrow scope of our present study, we can merely draw these issues to the reader's attention and encourage a deeper investigation of them elsewhere.

International Economic Justice

Economic justice refers to what people deserve economically. The question of moral obligation regarding world hunger is inseparable from the issue of economic justice. To see why, consider this simple example.

Suppose you're walking down a big-city street with a friend. You're approached by a beggar who asks, "You got some change for a meal, pal?" You fish into your pocket for a couple of quarters and hand them to the man. He thanks you and moves on.

Your friend is outraged. "Why did you do that?" she asks you, in a most disapproving tone.

"Because the guy needed to eat," you reply.

"But the guy was a bum!" she points out. "Let him get a job, not a handout!"

Presumably you feel you have an obligation to help the beggar, but your friend does not. In fact, she seems to think she has an obligation *not* to help him. But notice the reasons behind these judgments, reasons that imply full-blown views on what people deserve economically. You feel the beggar deserves something simply because he *needs* it. Your friend believes you should not give the beggar anything because of the kind of person he is (a "bum") and because he has done nothing to help himself. For her, *need* is not as much a determinant of economic desert as are *merit* and *effort*. For both of you, economic justice is associated with some view of distributive justice.

Distributive Justice

The subject of economic desert touches numerous areas, from jobs to income to taxes to world resources. Thus questions of economic justice would include: How ought jobs be awarded? How should income and taxes be determined? What is the fairest way to allocate the wealth of the world? Any answer to these questions inevitably implies a working principle of *distributive justice: an assumption about what is the proper way of passing out the wealth of a society.* For example, people commonly say: "Jobs should be awarded on the basis of merit"; "Income should be determined on the basis of contribution to society or on the degree of preparation for a job"; "Taxes should be assessed on the basis of ability to pay." Each statement implies some standard that should be considered in the distribution of society's wealth: merit, contribution and effort, capacity. Whether these or other principles should be taken into account is a basic concern of economic justice.

Such a question is also basic to the issue of worldwide hunger. To illustrate: Some argue that the affluent nations have a moral obligation to help feed the hungry nations simply because the latter need help. Others argue that the affluent nations do not have an obligation to share what they have because they have a proprietary right to what they have earned and may dispose of it however they choose. Still others argue that only starving nations that attempt to help themselves (as, for example, by controlling their populations) should receive help. Again, underlying each of these positions is a principle of distributive justice. Thus, in the matter of world hunger, some believe *need* ought to determine the distribution of aid; others feel that *merit* should; and still others that *effort* should.

Whether the entity under consideration is a business, a society, or the world, serious questions of distributive and economic justice arise as soon as we begin to speculate about how—on what basis—the wealth of the entity ought to be parceled out. Well, just what are the options? What are the vying principles on the basis of which we can mete out economic justice? There appear to be five likely candidates, which bear on world hunger: (1) equality, (2) need, (3) merit or achievement, (4) contribution, and (5) effort. The first two can be viewed as egalitarian principles, the last three as desert principles.

EQUALITY.   The principle of equality would give each individual an equal share in the distribution, for, it is claimed, as human beings they deserve to be treated equally. By this account, every individual in a society would be entitled to the same portion of a society's goods as every other individual in the society.

Notice that the principle of equality ignores individual merit, contribution, and effort. Most important, claim its critics, it overlooks need. Is a pattern of distribution that ignores individual differences fair? Is any distribution that results from it equitable?

To see the thrust of this criticism, consider that I may need more food than you; and you may need more money than I; and both of us may need less medical attention than somebody else. Under strict equality of distribution, each of us would receive identical shares of the goods and services available. Clearly, there would be no guarantee that any one of us would receive all that we need.

Applied to world hunger, the equality principle would lead to equal shares of the world's food for all the peoples of the world, presumably on a person-by-person basis. Conceivably, as a result of such equal distribution, some individuals who need more food than others might be left malnourished. Or possibly, those starving to death might, as a result of a greater share of food, not only live but add to their nation's population problems, which in turn would reduce the individual share. Operational problems such as these have caused some people who want some sort of egalitarian principle to turn to a different consideration.

NEED.   The principle of need would give to each individual according to his or her needs. Notice that this principle is, like the preceding, an egalitarian principle, in that it treats everyone equally. By the principle of need, each of us should get exactly what we require. Clearly, this principle, unlike the first, squarely faces the problem of differences among individuals. However, it too has several operational challenges.

In a world of limited resources, priorities must be set. Needs must be ranked. But what needs are to receive top priority? After we answer that question, how do we establish whose needs shall be met among those with similar needs when there is not enough to satisfy the needs of all? For example, suppose we give top priority to the need for enough food to maintain life. Taking a global view, let's suppose that a very needy nation will survive if given enough food because it is prepared to take population-control measures. In contrast, another even needier nation probably will not survive even with massive food aid, because it is not prepared to take any population-control measures. Now, let's say that if we fully satisfy the needs of the more desperate nation, we won't be able to satisfy the food needs of the less desperate one. Should we, nevertheless, give the lion's share of the available food to the nation that appears doomed?

As indicated, both the principle of equality and the principle of need rest on considerations of equality, on treating people the same way. The first claims that everyone should receive an equal share; the second holds that everyone should get the share he or she needs. In contrast, the next three principles emphasize desert, not equal treatment.

MERIT OR ACHIEVEMENT.   The principle of merit or achievement would give to each individual according to the kind of person he or she is or the characteristics he or she has. But just what types of characteristic should we consider? Skill, some say. But what kind of skills? If we introduce native skills (inherited aptitude) as a basis of desert, then we seem to reward and punish individuals for their genetic makeup. But since none of us has an opportunity to choose our genes, is it fair that we should be judged on them? Perhaps we should consider acquired or learned skills. While perhaps a fairer consideration than the genetic calculus, acquired skills to a large degree depend on native skills. True, the degree to which we develop our skills is greatly influenced by individual effort: practice, drill, perseverance. But to introduce *effort* as a principle of justice is to depart from the principle of merit or achievement. After all, effort refers to labor; merit to productivity.

Others who advocate merit or achievement want to evaluate merit in terms

of virtue: Those individuals who show character qualities such as kindness, courage, diligence, reliability, and the like should receive a greater share of the economic pie than those who are cruel, cowardly, careless, and irresponsible. But
by what standard are these traits to be isolated and measured? And even if we
can locate and calculate them, are such qualities the sort of things that we want
to make economic allotments for? Critics argue that by definition, acts of virtue
must result from motives other than pecuniary ones, that tying virtue to material
rewards undermines the nature of virtue itself.

Others who espouse principles based on desert focus their nonegalitarian
theories not on what one is, but on what one has done. The final two principles
typify these views.

CONTRIBUTION.   The principle of contribution would give each individual
exactly that portion of a society's wealth he or she has produced. But in as complex
a society and economy as ours, this is extraordinarily difficult to determine, if
possible at all. It requires not only a precise measurement of the contribution,
but an evaluation of its significance toward creating a society's wealth. In the
production, say, of a car, what is the comparable worth of the contribution of the
designer, the engineer, the assembler, the retailer, the stockholder, and the
numerous others involved in the production and sale of the automobile? How is
an artist's contribution to society to be measured? What about the people who
collect our garbage, wash our laundry, cut our hair?

It might be easier to evaluate the contribution of nations to the world's wealth.
Just look at their gross national products. Maybe the world resources should be
distributed on that basis: Nations will get back exactly the proportion of the
world's food supply that they themselves have created. But is this fair? Surely
there is a measure of fortune, of chance, in the development of nations. Like
individuals, some nations appear to have begun with a head start; they have had
more to work with, to develop and exploit. Also, there is always a line of social
factors stretching far back into a nation's history that help account for its present
economic status. In short, individuals have no say over the society or nations
they are born into. To expect them to reverse in their lifetimes the historical
interplay of natural and social forces, or to penalize them by neglect for the
decisions and actions of those long since dead, hardly seems fair.

EFFORT.   The principle of effort would give to each according to the degree
of his or her labor. Like the principle of contribution, effort focuses on what
people have done, not on what they are. But unlike contribution, the principle
of effort is not concerned with what individuals have produced, but on the effort
they make. By this account, the nature of one's job is irrelevant to justice. Equal
effort requires equal remuneration. But how is effort to be measured? Effort
appears to be relative to the individual who is doing the work. The effort you
expend in writing an essay might be far greater than someone else's because that
person happens to be a more "gifted" writer. Also, the degree to which we extend
ourselves is largely determined by genetic and early environmental factors.

As with compensation, we might apply the effort principle more easily to
nations than to individuals. For example, we might distribute food according to

the effort a nation has made to become self-sufficient, as, for example, by controlling its population, utilizing its natural resources, and modernizing its agriculture. Having identified nations who have made the greatest effort, we might evaluate individuals within those nations by the same criteria. It is difficult, however, in instances such as these to separate effort from results. In some cases, the results are appalling; but that does not necessarily mean that the effort was lacking. After all, birth-control programs often must struggle to take hold in the soil of superstition, social taboos, and invincible ignorance. True, a country may fail to control its population, but perhaps not for the lack of effort. The effort simply may be no match for the gargantuan obstacles to be overcome.

These, then, are some common candidates for principles of economic justice. Some people base their views of proper distribution on a single principle. Others appeal to a combination. Whatever one's approach, it will underlie one's position on the issue of moral obligation and world hunger.

But any discussion of international economic justice that focuses exclusively on distributive justice without considering the productive side of economic arrangements seems incomplete. After all, what good does it do to redistribute scarce resources if there simply aren't enough resources to go around? Increasing the supply so that no one suffers certainly is preferable to spreading misery about more equitably. But increasing the supply raises questions not about how goods should be distributed, but about what goods should be produced.

Productive Justice

Howard Richards, for one, believes that by recognizing the importance of the principle of productive justice, concerned individuals might make a more effective response to problems of hunger and malnutrition. In making his case, he provides five considerations he thinks will convince rational men and women of the need to supplement principles of distributive justice with principles of productive justice.[4]

(1) The practices responsible for keeping world food production at dismayingly low levels are unjust because they cause harm that minor, morally insignificant sacrifice could avert. (2) Unproductive practices kill people. They're unjust because they're analogous to homicide in the morally relevant respects. (3) The hungry of the earth have a right to a reasonably high level of agricultural production because, as inhabitants of the earth, they, as well as all other people, have a right to a planet that is as productive as people can reasonably be expected to make it. (4) Distributive justice cannot be achieved without production; hence justice requires production. In other words, if distributive justice, for whatever reasons, requires a minimum standard below which no one should fall, distributive justice cannot be achieved without production. Production, then, becomes a requirement of justice. (5) It is misleading to say the practices that sacrifice distributive justice in order to increase production are just without also saying production is required of justice.

4. *Howard Richards, "Productive Justice," in* World Hunger and Moral Obligation, *ed. William Aiken and Hugh LaFollette (Englewood Cliffs, N.J.: Prentice-Hall, 1977), pp. 165–179.*

It's not necessary here to lay out the arguments which underlie these principles as much as to identify the implications of introducing the notion of productive justice into discussions of world hunger. It is a common observation that even if the population explosion could be checked and the rich nations were to share their surpluses with the poor, world hunger wouldn't be solved because world need exceeds surpluses. Then it is concluded that apathy and inaction are justified because nothing can be done. Those arguing this way, however, overlook productive justice. For the point is not what would happen if we'd share what we *have*, but if we'd share what we can *produce*. Even if need exceeds surpluses, it's potential production, not current supplies, that sets the moral standard. Looking at the issue from the view of producing more of those foods that more efficiently satisfy human nutritional requirements, and assuming the population explosion can be brought under control, the world hunger problem seems soluble and the grounds for apathy and inaction shaky.

Considerations of productive justice also seem to properly focus moral sentiments and righteous indignation on the causes and not, as is more often the case, on the effects of world hunger. "It is not the starving child and the extravagant banquet that should awaken our moral sentiments," Richards writes, "but the underutilized land, the unemployed work force, and the factories that are closed waiting for passenger car sales to pick up when they could be making tractors."[5]

Of course, identifying what needs to be produced to meet survival needs of the world's hungry is one thing and designing the economic system to do it is another. The inclusion of productive justice, therefore, ultimately invites a full-scale study of our economic system, with special attention to how well that system fulfills its obligation to produce.

Arguments for an Obligation to Help

1.   *All human beings have equal rights to the necessities of life.*

POINT: "Where people are treated differently, the different treatment should be based on their freely chosen actions and not on accidents of birth. But look around you and what do you see? Millions of people who are starving, not because of some action of their own but because they were unlucky enough to be born in a hostile environment. To ignore their plight is the height of moral callousness. We have an obligation to help the starving for one reason and one reason only: They are human beings, and as human beings they have the same rights we all do to the necessities of life."

COUNTERPOINT: "What you say sounds fine until one realizes that it flies in the face of fact. Don't you see that if we equally shared what we have with the starving people of the world, *all* of us would end up suffering? There simply isn't enough food to go around. So if we did what you propose, everybody would end up malnourished."

5.   *Ibid., p. 178.*

2. *People are required to help prevent suffering.*

POINT: "I agree that it's irrational to ask people to help others when such help is going to create great hardship for the 'good samaritans' themselves. But it's altogether reasonable to expect people to help if by so doing they don't seriously injure themselves. This is precisely the situation with world hunger. Two-thirds of the world's people—the so-called Third World—are malnourished. The remaining one-third—the West—are consuming two-thirds of the world's resources. Now, surely that affluent one-third could share their resources and help feed the starving masses, without imperiling themselves. They could and they are obliged to—at least up to the point where any more help would cause them as much suffering as it would prevent. We in the West are far from having reached that point. Just where that point is, it's impossible to say. But surely, since we're dealing with millions of human lives, we are obligated to extend ourselves, even if it means great personal sacrifice and a radical change in our life-styles. After all, by no measure of decency can it be seriously and respectably argued that we are justified in feeding our cats and dogs each day enough protein to meet the daily requirements of thousands of people, who, for lack of protein, are contracting horrible diseases and even dying. We must give, and give until it hurts, to the degree commensurate with the suffering of those starving."

COUNTERPOINT: "I know I must sound like an arch-villain to criticize an argument in behalf of the starving masses, but criticize I must. Let's assume for argument's sake that the affluent Western nations share their food until every Westerner is just well-nourished, no more. At that point the surplus of food is distributed equally to the remaining two-thirds of the world's population. Even then the Third World peoples would still be malnourished. My point is that there simply isn't enough food currently available to feed everyone on an equal basis. And if you're suggesting that the affluent nations should share to the point of leaving themselves malnourished, what's the logic behind that? Is the world better off having four-fifths, five-sixths, maybe even 100 percent of its population malnourished rather than two-thirds? All this aside, why do you focus exclusively on the 'rights' of the starving? What about the rights of the affluent? They're human beings too, you know. On what grounds is it justifiable to expect them to 'give until it hurts, to a degree commensurate with the suffering of the starving'?"

3. *Human beings have a right to be saved from starvation.*

POINT: "Those who claim that the affluent nations have no obligation to help the starving forget what we're dealing with: individual, flesh-and-blood human beings. Human beings who have the same needs, fears, and pains as you or I. When they ask for help, they're not merely begging for charity or pleading for us to be benevolent. To insist that they are is to reduce the urgency of their plight to the level of a street-corner beggar's. But don't kid yourself—the need of these people is neither trivial nor manufactured. Their need is real and dire, and desperate need creates obligations and rights. The starving person has a moral right to get help from those in a position to provide it. This right derives from a more general right to be saved from preventable death due to deprivation, and this general right is based on human need. The bottom line is that anyone starving to death has a right to the goods and services that will prevent his or her death by deprivation. And if you or I happen to have the necessary goods and services, then we have an obligation to prevent the person's death. So it's quite clear that the affluent nations are obliged to help the world's starving masses. Should they not try to meet this obligation, they would be guilty of an act as morally reprehensible as if they had taken a direct action to kill these people."

COUNTERPOINT: "Although I can sympathize with the sincerity, even urgency, of your appeal, I can't get a handle on what you mean by a 'right based on need.' I can understand moral rights resulting from promises, or from special roles and relationships. But when you talk of a right based on need, you lose me. I'll grant that there could be such a category of 'need rights.' Even so, the whole concept is terribly vague. For example, I have a tough time distinguishing 'needs' from 'wants' or 'wishes.' Then there's the matter of how intense a need must be to be considered a right. Some people undoubtedly have a profound 'need' to be loved, and if this need is not met, they seem to languish. Does that mean they have a right to be loved, and that someone has an obligation to provide that love? Another thing: Assuming that a need can be the basis of a right, against whom, if anyone, is this right correctly claimed? Suppose, for example, we consider a person's need for medical care a right. Precisely who is responsible for providing it? If I didn't put the person in the condition of need, why should I be obligated? Then there's the matter of conflicting rights. It's generally acknowledged that individuals and nations have a right to control their resources and property. Does a right based on need automatically take precedence over such ownership rights? If so, why? It could very well be that your central argument is cogent. But until you clear up this concept of 'need right,' I'll remain unconvinced."

Arguments for an Obligation Not to Help

1. *Helping will actually damage some recipient nations.*

POINT: "There's no question that a number of Third World countries have exceeded their 'carrying capacity.' In simple English, that means their populations exceed their productivity. They neither are nor can be self-sufficient. So if we give aid to countries whose reproduction has outstripped their productivity, all we do is increase their population without increasing their rate of productivity. The ironic result is that we increase the number of starving people and produce a net increase in human misery. Now, don't misunderstand. I'm not objecting to our helping countries in biological balance, countries whose populations haven't so outpaced their production that they can never be self-sufficient. On the contrary, I think we ought to help such countries, and also of course those in need of emergency famine or disaster relief. But I don't think we have an obligation to help if by helping we actually increase the net suffering of a recipient country.

And this is precisely what we will do in the case of many countries. In fact, it would be immoral to help, since by 'helping' we would create more pain."

COUNTERPOINT: "First of all, how does one determine precisely the point at which a country has exceeded its 'carrying capacity'? What criteria do you use to determine that a country can never be self-sufficient? Your whole argument assumes we can clearly identify population trends that indicate major worldwide population growth. And it also assumes that these trends are irreversible. But why couldn't immediate food assistance together with developmental assistance aimed at improved food production contain and even wipe out widespread hunger? India is a case in point. Far from being hopelessly overpopulated, India actually reduced its population-growth rate in many areas as a result of a well-planned birth-control effort. Specifically, during India's third 'Five Year Plan' (1961–1966), the birth rate in Bombay actually declined to only 27 per 1,000 population, which is only slightly higher than the U.S. rate, 23 per 1,000.[6] True, this was the most impressive result in the country, but there were other promising signs. For example, in one rural district of West Bengal the birth rate dropped from 43 to 36 per 1,000. Such results suggest that the hopeless picture you paint grossly distorts the plights of these countries."

  2.   *Helping would ultimately threaten the human species.*

POINT: "Consider a couple of sobering facts. The population of the two-thirds of the world that we call the 'Third World' is increasing more than twice as fast as the population of the one-third we call 'affluent.' What's more, if you compare most Third World countries with just the United States, you'll find that their populations are doubling *three* or *four* times as fast as the U.S. population! Now, suppose we decide to share what we have with these starving nations. What do you think things would be like by the end of this century? Each one of us in the United States would be sharing our resources with about a dozen people. Even if there were still enough to go around, contemplate the miserable conditions we'd all be living under. Of course, ultimately it wouldn't be a question of quality of life; there simply wouldn't be any life left! That's right, the human species would die out. So not only do the affluent nations have *no* obligation to help the starving peoples of the world, they *must not* share their food or even provide developmental assistance. Their moral obligation is to the species, to future generations. Above everything else, we, the affluent, must ensure our own survival by retaining a safety factor of surplus and by preserving the environment for posterity."

COUNTERPOINT: "Again, you assume not only that population trends are identifiable but that they're not reversible. I remind you of India's experiences, and caution you about such distortive population projections as the ones you make. It wasn't too long ago, you know, that China faced widespread starvation. Many people termed China's plight 'hopeless.' But today China's huge population is adequately fed. What happened? To put it in the vernacular, China got its

---

6. *B. L. Raina, India," in* Family Planning and Populations Programs: A Review of World Developments, ed. *Bernard Berelson (Chicago: University of Chicago Press, 1966), pp. 111–22.*

agricultural act together. So your doomsday forecasts are very misleading. Even worse, they do a dreadful, and potentially fatal, disservice to the world's poor by making their plight appear hopeless, and thus futile to address. I'll give you an example of what I mean. Remember the starvation problem that Bangladesh faced a few years ago? Well, recall how the media represented it. The only pictures that ever appeared in our newspapers and on our television screens were of children and adults with bellies swollen with hunger. No wonder a lot of people in this country got the impression that Bangladesh was beyond hope. But the fact of the matter is that the majority of Bangladeshi have enough to get by and that Bangladesh potentially has some of the world's richest croplands. 'Potentially'—it all depends on whether a well-formulated aid program is forthcoming. But judging from the reporting on Bangladesh, we understandably considered their plight hopeless. In the last analysis, short-term relief programs coupled with long-range population-control programs and assistance to improve local agriculture could minimize if not eradicate starvation."

Argument for Helping as Morally Permissible but Not Obligatory

1. *Helping is an act of charity.*

POINT: "Helping the starving people of the world isn't something we must or must not do. It's something we can do, if we choose. In other words, we should look on such help as charity or benevolence. As with any act of charity, we are not obligated to perform it. Sure, it might be nice if we did, even desirable, noble. But it's not required of us. After all, we have a right to our property and can dispose of it pretty much however we choose. If we choose to share what we have, fine; but we have no duty to do so. Helping to feed the world's needy is an option that the well-fed have. In the last analysis, it's an act of charity or benevolence, but not a duty."

COUNTERPOINT: "Your argument ignores important aspects of the other two positions: (1) that we have a duty to help, (2) that we have a duty not to help. I think those people supporting the first position can legitimately ask: Why do you relegate something as important as preventing massive starvation to 'charity'? If we don't have a duty to help prevent human misery and death, just what duties do we have? To leave such a momentous issue to the benevolent impulses of individuals and nations is wholly unrealistic. Furthermore, you imply that personal property rights are extensive, if not unlimited. Maybe they are, but I find it hard to argue that I have a right to something that is not necessary, such as a second car or a swimming pool, when others will die unless they have the food that could be purchased with the money used to buy these things. If an affluent nation could save millions of people from starvation by diverting a fraction of its GNP into developmental assistance or hunger relief, would that country be morally justified in retaining that wealth? Besides, you don't for a minute consider how the affluent obtained their wealth, which may be morally suspect. Do we have moral rights to what we've acquired nefariously? Similarly, I think those supporting the second position are justified in pointing out that whether the help springs from charity or duty, the result is the same. And, according to the Neo-Malthusians, the result isn't good; in fact, it's calculated to cause overpopulation and increase human misery for recipients and donors alike. Are these dire futuristic projections mistaken, or irrelevant? You're going to have to deal with this question before you can convince any Neo-Malthusian of the merit of your argument."

Lifeboat Ethics: The Case against Helping the Poor

Garrett Hardin

In this essay, biologist Garrett Hardin rejects the claim, and the ethic entailing it, that affluent nations have an obligation to help the world's starving masses. Indeed, Hardin argues that the duty of the affluent nations is to not help. And he implies that this duty includes not providing even developmental assistance.

After criticizing the environmentalists' metaphor of the earth as a spaceship, Hardin sets up an extended metaphor of his own. He asks us to regard each rich nation as a lifeboat with limited capacity and full of relatively rich people. Outside the lifeboat, the sea is full of the poor and needy, who want to get in the boat. Hardin claims that unless the lifeboat's occupants maintain a safety factor—that is, keep people out—the boat will swamp.

But "swamping" is precisely what the "spaceship" or sharing ethic will lead to, Hardin believes. A good example, he feels, can be seen in the international food bank, which he considers nothing more than a device for moving the wealth of the rich, productive nations over to the poor, unproductive ones. Eventually, Hardin predicts, there will be nothing left to withdraw. In the end, the sharing ethic will undo us all.

Thus Hardin concludes that we must reject the sharing ethic. We owe it to future generations, to the species, not to help the starving masses.

Environmentalists use the metaphor of the earth as a "spaceship" in trying to persuade countries, industries and people to stop wasting and polluting our natural resources. Since we all share life on this planet, they argue, no single person or institution has the right to destroy, waste or use more than a fair share of its resources.

But does everyone on earth have an equal right to an equal share of its resources? The spaceship metaphor can be dangerous when used by misguided idealists to justify suicidal policies for sharing our resources through uncontrolled immigration and foreign aid. In their enthusiastic but unrealistic generosity, they confuse the ethics of a spaceship with those of a lifeboat.

A true spaceship would have to be under the control of a captain, since no ship could possibly survive if its course were determined by committee. Spaceship Earth certainly has no captain; the United Nations is merely a toothless tiger, with little power to enforce any policy upon its bickering members.

If we devide the world crudely into rich nations and poor nations, two thirds of them are desperately poor, and only one third comparatively rich, with the United States the wealthiest of all. Metaphorically each rich nation can be seen as a lifeboat full of comparatively rich people. In the ocean outside each lifeboat swim the poor of the world, who would like to get in, or at least to share some of the wealth. What should the lifeboat passengers do?

First, we must recognize the limited capacity of any lifeboat. For example, a nation's land has a limited capacity to support a population and as the current energy crisis has shown us, in some ways we have already exceeded the carrying capacity of our land.

Adrift in a Moral Sea

So here we sit, say fifty people in our lifeboat. To be generous, let us assume it has room for ten more, making a total capacity of sixty. Suppose the fifty of us in the lifeboat see 100 others swimming in the water outside, begging for admission to our boat or for handouts. We have several options: We may be tempted to try to live by the Christian ideal of being "our brother's keeper," or by the Marxist ideal of "to each according to his needs." Since the needs of all in the water are the same, and since they can all be seen as "our brothers," we could take them all into our boat, making a total of 150 in a boat designed for sixty. The boat swamps, everyone drowns. Complete justice, complete catastrophe.

Since the boat has an unused excess capacity of ten more passengers, we could admit just ten more to it. But which ten do we let in? How do we choose? Do we pick the best ten, the neediest ten, "first come, first served"? And what do we say to the ninety we exclude? If we do let an extra ten into our lifeboat, we will have lost our "safety factor," an engineering principle of critical importance. For example, if we don't leave room for excess capacity as a safety factor in our country's agriculture, a new plant disease or a bad change in the weather could have disastrous consequences.

Suppose we decide to preserve our small safety factor and admit no more to the lifeboat. Our survival is then possible, although we shall have to be constantly on guard against boarding parties.

While this last solution clearly offers the only means of our survival, it is morally abhorrent to many people. Some say they feel guilty about their good luck. My reply is simple: "Get out and yield your place to others." This may solve the problem

of the guilt-ridden person's conscience, but it does not change the ethics of the lifeboat. The needy person to whom the guilt-ridden person yields his place will not himself feel guilty about his good luck. If he did, he would not climb aboard. The net result of conscience-stricken people giving up their unjustly held seats is the elimination of that sort of conscience from the lifeboat.

This is the basic metaphor within which we must work out our solutions. Let us now enrich the image, step by step, with substantive additions from the real world, a world that must solve real and pressing problems of overpopulation and hunger.

The harsh ethics of the lifeboat become even harsher when we consider the reproductive differences between the rich nations and the poor nations. The people inside the lifeboats are doubling in numbers every eighty-seven years; those swimming around outside are doubling, on the average, every thirty-five years, more than twice as fast as the rich. And since the world's resources are dwindling, the difference in prosperity between the rich and the poor can only increase.

As of 1973, the U.S. had a population of 210 million people, who were increasing by 0.8 percent per year. Outside our lifeboat, let us imagine another 210 million people (say the combined populations of Colombia, Ecuador, Venezuela, Morocco, Pakistan, Thailand and the Philippines), who are increasing at a rate of 3.3 percent per year. Put differently, the doubling time for this aggregate population is twenty-one years, compared to eighty-seven years for the U.S.

Multiplying the Rich and the Poor

Now suppose the U.S. agreed to pool its resources with those seven countries, with everyone receiving an equal share. Initially the ratio of Americans to non-Americans in this model would be one-to-one. But consider what the ratio would be after eighty-seven years, by which time the Americans would have doubled to a population of 420 million. By then, doubling every twenty-one years, the other group would have swollen to 354 billion. Each American would have to share the available resources with more than eight people.

But, one could argue, this discussion assumes that current population trends will continue, and they may not. Quite so. Most likely the rate of population increase will decline much faster in the U.S. than it will in the other countries, and there does not seem to be much we can do about it. In sharing with "each according to his needs," we must recognize that needs are determined by population size, which is determined by the rate of reproduction, which at present is regarded as a sovereign right of every nation, poor or not. This being so, the philanthropic load created by the sharing ethic of the spaceship can only increase.

The Tragedy of the Commons

The fundamental error of spaceship ethics, and the sharing it requires, is that it leads to what I call "the tragedy of the commons." Under a system of private property, the men who own property recognize their responsibility to care for it, for if they don't they will eventually suffer. A farmer, for instance, will allow no more cattle in a pasture than its carrying capacity justifies. If he overloads it, erosion sets in, weeds take over, and he loses the use of the pasture.

If a pasture becomes a commons open to all, the right of each to use it may not be matched by a corresponding responsibility to protect it. Asking everyone to use it with discretion will hardly do, for the considerate herdsman who refrains from overloading the commons suffers more than a selfish one who says his needs are greater. If everyone would restrain himself, all would be well; but it takes only one less than everyone to ruin a system of voluntary restraint. In a crowded world of less than perfect human beings, mutual ruin is inevitable if there are no controls. This is the tragedy of the commons.

One of the major tasks of education today should be the creation of such an acute awareness of the dangers of the commons that people will recognize its many varieties. For example, the air and water have become polluted because they are treated as commons. Further growth in the population or per-capita conversion of natural resources into pollutants will only make the problem worse. The same holds true for the fish of the oceans. Fishing fleets have nearly disappeared in many parts of the world, technological improvements in the art of fishing are hastening the day of complete ruin. Only the replacement of the system of the commons with a responsible system of control will save the land, air, water and oceanic fisheries.

The World Food Bank

In recent years there has been a push to create a new commons called a World Food Bank, an international depository of food reserves to which nations would contribute according to their abilities and from which they would draw according to their needs. This humanitarian proposal has received support from many liberal international groups, and from such prominent citizens as Margaret Mead, U.N. Secretary General Kurt Waldheim, and Senators Edward Kennedy and George McGovern.

A world food bank appeals powerfully to our humanitarian impulses. But before we rush ahead with such a plan, let us recognize where the greatest political push comes from, lest we be disillusioned later. Our experience with the "Food for Peace program," or Public Law 480, gives us the answer. This program moved billions of dollars' worth of U.S. surplus grain to food-short, population-long countries during the past two decades. But when P.L. 480 first became law, a headline in the business magazine *Forbes* revealed the real power behind it: "Feeding the World's Hungry Millions: How It Will Mean Billions for U.S. Business."

And indeed it did. In the years 1960 to 1970, U.S. taxpayers spent a total of $7.9 billion on the Food for Peace program. Between 1948 and 1970, they also paid an additional $50 billion for other economic-aid programs, some of which went for food and food-producing machinery and technology. Though all U.S. taxpayers were forced to contribute to the cost of P.L. 480, certain special interest groups gained handsomely under the program. Farmers did not have to contribute the grain; the Government, or rather the taxpayers, bought it from them at full market prices. The increased demand raised prices of farm products generally. The manufacturers of farm machinery, fertilizers and pesticides benefited by the farmers' extra efforts to grow more food. Grain elevators profited from storing the surplus until it could be shipped. Railroads made money hauling it to ports, and shipping lines profited from carrying it overseas. The implementation of P.L. 480 required the creation of a vast Government bureaucracy, which then acquired its own vested interest in continuing the program regardless of its merits.

Extracting Dollars

Those who proposed and defended the Food for Peace program in public rarely mentioned its importance to any of these special interests. The public emphasis was always on its humanitarian effects. The combination of silent selfish interests and highly vocal humanitarian apologists made a powerful and successful lobby for extracting money from taxpayers. We can expect the same lobby to push now for the creation of a World Food Bank.

However great the potential benefit to selfish interests, it should not be a decisive argument against a truly humanitarian program. We must ask if such a program would actually do more good than harm, not only momentarily but also in the long run. Those who propose the food bank usually refer to a current "emergency" or "crisis" in terms of world food supply. But what is an emergency? Although they may be infrequent and sudden, everyone knows that emergencies will occur from time to time. A well-run family, company, organization or country prepares for the likelihood of accidents and emergencies. It expects them, it budgets for them, it saves for them.

Learning the Hard Way

What happens if some organizations or countries budget for accidents and others do not? If each country is solely responsible for its own well-being, poorly managed ones will suffer. But they can learn from experience. They may mend their ways, and learn to budget for infrequent but certain emergencies. For example, the weather varies from year to year, and periodic crop failures are certain. A wise and competent government saves out of the production of the good years in anticipation of bad years to come. Joseph taught this policy to Pharaoh in Egypt more than 2,000 years ago. Yet the great majority of the governments in the world today do not follow such a policy. They lack either the wisdom or the competence, or both. Should those nations that do manage to put something aside be forced to come to the rescue each time an emergency occurs among the poor nations?

"But it isn't their fault!" some kindhearted liberals argue. "How can we blame the poor people who are caught in an emergency? Why must they suffer for the sins of their governments?" The concept of blame is simply not relevant here. The real question is, what are the operational consequences of establishing a world food bank? If it is open to every country every time a need develops, slovenly rulers will not be motivated to take Joseph's advice. Someone will always come to their aid. Some countries will deposit food in the world food bank, and others will withdraw it. There will be almost no overlap. As a result of such solutions to food shortage emergencies, the poor countries will not learn to mend their ways, and will suffer progressively greater emergencies as their populations grow.

Population Control the Crude Way

On the average, poor countries undergo a 2.5 percent increase in population each year; rich countries, about 0.8 percent. Only rich countries have anything in the way of food reserves set aside, and even they do not have as much as they should. Poor countries have none. If poor countries received no food from the outside, the rate of their population growth would be periodically checked by crop failures and famines. But if they can always draw on a world food bank in time of need, their population can continue to grow unchecked, and so will their "need" for aid. In the short run, a world food bank may diminish that need, but in the long run it actually increases the need without limit.

Without some system of worldwide food sharing, the proportion of people in the rich and poor nations might eventually stabilize. The overpopulated poor countries would decrease in numbers, while the rich countries that had room for more people would increase. But with a well-meaning system of sharing, such as a world food bank, the growth differential between the rich and the poor countries will not only persist, it will increase. Because of the higher rate of population growth in the poor countries of the world, 88 percent of today's children are born poor, and only 12 percent rich. Year by year the ratio becomes worse, as the fast-reproducing poor outnumber the slow-reproducing rich.

A world food bank is thus a commons in disguise. People will have more motivation to draw from it than to add to any common store. The less provident and less able will multiply at the expense of the abler and more provident, bringing eventual ruin upon all who share in the commons. Besides, any system of "sharing" that amounts to foreign aid from the rich nations to the poor nations will carry the taint of charity, which will contribute little to the world peace so devoutly desired by those who support the idea of a world food bank.

As past U.S. foreign-aid programs have amply and depressingly demonstrated, international charity frequently inspires mistrust and antagonism rather than gratitude on the part of the recipient nation.

Chinese Fish and Miracle Rice

The modern approach to foreign aid stresses the export of technology and advice, rather than money and food. As an ancient Chinese proverb goes: "Give a man a fish and he will eat for a day; teach him how to fish and he will eat for the rest of his days." Acting on this advice, the Rockefeller and Ford Foundations have financed a number of programs for improving agriculture in the hungry nations. Known as the "Green Revolution," these programs have led to the development of "miracle rice" and "miracle wheat," new strains that offer bigger harvests and greater resistance to crop damage. Norman Borlaug, the Nobel Prize winning agronomist who, supported by the Rockefeller Foundation, developed "miracle wheat," is one of the most prominent advocates of a world food bank.

Whether or not the Green Revolution can increase food production as much as its champions claim is a debatable but possibly irrelevant point. Those who support this well-intended humanitarian effort should first consider some of the fundamentals of human ecology. Ironically, one man who did was the late Alan Gregg, a vice president of the Rockefeller Foundation. Two decades ago he expressed strong doubts about the wisdom of such attempts to increase food production. He likened the growth and spread of humanity over the surface of the earth to the spread of cancer in the human body, remarking that "cancerous growths demand food; but, as far as I know, they have never been cured by getting it."

Overloading the Environment

Every human born constitutes a draft on all aspects of the environment: food, air, water, forests, beaches, wildlife, scenery and solitude. Food can, perhaps, be significantly increased to meet a growing demand. But what about clean beaches, unspoiled forests, and solitude? If we satisfy a growing population's need for food, we necessarily decrease its per-capita supply of the other resources needed by men.

India, for example, now has a population of 600 million, which increases by 15 million each year. This population already puts a huge load on a relatively impoverished environment. The country's forests are now only a small fraction of what they were three centuries ago, and floods and erosion continually destroy the insufficient farmland that remains. Every one of the 15 million new lives added to India's population puts an additional burden on the environment, and increases the economic and social costs of crowding. However humanitarian our intent, every Indian life saved through medical or nutritional assistance from abroad diminishes the quality of life for those who remain, and for subsequent generations. If rich countries make it possible, through foreign aid, for 600 million Indians to swell to 1.2 billion in a mere twenty-eight years, as their current growth rate threatens, will future generations of Indians thank us for hastening the destruction of their environment? Will our good intentions be sufficient excuse for the consequences of our actions?

My final example of a commons in action is one for which the public has the least desire for rational discussion—immigration. Anyone who publicly questions the wisdom of current U.S. immigration policy is promptly charged with bigotry, prejudice, ethnocentrism, chauvinism, isolationism or selfishness. Rather than encounter such accusations, one would rather talk about other matters, leaving immigration policy to wallow in the crosscurrents of special interests that take no account of the good of the whole, or the interest of posterity.

Perhaps we still feel guilty about things we said in the past. Two generations ago the popular press frequently referred to Dagos, Wops, Polacks, Chinks and Krauts, in articles about how America was being "overrun" by foreigners of supposedly inferior genetic stock. But because the implied inferiority of foreigners was used than as justification for keeping them out, people now assume that restrictive policies could only be based on such misguided notions. There are other grounds.

A Nation of Immigrants

Just consider the numbers involved. Our Government acknowledges a net inflow of 400,000 immigrants a year. While we have no hard data on the extent of illegal entries, educated guesses put the figure at about 600,000 a year. Since the natural increase (excess of births over deaths) of the resident population now runs about 1.7 million per year, the yearly gain from immigration amounts to at least 19 percent of the total annual increase, and may be as much as 37 percent if we include the estimate for illegal immigrants. Considering the growing use of birth-control devices, the potential effect of educational campaigns by such organizations as Planned Parenthood Federation of America and Zero Population Growth, and the influence of inflation and the housing shortage, the fertility rate of American women may decline so much that immigration could account for all the yearly increase in population. Should we not at least ask if that is what we want?

For the sake of those who worry about whether the "quality" of the average immigrant compares favorably with the quality of the average resident, let us assume that immigrants and nativeborn citizens are of exactly equal quality, however one defines that term. We will focus here only on quantity; and since our conclusions will depend on nothing else, all charges of bigotry and chauvinism become irrelevant.

Immigration vs. Food Supply

World food banks *move food to the people*, hastening the exhaustion of the environment of the poor countries. Unrestricted immigration, on the other hand, *moves people to the food*, thus speeding up the destruction of the environment of the rich countries. We can easily understand why poor people should want to make this latter transfer, but why should rich hosts encourage it?

As in the case of foreign-aid programs, immigration receives support from selfish interests and humanitarian impulses. The primary selfish interest in unimpeded immigration is the desire of employers for cheap labor, particularly in industries and trades that offer degrading work. In the past, one wave of foreigners after another was brought into the U.S. to work at wretched jobs for wretched wages. In recent years the Cubans, Puerto Ricans and Mexicans have had this dubious honor. The interests of the employers of cheap labor mesh well with the guilty silence of the country's liberal intelligentsia. White Anglo-Saxon Protestants are particularly reluctant to call for a closing of the doors to immigration for fear of being called bigots.

But not all countries have such reluctant leadership. Most educated Hawaiians, for example, are keenly aware of the limits of their environment, particularly in terms of population growth. There is only so much room on the islands, and the islanders know it. To Hawaiians, immigrants from the other forty-nine states present as great a threat as those from other nations. At a recent meeting of Hawaiian government officials in Honolulu, I had the ironic delight of hearing a speaker, who like most of his audience was of Japanese ancestry, ask how the country might practically and constitutionally close its doors to further immigration. One member of the audience countered: "How can we shut the doors now? We have many friends and relatives in Japan that we'd like to bring here some day so that they can enjoy Hawaii too." The Japanese-American speaker smiled sympathetically and answered: "Yes, but we have children now, and someday we'll have grandchildren too. We can bring more people here from Japan only by giving away some of the land that we hope to pass on to our grandchildren some day. What right do we have to do that?"

At this point, I can hear U.S. liberals asking: "How can you justify slamming the door once you're inside? You say that immigrants should be kept out. But aren't we all immigrants, or the descendants of immigrants? If we insist on staying, must we not admit all others?" Our craving for intellectual order leads us to seek and prefer symmetrical rules and morals: a single rule for me and everybody else; the same rule yesterday, today, and tomorrow. Justice, we feel, should not change with time and place.

We Americans of non-Indian ancestry can look upon ourselves as the descendants of thieves who are guilty morally, if not legally, of stealing this land from its Indian owners. Should we then give back the land to the now living American descendants of those Indians? However morally or logically sound this proposal may be, I, for one, am unwilling to live by it and I know no one else who is. Besides, the logical consequence would be absurd. Suppose that, intoxicated with a sense of pure justice, we should decide to turn our land over to the Indians. Since all our wealth has also been derived from the land, wouldn't we be morally obliged to give that back to the Indians too?

Pure Justice vs. Reality

Clearly, the concept of pure justice produces an infinite regression to absurdity. Centuries ago, wise men invented statutes of limitations to justify the rejection of such pure justice, in the interest of preventing continual disorder. The law zealously defends property rights, but only relatively recent property rights. Drawing a line after an arbitrary time has elapsed may be unjust, but the alternatives are worse.

We are all descendants of thieves, and the world's resources are inequitably distributed. But we must begin the journey to tomorrow from the point where we are today. We cannot remake the past. We cannot safely divide the wealth equitably among all peoples so long as people reproduce at different rates. To do so would guarantee that our grandchildren, and everyone else's grandchildren, would have only a ruined world to inhabit.

To be generous with one's own possessions is quite different from being generous with those of posterity. We should call this point to the attention of those who, from a commendable love of justice and equality, would institute a system of the commons, either in the form of a world food bank, or of unrestricted immigration. We must convince them if we wish to save at least some parts of the world from environmental ruin.

Without a true world government to control reproduction and the use of available resources, the sharing ethic of the spaceship is impossible. For the foreseeable future, our survival demands that we govern our actions by the ethics of a lifeboat, harsh though they may be. Posterity will be satisfied with nothing less.

Questions for Analysis

1. *Why does Hardin object to the environmentalists' metaphor of the earth as a spaceship?*

2. *Hardin seems opposed even to developmental assistance. Why?*

3. *In Hardin's view, "pure justice" is not compatible with survival. What does he mean? Do you agree?*

4. *Do you agree that future generations have a claim against us? If they do, what is the nature of this claim?*

5. *Explain why Hardin's argument can be called utilitarian.*

Famine, Affluence, and Morality

Peter Singer

Unlike Garrett Hardin, professor of philosophy Peter Singer believes that the affluent nations of the world have an obligation to help the poor nations. Singer opens his argument with what he considers are two uncontroversial principles. The first is that suffering and death from lack of food, shelter, and medical care are bad. The second is that if we can prevent something bad from

Peter Singer, "Famine, Affluence, and Morality," Philosophy and Public Affairs, Vol. 1, No. 3 (Spring 1972). Copyright © 1972 by Princeton University Press. Reprinted by permission of Princeton University Press.

happening "without thereby sacrificing anything of comparable moral importance," then we should do it. (While Singer believes that this principle is correct, he does offer a "weaker" version of it as well: We ought to prevent something bad from happening unless we have to sacrifice something morally significant.)

Basing his argument on these principles, Singer concludes that help or relief for the starving masses is a duty, not charity. Affluent nations are morally obliged to help; to refrain from helping is not merely uncharitable, it is immoral.

In addition to drawing a philosophical distinction between charity and duty, Singer raises a number of practical concerns. One is whether help to poor nations should be a government responsibility and not a personal one. Another is whether relief to countries lacking effective population-control measures merely postpones starvation.

Still another concern is just how much individually and collectively we ought to be giving away.

In the postscript to his essay, written several years afterward, Singer concedes that there is a serious case to be made for denying aid to countries that refuse to take any population-control measures. He also admits definitional problems with the phrase "moral significance," which, of course, is crucial in his second principle.

As I write this, in November 1971, people are dying in East Bengal from lack of food, shelter, and medical care. The suffering and death that are occurring there now are not inevitable, not unavoidable in any fatalistic sense of the term. Constant poverty, a cyclone, and a civil war have turned at least nine million people into destitute refugees; nevertheless, it is not beyond the capacity of the richer nations to give enough assistance to reduce any further suffering to very small proportions. The decisions and actions of human beings can prevent this kind of suffering. Unfortunately, human beings have not made the necessary decisions. At the individual level, people have, with very few exceptions, not responded to the situation in any significant way. Generally speaking, people have not given large sums to relief funds; they have not written to their parliamentary representatives demanding increased government assistance; they have not demonstrated in the streets, held symbolic fasts, or done anything else directed toward providing the refugees with the means to satisfy their essential needs. At the government level, no government has given the sort of massive aid that would enable the refugees to survive for more than a few days. Britain, for instance, has given rather more than most countries. It has, to date, given £14,750,000. For comparative purposes, Britain's share of the non-recoverable development costs of the Anglo-French Concorde project is already in excess of £275,000,000, and on present estimates will reach £440,000,000. The implication is that the British government values a supersonic transport more than thirty times as

highly as it values the lives of the nine million refugees. Australia is another country which, on a per capita basis, is well up in the "aid to Bengal" table. Australia's aid, however, amounts to less than one-twelfth of the cost of Sydney's new opera house. The total amount given, from all sources, now stands at about £65,000,000. The estimated cost of keeping the refugees alive for one year is £464,000,000. Most of the refugees have now been in the camps for more than six months. The World Bank has said that India needs a minimum of £300,000,000 in assistance from other countries before the end of the year. It seems obvious that assistance on this scale will not be forthcoming. India will be forced to choose between letting the refugees starve or diverting funds from her own development program, which will mean that more of her own people will starve in the future.[1]

These are the essential facts about the present situation in Bengal. So far as it concerns us here, there is nothing unique about this situation except its magnitude. The Bengal emergency is just the latest and most acute of a series of major emergencies in various parts of the world, arising both from natural and from man-made causes. There are also many parts of the world in which people die from malnutrition and lack of food independent of any special emergency. I take Bengal as my example only because it is the present concern, and because the size of the problem has ensured that it has been given adequate publicity. Neither individuals nor governments can claim to be unaware of what is happening there.

What are the moral implications of a situation like this? In what follows, I shall argue that the way people in relatively affluent countries react to a situation like that in Bengal cannot be justified; indeed, the whole way we look at moral issues—our moral conceptual scheme—needs to be altered, and with it, the way of life that has come to be taken for granted in our society.

In arguing for this conclusion I will not, of course, claim to be morally neutral. I shall, however, try to argue for the moral position that I take, so that anyone who accepts certain assumptions, to be made explicit, will, I hope, accept my conclusion.

I begin with the assumption that suffering and death from lack of food, shelter, and medical care are bad. I think most people will agree about this, although one may reach the same view by different routes. I shall not argue for this view. People can hold all sorts of eccentric positions, and perhaps from some of them it would not follow that death by starvation is in itself bad. It is difficult, perhaps impossible, to refute such positions, and so for brevity I will henceforth take this assumption as accepted. Those who disagree need read no further.

My next point is this: If it is in our power to prevent something bad from happening, without thereby sacrificing anything of comparable moral importance, we ought, morally, to do it. By "without sacrificing anything of comparable moral importance" I mean without causing anything else comparably bad to happen, or doing something that is wrong in itself, or failing to promote some moral good, comparable in significance to the bad thing that we can prevent. This principle seems almost as uncontroversial as the last one. It requires us only to prevent what is bad, and not to promote what is good, and it requires this of us only when we can do it without sacrificing anything that is, from the moral point of view, comparably important. I could even, as far as the application of my argument to the Bengal emergency is concerned, qualify the point so as to make it: If it is in our power to prevent something very bad from happening, without thereby sacrificing anything morally significant, we ought, morally, to do it. An application of this principle would be as follows: If I am walking past a shallow pond and see a child drowning in it, I ought to wade in and pull the

child out. This will mean getting my clothes muddy, but this is insignificant, while the death of the child would presumably be a very bad thing.

The uncontroversial appearance of the principle just stated is deceptive. If it were acted upon, even in its qualified form, our lives, our society, and our world would be fundamentally changed. For the principle takes, firstly, no account of proximity or distance. It makes no moral difference whether the person I can help is a neighbor's child ten yards from me or a Bengali whose name I shall never know, ten thousand miles away. Secondly, the principle makes no distinction between cases in which I am the only person who could possibly do anything and cases in which I am just one among millions in the same position.

I do not think I need to say much in defense of the refusal to take proximity and distance into account. The fact that a person is physically near to us, so that we have personal contact with him, may make it more likely that we *shall* assist him, but this does not show that we *ought* to help him rather than another who happens to be further away. If we accept any principle of impartiality, universalizability, equality, or whatever, we cannot discriminate against someone merely because he is far away from us (or we are far away from him). Admittedly, it is possible that we are in a better position to judge what needs to be done to help a person near to us than one far away, and perhaps also to provide the assistance we judge to be necessary. If this were the case, it would be a reason for helping those near to us first. This may once have been a justification for being more concerned with the poor in one's town than with famine victims in India. Unfortunately for those who like to keep their moral responsibilities limited, instant communication and swift transportation have changed the situation. From the moral point of view, the development of the world into a "global village" has made an important, though still unrecognized, difference to our moral situation. Expert observers and supervisors, sent out by famine relief organizations or permanently stationed in famine-prone areas, can direct our aid to a refugee in Bengal almost as effectively as we could get it to someone in our own block. There would seem, therefore, to be no possible justification for discriminating on geographical grounds.

There may be a greater need to defend the second implication of my principle—that the fact that there are millions of other people in the same position, in respect to the Bengali refugees, as I am, does not make the situation significantly different from a situation in which I am the only person who can prevent something very bad from occurring. Again, of course, I admit that there is a psychological difference between the cases; one feels less guilty about doing nothing if one can point to others, similarly placed, who have also done nothing. Yet this can make no real difference to our moral obligations.[2] Should I consider that I am less obliged to pull the drowning child out of the pond if on looking around I see other people, no further away than I am, who have also noticed the child but are doing nothing? One has only to ask this question to see the absurdity of the view that numbers lessen obligation. It is a view that is an ideal excuse for inactivity; unfortunately most of the major evils—poverty, overpopulation, pollution—are problems in which everyone is almost equally involved.

The view that numbers do make a difference can be made plausible if stated in this way: If everyone in circumstances like mine gave £5 to the Bengal Relief Fund, there would be enough to provide food, shelter, and medical care for the refugees; there is no reason why I should give more than anyone else in the same circumstances as I am; therefore I have no obligation to give more than £5. Each premise in this argument is true, and the argument looks sound. It may convince us, unless we notice that it is based on a hypothetical premise, although the conclusion is not stated hypothetically. The argument would be sound if the conclusion were: if everyone in circumstances like mine were to give £5, I would have no obligation to give more than £5. If the conclusion were so stated, however, it would be obvious that the argument has no bearing on a situation in which it is not the case that everyone else gives £5. This, of course, is the actual situation. It is more or less certain that not everyone in circumstances like mine will give £5. So there will not be enough to provide the needed food, shelter, and medical care. Therefore by giving more than £5 I will prevent more suffering than I would if I gave just £5.

It might be thought that this argument has an absurd consequence. Since the situation appears to be that very few people are likely to give substantial amounts, it follows that I and everyone else in sim-

ilar circumstances ought to give as much as possible, that is, at least up to the point at which by giving more one would begin to cause serious suffering for oneself and one's dependents—perhaps even beyond this point to the point of marginal utility, at which by giving more one would cause oneself and one's dependents as much suffering as one would prevent in Bengal. If everyone does this, however, there will be more than can be used for the benefit of the refugees, and some of the sacrifice will have been unnecessary. Thus, if everyone does what he ought to do, the result will not be as good as it would be if everyone did a little less than he ought to do, or if only some do all that they ought to do.

The paradox here arises only if we assume that the actions in question—sending money to the relief funds—are performed more or less simultaneously, and are also unexpected. For if it is to be expected that everyone is going to contribute something, then clearly each is not obliged to give as much as he would have been obliged to had others not been giving too. And if everyone is not acting more or less simultaneously, then those giving later will know how much more is needed, and will have no obligation to give more than is necessary to reach this amount. To say this is not to deny the principle that people in the same circumstances have the same obligations, but to point out that the fact that others have given, or may be expected to give, is a relevant circumstance: Those giving after it has become known that many others are giving and those giving before are not in the same circumstances. So the seemingly absurd consequence of the principle I have put forward can occur only if people are in error about the actual circumstances—that is, if they think they are giving when others are not, but in fact they are giving when others are. The result of everyone doing what he really ought to do cannot be worse than the result of everyone doing less than he ought to do, although the result of everyone doing what he reasonably believes he ought to do could be.

If my argument so far has been sound, neither our distance from a preventable evil nor the number of other people who, in respect to that evil, are in the same situation as we are, lessens our obligation to mitigate or prevent that evil. I shall therefore take as established the principle I asserted earlier. As I have already said, I need to assert it only in its qualified form: If it is in our power to prevent something very bad from happening, without thereby sacrificing anything else morally significant, we ought, morally, to do it.

The outcome of this argument is that our traditional moral categories are upset. The traditional distinction between duty and charity cannot be drawn, or at least, not in the place we normally draw it. Giving money to the Bengal Relief Fund is regarded as an act of charity in our society. The bodies which collect money are known as "charities." These organizations see themselves in this way—if you send them a check, you will be thanked for your "generosity." Because giving money is regarded as an act of charity, it is not thought that there is anything wrong with not giving. The charitable man may be praised, but the man who is not charitable is not condemned. People do not feel in any way ashamed or guilty about spending money on new clothes or a new car instead of giving it to a famine relief. (Indeed, the alternative does not occur to them.) This way of looking at the matter cannot be justified. When we buy new clothes not to keep ourselves warm but to look "well-dressed" we are not providing for any important need. We would not be sacrificing anything significant if we were to continue to wear our old clothes, and give the money to famine relief. By doing so, we would be preventing another person from starving. It follows from what I have said earlier that we ought to give money away, rather than spend it on clothes which we do not need to keep us warm. To do so is not charitable, or generous. Nor is it the kind of act which philosophers and theologians have called "supererogatory"—an act which it would be good to do, but not wrong not to do. On the contrary, we ought to give the money away, and it is wrong not to do so.

I am not maintaining that there are no acts which are charitable, or that there are no acts which it would be good to do but not wrong not to do. It may be possible to redraw the distinction between duty and charity in some other place. All I am arguing here is that the present way of drawing the distinction, which makes it an act of charity for a man living at the level of affluence which most people in the "developed nations" enjoy to give money to save someone else from starvation, cannot be supported. It is beyond the scope of my argument to consider whether the distinction should be redrawn or abolished altogether. There would be many other possible ways of drawing the distinction—for instance, one might decide that it is good to make other people as happy as possible, but not wrong not to do so.

Despite the limited nature of the revision in our moral conceptual scheme which I am proposing, the revision would, given the extent of both affluence and famine in the world today, have radical implications. These implications may lead to further objections, distinct from those I have already considered. I shall discuss two of these.

One objection to the position I have taken might be simply that it is too drastic a revision of our moral scheme. People do not ordinarily judge in the way I have suggested they should. Most people reserve their moral condemnation for those who violate some moral norm, such as the norm against taking another person's property. They do not condemn those who indulge in luxury instead of giving to famine relief. But given that I did not set out to present a morally neutral description of the way people make moral judgments, the way people do in fact judge has nothing to do with the validity of my conclusion. My conclusion follows from the principle which I advanced earlier, and unless that principle is rejected, or the arguments shown to be unsound, I think the conclusion must stand, however strange it appears.

It might, nevertheless, be interesting to consider why our society, and most other societies, do judge differently from the way I have suggested they should. In a well-known article, J. O. Urmson suggests that the imperatives of duty, which tell us what we must do, as distinct from what it would be good to do but not wrong not to do, function so as to prohibit behavior that is intolerable if men are to live together in society.[3] This may explain the origin and continued existence of the present division between acts of duty and acts of charity. Moral attitudes are shaped by the needs of society, and no doubt society needs people who will observe the rules that make social existence tolerable. From the point of view of a particular society, it is essential to prevent violations of norms against killing, stealing, and so on. It is quite inessential, however, to help people outside one's own society.

If this is an explanation of our common distinction between duty and supererogation, however, it is not a justification of it. The moral point of view requires us to look beyond the interests of our own society. Previously, as I have already mentioned, this may hardly have been feasible, but it is quite feasible now. From the moral point of view, the prevention of the starvation of millions of people outside our society must be considered at least as pressing as the upholding of property norms within our society.

It has been argued by some writers, among them Sidgwick and Urmson, that we need to have a basic moral code which is not too far beyond the capacities of ordinary man, for otherwise there will be a general breakdown of compliance with the moral code. Crudely stated, this argument suggests that if we tell people that they ought to refrain from murder and give everything they do not really need to famine relief, they will do neither, whereas if we tell them that they ought to refrain from murder and that it is good to give to famine relief but not wrong not to do so, they will at least refrain from murder. The issue here is: Where should we draw the line between conduct that is required and conduct that is good although not required, so as to get the best possible result? This would seem to be an empirical question, although a very difficult one. One objection to the Sidgwick-Urmson line of argument is that it takes insufficient account of the effect that moral standards can have on the decisions we make. Given a society in which a wealthy man who gives 5 percent of his income to famine relief is regarded as most generous, it is not surprising that a proposal that we all ought to give away half our incomes will be thought to be absurdly unrealistic. In a society which held that no man should have more than enough while others have less than they need, such a proposal might seem narrow-minded. What it is possible for a man to do and what he is likely to do are both, I think, very greatly influenced by what people around him are doing and expecting him to do. In any case, the possibility that by spreading the idea that we ought to be doing very much more than we are to relieve famine we shall bring about a general breakdown of moral behavior seems remote. If the stakes are an end to widespread starvation, it is worth the risk. Finally, it should be emphasized that these considerations are relevant only to the issue of what we should require from others, and not to what we ourselves ought to do.

The second objection to my attack on the pres-

ent distinction between duty and charity is one which has from time to time been made against utilitarianism. It follows from some forms of utilitarian theory that we all ought, morally, to be working full time to increase the balance of happiness over misery. The position I have taken here would not lead to this conclusion in all circumstances, for if there were no bad occurrences that we could prevent without sacrificing something of comparable moral importance, my argument would have no application. Given the present conditions in many parts of the world, however, it does follow from my argument that we ought, morally, to be working full time to relieve great suffering of the sort that occurs as a result of famine or other disasters. Of course, mitigating circumstances can be adduced—for instance, that if we wear ourselves out through overwork, we shall be less effective than we would otherwise have been. Nevertheless, when all considerations of this sort have been taken into account, the conclusion remains: We ought to be preventing as much suffering as we can without sacrificing something else of comparable moral importance. This conclusion is one which we may be reluctant to face. I cannot see, though, why it should be regarded as a criticism of the position for which I have argued, rather than a criticism of our ordinary standards of behavior. Since most people are self-interested to some degree, very few of us are likely to do everything that we ought to do. It would, however, hardly be honest to take this as evidence that it is not the case that we ought to do it.

It may still be thought that my conclusions are so wildly out of line with what everyone else thinks and has always thought that there must be something wrong with the argument somewhere. In order to show that my conclusions, while certainly contrary to contemporary Western moral standards, would not have seemed so extraordinary at other times and in other places, I would like to quote a passage from a writer not normally thought of as a way-out radical, Thomas Aquinas.

> Now, according to the natural order instituted by divine providence, material goods are provided for the satisfaction of human needs. Therefore the division and appropriation of property, wich proceeds from human law, must not hinder the satisfaction of man's necessity from such goods. Equally, whatever

a man has in superabundance is owed, of natural right, to the poor for their sustenance. So Ambrosius says, and it is also to be found in the *Decretum Gratiani*: "The bread which you withhold belongs to the hungry; the clothing you shut away, to the naked; and the money you bury in the earth is the redemption and freedom of the penniless."[4]

I now want to consider a number of points, more practical than philosophical, which are relevant to the application of the moral conclusion we have reached. These points challenge not the idea that we ought to be doing all we can to prevent starvation, but the idea that giving away a great deal of money is the best means to this end.

It is sometimes said that overseas aid should be a government responsibility, and that therefore one ought not to give to privately run charities. Giving privately, it is said, allows the government and the noncontributing members of society to escape their responsibilities.

This argument seems to assume that the more poeple there are who give to privately organized famine relief funds, the less likely it is that the government will take over full responsibility for such aid. This assumption is unsupported, and does not strike me as at all plausible. The opposite view—that if no one gives voluntarily, a government will assume that its citizens are uninterested in famine relief and would not wish to be forced into giving aid—seems more plausible. In any case, unless there were a definite probability that by refusing to give one would be helping to bring about massive government assistance, people who do refuse to make voluntary contributions are refusing to prevent a certain amount of suffering without being able to point to any tangible beneficial consequence of their refusal. So the onus of showing how their refusal will bring about government action is on those who refuse to give.

I do not, of course, want to dispute the contention that governments of affluent nations should be giving many times the amount of genuine, no-strings-attached aid that they are giving now. I agree, too, that giving privately is not enough, and that we ought to be campaigning actively for entirely new standards for both public and private contributions to famine relief. Indeed, I would sympa-thize with someone who thought that campaigning was more important than giving oneself, although I doubt whether preaching what one does not practice would be very effective. Unfortunately, for many people the idea that "it's the government's responsibility" is a reason for not giving which does not appear to entail any political action either.

Another, more serious reason for not giving to famine relief funds is that until there is effective population control, relieving famine merely postpones starvation. If we save the Bengal refugees now, others, perhaps the children of these refugees, will face starvation in a few years' time. In support of this, one may cite the now well-known facts about the population explosion and the relatively limited scope for expanded production.

This point, like the previous one, is an argument against relieving suffering that is happening now, because of a belief about what might happen in the future; it is unlike the previous point in that very good evidence can be adduced in support of this belief about the future. I will not go into the evidence here. I accept that the earth cannot support indefinitely a population rising at the present rate. This certainly poses a problem for anyone who thinks it important to prevent famine. Again, however, one could accept the argument without drawing the conclusion that it absolves one from any obligation to do anything to prevent famine. The conclusion that should be drawn is that the best means of preventing famine, in the long run, is population control. It would then follow from the position reached earlier that one ought to be doing all one can to promote population control (unless one held that all forms of population control were wrong in themselves, or would have significantly bad consequences). Since there are organizations working specifically for population control, one would then support them rather than more orthodox methods of preventing famine.

A third point raised by the conclusion reached earlier relates to the question of just how much we all ought to be giving away. One possibility, which has already been mentioned, is that we ought to give until we reach the level of marginal utility—that is, the level at which, by giving more, I would cause as much suffering to myself or my dependents as I would relieve by my gift. This would mean, of course, that one would reduce oneself to very near the material circumstances of a Bengali refugee. It will be recalled that earlier I put forward both a strong and a moderate version of the principle of preventing bad occurrences. The strong version, which required us to prevent bad things from happening unless in doing so we would be sacrificing something of comparable moral significance, does seem to require reducing ourselves to the level of marginal utility. I should also say that the strong version seems to me to be the correct one. I proposed the more moderate version—that we should prevent bad occurrences unless, to do so, we had to sacrifice something morally significant—only in order to show that even on this surely undeniable principle a great change in our way of life is required. On the more moderate principle, it may not follow that we ought to reduce ourselves to the level of marginal utility, for one might hold that to reduce oneself and one's family to this level is to cause something significantly bad to happen. Whether this is so I shall not discuss, since, as I have said, I can see no good reason for holding the moderate version of the principle rather than the strong version. Even if we accepted the principle only in its moderate form, however, it should be clear that we would have to give away enough to ensure that the consumer society, dependent as it is on people spending on trivia rather than giving to famine relief, would slow down and perhaps disappear entirely. There are several reasons why this would be desirable in itself. The value and necessity of economic growth are now being questioned not only by conservationists, but by economists as well.[5] There is no doubt, too, that the consumer society has had a distorting effect on the goals and purposes of its members. Yet looking at the matter purely from the point of view of overseas aid, there must be a limit to the extent to which we should deliberately slow down our economy; for it might be the case that if we gave away, say, 40 percent of our Gross National Product, we would slow down the economy so much that in absolute terms we would be giving less than if we gave 25 percent of the much larger GNP that we would have if we limited our contribution to this smaller percentage.

I mention this only as an indication of the sort of factor that one would have to take into account in working out an ideal. Since Western societies generally consider one percent of the GNP an acceptable level for overseas aid, the matter is entirely academic. Nor does it affect the question of how much an individual should give in a society in which very few are giving substantial amounts.

It is sometimes said, though less often now than it used to be, that philosophers have no special role to play in public affairs, since most public issues depend primarily on an assessment of facts. On questions of fact, it is said, philosophers as such have no special expertise, and so it has been possible to engage in philosophy without committing oneself to any position on major public issues. No doubt there are some issues of social policy and foreign policy about which it can truly be said that a really expert assessment of the facts is required before taking sides or acting, but the issue of famine is surely not one of these. The facts about the existence of suffering are beyond dispute. Nor, I think, is it disputed that we can do something about it, either through orthodox methods of famine relief or through population control or both. This is therefore an issue on which philosophers are competent to take a position. The issue is one which faces everyone who has more money than he needs to support himself and his dependents, or who is in a position to take some sort of political action. These categories must include practically every teacher and student of philosophy in the universities of the Western world. If philosophy is to deal with matters that are relevant to both teachers and students, this is an issue that philosophers should discuss.

Discussion, though, is not enough. What is the point of relating philosophy to public (and personal) affairs if we do not take our conclusions seriously? In this instance, taking our conclusion seriously means acting upon it. The philosopher will not find it any easier than anyone else to alter his attitudes and way of life to the extent that, if I am right, is involved in doing everything that we ought to be doing. At the very least, though, one can make a start. The philosopher who does so will have to sacrifice some of the benefits of the consumer society, but he can find compensation in the satisfaction of a way of life in which theory and practice, if not yet in harmony, are at least coming together.

Postscript

The crisis in Bangladesh that spurred me to write the above article is now of historical interest only, but the world food crisis is, if anything, still more serious. The huge grain reserves that were then held by the United States have vanished. Increased oil prices have made both fertilizer and energy more expensive in developing countries, and have made it difficult for them to produce more food. At the same time, their population has continued to grow. Fortunately, as I write now, there is no major famine anywhere in the world; but poor people are still starving in several countries, and malnutrition remains very widespread. The need for assistance is, therefore, just as great as when I first wrote, and we can be sure that without it there will, again, be major famines.

The contrast between poverty and affluence that I wrote about is also as great as it was then. True, the affluent nations have experienced a recession, and are perhaps not as prosperous as they were in 1971. But the poorer nations have suffered at least as much from the recession, in reduced government aid (because if governments decide to reduce expenditure, they regard foreign aid as one of the expendable items, ahead of, for instance, defense or public construction projects) and in increased prices for goods and materials they need to buy. In any case, compared to the difference between the affluent nations and the poor nations, the whole recession was trifling; the poorest in the affluent nations remained incomparably better off than the poorest in the poor nations.

So the case for aid, on both a personal and a governmental level, remains as great now as it was in 1971, and I would not wish to change the basic argument that I put forward then.

There are, however, some matters of emphasis that I might put differently if I were to rewrite the article, and the most important of these concerns the population problem. I still think that, as I wrote then, the view that famine relief merely postpones starvation unless something is done to check population growth is not an argument against aid, it is only an argument against the *type* of aid that should be given. Those who hold this view have the same obligation to give to prevent starvation as those who do not; the difference is that they regard assisting population control schemes as a more effective way of preventing starvation in the long run. I would now, however, have given greater space to the discussion of the population problem; for I now think that there is a serious case for saying that if a country refuses to take any steps to slow the rate of its population growth, we should not give it aid. This is, of course, a very drastic step to take, and the choice it represents is a horrible choice to have to make, but if, after a dispassionate analysis of all the available information, we come to the conclusion that without population control we will not, in the long run, be able to prevent famine or other catastrophes, then it may be more humane in the long run to aid those countries that are prepared to take strong measures to reduce population growth, and to use our aid policy as a means of pressuring other countries to take similar steps.

It may be objected that such a policy involves an attempt to coerce a sovereign nation. But since we are not under an obligation to give aid unless that aid is likely to be effective in reducing starvation or malnutrition, we are not under an obligation to give aid to countries that make no effort to reduce a rate of population growth that will lead to catastrophe. Since we do not force any nation to accept our aid, simply making it clear that we will not give aid where it is not going to be effective cannot properly be regarded as a form of coercion.

I should also make it clear that the kind of aid that will slow population growth is not just assistance with the setting up of facilities for dispensing contraceptives and performing sterilizations. It is also necessary to create the conditions under which people do not wish to have so many children. This will involve, among other things, providing greater economic security for people, particularly in their old age, so that they do not need the security of a large family to provide for them. Thus, the requirements of aid designed to reduce population growth and aid designed to eliminate starvation are by no means separate; they overlap, and the latter will often be a means to the former. The obligation of the affluent is, I believe, to do both. Fortunately, there are now so many people in the foreign aid field, including those in the private agencies, who are aware of this.

One other matter that I should now put forward slightly differently is that my argument does, of course, apply to assistance with development, particularly agricultural development, as well as to direct famine relief. Indeed, I think the former is usually the better long-term investment. Although this was my view when I wrote the article, the fact that I started from a famine situation, where the need was for immediate food, has led some readers to suppose that the argument is only about giving food and not about other types of aid. This is quite mistaken, and my view is that the aid should be of whatever type is most effective.

On a more philosophical level, there has been some discussion of the original article which has been helpful in clarifying the issues and pointing to the areas in which more work on the argument is needed. In particular, as John Arthur has shown in "Rights and the Duty to Bring Aid" . . . something more needs to be said about the notion of "moral significance." The problem is that to give an account of this notion involves nothing less than a full-fledged ethical theory; and while I am myself inclined toward a utilitarian view, it was my aim in writing "Famine, Affluence, and Morality" to produce an argument which would appeal not only to utilitarians, but also to anyone who accepted the initial premises of the argument, which seemed to me likely to have a very wide acceptance. So I tried to get around the need to produce a complete ethical theory by allowing my readers to fill in their own version—within limits—of what is morally significant, and then see what the moral consequences are. This tactic works reasonably well with those who are prepared to agree that such matters as being fashionably dressed are not really of moral significance; but Arthur is right to say that people could take the opposite view without being obviously irrational. Hence, I do not accept Arthur's claim that the weak principle implies little or no duty of benevolence, for it will imply a significant duty of benevolence for those who admit, as I think most nonphilosophers and even off-guard philosophers will admit, that they spend considerable sums on items that by their own standards are of no moral significance. But I do agree that the weak principle is nonetheless too weak, because it makes it too easy for the duty of benevolence to be avoided.

On the other hand, I think the strong principle will stand, whether the notion of moral significance is developed along utilitarian lines, or once again left to the individual reader's own sincere judgment. In either case, I would argue against Arthur's view that we are morally entitled to give greater weight to our own interests and purposes simply because they are our own. This view seems to me contrary to the idea, now widely shared by moral philosophers, that some element of impartiality or universalizability is inherent in the very notion of a moral judgment. (For a discussion of the different formulations of this idea, and an indication of the extent to which they are in agreement, see R. M. Hare, "Rules of War and Moral Reasoning," *Philosophy and Public Affairs* I, no. 2 [1972].) Granted, in normal circumstances, it may be better for everyone if we recognize that each of us will be primarily responsible for running our own lives and only secondarily responsible for others. This, however, is not a moral ultimate, but a secondary principle that derives from consideration of how a society may best order its affairs, given the limits of altruism in human beings. Such secondary principles are, I think, swept aside by the extreme evil of people starving to death.

Notes

1. There was also a third possibility: that India would go to war to enable the refugees to return to their lands. Since I wrote this paper, India has taken this way out. The situation is no longer that described above, but this does not affect my argument, as the next paragraph indicates.

2. In view of the special sense philosophers often give to the term, I should say that I use "obligation" simply as the abstract noun derived from "ought," so that "I have an obligation to" means no more, and no less, than "I ought to." This usage is in accordance with the definition of "ought" given by the *Shorter Oxford English Dictionary*: "the general verb to express duty or obligation." I do not think any issue of substance hangs on the way the term is used; sentences in which I use "obligation" could be all rewritten, although somewhat clumsily, as sentences in which a clause containing "ought" replaces the term "obligation."

3. J. O. Urmson, "Saints and Heroes," in *Essays in Moral Philosophy*, ed. Abraham I. Melden (Seattle: University of Washington Press, 1958), p. 214. For a related but significantly different view see also Henry Sidgwick, *The Methods of Ethics*, 7th edn. (London: Dover Press, 1907), pp. 220–21, 492–93.

4. *Summa Theologica*, II-II, Question 66, Article 7, in *Aquinas, Selected Political Writings*, ed. A. P. d'Entreves, trans. J. G. Dawson (Oxford: Basil Blackwell, 1948), p. 171.

5. See, for instance, John Kenneth Galbraith, *The New Industrial State* (Boston: Houghton Mifflin, 1967); and E. J. Mishan, *The Costs of Economic Growth* (New York: Praeger, 1967).

Questions for Analysis

1. *What is the difference between the strong and weak versions of the principle of preventing bad occurrences?*

2. *What does Singer mean by "without sacrificing anything of comparable importance"?*

3. *Why does Singer say the world would be fundamentally different if we followed his two principles?*

4. *Suppose someone said to Singer: "But I'm not responsible for the starvation that people experience. So why do I have a duty to prevent it?" How might Singer reply?*

5. *Why does Singer not regard helping as charity?*

6. *Suppose one accepts the argument that relief to countries without population-control measures merely postpones starvation. Does this absolve one of the obligation to do anything to prevent starvation?*

7. *Is it accurate to say that while Singer is inclined to the utilitarian view, his principles are essentially nonutilitarian or at least could appeal to nonutilitarians? Explain.*

8. *Does Singer's postscript undercut his original argument?*

Reason and Morality in a World of Limited Food

Richard A. Watson

The principle of equity is central to philosophy professor Richard A. Watson's thesis in this essay. The principle of equity refers to equal sharing. Watson's thesis is that, with respect to world hunger, there should be an equal sharing of food.

Watson is aware of the most trenchant objection to his position: Sharing food may turn out to be futile. Indeed, what if, as a result of sharing, the human species perishes? So be it, Watson answers. No matter how horrendous the consequences, the moral action is to share and share equally. As Watson says, "No principle of morality absolves one of behaving immorally simply to save one's life or nation."

Watson grants that such a suicidal course may be irrational. Nevertheless, he argues that the claims of morality supersede those of conflicting reason. In other words, the moral action may not necessarily be the reasonable or practical action. Where in fact the moral action is unreasonable, one nevertheless has a obligation to behave morally.

From Richard A. Watson, "Reason and Morality in a World of Limited Food," in World Hunger and Moral Obligation, *William Aiken and Hugh LaFollette, eds. (Englewood Cliffs, N.J.: Prentice-Hall, 1977). Reprinted by permission of the author.*

Watson believes his conclusion that we must equally share what we have follows inexorably from the assumption that every human life is equal in value. Accepting this assumption, presumably we must conclude that everyone deserves an equal share—no matter what the consequences, even if they be extinction.

Obviously Watson subordinates the principle of survival to the principle of equity. He feels that this is justified because "in the milieu of morality, it is immaterial whether or not the human species survives as a result of individual moral behavior."

Like Singer, Watson is arguing for an obligation to share. But while Singer's basis is utilitarian, Watson's is Kantian in its rejection of any consequential considerations as a basis for morality.

A few years ago, President Johnson said:

> There are 200 million of us and 3 billion of them and they want what we've got, but we're not going to give it to them.

In this essay I examine the conflict between reasonable and moral behavior in a world of limited food. It appears to be unreasonable—and conceivably immoral—to share all food equally when this would result in everyone's being malnourished. Arguments for the morality of unequal distribution are presented from the standpoint of the individual, the nation, and the human species. These arguments fail because, although it is unreasonable to share limited food when sharing threatens survival, the moral principle of equity ranks sharing above survival. I accept the principle of equity, and conclude by challenging the ideological basis that makes sharing unreasonable.

The contrast of the moral with the reasonable depends on distinguishing people from things. Moral considerations pertain to behavior of individuals that affects other people by acting on them directly or by acting on things in which they have an interest. The moral context is broad, for people have interests in almost everything, and almost any behavior may affect someone.

If reasonable and moral behavior were coextensive, then there would be no morality. Thus, there is no contrast at the extremes that bound the moral milieu, reason and morality being the same at one pole, and morality not existing at the other. These extremes meet in evolutionary naturalism: If it is moral to treat people as animals surviving, then reason augmenting instinct is the best criterion for behavior, and a separate discipline of morality is extraneous. Only between the extremes can reason and morality conflict.

Between the extremes, some moralists use "rational" to indicate conclusions that tend toward

moral behavior, and "practical" for conclusions that excusably do not. The use of these terms often constitutes special pleading, either to gain sympathy for a position that is not strictly reasonable but is "rational" (because it is "right"), or that is not strictly moral but is "practical" (because it "should" be done). These hedges hide the sharp distinction between people and things in the context of reason and morality. The rational and the practical are obviously reasonable in a way that they are not obviously either moral or immoral. Reasonable behavior is either moral, immoral, or amoral. When reason and morality conflict, there can be confusion, but no compromise.

Attacks on morality by reason disguised in practical dress are so common as to go almost without notice. The practical ousts morality as a determinant of behavior, particularly in industrialized nations. Many argue that the practical imperatives of survival preclude moral behavior even by those who want to be moral. If only it were practical to be moral, then all would gladly be so.

It is difficult to be moral in a world of limited food because the supreme moral principle is that of equity. The principle of equity is based on the belief that all human beings are moral equals with equal rights to the necessities of life. Differential treatment of human beings thus should be based only on their freely chosen actions and not on accidents of their birth and environment. Specific to this discussion, everyone has a right to an equal share of available food.

However, we find ourselves in a world about which many food and population experts assert the following:

1. One-third of the world's people (the West) consume two-thirds of the world's resources.

2. Two-thirds of the world's people (the Third World) are malnourished.

3. Equal distribution of the world's resources would result in everyone's being malnourished.

There is ample evidence that these statements are true, but for this discussion it is enough that many people in the West—particularly those who occupy positions of responsibility and power—understand and accept them.

These moral and factual beliefs drive one to this practical conclusion: Although morally we should share all food equally, and we in the West eat more than we need, equal sharing would be futile (unreasonable), for then no one would be well nourished. Thus, any food sharing is necessarily symbolic, for no practical action would alleviate the plight of the malnourished.

For example, practical action—moral as far as it goes—might be to reduce food consumption until every Westerner is just well nourished. But if the surplus were distributed equally to the other two-thirds of the world's people, they would still be malnourished. Thus, an easy excuse for not sharing at all is that it would neither solve the nourishment problem nor change the moral situation. Two-thirds would still be malnourished, and one-third would still be consuming more than equal shares of the world's food, to which everyone has equal rights.

Another argument for unequal distribution is as follows: All people are moral equals. Because everyone has a right to be well nourished, it would be immoral to take so much food from someone who has enough as to leave him without enough. Anyone who takes the food would be acting immorally, even if the taker is starving. This argument can go two ways. One could simply say that it would be immoral to deprive oneself of what one has. But if one wanted to discredit morality itself, one could claim that morality in this instance is self-contradictory. For if I behave morally by distributing food equally, I behave immorally by depriving someone (myself) of enough food to remain well nourished. And noticing that if all food were shared equally, everyone would be malnourished instead of just some, one might argue that it cannot be moral to deprive one person of his right to enough food so that two people have less than enough. Proper moral action must be to maintain the inequity, so at least one person can enjoy his rights.

Nevertheless, according to the highest prin-ciples of traditional Western morality, available food should be distributed equally even if everyone then will be malnourished. This is belabored by everyone who compares the earth to a lifeboat, a desert island, or a spaceship. In these situations, the strong are expected to take even a smaller share than the weak. There is no need for us to go overboard, however. We shall soon be as weak as anyone else if we just do our moral duty and distribute the food equally.

Given this, the well-nourished minority might try to buttress its position morally by attempting to solve the nourishment problem for everyone, either by producing enough food for everyone, or by humanely reducing the world's population to a size at which equal distribution of food would nourish everyone adequately. The difficulty with this is that national survival for the food-favored industrial nations requires maintenance of political and economic systems that depend on unequal distribution of limited goods.[1] In the present world context, it would be unreasonable (disastrous) for an industrialized nation to attempt to provide food for everybody. Who would pay for it? And after all, well-nourished citizens are obviously important to the survival of the nation. As for humanely reducing the world's population, there are no practical means for doing it. Thus, the practical expediencies of national survival preclude actions that might justify temporary unequal distribution with the claim that it is essential for solving the nourishment problem. Equal distribution is impossible without total (impractical) economic and political revolution.

These arguments are morally spurious. That food sufficient for well-nourished survival is the equal right of every human individual or nation is a specification of the higher principle that everyone has equal right to the necessities of life. The moral stress of the principle of equity is primarily on equal sharing, and only secondarily on what is being shared. The higher moral principle is of human *equity per se*. Consequently, the moral action is to distribute all food equally, *whatever the consequences*. This is the hard line apparently drawn by such moralists as Immanuel Kant and Noam Chomsky—but then, morality is hard. The conclusion may be unreasonable (impractical and irrational in conventional terms), but it is obviously moral. Nor should anyone purport surprise; it has always been understood that the claims of morality—if taken seriously—supersede those of conflicting reason.

One may even have to sacrifice one's life or one's nation to be moral in situations where practical behavior would preserve it. For example, if a prisoner of war undergoing torture is to be a (perhaps dead) patriot even when reason tells him that collaboration will hurt no one, he remains silent. Similarly, if one is to be moral, one distributes available food in equal shares (even if everyone then dies). That an action is necessary to save one's life is no excuse for behaving unpatriotically or immorally if one wishes to be a patriot or moral. No principle of morality absolves one of behaving immorally simply to save one's life or nation. There is a strict analogy here between adhering to moral principles for the sake of being moral, and adhering to Christian principles for the sake of being Christian. The moral world contains pits and lions, but one looks always to the highest light. The ultimate test always harks to the highest principle—recant or die—and it is pathetic to profess morality if one quits when the going gets rough.

I have put aside many questions of detail—such as the mechanical problems of distributing food—because detail does not alter the stark conclusion. If every human life is equal in value, then the equal distribution of the necessities of life is an extremely high, if not the highest, moral duty. It is at least high enough to override the excuse that by doing it one would lose one's own life. But many people cannot accept the view that one must distribute equally even if the nation collapses or all people die.

If everyone dies, then there will be no realm of morality. Practically speaking, sheer survival comes first. One can adhere to the principle of equity only if one exists. So it is rational to suppose that the principle of survival is morally higher than the principle of equity. And though one might not be able to argue for unequal distribution of food to save a nation—for nations can come and go—one might well argue that unequal distribution is necessary for the survival of the human species. That is, some large group—say one-third of the present world population—should be a least well-nourished for human survival.

However, from an individual standpoint, the human species—like the nation—is of no moral relevance. From a naturalistic standpoint, survival does come first; from a moralistic standpoint—as indicated above—survival may have to be sacrificed. In the milieu of morality, it is immaterial whether or not the human species survives as a result of individual moral behavior.

A possible way to resolve this conflict between reason and morality is to challenge the view that morality pertains only to the behavior of individual human beings. One way to do this is to break down the distinction between people and things. It would have to be established that such abstract things as "the people," "the nation," and "the human species" in themselves have moral status. Then they would have a right to survival just as human beings have a right to life: We should be concerned about the survival of these things not merely because human beings have an interest in them, but because it would be immoral *per se* to destroy them.

In the West, corporation law provides the theoretical basis for treating things as people.[2] Corporate entities such as the State, the Church, and trading companies have long enjoyed special status in Western society. The rights of corporate entities are precisely defined by a legal fiction, the concept of the corporate person. Christopher D. Stone says that corporate persons enjoy as many legal rights as, and sometimes more than, do individual human persons.[3] Thus, while most of us are not tempted to confuse ordinary things like stones and houses with people, almost everyone concurs with a legal system that treats corporate entities as people. The great familiarity and usefulness of this system supports the delusion that corporate entities have rights in common with, and are the moral equals of, individual human beings.

On these grounds, some argue that because of size, importance, and power of corporate entities, institutional rights have priority over the rights of individuals. Of course, to the extent that society is defined by the economy or the State, people are dependent on and subordinate to these institutions. Practically speaking, institutional needs come first; people's needs are satisfied perhaps coextensively with, but secondarily to, satisfying institutional needs. It is argued that to put individual human needs first would be both illogical and impractical, for people and their needs are defined only in the social context. Institutions come first because they are prerequisite to the very existence of people.

A difficulty with the above argument as a support for any given institution is that it provides merely for the priority of *some* institutions over human individuals, not, say, for the priority of the United States or the West. But it does appear to provide an argument for the priority of the human species.

Given that the human species has rights as a fictional person on the analogy of corporate rights, it would seem to be rational to place the right of survival of the species above that of individuals. Unless the species survives, no individual will survive, and thus an individual's right to life is subordinate to the species' right to survival. If species survival depends on the unequal distribution of food to maintain a healthy breeding stock, then it is morally right for some people to have plenty while others starve. Only if there is enough food to nourish everyone well does it follow that food should be shared equally.

This might be true if corporate entities actually do have moral status and moral rights. But obviously, the legal status of corporate entities as fictional persons does not make them moral equals or superiors of actual human persons. Legislators might profess astonishment that anyone would think that a corporate person is a *person* as people are, let alone a moral person. However, because the legal rights of corporate entities are based on individual rights, and because corporate entities are treated so much like persons, the transition is often made.

Few theorists today would argue that the state or the human species is a personal agent.[4] But all this means is that idealism is dead in theory. Unfortunately, its influence lives, so it is worth giving an argument to show that corporate entities are not real persons.

Corporate entities are not persons as you and I are in the explicit sense that we are self-conscious agents and they are not. Corporate entities are not *agents* at all, let alone moral agents. This is a good reason for not treating corporate entities even as fictional persons. The distinction between people and other things, to generalize, is that people are self-conscious agents, whereas things are not.

The possession of rights essentially depends on an entity's being self-conscious, i.e., on its actually being a person. If it is self-conscious, then it has a right to life. Self-consciousness is a necessary, but not sufficient, condition for an entity's also being a responsible moral agent as most human beings are. A moral agent must have the capacity to be responsible, i.e., the capacity to choose and to act freely with respect to consequences that the agent does or can recognize and accept as its own choice and doing. Only a being who knows himself as a person, and who can effect choices and accept consequences, is a responsible moral agent.

On these grounds, moral equality rests on the actuality of moral agency based on reciprocal rights and responsibilities. One is responsible to something only if it can be responsible in return. Thus, we have responsibilities to other people, and they have reciprocal rights. We have no responsibilities to things as such, and they have no rights. If we care for things, it is because people have interests in them, not because things in themselves impose responsibilities on us.

That is, as stated early in this essay, morality essentially has to do with relations among people, among persons. It is nonsense to talk of things that cannot be moral agents as having responsibilities; consequently, it is nonsense to talk of whatever is not actually a person as having rights. It is deceptive even to talk of legal rights of a corporate entity. Those rights (and reciprocal responsibilities) actually pertain to individual human beings who have an interest in the corporate entity. The State or the human species have no rights at all, let alone rights superior to those of individuals.

The basic reason given for preserving a nation or the human species is that otherwise the milieu of morality would not exist. This is false so far as specific nations are concerned, but it is true that the existence of individuals depends on the existence of the species. However, although moral behavior is required of each individual, no principle requires that the realm of morality itself be preserved. Thus, we are reduced to the position that people's interest in preserving the human species is based primarily on the interest of each in individual survival. Having shown above that the principle of equity is morally superior to the principle of survival, we can conclude again that food should be shared equally even if this means the extinction of the human race.

Is there no way to produce enough food to nourish everyone well? Besides cutting down to the minimum, people in the West might quit feeding such nonhuman animals as cats and dogs. However, some people (e.g., Peter Singer) argue that mere sentience—the capacity to suffer pain—means that an animal is the moral equal of human beings.[5] I argue that because nonhuman animals are not moral agents, they do not share the rights of self-conscious responsible persons. And considering the profligacy of nature, it is rational to argue that if nonhuman animals have any rights at all, they include not the right to life, but merely the right to fight for life. In fact, if people in the West did not feed grain to cattle, sheep, and hogs, a considerable amount of food would be freed for human consumption. Even then, there might not be enough to nourish everyone well.

Let me remark that Stone and Singer attempt to break down the distinction between people on the one hand, and certain things (corporate entities) and nonhuman animals on the other, out of moral concern. However, there is another, profoundly antihumanitarian movement also attempting to break down the distinction. All over the world, heirs of Gobineau, Goebbels, and Hitler practice genocide and otherwise treat people as nonhuman animals and things in the name of the State. I am afraid that the consequences of treating entities such as corporations and nonhuman animals—that are not moral agents—as persons with rights will not be that we will treat national parks and chickens the way we treat people, but that we will have provided support for those who treat people the way we now treat nonhuman animals and things.

The benefits of modern society depend in no small part on the institution of corporation law. Even if the majority of these benefits are to the good—of which I am by no means sure—the legal fiction of corporate personhood still elevates corporate needs above the needs of people. In the present context, reverence for corporate entities leads to the spurious argument that the present world imbalance of food and resources is morally justified in the name of the higher rights of sovereign nations, or even of the human species, the survival of which is said to be more important than the right of any individual to life.

This conclusion is morally absurd. This is not, however, the fault of morality. We *should* share all food equally, at least until everyone is well-nour-ished. Besides food, *all* the necessities of life should be shared, at least until everyone is adequately supplied with a humane minimum. The hard conclusion remains that we should share all food equally even if this means that everyone starves and the human species becomes extinct. But, of course, the human race would survive even equal sharing, for after enough people died, the remainder could be well-nourished on the food that remained. But this grisly prospect does not show that anything is wrong with the principle of equity. Instead, it shows that something is profoundly wrong with the social institutions in which sharing the necessities of life equally is "impractical" and "irrational."

In another ideological frame, moral behavior might also be practical and rational. As remarked above, equal sharing can be accomplished only through total economic and political revolution. Obviously, this is what is needed.

Notes

1. See Richard Watson, "The Limits of World Order," *Alternatives: A Journal of World Policy,* I (1975), 487–513.

2. See Christopher D. Stone, *Should Trees Have Standing? Toward Legal Rights for Natural Objects* (Los Altos, Calif.: William Kaufman, 1974). Stone proposes that to protect such things as national parks, we should give them legal personhood as we do corporations.

3. Ibid., p. 47: "It is more and more the individual human being, with his consciousness, that is the legal fiction." Also: "The legal system does the best it can to maintain the illusion of the reality of the individual human being." (footnote 125) Many public figures have discovered that they have a higher legal status if they incorporate themselves than they do as individual persons.

4. Stone (ibid., p. 47) does say that "institutions . . . have wills, minds, purposes, and inertias that are in very important ways their own, i.e., that can transcend and survive changes in the consciousness of the individual humans who supposedly comprise them, and whom they supposedly serve," but I do not think Stone actually believes that corporate entities are persons like you and me.

5. See Peter Singer, *Animal Liberation* (New York: The New York Review of Books/Random House, 1975).

Questions for Analysis

1. Describe the conflict between the "reasonable" and the "moral."

2. At one point in the essay, Watson invokes Kant to fortify his position. But surely Kant saw no conflict between the "reasonable" and the "moral." Do you think Watson is using the term reasonable in the sense of what is practical, useful, or productive of happiness and not in the sense of what is logically consistent? Explain.

3. Why does Watson feel that arguments for the morality of unequal distribution fail?

4. Why does Watson say: "It is difficult to be moral in a world of limited food because the supreme moral principle is that of equity"? Do you accept the supremacy of equity as a moral principle?

5. From what higher principle does Watson say people have a right to food sufficient for well-nourished survival?

6. Do you agree with Watson that morality in some cases may be irrational? Is it necessary first to clarify Watson's use of the term irrational?

7. If morality may be unreasonable, does this create any special problems for the moralist?

8. Do you think Kant would agree that "if one is to be moral, one distributes available food in equal shares (even if everyone then dies)"?

Equality, Entitlements, and the Distribution of Income

John Arthur

As indicated in the chapter, an alternative to the positions that argue for an obligation to share or not to share food is the position that views sharing as morally permissible but not obligatory. In this essay, professor of philosophy John Arthur argues that sharing ultimately is an act of benevolence. At the same time, he claims that there may be occasions when we have a duty to be so benevolent.

Arthur begins by observing an ambivalence in our moral code. Sometimes we feel obliged to help the needy; other times we feel justified in keeping what we have, even though our sacrifice might cause greater evil to be avoided. How can we resolve the tension?

Singer in his essay suggested a principle of greater moral evil: Any time we can prevent something bad without sacrificing anything of comparable moral significance, we ought to do it. Arthur rejects this response, arguing that it ignores the essential role of entitlements in our moral

Thanks to Aleta Arthur, Clement Dore, and William Shaw for helpful comments on an earlier version of this paper, and especially to Richard B. Brandt, whose influence is apparent throughout.

code. Arthur then goes on to discuss entitlements in terms of rights and desert and demonstrates how they are embedded in our moral outlook. Indeed, by dissecting the nature of morality, with special attention to the kind of morality we want to endorse, Arthur champions entitlements as a necessary part of an ideal moral code.

Be careful not to misconstrue Arthur. He is not *making entitlements absolute; he is* not *saying that individuals never have an obligation to help the needy. Quite the opposite: He acknowledges that we likely have obligations to help* where there is no substantial cost to ourselves. *By the same token, in Arthur's view it is at least sometimes moral to invoke rights and duties as justification for not giving aid.*

Introduction

My guess is that everyone who reads these words is wealthy by comparison with the poorest millions of people on our planet. Not only do we have plenty of money for food, clothing, housing, and other necessities, but a fair amount is left over for far less important purchases like phonograph records, fancy clothes, trips, intoxicants, movies, and so on. And what's more, we don't usually give thought to whether or not we ought to spend our money on such luxuries rather than to give it to those who need it more; we just assume it's ours to do with as we please.

Peter Singer, "Famine, Affluence, and Morality," and Richard Watson, "Reason and Morality in a World of Limited Food" [both reprinted in this volume] argue that our assumption is wrong, that we should not buy luxuries when others are in severe need. But are they correct? In the first two sections of this paper my aim is to get into focus just what their arguments are, and to evaluate them. Both Singer and Watson, it seems to me, ignore an important feature of our moral code, namely that it allows people who deserve or have rights to their earnings to keep them.

But the fact that our code encourages a form of behavior is not a complete defense, for it is possible that our current moral attitudes are mistaken. Sections 3 and 4 consider this possibility from two angles: universalizability and the notion of an ideal moral code. Neither of these approaches, I argue, requires that desert and rights be sacrificed in the name of redistribution.

1. Equality and the Duty to Aid

What does our moral code have to say about helping people in need? Watson emphasizes what he calls the "principle of equity." Since "all human

life is of equal value," and difference in treatment should be "based on freely chosen actions and not accidents of birth or environment," he thinks that we have "equal rights to the necessities of life." To distribute food unequally assumes that some lives are worth more than others, an assumption which, he says, we do not accept. Watson believes, in fact, that we put such importance on the "equity principle" that it should not be violated even if unequal distribution is the only way for anybody to survive. (Leaving aside for the moment whether or not he is correct about our code, it seems to me that if it really did require us to commit mass suicide rather than allow inequality in wealth, then we would want to abandon it for a more suitable set of rules. But more on that later.)

Is Watson correct in assuming that all life is of equal value? Did Adolph Hitler and Martin Luther King, for example, lead two such lives? Clearly one did far more good and less harm than the other. Nor are moral virtues like courage, kindness, and trustworthiness equally distributed among people. So there are at least two senses in which people are not morally equal.

Yet the phrase "All men are equal" has an almost platitudinous ring, and many of us would not hesitate to say that equality is a cornerstone of our morality. But what does it mean? It seems to me that we might have in mind one of two things. First is an idea that Thomas Jefferson expressed in the *Declaration of Independence*. "All men are created equal" meant, for him, that no man is the moral inferior of another, that, in other words, there are certain rights which all men share equally, including life and liberty. We are entitled to pursue our own lives with a minimum of interference from others, and no person is the natural slave of another. But, as Jefferson also knew, equality in that sense does not require equal distribution of the necessities of life, only that we not interfere with one another, allowing instead every person the liberty to pursue his own affairs, so long as he does not violate the rights of his fellows.

Others, however, have something different in mind when they speak of human equality. I want to develop this second idea by recounting briefly the details of Singer's argument in "Famine, Affluence, and Morality." He first argues that two general moral principles are widely accepted, and then that those principles imply an obligation to eliminate starvation.

The first principle is simply that "suffering and death from lack of food, shelter and medical care are bad." Some may be inclined to think that the mere existence of such an evil in itself places an obligation on others, but that is, of course, the problem which Singer addresses. I take it that he is not begging the question in this obvious way and will argue from the existence of evil to the obligation of others to eliminate it. But how, exactly, does he establish this? The second principle, he thinks, shows the connection, but it is here that controversy arises.

This principle, which I will call the greater moral evil rule, is as follows:

> If it is in our power to prevent something bad from happening, without thereby sacrificing anything of comparable moral importance, we ought, morally, to do it.[1]

In other words, people are entitled to keep their earnings only if there is no way for them to prevent a greater evil by giving them away. Providing others with food, clothing, and housing would generally be of more importance than buying luxuries, so the greater moral evil rule now requires substantial redistribution of wealth.

Certainly there are few, if any, of us who live by that rule, although that hardly shows we are *justified* in our way of life; we often fail to live up to our own standards. Why does Singer think our shared morality requires that we follow the greater moral evil rule? What arguments does he give for it?

He begins with an analogy. Suppose you came across a child drowning in a shallow pond. Certainly we feel it would be wrong not to help. Even if saving the child meant we must dirty our clothes, we would emphasize that those clothes are not of comparable significance to the child's life. The greater moral evil rule thus seems a natural way of capturing why we think it would be wrong not to help.

But the argument for the greater moral evil rule is not limited to Singer's claim that it explains our feelings about the drowning child or that it appears "uncontroversial." Moral equality also enters the picture. Besides the Jeffersonian idea that we share certain rights equally, most of us are also attracted to another type of equality, namely that like amounts of suffering (or happiness) are of equal significance, no matter who is experiencing them. I cannot reasonably say that, while my pain is no more severe than yours, I am somehow special and it's more important that mine be alleviated. Objectivity requires us to admit the opposite, that no one has a unique status which warrants such special pleading. So equality demands equal consideration of interests as well as respect for certain rights.

But if we fail to give to famine relief and instead purchase a new car when the old one will do, or buy fancy clothes for a friend when his or her old ones are perfectly good, are we not assuming that the relatively minor enjoyment we or our friends may get is as important as another person's lfe? And that is a form of prejudice; we are acting as if people were not equal in the sense that their interests deserve equal consideration. We are giving special consideration to ourselves or to our group, rather like a racist does. Equal consideration of interests thus leads naturally to the greater moral evil rule.

2. Rights and Desert

Equality, in the sense of giving equal consideration to equally serious needs, is part of our moral code. And so we are led, quite rightly I think, to the conclusion that we should prevent harm to others if in doing so we do not sacrifice anything of comparable moral importance. But there is also another side to the coin, one which Singer and Watson ignore. This can be expressed rather awkwardly by the notion of entitlements. These fall into two broad categories, rights and desert. A few examples will show what I mean.

All of us could help others by giving away or allowing others to use our bodies. While your life may be shortened by the loss of a kidney or less enjoyable if lived with only one eye, those costs are probably not comparable to the loss experienced by a person who will die without any kidney or who is totally blind. We can even imagine persons who will actually be harmed in some way by your not granting sexual favors to them. Perhaps the absence of a sexual partner would cause psychological harm or even rape. Now suppose that you can prevent this evil without sacrificing anything of comparable importance. Obviously such relations may not be pleasant, but according to the greater moral evil rule, that is not enough; to be justified in refusing, you must show that the unpleasantness you would experience is of equal importance to the harm you are preventing. Otherwise, the rule says you must consent.

If anything is clear, however, it is that our code does not *require* such heroism; you are entitled to keep your second eye and kidney and not bestow sexual favors on anyone who may be harmed without them. The reason for this is often expressed in terms of rights; it's your body, you have a right to it, and that weighs against whatever duty you have to help. To sacrifice a kidney for a stranger is to do more than is required, it's heroic.

Moral rights are normally divided into two categories. Negative rights are rights of noninterference. The right to life, for example, is a right not to be killed. Property rights, the right to privacy, and the right to exercise religious freedom are also negative, requiring only that people leave others alone and not interfere.

Positive rights, however, are rights of recipience. By not putting their children up for adoption, parents give them various positive rights, including the rights to be fed, clothed, and housed. If I agree to share in a business venture, my promise creates a right of recipience, so that when I back out of the deal, I've violated your right.

Negative rights also differ from positive in that the former are natural; the ones you have depend on what you are. If lower animals lack rights to life or liberty it is because there is a relevant difference between them and us. But the positive rights you may have are not natural; they arise because others have promised, agreed, or contracted to give you something.

Normally, then, a duty to help a stranger in need is not the result of a right he has. Such a right would be positive, and since no contract or promise was made, no such right exists. An exception to

this would be a lifeguard who contracts to watch out for someone's children. The parent whose child drowns would in this case be doubly wronged. First, the lifeguard should not have cruelly or thoughtlessly ignored the child's interests, and second, he ought not to have violated the rights of the parents that he help. Here, unlike Singer's case, we can say there are rights at stake. Other bystanders also act wrongly by cruelly ignoring the child, but unlike the lifeguard they do not violate anybody's rights. Moral rights are one factor to be weighed, but we also have other obligations; I am not claiming that rights are all we need to consider. That view, like the greater moral evil rule, trades simplicity for accuracy. In fact, our code expects us to help people in need as well as to respect negative and positive rights. But we are also entitled to invoke our own rights as justification for not giving to distant strangers or when the cost to us is substantial, as when we give up an eye or a kidney.

Rights come in a variety of shapes and sizes, and people often disagree about both their shape and size. Can a woman kill an unborn child because of her right to control her body? Does mere inheritance transfer rights to property? Do dolphins have a right to live? While some rights are widely accepted, others are controversial.

One more comment about rights, then we'll look at desert. Watson's position, which I criticized for other reasons earlier, is also mistaken because he ignores important rights. He claims that we must pay no attention to "accidents of birth and environment" and base our treatment of people on "what they freely choose." But think about how you will (or did) select a spouse or lover. Are you not entitled to consider such "accidents of birth and environment" as attractiveness, personality, and intelligence? It is, after all, your future, and it is certainly a part of our shared moral code that you have a right to use those (or whatever) criteria you wish in selecting a mate. It is at best an exaggeration to say we must always "ignore accidents of birth and environment" in our treatment of people.

Desert is a second form of entitlement. Suppose, for example, an industrious farmer manages through hard work to produce a surplus of food for the winter while a lazy neighbor spends his summer fishing. Must our industrious farmer ignore his hard work and give the surplus away because his neighbor or his family will suffer? What again seems clear is that we have more than one factor to weigh. Not only should we compare the consequences of his keeping it with his giving it away; we also should weigh the fact that one farmer deserves the food, he earned it through his hard work. Perhaps his deserving the product of his labor is outweighed by the greater need of his lazy neighbor, or perhaps it isn't, but being outweighed is in any case not the same as weighing nothing!

Desert can be negative, too. The fact that the Nazi war criminal did what he did means he deserves punishment, that we have a reason to send him to jail. Other considerations, for example the fact that nobody will be deterred by his suffering, or that he is old and harmless, may weigh against punishment and so we may let him go; but again that does not mean he doesn't still deserve to be punished.

Our moral code gives weight to both the greater moral evil principle and entitlements. The former emphasizes equality, claiming that from an objective point of view all comparable suffering, whoever its victim, is equally significant. It encourages us to take an impartial look at all the various effects of our actions; it is thus forward-looking. When we consider matters of entitlement, however, our attention is directed to the past. Whether we have rights to money, property, eyes, or whatever, depends on how we came to possess them. If they were acquired by theft rather than from birth or through gift exchange, then the right is suspect. Desert, like rights, is also backward-looking, emphasizing past effort or past transgressions which now warrant reward or punishment.

Our commonly shared morality thus requires that we ignore neither consequences nor entitlements, neither the future results of our action nor relevant events in the past. It encourages people to help others in need, especially when it's a friend or someone we are close to geographically, and when the cost is not significant. But it also gives weight to rights and desert, so that we are not usually obligated to give to strangers.

One path is still open as a defense of the greater moral evil rule, and it deserves comment. I have assumed throughout that Singer wants to emphasize the great disparity in the amount of enjoyment someone may get from, say, a new car, as compared with the misery that could be prevented by using the money to save another's life. The fact that the

two are not comparable means that the money should not be spent on the car. It is possible to interpret the rule differently, however. By admitting that having rights and deserving things are also of moral significance, Singer could accept what I have said so that the greater moral evil rule would survive intact.

The problem with this response, however, is that the greater moral evil rule has now become an almost empty platitude, urging nothing more than that we should prevent something bad unless we have adequate moral reason not to do so. Since rights and desert often provide such reasons, the rule would say nothing useful about our obligation to help others, and it certainly would not require us to "reduce ourselves to the level of marginal utility" so that the "consumer society" would "slow down and perhaps disappear" as Singer claims. I will therefore assume he would not accept such an interpretation of his view, that entitlements are not among the sacrifices which could balance off the suffering caused by failing to help people in need.

But unless we are moral relativists, the mere fact that entitlements are an important part of our moral code does not in itself justify such a role. Singer and Watson can perhaps best be seen as moral reformers, advocating the rejection of rules which provide for distribution according to rights and desert. Certainly the fact that in the past our moral code condemned suicide and racial mixing while condoning slavery should not convince us that a more enlightened moral code, one which we would want to support, would take such positions. Rules which define acceptable behavior are continually changing, and we must allow for the replacement of inferior ones.

Why should we not view entitlements as examples of inferior rules we are better off without? What could justify our practice of evaluating actions by looking backward to rights and desert instead of just to their consequences? One answer is that more fundamental values than rights and desert are at stake, namely fairness, justice, and respect. Failure to reward those who earn good grades or promotions is wrong because it's *unfair;* ignoring past guilt shows a lack of regard for *justice;* and failure to respect rights to life, privacy, or religious choice suggests a lack of *respect for other persons.*

Some people may be persuaded by those remarks, feeling that entitlements are now on an acceptably firm foundation. But an advocate of equality may well want to question why fairness, justice, and respect for persons should matter. But since it is no more obvious that preventing suffering matters than that fairness, respect, and justice do, we again seem to have reached an impasse.

3. Universalizability

It is sometimes thought that we can choose between competing moral rules by noting which ones are compatible with some more fundamental rule. One such fundamental standard is attributed to Kant, though it is also rooted in traditional Christian thought. "Do unto others as you would have them do unto you" and the Kantian categorical imperative, "Act only on maxims that you can will would become universal laws," express an idea some think is basic to *all* moral rules. The suggestion is that if you think what you're doing is right, then you have got to be willing to universalize your judgment, that is, to acknowledge that anyone in similar circumstances would be correct if he were to follow the same rule.

Such familiar reasoning can be taken in two very different ways. The first requires only that a person not make himself an exception, that he live up to his own standard. This type of universalizability, however, cannot help choose between the two rules. An advocate of rights and desert would surely agree that whether he were the deserving or undeserving one, whether he had the specific right or did not have it, entitlements still should not be ignored. Nothing about the position of those supporting rights and desert suggests that they must make exceptions for themselves; such rules are in that sense universalizable. But the advocate of the greater moral evil rule can also be counted on to claim that he too should not be made an exception, and that *ignoring* entitlements in favor of the greater moral evil rule is the proper course whether or not he would benefit from the policy. Both views, then, could be universalized in the first sense.

But if we understand universalizability in another sense, neither of the rules passes the test. If being "willing to universalize the judgment" means that a supporter of a particular moral rule would be equally happy with the result were the roles reversed, then there is doubt whether either is universalizable. The rights advocate cannot

promise always to like the outcome; he probably would *prefer*, were the tables turned and his life depended on somebody not keeping his rightfully owned income, that entitlements be ignored in that instance. But his opponent cannot pass the test either, since he would likely prefer that rights and desert *not* be ignored were he in a positon to benefit from them. But in any case it is not at all clear why we should expect people who make moral judgments to be neutral as to which position they occupy. Must a judge who thinks justice requires that a murderer go to jail agree that he would prefer jail if he were the murderer? It seems that all he must do to universalize his judgment is agree that it would be *right* that he go to jail if the tables were turned, that, in other words, he is not exempt from the rules. But that is a test, as I said, which supporters of entitlements can pass.

So the test of universalizability does not provide grounds for rejecting entitlement rules, and we are once again at an impasse. A second possibility is to view the egalitarian as a moral reformer. Then, perhaps, the criticism of entitlements can be defended as part of a more reasonable and effective moral system. In the final section I look in detail at the idea that rights and desert would not be part of a such ideal moral code, one which we would support if we were fully rational.

4. Entitlements and the Ideal Moral Code

The idea I want now to consider is that part of our code should be dropped, so that people could no longer invoke rights and desert as justification for not making large sacrifices for strangers. In place of entitlements would be a rule requiring that any time we can prevent something bad without sacrificing anything of comparable moral significance we ought to do it. Our current code, however, allows people to say that while they would do more good with their earnings, still they have rights to the earnings, the earnings are deserved, and so need not be given away. The crucial question is whether we want to have such entitlement rules in our code, or whether we should reject them in favor of the greater moral evil rule.

Universalizability, I argued, gives no clear answer to this. Each position also finds a certain amount of support within our code, either from the idea of equal consideration of interests or from our concerns about fairness, justice, and respect for other persons. The problem to be resolved, then, is whether there are other reasons to drop entitlement rules in favor of the greater moral evil rule.

I believe that our best procedure is not to think about this or that specific rule, drawing analogies, refining it, and giving counterexamples, but to focus instead on the nature of morality as a whole. What is a moral code? What do we want it to do? What type of code do we want to support? These questions will give us a fresh perspective from which to consider the merits of rules which allow people to appeal to rights and desert and to weigh the issue of whether our present code should be reformed.

We can begin with the obvious: A moral code is a system of rules designed to guide people's conduct. As such, it has characteristics in common with other systems of rules. Virtually every organization has rules which govern the conduct of members; clubs, baseball leagues, corporations, bureaucracies, profession associations, even *The* Organization all have rules. Another obvious point is this: What the rules are depends on why the organization exists. Rules function to enable people to accomplish goals which lead them to organize in the first place. Some rules, for example, "Don't snitch on fellow mafioso," "Pay dues to the fraternity," and "Don't give away trade secrets to competing companies," serve in obvious ways. Other times the real purposes of rules are controversial, as when doctors do not allow advertising by fellow members of the AMA.

Frequently rules reach beyond members of a specific organization, obligating everyone who is capable of following them to do so. These include costs of civil and criminal law, etiquette, custom, and morality. But before discussing the specific purposes of moral rules, it will be helpful to look briefly at some of the similarities and differences between these more universal codes.

First, the sanctions imposed on rule violators vary among different types of codes. While in our legal code, transgressions are punished by fines, jail, or repayment of damages, informal sanctions of praise, blame, or guilt encourage conformity to the rules of morality and etiquette. Another difference is that while violation of a moral rule is always a serious affair, this need not be so for legal rules

of etiquette and custom. Many of us think it unimportant whether a fork is on the left side of a plate or whether an outmoded and widely ignored Sunday closing law is violated, but violation of a moral rule is not ignored. Indeed, that a moral rule has lost its importance is often shown by its demotion to status of mere custom.

A third difference is that legal rules, unlike rules of morality, custom, and etiquette, provide for a specific person or procedure that is empowered to alter the rules. If Congress acts to change the tax laws, then as of the date stated in the statute the rules are changed. Similarly for the governing rules of social clubs, government bureaucracies, and the AMA. Rules of custom, morals, and etiquette also change, of course, but they do so in a less precise and much more gradual fashion, with no person or group specifically empowered to make changes.

This fact, that moral rules are *in a sense* beyond the power of individuals to change, does not show that rules of morality, any more than those of etiquette, are objective in the same sense that scientific laws are. All that needs to happen for etiquette or morality to change is for people to change certain practices, namely the character traits they praise and blame, or the actions they approve and disapprove. Scientific laws, however, are discovered, not invented by society, and so are beyond human control. The law that the boiling point of water increases as its pressure increases cannot be changed by humans, either individually or collectively. Such laws are a part of the fabric of nature.

But the fact that moral rules, like legal ones, are not objective in the same sense as scientific ones does not mean that there is no objective standard of right or wrong, that one code is as good as another, or even that the "right thing to do" is just what the moral code currently followed in our society teaches is right. Like the rules of a fraternity or corporation, legal and moral rules can serve their purposes either well or poorly, and whether they do is a matter of objective fact. Further, if a moral code doesn't serve its purpose, we have good reason to criticize all or part of it, to ignore it, and to think of a way to change it, just as its serving us well provides a good reason to obey. In important respects morality is not at all subjective.

Take, for example, a rule which prohibits homosexual behavior. Suppose it serves no useful purpose, but only increases the burdens of guilt, shame, and social rejection borne by 10% of our population. If this is so, we have good reason to ignore the rule. On the other hand, if rules against killing and lying help us to accomplish what we want from a moral code, we have good reason to support those rules. Morality is created, and as with other systems of rules which we devise, a particular rule may or may not further the shared human goals and interests which motivated its creation. There is thus a connection between what we ought to do and how well a code serves its purposes. If a rule serves well the general purposes of a moral code, then we have reason to support it, and if we have reason to support it, we also have reason to obey it. But if, on the other hand, a rule is useless, or if it frustrates the purposes of morality, we have reason neither to support nor to follow it. All of this suggests the following conception of a right action: Any action is right which is approved by an ideal moral code, one which it is rational for us to support. Which code we would want to support would depend, of course, on which one is able to accomplish the purposes of morality.

If we are to judge actions in this way, by reference to what an ideal moral code would require, we must first have a clear notion of just what purposes morality is meant to serve. And here again the comparison between legal and moral rules is instructive. Both systems discourage certain types of behavior—killing, robbing, and beating—while encouraging others—repaying debts, keeping important agreements, and providing for one's children. The purpose which both have in discouraging various behaviors is obvious. Such negative rules help keep people from causing harm. Think, for example, of how we are first taught it is wrong to hit a baby brother or sister. Parents explain the rule by emphasizing that it hurts the infant when we hit him. Promoting the welfare of ourselves, our friends and family, and to a lesser degree all who have the capacity to be harmed is the primary purpose of negative moral rules. It's how we learn them as children and why we support them as adults.

The same can be said of positive rules, rules which encourage various types of behavior. Our own welfare, as well as that of friends, family, and others, depends on general acceptance of rules which encourage keeping promises, fulfilling con-

tracts, and meeting the needs of our children. Just try to imagine a society in which promises or agreements mean nothing, or where family members took no concern for one another. A life without positive or negative rights would be as Thomas Hobbes long ago observed: nasty, brutish, and short.

Moral rules thus serve two purposes. They promote our own welfare by discouraging acts of violence and promoting social conventions like promising and paying debts, and second, they perform the same service for our family, friends, and others. We have reason to support a moral code because we care about our own welfare, and because we care about the well-being of others. For most of us the ideal moral code, the one we would support because it best fulfills these purposes, is the code which is most effective in promoting general welfare.

But can everyone be counted on to share these concerns? Think, for example, of an egoist, who only desires that *he* be happy. Such a person, if he existed, would obviously like a code which maximizes his own welfare. How can we hope to get agreement about which code it is rational to support, if different people expect different things from moral rules?[2]

Before considering these questions, I want to mention two preliminary points. First, the problem with egoism is that it tends to make morality relative. If we are going to decide moral disputes by considering what would be required by the code which it is rational for people to support, then we must reach agreement about what that code is. Otherwise the right action for an altruist, the one which is required by the code which it's rational for him to support, may be the wrong act for the egoist. Yet how can the very same act done in identical circumstances be wrong for one person yet right for another? Maybe morality is relative in that way, but if so the prospects for peaceful resolution of important disputes is lessened, a result not to be hoped for.

My second point is that while we certainly do not want to assume people are perfect altruists, we also do not want to give people less credit than they deserve. There is some evidence, for example, that concern for others in our species is part of our biological heritage. Some geneticists think that many animals, particularly higher ones, take an innate interest in the welfare of other members of their species.[3] Other researchers argue that feelings of benevolence originate naturally, through classical conditioning; we develop negative associations with our own pain behavior (since we are then in pain) and this attitude becomes generalized to the pain behavior of others.[4] If either of these is true, egoism might be far more unusual than is commonly supposed, perhaps rare enough that it can be safely ignored.

There is also a line of reasoning which suggests that disagreement about which moral code to support need not be as deep as is often thought. What sort of code in fact *would* a rational egoist support? He would first think of proposing one which allows him to do anything whatsoever that he desires, while requiring that others ignore their own happiness and do what is in his interests. But here enters a family of considerations which will bring us back to the merits of entitlements versus the greater moral evil rule. Our egoist is contemplating what code to *support*, which means going before the public and trying to win general acceptance of his proposed rules. Caring for nobody else, he might secretly prefer the code I mentioned, yet it would hardly make sense for him to work for its public adoption since others are unlikely to put his welfare above the happiness of themselves and their families. So it looks as if the code an egoist would actually support might not be all that different from the ideal (welfare maximizing) code; he would be wasting his time to advocate rules that serve only his own interests because they have no chance of public acceptance.

The lesson to be learned here is a general one: The moral code it is rational for us to support must be practical; it must actually work. This means, among other things, that it must be able to gain the support of almost everyone.

But the code must be practical in other respects as well. I have emphasized that it is wrong to ignore the possibilities of altruism, but it is also important that a code not assume people are more unselfish than they are. Rules that would work only for angels are not the ones it is rational to support for humans. Second, an ideal code cannot assume we are more objective than we are; we often tend to rationalize when our own interests are at stake, and a rational person will also keep that in mind when choosing a moral code. Finally, it is not rational to support a code which assumes we have perfect knowledge.

We are often mistaken about the consequences of what we do, and a workable code must take that into account as well.

I want now to bring these various considerations together in order to decide whether or not to reject entitlements in favor of the greater moral evil rule. I will assume that the egoist is not a serious obstacle to acceptance of a welfare maximizing code, either because egoists are, like angels, merely imaginary, or because a practical egoist would only support a code which can be expected to gain wide support. We still have to ask whether entitlements would be included in a welfare maximizing code. The initial temptation is to substitute the greater moral evil rule for entitlements, requiring people to prevent something bad whenever the cost to them is less significant than the benefit to another. Surely, we might think, total welfare would be increased by a code requiring people to give up their savings if a greater evil can be prevented.

I think, however, that this is wrong, that an ideal code would provide for rights and would encourage rewarding according to desert. My reasons for thinking this stem from the importance of insuring that a moral code really does, in fact, work. Each of the three practical considerations mentioned above now enters the picture. First, it will be quite difficult to get people to accept a code which requires that they give away their savings, extra organs, or anything else merely because they can avoid a greater evil for a stranger. Many people simply wouldn't do it: they aren't that altruistic. If the code attempts to require it anyway, two results would likely follow. First, because many would not live up to the rules, there would be a tendency to create feelings of guilt in those who keep their savings in spite of having been taught it is wrong, as well as conflict between those who meet their obligations and those who do not. And, second, a more realistic code, one which doesn't expect more than can be accomplished, may actually result in more giving. It's a bit like trying to influence how children spend their money. Often they will buy less candy if rules allow them to do so occasionally but they are praised for spending on other things than if its purchase is prohibited. We cannot assume that making a charitable act a requirement will always encourage such behavior. Impractical rules not only create guilt and social conflict, they often tend to encourage the opposite of the desired result. By giving people the right to use their savings for themselves, yet praising those who do not exercise the right but help others instead, we have struck a good balance; the rules are at once practical yet reasonably effective.

Similar practical considerations would also influence our decision to support rules that allow people to keep what they deserve. For most people, working is not their favorite activity. If we are to prosper, however, goods and services must be produced. Incentives are therefore an important motivation, and one such incentive for work is income. Our code encourages work by allowing people to keep a large part of what they earn, indeed that's much the point of entitlements. "I worked hard for it, so I can keep it" is an oft-heard expression. If we eliminate this rule from our code and ask people to follow the greater moral evil rule instead, the result would likely be less work done and so less total production. Given a choice between not working and continuing to work knowing the efforts should go to benefit others, many would choose not to work.

Moral rules should be practical in a third sense, too. They cannot assume people are either more unbiased or more knowledgeable than they are. This fact has many implications for the sorts of rules we would want to include in a welfare maximizing code. For example, we may be tempted to avoid slavish conformity to counterproductive rules by allowing people to break promises whenever they think doing so would increase total welfare. But again we must not ignore human nature, in this case our tendency to give special weight to our own welfare and our inability to be always objective in tracing the effects of our actions. While we would not want to teach that promises must never be broken no matter what the consequences, we also would not want to encourage breaking promises any time a person can convince himself the results of doing so would be better than if he kept his word.

Similar considerations apply to the greater moral evil rule. Imagine a situation where someone feels he can prevent an evil befalling himself by taking what he needs from a large store. The idea that he's preventing something bad from happening (to himself) without sacrificing anything of compara-

ble moral significance (the store won't miss the goods) would justify robbery. Although sometimes a particular act of theft really is welfare maximizing, it does not follow that we should support a *rule* which allows theft whenever the robber is preventing a greater evil. Such a rule, to work, would require more objectivity and more knowledge of long-term consequences than we have. Here again, including rights in our moral code serves a useful role, discouraging the tendency to rationalize our behavior by underestimating the harm we may cause to others or exaggerating the benefits that may accrue to ourselves.

The first sections of this paper attempted to show that our moral code is a bit schizophrenic. It seems to pull us in opposite directions, sometimes toward helping people who are in need, other times toward the view that rights and desert justify keeping things we have even if greater evil could be avoided were we to give away our extra eye or our savings account. This apparent inconsistency led us to a further question: Is the emphasis on entitlements really defensible, or should we try to resolve the tension in our own code by adopting the greater moral evil rule and ignoring entitlements? In this section I considered the idea that we might choose between entitlements and the greater moral evil rule by paying attention to the general nature of a moral code; and in particular to the sort of code we might want to support. I argued that all of us, including egoists, have reason to support a code which promotes the welfare of everyone who lives under it. That idea, of an ideal moral code which it is rational for everyone to support, provides a criterion for deciding which rules are sound and which ones we should support.

My conclusion is a conservative one: Concern that our moral code encourages production and not fail because it unrealistically assumes people are more altruistic or objective than they are means that our rules giving people rights to their possessions and encouraging distribution according to desert should be part of an ideal moral code. And since this is so, it is not always wrong to invoke rights or claim that money is deserved as justification for not giving aid, even when something worse could be prevented by offering help. The welfare maximizing moral code would not require us to maximize welfare in each individual case.

I have not yet discussed just how much weight should be given to entitlements, only that they are important and should not be ignored as Singer and Watson suggest. Certainly an ideal moral code would not allow people to overlook those in desperate need by making entitlements absolute, any more than it would ignore entitlements. But where would it draw the line?

It's hard to know, of course, but the following seems to me to be a sensible stab at an answer. Concerns about discouraging production and the general adherence to the code argue strongly against expecting too much; yet on the other hand, to allow extreme wealth in the face of grinding poverty would seem to put too much weight on entitlements. It seems to me, then, that a reasonable code would require people to help when there is no substantial cost to themselves, that is, when what they are sacrificing would not mean *significant* reduction in their own or their families' level of happiness. Since most people's savings accounts and nearly everybody's second kidney are not insignificant, entitlements would in those cases outweigh another's need. But if what is at stake is trivial, as dirtying one's clothes would normally be, then an ideal moral code would not allow rights to override the greater evil that can be prevented. Despite our code's unclear and sometimes schizophrenic posture, it seems to me that these judgments are not that different from our current moral attitudes. We tend to blame people who waste money on trivia when they could help others in need, yet not to expect people to make large sacrifices to distant strangers. An ideal moral code thus might not be a great deal different from our own.

Notes

1. Singer also offers a "weak" version of this principle which, it seems to me, is *too* weak. It requires giving aid only if the gift is of *no* moral significance to the giver. But since even minor embarrassment or small amounts of happiness are not completely without moral importance, this weak principle implies little or no obligation to aid, even to the drowning child.

2. This difficulty leads many to think the choice of a code should be made behind a "veil of ignorance" about one's particular station in life, talents, class, and religious or other moral values. The major proponent of this view is John Rawls, *A Theory of Justice* (Cambridge: Harvard University Press, 1971).

3. Stephen Jay Gould, "So Cleverly Kind an Animal" in *Ever Since Darwin* (New York: W. W. Norton Co., 1977).

4. Richard B. Brandt, *Theory of Right and Good* (New York: Oxford University Press, 1979).

Questions for Analysis

1. What is the "greater moral evil principle"?

2. What does Arthur mean by "entitlements"?

3. What is the difference between negative and positive rights?

4. Arthur claims that the greater moral evil principle is forward-looking, while matters of entitlement are directed to the past. What does he mean?

5. In what sense can both the greater moral evil rule and the rights-and-desert rule be universalized? In what sense can they not?

6. Explain how a consideration of the nature of morality demonstrates the need for entitlements.

7. According to Arthur, what two purposes do moral rules serve?

8. Are there features of Arthur's presentation that remind you of Rawls's ethics? Explain.

CASE PRESENTATION
To Aid or Not to Aid

The conference on world hunger had promised to be uneventful. Such confer-
ences had convened periodically over the past forty years. Invariably they did
little more than tell those assembled what they already knew: World hunger is
still with us.

The first hint that this conference would be different came when the secretary
of the U.S. Commission on World Hunger injected a political note. He suggested
that the declining trend in U.S. foreign assistance had to be reversed if American
leadership in the world was to continue.

"Intelligently administering foreign aid," the secretary pointed out, "is in
America's self-interest and in the interest of world security." Then, as if to reinforce his point, he added, "Make no mistake about it. The purpose of our international aid program is self-serving. It's an approach that makes sense not only
in international relations, but also in managing our families, businesses, and
other aspects of our lives. That approach recognizes that it's safer and cheaper
to anticipate a problem than to wait for it to become a crisis."

Thus the secretary concluded that it was in our national interest to do all we
could to combat the conditions that would otherwise likely drive people to des-
peration. By slashing international programs, he said finally, we're not saving
money but merely postponing, even raising, the costs that we'll one day have to
pay.

Not everyone agreed, however. In fact, one panel member strongly objected
to the secretary's remarks. She suggested that our international aid might actually
be hurting the very people we want to help.

"Our aid fails to help," she argued, "because it assumes that aid can reach
the powerless, even though it's funneled through the powerful. Well, it can't."
She went on to insist that our aid to those countries where economic control is
concentrated in the hands of a few merely underwrites the local, national, and
international elites whose control over the land and other productive resources
is generating the poverty and hunger we are trying to eradicate.

The secretary listened attentively to her remarks. When she finished, he said,
"What would you propose we do?"

"Cut aid to all countries where a genuine redistribution of control over productive resources isn't under way," she shot back.

"Do you know how many countries that would involve?" the secretary asked
her.

"Dozens," she said. "Perhaps scores."

The secretary agreed. "And do you know how many people would starve?"

"Millions," she said without hesitation. Then she asked the secretary, "Do
you know how many people we're sentencing to a life of suffering and to a death
by starvation through our well-intentioned but tragically misguided aid?"

Questions for Analysis

1. *How would Kant evaluate aid given primarily out of self-interest?*

2. *Do you think it would be moral to allow people to starve so long as their nation was not taking measures to redistribute control of its productive resources?*

3. *Would it be accurate to describe both the secretary's and the panel member's positions as utilitarian?*

4. *If the secretary agreed that the panel member is correct in her assessment of the impact of U.S. aid, could he continue to argue that it is still in our best interest to provide aid?*

5. *Do you think a rich nation such as the United States is morally justified in using its aid program as a weapon for molding the social and economic infrastructures of recipient nations?*

CASE PRESENTATION
The Way Out

"You know the worst of it?" Lila Robbins asked her companion Walter Moore, who was decrying the grayish-brown poison that passed for air in the Los Angeles basin.

"Sure," said Walt. "It's killing us." With that he honked the car's horn. Not that it would do any good. As usual during rush hour, the freeway traffic had backed up. Walt knew that at best they'd crawl at a snail's pace for the next thirty minutes or so. But it always made him feel better to honk the horn, as if he still had some control over things.

"No," Lila said. "The worst thing is that there is absolutely nothing anyone of us can do to stop its spread."

"How depressing!"

"Depressing but true. An individual act of renunciation would be meaningless."

"Unless everyone else did the same thing," Walt said.

Lila wagged her head from side to side and said, "It'll never happen."

The young couple took on the gloom of the day. Unconsciously they checked to see if their windows were sealed.

"So what's the solution?" Walt asked with a sigh.

"Control the behavior that's causing the problem," Lila answered firmly.

"You mean get people off the roads?"

"I'm not just talking about smog," Lila said. "The smog's just a symptom of a far more serious problem."

"Which is?"

"The pursuit of private gratification. That's what's responsible for pollution, world hunger, dwindling resources—what environmentalists call 'ecological scarcity.'"

She went on to explain that ecological scarcity is upon us. We live on a finite planet containing limited resources, and we appear to be approaching those limits at breakneck speed. In short, "We're about to overtax the carrying capacity of our planet."

Walt disagreed. "What you fail to take note of," he told Lila, "is that technology is simultaneously expanding the limits."

Lila shook her head. "Look," she said. "We're like fish in a pond where all life is rapidly being suffocated by a water lily that doubles in size every day and will cover the whole pond in a month."

"I don't deny that the lily—to use your metaphor—is growing really fast. But the pond can be made to grow even faster. We'll never run out of resources because economics and technology will always keep finding ways for us to meet our needs."

"You miss the point."

"What point?"

"That either way we lose." Walt didn't catch her drift. "If," Lila said, "I'm right, then sooner or later—probably sooner—we'll reach the physical limits and all hell will break loose. It'll be every person for himself, dog-eat-dog, sheer anarchy. The only way to restore order will be through dictatorship."

"And if I'm right?" Walt asked her.

"If you're right, the result will be much the same. Think about it. If we can save ourselves technologically, we'll still have to vigilantly guard our resources, and that means we must control human behavior—through strong-arm tactics, if necessary. In the end, the measures we'll have to adopt to survive won't be much different from the future that I'm predicting when we reach our physical limits."

The traffic inched forward and then stopped. Walt craned his head out his window, but he couldn't see much. Up ahead the smog hung thicker. He rolled his window up again and dabbed his stinging eyes. "So what's the way out?"

"We have to abandon our political corruption. We must stop using liberty as a license for self-indulgence. We must recognize that we can lead a very good life, even an affluent one, without wasteful use of our resources. When we recognize that the pursuit of happiness doesn't mean an insane, lustful quest for material gain, then we'll start dealing with the crisis of ecological scarcity. Then we'll seriously start dealing with problems like world poverty, sickness, and starvation."

Walt mulled over what Lila had said. After several minutes he spoke. "You make it sound like our real shortage is in moral resources."

"Exactly!" Lila was quick to agree. "There's no real scarcity in nature. It's just that our wants have outstripped nature's bounty. If we're to avoid a grim future, we must assume full moral responsibilities."

"Thank God!" Walt blurted as the traffic bolted forward. He turned on the headlights and started to think about something to eat. "I'm famished!" he said.

But Lila wasn't listening. She was recalling a quotation from the Chinese sage Lao-tzu:

> Nature sustains itself through three precious principles, which one does well to embrace and follow. These are gentleness, frugality, and humility.

Questions for Analysis

1. *Do you agree with Lila?*
2. *What do you think Lila means by "assuming full moral responsibilities"?*
3. *What connection, if any, do you see between ecological scarcity and our alleged failure to assume moral responsibilities?*
4. *How is ecological scarcity related to world hunger?*
5. *An essay entitled "The Scarcity Society" inspired this case presentation. In it the author, William Ophuls, writes: "If this inexorable process is not controlled by prudent and, above all, timely political restraints on the behavior that causes it, then we must resign ourselves to ecological self-destruction."[7] What political restraints do you think are necessary?*

Selections for Further Reading

Aiken, William, and Hugh LaFollette. *World Hunger and Moral Obligation.* Englewood Cliffs, N.J.: Prentice-Hall, 1977.

Bauer, P. T. *Equality, the Third World and Economic Delusion.* Cambridge, Mass.: Harvard University Press, 1981.

Bayles, Michael D. *Morality and Population Policy.* Birmingham: University of Alabama Press, 1980.

Brown, Peter R., and Erik P. Eckholm. *By Bread Alone.* New York: Praeger, 1974.

Brown, Peter, and Henry Shue. *Boundaries.* Totowa, N.J.: Rowman and Littlefield, 1981.

Ehrlich, Paul. *The Population Bomb.* New York: Ballantine, 1971.

Hardin, Garrett. *Promethean Ethics.* Seattle: University of Washington Press, 1980.

Kahn, Herman; William Brown; and Leon Martel. *The Next 200 Years.* New York: William Morrow, 1976.

Lucan, George R., Jr., and Thomas W. Ogletree. *Lifeboat Ethics.* New York: Harper and Row, 1976.

Partridge, Ernest. *Responsibilities to Future Generations.* Buffalo, N.Y.: Prometheus, 1981.

---

7. *William Ophuls, "The Scarcity Society," Harper's, April 1974, pp. 29–37.*

Sikora, R. I., and Brian Barry. *Obligations to Future Generations*. Philadelphia: Temple University Press, 1978.

Simon, Arthur, and Paul Simon. *The Politics of World Hunger*. New York: Harper's Magazine Press, 1973.

Wortman, Sterling, and Ralph Cummings, Jr. *To Feed This World*. Baltimore: Johns Hopkins University Press, 1978.

9
WAR[1]

In 1979, members of NATO (the North Atlantic Treaty Organization) decided to install in Europe medium-range nuclear missiles targeted on the Soviet Union. In range and accuracy, these would match the SS-20 missiles the Soviet Union already had targeted on Western Europe.

Because the missiles were relatively small and thus less inhibiting to use, the NATO decision seemed to some to make war more likely. That impression was strengthened when President Reagan later spoke casually to reporters about a "limited war" in Europe. Believing their worst fears confirmed, hundreds of thousands of Europeans took to the streets in the spring and summer of 1980, and since then anti-nuclear demonstrators have become a formidable force in some countries (e.g., West Germany). While different groups of demonstrators proposed different things—the repeal of the NATO decision, the creation of nuclear-free zones in Europe, unilateral nuclear disarmament, multilateral nuclear disarmament—they were united in their opposition to war between the nuclear powers.

In the U.S., President Reagan's view of the world and the U.S. position in it occasioned similar fears of nuclear war. Shortly after his election in 1980, Reagan spoke of controlling nuclear war, not of controlling arms. He apparently thought that a nuclear war can be won. More generally, the President expressed a vision of a powerful, some would say invincible, America. He expressed this vision in a budget that called for a radical expansion of military expenditures and a contraction of just about everything else. Secretary of State Alexander Haig spoke to Congress about a "nuclear demonstration shot," and Secretary of Defense Caspar Weinberger drafted plans called the "Defense Guidance" for a "protracted" nuclear war.

---

1. *In a recent publication, Leon Wieseltier, a scholar of medieval Jewish history, traces the immediate events that have produced the current peace movement throughout the world. [Leon Wieseltier,* Nuclear War, Nuclear Peace *(New York: Holt, Rinehart and Winston, 1983) pp. 9–12.]*

In the face of what they perceived as a cavalier and benighted attitude toward nuclear war, hundreds of thousands of Americans turned out to protest. As in Europe, the result was a change in the political climate. Politicians no longer could ignore the anti-nuclear sentiment of the people. Several legislators offered anti-nuclear proposals, the most popular of which was the Kennedy-Hatfield resolution calling for "a mutual and verifiable freeze on the testing, production, and future deployment of nuclear warheads, missiles, and other delivery systems." In the election of 1982, freeze referenda were approved in eight states out of nine and in twenty-eight cities and counties. A genuine peace movement had emerged, and is continuing.

Unlike the peace movement of the '60s, which aimed to stop a war, this one aims to prevent one—one which in the view of many would at the very least destroy millions of human beings, and at worst exterminate all life on the planet. The peace movement has brought together individuals of divergent political ideas and interests who share one overarching assumption: that the existence of nuclear weapons unites U.S. citizens and all peoples of the world in a single community of fate. They share a presentiment of nuclear holocaust.

While their fear is well-founded, it is not only fear that fires the peace movement. Its representatives advance certain moral judgments about nuclear war: that it is inherently evil; that no matter the ends, nuclear war can never be morally justified; that even a policy based on nuclear deterrence is immoral. Indeed, more than just a few in the peace movement claim that any war today between nuclear powers is immoral, inasmuch as it will invite the use of nuclear weapons.

The development and spread of nuclear weapons, then, not only has made ours a most perilous time but has compelled us to examine the morality of nuclear war, and to re-examine the morality of war generally. While the morality of war has concerned philosophers in the past, the issue takes on great moment today because of the unspeakable destructiveness of modern nuclear weapons.

Definition of War

Although war has been defined in various ways throughout history, there do seem to be at least three characteristics that distinguish war from other kinds of violent activities: (1) participation of countries, (2) a variety of forms of violence under a claim of right, and (3) some operational concept of war.[2]

Participation of Countries

War is something that takes place between countries or nations, rather than between lesser groups or individuals. So characterized, war would include so-called civil wars, since they involve a claim that what has been one country is more properly two; or possibly even that what has been two countries is more properly one (some would consider the conflict in Ireland a civil war).

---

2.   See Richard A. Wasserstrom, "On the Morality of War: A Preliminary Inquiry," in War and Morality, ed. Richard A. Wasserstrom (Belmont, Calif: Wadsworth, 1970), pp. 78–101. Wasserstrom is a professor of law and philosophy.

On the other hand, this characteristic of war would not include insurrections, which are rebellions against the enforcement of law and not, like civil wars, attempts to resolve rival claims of nationhood. Excluded also would be revolutions, in which nation status isn't the issue, but rather who will govern and how. Some would point to Nicaragua, El Salvador, and the Philippines as sites of contemporary revolutions.

Various Forms of Violence under a Claim of Right

For a conflict to be called a war, it must also involve a variety of forms of violence that countries believe they have a right to use. These methods of violence ordinarily are carried out by a specialized group, an army, prepared to use deadly force in various contexts in order to subdue or even kill the forces of another country.

A Concept of War

While it's arguable that the preceding characteristics capture the minimally necessary characteristics of war, nations almost always harbor some concept of war that, in effect, prescribes the extent of violence they are prepared to engage in. Some countries conceive of war as a circumscribed, clearly definable instrument of foreign policy. By this account, war has rules delimiting the means that can be rightly used in subduing another country. Two famous examples of the rules about when and how a war is to be fought are the Hague Conference of 1907 and the Geneva Convention of 1929. These prohibit, among other things, the inhumane treatment of prisoners, the use of poisoned weapons, and the improper use of flags of truce.

But countries have not always shared the view of war as clearly definable. Indeed, some have viewed it as an indeterminate, indefinable, and unlimited conflict between countries. The best modern examples are the Nazi leaders who seemed to embrace the concept of total war. In the words of the Nuremberg Tribunal:

> In this concept of "total war," the moral ideas underlying the conventions which seek to make war more humane are no longer regarded as having force or validity. Everything is made subordinate to the overmastering dictates of war. Rules, regulations, assurances, and treaties, all alike are of no moment; and so freed from the restraining influence of international law, the aggressive war is conducted by the Nazi leaders in the most barbaric way. Accordingly, war crimes were committed when and wherever the Fuehrer and his close associates thought them to be advantageous.[3]

For their part, the Allies themselves flirted with the concept of total war. The United States, for example, seemed to ignore whatever laws of war seemed imprudent to follow: thus the saturation bombings of the cities of Europe and the dropping of two atomic bombs on the Japanese cities of Hiroshima and Nagasaki. These tactics qualify as "obliteration bombing," which refers to the

3. *"Opinion and Judgment of the Nuremberg Tribunal,"* 56–57 (1947), *reprinted in* American Journal of International Law, *172, 1947.*

strategic bombing of industrial centers of population, where the target to be wiped out is not a specific factory, bridge, or similar object, but a large section of a whole city, including by design the residential districts. Perhaps such tactics were not explicitly prohibited by international covenant, but by the same token neither were many of the Nazi and Japanese atrocities.

A similar analysis applies to the Vietnam War. The atrocities committed by the North Vietnamese and the Vietcong are well documented. For its part, the U.S. again engaged in saturation bombing, and introduced the use of napalm and Agent Orange, which contained what some consider the most deadly chemical every synthesized, dioxin.

The moral difference between the rules of war and notions of unlimited war is admittedly uncertain. In fact, both conceptions are sometimes endorsed, as they are in these passages from the work of the famous German writer on war Karl von Clausewitz:

> We shall not begin with a pedantic definition, but confine ourselves to war's essence: the duel. War is nothing but a duel on a larger scale. Each [side] seeks by physical force to overthrow the other, render him incapable of further resistance, and compel his opponent to do his will. . . . War is an act of force, and there is no limit to the application of that force. . . . Thus, there can be wars of all degrees of importance and energy, from a war of extermination down to a mere state of armed observation.[4]

Even though the moral difference between the two vying concepts of war is ambiguous, it's important to keep the concepts in mind. The reason is that the moral assessment of a war conceived as governed by laws would be different from one conceived of as ruleless. Thus if rules prevail, then generally speaking those who violate the rules act immorally. A ruleless war, on the other hand, would preclude such an assessment. Of course, in both instances it is assumed that war is not in itself immoral—an assumption that many today would reject when the war involves nuclear powers.

In any event, the definition of war that we will use here is the following: *War is something that takes place between countries, involves the use of a variety of forms of violence under a claim of right, and is conceived of in some particular way.*

War and Morality

Before we discuss the morality of war, we should address a question that is logically prior to any moral assessment: Is it possible to assess war in moral terms?[5] If it isn't, there's no point in asserting that war is good or bad, or that some particular war is. But if it is possible to assess it in moral terms, the morality of war or of any particular war is an authentic question.

Some claim that war, or at least some particular war, cannot be morally assessed because moral practices—"good-bad," "right-wrong," "moral-immoral," "justified-unjustified"—either can't be meaningfully applied or shouldn't be applied.

4.   Karl von Clausewitz, "On War," in War, Politics and Power, E. Collins, trans. (Chicago: Regnery-Gateway, 1962), pp. 63–72.

5.   Wasserstrom, "On the Morality of War: A Preliminary," pp. 78–85.

Can Moral Predicates Be Applied?

For some, moral predicates simply cannot be applied meaningfully to war. (Unless otherwise stated, "war" will be taken to refer to war in general, rather than a specific war, since it's theoretically possible to say that moral predicates can be applied meaningfully to this war, but not to that.) One basis for such a judgment is the distinction between personal and national behavior. While there are laws governing the behavior of individuals, the claim goes, there really aren't any clearly defined laws governing the behavior of countries. True, there is something called international law, but international law is often vague and loose enought to allow diverse interpretations.

Skepticism about the lawlike quality of international law leads some to divorce morality from war, though it's not exactly obvious how they make this leap. However, implied seems to be the notion that moral predicates are meaningless in the absence of clearly defined laws or rules. But this assumption so mixes the categories of law and morality as to make them indistinguishable. Adherence to law does not necessarily define morality; nor does flouting law define immorality. If international laws aren't explicit, comprehensive, and positive enough, that does not of itself make a moral appraisal of war impossible.

Another basis for saying moral predicates cannot be meaningfully applied to war is that no machinery exists for punishing those who commit war atrocities. Like the first basis, this one rests on a most dubious assumption: that morality depends on the existence of guarantees of moral conformity by others. This assumption simply does not reflect the general understanding of morality as conformity with some norm, regardless of whether the norm can be enforced.

Much can be said against a law that cannot be enforced—perhaps even that it is meaningless. But that doesn't mean that the behavior it proscribes is nonmoral. For example, the law that prohibits suicide cannot be enforced, or at best it can be enforced only on those who tried but failed to commit suicide. Even in cases of attempted suicide, the "perpetrators of the crime" typically are not punished but turned over for psychiatric examination. Are we to say, then, that it's meaningless to attribute moral predicates to suicide? Certainly not.

A third basis for the claim that no moral judgments of war are possible involves the concept of "total war." If war is an activity in which anything goes, then by definition it's meaningless to talk of war as good or bad, right or wrong, justified or unjustified. But, as we've seen, it is possible to conceive of war in other than "anything goes" terms. Totality or unlimitedness is not a necessary feature of war. Yes, war is a unique activity, because it makes killing and violence permissible that would otherwise be impermissible. But that's different from saying war is unique because anything connected with it is morally permissible.

Should Moral Predicates Be Applied?

There are those who would say that although moral predicates can be meaningfully applied to war, they *shouldn't* be. The two main bases for this position are appeal to national interest and to the "logic of war."

NATIONAL INTEREST.   To say that national interest should determine whether and how war will be waged seems tantamount to making national interest the moral norm. Hence if a country starts or prosecutes a war strictly on its perception of national interest, it's acting rightly; if not, it's acting wrongly. The same analysis could be applied to the principals involved: presidents, high government officials, combatants, etc. If they act in their nation's interest, they act morally; if not, they act immorally. Looked at this way, national interest functions roughly like egoism: What's the best for the nation is used as the yardstick of morality. As such, the appeal to national interest would be vulnerable to the kinds of criticisms that egoism is.

Of course, those who espouse national interest as the determining factor for and in war presumably wish to distinguish it from any moral considerations. But even if national interest is divorced from moral considerations—that is, it is not functioning as a species of egoism—national interest, as a goal, still must be justified. On what grounds are we to accept national interest as the determinant of war policies? Some would argue that the position of a great international power like the U.S. imposes on it duties beyond national concern—for example, promoting international stability. When national interest is defined in narrowly provincial terms (as it typically is), it rules out a consideration of other obligations.

Besides the problem of justification, there is the issue of determining national interest. In defining national interest with respect to war, countries inevitably invoke all manner of principles: self-defense, independence, the preservation of a way of life, the safeguarding of territory to which they have a rightful claim, the honoring of treaty obligations, the liberation of oppressed peoples, and, to be sure, sheer adventure and the promise of lucre. Moreover, countries inevitably treat these principles or ideals as moral imperatives.

In short, "national interest" is inevitably explained and defined with reference to some ideal that's perceived as imposing a moral imperative: "We must defend ourselves"; "We must liberate oppressed peoples"; "We must halt aggression"; and so on. If this analysis is correct, then national interest, far from being divorced from morality, is very much tied to moral ideals and imperatives— indeed, to a whole cluster of ideals a nation embraces and that, to a large extent, characterize that nation.

But what about war policies of specific government officials? It's commonplace, for example, to assert that the President of the U.S. must make decisions based not on moral considerations but on national interest. A graphic example of this is President Truman's decision to drop atomic bombs on Japan during World War II. "We have used it [the atomic bomb]," Truman told the nation on August 9, 1945, "in order to shorten the agony of war, in order to save the lives of thousands and thousands of young Americans."[6] Presumably Truman based his decision on national interest. Let's assume that in this context national interest means taking action that will save American lives, even though a great number of *total* lives might be spared if that action, the atomic bombing, were not taken. On this interpretation—and it may be an incorrect one—American lives clearly are assumed to have more qualitative value than non-American lives. And that is as it should be, most Americans probably would say even today. After all, they'd point out, Truman was the President of the U.S. and as President he had a duty

---

6.   *Address to the nation by President Harry S Truman, August 9, 1945. Quoted in Wasserstrom, p. 83. The following discussion of Truman's defense is based on Wasserstrom's lengthier treatment, pp. 82–85.*

to favor Americans over non-Americans. He was *obliged* to take action, no matter how extreme, to preserve the lives of his soldier-citizens.

Few would deny that a President and those who hold high public office have special obligations imposed on them by virtue of the position they fill. However, as professor of law and philosophy Richard Wasserstrom points out, it's one thing to recognize a category of special obligations borne by public officials; it's quite another to assert that these obligations always and under all circumstances override all other obligations any ordinary person might have. This is not at all to imply Truman's action was unjustified, but merely to point out that embedded in the argument from national interest is the highly debatable assumption that in a showdown between national interest and other obligations, national interest should prevail.

LOGIC OF WAR.   Besides the national-interest argument that moral judgments shouldn't be applied to war, there is the argument that once war has begun it becomes a nightmare of brutality committed by all participants in one form or another. In effect, there are no moral bounds, only practical ones. Only the limitations of force itself and the "logic of war" operate. The logic of war is such that violence and brutality inevitably escalate, with each side becoming equally vicious. To try to distinguish the more vicious is to fail to recognize the logic of war. Given this characterization, logic-of-war theorists conclude that no moral judgments should be made regarding war.

The basic and recurring criticism of this view is that even if the logic of war is a proper characterization of war, it remains just that: a *description*. But it doesn't necessarily follow that because atrocities are an unavoidable part of war, moral assessments of them shouldn't be made.

More specifically, even though war is hell, there is a point where the means employed for the sake of a political goal come into conflict with a moral general human purpose: the maintenance of moral standards and the survival of some sort of international community.[7] The claim that all acts in war are of comparable brutality, thus rendering moral judgments irrelevant, erases the line that international law as well as our own moral intuitions draw between licit and illicit behavior.

Consider the case of prisoners of war, ex-combatants helpless in the hands of enemies. According to explicit international agreements, prisoners are entitled to benevolent quarantine for the duration of the war. In recent times, for example during the Vietnam War, the tendency has been to deny quarantine and maintain a state of warfare, which often takes the form of a struggle for the minds of prisoners, even in prison camps. Virtually every form of violence short of murder has been used. Even the United States, which prides itself on humane treatment of prisoners and righteously protests when its own soldiers are abused as prisoners, engaged in "unorthodox treatment" of Vietcong prisoners, which it seemingly adapted from the Chinese communists.[8] What are we to say of brutal treatment of prisoners? That the logic of war requires it? This is a justification that even the least scrupulous of moralists couldn't accept.

7. See Michael Walzer, "Moral Judgment in Time of War," in War and Morality, *pp. 54–58.*

8. See Marshall Sahlins, "The Destruction of Conscience in Vietnam," Dissent, *January-February 1966.*

Logic-of-war theorists probably would say that the brutal treatment of prisoners, in fact, makes their very point, as do other war atrocities. Each side will be as brutal as it can be. And the brutality stops only when force is limited, or when it encounters superior force. The logic of war is that each side will and must do what the other side does. Yes, in every war mostly informal agreements exist that rule out certain actions. But these are enforced by mutual deterrence and self-restraint. When mutual deterrence fails, self-restraint breaks down. Besides, the very purpose of fielding an army is to make the most of its superiority. This is precisely what Lieutenant William L. Calley, Jr., did when he killed twenty-two My Lai villagers on March 16, 1972. Calley's actions as well as all other war atrocities attest that the logic of war, whether we like it or not, begets ugly deeds.

But even if opponents in war operate from identical brutal intentions, how does it follow that we shouldn't make any moral judgments? After all, there are different ways of exploiting one's strength. Calley chose one way (which, incidentally, a military court judged premeditated murder), but he could have chosen others. He could have selected to preserve the lives of the villagers, or to torture them, perhaps maiming them and thereby precluding their participation in combat. Are we to treat these and other possibilities as morally identical?

In fact, it's this very attempt to obliterate moral assessments in war that many Vietnam veterans claim is at the root of their struggle to readjust to civilian life. "Anything goes in Vietnam, but not back home. Once returned to civilian life, you must adhere to its civilities and moral conventions; if you don't, society is justified in punishing you." There's no question that unthinkable acts are committed in war by individuals who elsewhere wouldn't dream of doing such things. But why does that rule out moral assessments of such acts? Indeed, it seems ruling out moral judgments invites those very acts that we consider too brutal to contemplate, because it makes one act morally indistinguishable from another. If precedents are established that make more brutal wars and more brutal civilian behavior likelier, why shouldn't we condemn the initiating party? To reply that the other side would have done the same things had they the chance is irrelevant, for people are judged on the crimes they commit, not on the ones they wished to commit.

In the final analysis, the logic-of-war argument seems to overlook the fact that war is never an end in itself but a means to happiness, freedom, security, or some other ideal. As such, war policies and actions can and should be, at the very least, evaluated as to whether they promote those ends. Even more important, the long-term effects of war in part depend on the ways it was fought. Postwar life can be profoundly shaped by people's perceptions of the justifiability of a war and how it was waged, as dramatically demonstrated by the Vietnam War. As Michael Walzer points out, to appeal to a logic of war ignores this fact by treating war as a permanent state of affairs, rather than what it is: a temporary rupture in international society.[9]

The preceding discussion leads us to conclude that those who say moral assessments cannot or should not be applied to war have not made their case.

9. Walzer, "Moral Judgment in Time of War," p. 62.

Indeed, if the preceding analyses are fair, they point to the opposite position: that moral assessments of war are possible. Assuming that they are, we can now turn to the morality of war.

It's possible to hold one of two broad positions concerning the morality of war: (1) At least some wars are morally justifiable. (2) No war is ever morally justifiable. Regarding the first view, there are a number of different perspectives and criteria that can come into play in assessing particular wars. Regarding the second, it is thought that all wars, and especially modern ones, share a feature that makes them a moral abomination.

Arguments for the Morality of War

1.   *A war that conforms to the laws of war is moral.*

POINT: "There are rules which, though perhaps incomplete and imprecise, nonetheless do indicate when a war may be rightly undertaken. I won't spell out the conditions here, except to say that a war initiated in accordance with international conventions is justified.

"I'll admit that once a war begins, all sorts of horrors occur. General Sherman's description of war as hell couldn't be more accurate. But that doesn't mean individuals can't act morally in war, or that war policies can't be moral. In fact, acts in war and war policies are moral if they accord with the laws of war. Again, I needn't spell out these laws here; if you're interested, read for yourself the body of international law that deals with war. But I should point out that the morally most important rule is not to inflict *unnecessary* harm on others. Those who do— for example, by slaughtering innocents or torturing prisoners—act immorally. On the other hand, those who avoid, or at least try to avoid, unnecessary harm act morally in war. So when nations and individuals take actions that conform to the laws and rules governing war, they're acting morally."

COUNTERPOINT: "I can agree that some wars are moral, others not; that some acts in war are justifiable, others not. But I don't see how conformity to law makes them so. First of all, I doubt that these laws you speak of preclude any significant behavior. For example, no law of war prohibited the use of napalm and Agent Orange in Vietnam. Nor does any law make it illegal to drop an atomic or hydrogen bomb. To me this means the moral status of war acts that conform to law could still be in question. Furthermore, simply that international agreement permits war under certain conditions no more makes a particular war necessarily moral than a law that permits the stockpiling of nuclear weapons makes such a policy moral. Law doesn't determine morality; morality determines law.

"Besides, the legal character of these laws of wars is suspect in several respects. First, there is no authoritative body to make and decide them. Second, the distinctions made by these so-called laws are questionable. For example, the use of irregular-shaped bullets and projectiles filled with glass violates our standards of land warfare, but the use of nuclear bombs doesn't. Third, generally speaking only the losing side is punished for violating laws of war. And finally, countries usually regard their own behavior as an exception to the rules, and thus lawful. So, frankly, I can't see how the so-called laws of war are to be taken as laws or even binding rules. And therefore I can't accept them as a basis for assessing the morality of war."

   2.   *A war that's a response to aggression is moral.*

   POINT: "Wars are undertaken for all sorts of reasons. But not every reason justifies the war. For example, I don't believe that a war of aggression is moral. By that I mean that the initiation of a war is always wrong. On the other hand, a country surely is justified in fighting back when an aggressor has struck first. Everyone knows that aggression is wrong, and that it deserves to be thwarted and punished. There can be no question, then, that a warlike response to aggression is justified."

   COUNTERPOINT: "If aggression means something like 'striking the first blow,' I have serious doubts that aggression can always be conclusive in a moral assessment of war. What about a war undertaken to free innocent people from concentration camps, or from slavery? Should such wars be considered immoral because they were acts of aggression? Why must it be wrong to strike the first blow? And why is it right to strike the second blow? It seems to me that the only question is: Who is right? And that can't be answered simply by saying: Those responding to aggression are right, the aggressor is wrong."

   3.   *A war based on self-defense is moral.*

   POINT: "When a country goes to war in order to defend itself from immediate harm, it acts justifiably. The doctrine of self-defense applies to war the same as it does to criminal law. That doctrine rests on the notion that people are entitled to defend themselves from serious attacks. To me this means there is a natural, almost inevitable reaction when attacked. Something that instinctive certainly must be right. By the same token, a country that reacts self-defensively to an attack is acting properly."

   COUNTERPOINT: "You forget, or ignore, that individuals are not countries. Besides the obvious differences between individuals and countries, countries aren't harmed or killed in the same way individuals are. I admit that individuals can be harmed or killed as a result of war, and perhaps self-defense would justify a war in such cases. But it's possible for an attack by a country not to harm people physically so long as those people don't resist the attack. Of course, the country as a political entity might disappear. But that's my point. Would you call the loss of political autonomy the equivalent of death? Would you say it's just as harmful, more harmful, or less harmful? It seems to me you must address these issues before claiming that self-defense justifies war.

   "One other thing. You make no mention of the degree of force a country can use in defending itself. Since you introduced the doctrine of self-defense as it operates in criminal law, it's fair to point out that the doctrine limits the degree of force that's permissible to no more than is reasonably necessary to prevent the inflicting of comparable harm.[10] If this applies equally to national self-defense, that doctrine cannot be invoked by a country to justify waging unlimited defensive war or insisting on unconditional surrender. I think it would also limit acts of war to those undertaken to prevent immediate harm to combatants or their country.

"Finally, I think that for 'self-defense' to be taken as justification of war, it must, on the whole, work well. It must preserve human life and prevent human injury better than any other possible alternative. The historical record suggests that it doesn't. Self-defense typically is misapplied in practice. Nations almost always exaggerate the imminence and severity of a threat. As a result, they use force prematurely and inevitably more than is needed to protect themselves. The shooting down of a Korean Airlines commercial jet in September 1983 is a case in point. Granted, this was not an act of war, but it does point up how countries typically misconstrue or magnify a threat; for, according to the Soviet Union, in breaching its airspace the plane posed a direct and immediate threat to its national security. I'm not saying that where a threat is clear and present and only the force needed to prevent injury or death is used, a war is immoral. Only that in practice, the self-defense principle usually is misapplied."

Arguments against War

By far the most important argument against war is based on the observation that war inevitably takes innocent lives: Any war that results in the death of innocent people is immoral. Inasmuch as any modern war will destroy innocent lives in air attacks, a natural extension of this position is that all modern war is immoral. So important and intricate is this argument that we will extend the dialogue in exploring it.

POINT: "Innocent people always have a right to life and limb. To violate that right is always wrong. That the violation occurs in war is immaterial. Anything that results in the death of innocent people is always immoral.

"Does this include wars undertaken in self-defense, or acts of war that kill innocents not intentionally but accidentally? Absolutely. We don't say, 'The innocent have a right to life and limb, except in war undertaken for self-defense, or to repel an aggressor, or except when they happen to get in the way.' No matter how seemingly noble the cause of a particular war, if it kills or harms innocent people, it's immoral.

"Some will say there has never been a war that hasn't killed some innocent people. If so, then there has never been a moral war. Others might point out that no modern war can avoid killing some innocents. Then so much the worse for those trying to justify modern war. If innocents must perish in modern war— and I believe they must—then modern war is never morally justifiable."

COUNTERPOINT: "I'm certainly sympathetic to the plight of the innocent in times of war, and consider their victimization a profound tragedy and of the

---

10.   *Wasserstrom, "On the Morality of War: A Preliminary Inquiry," pp. 90–94.*

utmost moral concern. But, frankly, I'm having trouble understanding whom you mean by 'innocent' and what you mean by 'innocence.'

"Are innocents noncombatants? If so, precisely who is a noncombatant? Many of those who are not in a country's army or are not actually doing the fighting can't really be distinguished from combatants in any meaningful sense: for example, those who manufacture munitions, build aircraft, or write propaganda, and even those who pay the taxes used to prosecute the war.

"Of course, you may prefer to define 'innocent' in terms of a person's causal connection to the war rather than his or her status as combatant or noncombatant. But what causal connections do you have in mind? Would someone's voting record, for example, be enough to connect the person causally to the war if he or she voted in support of the war? Are there degrees of causal connectedness? Would a munitions worker be more closely connected than a journalist?

"Maybe you don't have either of these concepts of innocence—combatant vs. noncombatant, or causal connection—in mind. Maybe you're defining innocence in terms of blameworthiness. Individuals are innocent if their behavior can't fairly be held responsible either for the war's initiation or for its conduct. Even so, some combatants could, in theory, be not guilty and some civilians could be."

POINT: "Okay, I agree that defining 'innocent' is troublesome. But surely you must admit that, by whatever standards, there will always be some innocents who will meet the test we set up: children, for example."

COUNTERPOINT: "Agreed. But even if war kills innocents, under what circumstances is the death of innocents immoral? As awful as killing innocents is, I can't see how it alone makes war immoral. It seems to me that even the intentional killing of innocents could be justified under certain conditions—for example, if a failure to do so would bring about the death of even more innocents."

POINT: "I'm not convinced that would justify it, but I do admit my position doesn't allow for exceptions like the one you raise. So for the sake of argument, let me modify it to allow for such cases, and say that *in the absence of special overriding circumstances,* the knowing or intentional killing of innocents is immoral."

COUNTERPOINT: "But that means war can be justified, at least in theory. In which case your argument against war isn't very convincing."

POINT: "What I'm saying is that the killing of innocents is a most serious evil whenever it occurs. As with any serious evil, there is a strong presumption against its justifiability. So if you agree that harming and killing innocents is always a serious evil, then the burden is on you, not me, to justify behavior that leads to it. You, not I, have to justify a modern war, which will inevitably result in the death of innocents. And when you try to justify it, remember that air warfare, which is a standard feature of modern war, will result in the death not of a few innocent people, but thousands of them. And if the war in question is thermonuclear, the potential number of innocents who will die or be harmed runs into the millions. Therefore, I believe no major war that would be fought today can be justified by the typical considerations. In fact, I can't imagine any justification, typical or otherwise."

Nuclear War

Most conventional bombs produce only one destructive effect, the shock wave. But nuclear weapons produce many. Before turning to the morality of nuclear war, let's consider some of its effects.[11]

The first effect of a nuclear explosion is the emission of *radiation,* consisting mostly of gamma rays. It's estimated that in an air blast of a one-megaton bomb (a bomb with the explosive yield of a million tons of TNT, which is the average-size bomb in a modern nuclear arsenal), the initial radiation can kill unprotected human beings in an area of about six square miles.

There occurs simultaneously with the initial radiation an *electromagnetic pulse,* which is generated by the intense gamma radiation acting on the air. In a high-altitude detonation, the pulse can knock out electrical equipment over a wide area by inducing a powerful surge of voltage through various conductors: antennas, overhead power lines, pipes, railroad tracks, and so on. For example, by the Defense Department's own reckoning, one multiple-kiloton nuclear weapon detonated 125 miles over Omaha, Nebraska, could generate an electromagnetic pulse strong enough to damage solid-state electrical circuits throughout the entire continental United States and in parts of Canada and Mexico. As a result, the economies of these countries could be expected to halt.

After the initial radiation and the electromagnetic pulse have blown themselves out, a fireball takes shape. As it expands, the surrounding air absorbs energy in the form of X rays. The air then re-radiates a portion of that energy into the environment in the form of a *thermal pulse,* a wave of blinding light and intense heat. Lasting about ten seconds, the thermal pulse of a one-megaton bomb can cause second-degree burns in unprotected humans at a distance of 9½ miles. The thermal wave of a twenty-megaton bomb lasts about twenty seconds and produces the same effect at a distance of 28 miles.

As the thermal pulse expands, it also sends out a *blast wave* in all directions. The blast wave produced by a one-megaton bomb can flatten or severely damage all but the strongest buildings within a radius of 4½ miles, and that of a twenty-megaton bomb has the same effect within a radius of 12 miles.

As the fireball burns, it rises, condensing water from the surrounding atmosphere to form the characteristic mushroom cloud. If set off close to the ground, the bomb will produce a crater, and tons of dust and debris will be fused with the highly radioactive products and sucked up into the clouds, from which they return to the earth in the form of radioactive ash.

Anywhere from 40 to 70 percent of this early or local fallout descends to the earth within about a day of the explosion near the blast or downwind from it. Weather and other factors affect the lethal range of this local fallout, "lethal" being defined as the amount of radiation that if delivered over a short period of time would kill half the able-bodied young adult population. According to a report by the Office of Technology Assessment, one-megaton ground burst would, under any conditions, lethally contaminate over 1,000 square miles.

The initial radiation, the electromagnetic pulse, the thermal pulse, the blast wave, and the local fallout, then, are the immediate, primary effects of a nuclear

11.   See Jonathan Schell, The Fate of the Earth (*New York: Knopf, 1982) pp. 17–26.*

explosion. But these effects themselves produce numerous others. As one example, nuclear explosions generate mass fires, which may kill more people than the original thermal pulse and blast wave. Perhaps of greatest concern are the global effects that could be produced by the detonation of thousands of nuclear bombs around the world—that is, a nuclear holocaust.

At least three grave, direct blows to the ecosphere are anticipated: (1) Delayed or worldwide fallout, a kind of protracted afterburst, would be dispersed into the land, air, and sea, and into the tissues, bones, roots, stems, and leaves of all living things, where in effect it would go on detonating almost indefinitely. (2) Millions of tons of dust would be lofted into the stratosphere, drastically cooling the earth's surface. Indeed, some scientists, among them Cornell University astronomer Carl Sagan, talk about "nuclear winter," in which temperatures throughout the world would drop so far below zero as to be unsurvivable. (3) The layer of ozone that surrounds the entire earth in the stratosphere would be partially destroyed. The ozone layer is crucial to life, because it shields the earth's surface from deadly levels of the sun's ultraviolet radiation.

In judging the global effects of a nuclear holocaust, then, the overriding question that emerges is not how many people would be irradiated, burned, or crushed to death, but whether the earth would remain habitable. In short, a nuclear holocaust raises the question of the survival of all life forms.

The Moral Question

Given its potential for vast, even total destruction, nuclear war emerges as the most important moral issue of our time, and probably of any time. Those who deny that any war can ever be morally justified would naturally say nuclear war is never permissible. But many who believe that at least some wars are permissible think nuclear war can never be justified. Because nuclear war is potentially so destructive, they say, the ordinary justifications for war simply don't apply. Furthermore, since any conflict between the nuclear powers carries the implicit threat of a nuclear war and holocaust, these people conclude that not even a conventional war between the nuclear powers can be justified. As an extension of this argument, they often claim that all modern war is indefensible, because virtually every country is today associated, formally or informally, with one nuclear camp or another.

Not everyone agrees that a nuclear war must be a holocaust, in which thousands of nuclear devices are detonated worldwide. They suggest that a limited area could become the target for a specific number of nuclear devices used to attain some carefully circumscribed and immediate objective, such as deterrence, stalemate, or capitulation. If nuclear weapons can be used with such restraint and specificity, then seemingly the stock arguments for the justification of war can be applied.

But since nuclear weapons pose an immensely greater threat to innocents than do conventional weapons, the presumption against the justifiability of killing innocents looms as an even greater obstacle to justifying even a limited nuclear war. Moreover, a limited nuclear war carries the implicit threat of escalating into a nuclear holocaust, which would cause unprecedented suffering, death, and destruction; these effects would extend indefinitely into the future. Even limited nuclear war, therefore, or a conventional war between the nuclear powers carries a unique and unprecedented danger, in the face of which even the most compelling ordinary justifications for war lose some of their force, perhaps most of it.

Whatever one's view of the morality of nuclear war, all agree that the invention of nuclear weapons has brought with it the specter of global doom. The means the world has chosen to escape its doom—or the superpowers have chosen for it—is the doctrine of nuclear deterrence, which recently has raised almost as much moral debate as nuclear war itself—and for good reason.

Nuclear Deterrence

The crux of the deterrence doctrine is that a nuclear holocaust can best be prevented if each nuclear power, or bloc of powers, holds in readiness a nuclear force with which it credibly threatens to destroy the entire society of an attacker, even after suffering the worst possible first strike that the attacker can launch. As the current peace movement builds steam and anti-nuclear activists marshal their forces, the very morality of this doctrine has been called into question.

Some, like Fred C. Ilke, the Reagan administration's Undersecretary for Policy in the Defense Department, claim that nuclear deterrence is, in fact, mutually assured genocide. Inasmuch as the calculated decisions deterrence seeks to prevent aren't the sole processes that could lead to nuclear war, Ilke concludes there's no rational basis for deterrence. In a similar vein, British social historian E. P. Thompson claims that proponents of nuclear deterrence attribute a rationality to states which can rarely be found in history. In fact, says Thompson, the historical record shows that, as often as not, countries operate from nonrational urges of passion or national self-assertion. (It should be noted that while Ilke and Thompson agree the deterrence doctrine is immoral, they take radically different approaches in trying to trash deterrence. Ilke works within the Pentagon to find ways to win nuclear war. Thompson has taken to the streets to gain support for the abolition of nuclear weapons.[12])

Still others condemn the deterrence doctrine as a promise of murder: The U.S. prevents the Soviet Union from using its nuclear weapons by threatening to kill millions of Russians and by making the Soviets believe the threat is serious. And the Soviet Union does the same. If nuclear war can't be called moral, so the argument goes, neither can the promise of nuclear war.

This position is the essence of the objections made in the pastoral letter on nuclear weapons that the National Conference of Catholic Bishops drafted in 1983. Drawing on the congressional testimony of Cardinal Krol of Philadelphia against SALT II (Strategic Arms Limitation Treaty), the letter states:

> Not only the *use* of strategic nuclear weapons, but the *declared intent* to use them involved in our deterrence policy, are both wrong. . . . Under no

---

12.   Leon Wieseltier, Nuclear War, Nuclear Peace. *New York: Holt, Rinehart and Winston, 1983, p. 73.*

circumstances may nuclear weapons or other instruments of mass slaughter be used for the purpose of destroying population centers. . . . Our condemnation applies especially to the retaliatory use of weapons striking enemy cities after our own have already been attacked.

Although the bishops did acknowledge deterrence as a lesser evil than nuclear war itself, they left no doubt about the intrinsic evil of the nuclear-deterrence doctrine.

Finally, it is argued that a policy of nuclear deterrence is actually causing immense social harm. To the extent that the U.S., for example, continues to devote a large portion of its financial and human resources to manufacturing nuclear weapons in order to deter the Soviet Union from making war, it has that much less to spend on the pressing social-service needs of its people, such as education, health care, law enforcement, pollution control, conservation.

But perhaps the most common reason given for considering deterrence immoral is that, in effect, it makes nuclear war more likely, not less. If nuclear war is an abomination, then whatever makes it likely, by either accident or design, is equally repugnant morally. Nuclear deterrence, it is argued, has the effect of escalating the arms race, often encouraging superpowers to develop more sophisticated killing machines. Since humans have never invented a weapon they haven't used, it's inferred they will eventually use the nuclear weapons that the deterrence doctrine has induced them to develop and stockpile.

Counter to these arguments, especially the last one, is the argument that deterrence, in fact, is moral and obligatory because it makes war less likely. Those advancing this argument point out that the Soviet Union and the U.S. have not directly clashed since the advent of the deterrence doctrine. The reason, they say, is that each side realizes initiating or conducting nuclear war would be suicidal.

One problem with this claim is it assumes that since deterrence has worked in the past, it will continue to. Obviously, there's no guarantee of this. In fact, if we assume that nuclear deterrence will continue to operate as an international policy far into the future, then the quarter-century for which it has "worked" does not provide clinching evidence that it will continue to.

In the final analysis, the deterrence doctrine is what logicians would term a "counterfactual proposition," one that does not admit proof. It's a proposition that may be known to be false, but it cannot be known to be true. If nuclear war breaks out, we will know the doctrine was false. But even if nuclear war never breaks out, we can't know the deterrence policy is true, in the sense of having, of itself, prevented nuclear war. The counterfactual nature of the policy wouldn't necessarily make it immoral, but it would call into question an argument for its morality based on the assertion that deterrence makes nuclear war less likely.

If deterrence is immoral, countries seemingly must abandon it. After all, moralists are agreed that individuals have a prima facie obligation to avoid and correct what is immoral. If nations are under the same moral imperative as individuals, then presumably they too must so act. But at this point, the moral clashes with the prudential.

Suppose, for example, the U.S. recognizes a moral obligation to abandon its deterrence policy. Should it act unilaterally? Or, better, does it have a moral obligation to? If its policymakers did act unilaterally, they probably would be leaving their population in jeopardy. Any plan by one side but not another to junk nuclear deterrence apparently would leave that side more exposed, not less, at least to destruction as a political entity.

But the most this hypothesis would argue against is unilateralism with respect to deterrence, and not deterrence itself. In fact, if nuclear deterrence is immoral, then nations have an obligation to work in concert to scrap it as a policy of national defense. Precisely how this can be done emerges as the paramount political challenge of our times. Whether we succeed could well determine whether we continue to exist.

Just and Unjust Wars

Michael Walzer

In the following selection from his book Just and Unjust Wars: A Moral Argument with Historial Illustrations, *professor of philosophy Michael Walzer first tries to determine whether the threat of massive nuclear destruction is morally defensible. He decides that it might be. But nuclear war itself—even a limited one—cannot be justified because: (1) The collateral damage from such a war would likely be disproportionate, and in order to deter would have to be expected to be disproportionate. (2) Such a war would likely lead to escalation. (3) The collateral damage would have to be intended.*

The Problem of Immoral Threats

Truman used the atomic bomb to end a war that seemed to him limitless in its horrors. And then, for a few minutes or hours in August 1945, the people of Hiroshima endured a war that actually was limitless in its horrors. "In this last great action of the Second World War," wrote Stimson, "we were given final proof that war is death." *Final proof* is exactly the wrong phrase, for war had never been like that before. A new kind of war was born at Hiroshima, and what we were given was a first glimpse of its deadliness. Though fewer people were killed than in the fire-bombing of Tokyo, they were killed with monstrous ease. One plane, one bomb: with such a weapon the 350 planes that raided Tokyo would virtually have wiped out human life on the Japanese islands. Atomic war was death indeed, indiscriminate and total, and after Hiroshima, the first task of political leaders everywhere was to prevent its recurrence.

The means they adopted is the promise of reprisal in kind. Against the threat of an immoral attack, they have put the threat of an immoral response. This is the basic form of nuclear deterrence. In international as in domestic society, deterrence works by calling up dramatic images of human pain. "In the groves of *their* academy," wrote Edmund Burke of the liberal theorists of crime and punishment, "at the end of every vista, you see nothing but the gallows." The description is uncomplimentary, for Burke believed that domestic peace must rest upon some other foundation. But there is this much to be said for the gallows: in principle, at least, only guilty men need fear the death it brings. About the theorists of deterrence, however, it must be said: "In the groves of *their* academy, at the end of every vista, you see nothing but the mushroom cloud"—and the cloud symbolizes indiscriminate slaughter, the killing of the innocent (as in Hiroshima) on a massive scale. No doubt, the threat of such slaughter, if it is believed, makes nuclear attack a radically undesirable policy. Doubled by a potential enemy, the threat produces a "balance of terror." Both sides are so terrified that no further terrorism is necessary. But is the threat itself morally permissible?

The question is a difficult one. It has generated in the year since Hiroshima a significant body of literature exploring the relation between nuclear deterrence and just war. This has been the work mostly of theologians and philosophers, but some of the strategists of deterrence have also been involved; they worry about the act of terrorizing much as conventional soldiers worry about the act of killing. I cannot review this literature here, though I shall draw upon it freely. The argument against deterrence is familiar enough. Anyone committed to the distinction between combatants and noncombatants is bound to be appalled by the specter of destruction evoked, and purposely evoked, in deterrence theory. "How can a nation live with its conscience," John Bennett has asked, "and know that it is preparing to kill twenty million children in another nation if the worst should come to the worst?" And yet, we have lived with that knowledge, and with our consciences too, for several decades now. How have we managed? The reason for our acceptance of deterrent strategy, most people would say, is that preparing to kill, even threatening to kill, is not at all the same thing as killing. Indeed it is not, but it is frighteningly close—else deterrence wouldn't "work"—and it is in the nature of that closeness that the moral problem lies.

The problem is often misdescribed—as in the following analogy for nuclear deterrence first suggested by Paul Ramsey and frequently repeated since:

> Suppose that one Labor Day weekend no one was killed or maimed on the highways; and that the reason for the remarkable restraint placed on the recklessness of automobile drivers was that suddenly everyone of them discovered he was driving with a baby tied to his front bumper! That would be no way to regulate traffic *even if it succeeds* in regulating it perfectly, since such a system makes innocent human lives the *direct object* of attack and uses them as a mere means for restraining the drivers of automobiles.

No one, of course, has ever proposed regulating traffic in this ingenious way, while the strategy of deterrence was adopted with virtually no opposition at all. That contrast should alert us to what is wrong with Ramsey's analogy. Though deterrence turns American and Russian civilians into mere means for the prevention of war, it does so without restraining any of us in any way. Ramsey reproduces the strategy of the German officers during the Franco-Prussian War who forced civilians to ride on military trains in order to deter saboteurs. By contrast with those civilians, however, we are hostages who lead normal lives. It is in the nature of the new technology that we can be threatened without being held captive. That is why deterrence, while in principle frightening, is so easy to live with. It cannot be condemned for anything it does to its hostages. It is so far from killing them that it does not even injure or confine them; it involves no direct or physical violation of their rights. Those critics of deterrence who are also committed consequentialists have had to imagine psychic injuries. Thus Erich Fromm, writing in 1960: "To live for any length of time under the constant threat of destruction creates certain psychological effects in most human beings—fright, hostility, callousness . . . and a resulting indifference to all the values we cherish. Such conditions will transform us into barbarians. . . ." But I don't know of any evidence that bears out either the assertion or the prediction; surely we are no more barbarians now than we were in 1945. In fact, for most people, the threat of destruction, though constant, is invisible and unnoticed. We have come to live with it casually—as Ramsey's babies, traumatized for life in all probability, could never do, and as hostages in conventional wars have never done.

If deterrence were more painful, we might have found other means of avoiding nuclear war—or we might not have avoided it. If we had to keep millions of people under restraint in order to maintain the balance of terror, or if we had to kill millions of people (periodically) in order to convince our adversaries of our credibility, deterrence would not be accepted for long. The strategy works because it is easy. Indeed, it is easy in a double sense: not only don't we do anything to other people, we also don't believe that we will ever have to do anything. The secret of nuclear deterrence is that it is a kind of bluff. Perhaps we are only bluffing ourselves, refusing to acknowledge the real terrors of a precarious and temporary balance. But no account of our experience is accurate which fails to recognize that, for all its ghastly potential, deterrence has so far been a bloodless strategy.

So far as consequences go, then, deterrence and mass murder are very far apart. Their closeness is a matter of moral posture and intention. Once again, Ramsey's analogy misses the point. His babies are not really the "direct object of attack," for whatever happens on that Labor Day weekend, no one will deliberately set out to kill them. But deterrence depends upon a readiness to do exactly that. It is as if the state should seek to prevent murder by threatening to kill the family and friends of every murderer—a domestic version of the policy of "massive retaliation." Surely that would be a repugnant policy. We would not admire the police officials who designed it or those pledged to carry it out, even if they never actually killed anybody. I don't want to say that such people would necessarily be transformed into barbarians; they might well have a heightened sense of how awful murder is and a heightened desire to avoid it; they might loathe the work they were pledged to do and fervently hope that they never had to do it. Nevertheless, the enterprise is immoral. The immorality lies in the threat itself, not in its present or even its likely consequences. Similarly with nuclear deterrence: it is our own intentions that we have to worry about and the potential (since there are no actual) victims of those intentions. Here Ramsey has put the case very well: "Whatever is wrong to do is wrong to threaten, if the latter means 'mean to do' . . . If counter-population warfare is murder, then counter-population deterrent threats are murderous. No doubt, killing millions of innocent people is worse than threatening to kill them. It is also true that no one wants to kill them, and it may well be true that no one expects to do so. Nevertheless, we intend the killings under certain circumstances. That is the stated policy of our government; and thousands of men, trained in the techniques of mass destruction and drilled in instant obedience, stand ready to carry it out. And from the perspective of morality, the readiness is all. We can translate it into degrees of danger, high and low, and worry about the risks we are imposing on innocent people, but the risks depend on the readiness. What we condemn in our own government, as in the police in my domestic analogy, is the commitment to murder.[1]

But this analogy, too, can be questioned. We don't prevent murder any more than we control traffic in these bizarre and inhuman ways. But we do deter or seek to deter our nuclear adversaries. Perhaps deterrence is different because of the danger its advocates claim to avoid. Traffic deaths and occasional murders, however much we deplore them, do not threaten our common liberties or our collective survival. Deterrence, so we have been told, guards us against a double danger: first, of atomic blackmail and foreign domination; and second, of nuclear destruction. The two go together, since if we did not fear the blackmail, we might adopt a policy of appeasement or surrender and so avoid the destruction. Deterrence theory was worked out at the height of the cold war between the United States and the Soviet Union, and those who worked it out were concerned above all with the political uses of violence—which are not relevant in either the traffic or police analogies. Underlying the American doctrine, there seemed to lurk some version of the slogan "Better dead than Red" (I don't know the Russian parallel). Now that is not really a believable slogan; it is hard to imagine that a nuclear holocaust was really thought preferable to the expansion of Soviet power. What made deterrence attractive was that it seemed capable of avoiding both.

We need not dwell on the nature of the Soviet regime in order to understand the virtues of this argument. Deterrence theory doesn't depend upon a view of Stalinism as a great evil (though that is a highly plausible view) in the same way that my argument about terror bombing depended upon an assertion about the evils of Nazism. It requires only that we see appeasement or surrender to involve a loss of values central to our existence as an independent nation-state. For it is not tolerable that advances in technology should put our nation, or any nation, at the mercy of a great power willing to menace the world or to press its authority outwards in the shadow of an implicit threat. The case here is very different from that which arises commonly in war, where *our* adherence to the war convention puts us, or would put us, at a disadvantage vis-à-vis *them*. For disadvantages of that sort are partial and relative; various counter-measures and compensating steps are always available. But in the nuclear case, the disadvantage is absolute. Against an enemy actually willing to use the bomb, self-defense is impossible, and it makes sense to say that the only compensating step is the (immoral) threat to respond in kind. No country capable of making such a threat is likely to refuse to make it. What is not tolerable won't be tolerated. Hence any state confronted by a nuclear adversary (it makes little difference what the adversary relationship is like or what ideological forms it assumes), and capable of developing its own bomb, is likely to do so, seeking safety in a balance of terror.[2] Mutual disarmament would clearly be a preferable alternative, but it is an alternative available only to the two countries working closely together, whereas deterrence is the likely choice of either one of them alone. They will worry about one another's readiness to attack; they will each assume their own commitment to resist; and they will realize that the greatest danger of such a confrontation would not be the defeat of one side or the other but the total destruction of both—and possibly of everyone else too. This in fact is the danger that has faced mankind since 1945, and our understanding of nuclear deterrence must be worked out with reference to its scope and imminence.

Supreme emergency has become a permanent condition. Deterrence is a way of coping with that condition, and though it is a bad way, there may well be no other that is practical in a world of sovereign and suspicious states. We threaten evil in order not to do it, and the doing of it would be so terrible that the threat seems in comparison to be morally defensible.

Limited Nuclear War

If the bomb were ever used, deterrence would have failed. It is a feature of massive retaliation that while there is or may be some rational purpose in threatening it, there could be none in carrying it out. Were our "bluff" ever to be called and our population centers suddenly attacked, the resulting war could not (in any usual sense of the word) be *won*. We could only drag our enemies after us into the abyss. The use of our deterrent capacity would be an act of pure destructiveness. For this reason, massive retaliation, if not literally unthinkable, has always seemed undo-able, and this is a source of considerable anxiety for military strategists. Deterrence only works, they argue, if each side believes that the other might actually carry out its threat. But would we carry it out? George Ken-

nan has recently given what must be the moral response:

> Let us suppose there were to be a nuclear attack of some sort on this country and millions of people were killed and injured. Let us further suppose that we had the ability to retaliate against the urban centers of the country that had attacked us. Would you want to do that? I wouldn't . . . I have no sympathy with the man who demands an eye for an eye in a nuclear attack.

A humane position—though one that should probably be whispered, rather than published, if the balance of terror is to be sustained. But the argument might look very different if the original attack or the planned response avoided cities and people. If a limited nuclear war were possible, wouldn't it also be do-able? And might not the balance of terror then be re-established on the basis of threats that were neither immoral nor unconvincing?

Over a brief timespan, in the late 1950s and early 1960s, these questions were answered with an extraordinary outpouring of strategic arguments and speculations, overlapping in important ways with the moralizing literature I described earlier. For the debate among the strategists focused on the attempt (though this was rarely made explicit) to fit nuclear war into the structure of the war convention, to apply the argument for justice as if this sort of conflict were like any other sort. The attempt involved, first, a defense of the use of tactical nuclear weapons in deterring and, if that failed, in resisting conventional or small-scale nuclear attacks; and it involved, secondly, the development of a "counterforce" strategy directed at the enemy's military installations and also at major economic targets (but not at entire cities). These two had a similar purpose. By holding out the promise of a limited nuclear war, they made it possible to imagine actually fighting such a war—they made it possible to imagine *winning* it—and so they strengthened the intention that lay behind the deterrent threat. They transformed the "bluff" into a plausible option.

Until the late 1950s, the tendency of most people was to regard the atomic bomb and its thermonuclear successors as forbidden weapons. They were treated on analogy with poison gas, though the prohibition on their use was never legally established. "Ban the bomb" was everyone's policy, and deterrence was simply a practical way of enforcing the ban. But now the strategists suggested (rightly) that the crucial distinction in the theory and practice of war was not between prohibited and acceptable weapons but between prohibited and acceptable targets. Massive retaliation was painful and difficult to contemplate because it was modeled on Hiroshima; the people we were planning to kill were innocent, militarily uninvolved, as removed from and ignorant of the weapons with which their leaders threatened us as we were of the weapons with which our leaders threatened them. But this objection would disappear if we could deter our adversaries by threatening a limited and morally acceptable destruction. Indeed, it might disappear so entirely that we would be tempted to give up deterrence and initiate the destruction ourselves whenever it seemed to our advantage to do so. This was certainly the tendency of much strategic argument, and several writers painted rather attractive pictures of limited nuclear war. Henry Kissinger likened it to war at sea—the very best kind of war, since no one lives in the sea. "The proper analogy . . . is not traditional land warfare, but naval strategy, in which self-contained, [highly mobile] units with great fire power gradually gain the upper hand by destroying their enemy counterparts without physically occupying territory or establishing a front line." The only difficulty is that Kissinger imagined fighting a war like that in Europe.

Tactical and counter-force warfare meets the formal requirements of *jus in bello*, and it was seized upon eagerly by certain moral theorists. That is not to say, however, that it makes moral sense. There remains the possibility that the new technology of war simply doesn't fit and cannot be made to fit within the old limits. This proposition can be defended in two different ways. The first is to argue that the collateral damage likely to be caused even by a "legitimate" use of nuclear weapons is so great that it would violate both of the proportionality limits fixed by the theory of war: the number of people killed in the war as a whole would not be warranted by the goals of the war—particularly since the dead would include many if not most of the

people for whose defense the war was being fought; and the number of people killed in individual actions would be disproportionate (under the doctrine of double effect)* "to the value of the military targets directly attacked. "The disproportion between the cost of such hostilities and the results they could achieve," wrote Raymond Aron, thinking of a limited nuclear war in Europe, "would be colossal." It would be colossal even if the formal limits on targeting were in fact observed. But the second argument against limited nuclear war is that these limits would almost certainly not be observed.

At this point, of course, one can only guess at the possible shape and course of the battles; there is no history to study. Neither moralists nor strategists can refer to cases; instead they design scenarios. The scene is empty; one can fill it in very different ways, and it is not impossible to imagine that limits might be maintained even after nuclear weapons had been used in battle. The prospect that they would be maintained and the war extended over time is so frightening to those countries on whose soil such wars are likely to be fought that they have generally opposed the new strategies and insisted upon the threat of massive retaliation. Thus, as André Beaufre has written, "Europeans would prefer to risk general war in an attempt to avoid war altogether rather than have Europe become the theater of operations for limited war." In fact, however, the risks of escalation will be great whatever limits are adopted, simply because of the immense destructive power of the weapons involved. Or rather, there are two possibilities: either nuclear weapons will be held at such low levels that they won't be significantly different from or of greater military utility than conventional explosives, in which case there is no reason to use them at all; or their very use will obliterate the distinction between targets. Once a bomb has been aimed at a military target but has, as a side effect, destroyed a city, the logic of deterrence will require the other side to aim at a city (for the sake of its seriousness and credibility). It is not necessarily the case that every war would become a total war, but the danger of escalation is so great as to preclude the first use of

---

*Editor's note: *Often in moral decision making we are faced with the choice of an action that will produce both good and bad effects. Considering only the good effect, we are inclined to perform the action; considering only the bad effect, we are inclined to avoid it. The principle of double effect aims at resolving such conflicts. Essentially, the principle of double effect holds that an action should be performed only if the intention is to bring about the good effect and only if the good effect is at least equivalent in importance to the bad effect.*

nuclear weapons—except by someone willing to face their final use. "Who would even launch such hostilities," Aron has asked, "unless he was determined to persist to the bitter end?" But such a determination is not imaginable in a sane human being, let alone in a political leader responsible for the safety of his own people; it would involve nothing less than national suicide.

These two factors, the extent even of limited destruction and the dangers of escalation, seem to rule out any sort of nuclear war between the great powers. They probably rule out large-scale conventional war, too, including the particular conventional war about which the strategists of the 1950s and 1960s were most concerned: a Russian invasion of western Europe. "The spectacle of a large Soviet field army crashing across the line into western Europe in the hope *and expectation* that nuclear weapons would not be used against it— thereby putting itself and the USSR totally at risk while leaving the choice of weapons to us—would seem to be hardly worth a second thought. . . ." It is important to stress that the bar lies in the totality of the risk: not in the possibility of what the strategists called a "flexible response," finely adjusted to the scope of the attack, but in the stark reality of ultimate horror should the adjustments fail. It may well be that "flexible response" enhanced the value of a counter-population deterrent by making it possible to reach that final point in "easy" stages, but it is also and more importantly true that we have never begun the staged escalation and are never likely to begin it, because of what lies at the end. Hence the persistence of counter-population deterrence, and hence also the virtual end of the strategic debate, which petered out in the middle 1960s. At that point, I think, it became clear that given the existence of large numbers of nuclear weapons and their relative invulnerability, and barring major technological breakthroughs, *any imaginable strategy* is likely to deter a "central war" between the great powers. The strategists helped us to understand this, but once it was understood it became unnecessary to adopt any of their strategies—or at least, any particular one of them. We continue to live, then, with the paradox that preexisted the debate: nuclear weapons are politically and militarily unusable only because and insofar as we can plausibly threaten to use them in some ultimate way. And it is immoral to make threats of that kind.

The Argument of Paul Ramsey

Before deciding (or refusing) to live with this paradox, I want to consider in some detail the work of the Protestant theologian Paul Ramsey, who has over a period of years argued that there exists a justifiable deterrent strategy. From the beginning of the moral and strategic debates, Ramsey has been a sharp opponent of the advocates of counter-city deterrence and also of those of its critics who think that it is the only form of deterrence and therefore opt for nuclear disarmament. He has condemned both these groups for the all-or-nothing character of their thinking: either total and immoral destruction or a kind of "pacifistic" inertia. He argues that these twin perspectives conform to the traditional American view of war as an all-out conflict, which must therefore be avoided whenever possible. Ramsey himself, I think, is a Protestant soldier in a different tradition; he would have Americans gird themselves for a long, continuous struggle with the forces of evil.

Now if there is to be a justified deterrent strategy, there must be a justified form of nuclear war, and Ramsey has conscientiously argued "the case for making just war possible" in the modern age. He takes a lively and well-informed interest in the strategic debates and has at various times defended the use of tactical nuclear weapons against invading armies and of strategic weapons against nuclear installations, conventional military bases, and isolated economic objectives. Even these targets are only "conditionally" permissible, since the proportionality rule would have to be applied in each case, and Ramsey does not believe that its standards will always be met. Like everyone (or almost everyone) who writes about these matters, he has no zest for nuclear combat; his main interest is in deterrence. But he needs at least the possibility of legitimate warfare if he is to maintain a deterrent posture without making immoral threats. That is his central purpose, and the effort to achieve it involves him in a highly sophisticated application of just war theory to the problems of nuclear strategy. In the best sense of the word, Ramsey is engaged with the realities of his world. But the realities in this case are intractable, and his way around them is finally too complex and too devious to provide a plausible account of our moral judgments. He multiplies distinctions like a Ptolemaic astronomer with his epicycles and comes very close at the end to what G.

E. M. Anscombe has called "double-think about double effect." But his work is important; it suggests the outer limits of the just war and the dangers of trying to extend those limits.

Ramsey's central claim is that it is possible to prevent nuclear attack without threatening to bomb cities in response. He believes that "the collateral civilian damage that would result from counter-force warfare in its maximum form" would be sufficient to deter potential aggressors. Since the civilians likely to die in such a war would be the incidental victims of legitimate military strikes, the threat of counter-force warfare plus collateral damage is also morally superior to deterrence in its present form. These are not hostages whom we intend to murder (under certain circumstances). Nor are we planning their deaths; we are only pointing out to our possible enemies the unavoidable consequences even of a war justly fought—which is, we could honestly say were we to adopt Ramsey's proposal, the only sort of war we were preparing to fight. Collateral damage is simply a fortunate feature of nuclear warfare; it serves no military purpose, and we would avoid it if we could, though it is clearly a good thing that we cannot. And since the damage is justifiable in prospect, it is also justifiable here and now to call that prospect to mind for the sake of its deterrent effects.

But there are two problems with this argument. First, the danger of collateral damage is unlikely to work as a deterrent unless the damage expected is radically disproportionate to the ends of the war or the value of this or that military target. Hence Ramsey is driven to argue that "the threat of something disproportionate is not always a disproportionate threat." What that means is this: proportionality in combat is measured, let's say, against the value of a particular missile base, while proportionality in deterrence is measured against the value of world peace. So the damage may not be justifiable in prospect (under the doctrine of double effect), and yet the threat of such damage may still be morally permitted. Perhaps that argument is right, but I should stress that its result is to void the proportionality rule. Now there is no limit on the number of people whose deaths we can threaten, so long as those deaths are to be caused "collaterally" and not by taking direct aim. As we have seen before, the idea of proportionality, once it is worked on a bit, tends to fade away. And then the entire burden of Ramsey's argument falls on the idea of

death by indirection. That is indeed an important idea, central to the permissions and restraints of conventional war. But its standing is undermined here by the fact that Ramsey relies so heavily on the deaths he supposedly doesn't intend. He wants, like other deterrent theorists, to prevent nuclear attack by threatening to kill very large numbers of innocent civilians, but unlike other deterrent theorists, he expects to kill these people without aiming at them. That may be a matter of some moral significance, but it does not seem significant enough to serve as the cornerstone of a justified deterrent. If counter-force warfare had no collateral effects, or had minor and controllable effects, then it could play no part in Ramsey's strategy. Given the effects it does have and the central part it is assigned, the word "collateral" seems to have lost much of its meaning. Surely anyone designing such a strategy must accept moral responsibility for the effects on which he is so radically dependent.

But we have not yet seen the whole of Ramsey's design, for he doesn't pull back from the hardest questions. What if the likely collateral damage of a just nuclear war isn't great enough to deter a would-be aggressor? What if the aggressor threatens a counter-city strike? Surrender would be intolerable, and yet we cannot ourselves threaten mass murder in response. Fortunately (again), we don't have to. "We do not need . . . to threaten that we will use [nuclear weapons] in case of attack," Bernard Brodie has written. "We do not need to threaten anything. Their being there is quite enough." So it is, too, according to Ramsey, with counter-city strikes: the mere possession of nuclear weapons constitutes an implicit threat which no one actually has to make. If the immorality lies in uttering the threat, then it may in practice be avoided—though one may wonder at the ease of this solution. Nuclear weapons, Ramsey writes, have a certain inherent ambiguity: "they may be used either against strategic forces or against centers of populations," and that means that "*apart from intention, their capacity to deter cannot be removed from them. . . . No matter how often we declare, and quite sincerely declare, that our targets are an enemy's forces, he can never be quite certain* that in the fury or the fog of war his cities may not be destroyed." Now, the possession of conventional weapons is both innocent and ambiguous in exactly the way Ramsey suggests. The fact that I am holding a sword or a rifle doesn't mean that I am going to use it against innocent people, though it is quite effective against them; it has the same "dual use" that Ramsey has discovered in nuclear weapons. But the bomb is different. In a sense, as Beaufre has said, it isn't designed for war at all. It is designed to kill whole populations, and its deterrent value depends upon that fact (whether the killing is direct or indirect). It serves the purpose of preventing war only by virtue of the implicit threat it poses, and we possess it for the sake of that purpose. And men and women are responsible for the threats they live by, even if they don't speak them out loud.

Ramsey presses on. Perhaps the mere possession of nuclear weapons won't be enough to deter some reckless aggressor. Then, he suggests, we must distinguish "between the appearance and the actuality of being . . . committed to go to city exchanges. . . . In that case, only the appearance should be cultivated." I am not sure exactly what that means, and Ramsey (for once) seems reluctant to say, but presumably it would allow us to hint at the possibility of massive retaliation without actually planning for it or intending to carry it out. Thus we are offered a continuum of increasing moral danger along which four points are marked out: the articulated prospect of collateral (and disproportionate) civilian deaths; the implicit threat of counter-city strikes; the "cultivated" appearance of a commitment to counter-city strikes; and the actual commitment. These may well be distinct points, in the sense that one can imagine policies focused around each of them, and these would be different policies. But I am inclined to doubt that the differences make a difference. To rule out the last for moral reasons, while permitting the first three, can only make poeple cynical about one's moral reasons. Ramsey aims to clear our intentions without prohibiting those policies that he believes necessary (and that probably are necessary under present conditions) for the dual prevention of war and conquest. But the unavoidable truth is that all these policies rest ultimately on immoral threats. Unless we give up nuclear deterrence, we cannot give up such threats, and it is best if we straightforwardly acknowledge what it is we are doing.

The real ambiguity of nuclear deterrence lies in the fact that no one, including ourselves, can be sure that we will ever carry out the threats we make. In a sense, all we ever do is to "cultivate the appearance." We strain for credibility, but what we are putatively planning and intending remains incredible. As I have already suggested, that helps make deterrence psychologically bearable, and perhaps also it makes a deterrent posture marginally better from a moral standpoint. But at the same time, the reason for our hesitancy and self-doubt is the monstrous immorality that our policy contemplates, an immorality we can never hope to square with our understanding of justice in war. Nuclear weapons explode the theory of just war. They are the first of mankind's technological innovations that are simply not encompassable within the familiar moral world. Or rather, our familiar notions about *jus in bello* require us to condemn even the threat to use them. And yet there are other notions, also familiar, having to do with aggression and the right of self-defense, that seem to require exactly that threat. So we move uneasily beyond the limits of justice for the sake of justice (and of peace).

According to Ramsey, this is a dangerous move. For if we "become convinced," he writes, "that in the matter of deterrence a number of things are wicked which are not," then, seeing no way of avoiding wickedness, we will "set no limits on it." Once again, this argument is precisely right with reference to conventional warfare; it catches the central error of what I have called the "war is hell" doctrine. But it is persuasive in the case of nuclear warfare only if one can describe plausible and morally significant limits, and that Ramsey has not done; nor have the strategists of "flexible response" been able to do it. All their arguments depend upon the ultimate wickedness of counter-city strikes. The pretense that this is not so carries with it dangers of its own. To draw insignificant lines, to maintain the formal categories of double effect, collateral damage, noncombatant immunity, and so on, when so little moral content remains is to corrupt the argument for justice as a whole and to render it suspect even in those areas of military life to which it properly pertains. And those areas are wide. Nuclear deterrence marks their outer limits, forcing us to contemplate wars that can never be fought. Within those limits there are wars that can and will and perhaps even should be fought, and to which the old rules apply with all their force. The specter of a nuclear holocaust does not invite us to act wickedly in conventional wars. Indeed, it probably is a deterrent there, too; it is hard to imagine a repetition of Dresden or Tokyo in a conventional war between nuclear powers. For destruction on such a scale would invite a nuclear response and a drastic and unacceptable escalation of the struggle.

Nuclear war is and will remain morally unacceptable, and there is no case for its rehabilitation. Because it is unacceptable, we must seek out ways to prevent it, and because deterrence is a bad way, we must seek out others. It is not my purpose here to suggest what the alternatives might look like. I have been more concerned to acknowledge that deterrence itself, for all its criminality, falls or may fall for the moment under the standard of necessity. But as with terror bombing, so here with the threat of terrorism: supreme emergency is never a stable position. The realm of necessity is subject to historical change. And, what is more important, we are under an obligation to seize upon opportunities of escape, even to take risks for the sake of such opportunities. So the readiness to murder is balanced, or should be, by the readiness not to murder, not to threaten murder, as soon as alternative ways to peace can be found.

Notes

1. Would it make any difference if this commitment were mechanically fixed? Suppose we set up a computer which would automatically respond to any enemy attack by releasing our missiles. Then we informed our potential enemies that if they attacked our cities, theirs would be attacked. And they would be responsible for both attacks, we might say, since in the interval between the two, no political decision, no act of the will, would be possible on our side. I don't want to comment on the possible effectiveness (or the dangers) of such an arrangement. But it is worth insisting that it would not solve the moral problem. The men and women who designed the computer program or the political leaders who ordered them to do so would be responsible for the second attack, for they would have planned it and organized it and intended that it should occur (under certain conditions).

2. This is obviously the grim logic of nuclear proliferation. So far as the moral question goes, each new balance of terror created by proliferation is exactly like the first one, justified (or not) in the same way. But the creation of regional balances may well have general effects upon the stability of the great power equilibrium, thereby introducing new moral considerations that I cannot take up here.

Questions for Analysis

1. *What does Walzer feel is wrong with Ramsey's analogy? What analogy does he substitute, and why does he think that it, too, is inadequate for understanding nuclear deterrence?*

2. *What are some of the common arguments cited by Walzer against policies of nuclear deterrence?*

3. *What "double danger" does deterrence supposedly guard against?*

4. *Why does Walzer believe that the threat of nuclear destruction is morally defensible? Do you agree?*

The Fate of the Earth

Jonathan Schell

In his book The Fate of the Earth, *a selection from which follows, author Jonathan Schell attacks the doctrine of nuclear deterrence as contradictory. Hoping to avoid extermination of the human race, we threaten a massive nuclear attack that could in fact bring about that fate. Inasmuch as*

*threatening implies an intention to implement the threat, we therefore find ourselves both
intending and not intending to do something. Schell points out that although traditional military
doctrine says that given the limited forces available to each side, one side would be exhausted
before both were annihilated, nuclear deterrence is based on the premise that the opponents and
possibly the human species will be annihilated before either side exhausts its forces. In Schell's
view, there is no question that at present the nuclear premise is the accurate one, and that it runs
counter to traditional military thinking.*

The central proposition of the deterrence doctrine—the piece of logic on which the world theoretically depends to see the sun rise tomorrow—is that a nuclear holocaust can best be prevented if each nuclear power, or bloc of powers, holds in readiness a nuclear force with which it "credibly" threatens to destroy the entire society of any attacker, even after suffering the worst possible "first strike" that the attacker can launch. Robert McNamara, who served as Secretary of Defense for seven years under Presidents Kennedy and Johnson, defined the policy, in his book *The Essence of Security*, published in 1968, in the following terms: "Assured destruction is the very essence of the whole deterrence concept. We must possess an actual assured-destruction capability, and that capability also must be credible. The point is that a potential aggressor must believe that our assured-destruction capability is in fact actual, and that our will to use it in retaliation to an attack is in fact unwavering." Thus, deterrence "means the certainty of suicide to the aggressor, not merely to his military forces, but to his society as a whole." Let us picture what is going on here. There are two possible eventualities: success of the strategy or its failure. If it succeeds, both sides are frozen into inaction by fear of retaliation by the other side. If it fails, one side annihilates the other, and then the leaders of the second side annihilate the "society as a whole" of the attacker, and the earth as a whole suffers the consequences of a full-scale holocaust, which might include the extinction of man. In point of fact, neither the United States nor the Soviet Union has ever adopted the "mutual-assured-destruction" doctrine in pure form; other aims, such as attempting to reduce the damage of the adversary's nuclear attack and increasing the capacity for destroying the nuclear forces of the adversary, have been mixed in. Nevertheless, underlying these deviations the concept of deterring a first strike by preserving the capacity for a devastating second strike has remained constant.

The strategists of deterrence have addressed the chief issue in any sane policy in a nuclear-armed world—the issue of survival—and have come up with this answer: Salvation from extinction by nuclear weapons is to be found in the nuclear weapons themselves. The possession of nuclear weapons by the great powers, it is believed, will prevent the use of nuclear weapons by those same powers. Or, to put it more accurately, the threat of their use by those powers will prevent their use. Or, in the words of Bernard Brodie, a pioneer in nuclear strategy, in *The Absolute Weapon: Atomic Power and World Order*, a book published in 1946: "Thus far, the chief purpose of our military establishment has been to win wars. From now on its chief purpose must be to avert them. It can have almost no other useful purpose." Or, in the classic, broad formulation of Winston Churchill, in a speech to the House of Commons in 1955: "Safety will be the sturdy child of terror, and survival the twin brother of annihilation."

This doctrine, in its detailed as well as its more general formulations is diagrammatic of the world's failure to come to terms with the nuclear predicament. In it, two irreconcilable purposes clash. The first purpose is to permit the survival of the species, and this is expressed in the doctrine's aim of frightening everybody into holding back from using nuclear weapons at all; the second purpose is to serve national ends, and this is expressed in the doctrine's permitting the defense of one's nation and its interests by threatening to use nuclear weapons. The strategists are pleased to call this clash of two opposing purposes in one doctrine a paradox, but in actuality it is a contradiction. We cannot both threaten ourselves with something and hope to avoid that same thing by making the threat—both intend to do something and intend not to do it. The head-on contradiction between these aims has set up a crosscurrent of tension within the policies of each superpower. The "safety" that Churchill mentions may be emphasized at one moment, and at the next moment it is the "terror" that comes to the fore. And since the deterrence doctrine pairs the safety and the terror, and makes the former depend on the latter, the world is never quite sure from day to day which one is in the ascendant—if, indeed, the distinction can be maintained in the first place. All that the world can know for certain is that at any moment the fireballs may arrive. I have said that we do not have two earths, one to blow up experimentally and the other to live on; nor do we have two souls, one for reacting to daily life and the other for reacting to the peril to all life. But neither do we have two wills, one with which we can intend to destroy our species and the other with which we can intend to save ourselves. Ultimately, we must all live together with one soul and one will on our one earth.

For all that, the adoption of the deterrence doctrine represented a partial recognition that the traditional military doctrine had become an anachronism—a doctrine that was suited well enough to the pre-nuclear world but lost all application and relevance when the first nuclear bomb flashed over the New Mexican desert. In assessing the advance made by deterrence, we must acknowledge how radically it departed from traditional military doctrine. Traditional military doctrine and nuclear doctrine are based on wholly different factual circumstances, each set of which corresponds to the technical realities of its period. Traditional military doctrine began, as I have suggested, with the premise that the amounts of force available to the belligerents were small enough to permit one side or the other to exhaust itself before both sides were annihilated. Nuclear doctrine, on the other hand, begins with the premise that the amounts of force are so great that both sides, and perhaps all mankind, will be annihilated before either side exhausts its forces. Like postulates in geometry, these two premises determine the entire systems of thought that follow, and no discussion of military strategy can make any sense unless one clearly specifies which premise one is starting from. But . . . there is no longer room for doubt that in our time the second premise is the correct one.

The chief virtue of the doctrine of nuclear deterrence is that it begins by accepting this basic fact of life in the nuclear world, and does so not only on the rhetorical plane but on the practical plane of strategic planning. Hence, it acknowledges that victory can no longer be obtained in a contest between two well-armed nuclear powers, such as the United States and the Soviet Union. Senator Barry Goldwater wrote a book, published in 1962, whose title was *Why Not Victory?* To this question the strategists of deterrence have a decisive answer: Because in the present-day, nuclear world "victory" is oblivion. From this recognition flows the conclusion, arrived at by Brodie in 1946, that the sole purpose of possessing nuclear strategic arms is not to win war but to prevent it. The adoption of the aim of preventing rather than winning war requires the adoption of other policies that fly in the face of military tradition. One is abandonment of the military defense of one's nation—of what used to be at the center of all military planning and was the most hallowed justification of the military calling. The policy of deterrence does not contemplate doing anything in defense of the homeland; it only promises that if the homeland is annihilated the aggressor's homeland will be annihilated, too. In fact, the policy goes further than this: it positively requires that each side leave its population open to attack, and make no serious effort to protect it. This requirement follows from the basic logic of deterrence, which is that safety is "the sturdy child of terror." According to this logic, the safety can be only as great as the terror is, and the terror therefore has to be kept relentless. If it were to be diminished—by, for example, building bomb shelters that protected some significant part of the population—then safety would be diminished, too, because the protected side might be tempted to launch a holocaust, in the belief that it could "win" the hostilities. That is why in nuclear strategy "destruction" must, perversely, be "assured," as though our aim were to destroy, and not to save, mankind.

In strategic terms, the requirement that the terror be perfected, and never allowed to deteriorate toward safety, translates into the requirement that the retaliatory force of both sides be guaranteed—first, by making sure that the retaliatory weapons cannot be destroyed in a first strike, and, second, by making sure that the society of the attacking power *can* be destroyed in a second strike. And since in this upside-down scheme of things the two sides will suffer equally no matter which one opens the hostilities, each side actually has an interest in maintaining its adversary's retaliatory forces as well as its own. For the most dangerous of all the configurations of forces is that in which one side appears to have the ability to destroy the nuclear forces of the other in a first strike. Then not only is the stronger side theoretically tempted to launch hostilities but—what is probably far more dangerous—the other side, fearful of completely losing its forces, might, in a crisis, feel compelled to launch the first strike itself. If on either side the population becomes relatively safe from attack or the retaliatory strike becomes vulnerable to attack, a temptation to launch a first strike is created, and "stability"—the leading virtue of any nuclear balance of power—is lost. As Thomas Schelling, the economist and noted nuclear theorist, has put it, in *The Strategy of Conflict*, a book published in 1960, once instability is introduced on either side, both sides may reason as follows: "He, thinking I was about to kill him in self-defense, was about to kill me in self-defense, so I had to kill him in self-defense." Under deterrence, military "superiority" is therefore as dangerous to the side that possesses it as to the side that is supposedly threatened by it. (According to this logic, the United States should have heaved a sigh of relief when the Soviet Union reached nuclear parity with it, for then stability was achieved.) All these conclusions follow from the deterrence doctrine, yet they run so consistently counter to the far simpler, more familiar, and emotionally more comprehensible logic of traditional military thinking—not to mention instinct and plain common sense, which rebel against any such notion as "assuring" our own annihilation—that we should not be surprised when we find that the deterrence doctrine is constantly under challenge from traditional doctrine, no matter how glaringly at odds with the facts traditional doctrine may be. The hard-won gains of deterrence, such as they are, are repeatedly threatened by a recrudescence of the old desire for victory, for national defense in the old sense, and for military superiority, even though every one of these goals not only would add nothing to our security but, if it should be pursued far enough, would undermine the precarious safety that the deterrence doctrine tries to provide.

If the virtue of the deterrence policy lies in its acceptance of the basic fact of life in the nuclear world—that a holocaust will bring annihilation to both sides, and possibly the extinction of man as well—its defect lies in the strategic construct that it erects on the foundation of that fact. For if we try to guarantee our safety by threatening ourselves with doom, then we have to mean the threat; but if we mean it, then we are actually planning to do, in some circumstance or other, that which we categorically must never do and are supposedly trying to prevent—namely, extinguish ourselves. This is the circularity at the core of the nuclear-deterrence doctrine; we seek to avoid our self-extinction by threatening to perform the act. According to this logic, it is almost as though if we stopped threatening ourselves with extinction, then extinction would occur. Brodie's formula can be reversed: if the aim of having nuclear forces is to avert annihilation (misnamed "war" by him), then we must cling for our lives to those same forces. Churchill's dictum can be reversed, too: If safety is the sturdy child of terror, then terror is equally the sturdy child of safety. But who is to guarantee which of the children will be born? And if survival is the twin brother of annihilation, then we must cultivate annihilation. But then we may *get* annihilation. By growing to actually rely on terror, we do more than tolerate its presence in our world: we place our trust in it. And while this is not quite to "love the bomb," as the saying goes, it decidedly is to place our faith in it, and to give it an all-important position in the very heart of our affairs. Under this doctrine, instead of getting rid of the bomb we build it ever more deeply into our lives.

The logical fault line in the doctrine runs straight through the center of its main strategic tenet—the proposition that safety is achieved by assuring that any nuclear aggressor will be annihilated in a retaliatory strike. For while the doctrine relies for its success on a nuclear-armed victim's resolve to launch the annihilating second strike, it can offer no sensible or sane justification for launching it in the event. In pre-nuclear military strategy, the deterrent effect of force was a useful by-product of the ability and willingness to wage and win wars. Deterrence was the shadow cast by force, or, in Clausewitz's metaphor, the credit that flowed from the ability to make the cash payment of the favorable decision by arms. The logic of pre-nuclear deterrence escaped circularity by each side's being frankly ready to wage war and try for victory if deterrence failed. Nuclear deterrence, however, supposedly aims solely at forestalling any use of force by either side, and has given up at the outset on a favorable decision by arms. The question, then, is: Of what object is nuclear deterrence the shadow? Of what cash payment is it the credit? The theoretical answer, of course, is: The retaliatory strike. Yet since in the nuclear-deterrence theory the whole purpose of having a retaliatory capacity is to deter a first strike, one must ask what reason would remain to launch the retaliation once the first strike had actually arrived. Nuclear deterrence requires one to prepare for armed conflict not in order to "win" it if it breaks out but in order to prevent it from breaking out in the first place. But if armed conflict breaks out anyway, what does one do with one's forces then? In pre-nuclear times, the answer would have required no second thought: it would have been to strive for the decision by arms—for victory. Yet nuclear deterrence begins by assuming, correctly, that victory is impossible. Thus, the logic of the deterrence strategy is dissolved by the very event— the first strike—that it is meant to prevent. Once the action begins, the whole doctrine is self-cancelling. In sum, the doctrine is based on a monumental logical mistake: one cannot credibly deter a first strike with a second strike whose *raison d'être* dissolves the moment the first strike arrives. It follows that, as far as deterrence theory is concerned, there is no reason for either side not to launch a first strike.

What seems to be needed to repair the doctrine is a motive for retaliation—one that is not supplied by the doctrine itself and that lies outside its premises—but the only candidates are those belonging to traditional military doctrine; namely, some variation of victory. The adherents of nuclear victory— whatever that would be—have on occasion noted the logical fallacy on which deterrence is based, and stepped forward to propose their solution: a "nuclear-war-fighting" capacity. Thus, the answer they give to the question of what to do after the first strike arrives is: Fight and "win" a "nuclear war." But victory does not suddenly become possible simply because it offers a solution to the logical contradiction on which the mutual-assured-destruction doctrine rests. The facts remain obdurately what they are: an attack of several thousand megatons will annihilate any country on earth many times over, no matter what line of argument the strategists pursue; and a "nuclear exchange" will, if it is on a large scale, threaten the life of man.

Indeed, if victory were really possible there would have been no need for a deterrence strategy to begin with, and traditional military strategy would have needed no revision. This "solution" is therefore worse than the error it sets out to remedy. It resolves the contradiction in the deterrence doctrine by denying the tremendous new reality that the doctrine was framed to deal with, and that all of us now have to deal with on virtually every level of our existence. Consequently, this "solution" could lead us to commit the ultimate folly of exterminating ourselves without even knowing what we were doing. Aiming at "victory," we would wind up extinct.

In the last analysis, there can be no credible threat without credible use—no shadow without an object, no credit without cash payment. But since use is the thing above all else that we don't want, because it means the end of all of us, we are naturally at a loss to find any rationale for it. To grasp the reality of the contradiction, we have only to picture the circumstances of leaders whose country has just been annihilated in a first strike. Now their country is on its way to becoming a radioactive desert, but the retaliatory nuclear force survives in its silos, bombers, and submarines. These leaders of nobody, living in underground shelters or in "doomsday" planes that could not land, would possess the means of national defense but no nation to defend. What rational purpose could they have in launching the retaliatory strike? Since there was no longer a nation, "national security" could not be the purpose. Nor could defense of other peoples be the purpose, since the retaliatory strike might be the action that would finally break the back of the ecosphere and extinguish our species. In these circumstances, it seems to me, it is really an open question whether the leaders would decide to retaliate or not.

This conclusion is not one that is likely to be breathed aloud by anyone in or near power in either the Soviet Union or the United States. Since deterrence depends fully as much on one's adversary's perception of one's "unwavering" will to retaliate as on one's technical ability to do it, an acknowledgment that retaliation is senseless would in a way amount to unilateral disarmament by verbal means. The doctrine of nuclear deterrence thus deters debate about itself, and this incidental "deterrence" may have been no small factor in the

sharp limits placed on the definition of "respectable," so-called "realistic" thinking about nuclear
strategy. Nevertheless, the contradiction at the heart
of the doctrine has occasioned considerable indirect intellectual twisting and turning among the
nuclear theorists, and the resulting recommendations lead one into byways of the maze of strategic
theory which stand out as bizarre and frightening
even for the catalogues of nuclear strategic "options."
The commonest solution to the problem of the
missing motive for retaliation is to suggest that the
policymakers try to cultivate an appearance of
unreason, for if one is insane one doesn't need to
supply any motive for retaliating—one might do it
simply out of madness. The nuclear theorist Herman Kahn, for example, suggests that "it might
best deter the attack" by an *appearance* of irrationally inexorable commitment." Kahn first wonders
whether it might not be enough merely to "pretend" to be irrationally committed, but he concludes that a pretense of unreason is not reliable,
and that one must *really intend to do it."* The prescription, then, which he calls the policy of "the
rationality of irrationality," is to coolly resolve to be
crazy. How statesmen are to go about this, Kahn
does not say. Another solution, quite closely related,
is to try to create either the appearance or the reality of being out of control. Uncontrol, like insanity,
removes the need for a rational motive in retaliating, this time by arranging for the retaliation to
occur "by accident." Thomas Schelling, addressing
the general question "How can one commit himself
in advance to an act that he would in fact prefer
not to carry out in the event?" suggests the tactic
either of pretending that the crucial decisions will
be in part up to "chance" or of actually arranging
things so that this is true, thus adding to Kahn's
concept of reasoned insanity the planned accident.
With this strategy in effect, he writes, "the brink is
not . . . the sharp edge of a cliff, where one can
stand firmly, look down, and decide whether or
not to plunge." Rather, "the brink is a curved slope
that one can stand on with some risk of slipping."
Therefore, "brinkmanship involves getting onto the
slope where one may fall in spite of his own best
efforts to save himself, dragging his adversary with
him." That these astonishing remedies are no less
consequential in the real world than the doctrinal
illogicality they try to remedy is testified to by, among
other things, a statement in the memoirs of Presi-

dent Richard Nixon's chief of staff H. R. Haldeman
that Nixon believed in the "Madman Theory" of
the Presidency, according to which the nation's foes
would bow to the President's will if they believed
that he had taken leave of his senses and was ready
to risk a holocaust in order to secure some limited
national gain. Whether or not Nixon had read the
writings of Kahn and Schelling, he was following
their counsel to the letter.

The recommendation of these tactics naturally
raises the question of whether, with the life of our
species at stake, we want our nuclear decision-
makers to be cultivating irrationality and uncontrol, and whether a slippery slope over the nuclear
abyss is where we all want to be. But these questions, which I think must be answered with a
resounding "no," come up only as a consequence
of our reliance on "terror" to provide "safety," and
on the threat of "annihilation" to provide "survival." For it is in an effort to strengthen and shore
up the terror and make annihilation more certain
that the strategists and statesmen are forced into
these appalling postures. Their problem is to find
a way of appearing "inexorably" resolved to do
things that can never make any sense or ever be
justified by any moral code, and irrationality and
uncontrol fulfill the requirements for the very reason that they represent the abandonment of morality and sense. Adopted as policy, they lend credibility to actions that are—conveniently for strategic
purposes, if not for the safety of mankind—immoral and insane.

It must be added that there is another extreme
solution, which would entirely remove the defect
in the doctrine of nuclear deterrence. This solution,
described (but not recommended) by Kahn, would
be to construct a literal doomsday machine, which
would blow up the whole world as soon as an
adversary engaged in some activity that had previously been defined as "unacceptable" by the
machine's possessor. Kahn, who estimated in 1960
that a doomsday machine might be built for as little
as ten billion dollars, points out that the machine
would eliminate any doubt concerning the retaliatory strike by making it fully automatic. The retaliatory strike would still be senseless, but this sense-
lessness would no longer cloud its "credibility,"
since the action would have been predetermined:
the foundation would have been provided for a
fully consistent policy of nuclear deterrence, under

which nations would be deterred from launching nuclear attacks by the prearranged certainly that their own countries would perish in the ensuing global annihilation. But Kahn is also quick to point out a disadvantage of the doomsday machine which makes its construction immediately repugnant and intolerable to anyone who thinks about it: once it is in place, "there is no chance of human intervention, control, and final decision." And behind this objection, we may add, is an even simpler and more basic one: the chief reason we don't want a doomsday machine is that we don't want doom—not in any circumstances. Doom doesn't become any more acceptable because it comes about as someone's "final decision." And, of course, even though no enemy attack has been launched, in a moment of computer confusion the doomsday machine might make its own "final decision" to go off.

Because deterrence, on which we all now rely for whatever safety we have, is a psychological strategy, which aims at terrorizing the adversary into holding back from attacking us, it might seem that the discovery in one or the other command center of the logical absurdity of the policy would lead to the breakdown of the system—or, at least, to the abandonment of the doctrine. That this has not occurred is an indication that, even in the abstruse realm of nuclear doctrine, theory and practice, thought and reality are still different. In the real world, there are several stand-ins for the missing motive for the crucial retaliatory strike. The first stand-in is revenge, which, even though retaliation is not a rational action, might cause it to be carried out anyway. According to the emotional logic of revenge, the living act to right the wrong inflicted on the unjustly slain, who, being dead, cannot themselves realign the unbalanced scales of justice. Revenge is neither sensible nor constructive—especially not in a nuclear holocaust—but it is human, and the possibility that it would well up in the breasts of the leaders of a country that has just been effaced from the earth can by no means be ruled out by an aggressor; he has to consider that, even without any irrationality of the planned sort, a "rational" response to a nuclear attack can hardly be counted on. The second, and perhaps more important, stand-in for the missing motive is the irreducible unpredictability of events once the nuclear threshold is crossed. At this verge, with the survival of the species at stake, the human mind

falters. The leaders of the nuclear powers have no choice, as they stare into McNamara's "vast unknown," but to assume that the stakes are total. Certainly there is no need for anyone to strain to appear irrational, as Kahn suggests, or out of control, as Schelling suggests: a world that has embarked on a holocaust is in its nature irrational and out of control.

Our experience of nuclear crises leads us to believe that when the leaders of nuclear powers are forced to contemplate the reality of a holocaust at close quarters they have looked on it in this light. That is, they have assumed that if a limited nuclear war, or even conventional war between the superpowers, breaks out, a holocaust is the likely result. Michael Mandelbaum, in his history of nuclear strategy and experience, *The Nuclear Question*, published in 1979, observes that when the Soviet and American leaders confronted one another in the Cuban missile crisis they discovered that the fearful nature of a holocaust, which during the days of the crisis partly emerged from abstraction and unreality to become almost palpable in people's emotions, strongly deterred them from inaugurating hostilities at no matter how minor a level. Brought face to face with the beast, both sides realized that "there was no way to fight a nuclear war." Thus, "in striving to avoid having to fight a nuclear war they took great care not to start a war of any kind, which they feared would become nuclear." This lesson of experience offered some complementary lessons. One was that although no one had decided to establish a doomsday machine, people had to act as though one were in place. They had to assume that one misstep could be the misstep that ended the world. The notion that there was a middle ground of "tactical" nuclear hostilities of a limited kind, or even of conventional hostilities, disappeared under the awful pressure of the crisis. The doorway to the "vast unknown" seemed always right at hand, and all the scenarios of "limited war" and the like tended to crumble.

A final "deterrent," which, although fallible, is both rational and human, but which goes unmentioned in deterrence theory, is the humanity of the leaders of nuclear powers. History is crowded with ruthless, berserk actions, yet there are none that have attained the horror and insanity of a nuclear holocaust, and very few that have gone as far as the worst crime of which we do have experience—

genocide. I believe that without indulging in wishful thinking we can grant that the present leaders of both the Soviet Union and the United States are considerably deterred from launching a nuclear holocaust by sheer aversion to the unspeakable act itself.

Questions for Analysis

1. In Schell's view, what are the two "irreconcilable purposes" involved in the world's failure to resolve the nuclear predicament?

2. Would you agree with Schell that the deterrence premise is the correct one, and not the traditional military premise?

3. Why does Schell believe that the nuclear doctrine "positively requires that each side leave its population open to attack and make no serious effort to protect it"? Do you agree?

4. What leads Schell to conclude: "As far as deterrence theory is concerned, there is no reason for either side not to launch a first strike"? Do you agree?

5. One solution to the contradiction in the deterrence doctrine is to develop a capacity to fight and "win" a "nuclear war"—that is, develop a motive for retaliation. Why does Schell consider this "solution" worse than the error it attempts to remedy? (Incidentally, what does Schell imply by putting the quotation marks around the words in the preceding sentence?)

6. Schell says the most common solution to the problem of the missing motive for retaliation is that policymakers try to cultivate an appearance of unreason. What does this mean, and why does Schell object to it?

7. What is the "doomsday machine"? How would it remove the defect in the nuclear doctrine, and why does Schell consider it repugnant?

8. Evaluate the moral justifiability of the deterrence doctrine from the viewpoints of rational development, natural law (both religious and secular), Kantian ethics, and utilitarianism.

The Great Nuclear Debate

Leon Wieseltier

In the following excerpt from a lengthy article entitled "The Great Nuclear Debate," author Leon Wieseltier concedes there is a sense in which nuclear deterrence is immoral and irrational. While the criticisms may be well-founded, the conclusions often drawn from them are, according to Wieseltier, groundless. The apparent shortcomings of deterrence, he says, indicate not that deterrence must be scrapped, but that deterrence alone is insufficient without disarmament.

There is a sense in which deterrence is certainly immoral. It is a promise of murder. We prevent them from using their weapons by threatening to kill millions of innocent people, and by making them believe that we mean it; and they do the same. If the deed cannot be called moral, the threat cannot be called moral. This is the objection that is made in the pastoral letter on nuclear weapons drafted for the National Conference of Catholic Bishops. "The nature of deterrence in the nuclear age has raised the most severe moral questions," it warns. "Under no circumstances may nuclear weapons or other instruments of mass slaughter be used for the purpose of destroying population centers. . . . Our condemnation applies especially to the retaliatory use of weapons striking enemy cities after our own have been already struck." Such a retaliatory strike, or rather the plausible threat of it, is of course the essence of deterrence. It must be said to the credit of the bishops that they have correctly decoded the Pentagon's present counter-political strategy, which is the murder of innocents by another name; and it must be said to the discredit of the Pentagon that its plans for the fighting of a nuclear war have been so deceitfully disguised as deterrence that doubts about the one have led many to doubts about the other.

There is a sense, too, in which deterrence is irrational. It is irrational to think highly of human nature. Our intelligence has placed intercontinental missiles at the disposal of our instincts. Nothing in the past can have been so attractive to the aggressive drives of men, so seductive to their desire for self-destruction, as nuclear weapons. "Men have gained control over the forces of nature to such an extent that with their help they would have no difficulty in exterminating one another to the last man": Freud made this observation a full fifteen years before the explosion at Almagordo. No policy on nuclear weapons except for the immediate unscrewing of every one of them, can guarantee against an accidental war, but there is something even worse to consider. Who can say with any certainty that there will never be somebody with a finger on the button who will not want to push it? The world may one day pay dearly for somebody's experience of his or her parents. This is the happiest time in history for sick minds.

Deterrence, moreover, is not peace. It is a condition of crisis. Indeed, deterrence is another word for danger, a brief expression for the first stage of nuclear confrontation, for the fact that what we fear most may have already begun. Deterrence is often said to have "worked," and if anything has "worked," it has: but we cannot be sure. Even if it "worked" in the past, we cannot be confident that it will "work" in the future. (Deterrence must be the only public arrangement that is a total failure if it is successful 99.9 percent of the time.) Thompson [British social historian E. P. Thompson] is correct that deterrence is "a counter-factual proposition that does not admit of proof." To be a little more precise, deterrence is a proposition that may be known to be false, but not to be true. When it fails, we will know that it was false, or a few of us will. Until then we will persist in believing that it is true, and not entirely without reason. Deterrence is probably more than a necessary fiction and probably less than a law of history.

The criticism of deterrence, then, is not quite groundless. But many of the conclusions drawn from this criticism are. The alternatives to deterrence that have been proposed are no more moral or rational; they are in fact much less so. The razing of Moscow known as "decapitation" is ethically no more satisfactory than the razing of Moscow known as "mutual assured destruction." Nor is it particularly moral to place our populations in still greater peril simply by taking back the threat, as some suggest, or taking back the weapons; the only thing more menacing to our security than nuclear strength is nuclear weakness. Any scheme for dealing with the nuclear danger that would disarm only one side, or upset the balance between the two sides, would leave us more exposed, not less. It is just as irrational to invite a war with ICBMS as it is to fight a war with ICBMS.

The proper conclusion to be drawn from the shortcomings of deterrence is, rather, that deterrence is not enough. It must not be rejected. It must be completed. And it is completed by disarmament, in the form of arms control. Deterrence and disarmament are complementary concepts. The proper policy for the nuclear powers may be put this way: no deterrence without disarmament, no disarmament without deterrence. But this is a slogan whose meaning must be spelled out.

The need of deterrence for disarmament is pretty plain. The existence of such weapons means that we already exist in a state of emergency. They simply cannot be left to the pacific tendencies of people in power. They must be controlled, limited, reduced, and abolished—that is, they must be more than deterred. It follows from the nature of the emergency, furthermore, that all this must happen bilaterally. Anybody who is sincerely concerned about the nuclear danger will agree that the world will be no safer if cuts are made in only one arsenal. Nuclear superiority does not lessen the possibility of nuclear use; the United States dropped the bomb on Hiroshima when it had a nuclear monopoly. (It is worth noting, too, that if Japan had had the bomb, Hiroshima would not have been hit, because the United States would have been deterred.) The only real disarmament, then, is mutual disarmament. It is the only form of disarmament that will not advance the national interests of one side at the expense of the other's, and the only form of disarmament that will advance the higher interests of both.

The need of disarmament for deterrence is perhaps less plain. Put simply, deterrence serves as the proper regulating principle for arms control. It determines how many weapons, and of what kind, may be limited or reduced without upsetting the balance—without tempting either side to think that there would be a greater advantage in using force than in controlling it. There follows from deterrence the ideal for disarmament, which is the ideal of stockpiles shrinking more or less symmetrically. They continue to deter each other as they are diminished; and if they did not deter, they would not be diminished. This is not very rousing—unlike, say, Schell's summons to "rise up to cleanse the earth of nuclear weapons"—but it is very responsible.

Some say that the reliance upon negotiations to rid us of the risk is a counsel of despair. As anybody knows who has read Gerard Smith's comfortless account of the SALT I talks, there is some truth to this. Arms control talks have almost always smothered their purpose with the political ends of the parties. In such critical areas as strategic nuclear weapons they have not been able to agree even upon the definition of the reality that they have been mandated to modify; different measures of nuclear strength are proposed in order to disguise advantages that nobody is prepared to give away. The effort at the table has often been not to renounce, but to retain, as many weapons as possible. To be

sure, SALT I and SALT II were not exactly futile; there are fifty thousand nuclear weapons alive in the world, and every cut counts. The symbolic significance of nuclear negotiations, furthermore, should not be sacrificed. But arms control is not the solution to the nuclear problem, at least not for a long time to come. Ronald Reagan has called for the reduction by a third of the nuclear warheads in the land-based and sea-based missiles of both superpowers to be followed by an "equal ceiling" on the number of land-based warheads. George Kennan has called for "an across-the board reduction by 50 percent of the nuclear arsenals now being maintained." Both are fine proposals, and both would leave intact the power to destroy the world. That is the most pressing reason for preserving the doctrine of deterrence—these missiles and warheads are not going away. If you do not believe that we should unilaterally disarm, and you do not believe that we should fight a war, and you do not believe that the arms race should forever be run, then you must believe in deterrence.

This last point should be clarified. The relationship of deterrence to the arms race is a matter of dispute. It is true that there has been no military buildup in the atomic age that has not been made in the name of deterrence, and in many cases (the "bomber gap" and the "missile gap") its name was taken in vain. Deterrence has become an idea behind which a major sector of the American economy frequently hides. This is the version of deterrence that does not include a principle of limits. It is, in this version, a purely relative idea—we must have whatever they have. And if they have more, then so must we. Such a doctrine of keeping up is a perfect rationale for an arms race. Strategic stability is a worthy goal, but strategic stability applies also to the most swollen arsenals, which is exactly the present predicament. The other side is allowed to raise the ante, and to dictate the size and style of our forces. It is not on the basis of this version of deterrence, then, that the arms race may be restrained.

There is another version of deterrence, however, which flies in the face of the arms race. This version originates not in the idea of strategic stability, but in the idea of mutual assured destruction, which it takes very seriously. The strategic criterion for the research, development, and production of nuclear weapons is taken to be simply the capacity to inflict an unacceptable degree of damage upon any aggressor. During the McNamara administration at the Pentagon, when the idea of mutual assured destruction was adopted as American policy, such unacceptable damage was deemed to be 20 to 33 percent of the Soviet population and 50 to 75 percent of Soviet industry. Obviously a lower level of damage would be equally unacceptable. The point is that whatever the definition of unacceptable damage, the capacity to inflict it already exists. It existed twenty years ago. The manufacture of nuclear weaponry beyond the requirements of assured destruction is redundant; and according to this version of deterrence, the arms race is exactly that—an exercise in redundancy.

There is a kind of redundancy, of course, that deterrence requires. The United States must ready itself with the ability to strike at the Soviet Union after it has itself been struck, and so its forces are structured in a "triad" of land, sea, and air forces, each of which can do the deadly work of the other. But the arms race is a redundancy not of structure, which is necessary for security, but of numbers, which is necessary for business. "And the result," as Kennan remarked, "is that today we have achieved, we and the Russians together, in the creation of these devices and their means of delivery, levels of redundancy of such grotesque dimensions as to defy rational understanding." Kennan then scoffs at "something called deterrence," again from the perfectibilian point of view, but it is precisely the technological and military situation to which he points that is deterrence's reason for being. Unless a weapon must be made it must not be made. This is what is known as "minimal deterrence." In the early Nixon years it was known as "sufficiency." It would lead to a kind of selective freeze, with some projects of research and development properly frozen.

Deterrence, finally, is more than a military dispensation. It is a political dispensation, too. It permits nations that have the power to kill each other to prosecute their interests without killing each other. This is part of its offense to many in the peace movement, who want everything called off until the nuclear problem is solved. The most prominent spokesman for the suspension of politics due to the nuclear peril is George Kennan. In a recent speech in Frankfurt, Kennan succinctly delivered his well-known views on the way in which American policy toward the Soviet Union must adapt to the nuclear condition. "We must immediately stop every type of economic warfare . . . these are means for preparing a new war, not the means for preventing one." And "we have to put an end to the often systematic condemnation of another great people and its government—a condemnation which if not stopped will really make war inevitable by making it seem inevitable." And we must "exercise restraint in the tragic question of human rights and national independence," bearing in mind always "that a new war would not help those who are considered victims of Communist arbitrariness." The argument is simple. Because of the possibility of nuclear war, the United States may do nothing, in words or in deeds, to express its profound philosophical differences with the Soviet Union. It may challenge Soviet influence, and the Soviet ideal of life, only in ways that will not matter.

To "put an end to the systematic condemnation" of the Soviet Union, however, is to put an end to the telling of the truth. (Kennan disagrees. In 1976 he told an interviewer that "I can see very little merit in organizing ourselves to defend from the Russians the porno shops in central Washington. In fact, the Russians are much better in holding pornography at bay than we are." They certainly are.) Furthermore, to "exercise restraint in the tragic question of human rights" is to deprive the victims of "Communist arbitrariness" of their only hope. The course that Kennan counsels is the compromise of America's deepest convictions. It is also political paralysis. A "tragic question" is a question you can do nothing about. Kennan is a man unnerved by a nightmare. He would unnerve his countrymen, too. He would have them believe that the tightening of credit to the Russians, or the public support of Soviet dissidents, or the linkage of favorable trade agreements to the free emigration of Jews and others from the Soviet Union, will lead to war. This is especially odd in a man who denies that the Soviets are "aggressively disposed."

There is a part of politics, to be sure, that must never be linked to the rivalry between the superpowers, and that is nuclear politics. Arms control must not be a pawn in the game. It must be recognized as a different dimension, and dissociated from the ordinary political world. But ordinary politics must go on. Just as the bomb must not become a tool of political principle, political principle must not become a tool of the bomb. It is the divorce of the two that deterrence accomplishes. Deterrence does not depart from the consideration of the Soviet Union as an enemy—as an enemy of which the United States may be proud. Deterrence and arms control are quite compatible with the cold war. Their objective is simply to keep the cold war cold.

There is no contradiction between anti-Communism and arms control. But it works both ways. If anti-Communists must not be daunted by arms controllers, arms controllers must not be daunted by anti-Communists. For the ultimate reason for the absence of a contradiction between anti-Communism and arms control is the grotesque size of the nuclear arsenal itself. The United States has 1,052 intercontinental ballistic missiles, on which there are 2,152 warheads; and 520 submarine-launched ballistic missiles, on which there are 4,768 warheads; and 316 long-range bombers. In this decade, furthermore, the United States will deploy air-launched cruise missiles and sea-launched cruise missiles, making its strategic triad into a strategic pentad. The requirements of deterrence, then, are

well satisfied. This means that a good deal of arms controlling may take place before this country, and the campaign against totalitarianism, is put in jeopardy. Because the numbers are so great, we have room in which to move. Let us, to show that we are serious about arms control, volunteer to take apart some of what we have, because the gesture may make a change in the hearts of Americans and in the hearts of Russians, and let us default on the Polish debt. These actions will cost us nothing in security. They will profit us much in morality.

This, then, is the situation. There is the party of peace, and the party of war, and the party of deterrence. The party of deterrence is too little esteemed by the public. This is not surprising; no masses ever marched in the name of realism. But the public must be made to see that freedom's immediate future lies with this party, and that there is much work to be done. "It is not for you to finish the work," said a rabbi of the second century, "but neither are you free to desist from it." The rabbi was martyred by the Romans, but he spoke like a man who knew he would be survived.

Questions for Analysis

1. *In what sense does Wieseltier believe deterrence is immoral? In what sense does he believe it is irrational?*

2. *How does deterrence serve as the proper regulating principle for arms control?*

3. *Why does Wieseltier believe deterrence will limit rather than extend the arms race?*

4. *What does he mean by calling deterrence a "political dispensation"?*

5. *Would it be accurate to describe Wieseltier's argument as largely utilitarian? Explain.*

CASE PRESENTATION
The Grenada Invasion (a.k.a. "Rescue Mission")

On the morning of Tuesday, November 1, 1983, some 600 United States Marines aboard troop helicopters from the amphibious assault ship *Guam* roared into Pearls airport, the only functioning airstrip on the Caribbean island of Grenada. A half hour later, hundreds of U.S. Rangers, the army's elite special forces, parachuted onto the barricaded, uncompleted 1,000-foot airstrip at Point Saline on Grenada's southeastern tip. For the first time since the end of the Vietnam War, the U.S. had committed its troops to a combat action.

The sudden use of force drew immediate and worldwide shouts of protest. U.S. allies deplored the violation of international law and of Grenada's sovereignty. Latin Americans saw the intervention as a revival of the type of gunboat diplomacy associated for a century with "Yankee imperialism." On Capitol Hill and Main Street, Americans still reeling after the death of at least 229 Marines just two days before in Beirut, Lebanon, wondered what had prompted President Reagan to take such drastic action against the tiny, obscure island.

In the wake of the operation, the administration provided a string of justifications for its assault on a sovereign nation. The primary consideration, President Reagan told the nation, was the safety of the 1,000 U.S. citizens, mostly medical students, who had become trapped on the island after the bloody leftist military coup that had toppled the less radically leftist regime of Maurice Bishop. Foremost in the minds of U.S. officials was an event that happened four years earlier: the taking of hostages at the U.S. embassy in Tehran, Iran. The administration saw in Grenada the potential for a replay of that sorry tale.

But if the safety of U.S. citizens was the primary motivation, skeptics wondered, why couldn't far more limited and less inflammatory rescue and evacuation have been attempted? The implication was clear: If a straightforward rescue mission had been the goal, as the President claimed, there would have been no need, and no opportunity, to wrest control of the island from its Marxist rulers, which in fact U.S. troops had done. So the administration put forth other reasons for the action.

The little-known Organization of Eastern Caribbean States (OECS), said administration officials, had requested the intervention. But this legal basis seemed most tenuous. After all, Grenada was one of the seven members of the OECS, whose charter called for unanimous approval of any military action. Just as important, it was not at all certain that the OECS, formed in 1981, had any provisions, or right, to authorize military intervention in one of its member states.

The organization designated to handle matters of collective security in the region was, and continues to be, the Organization of American States (OAS), formed in 1948 expressly to protect the principles of nonintervention and national sovereignty. The OAS charter is explicit: "The territory of a State is inviolable; it may not be the object, even temporarily, of military occupation or other measures of force taken by another State, directly or indirectly, on any grounds whatever." The administration had not consulted the OAS prior to the invasion, and most of the organization's members subsequently called the action a violation of international law and the principles of nonintervention.

The administration, along with OECS members, claimed that the breakdown of order and authority on Grenada required some military intervention. In the days following the invasion, officials, including the President himself, pointed to the many Grenadians applauding the action as clear vindication of it.

But it was no secret that deeper reasons underlay the U.S. action. Addressing the nation, President Reagan provided one. "Grenada," said the President, "was a Soviet-Cuban colony being readied as a military bastion to export terror and undermine democracy." Evidently the nation could now rest easy, for, in the President's words, "We got there just in time." Reagan highlighted his comments by referring to the cache of Cuban and Soviet weapons and numbers of military personnel found on the island.

The action also seemed intended to send a clear message to friend and foe that the U.S. was willing to use its military power in resisting Cuban and Soviet influence. Such a willingness to use military force in the superpower struggle seemed the U.S. counterpart of the late Soviet President Brezhnev's determination that Moscow had the right to use military force to prevent pro-Soviet governments such as Poland from drifting or being pulled out of its sphere. Presumably the U.S. position, evidenced by Reagan's rationale for the Grenada invasion, was that the U.S. could and might use force to challenge regimes that threatened American security.

Questions for Analysis

1. Does the Grenada invasion qualify as a war? Explain.

2. Presumably President Reagan operated out of a sense of national interest. What other obligations, if any, did he possibly overlook?

3. In what sense was the Grenada action in the U.S. national interest? In what sense was it not?

4. Would you consider the intervention an act of aggression?

5. One reason given in attempting to justify the invasion was the restoration of authority and order. Do you think such an objective justifies military action taken by one country against another? What are the implications of such a rationale?

6. Vice President George Bush, for one, attempted to distinguish between the U.S. invasion of Grenada and seemingly similar Soviet military interventions. The objective in Grenada, Bush pointed out, would be democratic constitutional government. In contrast, he said, the Soviets seek to set up puppets that don't adhere to democratic institutions, as in Afghanistan. Do you think the installation of democratic constitutional governments provides moral justification for one nation sending its troops into another nation to fight against a ruling government?

7. Some would say an intervention of this sort is justifiable only if there is very strong evidence that the regime in power has begun actively to subvert its neighbors. Would you agree?

8. Would you say the Grenadian government was morally justified in defending its land against the U.S. military action? Would another nation—for example, Cuba—have been justified in rallying to Grenada's assistance?

9. A number of institutionalized mental patients on Grenada were killed by a U.S. air strike. Would these people be "innocents"? If so, what would you say of the morality of their deaths? What bearing, if any, would this have on the morality of the intervention?

CASE PRESENTATION
Ways Out of the Nuclear Dilemma

A few hundred megatons is more than enough to destroy several hundred cities, constituting a death blow to either the U.S. or the Soviet Union. In fact, in the 1950s, when there were only a few hundred deliverable strategic weapons in the world, each nation announced that this was adequate to deter the other side from starting a nuclear war. What's more, a few hundred strategic weapons is roughly all that's needed for triggering environmental catastrophe. So is it really prudent or moral to have the 13,000 megatons and 50,000 nuclear weapons that make up the modern world's nuclear arsenal?

Several serious proposals have been made to moderate or reverse the nuclear arms race. Each, according to its advocates, is bilateral, verifiable by treaty, and doesn't compromise the security of the U.S. or USSR. The three that have gained widest attention are deep cuts, build-down, and nuclear freeze. While differing from each other in important ways, they are not mutually exclusive.

Deep Cuts.   An agreement under which each nation would turn in to a bilateral or multilateral commission equal numbers or equal yields of the plutonium triggers that ignite the H-bombs. The triggers would then be consumed in nuclear power plants. This proposal is advocated by Admiral Noel Gayler (ret.), former director of the National Security Agency, and George Kennan, former ambassador to the USSR.

Build-Down.   An agreement under which each nation would destroy some number—two or three, say—of its nuclear warheads for every new one it develops. Among its supporters are Senators Sam Nunn (D-Ga.), Charles Percy (R-Ill.), and Gary Hart (D-Col.) as well as President Reagan.

Nuclear Freeze.   An agreement aimed at preventing any further growth in the strategic arsenals. Senators Kennedy and Hatfield have sponsored the nuclear freeze proposal, which is reproduced here:

> Whereas the greatest challenge facing the earth is to prevent the occurrence of nuclear war by accident or design;
>
> Whereas the nuclear arms race is dangerously increasing the risk of a holocaust that would be humanity's final war; and
>
> Whereas a freeze followed by reductions in nuclear warheads, missiles, and other delivery systems is needed to halt the nuclear arms race and to reduce the risk of nuclear war;
>
> Resolved by the Senate and the House of Representatives of the United States of America in Congress assembled,
>
> 1. As an immediate strategic arms control objective, the United States and the Soviet Union should:
>
>   (a) pursue a complete halt to the nuclear arms race;
>
>   (b) decide when and how to achieve a mutual and verifiable freeze on the testing, production, and future deployment of nuclear warheads, missiles, and other delivery systems; and
>
>   (c) give special attention to destabilizing weapons whose deployment would make such a freeze more difficult to achieve.

2. Proceeding from this freeze, the United States and the Soviet Union should pursue major, mutual, and verifiable reductions in nuclear warheads, missiles, and other delivery systems, through annual percentages of equally effective means, in a manner that enhances stability.[13]

Questions for Analysis

1. *What objections would you raise to each of the proposals?*

2. *Which of the proposals do you think best addresses the nuclear dilemma? Explain. (If you think a combination is called for, explain and defend your view.)*

3. *Suppose someone said: "These proposals are all well and good, but they rest on the dubious assumptions that the agreements can be verified and that they don't jeopardize national security. I just don't think there can be such a foolproof solution." Do you think that because cheating on the agreement is always possible, one is morally justified in rejecting these or similar proposed ways out of the nuclear dilemma? Or do you think one is morally obligated to take a chance? Explain.*

Selections for Further Reading

Barton, John H., and Lawrence D. Weiler. *International Arms Control.* Palo Alto, Calif.: Stanford University Press, 1976.

Fallows, James. *National Defense.* New York: Vintage Books, 1981.

Ground Zero. *Nuclear War.* New York: Pocket Books, 1982.

Kahan, Jerome H. *Security in the Nuclear Age.* Washington, D.C.: The Brookings Institution, 1975.

Kennedy, Edward M., and Mark O. Hatfield. *Freeze.* New York: Bantam Books, 1982.

Lens, Sidney. *The Day before Doomsday.* Boston: Beacon Press, 1977.

Mandebaum, Michael. *The Nuclear Question.* Cambridge, England: Cambridge University Press, 1979.

Marrin, Albert. *War and the Christian Conscience.* Chicago: Henry Regnery Co., 1976.

Thompson, W. Scott. *From Weakness to Strength.* San Francisco: Institute for Contemporary Studies, 1980.

Wakim, Malham. *War, Morality, and the Military Profession.* Boulder, Colo.: Westview Press, 1979.

Walzer, Michael. *Just and Unjust Wars.* New York: Basic Books, 1977.

---

13.   *Senate Joint Resolution 163 and House Joint Resolution 434 (1982).*

INDEX

Economic and Philosophical Manuscripts (Marx), 80–81
Economic justice, 326–331
  defined, 326
  related to distributive justice, 327–331
  (*see also* World hunger)
Effort, as a principle of distributive justice, 329–330
Egalitarianism, 71
Egoism, 61–65
  Epicurus on, 61
  objections to, 62–65
Emerson, Ralph Waldo, 26
Emotivism, 12
Engels, Friedrich, 80, 82
Epicurus, 61
Equal Employment Opportunity Act (1972), 287
Equal Employment Opportunity Commission (EEOC), 283, 287, 288
Equality, as a principle of distributive justice, 74–77, 327–328
"Equality, Entitlements, and the Distribution of Income" (Arthur), 358–368
Equal-liberty principle, 74–75
Ethical absolutism, 10–11 (*see also* Normative ethics)
Ethical intuitionism, 40
Ethical relativism, 11
Ethics, 5–13
  defined, 5
  emotivism in, 12
  meta-, 11–12
  moral in, 5
  naturalism in, 11–12
  nonmoral in, 5
  nonnaturalism in, 12
  nonnormative, 10–12
  normative, 10, 12–13
  (*see also* Social ethics)
Etiquette, 6–7
Eudaimonia, 44
Euthanasia, 188–237
  active, 194
  arguments against, 198–200
  arguments for, 197–198
  concepts and issues of death and, 189–192
  defective newborns and, 201–202, 235–236
  hospices and, 204–205
  in institutional setting, 202–204
  killing vs. allowing to die in, 193–194

Euthanasia (*continued*)
  legal considerations of, 205–206
  living wills and, 205, 206
  meaning of, 194–195
  nonvoluntary, 195–196
  ordinary vs. extraordinary treatment, 192–193
  passive, 194
  personhood and, 189
  voluntary, 195–196
"Euthanasia" (Foot), 214–228
Euthyphro (Plato), 53
Ewing, A. C., 67
Ezorsky, Gertrude, 287n

Fallacies, 21–36
  ad hominem, 24–25
  ambiguity, 22–23
  argument from ignorance, 27–28
  begging the question, 26–27
  causal inference from statistical correlation, 35–36
  causal oversimplification, 33–34
  cause as a contributory condition, 33
  cause as a necessary condition, 32
  cause as a sufficient condition, 32–33
  defined, 21
  false appeal to authority, 28–29
  of faulty causation, 32–36
  genetic, 23
  hasty conclusion, 29
  inconsistency, 26
  invincible ignorance, 25
  is/ought, 31–32
  neglect of a common cause, 34
  popularity, 28–29
  post hoc, 34
  provincialism, 29
  questionable claim, 25–26
  slippery slope, 34–35
  straw man, 30–31
  traditional wisdom, 29
  two-wrongs-make-a-right, 29
False appeal to authority (*see* Fallacies)
"Famine, Affluence and Morality" (Singer), 342–352
"Fate of the Earth, The" (Schell), 398–405
Faulty causation (*see* Fallacies)
Fetus:
  development of, 141
  moral status of, 144–146